THE
PATTON
PAPERS

Books by Martin Blumenson

Breakout and Pursuit

The Duel for France: 1944

Anzio: The Gamble That Failed

Kasserine Pass

Sicily: Whose Victory?

Salerno to Cassino

Bloody River: The Real Tragedy of the Rapido

The Patton Papers: 1885–1940

"By perseverance and study and eternal desire any man can be great."

— *George S. Patton, Jr., Cadet Notebook, 1906–1909*

THE PATTON PAPERS

1885-1940

MARTIN BLUMENSON

ILLUSTRATED WITH PHOTOGRAPHS
AND WITH MAPS BY SAMUEL H. BRYANT

HOUGHTON MIFFLIN COMPANY BOSTON

Third Printing w

Library of Congress Catalog Card Number: 76-156490
ISBN: 0-395-12706-8
Printed in the United States of America

to June, Françoise and Steve,
with love

. . .

"*The history of war is the history of warriors; few in number, mighty in influence. Alexander, not Macedonia conquered the world. Scipio, not Rome destroyed Carthage. Marlborough, not the allies defeated France. Cromwell, not the roundheads dethroned Charles . . . Truly in war: 'Men are nothing, a man is everything' . . . the leader must be an actor . . . he is unconvincing unless he lives his part . . . The fixed determination to acquire the warrior soul and having acquired it to conquer or perish with honor is the secret of victory.*"

— George S. Patton, Jr.,
"The Secret of Victory," 1926

Preface

AFTER THE END of World War II and particularly after the death of General George S. Patton, Jr., many military historians interested in and concerned with the European side of the war talked and conjectured often about the Patton Papers, which, according to rumor and gossip, were supposed to be magnificent for one reason or another. Not only were the Papers said to be a remarkable collection of documents about the U.S. Army during the first half of the twentieth century; they were also thought to contain the private and controversial thoughts and opinions of the violent figure who was one of America's greatest and most colorful military leaders.

The existence of the Patton Papers was widely known. But very few people — if any at all, outside the Patton family and several close associates — had ever seen the collection. From time to time, publications revealed fragments of Patton's written work, for example, *War as I Knew It,* authorized by Mrs. Patton and published in 1947, which disclosed some of Patton's wartime letters home and a few of his diary entries. The quotations they presented from General Patton's papers were sparse. For the most part, the published extracts of his written work were limited to those dealing with World War II.

They only whetted the legitimate curiosity of historians, who were as much interested in the early years of George S. Patton, Jr., as in his war experience.

When I was asked whether I would like to work with the Patton Papers, I could hardly believe my good fortune.

On a beautiful summer morning shortly thereafter, Craig Wylie, who was then Managing Editor of Houghton Mifflin's Trade Books Division, and I drove from Boston to the North Shore of Massachusetts and to the place that had been General and Mrs. Patton's home. We met their son,

Colonel George S. Patton IV, and his lovely wife. They showed us through the house, which was filled with military books and war mementos.

In a locked room in the basement were at least fifty metal filing cases. In those cabinets were the Patton Papers.

I opened several drawers at random, pulled out a few files, and saw at once that the collection contained a wealth of material. It would be a joy to work in this priceless repository of facts about Patton and the Army he had served.

But I was concerned about the location of the Papers in a house that was hardly fireproof or burglarproof, and I suggested that the Patton heirs donate the Papers to an institution that would catalogue them professionally, keep them safely, and make them available to scholars and other interested researchers.

The Patton family had been thinking of giving the collection to a library in California, the general's birthplace. On the basis that General Patton was a figure of national importance rather than of local or regional significance, the family selected the Library of Congress.

The Patton Papers are there now, and the public may have access to them in 1975. They consist of 122 containers of diaries, journals, correspondence, military studies, articles, speeches, lectures, memoranda, reports, orders, notes, notebooks, articles, photographs, maps, poetry, newspaper clippings, scrapbooks, and fan mail. Some material was presented to the Library of Congress in 1955 by Mrs. Samuel J. Graham; the bulk was given in 1964 by Lieutenant Colonel George S. Patton IV, Mrs. James W. Totten, John Knight Waters, Jr., and George Patton Waters.

The Papers are a splendid collection of material about a unique American soldier and his times. They offer a surprisingly complete record of events in his lifetime.

The most illuminating sources are the letters Patton wrote to his wife. The two were frequently separated, and his letters — he wrote almost every day, sometimes twice a day — contain a marvelously detailed account of his activities, his concerns, his triumphs, his disappointments. Unusually self-centered, Patton wrote virtually wholly about himself. His prime subject was his military occupations. Thus, for example, his correspondence with his wife from Mexico and France paints a full-bodied picture of life from his personal point of view; at the same time, it throws

much light on the larger aspects of the operations in which he participated.

There are, to be sure, some gaps. Some letters have been lost, others
were discarded or destroyed. And, of course, when Patton was not absent
from his wife, there were no letters to her. During these periods, his correspondence with his father and with other persons is invaluable.

Patton was an inveterate diary keeper, and his journal entries, though
brief, are usually evocative. Similarly, his lectures and articles indicate
his mental outlook and his intellectual pursuits.

My aim throughout has been to show the personal development of
George S. Patton, Jr., and his professional growth. One without the other
would result in an incomplete and distorted portrait, for the man and
the soldier were inseparable. As for his private life, I have used those
passages that reveal the personality of the leader, who, quite aside from
the printed word and quite in addition to his thoughts and ideas, lived
and acted and commanded and dominated, all in a most energetic, enthusiastic, and, usually, engaging manner.

Because a man lives in a certain world, at specific places and during a
definite period of time, I have tried to give some idea of his environment
— his friends and associates, the Army, and the climate and events of his
times.

This book is based primarily on the documents in the Patton Papers.
It is supplemented by the official 201 (Personal) File of General Patton,
to which I obtained access through the kindness of Mrs. Totten and
Colonel Patton.

All passages taken directly from the sources are set off in the text by
quotation marks or otherwise indicated. Brackets in quotations enclose
words I have added to complete or summarize a sentence or thought, or
to explain what might otherwise be obscure. A series of three periods in
a quotation indicates the omission of words I judged to be irrelevant. In
the interest of brevity, I have paraphrased some diary entries and other
materials, but I have noted these exceptions in the text.

Every attempt has been made to preserve the flavor of Patton's spelling
and punctuation, but in some cases periods and capital letters have been
added to help the reader.

I have, ordinarily, deleted references to family matters, inquiries about
the children (which are rare), banal or perfunctory endearments (the

others are included), and what seemed to me to be trivial. Letters that appear here with the salutation and the closing phrase are generally complete.

The quotations on the title pages in this book are all from the Patton Papers; they were written by George S. Patton, Jr.

I thank the heirs of General Patton — his daughter Ruth Ellen, Mrs. James W. Totten; his son, Brigadier General George S. Patton IV; and John K. Waters, Jr., and George Patton Waters, the children of his deceased daughter Beatrice, Mrs. John K. Waters — for granting me permission to work in the Papers.

I wish to thank especially Ruth Ellen Totten for her many acts of kindness and her willingness to clarify obscure family matters; Craig Wylie for his wise counsel and steadfast support; Blanche Gregory for her encouragement and confidence; Philip Rich for his sensitive and creative editing.

I thank John Gordon and Beulah Lewallen of the U.S. Army Administrative Center Liaison Office, The Adjutant General's Office; Horace L. Hilb, Mary Wolfskill, Leslie Sabo, and Eric L. Munro of the Library of Congress Manuscript Reading Room; Detmar Finke and Hannah Zeidlik of the Army's Office of the Chief of Military History; Dr. Barry Yoell of Wolfville, Nova Scotia, and my brother, Dr. Walter Blumenson, who clarified certain medical points; Frances Carey of the Naval War College Library; Margot Murray, Ruth Scott, and Marjorie Wickwire of the Acadia University Library; and Stephen Ambrose, Hugh M. Cole, Joseph R. Friedman, George F. Hofmann, Brooks Kleber, Charles B. MacDonald, Brigadier General Hal C. Pattison, Forrest C. Pogue, James L. Stokesbury. I am indebted to Sylvia Cleveland, whose guidance went far beyond the normal demands of copy-editing, and to Billy C. Mossman, whose expert advice on maps was invaluable.

I want also to record my immense gratitude to my wife for her patience, understanding, and perception.

All the interpretations and opinions expressed in the book are mine alone, and all errors, both of omission and commission, are my responsibility.

Contents

X. THE MIDDLE YEARS

XI. THE APPROACH OF WAR

Illustrations

Unless otherwise noted, all illustrations herein
are reproduced by courtesy of the Patton family

Following page 300

Grandfather Patton, circa 1860

Grandmother Patton, circa 1872

Grandmother Wilson, circa 1865

Grandfather Wilson, circa 1860

Father, circa 1884

Mother, circa 1884

George S. Patton, Jr., 1892

Aunt Nannie

The family home, Lake Vineyard, 1898

Family dinner, 1900

Father and son, 1901

Cadet George S. Patton, Jr., VMI, 1903

Nita, 1905

West Point drawing class, 1907. *United States Military Academy
Archives*

Cadet Patton, Adjutant, 1909. *United States Military Academy
Archives*

Cadet Patton, West Point graduation, June 1909. *United States
Military Academy Archives*

Beatrice Patton and her father, wedding day, 1910

Following page 780

MAPS

I

Prologue

"... the historian ... is by nature a man of thoughtful and studious habits utterly incapable of appreciating the roaring energy of a soldier. ... In peace the scholar flourishes, in war the soldier dies; so it comes about that we view our soldiers through the eyes of scholars and attribute to them scholarly virtues."

George S. Patton, Jr.
"The Secret of Victory," 1926

The Man, the Warrior,
and the Legend

*"The character of Caesar — if a man of so profoundly complex
a nature can be said to have a character — is extremely difficult
to define."*

> George S. Patton, Jr., School
> Composition, around 1903

EVERYTHING that everyone has ever said about George S. Patton, Jr., is
probably true. He is remembered for his military genius, his profanity,
and his victories in World War II. But there was much more to him than
the blustering egomaniac frequently portrayed by the war correspondents, much more than the simplistic man of action recalled by the public.
He was, in fact, a complex, paradoxical, and many-faceted figure.

He was unpredictable, capricious, at the same time dependable, loyal
He was brutal yet sensitive. He was gregarious and a loner. Enthusiastic
and buoyant, he suffered from inner anguish. He displayed what Craig
Wylie once called, in another context, an astonishing mixture of arro-
gance and humility.

He was driven by ambition, tortured by self-doubt. "I am certainly
giving my future biographer," he wrote to his sister in 1930, "— if there
ever is one —" he had the modesty to add, "an easy job with all my papers
on war so nicely arranged."

Fourteen years later, when he had gained fame and was on the thresh-
old of immortality, when he wore the three stars of a lieutenant general,
when he was widely known for his driving toughness, he could write to his
daughter Ruth Ellen, "I don't feel any different than when I was a 2nd.
Lt except that perhaps I have less self-confidence."

Personifying the pitiless gladiator, regarded by many as the soldier
most responsible for victory in World War II, he came to symbolize the

ruthless strength and will required to vanquish Hitler's evil. He captured the imagination of people everywhere by his spirit and skill. He shaped his troops into the best and most efficient fighters, and he gave them the determination to win.

"You have made your Army," Eisenhower wrote him in March 1945, "a fighting force that is not excelled . . . by any other of equal size in the world."

Characterized in 1948 as "the outstanding exponent of . . . combat effectiveness in World War II," he had become a legend.

"Everywhere I go in the Army," John B. Spore, then editor of *Army* magazine, wrote in 1963, "at Fort Benning, [Fort] Knox, and various places in Europe, I am on to the trail of Georgie Patton. George Patton had his headquarters here, slept there and so on. There is a Patton Hall at Fort Myer [Virginia] and there is a Patton Hotel in Garmisch [Germany] . . . At Fort Benning the Commanding General . . . will tell you that his office was occupied by General Patton when he commanded a division there. At Bad Tolz, in Germany, the Commanding Officer . . . will tell you that his office was occupied by Patton . . . And so it goes . . . Patton is as much a legend today as Stonewall [Jackson] was in 1870."

Luxembourg issued a commemorative postage stamp in his honor. Belgium revered him as a liberator. Hundreds of communities in France have streets, squares, and other public places named for him. The Patton Museum at Fort Knox in 1948 was attracting as many as 1200 visitors in a single day.

He was a hero to teen-agers, girls who pinned his picture to their bedroom walls at home and at school, boys who saw him as the embodiment of virility and the other masculine virtues. He was, and remains, a hero to Americans everywhere who glory in his exploits. He was a hero even to the professional German officers who respected him as the adversary they most feared in battle.

What manner of man was this who took equal pleasure and pride in writing a poem and in killing an enemy soldier with his pistol? Could the man who slapped and cursed shell-shocked soldiers in a hospital be the same who was cherished by his close associates for his love of beautiful things and for his fairness to all?

Gorgeous Georgie, the soldiers called him in North Africa, and they hated him for the strict military discipline he imposed, for his insistence that the troops salute, that they be clean and neat, that they wear neckties and helmets whether in combat or in a rear area. But they thrilled to his presence too.

Old Blood and Guts, he was called in Sicily, a term supposedly pinned on him by reporters but actually a phrase he had coined himself in the 1930s. "Our blood, your guts," some soldiers said in disgust. But in the thousands they proudly said, "I rolled with Patton."

He was loved as well as detested. Throughout his lifetime he prompted intense devotion as well as instant dislike.

"All of his men, and that goes for all the correspondents," a newspaperman wrote during the war, "worship him, and would literally go through hell for him. For his part, I don't believe he ever asked any of his men to do anything that he himself would not be willing to do."

Shortly after the war, when he toured the United States, he appeared to some "as a grand-stander . . . wearing pistols when no other officer wears them off duty, wearing a tin hat for show far from the battlefields . . . cussing and showing off, he is a decided detriment to the Army."

Quite a few judged him hardly representative of the best in America. Someone called him the Huey Long of the armed forces, a swaggering, boastful blowhard, and thought it was tragic that his vulgarity and exhibitionism robbed his undoubted military genius of luster.

The fact is, some who knew him slightly or saw him from afar were repelled; those who knew him better were charmed.

When Sergeant E. W. Fansler of Winchester, Virginia, was discharged from the Army in 1919, he was unable to see Patton, his commanding officer, before he left for home. He wrote a few days later "to thank you for the pleasant times that you were responsible for my having while in France. I do not believe that it was possible for a man of your rank to treat one of my rank better than I was treated. I want you to know that I appreciate it, and my wishes for you are that some day I may see the Pierce [Arrow] or some other car, belonging to you, pass with [the] four stars [of a full general] on the wind shield."

About the same time, Charles H. McCann was writing from Worcester, Massachusetts, to Mrs. Patton: "Dear Madam: I formerly was a soldier who served in France . . . under your husband . . . I am desirous of re-enlisting in the army and as all former soldiers can pick what post they wish to go I want to find out what post Col. Patton is at because I want to serve under him again because I not only admire him as a soldier but as a man."

In 1940, Corporal Donald H. Baker wrote: "Dear Colonel Patton: I am leaving . . . tomorrow morning, Sunday, and probably will not have a chance to tell you how very pleasant, enjoyable and inspiring it has been serving under you . . . I know that I voice the feelings of every enlisted man at Fort Myer who knows you, when I say that you have been our best friend during your tour here . . . You have been an inspirational leader, a good friend and a wise counsellor . . . we are confident that the high command will soon recognize your true worth, as we have always known it. May the next time I see you, and I sincerely hope that it will be in the not-too-distant future, that your [colonels'] eagles have turned to [generals'] stars."

The kindly father figure implied in these letters was far from the fire-eating, fire-spewing general made familiar to millions of people by newsmen covering World War II. He was pictured — usually sympathetically, for it was that kind of war — as a monster, a brute, a hard-driving commander who transmitted to his troops his violent aggressiveness and his desire to tear the enemy to pieces.

His personal characteristics, widely reported, complemented his military image. He was moody, temperamental, savagely profane, and easily moved to tears. He flared up in anger for no apparent reason and was immediately and abjectly contrite. He was subject to uncontrollable rage and the next instant tendered his sincere apology. He said things on the spur of the moment that he later regretted. Impatient, sometimes querulous, he could show immense kindness.

There was a peculiar instability in his personality, and it made good copy for the war correspondents. It became part of the Patton flair. It may even have contributed to his genius in military judgment and field performance.

Was he always like this? No. During his earlier years, even though he sought to epitomize violence, force, and drive, he was relatively stable, well-balanced, and usually mild-mannered. He played and worked hard, he was outspoken and could be blunt, but he tried to live by the code of the gentleman, the creed of the knight. Courteous, urbane, and charming, he carried within himself seeds of his later appearance, and these had blossomed by World War II and turned him into an exaggeration, a caricature of himself.

What changed the youthful warrior into the hard-eyed general?

Part of the transformation was cultivated, self-willed. He undertook consciously to alter his image.

In some measure, the change came from his understanding of fear and his perception of the basic paradox of war. Men had to be compelled to conquer their natural instincts of self-preservation in order to perform deeds of valor in combat.

A large part of his own nature abhorred the disorder and chaos of battle. He loved the quiet countryside and the sea, the quiet excitement of climbing craggy hills to hunt mountain goats, the calm thrill of riding a horse across lovely land, of sailing a ship across wide waters, the joy of training ponies, the serene satisfaction of fishing, the quiet feeling of power while swimming, the loss of self in the concentration of fencing, the uninterrupted evenings in his study when he read and wrote far into the night.

These were essentially solitary pursuits.

To enjoy group activities, he first had to school himself to overcome his fears, his uncertainties, his lack of confidence. He could plunge wildly and recklessly into the team play of football and polo and war only by putting on his mask. In his anguished sensitivity, he adopted a protective callousness. By force of will and against his inner disposition, he created himself in the image to which he aspired.

That picture of vital masculinity happened to coincide with his idea of a soldier. Other leaders have been successful without the driving ruthlessness that marked Patton. Yet he cultivated the ferocious face because he was probably concerned and worried about his voice, which was high-pitched, almost like a woman's, and because he believed that only he-men inspired troops to fight. Like Indian war paint, the hideous masks of primitive people, the rebel yell, the shout of paratroopers leaping from their planes, the fierce countenance helped men in battle disguise and overcome their fear of death.

The appearance became the reality. "A coward dressed as a brave man," he once wrote, "will change from cowardice" and assume the courageous qualities of the hero. This was the function of the oversized generals' stars he carried on his vehicle and wore on his helmet and shoulders during

World War II. This was the reason for the ivory-handled pistols, the profanity and the vulgar posturing.

Part of his transformation he perhaps could not help. A man like Patton who was accident prone, who once informed his wife nonchalantly that he had just suffered his normal annual injury, who spent his life in strenuous physical exertion, was likely to show personality alterations for another reason. As horses butted him, kicked him, threw him, rolled over him, he probably developed what the doctors now call subdural haematoma.

Physicians had a vague idea of it during Patton's lifetime, and they know little more of it today. But they are generally convinced that injury and shock around the head may prompt changes in personality.

The activating agent is a thin layer of blood that forms between the skull and the coverings of the brain. This pool of blood exerts high osmotic pressure, meaning that it tends to draw fluids to it. The subsequent swelling may sometimes exert pressure on the brain.

This condition may produce extreme ups and downs in behavior, barely concealed irritation, irrational irascibility, and over-aggressiveness in personal relations. In Patton's case, it would have made him even more aggressive than he had always been. It would have turned him on occasion into an unpredictable, difficult, and demanding tyrant.

Thus, part of his personal behavior during World War II — if indeed it was stimulated by a haematoma — was not a calculated effort. He may well have exploited his outbursts of temper and the other manifestations of his condition to enhance what had become his public image. But the general was quite unlike the young warrior, who was engaging and likable in the extreme.

"I guess my trouble is," Patton once wrote, "that I can never realize that anyone should be interested in what I say . . . All I want to do is win the war and everyone seems to think that all I want is notoriety which I despise."

He must have been joking. From one who urged his father during an election campaign to promise anything for a vote, from one who advised Pershing to take advantage of his publicity and exploit "self-advertising," the words ring false.

Patton was always interested in glory, adulation, recognition, and approval. He believed passionately in the virtue of becoming well and widely known. What he wanted, above all, was applause.

And for him that meant winning. Not only wars, races, and competitions of every sort, but also winning out over himself, overcoming what he regarded as disabilities and weaknesses of character and desire.

Profane in his language, religious in his convictions, he believed, he once wrote, "in fate if not in destiny." Precisely what the difference was he probably could not have articulated. He might have said that an individual was born to greatness, but not necessarily destined for it — unless he worked with all his might to help fate achieve his destiny.

This he did; he drove himself, seeking perfection whatever the task, never satisfied with his performance, apprehensive that he would be found wanting, fearing always that he lacked the qualities to reach the goal he dreamed of attaining.

A few days after Patton's death, the Right Reverend W. Bertrand Stevens conducted a memorial service at the Church of Our Saviour in San Gabriel, California, Patton's birthplace. "General Patton's life," Father Stevens said, "had a fulness and richness that is denied to most of us. It was not merely the variety of things he did in his lifetime (which stagger the imagination) but in the fact that he seemed to have fulfilled his destiny."

Like O. Henry's "man about town" who strove to gain that reputation and who died believing he had failed, Patton was never quite sure of his place in American military life. He was in disgrace before his death, having been relieved of his command for impolitic public utterances. He had been personally vilified for intemperate remarks. He had made the headlines, paraded in the spotlight, marched across the stage of history, and the final triumph — whatever it was — seemed to have eluded him.

Everything suddenly turned sour. He was tired, worn out by a lifetime of strenuous physical activity, exhausted by the nervous demands of having to perform, out of his own needs, always at peak perfection, injured mortally in a freak automobile accident.

As he lay paralyzed and dying, yet flashing by habit his infectious grin to the doctors and nurses who attended — and, although he knew he could not fool her, to his wife who sat at his bedside — he must have been tormented by the thought that he had failed to attain the promise of greatness that had tantalized him all his life.

Unless he remembered what he himself had written, in almost biblical style, early in his career: "Like all things which one wants it usually becomes dust on the getting."

He must have wondered whether it had all been necessary or even worthwhile to have played the military game in peacetime to get ahead — to bear and suffer that often demeaning subservience to superiors in order to be remarked and recommended for advancement, promotion, a good assignment.

Or was it all right and to the point? Was the continual struggle within himself simply excellent discipline, superb preparation for his achievement? Was it all fated and destined to have occurred the way it did?

Horseman, hunter, racer, steeplechaser, football player, swordsman, sailor, polo player, student, writer, poet, pilot, and, above all, soldier, he yearned for perfection and never quite reached it. He strove for recognition and was never sure he had earned it. He searched for glory and was certain it had passed him by. He wanted desperately the plaudits of his countrymen, sustained, unreserved, and unstinting, and doubted that he merited any. Unless he sits watching from a cloud in heaven or a steam bath in hell, he never knew how much praise he received.

What drove him, what generated his tremendous energy and will? "George Patton," he wrote to himself in his cadet notebook when he was in his early twenties, "you have seen what the enthusiasm of men can mean for things done. As God lives you must of your self merit and obtain such applause by your own efforts and remember that though at times of quiet this may not seem worth much yet at the last it is the only thing and to obtain it life and happiness are small sacrifices. You have done your damdest and failed now you must do your damdest and win. Remember that is what you live for Oh you must! you have got to do some thing! never stop until you have gained the top or a grave."

What made him so fiercely ambitious?

He treasured every scrap of praise, even to the extent of recording in his notebook an incident during football practice. He was playing an end position on the scrubs, the second team. "I blocked Fowler and Scrubs made 16 yards. [The coach] Kinney (Yale) said [to me] good work end."

What was that awful insecurity? From where did it come?

As a child, he was loved with all the tenderness that anyone could ever have hoped for. Perhaps he was adored too much, pampered and spoiled, encouraged to believe he could always have his way and whatever he desired. Nothing would ever be out of reach.

Perhaps he later felt that he had never earned the rich affection his parents gave him without asking anything in return. What better way to repay that adulation than by "winning," by obtaining the prize, by achieving glory?

Perhaps the birth of his sister hurt him. Until then, he had been the unquestioned center of all attention. Suddenly he had to share it. Was he determined to regain pre-eminence?

Or was he motivated essentially by reasons of family? His mother remains, unfortunately, a shadowy figure; she was probably stable, strong, and capable, although she was obscured by her handsome and talented husband.

Patton's close attachment to and identification with his father were of the strongest nature. An undated note suggests that he persisted in his poor spelling to please his father. "Christmas 1926 I brought this article . . . home and showed it to Papa. He read it over and corrected the spelling . . . Much of the pleasure I got out of writing was in showing the articles to papa."

Without Mr. Patton, who was an attorney, to draw the papers, to comply with the regulations, to exert pressures on the influential, it is doubtful that his son would have entered West Point. In those days it took virtually a lawyer, as well as a dedicated father, to follow the maze of paper and red tape into the Military Academy. It was, actually, Mr. Patton's glorious achievement, probably the most important contribution he made in his life. Perhaps he worked so hard to get his son admitted to West Point because he had little wish to see his own superb record at the Virginia Military Institute equaled or surpassed. On the other hand, perhaps young Patton could not bear to think he could measure up to his father's performance and attainments or, on the contrary, had no wish to compete — and for that reason desired so intensely to leave the Virginia Military Institute and enter West Point.

Patton's devotion to and admiration for his father were mixed with pity. He saw clearly his father's strengths and weaknesses, virtues and deficiencies. He tried to ignore his father's defects and overlook the failures. Perhaps, at least to some extent, he worked hard for accomplishment in order to redress and compensate for that lack in his father's life.

The Wilsons, his mother's family, were hardy southern farmers transplanted to California, where they were pioneers, well integrated and secure in their social position. The Pattons were southern aristocrats uprooted and shifted to California, where they had no solid standing. Their society had been discredited and destroyed in the Civil War, and they were never quite sure of their status. Even before the upheaval of the Civil War, although Patton men had earned distinction — one was a governor of Virginia, others were lawyers and military leaders — they had gained and enhanced their social prominence by marriage. The first Patton to come to the New World was of unknown antecedents, and the pride that members of the family had in their relation to the Mercers, Slaughters, and Washingtons came from the Patton wives.

Like the earlier Pattons, Patton's father married well. His wife belonged to a well-known California family and he thereby secured not only the benefit of social acceptability but also the very tangible advantage of land ownership. It was Mrs. Patton who provided the family with wealth in the form of land inherited from her father, who, by a strange coincidence, had come into possession of his estates through his first wife.

Mr. Patton, the general's father, administered the land holdings and eventually sold building lots to which he brought, at profit, water, sewage, roads, electricity, and the rest of the appurtenances of land development. He was well known locally as a lawyer and district attorney, but in the eyes of his son, who constantly found excuses for him, he never quite measured up to the romantic figure of the Patton grandfather who died in battle during the Civil War. *There* was a progenitor!

Was it to restore the Patton family name, to give it aristocratic validity, that impelled Patton to seek glory? Was he carrying on the tradition of his grandfather that his father had failed to perpetuate?

Trapped between the decayed fortunes of the Virginia Pattons and the natural vitality of the Wilsons, Mr. Patton Senior insisted on gentility. "Until the last year of his life when he was too ill," his son wrote, "Papa always dressed for dinner and I have followed his example both here [in California] and in the Army." Both Pattons, father and son, were autocrats who believed in the precepts of the gentleman warrior.

Patton was never interested in his father's political speeches to the extent of leaving a recorded remark about their substance. As a youngster he sometimes accompanied his father when he was campaigning. What he learned during those trips was how to look after the horses while his father talked. Perhaps he found his father's views and thoughts banal, uninteresting; and they probably were.

But he too lived in an ordered world where the differences, for example, between ladies and women were obvious. Breeding and wealth went hand in hand in his Anglo-Saxon, Protestant world. Character and work led inevitably to success. Ethnic minorities, whether Indian, Mexican, or whatever, played minor roles in his universe. Those persons of dubious background and questionable religion who performed loyally were treated with kindness, affection, even love. Those who drank too much, loved too freely, or aspired to goals beyond their station deserved disdain and contempt.

Patton was, therefore, comfortable in the Army, where all was orderly, where members were instantly graded by rank, where the prerogatives, privileges, duties, and responsibilities of each individual were clear and understood.

He attracted his superiors by his enthusiasm, his devotion to his profession, his willingness to learn, his serious application, his loyalty to his seniors, his concern for the welfare of his subordinates, his meticulous attention to orders and the job, his neatness in dress and appearance, his military bearing and good looks, his pleasant personality, and his adaptability.

He knew many of the important people in the Army, including every Army Chief of Staff from Leonard Wood to George C. Marshall — Hugh L. Scott, Tasker Bliss, Peyton March, John J. Pershing, John L. Hines, Charles P. Summerall, Douglas MacArthur, and Malin Craig. He was a friend of Henry L. Stimson and of Dwight D. Eisenhower.

Far from brilliant in his early days, Patton was quite aware that many others were quicker in mind than he. But he considered this to be merely a handicap to overcome — by will power, study, serious application, practice, and perseverance.

Eventually he outdid and outshone his classmates and colleagues. He was a late bloomer, a man who developed the habit of study and who learned to think and to analyze. It took him five years to graduate from West Point, and academically he stood in the center of his class. In his middle years he was an honor graduate of the Command and General Staff College and a distinguished graduate of the Army War College.

He owed much of his success in the Army to his wife. In fact, it might be said that Patton was, as man and legend, to a large degree, the creation of his wife.

She came from an immensely wealthy family, and he was keenly aware of what she had renounced to become the wife of an Army officer, particularly in those days early in the century when the typical Army post was distant from the centers of population, remote from metropolitan areas, and peopled by officers with pretensions of one sort or another and by enlisted men who were commonly uneducated and uncouth. To take his young and fragile bride who had lived in mansions surrounded by servants, who had been brought up to be charming, who was educated largely in Europe, who spoke French fluently, who sang and recited, who was delightfully poised and socially adept — to take her to camps, posts, and stations too hot in the summer, too cold in the winter, where it was dusty during the dry season and muddy when it rained, this was asking a great deal.

And yet she wanted to go with him and be part of his life, and this continually filled him with wonder.

The only way he could make her sacrifice worthwhile was to achieve the extraordinary. He had always aspired to greatness, and her abnegation of her way of life in favor of his reinforced his dedicated ambition.

She was determined to help her husband make it — whatever it was he was destined or fated to accomplish — among other reasons, in order to prove that she had been right to marry him. She provided immense assistance to him. She corrected his poor spelling, which had become second nature, his punctuation, his grammar, his translations of military studies from the French. She taught him the art of flattery. She encouraged him to believe in his destiny and fate. She collected his aphorisms and nurtured his myth. She saved his papers, catalogued them, and, shortly after his death, published a book about him.

And she was good in her own right, complementing his occasional roughness and awkwardness with patience and the glamor of her Boston background. She became a champion sailor and horsewoman, she translated Hawaiian legends into French and had them published, and she constantly delighted her husband's superiors and colleagues with her friendliness, kindness, and thoughtfulness.

He had to make good. He had to make it big. For her sake.

And yet, without meaning to do so, she robbed him of an essential facet of his masculinity. They lived on her income. He needed neither his Patton inheritance nor his Army pay. That too spurred him to achieve greatness, something that no amount of money could purchase. And that too is probably why he needed to project an image so strong and aggressive and masculine, an image that might otherwise be suspect.

In the popular mind, he was a flamboyant swashbuckler blessed with boldness, courage, drive, and luck. But it took more than that to become a four-star general. The showmanship that impressed the public with his toughness and the braggadocio that assaulted the ears of his troops only camouflaged his high professional competence. Constantly interested in technological advance, he strove to anticipate the effect of new weapons and equipment on the methods of waging warfare. He had a wide range of interests, a sharp discernment of the contemporary scene, and a profound sense of history.

In the thirty years from 1913, sixteen articles of his were published in the *Cavalry Journal*. All were distinguished by clarity of expression, exuberance, and humor. "When Samson took the fresh jawbone of an ass and slew a thousand men therewith, he probably started such a vogue for the weapon . . . that for years no prudent donkey dared to bray."

As a result of his close rapport with history, he liked to apply to contemporary problems his knowledge of warfare from the times of antiquity. He discoursed easily on such matters as scale, chain, and plate armor, German mercenaries in the Italian wars, Cossacks, Polish and Turkish horsemen, Arabian and Oriental military techniques, the Peninsular War, and Marshal Saxe. He wrote knowingly on the phalanxes of Greece, the legions of Rome, the columns of Napoleon, and the mass armies of World War I. He could compare the tank to the heavy cavalry of Belisarius.

"A picture without a background," he wrote, "is both uninteresting and misleading. Hence, in order to paint you an intelligent picture . . . as it exists today, we must provide an historical background." And to discuss the development of mechanized forces, he started with the Trojan War in 1096 B.C.

He never shut his eyes to the bloodshed involved in war. "Unfortunately," he wrote, "war means fighting and fighting means killing." The real aim of training was to learn "to be able to fight anywhere, any time, and to do it better than our opponents."

The intense desire for physical contact with the enemy rather than the threat of armed force alone produced victory. "Offensive, mordant troopers imbued with the fierce desire to destroy the enemy by always attacking him, will beat troops who . . . [are] more desirous of escaping alive . . . than of remaining victorious surrounded by slain opponents."

What made triumph possible was the individual. "The fierce frenzy of hate and determination flashing from bloodshot eyes squinting behind glittering steel is what wins."

"Ever since man banded together with the laudable intention of killing his fellows," he said in grim humor, "war has been a dirty business." But it was also an exhilarating contest, a fight for the highest possible stakes — for the warrior as for the nation — "life and the sweet triumph of victory."

"New weapons," he said, "are useful in that they add to the repertoire of killing, but, be they tank or tomahawk, weapons are only weapons after all. Wars are fought with weapons, but they are won by men . . . It was the spirit of the Lord, *courage,* that came mightily upon Samson at Lehi which gained victory — not the jawbone of an ass."

Always practical, he eschewed the unattainable, whether in his plans for military exercises or in his conduct of combat. He worked with what was present, what was at hand. Always, he maintained, "we are dealing with what actually exists" — whether it was types of weapons, numbers of men, or gallons of gasoline.

A cavalryman at heart, Patton achieved fame as a tanker. The principles he utilized in armored warfare came from the cavalry. He constantly sought surprise, mobility, maneuver — that is, the outflanking movement, the envelopment, the encirclement — and the relentless pursuit. For these, as well as for his understanding of space and time in warfare, he was indebted to Napoleon.

He owed more to Ardant du Picq who had postulated the belief that as two enemy lines approached, the soldiers with the lesser determination would break and run to the rear before the actual collision of bodies. Thus, Patton insited on morale, élan, and the spirit of the attack.

Above all, he learned from Pershing, who was his hero. He modeled himself deliberately on Pershing's bearing and command presence. He observed carefully how Pershing carried out inspections, gave orders, and handled men; and tried to do the same. He realized, after watching Pershing, that perfection emerged as the result of meticulous personal attention to detail, and remembered to do the same. Pershing showed no mercy to the inefficient, and neither did Patton. Pershing expected unswerving loyalty from his subordinates and Patton gave it — and accepted nothing less than the same from those under him. Pershing was a ruthless trainer of troops and a driving field commander; and Patton cast himself in the same mold.

It was Pershing himself, as well as the officers around him — Hines, Fox Conner, James G. Harbord, Hugh A. Drum, Malin Craig, Summerall, and others — who most shaped Patton's professional growth and his mastery of the complex art of waging war.

A man of action, Patton was no less a man of culture, knowledge, and wit. A man of erudition, he found his highest calling and genius in execution. A throwback to the Teutonic Knight, the Saracen, the Crusader, he was, in the final analysis, one of America's greatest soldiers, one of the world's great captains.

What sort of man he was, what impelled him to achievement, what thoughts, beliefs, convictions he had, what impressed him, he himself revealed in his Papers. They show, and particularly in his early years of preparation, a man of enormous sensitivity, perception, compassion. They record his self-depreciation and self-doubt. They make clear his happiness in action, for activity kept him from having the time to be nervous; it prevented him from worrying about his supposed disabilities. They report his strict attention to appearances. They reflect his humor, usually applied at his own expense. They underscore his complete focus on himself — he was the center and substance of his universe.

The Papers disclose the foibles, disappointments, hopes, and successes of a warm human being. Above all else, in the infinite complexity of his character, he was intensely human.

"The story of Patton, the man and warrior," someone said, "is a legend."

From the Patton Papers, it would appear that Patton the legend is the story of the warrior and, more especially, the man.

II

The Impetus

"We were all very proud."

CHAPTER 1

Ancestry and Family

"... men of my blood ... have ever inspired me ... Should I falter I will have disgraced my blood."

GSP, Jr., Notebook, July 11, 1913

Facts, dates, and incidents of my life which I hope will be of interest to posterity but which I fear will not.

Name George Smith Patton, Jr.

I was born on the eleventh (11th) of November 1885 in my family house at San Gabriel California. I was born in the same room in which my mother had been born.

The house was built by my grandfather Benjimen Davis Wilson in about 1830. It had been his ranch house, i.e. residence when his cattle ranch extended down the Valley from Redlands to Los Angeles and from the mountains to the hills.

This ranch he bought and did not get by grant as so many did later.

The city of Pasadena Cal. now occupies in part the sight [site] of his cattle pens. He gave the ground for this city to an Ohio company for nothing so that people would come west to settle. Mr. Wilson was from Kentuckey and was in the second party to cross the Santa Fe trail.

My mother Ruth Wilson was his youngest daughter. He had one son who died with out children one daughter, Mrs. Shorb who had a great many children who were all bad and one [un]married daughter Annie Wilson my aunt.

My grand mother was Mrs. Margaret Hereford Wilson.

She was among the first American women and the first lady to cross the plains to California. Her first husband and cousin Dr. Hereford was rich and lived in St. Louis Mo. He took the trip for his health and died in Los Angeles some time between 1850 and 58. He had one son Edward who was no good and died in San Gabriel Cal. in 1913.

My grandfather died long before I was born, my grandmother when I was twelve.

The eldest daughter married a man named Shorb who in foolish speculation spent and wasted a great part of my grandfathers money.

My father was the eldest son of George Smith Patton and Susan Thornton Glassell. He was born in Charlston Virginia (now West Virginia) . . .

[my grandfather's] commission as Brigadier General [in the Confederate Army] reached him several days after his death though it left Richmond before that time.

He commanded the advance guard in Earlies Raid on Washington and his command was the only Southern force which ever camped with in the city limits of Washington D.C.

My father accompanied his mother and two younger children one girl and one boy from place to place in Virginia [during the Civil War]. At one time during Stonemans raid they almost starved to death.

After the war his mother went to live in Los Angeles Cal. My father helped support the family from the time he was about seven.

Later he went back to his father's brother John Patton in Virginia and from there entered the Virginia Military Institute. His father had graduated there also in 1852. My father graduated from the V.M.I. in 1877. He was assistant professor of French there for one year then went to California and studied law.

At this time he had made all his arrangements to enter Hicks Pasha's expidition in Egypt. He did not [go] as he had to help his mother. The expidition was wiped out.

The first Patton in America came probably from Scotland through Bermuda. Some mystery attaches to him, his reason for emigrating, even his family name. Settling in Fredericksburg, Virginia, in the 1770s, Robert Patton married Mary Gordon Mercer, daughter of Dr. Hugh Mercer, who had accompanied George Washington on Braddock's Expedition and who was killed during the American War for Independence at the battle of Princeton.

One of their sons, John Mercer Patton, became governor of Virginia. He and his wife, Peggy French Williams, daughter of Colonel Isaac Hite

Williams, had nine sons, one of them being George Smith Patton. The first to carry this name, he was General Patton's grandfather.

Born in 1833, George Smith Patton graduated from the Virginia Military Institute in 1852, practiced law, and organized and commanded a volunteer militia company called the Kanawha Rifles. During the Civil War he was a colonel in command of the 22d Virginia Infantry. He died of wounds suffered at the third battle of Winchester, sometimes called the battle of Opequon, in September 1864.

General Philip H. Sheridan, in a letter from Cedar Creek, Virginia, on October 27, 1864, to Major General E. O. C. Ord, who was at Belair, Ohio, recuperating from a severe wound, documented Patton's death: "Colonel George S. Patton was mortally wounded at the battle of Opequon Sept. 19th, 1864 and died at the house of Mr. Williams in Winchester shortly afterwards." Lieutenant General Jubal A. Early, in his book *A Memoir of the Last Year of the War for Independence in the Confederate States of America* (Lynchburg, 1867), mentioned that Colonel G. W. [sic] Patton commanded a brigade, was mortally wounded, and fell into the hands of the enemy.

According to his grandson writing in 1927, more than sixty years after the event:

> [Grandfather's] nigro body servant who had followed him throughout the war took his horse saddle and saber and got them through the lines of both armies to my grand mother. Papa supported this man until he died.
>
> In this raid to Washington Col. Patton commanded the advance guard [of Early's forces] and actually camped within the district of Columbia near the present site of the soldiers' home. In 1919 I met an old lady on the road there who told me that in 1864 she had had two wounded soldiers of Col Patton's brigade in her house.

He left a widow, Susan Thornton Glassell Patton, and four children. The oldest child, born in 1855, was George William Patton, General Patton's father. According to his recollections, which he dictated in 1927 to his son, his mother and her four children lived during the Civil War with a brother of Mrs. Patton's, William Glassell, who had served as a captain in the Confederate Navy. About a year after the end of the Civil War, another brother, Andrew Glassell, "a man of means" who lived in California,

sent his sister $600.00 to pay the way of her father, old and blind, her
self and the children to California by way of Panama . . . They
landed in San Francisco and took another ship to San Pedro.

On reaching Los Angeles the family lived with Uncle Andrew for a
while, then Grandmother [Susan Thornton Glassell Patton] secured
a small adobe house where she supported her self by teaching a school
for girls. Papa [George William Patton] then ten or eleven [years
old] helped support the family by cleaning out a public school on
weekdays and a church on Sunday. At this time he developed an
intense aversion to poverty . . .

Through Susan Thornton Glassell Patton, the family traced its lineage
to Colonel William Thornton, a son of Mildred Washington, daughter of
Lawrence Washington, who was a son of John Washington, the great-
grandfather of George Washington. Beyond these progenitors were other
distinguished forebears. Some lines went back to Edward I, king of England, and his wife Margaret, daughter of Philip III of France. Even farther in the dim recesses of time were sixteen barons who signed the
Magna Charta, all of whom the Pattons believed were their direct ancestors.

The Pattons of the twentieth century were extremely proud of these
noble beings, who were deemed chivalrous and courageous, as well as in-
nately superior to other men. In feudal fashion, the Pattons felt that
their blood conveyed the birthright of leadership, together with a sense of
honor and an obligation to responsibility. They consciously modeled
themselves on their idealized heroes and strove to emulate them in manner and achievement.

The widow of George Smith Patton remarried in 1870. Her second
husband was her late husband's first cousin and schoolmate at VMI,
George Hugh Smith. He too was from an old Virginia family rooted in
the Alexandria area and distinguished for preachers and lawyers. Born in
Philadelphia, in 1834, the son of an Episcopal minister, Smith was a colonel who commanded the 62d Virginia Cavalry during the Civil War.
Smith's and Patton's commands, called brigades or regiments, fought side
by side in May 1864, at the battle of New Market where the VMI Corps of
Cadets under Cadet Lieutenant Colonel Scott Ship achieved glory.

At the close of hostilities, Colonel Smith went to Mexico to grow cotton.
When the enterprise failed, he traveled to Los Angeles. He joined Andrew Glassell's law firm in 1869, and in the following year married Glas-

sell's sister, whom he had known in Virginia. He became a devoted step-
father to her four children. So well did he bring up these youngsters that
the eldest, George William Patton, legally changed his name to George
Smith Patton, Jr., the second to be so known, in order to honor both his
father and his stepfather.

The union of Smith and the former Mrs. Patton produced two children. The second, a son, died when a child, but the elder, Annie Ophelia
Smith, married Hancock Banning. This event would have significance in
the life of General Patton.

Colonel Smith, who died in 1915, was a thoroughly cultivated and urbane gentleman. Although he never took the oath of allegiance to the
United States required of ex-Confederate officers, he served as a state senator, as a state supreme court commissioner, and as a judge of the appellate
court for southern California. His writings on jurisprudence gained him
considerable reputation in the legal profession in the United States and
in England. At the same time, he carried on an extensive correspondence
with military comrades and historians on the battles of the Civil War in
which he had taken part. Universally adored and esteemed, he displayed
a breadth of interest and a depth of knowledge that his stepson never
acquired. An intellectual, he wrote in a flowing if somewhat archaic style,
using an impressive vocabulary, but never with pretension and always
with clarity. He transmitted his ability to write, together with his old-
fashioned courtesy and good manners, to his stepson.

George Smith Patton, Jr., the second to carry this name and the father
of General Patton, attended the Virginia Military Institute in Lexington.
How this came about was recorded in a memoir written in 1927 by his
son, who was then over forty years old. The paper, entitled "My Father as
I Knew Him and of Him from Memory and Legand," reads in part:

> The State of Virginia gives appointments to V.M.I. in the same
> way that the states do to West Point; some of these appointments
> were reserved for the sons of Confederate officers killed in action.
> Papa secured one of these appointments and . . . went to stay with
> his Uncle John Mercer Patton . . . [who had] commanded a regi-
> ment throughout the entire war, being in more battles than any of
> the EIGHT Patton brothers; and though his clothes were hit six
> times and his horse was killed under him he was never hit . . .
> Papa told me that though he studied latin . . . it was only the day
> before he started to Lexington that he noted CAESAR was not

spelled CEASAR. This was a comfort to me for I was not a good speller.

When Papa reported at V.M.I. he went to have his uniform made and Mr. Wingfield the tailor took out the old measure book and showed him the measures of Grandpa which were the same as Papa's.

When I went to V.M.I. in 1903 Mr. Wingfield was still tailor and showed me the two sets of measures, when he took mine they were again the same so that my first uniform was made to the measure of my father and grandfather.

At the time Papa was a cadet young men were scarce in Virginia, so resorts like the White Sulphur Springs used to give cadets board and room during the summer to come and dance with the girls. Papa spent at least one summer in this manner. While there he was out riding and a confederate General seeing him in his gray uniform called him and asked if he were not George Patton.

On another occasion he was escorting a young lady to a band concert when he gallantly took his folded handkerchief from his sleeve to spread on the grass for her to sit on. On so doing he saw to his horror that it was all hem and holes. Neither of them said any thing but the next day he received a nice new handkerchief from the lady.

Another time while with a young girl they were approached by a nigger boy selling peaches. The girl asked for some but Papa had no money so calling the boy to him he took a peach and bit it then said: "Be off you young rascal, how dare you offer me green fruit."

. . . Papa was third corporal, Cadet Sergeant Major, and expected to be Cadet Adjutant but was made First Captain. He was in command of the battalion at the Philadelphia Centennial in 1876. This was the first time southern troops had appeared in the North since the war and a great fuss was made over them. . . .

When I was trying for an appointment to West Point, a Major Lee who had fought through the war in the union artillery and was a strong republican asked Papa if he had had any relatives at Gettysburg.

Yes, his Uncle Tazewell had died there. It turned out that Major Lee had seen him meet his death.

Major Lee was a great help in getting me my appointment . . .

In writing these traditions of some of my ancestors I have told them as nearly as I remember them from what my father told me. It may well be that some of the deeds are applied to wrong names but the fact that they were performed by men of my blood remains; and it is these facts which have ever inspired me. It is my sincere hope that any of my blood who read these lines will be similarly inspired and ever be true to the heroic traditions of their race.

Should my own end be fitting, as I pray it may be, it will be to such traditions that I owe what ever of valor I may have shown. Should I falter I will have disgraced my blood.

His father, graduating from VMI in 1877, remained there for one more year to teach French.

On returning to California Papa studied law in the offices of his Uncle Glassell and his step-father Col. George Hugh Smith and later became a member of the firm . . .

Papa was district attorney for two terms and fought the Southern Pacific with great violence. Later he was a friend of Mr. H. E. Huntington.

He married my mother Ruth Wilson on December 28, 1884 and at first they lived at Lake Vineyard where I was born . . . Then they moved to Los Angeles and lived on the hill above the courthouse. Here [my sister] Nita was born. My earliest recollection is seeing the guards walking along the wall of the prison which was below the house.

Papa's health broke down and he had to give up the practice of law and move permanently to Lake Vineyard.

This was near Pasadena, in San Gabriel, and there George Smith Patton, Jr., the third to have that name, spent his boyhood.

He adored his father and his Patton ancestors. He seemed never to be quite aware of the extent to which he took after his mother's side of the family, particularly his maternal grandfather, Benjamin Davis Wilson, whom he resembled in appearance and in personality.

This family had at least one famous ancestor. He was Major David Wilson, who served in the War of Independence, emigrated from Pennsylvania to Sumner County in what was then North Carolina, and was later a member of the Tennessee Territorial Assembly and finally Speaker of the House.

Benjamin D. Wilson was born in Nashville, Tennessee, in 1811. When he was about fifteen years old, he opened a trading post at Yazoo City,

Mississippi, above Vicksburg, and did business with Choctaw and Chicka-
saw Indians. He traveled west and in 1833 reached Santa Fe, where he
worked as a trapper and Indian trader. In 1841 he arrived in southern
California, one of the relatively few Americans who had crossed the continent. A storekeeper and rancher, he later was a large landowner. He first
owned the Jurupa Ranch, which the city of Riverside occupies today. At
one time he was proprietor of the San Jose de Buenos Ayres Ranch in
Westwood, where the University of California is located. On acres that
once belonged to his Lake Vineyard home are the buildings of the California Institute of Technology. The Huntington Art Gallery stands on
the site of the home built by his son-in-law, J. de Barth Shorb, across a
small canyon from his own.

Wilson led an active life filled with danger, excitement, and achievement. He battled the Mojave Indians, commanded a company of troops
under the Pico brothers, Pio and Andres, against the revolutionary General Micheltorena, was mayor of Los Angeles, headed a force of American
Californians during the war between Mexico and the United States. He
accepted a temporary commission as an Army captain — probably a simulated rank — offered, strangely enough, by Commodore Robert F. Stock-
ton, U.S. Navy. He worked to make southern California a separate state.

One of the Yankee Dons of Southern California, Americans who refused to accept Mexican citizenship, Wilson was a founder of the orange
industry. With Judge B. S. Eaton, he planted the first great vineyards in
the San Gabriel valley. With Phineas Banning, he established the town
of Wilmington and tried to create a harbor there. In 1864, in search of
timber for wine casks and orange boxes, he cut a zigzag path up the hill
now known as Mount Wilson, and over this trail burros carried the first
astronomical instruments for the observatory. After the Civil War he
bought the Drum Barracks for presentation to the Southern Methodist
Church, which opened Wilson College there. He built the Church of Our
Saviour at San Gabriel, the first Episcopal church in southern California.
He was appointed Indian agent for southern California by President
Millard Fillmore, and elected twice to the state senate.

A self-made man of brave and adventurous spirit, he dealt justly
throughout the course of his romantic life. He was an example of the
most admirable type of pioneer on the western frontier.

In 1844, Wilson married Ramona Yorba, daughter of a wealthy

Mexican. Born of this marriage were John, who was murdered when a young man, and Maria, who married J. de Barth Shorb and had eight children.

Mrs. Wilson died in 1849, and in 1853 Wilson married Mrs. Margaret Short Hereford, a widow who had been born in Loudoun County, Virginia, in 1816, and who had a young son named Eddy. Two daughters resulted from this union, Annie and Ruth. Annie remained unwed and was known as Aunt Nannie. Ruth married George Smith Patton, Jr., on December 10, 1884, in the Church of Our Saviour, and eleven months later became the mother of the future general. A daughter was born in August 1887; named Anne, she was sometimes called Anita or Nita.

According to George S. Patton, Jr., writing in 1927,

On the death of Mr. B. D. Wilson [in 1878] his son-in-law Mr. J. de Barth Shorb, married to Mama's half sister, ran the estate. He was either a fool or a crook and in a little while more of his management Mama and Aunt Nannie would have been beggars. Papa took up the management of the property and made them eventually wealthy.

. . . when Mr. Shorb died the Farmers and Merchants Bank of Los Angeles foreclosed on the Shorb Ranch and Papa, much against his will, was induced to be executor. For this work he received $500.00 a month and though realy poor at the time he gave it all to Mrs. Shorb and also went on notes for her.

As a child, General Patton lived with his father, mother, sister Nita, Aunt Nannie, plus various servants. The family lacked for nothing in the way of food, clothing, and housing but had little cash.

George had measles, whooping cough, and chronic tonsillitis, the latter cured by a tonsillectomy.

In 1927, Patton wrote:

I remember very vividly playing with Nita at the mouth of Mission Cannon [Canyon] and seeing Papa come up on a Chestnut mare belonging to Aunt Nannie called Beta. I wanted to go with him but he told me to play fort and showed me how to build one out of rocks.

As he rode on up the Cannon Mary Scally, our Nurse, said "you ought to be proud to be the son of such a handsome western millionaire." When I asked her what a millionaire was she said a farmer.

GSP, Jr., School Composition, February 6, 1902

The house occupies the site of an old church which was burned by the Indians, then this house was built, but not all the house only the central part, the wings were added one twenty, and the other fifty years after ward.

The house and wings are made of wood which was cut from the forest that once covered the hill. They are unpainted or at least appear to be for what the rain has not washed off the moss has covored up. In front of the house is a wide stretch of green lawn which stretched nearly to the village and is separated from it by a road and a low stone wall. On the left hand side of the house looking towards the village is an orchard of fine old apple trees, and on the right is a garden filled with rose bushes and other ornamental plants, in the back of this [a] garden for vegetables. Behind the house is a barn and a wooded pasture. Almost half the first floor of the main building is kitchen, and almost half the kitchen is fire place. After looking at the fire place you would not wonder that the forrests of the country are being exhausted. The parlor, which is in one of the wings, is large and now seldom used, the carpet is thick and brilliant in color, hiding a fine floor of oak. There are many huge pictures on the walls, the chaires are of mahoginy and very beautiful. The attic is a real attic and not one of those modern closets at the to[p] of the house. If any one in the house wants or looses any thing he hunts in the attic. In the attic are, canes, swords, trunks, saddles, guns, beds, chaires, clothes, papaers, books and rats.

His mother was quiet and strong. His father was handsome, articulate, mannered, charming, and somewhat of a dandy. Aunt Nannie, who adored her brother-in-law, spoiled the children, especially Georgie.

GSP Jr., "My Father," 1927

When I went to tell Papa and Mama good night I used to kiss Papa many times and Mama only once. This was childish and thoughtless. Papa used to tell me that he was worried to death trying to keep out of the poor house. I told him that I was worried too and when he asked why I said it was from fear that he would sell Broken, a Standard Bred Stallion he had.

Nita and I had two blue coats with brass buttons we called reefers. Nita used to say she was a major while I claimed to be a private which I thought was superior. When Papa would drive away in the morning he would salute us and ask how the private and major were.

Occasionally Nita and I would wear each others clothes to dinner. One night when I was wearing Her clothes Papa began talking about [Robert E.] Lee and I got all excited and when he told me that since I was dressed as a girl I should not get so bloodthirsty I cried . . .

With his after dinner coffee papa used to pour brandy on a lump of sugar and holding it on a spoon set it on fire and then put it in the coffee. I remember also that he liked marrow and used to fish it out of bones with a coffee spoon.

We both hated mush and I can hear him say every morning: "Georgie eat your mush." He used salt instead of sugar on his and I did the same which was probably the reason I did not like it.

In 1892 Mama had to take Aunt Nannie east for an operation. While they were gone Papa read Nita and my self the Iliad and then the Oddesy aloud. There was a big chair near the fire in the parlor and one of us would sit on his lap and the other in the chair beside him.

He often wore at that time an old white and brown check dressing gown which Mama said he kept because it smelled of me as I had often thrown up on it when a baby.

He bought me a 22 rifle when I was very young and once when Papa Mama and I were walking on what is now my place he put an orange on the fence and I fired and hit it. We were all very proud . . .

One Christmas I got a steam Train and another time a stationary engine both of which he ran for me until I was old enough to do it my self. I also had a soldier suit with a black wooly hat and pompom which he called a busby. There was a sword with belt and sabatash and a rifle with a bolt action; this he told me was a needle gun. I used to walk about with him carrying it and two empty 22 shells with which I religiously loaded it to shoot at lions and robbers.

Some times he would take his father's sword and I my toy one. He would kneel down and we would fight. We used to do the same thing with some boxing gloves he gave me.

I had a carpenter shop with a bench and a nice set of tools the latter a present from Captain William Banning. Papa and I built a toy boat and one day he said he would make me a sword, so we took a lathe out of the chicken yard fence and he made me a cross handled sword. Mary [Scally] made me a ticking scabbard and I wore the sword. Later I made my self many more such weapons. Once while riding with papa accoutered with my sword and mounted on Peachblossom I decided to charge and the saddle turned . . . I had a bad fall but was not realy hurt. The saddle I then rode was the McClellan saddle . . . on which my grandfather had been killed, on the pommel was a stain which I thought was his blood. Papa had also learned to ride on this saddle.

When I was ten or eleven he gave me a good imported English saddle and double bridle . . .

I always saddled my own horse and groomed it to some extent. Papa gave me two horses. First a black named Galahad then a Brown named Marmion. They were both about ¾ bred. Marmion was a really fine horse. I had a dog named Polvo about this time and he slept by Marmion I remember once going to the stable at night when I was supposed to be studying and laying by Polvo looking at Marmion and thinking that I must be the happiest boy in the world. I was probably right.

Papa also bought me a 16 gage hammer shot gun when I was ten and later when I was twelve a twelve gage Le Favre this latter cost $125.00. The day we got it papa had to borrow the money from the bank. I told him that it was too expensive but he said that it would last all my life. It is as good as ever now. When it came to marking the case I made him leave the Junior off so that he could use it if he wanted to.

Papa never economised so far as his family were concerned but would get nothing for him self. I think that at this time we lived on about Three hundred dollars a month but we never wanted a thing we did not get.

When in 1894 Papa ran for Congress, Nita and I did not want him to be elected as we hated the thought of leaving home; so we said that if he was beaten we would celebrate by having a boat race. The day he was beaten he must have felt very badly but he took us to the reservoir and we had a race with two toy boats, the Alley and the Flamingo.

After he built the reservoir he decided to stock it with Bass, so we went to Mr Chapmans ranch and caught three fish which we put in a milk can and brought home. They multiplied rapidly and soon we had plenty of fish.

Either we could not afford to buy rods or else Papa thought home made ones were better for he bought some little brass reels and tips and leaders and we cut two thin poles from the bamboo on the place and he made two rods. We used to fish a lot . . . When I fished alone Papa used to come to the stable and call me for supper. Mr. Stanton from Catalina gave me a boat. The first time Mama Nita and I went rowing Mama fell in the water launching the boat.

I caught my first land and first sea fish with papa. One Sunday after dinner Papa Cousin Ike Cooper and I went to the Pitman Pond above the Huntington Japanese Garden and I caught a cat fish on a pole with the line tied to the end of it. We ate it next morning and even then I disliked fish.

On Easter Sunday about 1895 Papa Mama and I were at Catalina [Island]. It was my first visit. Mr. Stanton arranged with Harry Elms to take us fishing. We went in a small whale boat. I caught six grooper on one line at one time.

After we owned a house at Catalina some one gave Papa a yellow-tail rod which he gave me and bought me a reel to go with it. He Jim Gardner and I went fishing off Jewfish point just beyond Pebly Beach. I caught five or six yellowtail, one of which weighed 45 pounds — a record fish . . . This fish was almost as tall as I was but when Aunt Nannie took the picture Papa made me stand back of the fish so it would seem even larger, I have always remembered that trick. Papa never fished him self but just went with me.

When he was away from the Island on business he made me promise not to swim beyond the end of the wharf. Once I dived and went so deep that I came up outside the limit, I could not rest until he got back so I could confess to him; of course he was not displeased. He was very proud of my swimming and once got me to swim to Discanso, the next valley. It was over two miles . . .

Our first goat hunt [on Catalina Island] was to Middle Ranch. I had a 38 and Papa a 44 winchester carbine. On the way up I got one of the 44 shells jammed in the magazine of my gun so he gave me his. At the Ranch Mr Whitley, the manager, fixed the gun for me and sent his boy Tommy to guide us up Cape Cannon. Here at a place called Rockey Mountain I killed five goats. We had some of the hides tanned and Papa always had one of them in his office.

On another trip which he and I went on, we came down on the coach with some other hunters. When we got to Avalon a crowd gathered as usual and asked us how many goats we had killed. Each of the others had killed one while I had killed several, of which fact I boasted. Papa said "Son it would have been more like a sportsman not to have mentioned the extra goats."

When I was 13 Papa had me a sail boat, The Elaine, built; he went

out with me when ever he was on the Island. Once we sailed up to
Goat Harbor beyond Long Point and camped. We slept on the
beach and between the hard rocks and the foxes who barked at us all
night we had little rest. Next day we climbed the cliff and I killed a
fox. We got covered with fleas skinning it for mama.

Papa also used to take me to the Island in the winter to hunt quail.
These various hunting and fishing trips which he accompanied me
on were a great proof of his affection for me as he hated both hunting
and sea fishing but he went even when I was a grown man . . .

In the years before I went to school I used to accompany Papa
almost daily to the San Gabriel Winery of which he was manager;
and over all the Ranches, Winery, Winston, Shorb and his own of
which he had charge. Some times we rode horseback and then Nita
often accompanied us. More often we went in a Concord single-
seated wagon without top, called The Yellow Wagon. Papa had a
very fine driving horse called Pompey . . . Once in a while we drove
the Stallion Brocken, which thrilled me as he was a very handsome
horse . . .

When he and I came back from Catalina alone for a few days, he
bought me my first sword. A store in Los Angeles was having a sale of
1870 French Sword beyonets and I asked for one. I remember lying
on the grass when we got home admiring it. Later I attacked the
cactus with it and got well stuck . . .

Sometimes I accompanied him at night when he drove to nearby
towns to make speeches. I helped unharness the horse and learned in
a second hand way much about the care of horses.

We always had white wine for midday dinner on Sunday and Nita
and I were always given a little. When I was between eight and ten,
I was sitting in the office with papa. As usual before dinner he
poured him self a glass of whiskey from a cupboard where he kept
liquor in decanters. He then poured me a drink and said: "Son this
is not locked and you can get a drink when ever you want one." I
never took one without him and seldom then. I think he did this
because the two Wilson boys [John Wilson and Eddy Hereford] who
had been very strictly raised both became drunkards after they came
of age. Papa's idea was to make me think drinking common place
and so set less store by it. Also he used to impress on me that an
ambitious man could not afford to drink . . .

He also showed me how to catch ground squirls in box traps and
made the first trap for me. I got ten cents each for these squirls which

were then a pest. Once I caught a skunk but did not find it out until too late . . .

Another time when I was quite small the men were pulling up dead orange trees. One would not move and I suggested that they put the horses on the tackle and pull it. That night at dinner he told about it saying "If the boy had not been there we could not have moved the tree"

The same day he caught me throwing potato bugs in a brush fire and told me not to be cruel.

In 1893? the whole family and Mary Scally went east; Papa being sent as the representative of the Los Angeles chamber of commerce to fight for the harbor at San Pedro against Collis P. Huntington who wanted it at Santa Monica. Papa won. We went to Philadelphia, and Washington and spent the summer at the Old Sweet Springs in Virginia. Here I learned to swim . . .

In September 1897 when I was eleven years old Papa and Mama decided to send me to the Classical School for Boys on South Euclid Avenue [Number 59, in] Pasadena, run by Mr Stephen Cutter Clark. The day I entered we drove up in the old surrey and on the way back just after we had turned into Lake Avenue off California Street papa turned to me and said very sadly: "Son hence forth our paths diverge for ever." I have never forgotten that but though we lived more and more apart our hearts and minds never separated.

CHAPTER 2

Boyhood and Beatrice

"desirus of an early and glorious death'

DR. CLARK, assisted by his brother, G. M. Clark, and probably by other teachers, offered essentially a high school course but the curriculum was flexible enough to accommodate boys who needed to brush up on or to acquire grammar school learning. The subjects taught were arithmetic, algebra, and geometry; English, reading, spelling, composition, penmanship, and declamation; Greek, Latin, French, and German; ancient and modern history; geography and drawing.

Young Patton attended the school for six years, from September 1897, to June 1903. His spelling was always erratic, and his punctuation often left much to be desired. But he showed steady improvement. And his conduct in class was exemplary. What interested him most of all was history, his best subject.

Ancient history at the Classical School for Boys consisted of Rome's kingly and Republican periods, struggle for existence, conquest of Italy, foreign wars, civil contests, and imperial era — all containing a high incidence of war and strife. Greek and Oriental history included social life, war, and conquest, plus a concentration on fifteen decisive battles of the world.

To Dr. Clark and his brother, who "examined and approved" the students' papers, history was a panorama highlighted by the moral choices of the leading personages. History, as they taught it, was a long conflict and clash between the personal ambitions of men — Persians, Greeks, and Romans for the most part — who made good or bad decisions, who lived properly and righteously or improperly and meanly, men who contributed to their nations' welfare and progress or who betrayed human hopes by reason of base motivation or weak character. History, in short, was a story of real beings who had grappled with real dilemmas still present in the world, although perhaps in different form.

The teachers stressed patriotism and self-sacrifice as the correct attributes of citizens and emphasized that success or failure in life emerged inevitably from character. They expected their students to pass judgment on the historical figures in terms of the current Christian or Protestant ethic that flourished in southern California and in most of the United States at the turn of the century.

In Dr. Clark's private school, which catered to the best families in southern California, to the sons of senators, high Episcopal clergymen, and prosperous businessmen, young Patton learned to think with a measure of logic, to write with a degree of clarity, and, above all, to make moral choices. He received the fundamentals of a good education.

According to young Patton's description, the school was somewhat austere, yet perfectly adequate:

GSP, Jr., School Composition, January 17, 1902
The school room has two walls covered with blackboards, there are two windoes, a stove. The doore is rather large, with a transome over it. There is a dictionary on a stand, a waste-paper-basket; a table, and chare for the teacher, three benches, and three desks for the pupils. Some maps are over the black-board, these maps are let down when wanted. A large beam runs across the middle of the ceiling, there is a ledge running around the room about three feet from the floor.

Young Patton's compositions, revealing his perceptions and sensibilities, displayed several persistent themes: gaining credit and recognition, achieving fame and glory through heroism, and enjoying physical comfort and pleasure. There was also the recurring thought that the prizes in life went to those who aspired and who tried with all their might to reach their goals. Perseverance in particular was a virtue, and to Patton especially, for nothing in his studies came easily to him.

English papers keyed to his daily life and observations disclosed his love of the countryside, of nature and the sea. Throughout his written exercises shone his directness, his sense of humor, and, above all, his love of the military, including a more than rudimentary appreciation of tactics, the art of handling military formations on the battlefield.

GSP, Jr., School Compositions

January 28, 1900

Catiline. It seems infortunate that so fine a mind . . . could not have been placed in a body equiped with a better conscience.

1901 (?)

No man ever so truly wanted the title of great as did Alexandor. From his earliest years he always aspired to perfection in everything.

December 2, 1901

[Julius Caesar's system of intelligence to obtain information on enemy movements was excellent, and when Caesar learned that] all the bands of the enemy were being gathered in one place. "Then truly!" Caesar was no longer in doubt what to do.

December 5, 1901

[On Marathon] Most of the Credit belongs to Miltadeos who was the first to use Greek troops in open field in so thin a formation, and his use of the second line saved the Greeks from destruction and won the Battle for them.

December 5, 1901

Closer and closer everyday crept the besieging lines, till at last when all hope of rescue was despaired of, a highland girl said she heard the pibroch of her Clan. Every one listened, but for a long time heard only the booming of the guns of the mutineers, then almost indistinguishable by distance they caught the highland ware [war] notes. After hours of waiting they could destinguish through the dust the highlanders of the relief-column, and hear their ware cries; then the wild ware music, changed into softer straines, and even above the roar of battle, as the rescuers broke through the rebel lines, the besieged could hear the tune they liked so well; Auld Lang Syne.

December 6, 1901

The attack on the castle was begun by a heavy discharge of arrows: which kept the defendors under cuver, but from loop holes the Normans answered the fire with their crosboes, and killed many outlaws. Then the out laws lead by the black Knight attacked and took Barbacon after a fierce fight in which, the black Knight and Fron de Berf met in hand to hand combat; the Norman being mortaly wounded, The Templer rescued his body, and retreated to the main castle, destroying the draw bridge. After a brief rest, the attack was renued, a floating bridge built to reach the main gate of the castle; this, after a fierce resistance was forced, and the castle having been set on fire in their rear, and most of their number slain or taken prisoner, the Tempeler and a fiew of his men cut their way out, leaving the castle in the hands of the out-laws.

December 11, 1901

Rode home, on bycicle. Ate lunch. After lunch read book for half an hour. Rode horse back to Pasadena to get some tools. Saw pretty horse in stable there. Got home at four studied algebra till supper ate lots. Studdied French.

1902

this reverence for the ancients is a great misfortune as it prevents progress.

January 7, 1902

[Tom hit the ball over the center fielder's head] securing an easy run and a great deal of credit.

Frank is a great carpenter, he is alwaies making something which is of no use to anyone. today he is making a book-case for his mother and she realy needs one.

January 8, 1902

When we arrived at the house . . . we found every thing ready; the rooms decoraited, the table set, and everything which could give comfort or pleasure provided.

[A bird in hand is worth two in the bush] is usualy true, especially when you are not a good shot.

January 10, 1902

[Describing a swimming race of endurance] the one who at first appeared the strongest gave up and the one who at first seemed the weakest got the prize.

January 11, 1902

[On Themistocles] He was eggotistical and had a right to be. He was unscrupiolos in ataining his ends and did not hesitate to decieve his best friends.

Cimon — His ideals were greater than Themistocles' but he was not.

January 27, 1902

[Describing a hunting trip] after an hour climeing over steep hills where I often had to crawl, I got three quail.

Last vacation I did not do very much out of the ordinary, so had rather a quiet time, riding, hunting, and playing tennis, towards the end of the vacation how ever, several of my cousins came to see me and we played football.

January 31, 1902

Dear aunt Kathren, Your letter arrived yesterday, and was very interesting, especially the description of the castle. I enjoyed it very much, and should like to see it for my self. Perhaps when I get my new Yacht, I shal come over and sail up the Rhine . . . but the Rhine may be too small to float my boat and my self. I am sure it will be If my feet continue to grow, and they have given no signs of stopping . . .

All the horses, dogs, cats, chickens, children, and relatives; are well and growing bigger every day. Write again soon the dogs and children want to hear from you.

Your loving nephew,

February 3, 1902

Dear Mr. Smith, The pony you sent me is simply fine . . . I played [with] him to day for the first time, and never enjoyed a game so much in my life. He is perfectly trained and bitted. It is of course impossible for me to express my thanks in words, so I wont try, but I am awfully greatful for your extreme generosity.

Your devoted friend,

February 7, 1902

[John Alden was a weak character and timid] as is shown by his not having told Standish at first that he was in love with Priscilla.

[A short story described a boy who confessed to his teammates after the football game that he had not fallen accidentally at a critical moment but] was affraid to charge the line and stumbeled on purpose.

February 28, 1902

[Upon seeing a blue-jay's nest with five eggs punctured] It looked like a case of revenge . . . An egg for an egg.

March 4, 1902

Epaminondas was next to, "Alexander the great," the best soldier in greece. For him self he had little or no ambition, but for his country and city he was very ambitious. He, in my mind seemes to have had the best character of all the Famous greeks up to his time.

[Mantineia was a battle where Epaminondas] used the same tactics which had wone Leuctra . . . the tactics were in general the same, but it would be too much to say they were exactly alike, for the flying colom was changed from an oblong to a V shaped body.

March 19, 1902
A peculiarly touching little incedent of bird life occurred to a caged female canary. Though unmated, it laid some eggs, and the happy bird was so carried away by her feelings that she would offer food to the eggs, and chatter and twitter, trying as it seemed, to encourage them to eat! The incident is hardly tragic, neither is it comic.

March 20, 1902
Periclise . . . as a soldier he did not destinguish him self, because he never chanced to be in battle, if he had fought it is probable he would have made a success.

Cleon, un like Periclese, was a man of violent passions. A great baster.

April 16, 1902
A pair of the least fly-catcher, the bird which says chebec, chebec, and is a small edition of the pewee one season built their nest where I had them for many hours each day under my observation.

May 5, 1902
[On the Sicilian expedition undertaken by the Athenians] the procrastonation of Nicias had already proved fatal and the whole Athenian army was captured.

May 20, 1902
[Epaminondas] was with out a doubt the best and one of the greatest greeks who ever lived, with out ambition, with great genius, great goodness, and great patriotism; he was for the age in which he lived almost a perfect man.

June 12, 1902
The Pieace of Antalcidos Was one of the most disgraceful things into which the Greeks ever entered, for after they had crushed the power of Persia . . . they . . . seemed to forget their former courage and fortitude.

Alexandor . . . in a fit of drunkardness he took his own life and his empire fell to pieces.

The chief book of the Jews is our own Old Testiment, which is in reality the history of the Jewish nation up to the Christian era. There is also another collection of books written, it is by the Heigh Priests called the Hipostrophel; at one time this was connected with the Bible but it has lately been left out.

June 13, 1902

the comon people of ancient times were very ignorant, as is the case with many in modern tims also.

June 18, 1902

Alexander the Great was one of the most ambitious men who ever lived. From his early youth he always tried to excell . . .

June 19, 1902

Leuctra. This battle was fought in Boeotia in the year 371 B.C. and was the first battle in which the formation of the troops was changed from a uniform depth of formation; to one in which a large mass was concentrated on one point in the opposite line. This new and extremely wise style of attack was invented by the Great Epaminonds . . .

[Alexander defeated the Persians at Issus] by use of the Phalanx, a modified form of that formation which Epaminondas had invented and which Philip perfected.

[Alexander defeated Darius at Arbela] as on all former occasions, by use of the Phalanx, and also by a dashing cavelry charge.

There was some talk in the family that summer of sending George to a private school away from home, and Mr. Patton investigated the facilities of nearby St. Mathew's. But he and Mrs. Patton decided, finally, to have George continue at Dr. Clark's. George was still too young, too immature, to go away to school, and perhaps they could not bear to part with him.

The whole family spent a good part of the summer at Santa Catalina Island, off the shore of southern California. A ship named the *Hermosa* made daily voyages between island and mainland. In 1903, the steamer *San Salvador*, about twice as large and with more power, reduced the duration of the trip from two hours to an hour and forty minutes.

The island had a small permanent population, some Indians and a few fishermen, and it was beautiful and unspoiled, with excellent beaches for swimming, boating, and fishing, as well as mountains with rocky ledges where wild goats could be hunted.

Several wealthy mainland families built substantial vacation homes there. The Hotel Metropole in the village of Avalon accommodated more transient tourists. A pier near the hotel jutted into a lovely bay with curving beach and received the ferry. Called "California's unique summer and winter resort," Catalina provided rest and quiet, as well as the opportunity for strenuous activity. In the evenings there were parties, where young people danced while their parents watched approvingly.

Mr. Patton owned some land on Catalina. So did the Bannings, who were friends of the Wilsons and the Pattons. Not only were there business connections among them — in addition to other enterprises, mainly in land development, they owned and operated the ferry; but there was also at least one family connection — Ophelia Smith, Mr. Patton's half sister, married a Banning.

The Banning family had two main branches. Some members lived in Delaware, others in California. Ellen Barrows Banning of the Delaware group had married Frederick Ayer, a wealthy industrialist from Massachusetts. She was his second wife and much younger than he. During the summer of 1902, Mr. Ayer, who was then eighty years old, his wife, and their three children, Beatrice, Katharine, and Frederick Jr., took a vacation trip to the West. Eventually they reached Catalina where they stayed with relatives.

Since the Pattons were on the island, it was inevitable that George Patton and Beatrice Banning Ayer should meet. They did so on August 26. He was seventeen; she was sixteen. For both it was love at first sight.

Early that September, in the living room of Joseph Banning's summer house on Sumner Avenue in Avalon, children of the Ayer, Banning, and Patton families presented a play, Caro Atherton Dugan's *Undine*. The company of players, who called themselves The Eight Cousins, put on a production that a Los Angeles newspaper society reporter termed "a pretty feature of the prettiest society function of the season."

Beatrice Ayer played Undine, a water spirit, Katharine Banning played a lady of rank, Katharine Ayer was the wife of a fisherman, Anita Patton played a knight, Joseph Banning, Jr., a fisherman, Frederick Ayer, Jr., a priest, and George Patton, Jr., was a water spirit named Kuhlborn.

Those who were present acclaimed Beatrice Ayer for her grace and her charming voice in song. George Patton, according to the reporter, "filled the difficult role to the huge satisfaction of his admiring audience."

When the play was over and the cast answered the curtain call, the performers were "loaded down with rare flowers brought all the way from the city florists" in Los Angeles. Music and dancing followed.

It was, as the headline on the story remarked, "a pretty society event." Mr. Banning's broad veranda had been converted into a punch room brightened with flowers and Japanese lanterns. The host and his family, as well as their guests, were handsome and well-to-do. They probably had no doubt that they were quite the best people in California and Massachusetts, indeed in the United States, and therefore the world.

When the Ayers departed from Catalina, they traveled to Glenwood Springs, Colorado. From the Hotel Colorado, Beatrice wrote to Aunt Nannie on October 1. "We are having a good time here," she said. But they were leaving for home soon because school was about to begin. "I am thinking particularly of Nita today because it is the first day of her school." But actually she was thinking more particularly of George. "I wonder if Georgie shot any very large goats at the island, and when he is going to St. Mathews. I hope that he will like it and that he won't get homesick."

That was all she dared say about him, for she went on: "My school begins just a week from today and I am beginning to dream of declensions, theorems and new girls, harmlessly swearing to myself the while (Hm! That doesn't sound very nice, does it?)." She closed with "Please give my love to everyone in your family." And having adopted Aunt Nannie, she signed, "Your affectionate Niece, Beatrice."

Young Patton was at Dr. Clark's school for what would be his final year.

GSP, Jr., School Compositions, autumn 1902

[Pyrrhus] always showed him self a true knight, courteous and gentle to friend and foe alike.

[Augustus was] the first of the world's great men to show that indispensable quality called tact; that quality with out which all is brute force, and with which all is courteous reason.

Carthage stood for eastern slavery wealth and all the evils that accompany it: while Rome stood for Freedom and purity of mind and body. Also these states were commercial Rivals. No wonder they fought.

At Christmas, Beatrice sent George a tie pin. Shortly thereafter she wrote him a letter. He replied awkwardly in a rather self-conscious manner.

Letter, GSP, Jr., to Beatrice, January 10, 1903

Dear Beatrice. It was very kind of you all to send me that pretty pin and I thank you very much for it. Please believe me when I say that it was the very thing I most wanted and that when I first wore it and looked into a glass to see if it was in straight, I involuntarily raised my hat "Unknowing whom it was upon whose cravat a pin had written 'sport.' "

As to Kuhlborns self there is little to say except that owing to his immortal nature he lived through the foot-ball season and did not even brake a bon[e] (worse luck) and that he is now devoting more time than he should to making a polo team; (for above all things he is desirus of an early and glorious death). He did not go hunting in the last part of the summer as he hoped, but a few days ago he left his native river and taking on him self mortal form destroyed 19 poor innocent goats and a fox; but the hour draws near when he must return to his spiritual form and wat'ry home, where there are no writing materials so he must now stop and thanking you again for the fox head [pin] he remains.

Your faithful friend Kuhlborn or Geo. S. Patton Jr.

There is a P.S. next page.

January 16, 1903

Dear Beatrice. Your letter got here and I — I *read* it. And was glad to see you are so well versed in the Bible. My hard study is making me fat and stupid so that I have come to the conclusion that the only way to pass an Ex[am] is to try not to. The reason this letter is so long coming is because I wanted [to] send K's and Fred's at the same time and as I only have Saturday I only had time for one letter I put off the writing of theirs till the middle of the week but falling behind on math. was not able to get theires written, and so fearing that yours will get too shop — I mean desk worn I send it now.

Please excuse this long yet truthful excuse, and in your liesure moments think of some [awful] name to call the man who invented this pen [which writes so badly]. Give my love to all.

Your faithful friend Geo. S. Patton Jr.

Their next exchange of correspondence would occur a year and a half later.

GSP, Jr., School Compositions
January 28, 1903

Jugurtha seems to have been an ambitious, cruel, but a brilliant man. It is hard to blame him for seizing power, yet the means he used to do this are worthy of the severest censure.

February 16, 1903

Please do not think it presumptious in me to introduce my Young friend [by this letter] . . . It would seem almost as rong for Mr. Taylor to visit here without seeing you; as to visit Egypt without seeing the Pyramids.

February 23, 1903

Mr. S. C. Clark: — Dear Sir, This letter is in reply to your request, to know what I did on last Friday and Saturday. As soon as I finished my lunch, I went to my shop and worked several hours. I then returned to the house, where I played several sets of Ping-Pong with a friend, by this [time] it was dinner time. After dinner I read for some hours and then went to bed.

On Saturday I started out to ride a horse which had never been riden. All went well till we came to a crossroads then the horse wished to go one way while I preferred the other. We argued with one another for nearly half an hour. During the course of this debate, he sat down twice, backed into a fence, and backed nearly a mile. in fact [I] was nearly forced to back him home for he utterly refused to go forward, at last however he decided to go my way.

In the afternoon I tried to play some more Ping-Pong but was almost too stiff, still I managed farely well. Towards the latter part of the after noon I wrote a composition and did some algebra. I am sorry that (I) comes in so much but there was no one else around, except one boy, with whom I played Table-Tennis. And now I must close this letter, which I fear is very stupid.

So I remain Your faithful pupil —

March 21, 1903

[Mithridates, a Persian general, successful against orientals but not against Romans] lacked one thing and that one thing is the undefinable difference which makes a good or a great general.

Soon he himself would be working hard to learn how to overcome that "undefinable difference" that separated a merely good general from a great one.

CHAPTER 3

Career Decision

"I feared that I might be cowardly."

BY THE SUMMER and early fall of 1902, George S. Patton, Jr., soon to be seventeen years old, had decided that he wished to become a soldier. Given the social prominence of the Patton family, enlistment in the Army was out of the question. The only acceptable career was the honorable profession of Regular Army officer.

Mr. Patton agreed that this suited his son's capacities. The best road to that goal, then, was an education at the Military Academy at West Point, New York, for graduation meant immediate entrance into the Regular Army as a second lieutenant.

Yet it was difficult to gain admission to West Point. Entrance requirements were rigorously prescribed by law. The student body was extremely small. About 150 cadets were admitted each year.

Each U. S. Congressman was entitled to have one cadet from his district at the Academy at any given time. Each U. S. Senator could appoint a cadet from the state at large. Each territorial delegate was allowed one cadet at the Academy. The President was permitted to have thirty cadets in residence.

An applicant wishing appointment could write at any time to the War Department Adjutant General and request that his name be placed on a register and furnished to the proper senator, representative, or delegate whenever a vacancy occurred. The candidates selected had to appear for a mental and physical examination before boards of Army officers.

Cadets had to be between seventeen and twenty-two years of age. They were expected to be well versed in reading, writing, and spelling; English grammar, composition, and literature; arithmetic, algebra (through quadratic equations), and plane geometry; descriptive and physical geography (especially of the United States); United States and general history; and the principles of physiology and hygiene. A certificate of graduation from a public high school or from a state normal school or the fact of regular enrollment at any college or university would be ample proof of mastery of these subjects.

Without being aware of the specific regulations, knowing vaguely that entrance depended on the good offices of a senator or congressman, Mr. Patton wrote two letters on September 29, 1902 — the beginning of young Patton's last year at the Classical School for Boys.

One was to the Superintendent of the Military Academy requesting information on admission procedures, the course of study, and the appointments that could be expected from California and the Territory of Arizona in the near future.

The other letter from Mr. Patton went to Senator Thomas R. Bard, a Republican who was in his sixties and who would, as it turned out, serve in the Senate only from 1900 to 1905. A native of Pennsylvania, he had been a railroad agent in Maryland during the Civil War. He had traveled to southern California immediately afterward to look after his employer's land interests, and he had remained in Ventura County, becoming himself involved in land development affairs and politics.

Mr. Patton informed the senator that he was interested in securing an appointment to West Point for his son.

Letter, Bard to Mr. Patton, October 6, 1902

It will afford me pleasure to notify you whenever it may become incumbent upon me to recommend another candidate for admission to the West Point Military Academy; with the view of giving your son an opportunity of presenting himself for examination in competition with other applicants for my recommendation.

Upon receipt of this noncommittal reply, Mr. Patton asked his friend Judge Henry T. Lee of Los Angeles, a well-known Republican who had been a major in the Union forces during the Civil War and who was a close friend of the senator, to recommend young Patton to Bard.

Letter, Lee to Bard, October 11, 1902

My Dear Mr. Bard: — Mr. George S. Patton of San Gabriel, who is doubtless well known to you, asked me the other day to see you or write you in regard to the appointment of his son, George S. Patton, Jr. to West Point, and I take very great pleasure in acceding to Mr. Patton's request.

The young man is about seventeen years of age and I think, has been a school mate of your son Tom, at Mr. Clark's school. I have not seen him for some years, but I know that he is a well bred and a well brought up young fellow, and his father tells me that he has developed a great taste and aptitude for the study of military history and sciences.

If blood counts for anything, he certainly comes of fighting stock, being a descendant of John Washington of Virginia, and counting among his forebears, Gen. Mercer of Revolutionary fame; while his grandfather, General Patton of Virginia, achieved wide renown in the Army of Northern Virginia for his skill and bravery, and was killed upon one of the battle fields of the Civil War. On his mother's side, he is, as you probably know, a grandson of the late Hon. B. D. Wilson.

I most heartily commend the claims of Mr. Patton to your attention.

Yours very truly,

An excellent recommendation, it applied some subtle pressure on Senator Bard, who, compared to B. D. Wilson, was a relative newcomer to California, and who had no military record of his own. Obviously, Mr. Patton had supplied some of the information for Judge Lee's communication.

On December 2, Mr. Patton wrote the Superintendent of the Military Academy again. He learned that Senator Bard was the best possibility for securing an appointment for young George. Bard was a Republican, whereas Mr. Patton was a Democrat. But perhaps Bard would be susceptible to the influence of Mr. Patton's many friends.

Mr. Patton was relatively sure, in fact absolutely certain, he could get George into the Virginia Military Institute, where he had close connections. But graduation was no automatic step into the Regular Army.

He also considered the University of Arizona in Tucson, where a cousin of his was professor of modern languages and the Commandant of Cadets.

If a military career eluded his son, he would have to think of a civilian college, perhaps Princeton University or Cornell. In that case, the Morristown School in New Jersey, a fine preparatory institution, would probably first be required.

And so Mr. Patton wrote some letters.

From the University of Arizona, Major J. M. Patton — Cousin Mercer — answered. He was sending a catalogue. Students could take a college, a preparatory, or a high school course. College graduates were automatically admitted to the senior class of the University of California at Berkeley. A certificate from Mr. Clark would enable George to enter classes suitable to him, either in the university or the subcollegiate department. Cousin Mercer would be able to help him, particularly in spelling, which Mr. Patton had written was his greatest weakness. The room accommodations were good, the "grub" was a shade better than he and Mr. Patton had had at VMI, and the boys at Arizona would be

> a good lot for Georgie to "break in" with. I agree with you and Ruth that it would be well for Georgie to be "broken in" . . . [he would] be able to judge for himself as to whether absence from home at West Point is his permanent desire. His Mama & Papa would also have an opportunity to consider the matter . . . I think the experience [at Arizona] would do him good.

Cousin Tim, who was attending Arizona, wrote on the same day to George, encouraging him to come. Tim was sure he could work Cousin Mercer for a room together with George, "and then I can sleep better, as my room mate stays up all night studying . . . Well come down and look at our big university, and see your cousin Tim."

Francis Call Woodman, headmaster of the Morristown School, said that he was obliged to Bishop Johnson for having referred Mr. Patton to his school. But, he wrote, "we distinctly shrink" from George's case because of his age, training, and experience. Nevertheless, the bishop's son had spoken so favorably of George and of the Patton family that Mr. Woodman was pleased to consider taking George as a special student to prepare him in two years or less for West Point or a university, probably an eastern college where the bulk of his students went. He therefore suggested that George review his mathematics and concentrate on languages to prepare for either alternative.

Princeton University mailed an examination to Dr. Clark for him to administer to young Patton to see whether he was qualified to enter the college.

All these were tempting possibilities, but if George wanted to be an Army officer, West Point was the place for him to go. In February 1903, Mr. Patton came to a firm decision. From that flowed three actions.

First, he sent a telegram to the Superintendent of the Military Academy to confirm the accuracy of the information he had earlier received. The Superintendent assured Mr. Patton that Senator Bard's appointee was a cadet in the second class or junior year and would graduate in 1904.

Second, he had George send a letter to the War Department Adjutant General, who duly acknowledged receipt and said that his name would be registered and presented to the proper representative and senators when vacancies occurred at the Military Academy from the Seventh Congressional District of California and from the state at large.

Third, Mr. Patton composed an impressive letter, wrote it in an elegantly flowing penmanship, and dispatched it to Senator Bard.

Letter, Mr. Patton to Bard, February 22, 1903

Dear Sir, I understand that in the course of the next few months it will be incumbent upon you to name a cadet to West Point to succeed your cadet who is to graduate in June 1904. Last Fall during your illness I applied to you in behalf of my son George S. Patton Jr — and also asked Bishop Johnson and Judge H. T. Lee to endorse my application.

In view of the near approach of the time for the appointment to be made, I venture to renew the application, and to ask your indulgence for stating certain facts, which in consideration of the dignity and honor of the position sought may be considered to have a certain relevancy.

I beg to assure you that in making the statement to follow, I am actuated by no foolish sentiment of pride of ancestry, but because it seems to me that to some extent it may properly carry some weight with you in making your decision.

My son is a direct lineal descendant of that John Washington who came to Virginia in 1657, and who was the grandfather of George Washington. He is also a direct descendant of General Hugh Mercer a friend and comrade of Geo. Washington in Braddock's expedition & who as a General in the Colonial Army led the advance and was killed at Princeton. In more recent times my son's immediate grandfather (my father) fell while in command of the Confederate division that sustained the historic charge of Sheridan at Winchester in 1864.

His maternal grandfather was B. D. Wilson who served in the Indian wars, and was a well known pioneer of this State.

Since his earliest boyhood my son has been possessed by the ambition to enter the army, an instinct that may possibly be accounted for by the hereditary effect of these strains of blood. He is a well grown, athletic manly boy, now in his 18th year — he has a good head, a sound heart, and is, I believe, a clean minded gentleman.

I have invoked and will have the cordial endorsement of the leading men of Los Angeles in business and politics and I earnestly ask your favorable consideration.

Upon your return home [to California] I hope I may have the honor of presenting my son to you that you may judge of his fitness to receive the honor sought at your hands.

All that Senator Bard could promise at the moment was to keep George on his list of the young men to be invited to compete for his recommendation. "I recognize," he added,

that he possesses a strain of blood which ought to result in a successful Army career. At the proper time, I will write him to appear before me, among other candidates for my nomination.

This was good news but ominous too. If the senator planned to administer an examination impartially to all the young men who sought appointment, George might be outclassed. His spelling was defective, his book learning relatively poor, his mental agility unimpressive. It would be well if the appointment did not depend entirely on the results of the test. On the other hand, if the senator administered the test solely as a matter of form, he would be vulnerable to the pressure of influence. In either case, Mr. Patton would do well to bestir himself.

Having been elected district attorney of Los Angeles County and having run for the state senate, Mr. Patton was a man of substance. He belonged to the California Club in Los Angeles, and numbered in this organization were many of the leading businessmen and political figures in the area. Mr. Patton addressed several of these friends, as well as his stepfather, Colonel Smith, who lived in San Francisco, to gain support for George's candidacy. The response was rapid and affirmative.

J. M. Elliott, president of the First National Bank of Los Angeles, wrote to Senator Bard and testified to the moral character and the intellectual abilities of young George. He had known the youngster all his life and was well acquainted with the family.

Bard personally replied to this prominent citizen and thanked him for his valuable testimonial, which assured Bard, without the usual inquiry, that the candidate possessed these important attributes. All that was now necessary was the need for Bard to compare him, physically and mentally, with the other applicants. He added:

I shall not omit to consider the important factor of heredity when making my choice. A young man who has reason to be proud of the military services of his ancestors may be depended upon for trying to maintain the honorable reputation of this family.

Lewis A. Groff, the Los Angeles postmaster, recommended to Bard

the son of our esteemed neighbor, George S. Patton, Sr., one of the foremost citizens of Los Angeles County. The young man comes of excellent stock on both sides of the family, and has a fine physique. I feel confident that if given the appointment he will in due time make a good officer.

From San Francisco, where he was one of five commissioners of the California Supreme Court, George H. Smith advised his stepson that he had attended to the request. Smith had written two letters, one from himself, the other for Judge Beatty to sign.

Tell George not to be puffed up with what I say of him. When a man undertakes to help his friends, he mustn't stand on trifles — Love to all — Affectionately yours George H. Smith. P.S. Don't you think a letter from Mrs. Shorb ought to do some good; also a letter from Bishop Nichols.

What Colonel Smith wrote to Bard was a tribute to family. He described young George's military ancestors, dwelt particularly on his grandfather, and predicted that the young man would not disappoint the hopes of his friends.

If inheritance counts, the young man ought to have all the qualifications required in a soldier . . .

[His grandfather] was a man of great gifts as a soldier and otherwise, and of a most noble and loveable character, and I am happy to
think I can see in the grandson many of the traits of character that
endeared the grandfather to his comrades, and excited the admiration of every one with whom he came in contact. The young [man] I
think is in every respect unusually qualified for a military life — on
which from his earliest years he has set his heart . . . Especially he
has one trait of great promise in one hoping to be a soldier, — and
one I am afraid very unusual. This is a strongly developed taste for
military history, in the study of which, in my opinion, is to be found
more than in any other kind of knowledge, the source of all superior
military capacity.

Judge W. N. Beatty, who signed the letter Smith had prepared, acknowledged that he did not know the young man personally, "though his
father and other connections are well and favorably known to me," and
he wrote in glowing terms of George's military forebears, including Mercer, Captain Philip Slaughter of the Continental Army, and his grandfather and seven great uncles who had fought in the Civil War.

Walter Van Dyke, associate justice of the California Supreme Court,
wrote Bard:

From my long acquaintance with Mr. Patton, the father, and others
of his family connection, I have no hesitation in acceding to his request and recommending to you the appointment of his son as desired . . .

Dr. W. G. Cochran, a physician, certified that George was six feet tall,
weighed 165 pounds, had good eyes and teeth, sound hearing, and was a
fine specimen of young manhood. He stood erect and had an ideal physical makeup for an Army officer. In addition, Dr. Cochran had served on
the Board of Education with Mr. Patton,

and never knew him to be governed by a motive other than the best.
He is a high-toned, brilliant, honorable gentleman, and if "blood
tells" in boys as it does in colts, you will always be proud of having
nominated his son, if the way is clear and you see fit to do so.

Commander Randolph Hollins, naval aide to the Governor of California, informed Senator Bard:

It is commonly the case that these appointments are the result of accident . . . but I have the opportunity of knowing that young Mr. Patton, a gentleman of the finest kind by birth and instincts, who inherits the traits of a distinguished father has a truly martial ambition which he has obtained by ardent study and I am sure that he will do credit to this vicinity and the State if you see fit to appoint him.

The president of the Newhall Oil and Development Company of San Francisco took "great pleasure in calling to your notice the son of our friend, Mr. George S. Patton." George J. Denis, a Los Angeles lawyer, stated: "I have known this young man since his infancy, and have watched him with the interest which is born of a life-long friendship with his parents." John S. Cravens of Los Angeles attested that Mr. Patton was "a prominent citizen of the state. The appointment of young Patton would gratify the leading men of this end of the state . . . I predict for him a distinguished military career."

Bradner W. Lee, an eminent Los Angeles attorney, endorsed young George "with great pleasure." William G. Kerckhoff, Randolph H. Miner, and Judge Lucien Shaw supported him in a similar manner. There were others.

By the end of March 1903, Senator Bard's private secretary, R. Woodland Gates, was wearily acknowledging the flood of letters. "Senator Bard," he wrote without further need of the senator's instructions or dictation, "has received numerous letters in behalf of the young man . . . to all of which he has replied."

Judge Henry T. Lee had also written his friend Bard again, and to him the senator had to make an acknowledgment:

I have already informed Mr. George S. Patton that I will give his son the opportunity of competing with other applicants for my recommendation for appointment to West Point. His many endorsements from gentlemen, for whom, like yourself, I have high regard, will prepare me for expecting the young man to impress me favorably. The examination which I will undertake is for the purpose of enabling me to determine by a personal conversation the relative merits of the candidates, particularly with reference to their natural mental abilities and moral character and physical qualities. I regard the hereditary history of an applicant as an important consideration.

Beyond that the senator refused to go. If he had bent at all under the pressure, it was in his admission that the examination would probably be informal.

In mid-April, J. R. Scott, a mutual friend of Mr. Patton and Judge Lee, informed Mr. Patton that Lee was persisting in his attempts to get the appointment for George. He was doing all he could. Yet Bard was holding firmly to his rule — he would see every applicant personally. If any person showed "a peculiar fitness" for military life, the senator would appoint him at once. Otherwise, Bard would make his decision on the results of a competitive examination. He would select the one who came out first. But Judge Lee had now met young George "and is highly pleased with him, and has great hopes of his preferment when the appointment comes to be made."

Apparently on the basis of this optimistic assessment, Mr. Patton followed the advice of a nephew, George Brown, who had graduated from the Naval Academy and was serving on active duty. Brown suggested two schools that had the reputation of successfully preparing candidates for West Point — Braden's Preparatory School at Highland Falls, New York, and the Berkeley School in Washington, D.C.

Mr. Patton wrote to the latter. The principal confirmed his specialty of preparing young men for West Point and Annapolis. He coached his pupils according to old examination papers. His terms were 40 dollars monthly or 100 dollars half-yearly in advance. No gymnasium was connected to the school, but George could join the Y.M.C.A. There was no set day for opening the fall term, and the young man could come any time.

Meanwhile, Mr. Patton had asked the Superintendent of the Military Academy whether it was advisable to send his son to a school to prepare him specifically for admission to West Point.

The Superintendent thought that would be unnecessary.

Any young man who has availed himself of the school opportunites afforded throughout our country need not fear the entrance examination for West Point, as it accords with the subjects covered in the public schools of the country at the minimum age of admission.

This was hardly reassuring, for George had had only six years of schooling and that at a private institution.

But there was a way out. If a candidate was a regular student at an incorporated college or university, he could enter West Point "upon presentation to the Academic Board of a proper certificate, without the usual mental exam."

The Virginia Military Institute happened to be an incorporated college.

Mr. Patton then received a letter from the headmaster of the Morristown School. Should he definitely reserve a place for George for the fall term? The school took only 75 boys. George could enter as a special student to prepare for West Point. He would take the same course as the son of Mr. Pritchett, president of the Boston Institute of Technology.

Always impressed by men of wealth and prominence and trying to keep all his options open, Mr. Patton sent a deposit of 25 dollars to insure a place for George. After acknowledging the check and saying he would welcome the boy "with much pleasure," the headmaster sent a certificate entitling George to admission as a special student in the sixth form. He advised the young man to prepare himself during the summer for an entrance examination to be administered at Morristown at 10:30 A.M., September 30. To get ready, George should read a book of Caesar; study 50 pages of *L'Abbé Constantin,* a simply written, popular French novel, or some similar text; and have some knowledge of French grammar.

In June 1903, Princeton University sent the results of the entrance examination. George had failed plane geometry but had passed English, algebra to quadratics, algebra from quadratics, and American history. He was admitted to the freshman class in the School of Sciences.

In mid-July, a cousin of George's age named Ormsby wrote in high spirits that he would enter Cornell University in the fall. "But I say George! What's this I hear about your taking Princeton Exams? . . . why [not] come to Cornell and room with me."

By then the matter was settled. Mr. Patton had finally enrolled George in the Virginia Military Institute. There was no problem of admission. Two generations of Pattons had preceded him. Friends and relatives of the family were members of the faculty and staff.

Attending VMI made a great deal of sense. If George received Senator Bard's appointment to the Military Academy, a year at VMI would help prepare him for his studies at West Point, accustom him to living away from home, and guarantee his entrance into West Point without the necessity of taking the mental examination. If George failed to secure Senator Bard's blessing, he could complete his studies at VMI and, with luck, enter the Regular Army from there. Honor graduates from the Institute usually, though not always, received commissions as Regular Army officers.

As a consequence of this decision, George spent a good part of the summer of 1903 studying, at home and at Catalina Island, where he stayed at the Hotel Metropole in Avalon with his sister Nita.

Letter, GSP, Jr., to his father, August 14, 1903
   Dear Papa, I believe that I am doing better this week and it is my opinion that with three or four weeks as good as the one which is now drawing to a close I might if the examiners are lenient and I am luckey succeed in becoming a star member of [my class at VMI] . . . But realy I think I am doing better . . . be sure and remind mama that Nita wants some one to play with . . . This is rottin writing but I am trying to get it in time for the boat. There was a big crowd at the dance last night.

The following month his mother and father took him east to enter VMI. Before school started, they stayed for a while with relatives. Twenty-four years later, Patton recalled:

   Just before I went away to the V.M.I. I was walking with Uncle Glassell Patton and told him that I feared that I might be cowardly. He told me that no Patton could be a coward. He was a most recklessly brave man. I told this to Papa and he said that while ages of gentility might make a man of my breeding reluctant to engage in a fist fight, the same breeding made him perfectly willing to face death from weapons with a smile. I think that this is true.

III

Formation

"I know that my ambition is selfish and cold yet it is not a selfish selfishness for instead of sparing me, it makes me exert my self to the utter most to attain an end which will do neither me nor any one else any good . . . I will do my best to attain what I consider — wrongly perhaps — my destiny."

CHAPTER 4

VMI

"with the help of God and a vigerous use of your influence"

GSP, Jr., "My Father," 1927

In 1903 Papa and Mama took me east to enter the V.M.I. We went by way of San Francisco and Salt Lake [City]. Papa went with me to report. The First Captain, Ragland, was in the room on the left of the salley port which had been Papa's when he was Sergeant Major. When I had signed up Ragland said "Of Course you realize Mr Patton that now your son is a cadet he cannot leave the grounds" Papa said "Of course." I never felt lower in my life.

Letter, Mr. Patton to GSP, Jr., September 27, 1903

. . . glad to hear from you. That must have been pretty embarrassing when you could not read the "no hazing pledge." How did you get out of it? I hope you managed some way to pass it off. I do not see how you are going to over-come this difficulty except by practicing reading all kinds of writing. Do not give it up, but when you start to read any thing keep at it till you work it out. You mis-spelled hazing. The verb is "to haze" and you should remember the general rule — to drop the final "e" before "ing."

We are all anxious to get your picture and see how you look in your uniform.

I am glad you have a seat at the first sergeant's table. What other rats sit at the table. You must bear in mind that it is not good for you to run with old cadets. It always hurts a Rat not only with his own class but with the old Cadets themselves. *Make your friends among your own class-mates.* Of course be polite and appreciative when older men notice you but hold yourself aloof and do not seek their society . . .

How are you getting on at foot-ball? Did you make the team? I
hope not. You would be better and harder next year.

GSP, Jr., "My Father," 1927
Papa told me that the first thing was to be a good soldier, next a
good scholar; that on the nights before I was to march on guard I was
to get my gun and brasses spotless and then if there was time, study.
The result was that I never walked but one tour of Quarter Guard.
On all other occasions [I succeeded in] getting Orderly; on the time
I did walk I had tied with another cadet and lost the toss.

George followed his father's advice, and it worked. The first class and
conduct marks he received — for September and October, 1903 — were
excellent. According to a scale where 10 was perfect, 8 was good, 6 fair, 4
bad, and 2 very bad, George had 9.7 in mathematics (algebra-geometry),
8.2 in Latin, 9.6 in English, and 9.8 in history. For personal appearance
and behavior, he had received no demerits.

Letter, GSP, Jr., to his father, November 28, 1903
Dear Papa; We did have vacation on Thanksgiving and Rowe and
I went to Thanksgiving dinner at Col Mar's [Colonel Marr was a
VMI schoolmate of Mr. Patton's]; we ate so much that we could
hardly get on our dikes for dress-parade . . . I still have five dollars
of that money left besides a couble of dollars in change and am
thinking of starting a banking room at the V.M.I. and of chargeing
third class men 50% interest on all loans . . . That fat Dunbar has
an appointment to West Point, and *I* cadet Private Patton have not.
Doesn't that show the rottinness of the government. I believe I will
get "Fat" to appoint me as his alternate for they are sure to kill him
at the Point. I got a letter from Young Tom Bard yesterday but he
did not even mention West Point. If I do get [appointed] send a
rush telegraph . . . I think I said that I got a letter from Beatrice
asking Mama and I to spend Thanksgiving with them.

Letter, GSP, Jr., to his father, December 13, 1903
I am now a K.A. [member of a secret fraternity] and here at least
it has and will be of use to me. But when I go to WP I am afraid that
it will be of little or no service as K.A. is very week up there. I do not
know whether or not I should tell you this next or not; but as I have
not heard any thing to the contrary I think I am safe in doing so
particularly as you will not let it go any further. The society of

K.A.'s here is not a real branch but only a sub branch; that is as long as they stay at the V.M.I. they do not know all the rot or the true grip but merely part of it, and they [use] a grip of their own which while it is known to all the frat is only used in the sub members. The only thing you do when you join a branch is to swear that you will not ever join any other "frat" after leaving here but you are not bound . . .

Maybe I have said too much but do not let any one else know for if news of it got out it might ruin [me] . . .

I am very glad my boat has been sold and also at the very good price she brought, who was the fool and what did he buy her fore. She realy was of little more use as she was too small for a sail boat and not the right build for a launch, still I had lots of fun out of her . . . I wish quite often that I were home, but realy I have very little time to get homesick and as yet have only hade it in very mild form. Of course I want to see you all very much but that is only natural so dont get to worrying about me in that account.

These darned K.A.'s struck me for another five [dollars] but I suppose that is only natural as a sort of initiation fee and as I am one of the capotolists of lexington I can very well stand it . . . since I was the first rat [fourth class man or freshman] to become a "K.A." I am treated almost as an equal. Theoretically I do not approve of this but practically I do.

Conserning Bard. Rowe says that if a man has been suspended the vacancy which his graduation would leave open is carried over another year. That is if Bards man who is supposed to graduate has for any reason been suspended for a year the vacancy would not come until June '05. I dont see how such a thing could have happened with out you hearing about it. But please try to find out about it because I *must* get that appointment but don't bother your self to much about it because you have enough to do any way with out worrying about any thing else. The only reason I am so anxious to get in next year is that the joys of cadet life are not so grate as to make me wish to spend six years in the enjoyment of them [meaning two years at VMI and four at West Point]. Five years will be bad enough but six o Lord. At the end of that time I would be so military that it would be impossible for me to either lounge or sleep. The only thing in which I could possibly find Pleasure would be to get a gun and walk up and down pretending to do sentry duty. While if I attempted to wash in hot water I would surly take cold.

Now to avoid this horrible contingency you must get me an appointment. Please do not spend too much time making money for Huntington and dont stay in your office after twelve but go out home and either ride or play golf.

His reference to spending six years as a cadet would turn out to be prophetic.

Letter, GSP, Jr., to his father, December 19, 1903
[Received six letters from home, and there was much excitement among the rats.] Rowe thought that the big envelope containing the Christmas cards was my appointment and I kind of hoped so myself. I *feel* quite like a college man tonight as I sit facing Curtis — Rowe is on guard — with nothing to do save discus the contense of a box of apples and candy which Mrs. Mar gave me . . . I don't see what makes me spell so badly, I seem to make always the same mistakes.

What do you think of this writing paper. It only cost a quarter, but I thought it plenty good enough to write home on while I saved my monogram-paper for strangers . . . I bought a silk V.M.I. flag for Beatrice and a V.M.I. pillow case for Katharin [her sister]. I fancy they will think I am running an advertising scheme; but they are the only things people seem to have in Lexington . . . Don't put that money I got from my boat in any place where I cant draw it out when I want it . . . P.S. Merry Christmas.

No doubt in response to George's letter, Mr. Patton wrote to the Superintendent of the Military Academy. You have kindly informed me, he said, that Senator Bard's cadet will graduate in June 1904, and that the senator would be notified of the approaching vacancy. But who, Mr. Patton asked, notified the senator — West Point or the War Department?

The West Point Adjutant replied simply that the senator's appointee would graduate in June 1904.

Letter, Mr. Patton to the Honorable H. T. Lee, January 5, 1904
My dear Mr. Lee: — Referring to my several conversations with you, concerning the West Point Cadetship and the possibility of receiving the appointment to the same for my son, I find myself somewhat perplexed in regard to the matter from the following considerations. In stating these, however, I am naturally anxious that my

anxiety shall not be construed as arising from a disposition to unduly press the Senator for a determination of the matter before it suits his own convenience. In the hope that my son's application would be favorably considered I sent him at the first of the year to the Virginia Military Institute at Lexington where he is now a cadet, and where his standing in his class up to this time indicates that he will stand very near the head of the class of nearly a hundred young men . . .

My son writes me that several of his class-mates who expect to go to West Point from the Virginia Military Institute have already received their appointments, and he naturally feels anxious to know whether or not he will be able to do likewise. He is now rooming with two young men from New York both of whom expect to enter the Military Academy at West Point, upon certificates from the Virginia Military Institute, and as I stated, his standing in his class at the present time indicates that he is much in earnest in his wish to prove himself worthy of an appointment to the latter academy. It has occurred to me that it was possible that the notification from the war department to Senator Bard may have been received during his absence in Europe, and either miscarried or been overlooked.

Without desiring to hurry the matter or to assume that my son is to receive the appointment, but desiring that the full circumstances may be understood by the senator, I have taken the liberty of addressing you this communication with a request that you use your own judgment as to the propriety of laying the matter before Mr. Bard at Washington.

Thank you for the great personal interest which you have taken in this matter, I am very truly Your friend, George S. Patton.

George was indeed doing well at VMI. His marks, as noted on January 8, 1904, were 9.1 in mathematics, 6.6 in Latin, 9 in English, 10 in history, and 9.1 in drawing. He had received no demerits since entering the college.

Letter, GSP, Jr., to his father, January 10, 1904

[Apologized for the wide intervals between his letters and explained that he had to write to many people after Christmas] thanking them for things I did not want . . . I got a 100 in math 99 in English 95 in history and 81 in latin last week my latin is pretty po[o]r but still it is better than it was . . . When you write next send me some stamps for I hate to buy them for my self. From what you say in your last letter I suppose my appointment is pretty sure and I am glad of it because I wont have to study Latin here next year. Still if I staied here I would get a good corp [a high appointment as a corporal] but then even if I go to West Point they will give me a corp here, and really the only advantage in being a corp is the honor for there is more work in it than in being a private. Mama asked in her last letter if I would not like to go in the army from here. I would like to but since I am to be a military man it would be much better for me to go to W.P. . . . Is my spelling still as bad as it was. I hope not for I heare W.P. is getting more and more strict about that.

Judge Lee wrote to Senator Bard, pressing George's candidacy. In reply the senator said that since he would be unable to return to California in time himself, he was going to appoint a committee to conduct the examination of applicants for his West Point recommendation. He promised to invite all applicants. Was this, he asked Lee, inconsistent with any statement he had formerly made?

Telegram, Lee to Bard, January 16, 1904
As I understand it, you made no positive promise to appoint Patton. After you had seen the boy you gave me the impression that you would appoint him during your absence when you received notification from War Department about June. On strength of this understanding Mr. Patton, after consulting with authorities, sent boy to Virginia Military Institute. If competitive examination is had cannot time be set so as to enable Patton to get furlough and also so that he can claim entrance under certificate from his school, if he is appointed. If you deem it proper to appoint without competitive examination I am sure you will make no mistake in appointing Patton. If you care to communicate with Major Strother Commandant Virginia Military Institute, Lexington, Virginia, he will assure you as to Patton's fitness and standing.

Letter, Major L. Harvie Strother to Mr. Patton, January 16, 1904
My dear George. I have a telegram from Senator Bard asking if I would grant George a furlough to attend informal competitive examination in Los Angeles in February. I answered yes if you requested. I am glad that George is going to be successful in his appointment. Don't you think if he is going to have to compete for the appoint-

ment, that he had better get him a tutor, who is familiar with the subjects on which he will be examined, and devote himself to that exclusively. It would be better if Bard would give him the appointment outright.

George is going well. He must have gained ten pounds or more. He seems to have the esteem and respect of all. *Must* resemble his *mother*. With love to you all.

Telegram, GSP, Jr., to his father, January 17, 1904

Commandant received this from Senator Bard: "Will you grant Cadet Patton furlough in February to attend informal competitive examination at Los Angeles of applicants for my recommendation of candidates for West Point appointment." Now suppose you see Mr Lee and arrange if possible for my examination at Washington. George.

Telegram, Mr. Patton to GSP, Jr., January 18, 1904

[Your] telegram received. I have wired Senator. Make no application for furlough till you hear from me.

Letter, Mr. Patton to GSP, Jr., January 19, 1904

After consulting Major Lee, I yesterday sent the Senator a telegram as follows.

"Telegram from my son stating that you asked Commandant if he could have furlough to attend competitive examination in February. I assume he can have furlough if desired, and will request it for him if necessary, but from personal knowledge, I know that three or four weeks absence from severe course at Lexington would be great detriment whether he would succeed in competitive test or not. Would it be possible for you to have examiners, in cases where applicant is actively pursuing his studies in a school outside of the state, to receive and consider official reports of standing in scholarship and conduct, covering his scholastic career, and excuse him from personal appearance?"

I have no reply to this as yet, but if one comes after this is mailed, I will mail a copy to you. In the meantime I am writing you this so that you may fully understand what is going on, and be prepared to decide on your course at the proper time. As I take it, the Senator must have received so many applicants that he finally decided on an informal competitive examination instead of an appointment as he of course has a perfect right to do. At the same time Major Lee and I feel that in acting on the assumption that the Senator had decided to appoint you, before he left for Europe, we were perhaps too sanguine, but feel justified under the circumstances. To compel you now, to leave V.M.I. for three or four weeks and stand competitive examination here is a hardship in many ways. I feel quite sure you can successfully pass the test, but still it is possible you would not do so, and in that event you would have lost that much out of your V.M.I. course, and it would inevitably affect your standing in your class. Of course if you got the West Point appointment, this would not make any material difference. The question, from all this, has presented itself to my mind, whether or not you would prefer to definitely give up the West Point Plan, and stay at the V.M.I., seeking to enter the army after graduation, there, by civil appointment, if you could get a civil appointment. There are some very obvious advantages about this plan, viz., you would gain one year in time, and you would have, at Lexington for the next three years, very much pleasanter conditions and surroundings than you can possibly have at West Point.

On the other hand, it may be assumed that if you have definitely settled on a military career, the West Point Diploma will be a benefit to you all through your military life. I do not like to determine the matter for you; think it all over and decide after mature consideration and consultation with Major Strother to whom you will show this letter. If Senator Bard decides he cannot permit you to be examined in the East, or to take your class marks in lieu of an actual examination, I think you need not greatly fear to come home in February and stand your chance. You might have to brush up a little on arithmetic and geography, but on all other subjects you would be mostly likely to stand all right; and besides, Senator Bard explained to me when I saw him, that his competitive examinations are informal in character, and only advisory to his own judgment, and that he takes into consideration many elements besides mere ability to pass competitive mental test.

Major Lee concurs with me in thinking you would have a very good show of coming out all right. If, therefore, you hear from me that there is no other course but to come home in February, and you make up your mind that you really want the West Point Career, you can apply, with my authority, to General Ship [Superintendent of VMI] for a thirty day furlough, and ask the General to make sight draft on me for money necessary to get you home. Get from the Agent at Lexington, a written itinerary by way of Chicago and the Santa Fe, and you will have no difficulty. You can wear your blouse uniform and overcoat all the way if you like.

Now, my dear boy, do not worry yourself over this matter, keep right on studying hard and doing as well as you have been. Consider the matter in all its bearings and when you decide, have no misgivings or after thoughts. You have done well always, and both your mother and I are proud of you, and our thoughts and prayers will be with you every moment as you consider the problem now presented. I feel perfectly confident that if you come home you will pass all right and get your appointment. I will telegraph fully all that is necessary.

Your mother and all at home join me in sending love and blessing. Your affectionate father, George S. Patton.

P.S. Since writing the foregoing and before mailing, I have received the following telegram from Senator Bard, "Washington, D.C. January 19, Your telegram 18th received. Commandant promises furlough when requested by you. Proposed informal examination will not involve absence for more than twelve days . . . Impracticable for committee to judge unless candidate personally present. Lee will have earliest possible notice of time of examination." This settles the matter as far as the necessity of returning home required is concerned, if you feel decided to persist in your determination to go through West Point. As I have stated in the foregoing letter, I do not like to decide this for you, but if you feel as I have always understood you did in reference to this matter, I do not think that you should fear to subject yourself to the required test. Doubtless the examination will be set for some time in February; as soon as I know the date I will request a furlough by telegram, and advise the Superintendent to supply you with necessary funds, and I will so arrange it, if possible, that you will have at least a week at home before the examination, during which you may recover from the fatigue of the trip as well as refresh yourself upon the subjects in which you may be examined. In the meantime make no change in your present course of hard work, and do not allow yourself to be upset or disconcerted by this matter. Perhaps it would be well for you to purchase, before starting upon your railway journey, a physical geography of the United States and an arithmetic, with which you can occupy your time on the way home. I believe that particular stress is laid upon the geography of our own country, and would advise you to go over this carefully state by state, refreshing yourself upon the names and location of the principal mountain ranges, rivers, capitols and such subjects as you know are usually required in examinations of this kind. Please show this letter to Col. Strother and General Ship, both of whom I feel sure will give you good advice in the matter.

Again with love from us all, I am your affectionate father

Letter, Mr. Patton to Colonel Strother, January 20, 1904

My dear Strother: I am presuming on kinship and "Auld Lang Syne" in calling upon you to give the benefit of your counsel and advice to my son George in the problem which has presented itself owing to the unexpected action of Senator Bard. I wrote George yesterday, a very full letter instructing him to show it to you. I desire to supplement this by a little more fully and confidential statement of the existing conditions. All of the circumstances point to the fact that the Senator unexpectedly found himself envolved in a political dilemma out of which he would be glad to extricate himself.

I had every reason to suppose that he had definitely made up his mind to appoint my son, and in fact, acted upon that impression when I sent him to Lexington. The senator explained to me and his attorney and most intimate friend here has also explained to me that he always regarded these competitive examinations as purely informal and simply intended to be advisory to his own judgment, in other words, if a candidate otherwise acceptable should prove himself glaringly deficient mentally, it would settle the matter. On the other hand, should one prove himself remarkably proficient mentally, and not otherwise suited to be an officer of the army, the decision would be otherwise. Under all the circumstances that exist, I feel very certain that George will be able to pass the competitive test required, the whole question remaining, is he sufficiently set in his determination to go into the army as a permanent career. If he is, I presume that you will concur with me in advising him that there is no doubt he should make every effort for the West Point Cadetship. If on the other hand, he felt willing to abandon his army idea, it would be much better for him to remain at the institute, but my fear, knowing him as I do, is that set notion which has persisted for so many years, will not be lightly abandoned and that if he did not abandon it in a moment of doubt or hesitation [meaning, rather, if he *did* abandon it], it would be a source of lasting regret to him thereafter. Therefore, I have refrained, in my letter as you will notice, from definitely deciding the matter for him. I am strongly of the opinion that he should be advised when he receives the proper notice, to come home and stand the test. Please talk fully with him and also make necessary explanations on his behalf to the Superintendent, so that when he receives my telegram he will be prepared to start at once. I presume that this letter will reach you before it becomes necessary for me, on account of the date of the examination, to notify him to return.

Thanking you for what you have done and will do in this matter, I am very truly

your kinsman, George S. Patton.

Telegram, Mr. Patton to GSP, Jr., January 22, 1904

Senator decides impracticable to make exception and sets February 15 for informal examination Los Angeles. Letter dated 19th should reach you Monday will explain fully. Am writing again today advising you to come on. Have great confidence in result. Am also writing superintendent to grant furlough from February 3d. And supply money. These should reach you by thirteenth [meaning, rather, the thirtieth]. Meantime stick to work and keep stand[ing in your class]. GSP.

Letter, Mr. Patton to GSP, Jr., January 22, 1904

The conditions are such that he is obliged to have competitive examination here on the 15th of February, and that it is impracticable to make any exceptions in your favor and permit you to be examined in the East.

. . . after very full consideration of the whole subject, and with the strong concurrence of Major Lee, [I am writing] to advise you to ask for a furlough, and to come home and stand the informal examination which has been decided upon. I have great confidence that you will be successful, and in view of your strong wish to enter the army, I do not feel that you should deprive yourself of the opportunity of entering it through West Point.

[He had written a full letter to General Ship, and was enclosing a copy of that letter.] After reading everything together, I feel sure that your judgment will coincide with mine that you should take the course I have suggested.

Then followed specific instructions. Make application to the Superin-

tendent for a 30-day furlough from around February 1; the Superintendent would supply the money Mr. Patton had forwarded. Purchase a
through ticket from Lexington to Pasadena via Cincinnati, Chicago, and
the Santa Fe Railroad; Mr. Patton enclosed an itinerary of the trip, together with suggestions on what to do if the trains were delayed because
of failure to make connections, a contingency possible at that time of year.
Get the ticket from the Agent at Lexington. Wire ahead for a sleeping
berth from Chicago to Pasadena on the limited train. Wire also for a
sleeping berth on the regular train following in case he failed to make
connections with the limited. Check trunk through from Lexington to
Pasadena on the ticket. Telegraph home the day he started from Lexington, and again when he made connections at Chicago, and later if any
delay ensued — so that Mr. Patton would know when to meet him. By
starting on February 2 or 3, George would have four or five days before
the examination to rest and study. By starting back for Lexington on the
16th, he would be back on the 22nd, so that if George failed to secure the
appointment, he would lose only about three weeks, which he could easily
make up without detriment to his class standing. If he received the appointment, Mr. Patton would instruct him on how to make the proper
application through General Ship for admission to West Point upon the
Superintendent's certification. In that case, George would remain in Lexington until June.

He continued:

It is highly probable that your Aunt Nannie will accompany you on
the trip East, and that your mother will join her later in the spring, so
that you will have quite a family party to see you off to West Point . . .
We are all looking forward with great joy and pleasure at the expectation of seeing you so soon.

In his letter to General Ship, Mr. Patton explained that he had confidently anticipated that George would receive the senatorial appointment
from California to West Point last fall and he hoped that George could
enter upon his certification from VMI, "which you stated was possible if
his standing should prove to justify it." Mr. Patton was virtually certain
that, according to the reports received from the school, George's standing
was sufficiently high to warrant the certification. Unfortunately, a complication had arisen. The senator felt obliged, instead of making an

"outright appointment," to call for an informal competitive examination. "From all the circumstances in the matter, and from some knowledge of the other applicants," Mr. Patton felt justified in believing that George stood "certainly the best chance of passing the required test," which had only advisory importance, along with such qualifications as "dignity, bearing and antecedence indicating the probability of a successful applicant as a useful officer in the army." He had advised George to apply for a furlough. George would return to VMI immediately after the exam.

Mr. Patton enclosed a draft on a New York bank to the treasurer of VMI in the amount of $290 — $165 to be applied to the bill rendered with the last report of his son, and $125 to be handed to George to buy his ticket and to pay for his traveling expenses.

If George obtained the appointment to West Point,

> I shall regret, in many ways, that he is not able to continue the full course at Lexington, but as he has definitely decided upon an army career, I feel that he should not be denied the benefit which is conferred by graduation from West Point if it is possible for him to secure this advantage.

Finally, Mr. Patton said he assumed there would be no difficulty securing the Superintendent's certification to avoid the necessity for George to take the entrance examination at the Military Academy. But if he was wrong in his assumption, would the Superintendent so notify him in order to permit Mr. Patton to arrange to have George prepared for the entrance exam to be held in May.

On January 23, 1904, Colonel R. A. Marr, the professor in charge of engineering, had a letter typed from George to Mr. E. O. Gerberding of Hueneme, Ventura County, California. Mr. Gerberding was Senator Bard's brother-in-law and looked after the senator's office at home. "Dear Sir," George wrote, "I am a candidate for appointment as Cadet at the U.S. Military Academy at West Point and in according with the instructions furnished me by United States Senator Thomas R. Bard I forward herewith the information desired." He gave his name and address, then stated: "Not only a bona fide resident but a native of California: born and raised at San Gabriel and have lived there over seventeen years." In his excitement he marked his birth date incorrectly as November 11, 1886, instead of 1885, but no one caught the error. He was 6 feet 1 inch tall, weighed 167 pounds. "I expect to appear in person before the Committee selected at such time between the dates of February 15th and 18th in Los Angeles, California and trust the Chairman of the Committee" — no doubt Mr. Gerberding — "will inform me at San Gabriel of the time and place it is desired to have candidates present themselves."

Attached to George's communication was a paper "To whom it may concern" signed by Colonel Marr:

I most heartily endorse the application of George S. Patton, Jr. . . . I have known Mr. Patton for seventeen years and have had him under close observation for some months and say without hesitation that he is far above the average young man. Mr. Patton will represent his State and district creditably at West Point as he is well endowed mentally, is in perfect health, is, in fact, a thoroughly wide-awake young man with a distinct and quiet personality. He does not use tobacco nor intoxicants and is moral and upright in character. Meeting and knowing as many young men as I do I desire to say that Mr. Patton will hold his own in a set of selected young men with dignity and ability.

Also attached was another commendation by Colonel Marr.

His rating in his class is very high. He will doubtless come out "distinguished" at the end of the session should he remain till that time a cadet. His average class mark in Algebra, English, History, and Drawing [nothing was said about Latin] is well above 90. His appearance and manner are pleasing and soldierly, and he is regarded as eminently trustworthy and promising by his Instructors and officers here.

Finally, the VMI surgeon wrote out his certificate. George was

entirely sound physically and of excellent physical development. Height 6 feet and 1 inch; weight 167 pounds. Chest 38. Age 18 years 2 months and will continue development rapidly. His eyes are normal. Has slight catarrh, no other weakness.

On the evening of January 26, George fell out from dinner roll call and brought certificates to the Marrs. The colonel had them typed, mailed the originals to Mr. Gerberding, and sent copies to San Gabriel in case the originals were lost in transit and "also that you [Mrs. Patton] and George [Mr. Patton] may see what has been sent." On the following day, young George carried all the papers to Colonel Strother, who was also preparing a letter for Mr. Gerberding.

Letter, G. A. Dewey to Mr. Patton, January 26, 1906
   I have a bill against your son for one month's coaching in Latin, which he requests me to send you: month ending January 21. Same amounts to fifteen dollars.

The VMI Superintendent wrote Mr. Patton that everything was being attended to, George would have his furlough, and the Pattons were, in his opinion, following the right course.

   Of course if George is to go into the Army, he should if possible pass through West Point. I had a talk with him last week. If he maintains his past record — and I doubt not he will — he can get certificate . . . George is clever, and I believe he will win in the competitive. While I shall be sorry to lose him, I wish him success — Kind regards to Mrs. Patton.

Still worrying that something might go wrong, Mr. Patton played one more card. He wrote on January 28 to the Honorable James McLachan, a member of the U. S. House of Representatives from California, marking the envelope personal and confidential. "My dear McLachan," Mr. Patton wrote, the generous offer McLachan had made of an appointment to Annapolis had been refused because of George's strong determination to enter West Point. At that time, Mr. Patton had strong hopes that Senator Bard had made up his mind to give his son the appointment. "I remember that you asked me whether Senator Bard had promised to make the appointment, to which I replied that he had not, but that from the circumstances of his interview and of his departure for Europe, I permitted myself to believe that he had definitely made up his mind [to do so]." In that belief, Mr. Patton had sent his son to "a Military School in Virginia a certificate from which admits him to West Point under very favorable circumstances."

Unfortunately, Mr. Patton continued, his assumption was in error.

Senator Bard had determined not to make an outright appointment but was calling a competitive examination.

> In doing this Senator Bard is perfectly consistent with anything he has ever said to me, and I have no right or disposition to complain of it . . . [But] believing as I did that the matter was practically settled, I made no further efforts in other directions, and of course at this time it is too late to expect that there are any existing vacancies to be filled this year which would be available to me, with one possible exception; you stated to me in our interview to which I have referred, that in case your appointee should fail to enter, or having entered, should fail to pass the first years examination, that it would again place in your hands an appointment to West Point. I do not know whether either of these contingencies has occurred or is likely to occur, but if either has, I wish to ask you to give me this appointment. If you are in a position to do so, I can give you, as I explained to you before, the very highest personal, business and political endorsements . . .
>
> It is needless for me to add, that until a definite occasion arises, I would ask you to regard this request as confidential. With personal regards and best wishes, I am Sincerely your friend, George S. Patton.

Mr. Gerberding notified George on January 30 that an informal, competitive exam would be held at the Hotel Van Nuys, Broadway, Los Angeles, on Monday, February 15, 1904, at 10 A.M. Since the West Point Academic Board might accept in lieu of the regular entrance examination for West Point a certificate of qualification, a candidate who contemplated using certification instead of the regular examination — which would be held at the Presidio, San Francisco, on May 3 — was to ask the Adjutant of the Military Academy whether the Academic Board would probably accept the certification he planned to present.

On the same day, Stephen Cutter Clark informed Mr. Patton that George had written to ask for certification in plane geometry, physiology, and ancient history. Mr. Clark enclosed the certificate, which stated that George had studied "the five books of Plane Geometry, Ancient History, and physiology . . . in these subjects he received above the average marks, and excelled in History." Mr. Clark wanted to add a testimonial to his character, but George had said he would have that from the VMI, and consequently Mr. Clark had refrained from doing so. If Mr. Patton wanted a fuller report, Mr. Clark would be more than glad to send one.

Letter, Col. L. H. Strother, Commandant of Cadets, VMI, to Mr. Patton, January 30, 1904

My dear George. I have your letter and you don't know what a pleasure it will be to do any thing for George. He seems very capable of taking care of himself and his views quite agree with mine, which makes me feel that they are quite correct: I think your idea of his spending the time en route [home] in studying is excellent. I fear and do not like these competitive examinations but I trust that every thing will come out well, and feel sure that it will . . . The fourth class or rather some of them distinguished themselves the other night, but George had the good sense not to be in it, or the good luck not to be caught. With love for you all.

Letter, L. H. Strother, Major, 28th U.S. Infantry, Commandant of Cadets, VMI, to Gerberding, January 31, 1904

As Commandant of cadets, Virginia Military Institute, George S. Patton Jr Has come under my special observation. He is a young man of exemplary habits and excellent mental ability and attainments. If he is appointed to the U.S. Military Academy he will acquit himself with credit to his state. He has an aptitude for a military life.

Certificate, Stephen Cutter Clark, Principal, Classical School for Boys, February 1, 1904

During his [young Patton's] attendance at the school he was attentive to his duties and was proficient in the studies pursued by him excelling in History. In his recitations and examinations he showed himself an earnest and conscientious student. He was always very gentlemanly in his behavior to all the teachers and to his fellow students; a thoroughly clean, pure, conscientious young man, deservedly a favorite with all.

Early in February, someone prepared a letter for George's signature to Colonel Albert L. Mills, the West Point Superintendent. George had the honor to request that a properly attested certificate from the VMI Superintendent be accepted in lieu of a regular entrance examination. He also asked permission to take the physical examination somewhere in the east in order to avoid the long journey to the Presidio in San Francisco.

On February 4, 1904, Mr. Gerberding, signing himself "of the Committee," informed Mr. Patton that all the necessary certificates and recommendations had been "duly received by me" and all would be placed before the committee on the 15th.

Mr. Patton wrote Colonel Mills on February 11 and explained the fact of the committee. Since it would be impossible for the senator, who was in Washington, to receive the committee's report before the 20th, even if the senator made the appointment immediately, there would be only about 20 days before March 15. Mr. Patton understood "from the circular forwarded to me by you" that an appointee had to have his certification accepted by the Academic Board before that date. His son would be entitled to a good certificate because of "his stand in his class (the fourth) being distinguished at the semi annual examinations just held." If his son obtained the appointment, Mr. Patton was anxious to have the application transmitted in the proper form. If his appointment was made and certification accepted, would it be possible for his son to pass his physical examination somewhere near Lexington, and if so, to whom should he apply?

> I trust that you will excuse me for the trouble that I am giving you in this matter, and attribute it to my anxiety, in case my son receives this appointment, that he shall comply with all the requirements of West Point with regard to his entrance thereto.

Colonel Mills answered promptly. If George secured the appointment, "a satisfactory certificate that he is a regular student of the Virginia Military Institute in good standing" would be accepted, and "you can arrange for his physical examination at any Army Post near Lexington" by applying to the Adjutant General.

George's class standing was highly satisfactory according to the report of February 15 to his parents. There were 93 students in his class, and among them George stood 9 in mathematics, 10 in Latin, 2 in English, 2 in history, and 6 in drawing. His "General Standing" was "Excellent." He had received no demerits for behavior since he had arrived the previous September.

Meanwhile, George studied on the train as he traveled toward California. He memorized the list of American colonies and the dates of their founding, the Presidents of the United States and their parties and terms, the Confederate States that had seceded, and Confederate and Union (in that order) generals. He also practiced his spelling of geographical terms, among them Algiers, Esquimaux, Cairo, Canandaigua, Dubuque, Chautauqua, Bologna, Honolulu, Himalaya, Gibraltar, Mediterranean, Schuylkill, Thames, and Morocco (sic).

On the day before the informal examination, Mr. Patton was still carefully reading the West Point circular. He was still worrying about whether all the intricate details had been properly attended to. He was still nervous even though his friend Judge Lee, formerly Major Lee, was a member of Senator Bard's examining committee. His uneasiness was hardly lessened when the examination was postponed one day.

Letter, Mr. Patton to L. H. Strother and R. A. Marr, February 16, 1904

Dear Fellows: I want to thank you for all the trouble you took in sending on George's certificate, and for your other many acts of kindness to him all of which I assure you is deeply appreciated both by his mother and myself. The competitive examination (informal) was held this morning, and George starts for Lexington tomorrow and I am sending this with him.

If George received the appointment, Mr. Patton continued, he would undoubtedly be informed by telegram. It would then be necessary to forward promptly an application asking for consideration of a certificate from VMI. Mr. Patton had written a letter to General Ship, which George was to deliver, and he was sending several suggested forms of application

for your consideration . . . I am so far away from the scene of action, and am so deeply interested in seeing that there is no hitch in case he gets the appointment that I am asking you two to please take this matter in charge for me and look over the printed circular of West Point requirements and all matters in connection with it, and see that everything is done in proper order . . . Again thanking you both for what you have done and for what I know you will do in this matter, I am Your friend and fellow-cadet.

The morning paper in Los Angeles on February 18 carried the news that the informal examining committee had recommended three young men to Senator Bard.

Letter, John B. Miller, President of the Edison Electric Company of Los Angeles, to Senator Bard, February 18, 1904

I see by this morning's paper that George Patton, son of George S. Patton who lives near me, is one of the three young men from whom you will select an appointee for West Point. I have known the young man in question ever since I have lived in California, and know him to be not only remarkably intelligent but also of strong character, and with absolutely irreproachable habits . . . George Patton is over six feet high, admirably proportioned, and in perfect robust health. He looks like a soldier and, while he is young and extremely modest, he has the self-possession and the habit of self-control which come with good birth, good breeding and good character. For all of these reasons I wish to commend him to you as eminently fitted to do great credit to you as your appointee, and I know that a great number of the very best known men of Los Angeles and Pasadena share this opinion with me.

I am writing this letter at the request or suggestion of no one, and trust you will not feel that I am intruding in doing so, but, on the other hand, hope that the letter may be of some service to you, and I know that if it, in any way, leads you to select George Patton for this appointment that it will always be a matter of congratulation to everybody concerned.

With kindest personal regards, I am Yours faithfully.

Letter, John B. Miller to Mr. Patton, February 18, 1904

My dear Mr. Patton: — I have just sent this off to Senator Bard as I felt it was my duty as a patriotic citizen to do so. I hope that other men who are acquainted with George, and are as well posted as I am, will do likewise; at least it can do no harm. Wishing you and George all success, I am Yours faithfully.

H. E. Huntington, president of the Los Angeles Railway Company, wrote to Senator Bard on the same day. He was taking the liberty of and asking pardon for speaking a good word in behalf of young George Patton, entirely unsolicited and only because Mr. Huntington had observed the young man personally and had been strongly impressed with his good habits and promising character. "He is unquestionably of the kind of timber that we want to train up for the future defense of our country." He would, of course, hardly urge George's appointment over others more deserving or over others who had passed the examination with higher grades. But there were many qualities besides mere book knowledge that were important for future officers, and besides, Huntington had the impression that George had stood well in the examination too.

Letter, Bard to Huntington, February 24, 1904

I note your statements commendatory of Mr. George S Patton Jr. . . .

The report of the board appointed by me to examine the various applicants has not as yet been received; but I have noticed in the Los Angeles papers a reference to the examination and also that Mr. Patton's name is among three from whom I shall select the principal candidate.

I am pleased to receive your commendation of young Mr. Patton, as it tends to confirm a favorable impression which I have formed concerning him. The matter will be given early consideration.

Letter, Mr. Patton to General Scott Ship, February 26, 1904

I am very anxious, if he receives this appointment, that there shall be no slip in the filing of his certificate before the 15th of March, and I will be very grateful to you if you will see that there is no delay in this matter, and will telegraph me fully that you have taken the necessary steps.

Letter, GSP, Jr., to Mr. Patton, probably late February 1904

I am feeling quite well but this week have not done very well in algibra I hope to do better next week as I will be back in the swing again . . . I went down to see Miss Maggie last night and she told me to tell mama that Louis is able to sit up and eat quite a few solid things. How should [I] envite myself down to Miss Maggies for dinner? Tell mama to write and tell me how but *do not* let miss M. know that I asked you such a thing for she would be terribly insulted, be sure and remember not to even mention such a thing if you write to her. And as for not trying to get that appointment why that is utter nonsense; for if I should have to study Latin here for another year I would surly die, or go crazy. Be sure and both[er] Mr. Bard until he gives it to me. To day is the second Saturday I have been back . . . Dikeman, Caffy, Owens the sergeant major, and half a dozen others are under arrest for gambling and Dikeman and Caffy have 25 [demerits] each becas the playing was in their room. I guess that this will kill Dikemans last chance for corp. Tuesday I was on guard for the first time since my return and I succeeded in getting commendants orderley the highes choice you can get for you do not have to do any thing except carry one dispatch from the sergeant Major to the O.C. [officer in charge]. Infact Com. orderely is merely an honorary position given as an insentive for the men to dress up well . . . I must now stop and shave; Your loving son George S. Patton, Jr. "The coming corp"

Telegram, Bard to Mr. Patton, March 3, 1904

I have today nominated your son as principal West Point. Will he return Virginia. Telegraph me where [War] Department may address him later.

Telegram, Mr. Patton to Bard, March 3, 1904

Please accept grateful thanks. Son is now at Virginia Military Institute Lexington. Please ask War Department to forward notification to him there as soon as possible so he may have time before March fifteenth to file required certificate at West Point.

The Los Angeles *Times,* by direct wire from Washington, announced on March 4, 1904, that Senator Bard had nominated George S. Patton of San Gabriel to be a cadet at West Point. Milton S. Stewart of Santa Barbara and Charles McHenry Pond of San Francisco were the alternates. "These young men secured the highest percentages at the examination held February 16 at Los Angeles."

Letter, Bard to Mr. Patton, March 4, 1904

I have reason to be confident that your son's career at school and as an army officer will be such as to commend my nomination.

Letter, Mr. Patton to GSP, Jr., March 4, 1904

My dear Son: I am unable to tell you how much gratified we all were this morning by the receipt of the following telegram from Senator Bard . . . I immediately telegraphed to you . . . and also wired Senator Bard, as follows . . . I suppose that before this reaches you, you will have received notification from the War Department, and will have presented the letter to General Ship, asking him to see to the proper filing of your request for consideration of certificate before the 15th of March . . . you should make application to the War Department to have the place of your physical examination designated somewhere in the East, as suggested by Colonel Mills.

I don't see now how there can be any further difficulty in your way. In case anything should arise which seems to jeopardize matters, you must telegraph me fully and consult freely with Colonel Strother, who I know will do anything in his power for you.

It has been a long and tiresome quest, but in your success I am sure that you will be more than compensated. It is a serious step that you have taken, thus fixing your future career for life, and I am sure that you have done so with a full appreciation of all that it means. While your mother and myself will naturally regret to have your life practically separated from our own, yet we both feel that in the gratification of your ambition in this respect, we are satisfied, because that which a man desires most strongly to do in this world, if he has really given it careful consideration, is what he is generally most fitted to do.

Of course, you will write a proper and appreciative letter to Senator Bard as soon as you receive the notice of your appointment. The proper manner of addressing such a letter would be, — Hon. Thomas R. Bard, U. S. Senator, Washington, D.C. I wish you would send me a copy of your letter to him. I wish you would also write a letter to Hon. H. T. Lee, Trust Building, Los Angeles, California, expressing to him your gratitude for the strong interest which he has taken in this matter . . .

Do not let this appointment interfere in any way with your duties at the V.M.I., it will stand you in good stead, both in the matter of your certificate and in many other ways if you attend to your duties up to the last moment there as if you intended to stay there permanently.

Your mother and sister join me in sending love and congratulations.

Your affectionate father, George S. Patton.

My dear Boy — I dictated the foregoing before going to lunch — and now I am writing to tell you all about it. It seems it was in the [Los Angeles] Times — and everybody at the [California] Club knew about it — I opened Champagne — and we all drank to your health — It seems that after the examination here — Several men — among others Mr. Huntington, and others wrote to Senator Bard and strongly urged your appointment.

I enclose newspaper clippings to show you how famous you are.

You cannot know how proud we feel — and how gratified that you have won your first promotion in the battle of life. If you keep your head level — and work hard — avoiding the pitfalls of dissipation into which so many fall — you may look forward to an honorable career — as a soldier of your country. All signs seem to indicate that the world is about to enter upon one of those periods of war, that mark the transition from one stage to another in the march of progress. — It is the decree of Providence that our own country shall play a leading — and probably a decisive part in the events which are to usher in the new era — You have in you good soldier blood — and the opportunity before you is one to inspire your earnest effort. Be honorable — brave — clean — and you will reap your merited reward. Love to Aunt Nannie [at Lexington] — and a thousand blessings from your father — George S. Patton.

On March 5, Senator Bard's private secretary sent George a communication from the Adjutant General's office, invited George's attention to the War Department circular concerning candidates, and sent a blank form for him to indicate his acceptance. There was a space on the latter for his father's signature signifying consent, but since it was impossible to send the form back to the west coast in time, Mr. Gates suggested that the acceptance be sent immediately with an explanation of the circumstances that prevented Mr. Patton from signing. Perhaps George could attach as evidence of his father's assent the telegram from Mr. Patton, which Gates enclosed, and a recent letter from Mr. Patton, also enclosed. George was also to say he could get formal consent later if necessary.

On the same day, the Acting Adjutant General sent Bard a telegram saying that young Patton could be examined at Fort McHenry, Maryland.

Letter, GSP, Jr., to Senator Bard, March 6, 1904

I have the honor to acknowledge your letter of the fourteenth inst. [meaning, rather, the fourth] and I wish to express to you my deep sense of gratitude for the honor you have done me. I believe that I realize the gravity of the position in which this appointment places me and I will try to do my duty both at West Point and afterwards in the army to the best of my ability. Thanking you again for this appointment. I am Very Respectfully

Letter, GSP, Jr., to his father, March 13, 1904

Dear Papa: Well I guess I have got it. And I am beastly glad and am sure you are. As for Mr. Bard I rank him and the pope on an equal plane of hollyness.

Everything is fixed, the certificate as you already know has been sent, but as yet I have received no answer. We hade to fill out and send the old certificate which you sent to Gen. Ship. It is not exactly the same form as the new ones but the General wrote a personal litter to Mills explaining that it was only the short ness of the time which prevented our using a new form and he said that in his opinion there would be no complications. As soon as I get an answer I will telegraph you. The paper for which I required your signature was my acceptance of the appointment. The department received it all right and also in accordance with my request changed the place of my examination from San Francisco to Fort McHenry Baltimore Maryland. The examination will take place on the third of May before nine o'clock in the morning. If I pass I think that it might be a good idea for me to resign from this place about the 25th of that month in order that I may get rested for the Hell to come. Of course I only suggest this course and have not yet looked into it. If I would miss much solid geometry by adopting it, why I would refrain.

To day I was premoted from the second to the first section of Latin but I fear that my premotion was due more to the extreme bumness of the rest of the section than to my own brilliancy. Though I did succeed in getting a mark of over 90 in it last week.

Here is a copy of the letter I wrote Mr. Bard . . . (It was composed without help and corrected by Curtis [a classmate]) . . .

In extenuation of this litter it must be remembered that at the time of its composition I was very much excited. It is nearly time for tattoo so I must stop. I have a strong belief that my certificate will be accepted all right or even if it is not in correct form that I will be given an opportunity to send another. Don't you bother about it for old Billy will fix it all right. He has been very kind indeed and so has the "Beam."

With love to all Your loving son George S. Patton Jr.

(Correct Spilling please).

Letter, GSP, Jr., to his father, March 18, 1904

Dear Papa; At last after all these many years this thing is finally setteled. I have just at this moment received the acceptance of my certificate, and now it only remains for the government inspectors to examin this hundred and seventy pounds of meat (which forms the

earthly cage of my imortal soal.) and if they consider that I am sufficiently sound to be killed, I suppose that like the Christmas turkey I
will be admitted to the mental fatning pen at the point [West
Point].

You see that tonight is the first time that I have felt realy sure of
getting through, and can at last stop worrying; I say "can stop" but I
wont for already I have begun to fear lest I fail in the physical which
up til now I have felt sure of. I guess that I inherit a good deal of
your sanguine character . . .

I was worried, fearing that the infernal red tape of this intensely
democratic Gov. might not allow the acceptance of a certificate a year
old: But it did.

I am sorry that I have been such a nusance to you about this business but according to that paper I signed I guess you will be freed
from care on my account for at least eight years.

Please thank the California Club. for the literary effort on their
part on my behalf and tell them that when I become dictator I will
send them my picture and authograph to be hung up along with the
moose head fish and the bear . . .

The study here is a lot harder than it wase before I went away. The
first week I got back I only got 7.8 in geometry (the worst mark I ever
got here) and that scared me so that I began to study hard and I have
had no time to do any thing else. I should have written but I kept
putting it off. Well every thing is now settled And with the help of
God and a vigerous use of your influence I have the appointment.

Your loving and greatful son

Letter, GSP, Jr. (from The Stafford Hotel, Washington Place, Balti-
more, Maryland) to Miss A. Wilson (c/o Miss Maggie Freeland, Lex-
ington, Va.), May 4, 1904

Dear Aunt Nannie I got here all right. Two other cadets are here
with me. My eyes are better I am now spraying my throat. Good
night Your loving nephew G S Patton Jr

Letter, GSP, Jr. (from V.M.I.), to Thomas R. Bard, May 7, 1904

On last Tuesday I stood at Fort McHenry Baltimore the Physical
Examination for West Point, and the Surgeon who gave it, told me
that I had passed. His statement of course is not official for he has to
forward his report to West Point and it is from there that I shall
receive my final statement. I do not believe that the authorities there

ever reverse the decision of any of the examining Surgeons. This being the case I think that I am entirely certain of entering the Academy in June. When I do enter I hope that I shall be able to maintain the reputation of California and by my conduct there repay you at least in some small measure for your goodness in appointing me. Trusting that my desire be fulfilled I am Very Respectfully George S. Patton, Jr.

Letter, Assistant Adjutant General, War Department to GSP, Jr., May 24, 1904

The report of recent examination received in Washington, informs me that you have met the requirements for admission and that you will be regularly admitted as a Cadet upon reporting in person to the Superintendent of the Academy on 16 June 1904, between 8 a.m. and 12 m. This notification confers no right to enter the Academy unless you report for admission on the date specified. Please acknowledge receipt.

CHAPTER 5

West Point: Turned Back

"running with my usual eagerness"

GSP, Jr., "My Father," *1927*

I left for West Point before graduation [exercises at Virginia Military Institute] but was told by Colonel Strother the commandant that I was to be first Corporal [the highest cadet appointment for second year students].

Between V.M.I and West Point we visited Richmond and went to the scene of the seven days battle [during the Civil War]. In Richmond Papa showed me the statue of Washington looking at the Capitol and pointing to the Prison and said it was prophetic of the future of legislators.

Papa went up to West Point with me the day before I entered. That afternoon while walking around, all the cadets saluted thinking from his bearing that he must be an officer.

George Patton hoped to be the cadet adjutant in his senior year at West Point. This position was conferred by the tactical officers on the cadet who exemplified soldierly conduct and who had demonstrated the ability to command and to impose discipline. Usually a tall and handsome fellow who dressed to perfection, the adjutant was a "showboat." He was at the center of the stage during cadet parades, the person who lined up the companies marching onto the field, took the reports of the company commanders, transmitted them to the First Captain, and read orders and announcements to the members of the cadet corps standing in ranks.

Mr. Patton had expected to have this appointment when he had been a student at VMI, but instead had been named First Captain, the highest cadet rank. Perhaps George wished the same thing would happen to him. More likely, he aspired to the lesser position of adjutant for he probably felt he could hardly equal his father's performance as a cadet.

Letter, GSP, Jr., to his mother, June 21, 1904

Dear Mama; West Point is pretty nice and so far I have been treated a lot better than at V.M.I. The corps are quite nice and they never touch you or sware. We have to take a bath every night and have but eight minutes to take it in. They make us shave every day and the only time we get to do this is before rev[eille]. This is also the only time we are allowed or have time to write except on Sunday. So you musent expect a very copious correspondence on my part for I dont like to get up at five o'clock. The food here is fine. There is lots of variety and we have dessert twice a day, chocolate and coffee in the morning and ice tea and milk at night. The table-cloth is changed every day.

There will be three plebes in a room this year. The two fellows who I am in with now are very nice and work hared and try to keep the room and them selves clean but they are not gentlemen in the sence of being refined and using good grammar. They are just very respectable middle class fellows. Still unless I can find some other fellows who are gentlemen and also students, I may room with these two all year. None of the things I brought were of any use to me except my under clothes and I wish I new some way of getting rid of them so that I could have an empty trunk . . . Did Beatrice get the flowers. I was sorry that I did not get a twenty dollar bunch as I had to turn in all my money here and so might just as well have spent it. Dont send me any money or any thing else as we have no place or room to keep or use it. Besides cadets are not permitted to receive bundles of any kind. It is nearly rev. now and I have to shave so good by. Your loving son Geo. S. Patton Jr.

Letter, GSP, Jr., to his father, July 3, 1904

Dear Papa; Your letter came last night and I was very glad to see that you had gotten home safe. I have written to mama or Aunt Nannie every Sunday. It is the only time I have as when ever we have nothing else to do we have cleaning formation. That is the most disagreeable thing to me in all of the drill.

We had a military funeral for the dead proffessor in mathematic and it was fine all the cadets and troops stationed here were in it besides about sixty officers of a Mass[achusetts] militia regement and the plebes. The body was born on a gun carriage and general Mills and all the officers walked behind it while a soldier led his horse all draped in black behind them. The boots sword and gloves and saddle were on the horse. When the three vollies were fired they were pretty bad I think the V.M.I. can do it much better.

To day we went to Cullum Hall to hear a Fourth of July oration by a cadet. It was good and described what the modern soldier was and what he stood for. Every one clapped and I believe they all agreed with the speaker. I didn't. Infact from what I have seen here and at the Institute I belong to a different class a class perhaps almost extinct or one which may have never existed yet as far removed from these lazy, patriotic, or peace soldiers as heaven is from hell. I know that my ambition is selfish and cold yet it is not a selfishnes for instead of sparing me, it makes me exert my self to the utter most to attain an end which will do neither me nor any one else any good. Of course I may be a dreamer but I have a firm conviction I am not and in any case I will do my best to attain what I consider — wrongly perhaps — my destiny.

I have been catching a good deal of *hell* lately because in an unguarded moment I said that we braced [stood at attention] harder at V.M.I. than here. Ever since that accursed speech all the corps have been trying to show me my error and they have succeeded . . .

I must stop now and write a letter to mama.

Letter, GSP, Jr., to his father, July 10, 1904

Dear Papa; We are in plebe camp at last and it is raining but the tents are quite dry and nice; they are much more comfortable than the rooms in barracks for sleeping purposes and we have mosquito nets to keep off insects besides there are no bed-bugs, there were quite a few in barracks, I am tenting with Ayres and a fine fellow his mother is one of the Fairfaxes of Virginia and he is strong for ancestors.

They dont allow a upper classman to brace or even speak roughly to a plebe and one of the corps has been busted already, for merely bracing Marshal in ranks. I think that they are almost too easy on us for our own good. On the other hand we are never allowed to go out of camp and when ever we are not drilling we are forced to clean our guns mine is so clean that it is shocking already. To morrow we begin drill with cannons and machine guns also we continue Infantry drill. In the after noon we have dancing and some times lectures . . . If you can please get me a wrist-watch one of those that fit in a little case and straps to your wrist get as thin a watch as you can and get a nice looking strap. I would not ask for this watch but upperclassmen are always asking plebes for the time and there is no place to carry my own watch. I dont want an expensive one . . . That trouble I mentioned about bracing is all over and I am feeling fine.

Letter, GSP, Jr., to Beatrice, July 10, 1904

Dear Beatrice; At last, after all these many years I am in West Point and what is more in "plebe camp." At times I can scarcely believe my good luck, but at other moments particularly at drill it does not require much imigination to see an realize where I am. Infact drill here is very "bracing" . . . I am now resting upon the floor and writin this by the light of a single candle whose feeble light is almost hidden by a vast and ever growing clowd of mosquitoes. My tent mate is on guard and I am in solitary possession of a tent five feet by eight, indeed if General Sherman's definition of war be right west point *is* war. But perhaps you are not acquainted with the great soldiers views of war . . . I certainly am glad to know that I am missed and that you would like to see me and I hope that you know me so well as to make it needless for me to say how often I wish I were with you all.

Letter, GSP, Jr., to Beatrice, July 1904

You should see me dance [the part of the] girl. I am simply perfect. The dancing master stood in open mouthed admiration and watched me, or so I thought when all at once he grabbed his head and shouted in a terrible voice Mr. Moon, time, oh time! Mr. Moon was standing about ten feet behind me, and as he looks like he is trying to walk a tight-rope when he dances I fear that the Masters attention was attracted by him more than by my dancing.

Letter, GSP, Jr., to his father, July 17, 1904

I dont much like the prospect of parade. The dress hats are very heavy and uncomfortable especially in hot weather . . . the betallion went out on practice march. When we got out in the hills we formed a line of skirmishers about two miles long and some men were detailed to break through it. I was stationed at a salient formed by a hill covered with brush with a road on the right of it. There was a deep gully with stones and brush running along the base of the hill, now the obvious place where a man would hide was in the brush on the side of the hill . . . but I knew that in that brush was just where the scout would look and according to the rules if he saw a sentinal and covered him with his gun before he was seen the sentinal would have to let him pass. Knowing this I crossed the gulley and lay down in some grass scarcely a foot high on the plain in front. I had been there about two hours when I saw a head jump up from behind a bush. I covered it and when it raised the third time I pulled the trigger — the click of the bolt scared [him] and he run for of course he did not know he was dead. When I finally came up to him he was very mad at being caught. I was highly praised for my remarkable hiding capacity . . .

I am rather sorry in a way that I went to V.M.I for I seem to have used up all my running capacity. I have gotten so I dont care whether I amount to any thing or not but I am trying to over-come this somnistic condition and work. Still two rat years in succession are very depressing . . .

The guard duty here is very hard we have to go on every six days for a 24 hour tour. Out of this we walk four reliefs of two hours each two at night and two in the day but though we are allowed to go to bed at night none of us can take off even so much as a glove and of course it is not very much fun sleeping in full uniform . . .

The corps goes back to barracks on the 28 of August and we begin studdying on the first of september I shall be rather glad when we do this and I at last find out just what my chances of being able to stick are . . . please send me a few five cent stamps to write to mama dont forget the stamps. Your loving son

Letter, GSP, Jr., to his father, July 24, 1904

Dear Papa; You have not written for nearly two weeks or at least I have not received a letter so please write soon . . . I have not received a letter from mama for some time but suppose she is alright. I am very well indeed and my stomach is in fine order, a state probably due to the fact that I have had no canday since the day I entered. This is the longest time I have ever gone with out it since I can remember and the effect certainly is good.

We went on another practice march yesterday but the enemy did not come my way so I got no glory but a lot of hard work.

. . . Most of the men here are nice fellows but very few indeed are born gentlemen infact the only ones of that type are Southerners. I have not yet settled on my roommates but believe I will live with Ayres and Marshal. Both are gentlemen both V.M.I. men and both are pretty studious, at least sufficiently so as not to bother me. I think it will be best to room with them, for if I were to room with some common man even if he were a student I could not go about with him and I would not like to live with one class and go with another . . .

In my last letter I said that I had lost the capacity for running. Well the mere expression of that thought in writing seemed to disepate it for ever since then I have been running with my usual eagerness. But to get a high corp here a man has to be in the first ten men or else be the sun of an officer and since I am afraid that I cant be the one and am not the other I am in rather a bad way. Still I hope that I get some office for I know with out a doubt that I will make a much better officer than any of the present third class do. Beatrice sent me a little silver soldier for my watch fob. I hope there was no hidden sarcasm in it and that she did not mean I was a tin soldier.

I must write to mama now

Letter, GSP, Jr., to his father, July 31, 1904

Dear Papa; I was very glad to get your letter and I am also glad that you did not get that wrist-watch as it will hardly be necessary this year and might seem out of place on a plebe. I would like two dollars in your next letter as I had to borrow some money and would like to pay it back as soon as possible. Don't forget to send me five *five cent* stamps in your next letter for if you dont I will not be able to write to mama . . .

I will be in confinement next week for not knowing an order on guard. The confinement does not make any difference as plebes have to stay in their tents any how but I hate to get reported especially as I knew the order but did not understand the O.D. [officer of the day] when he asked me . . . Our whole class will have more demerits than any preceding class for since the upper class-men are not allowed to speak to us or correct us, they naturally bone us [give demerits] and they are quite right. Indeed I think that the system which they have adopted here of absolute forbarence towards plebes, will ruin the academy in a very few years. I have not one fifth the respect for an upper class man here that I had at the institute, and with out respect it is impossible to have good discipline. To day I drew my first pay that is I signed some kind of a roll for it. I think that it is about fifty two dollars but dont know and care even less . . . please also send Dr. Campbell his money at once or write and ask him whether it has been paid or not. He sent me some thing I dont know whether it was a bill or a receipt and have lost it so am unable to assure my self. You had better write at once for I would not like people in Lexington to think I do not pay my bills. Well plebe camp is more than half over and soon we will be in barracks and to study which I hate more each day . . . With lots of love your loving son

Letter, GSP, Jr., to his father, August 7, 1904

They have almost stopped bracing us now and it is a lot easier than the V.M.I. was: when the second class returnes and we get back to barracks it may get bad again but I hardly think it will . . .

Yesterday we had a practice march in which the batalion formed the advance guard for a large army supposed to be advancing in rear. I was the leading man of the left flanking group . . . and you ought to have seen the pase I set. My corp was a city fellow and he nearly died . . . I try not to get boned but cant seem to manige it. I get skined for some foolish offense such as yawning in ranks or something equally foolish still I think that I am better off than the majority . . . Is the new steamer running yet and how are the crowds at the Island. It must be just about the hight of the season now. Has Mr. Huntington sold any of his numerous parks yet and is civilization still a[s] rampant as ever or has nature gained the upper hand and dryness reigns supreme. I must get ready for Perad [parade] now so good-by. Your loving son.

Letter, GSP, Jr., to his father, August 15, 1904

Dear papa: It is just two months to day since I first got to "hell-on-the Hudson," and it seemes nearly as many years . . . though the intervening time has passed very rapidly. Last monday we bueried another general and it was raining and we went in rain-coats. It was very impressive and the muffeled drums were great. Our vollies were pretty good too. I certainly think it is worth going in the army just to get a military funeral. I would like to get killed in a great victory and then have my body born between the ranks of my defeated enemy escorted by my own regiment and have my spirit come down and revil in hearing what people thought of me. But I am afraid that I have not got enough sence or persistance . . . I get put in the front rank all the time and have been complimented on several ocasions . . .

I had quite a little episode on guard the other night. I saw three cadets coming down the post. They spread out and prepaired to surround me. While I was watching one another rushed at me from behind. I turned and charged him and he dodged. I just missed him then they closed in and as I knew they were merely trying to bother me and get my gun I said "I will bayoned the first man who comes nearer than six pases" (which is the proscribed distance for talking at night) they talked a little more then one made a grab at me. I shook him off and drove my bayonet in to the second as hard as I could. Now these new bayonets slip down into a case behind the gun just like a ram-rod used to and when you fix them you merely pull them out and fasten them with a catch. Now before I had gone on post these fellows had opened the catch, so when I struck this man the bayoned slid down into its case and only the muzzle struck him but this had sufficient force to knock him about five feet. The party then went on and visited the rest of the sentinals but when they came back by my post they halted at the proper distance and did not fool with me. I think the incident gave me quite a reputation for when later in the evening a ghost came round he visited every post but mine. I am now rather glad that the bayonet was unfixed for I fear it might have killed the fool but when the thing happened I was mad and sleepy and ment business . . .

Our program of drill has been changed. We have no more artillery but in its place a two hour infantry drill from 7:30 to 9:30. It is pretty much hell especially as half of it is at double time. There is no use talking this place can out drill V.M.I. at double time. I only have nine demerits so far and only two this month. I am trying to run zero as of yore [at VMI] but 'it is hard work.

Letter, GSP, Jr., to his father, August 21, 1904

Dear Papa; The degeneration of the present plebean is simply incredible, the other day eleven of us went on a picnic in the woods. The function was given by a lady named Mrs. Watson. She had lots to eat and eleven young ladies. I was quite smiten with one of them, her daughter, but had the good sense not to show it, or at least not much instead I reverted to my old stunt of boning faver with the chaperone, I worked like a dog. There was one rather unique and I think very clever device employed to prevent confusion of names among people meeting one another for the first time. Each of us was given a slip of paper and a pin. We wrote our names on these slips and then pinned them on our coats so that all one had to do was to read the name and then address the person with perfect certainty: but one girl with a french name wrote so badly that I could scarcely read it.

I believe that some of the upper class men have begun to respect me, if not to like me and I am glad to say that this feeling is only apparent among the gentlemen for the rest I dont care and they know it . . .

I am in "A" Co. and . . . I will stay in it until I graduate unless I get some office which would place me in the next ranking Co. Thus if I got second corp (which is *impossible*) I would be put in "B" Co. . . . The absolute honor of this place is amazing yet so ever present that after a time it ceases to be noticible. There is nothing but truth here and even the worst of the rabble to whom the name "plebean" is *most* fitly applied soon learn this and conform to it.

As for the discipline it is equally good. In small things such as keeping eyes to the front and talking in ranks there is some laxity but in other details there is a corresponding strictness and there is never a question about obeying orders . . .

I have only three demerits this month so far and hope to hold them down. We go into barracks Saturday. We do not begin French until after Christmas so cheer up I may have learned to study by then . . .

I am making money at the rate of fifty two dollars a month but never see any of it . . .

P.S. Dont forget Dr Campbell's bill

Letter, GSP, Jr., to his father, August 28, 1904

Dear Papa; We are in barracks again . . . Breaking camp was quite impressive. All the tents went down at once. Ayers and I were the first to get our tent folded in the whole bettalion. Then we fell in and marched back to barracks. Just as we came opposite Trophy poin[t] I remembered the picture of the "Corp's marching from Camp to Barracks" and realized that all those people were looking at me and that I was part of the corps. I felt fine. The only draw back being that I was only part of the corps not the whole thing. Of a truth I am too ambitious, too much of a dweller in the future . . .

The Second Class got back to day and most of them were drunk or just recovering. One of them asked me what State he was from and when I did not know he said He was from the state of "Intoxication." But on the whole they are a nice lot and far more accomidating than the yearlings . . .

The doctor . . . said that though my eyes were not quite perfect he thought I had better not wear glasses. I had such long range sight that he got quite interested in me and gave me two examinations by different methods. We drew our books to day and they dont look very hard but of course they are.

When you get this letter, it will have been just a little over a year . . . since I started to learn the profession of killing my brothers. . . . And in this year of contact with the world my respect for man has dwindeled instead of increasing. For even among the best and the best are I take it those who devote them selves to the service of Mars, there is not the self sacrificing love of fame or self denying selfishness which I feel and which I had expected in others but rather a languid lacitude careless indiference or hazy uncertinty not becoming in my estimation a soldier or a man. But let this be: the fewer of a specis there are the greater is its individual worth. And if my nature prove incapable of the task I have set my self or if the opportunity never comes I can at least die happy in my own vanity knowing that I stood alone and that alone I fell.

Inspite of this letter I am quite well and happy.

Your loving son

Letter, GSP, Jr., to his father, September 4, 1904

We only have two lessons a day now namely mathematics and English. Neither would be at all hard if taught in the ordinary way but they are not. For instance when you go to the board in math you are only allowed to put down the figure in geometry and in Algibra only one or two equations. Then you must turn around and give your discussion in correct english that is; use well rounded sentences: besides this you are not permitted to erase any thing and you have to prove every rule. I fancy however that when once one gets familiar with this form of recitation that it is not hard: the lessons are pretty long but you have plenty of time to study. In English it is absolute memory you have to memorize word for word the entire lesson. Just now this subject is pretty hard for me because it is simply grammar and I know nothing of it but soon we will get in higher parts where my bluff will count. We also have every Saturday the study of tactics in regard to advance guards and the like. It is most interesting and for me at least easy. It is very imperative for a running [ambitious] man to get a good stand here for the only people who have a chance at corp. are the first twenty men in the class; sons of army officers where ever they stand and athletes. This being the case I fear that I will remain a private. I don't believe that there is any possibility of my being found [failed] at least this year for there are some absolute fools in the present third class who got through. You should see this place at night it is absolutely soundless yet there are five hundred men in it: and every one of them studying like hell . . . We drew our over coats the other day. They are beauties slightly different in cut from those of V.M.I. . . . I think that I had my first touch of home sickness the other day . . . I dont know whether you knew or not that I have always thought that I was a military genius or at least that I was or would be a great general. Well looking over the situation as it stands at present I see little in which to base such a belief. I am neither quicker nor brighter in any respect than other men nor do they look upon me as a leader as it is said Napolions class mates looked upon him. In fact the only difference between me and other people is that I have ideals with out strength of character enough to live up to them and they have not even got them [the ideals]. But this is all foolishness . . .

    With lots of love Your son, G. S. Patton Jr.

    Dont faint when you see this spelling. I haven't time to correct it.

Letter, GSP, Jr., to his father, September 11, 1904

    Dear Papa: — The lessons are pretty bad in that they take a lot of time and study. You have to absolutely memorize them especially the English . . . I think I did pretty well in Tactics but I studied that harder and also like it better . . . I am rooming on the first floor just by the front hall door. The only trouble with the room is that its window opens onto the stoop which has a low roof, this roof keeps out most of the light besides it is at the foot of the stairs and every one who has no time to go up to his room between classes throws his books in here. Still you don't have to get up early at reveille . . . Last Tuesday the International Peace Parliament came up here and we had a review for them, it seemed rather incongress [incongruous] to wealcom the creators of eternal Peace with the best trained fighting machine in the world but perhaps it was our Swan Song. The members of the Parliament were a curious looking set taken from the elect of all nations but giving a very poor example of what a Nations elect should be. On Labor Day there was a great big excursion up here to see us drill and parade. I suppose they had been reading about the war in China and wanted to see what soldiers looked like. It is queer what an effect a crowd has on a man. They did not say a word yet I could feel that we were drilling better the lines had more snap and I at least did not get tired at Double time . . . Have you heard any thing of Nita's school yet? I think it would be much better if she went home. Cultivation is a very poor thing after all and while it, like some varnishes, can hide the flaws in base wood it cannot improve that which is already perfect. Dont tell Nita I said that. It would make her vain.

Letter, GSP, Jr., to his father, September 18, 1904

    Dear Papa: — Mama, Nita and Aunt Nannie have just left . . . I saw them for two hours . . . they were all looking splendidly and Nita seemes to be quite grown up. I don't believe I ever will be. At this very moment I would lead a company against smokiless fire or roll marbles at lead soldiers with equal rediness and I hope with equal success. They brought me five swords and some daggers . . .

It has been quite exciting this week. On Tursday the "Royal british Engineers" were here and we gave them a review after which they inspected barracks: my room being on the first floor nearly all of them came into it. They were a fine looking set and very considerate not fingering every thing as the Americans do. I talked to one of them the commander he was a lord with several initials after his name he had a fat-gut. Some of them had their wives with them and one old lady who was rather near sighted said so that I heard it: "I suppose they have these figures (meaning myself and Ayers) to represent the cadets." This made me grin and one big Englishman said "My dear lad would you move if I were to thrust a pin into you"? . . . we began to laugh and all the English men did the same thing and went out. Yesterday the "National Bankers Association" came up and we gave them a Review they were also a very nice set and very appreciative clapping with much life when we came by.

Seeing mama makes me feel like being a W.P. cadet is a dream and that I will awake at home or at V.M.I. I did not do so well last week in math but was much better in English. I have been perfect so far in drill regulations. They count a good deal for a corp.

Letter, GSP, Jr., to his father, September 27, 1904

Dear Papa; Mama was here Sunday . . . I had a nice time and was darned glad to get out of that Infernal Mess Hall. It was the first time I had taken a meal out of it . . . though it is little over three months ago [that I arrived] it seemes much longer. It makes me shudder when I think how much I must have looked like the turists who come up here. We have been in barracks just a month to day and I am getting quite used to it but still like camp a great deal better. I have my old fault in studying. I don't consentrate but daudle along. Still I do fairly well though not well enough to get a good stand. I am also getting too many demerits for foolish things. I have not had any for realy important offences . . . [my room] is very near the company parade so is convenient and makes a "late" almost impossible, then there are no stairs to clime with water . . . and it is a good deal of trouble to carry it up stairs. We will be put into sections in two weeks now and I hope that when I wake up and realize that I am in the goats that I will do better than now when I am uncertain of my standing . . . a feeling of competition is a great help. Mama and Nita and Nannie brought me some beautiful swords and Beatrice brought me a Claymore. Nita brought me an English Engineer Officer's sword I suppose intending it for a hint that I should make that branch [usually taken by the graduates with the best academic averages]. It is needless to say that the hint was useless. I will miss them by at least a hundred files (unless I "buck-up") . . .

I am quite well and think that I will keep so.

Letter, GSP, Jr., to his father, October 5, 1904

Dear Papa; Mama was again the cause of my not writing. I had dinner with her last Sunday and was with her all afternoon. Nita seems to have aged visibly since she got into the four-hundred [high society] but she is looking very well.

I am doing rottin. I got into the third section from the bottom in english and unless I do much better will I much fear not even stop at the bottom. I got an instructor who in an evil moment found out my utter lack of knowledge about English Grammar so he has been questioning me on it with much regularity and I with equal exactness have flunked: still it is not all his fault for I dont spend enough time even on the part I know about. Infact I am afraid that I am in the same condition about my lessons as I was in camp about running "I don't seem to give a dam" I only hope that I will shake it off as I did in camp but I am absolutely worthless. I know that I should study and don't. I see my lack of preparation today but tomorrow will be in the same fix. My only hope is that now that mama has gone home I will have no more distractions and will study. I don't see how mama's being here could have effected me but it might have. If I were only my self of a year ago I would ask nothing better for then I tried and took a vital interest but now, *o! hell*

We began gymnastics this week but as yet have done but little. I think that I shall like it especially the fencing and I will try to do well at it as the best men are put on a team and fence with other colleges . . .

[Sham battles take place about three times a week; yesterday's was spectacular.] after severe fighting we were out flanked and driven in. I was not on the list of killed so am quite well.

Your loving son

Letter, GSP, Jr., to his father, October 15, 1904

[Played Harvard today, lost 4 to 0] but our team out played them from start to finish . . . there were four plebes in the team and I should have been one of them but unfortunately was not . . . Your idea that football is a game of bruits is disproved by this team and V.M.I. Here the captain of the team has second stand and one of the tackels has eighth. So next year I will play and in consequence desist from being a "goat" . . .

[Yesterday a practice battle with blank cartridges] I was nearly in the middle and when I looked down the line with every body either kneeling or lying down firing it looked fine . . .

I got my new blouse to day. It fits very well and looks fine. If I could only get a new cap I would be fixed but these fools are so afraid of a cadet becoming extravagant that they will only issue a certain number of caps a year so even though mine is so dirty that it stinks I cant get another . . .

[Every cadet gets tickets to football games and can invite people] even plebes can do this. I am going to invite Beatrice to next Saturdays game. It is mere a compliment as she cant possibly come but still I think I shall do it. One reason we got beaten to day was because the head coach was drunk and thought that the best man in our team was not playing well so took him out . . .

I am doing fairly well but hope to do better. With lots of love to you and mama. Your devoted son G. S. Patton Jr.

Where is my raizor strap. G.S.P. Jr.

Letter, GSP, Jr., to Beatrice, October 15, 1904

Dear Beatrice, Harvard was too much for us and we died by four to nothing but it was a fine game and very fiercely contested . . . I believe that I never was so excited in my life and towards the last when we began to break through their line I would have given my hope of Heaven and fear of the other place to have been in it if only for a minute . . .

. . . a great discovery to day [he could have 4 tickets for each game played at West Point.] So if you and any of your family who like foot ball were ever in New York or some where near here and would like to come I would be delighted. More than that it would be an act of charity if you would come . . .

Letter, GSP, Jr., to his father, October 30, 1904

Dear Papa; You need not worry too much about my stand in english. It is very bad indeed but I think there is little danger of its finding [failing] me [out of West Point] for I cannot find a case where a man has been found in english. Still I will try a lot harder and see if I can go up for though I am pretty lazy you know that I have never of my own volition stood low in my studies . . .

I would give a good deal to have the first two months of study here over again as I know very well that I would not occupy my present rottin position but it is an idle wish as foolish as would be a general to wish for the first hours of a battle to return again that he might profit by his experience and not make his initial errors a second time . . .

If I can only get a fairly good final stand say (thirty five) I am pretty sure of getting a corp . . . If I can get even goat corp I am sure that on the September make over I can get a good deal better one. For most of the sons of army officers who will in the first instance get corps are no good and will pretty surely loose them. I hope I can get a corp. and this while not the strongest motive will still have a great effect in making me work . . .

Don't let those pasadena boys shoot in the pasture. I can't hunt there myself but I would hate to think of my enemies doing it; but perhaps with Mr. Huntingtons civilization there is nothing left to shoot. Has Onianto Park ever developed any thing besides a name. That is are any of those Phantom houses imerging from the mysts of Mr. H's imagination into real bricks and wood. I met an English army officer a (captain of artillery) the other day and talked to him for a couple of hours. When he left he told me that he had expected to find all West Pointers like me but I was the only one who had come up to his expectations — and I am going to be found in english. We had ice cream for dinner to day . . . there was a piece left in the plate but I could not take it for fear of looking greedy so I nearly died from envy . . . With lots of love for you and ma your devoted son.

According to the class and conduct reports for October, in the fourth class totaling 153 members, George stood number 55 in mathematics, 139 in English, and 14 in drill regulations. He had accumulated a total of 19 demerits since his entrance in July.

Letter, GSP, Jr., to his mother, November 8, 1904
Dear Mama; I got your litter of the 30th this morning and your wish that I would do better made me feel rottin as the duce for I thought that I had just flunked in two subjects but when I came to look at my marks for the week I found that I had gotten 12.8 out of fifteen in english and that I had gone up a section in math. so that now I am in the fourth section in math. I certainly felt a lot better particularly as I had not expected to go up for I had not studied as hard as I should have. I certainly hope I can hold the fourth section and will study good and hard in trying to do so. The reason for my better mark in English is partly that I studied it harder and partly that I got a new instructor. My old instructor was a scoundril and did not like me so he consequently gave me low marks . . .

Princeton beat us to day by 11 to 6 so we are feeling pretty bad to night. The tigers played very dirty ball . . . [Our tackle, the] finest in America [got water on the knee and could not play, our best guard broke a blood vessel in his ear and had to be taken out, our center] got kicked in the head and nearly died . . . you would have liked the game.

Sometimes I get mad as thunder at this infernal place particularly when I think of the fun I might have at home. What I dislike most is the infernal "Well if you don't like it get out" way in which it treats you.

Letter, GSP, Jr., to his father, November 12, 1904

I am glad if I have been a comfort to you and mama and only wish that I had also been a comfort to my self; but I havent. I have lived 19 years yet it seemes to me that I have wasted them. I amount to very little more than when I was a baby. Even in games I have never been a great success. I am fare in every thing but good in nothing. It seems to me that for a person to amount to some thing they should be good at least in one thing. Other boys appear to make successes but though [I] want to I dont suc-ceed. Perhaps it is just that I lack that small fraction of courage, will power, or what ever it is which makes them succeed. Or perhaps I dont fail any worse than any one else only my jealousy makes me think I do. Still when I look at even my class mates I don't feel that sense of superior-ity which it seems to me should be felt by a (not great) but by a successful man. I some times fear that I am one of these darned dreamers with a willing spirit but a weak flesh a man who is always going to succeed but who never does. Should I be such an one it would have been far more merciful had I died ten years ago for I at least can imagine no more infernal hell than to be forced to live — a failure. If I ever seem to be degenerating into a commonplace American army officer please either nock me on the head or make me brace up. Of late I have lost I fear a good deal of that confidence which you prize so highly. I am not sure I will get a corp. I am not sure I will be a general. But now it is a new year in my life I will start out again I hope that this time the start will stay started. For as a rule I start every Sunday and by Monday night have slackened down again. Perhaps I show weakness to write this letter but for the past three weeks I have had such an overpowering sense of my own worthlessness that I had to give expression to it . . .

Did it bank rupt you for mama to come [east] or do you get more from Mr. H[untington]. I hope you do how are you hard up or not . . .

I am quite well.

Letter, GSP, Jr., to his mother, November 23, 1904

It will be impossible for me to get a permit for both Highland Falls and the hotel so I have put in for the Highland Falls . . . I am expecting that you are going to the Villa so will go straight there. Don't forget my *swords* or candy.

. . . As I have to get up before revellie to study tomorrow I expect I had better stop. I am well your devoted son.

Letter, GSP, Jr., to his father, November 25, 1904

Dear Papa: — You had better wake up and write, I haven't had a letter for over two weeks. Well the great Navy game is at last at hand. We leave here tomorrow in a nine car train (a special) and as soon as the game is over we get on it and come back arriving here about ten at night. On the way back we will have dining-cars . . . each cadet was issued a megaphone, a flag, and a lot of ribbons so we will look quite gay. The megaphones are painted with our collars, gold, black, and grey; and are fine for you can make a lot of noise with out loosing your voice.

I took dinner at Highland Falls with mama yesterday and had all my swords to play with . . . I saw a lot of candidates there; poor fools who are spending a year in pergitory preparitory to four in hell yet they looked happy and had the impudence to look at me their future master, that is unless I get found in English as you expect and I some times fear . . .

[Played left end on an intramural football team.] As a result . . . I am very stiff and skinned up some. Still I am going to try hard for the [varsity] team next year for it is a lot of more fun than I thought.

I have gained nearly fifteen pounds since I came here. I weighed to night in my blouse and trousers and weighed a hundred and seventy-seven. I must stop now and shave for tomorrow. I am quite well and confident that I wont get found.

Letter, GSP, Jr., to Beatrice, November 1904

You cant imagine how funny it seems to me that you are "coming out." Don't get angry but . . . you dont seem very old

You say that you feel as if . . . the world is so big that you will get lost. I don't blame you a bit. If I were as near my graduation . . . I should be frightened to death. . . .

Now please don't be made [mad] with me for if you want me to tell you that I think you are very old, sedate, and all the rest of it I will.

Letter, GSP, Jr., to Beatrice, November 1904

I predict that your mad career will be a great success . . .

I am either very lazy or very stupid or both for it is beastly hard for me to learn and as a natural result I hate to study.

Yesterday was the two hundredth day from June and to celebrate this fact every plebe had to make a speech at dinner in which he was supposed to make funn of all the upper class men

In mine I tried to imitate Shakespear's "Seven Ages of Man" only substituting the five ages of cadet life. It was a very poor attempt but it made most of the men laugh and that was all they wanted. Some of the fellows made realy mean speeches and as a result got into trouble but as I made as much fun of plebes as of any one else I escaped. You see the Liberty of the Press does not exist here and we have to be careful what we say.

Much obliged for your good wishes on my birth day. But I wish that instead of being for my nineteenth they had been for about my fifteenth for I just hate to grow old and be oppressed with the knowledge of how little I have done; it makes me feel absolutely worthless. It seems to me that I have spent my whole life having a good time and that I have not done one solitary thing worth doing. I often wonder if I am the only person who feels this way or if it is a common feeling of all people? Whether it is or not it is in my case, at least, very unplesant.

Still I made a good start this year for I got up at half past four to study . . . I made a good mark on my birth day. But this "Eulogy on the Death of a Mad Dog" cant be very interesting to you so I will stop it . . .

With the very best of wishes that you make a successful dive [coming out] on fifteenth of December

Geo. S. Patton Jr.

Letter, GSP, Jr., to his father, end of November 1904
Dear Papa: The weeks are going by with such wonderful rapidity that it scars me for the time in which I am to redeem my honor and get a good stand grows short and ever shorter. I have been trying my hardest for the last month to get to the fourth section in math, but to no purpose . . . it is disheartening and sickening to think that I am so stupid that though I study hard I don't go up while others who do not study yet do well. I also seem to have luck against me in the way of demerits. I was orderly and went a whole week with out being skinned on the room and today I swepped it to death washed some spots off the floor with soap and water and then got skinned for not having a towel hanging on the wash stand. While every one else who doesn't give a d— never gets skinned. I would almost like to get turned back [made to repeat the year — a prophetic wish] for then I could get a good stand and not get demerits and probably get a corp which I fear now is not possible . . . I actually think that

if I don't get a corp I will die so from the present out look you had better bring a coffin east in the Spring. It may be a method of developing my character to give me such hard luck but it certainly is awfully hard for I take such an intense interest in getting a corp and hate so not to be first. I fancy that there is no one in my class who so hates to be last or who tries so hard to be first and who so utterly fails. And what makes it worse the failure is partly my fault I still daudle a little in studdying and I cant seem to get over it. Infact the sum total of me is that I am a character-less, lazy, stupid yet ambitious dreamer; who will degenerate into a third rate second lieutenant and never command any thing more than a platoon. Gosh but it is a shame that I am so constituted as to have only ambition and now [no] power to carry out a single thing I like to do.

I will come off this rather cowardly line of discourse and try some more for a week when I will slacken as usual.

. . . Fencing with the sabre is fine and very pretty. I hit so sharp a blow that I cut mine in two the other day and it seemed quite realistic.

On December 1, the class and conduct reports showed George number 42 in mathematics, 71 in English, and 30 in drill regulations — in a class of 152 members. He had received 4 demerits in November, which gave him 23 from entrance in June.

Letter, GSP, Jr., to his father, December 10, 1904

[Has been in hospital since Wednesday] but don't be excited I was not sick [Had a slight attack of indigestion, which prevented him from studying well; because of the current general review in class, corresponding to the January examinations, he thought it better for his marks not to take written recitation.] With this end in view I went to the hospital and because I made a great speech and because I look like the Surgeons Godson he took me in but instead of excusing me from reciting he made me attend recitations with a result that . . . I got a very bad mark 1.9 out of 3. But having once got me in the hospital he would not let me out but still made me go to recitations. [The doctor also put him on a liquid diet. George was permitted to leave tonight] in a condition little short of starvation . . .

I am glad that you get $7200 [per year] but it should be $72000 and then you would be cheep, still you say you hope to get more I hope so too.

. . . I am quite well and getting fat.

Letter, GSP, Jr., to Beatrice, December 11, 1904

Dear Beatrice; It may be selfish but I certainly am sorry you are coming out. It makes me seem so old and then again it makes me feel so young. You see you are the first person of about my own age who I knew as a child that has come out . . . I have been in the hospital not that I have been very ill but simply because I got frightened at an examination that we are having and thought that I had better go to the hospital and not take it . . .

I have just gotten a new cap artistically trimmed with a brass shield in the front. It is of course not at all comperable to your hats but I expect that I like it nearly as much . . .

I hope that you will have the very best time in the world at your coming out and after it too and that you whirl your wings all over Boston, Harvard, and every where else . . .

Letter, GSP, Jr., to his father, December 17, 1904

I ordered a good pair of skates that will come tomorrow so when you get this litter I will probably be looking for a stand-up lunch. Still as I am to freeze for 4 years I had just as well learn how to enjoy frozen pleasures . . . [Fenced at gymnasium with a cadet who like Patton had not fenced before this year; they were both pretty poor and went to a corner to be inconspicuous. Mr. Barber, West Point's crack fencer and second best in America, came in with several ladies and politely asked George and his partner to fence for his friends. After a protest by George, they did so.] When ever we stuck one another the foolish girls would yell. Finally by mere accident I happened to nock the foil out of Kabee's hand and the[n] you should have heard them. I expect they thought I was master of the sword [a prophetic statement] or something of the sort. When I thought we had fenced enough I saluted Mr. Barber with "present-sword" and marched out. I bet that tickled him . . .

The [classroom] reviews ended to day. I dont have to take the exam [which meant that his academic average was passing].

Letter, GSP, Jr., to Beatrice, December 18, 1904

Dear Beatrice; Really the fact that you liked my flowers well enough to wear them [at your coming out party] gives me a great deal more pleasure than they could possibly have given you, so instead of your thanking me I should be greatful to you . . .

The December reviews are over at last and this place will have to stand me until next June for they did not "find" me or even com very near doing it . . .

It must be fine to be at home on Christmas and eat as much candy as you want and play games, and have a general good time. I havent done it for two years now so have partly forgotten how to laugh and play though I am still pretty good at eating.

Letter, GSP, Jr., to his father, December 26, 1904

I am afraid that you have an unjust idea of the *"hardships"* of this place and as a consequence an over rated notion of my merit in staying here. You must remember that I am not the only boy at west point on the contrary I am merely one of some 400 boy's and many of them very worthless ones who not with standing are doing well here some of them better than your own "young master." For after all habit is the strongest of human emotions as is evinced by the fact that though as you well know I was not of a studious nature yet now that I have no lessons I am at some loss to occupy my self. You said that I did well on my last report but I can hardly commend your judgement for to have more than forty men rank one in math and more than a hundred in English is to say the least not conducive to the "big head."

In fact in my own opinion I am pretty darned poor, not that I am in the least discouraged I am only ashamed; but sad to tell my shame only makes me cuss myself and does not make me work harder.

I also disagree with you about cultivating cheerfullness. It may be a good thing for a society star but I think that you will look in vain for a general who was a "laughing hiena." Still I am getting so much like other boys that it scares me and I think I will have to develop my old Puritanical sobriety . . .

I expect that we will have a good dinner to day and as many of the men at my table are absent we will have lots.

I think the little success and all the failures I have had are due to the same thing that is I continually live in the land of "tomorrow." This makes me work and again it keeps me from working. I continually say I will study harder tomorrow and make up for my lack of preperation to day. This same thing keeps me from considerable fun in the present for I am so egar after what is to come that I clean walk over what is at hand. If I could only live in the present in detail while at the same time live in the future in ideal I might amount to some thing so I guess I had better try to do it . . .

I carved the turkey and all said that I was a wonder. You see I learned some thing from watching you or maby I inherited the nack of carving . . .

Letter, GSP, Jr., to his mother, December 30, 1904

Dear Mama; The watch is a beauty and just the right size. I have been wearing it all day though I dident have any need to do so but simply to see how it felt. I am writing this letter with a stylographic pen that Beatrice gave me so you see I got quite a few presents. I also bought a big sweater with one of the fives I got on Christmas.

Letter, GSP, Jr., to his father, January 1, 1905

Dear Papa. This is nearly the prettiest day I have seen in this country and I only hope it presages a bright and successful year to come: though it will be a pretty hard six months . . . well filled with hard lessons but still they will not probably seem so hard as those over which I have just passed for as you say my mind is now in pretty good training. Infact I can notice a perceptable increase in my power to memorize a thing in a short space of time and after all the first years course here is simply to develop the memory. They dont care whether you realy know what you are talking about if only you can speak it off well. I may not carry out my present intention of hard study but I hope I shall for though you say you are satisfied with my report I am not. It is too much like the middle middle. I may not be good enough to be above the middle but it makes me sick to think it so I will try to go up and may succeede. We are going to have roast pig for dinner and I guess I will have to carve it, I dont much like the job . . .

[Visited] for the ferst time [the Ordnance museum]. It is fine and has a lot of things in it but the collection of swords is poor. [Saw the new entrenching knife.] As one of the tacks [tactical officers] said "You can make a darned good trench with your hands if there are only some men shooting at you" . . .

I expect I shall have to go in with new roommates but as long as they are studious and most of them are it dosent make much difference. I am very well and will try to study hard.

At the end of December 1904, he stood 51 in mathematics, 69 in English, 30 in drill regulations in a class of 150 members.

Letter, GSP, Jr., to his father, January 16, 1905

[After receiving a newspaper from home] They are playing the devil with things in the country arnt they. There were about fifty houses and streets (most of them were not called streets) that I had never seen. I am afraid that before I get home (unless I come in May [in the event he failed]) that Mr. H[untington] will have some of his picturesque flats in process of construction. And some of those spacious lots 200 × 100 with rare facilities for health and pleasure namely breathing crude oil dust and scraping the saim off the feloor. . . .

Trigonometry as yet has not been very hard and I expect to get on all right . . .

My mind of late has been so fixed on my math that I cant come down to letter writing and besides there is nothing to say.

Letter, GSP, Jr., to his father, January 27, 1905

That last run of demerits was pretty bad but fortunately I have not got any since. I am sorry that letter of mine was so blue but it is beastly discouraging to get worse marks than men who you know have less grey matter and not half the ambition . . . I got a valentine from B and cant make out what it means. If you will be careful not to mention it to any one I will tell you what it was . . . [Describes a rose leaf pasted on paper and beneath it a sprig of] that stuff that grows on either side of the front stips and gets frost bitten so easily . . . [Under that Beatrice had written] "Under the rose" What does it mean? . . .

As you see I have run out of good paper but have just ordered some with the class crest which I expect will be nice. You will expect the bill.

In his class of 146 members — 142 were actually present — George stood number 47 in mathematics, 100 in French, on February 1. A month later he had gone down three places in mathematics and up four in French; he was 8 in drill regulations.

He accompanied the Corps of Cadets to Washington, D.C., marched on March 4 in the Inaugural Parade for Theodore Roosevelt, and danced that evening at the Inaugural Ball with Beatrice.

Letter, GSP, Jr., to Beatrice, March 7, 1905

Dear Beatrice, If you had for the remainder of you[r] visit in Washington half as nice a time as I had the night of my visit with you, you must be dead with joy for actually I had the finest time in the world . . .

I certainly hope you can come up in June for realy it will be quite fine and there are lots of charming fellows in my class as well as in the others. Of course it would be much nicer for me at least could I go to that dance as a "corporal" (that is a kind of cadet officer) but unfortunately my chances of getting such an office are very small. So you will probably have to excuse my stupidity and dance with a private though really to any one but a cadet the fact of being an officer is of little moment.

We are having examinations here again but I do not dread them near so much as I used to for I have grown to have faith that foolish as I may be I have sufficient sense not to be found . . .

Geo. S. Patton

I forgot the Jr in this my new signature.

He described his trip to Washington in a letter to his father written March 18. The train was late, it was held up in Baltimore for two hours, but it finally arrived after dark. The corps marched through the night to the Washington Barracks, "just completed" at P and 4th Streets, Southwest. Each company was billeted in a huge room called a squad room, and they were "pretty nice." He reached Senator Bard's hotel a little after nine o'clock and found only his young daughters. Father, mother, and son Tom had already departed after having waited dinner for more than an hour for him. George had telegraphed them from the train, but the message never arrived. After staying there a short time, he went to the theater. He returned to the barracks to find a letter saying that Beatrice and her father and mother were at the

Shoram [Shoreham Hotel] and envited me to spend my entire spare time with them. Of course I nearly had a fit of joy and stipped out of the post next day to telephone my acceptance . . . We left barracks in full dress at 10:30 and marched in the face of a threatening storm and feirce wind through every back street in the city . . . When we came on the squair infront of the capitol it looked like the pit of an arena. On all sides were masses of people and one whole stand of cameras. The wind at this place was terrible . . . dust blew in our faces filling eyes nose and lungs. Our chin straps alone saved our hats . . . We stayed there for two hours then Teddy came out and barked and shook his fists and stuck out his chin but we could not hear a word . . . Then Teddy came down and got in his carriage and all the generals about fell in behind him . . .

[They then paraded down Pennsylvania Avenue.] The sun shown on the [trolley] car tracks and the people yelled. When we would change step or go from full to half step they simply burst. This kept up until we reached the turn just infront of the treasury here confronted by a huge stand we halted while Teddy ate. The street is a little elevated here and I could look back down the avenue to the foot of the Capitol and the whole avenue looked like one vast wave or human river . . . We halted at this place for an hour and a half then again the bugles blew attention and we were in motion. Now the great stands came and cheering that had gone before was as nothing to that which now burst from either side of the street rushed out ward . . . grew and grew untill at last all human energy was united and exhausted in one mighty shout as we executed eyes left to The President! Having passed him we emerged into comparitive quiet yet so great had been the excitement and so much are people effected by noise that we moved as machines for about a mile . . .

[After an excellent lunch in a big hall, the corps returned to barracks about 6:45.] I washed and left there at seven and got to the Shoram as fast as the [street] cars would take me . . . When arrived at the hotel I was just going to send up my card when B. grabbed me. She seemed realy very glad to see me, I was of course similarly effected. Pretty soon Mrs. Ayer came. She made me go in and get some more dinner while they dressed for the ball. As I was by my self I ordered all the deserts there were and nothing else then we went to the ball . . . and saw Teddy and the royal family. It was very pretty and gay. B. and I had a dance but it was pretty hard work and the floor was of stone. Still in my then state of mind I would have danced with equal eagerness on a hot stove that is if the above was not burning my partner. After the dance we went back to the hotel and had supper. And then twelve o'clock came and with it ended my permit so like a Sinderela (?) I had to go . . . Comeing out certainly had a wonderfully good effect on Beatrice for though she was nice before she is nicer and a lot prettier infact she is the prettiest girl I ever saw. Though you need not say that I said so as I am now probably suffering from a bad attack of puppy love even if it has lasted a long time.

After he returned to West Point "I was nearly dead and quite sick from having eaten too much candy on the train."

On April 1, he stood 60 in mathematics, 103 in French, and 5 in drill regulations.

Letter, GSP, Jr., to his father, early April 1905

I did not get turned out though I made pretty bad marks [in the March exams] . . .

I am the best or one of the best in the class [with the broadsword]. It is lots of fun and I practice it as much as possible . . . You should see the sparks fly on some of the parries also the blood if you chance to stick your unguarded left hand in the way. The other day I was fencing with a man who would not acknowledge my touches though they nearly nocked him down so I tried a dueling cut not supposed to be used in fencing at the right wrist. As a result he could not hold a pen for a day but will probably be a better sport in future . . .

I know that I am a better man in every way than Ayers for example yet he made the fencing team. I don't smoke yet men who when out of training are mere chimneys beat me at foot ball. Truely the ways of god are past human knowledge but every thing must have a definite meaning or else the human race is on a wrong track in belief and this latter seemes almost an untennible notion . . .

What is your translation of that Valentine?

Letter, GSP, Jr., to his father, April 9, 1905

I am nearly hopeless. I don't know what is the matter for I certainly work. Sometimes I think that it would be a good thing to get conditioned and turned back a year for then I would almost certainly get a corp and probably a very high stand. What do you think of the idea? My but I hate to be so low ranking for I still think that I am smarter than most of the men who rank me. My but it is exasperating to see a lot of fools who don't care beat you out when you work hard. I know that part of it is due to my lack of application and partly to other things but it is very trying . . .

I cant think of any thing but my own worthlessness so will stop writing

Your Goaty son

Letter, GSP, Jr., to his father, April 19, 1905

When you come [for the graduation exercises in June] don't forget to cultivate the Tacks [tactical officers]. The other officers don't count but if you can get on the good side of the tacks I might get a "make" that is a "corp."

What part of the [Catalina] Island do you propose selling and for how much. Sell it for enough so that you may turn into a sport and quit work it would be a lot better for you . . .

I am very well and eating like a horse.

Letter, GSP, Jr., to his father, April 24, 1905

Dear Papa; I am not going to be conditioned if I can help it . . . I am gowing to do my damdest . . .

Don't worry about me for it will do me no good and may make you sick. I know just the whole I am in and doing my *best* to get out of it.

Letter, GSP, Jr., to Beatrice, late April 1905

[After a lecture on the battle of Port Arthur] From the amount of mortality it must be a good deal safer to jump off a cliff than to be an infantry officer in a frontal attack . . . I shall take the artillery if I get a chance for while they get to wear badges and are called veterans they stay off at a respectable distance and eventually return to their loving families.

Perhaps what I have just said is not exactly true to my self for though I am not over desirous of being killed yet I think that should I want to go in the infantry the [prospect of] . . . being killed would not stop me for I would always think that I would be the fortunate one [who would survive].

On May 1, the fourth class totaled 138 members, but 6 were absent. Among the 132 who were present for classes, George stood 63 in mathematics, 108 in French, and 2 in drill regulations. He had received 22 demerits since December 1.

Letter, GSP, Jr., to Beatrice, early May 1905

[Tried to get rooms for Beatrice but was unable to because of reservations for the Board of Visitors. Asks her to write to the Villa at Highland Falls.] I would have gone there and not bothered you but it is off limits so I can't . . . Truly I am very sorry to have failed.

I am trying for the hundred and high hurdles.

Letter, GSP, Jr., to his father, May 14, 1905

I have been doing very well in math . . . as for french I will have to take the exam . . . yesterday I almost brought my fiery life to a sudden and tragic conclusion I tripped over a hurdle going at full speed and lit on my head about thirty feet further on taking all the skin off my bare knees so I can't run for a couple of day's I am well

Letter, GSP, Jr., to his father, May 21, 1905

I ran the other day when my legs were cold and broke a tendon near the ankle in my left one but though it hurts a good deal to run I still expect to make two entries in the out door meet. To continue my troubles I also cut a wisdom tooth, (about time isent it) and the darned thing has been hurting like hell particularly since I operated on my gum with a pocket knife to try to let the beast of a tooth through . . .

I certainly think that Beatrice likes me for she answers all my letters and in her last asked if I would mind if she stayed after graduation. Of course I hastened to tell her nothing would be finer. This is of course a secret. Don't tell any of those gushing Bannings or they will certainly tell her and I would have to end my unhappy life in a violent manner. The last reviews begin next week and I am confident of getting through. I am feeling very well and happy at the prospects of an end to study.

Letter, GSP, Jr., to his father, May 30, 1905

Don't worry about my french for I feel perfectly confident about it . . .
I still hope that I shall get a corp, but some times fear not for I am pretty low in studies. I am sorry that I am such a goat for my sake for yours and because B. will think I am stupid. It is true that if she thought other wise she would be mistaken but one never likes to be seen as he is.

Letter, GSP, Jr., to his father, June 3, 1905

Dear Papa: I seem to be destined to damnation. To day we had the track team meet and in the Hurdle race I got a fine start and was going like the divel when at the 7eventh hurdle with only two more to go and with second place sinched I tripped and fell and came out last. For an hour I would have gladly died . . . It was pretty hard for I hate to be beaten and try so hard and Fail. I missed the tackle in the foot-ball game and I got turned out in French and unless I make a 2.7 out of three Monday [in French I] will have to take the math. exam. too.

Pa I am stupid there is no use talking I am stupid. It is truly unfortunate that such earnestness and tenacity and so much ambition should have been put into a body incapable of doing any thing but wish . . .
Aside from my sprained ankle gotten this after noon I am well and sad

Letter, Mr. Patton to GSP, Jr., June 10, 1905

My dear Boy: Your letter of the 3rd came to-day and I can't tell you how my soul sympathized with you in your defeat in the hurdle race — but it was only because I knew how much you had set your heart on success. It is a good thing to be ambitious and to strive mightily to win in every contest in which you engage, but you must school yourself to meet defeat and failure without bitterness — and to take your comfort in having striven worthily and done your best . . . the real victor is he who strives bravely and *deserves* to win . . .

[He cited Kipling, Carlyle, Norse mythology, "that of our ancestors the Vikings," etc.]

So in all Life's battles you can find the real heroes among the *apparently* defeated. The honors which are bestowed upon the *apparently* successful ones — are most often the prizes of accident and circumstance . . .

If you do not get a "Corp" — take it with a smile — and keep on trying — your reward will come.

My dear boy, you do not know how I miss you — and wish I could be with you and help you bear your disappointments when they come, but I cannot — and indeed would not if I could. You have got to fight your battles alone — to meet victory or defeat as becomes a man and a gentleman . . .

I have no fears for you — I know you are doing your best — and that is all you can do. When you have done that — for me you have *won*.

Having failed to score 2.7 in the French examination, George had to take the examination in mathematics — although the relationship of the two subjects seems somewhat obscure.

Telegram, GSP, Jr., to his father, June 12, 1905
Did not pass math turned back to next class probably furlough this summer will wire definitely.

Telegram, Mr. Patton to GSP, Jr., June 13, 1905
It is all right my boy and all for best God bless you.

Telegram, Mr. Patton to Mrs. Patton (West Point Hotel, West Point, New York), probably June 13, 1905
Don't worry all for best wire if necessary I should come But I hope immediate furlough and all home.

Telegram, Mrs. Patton to Mr. Patton, June 14, 1905
George has leave [we] start [for] Rock Island Thursday.

There was one consolation. George was not a complete failure. He had been turned back, not turned out. He had obviously tried hard and his soldierly conduct had been excellent. He deserved another chance. After spending the summer at home, he would return at the beginning of September and join the new fourth class to do his plebe year over.

This the Academic Board recommended, and this the War Department accepted. A formal letter sent from Washington on June 16 to Cadet George S. Patton, Jr., through the Superintendent of the

Academy sealed the decision. Captain F. C. Marshall, the Acting Adjutant at West Point, placed the Superintendent's name on the 1st Indorsement on June 20. On the same day, Lieutenant Colonel Robert Howze, the Commandant of Cadets, added his 2d Indorsement and mailed it to young George.

CHAPTER 6

West Point: Corporal

"When I get out in front of them the foolish ness stops . . . some day I will show . . . them . . . I fear I will never be a general."

GSP, Jr., "My Father," 1927

In the spring of 1905 when I was turned back in Mathematics, Mama was there and we came home together. Neither she or Papa ever showed by word or deed their dissapointment at my failure.

George spent most of the summer at Catalina Island, hunting goats, fishing, helping on horseback to drive sheep into pens for shearing, and having a fine time.

Letter, GSP, Jr., to Beatrice, July 10, 1905

I killed the biggest goat of my life too and with a pistol . . .

I have been studying just a little to keep my hand in and to clear up some stuf I did not "hive" (understand) last year. Looking at it in cold blood I have pretty small chances of coming out one but hope that at least I can make the first ten. That would not be so bad would it.

I am awfully glad you all understand how it was with me at the last. I thought you did but wanted to be quite sure. I am now. Thanks for what you said about trying my hardest. I think I did but results do not seem to confirm my opinion so to have you say so is very nice.

Letter, GSP, Jr., to Beatrice, August 9, 1905

Dear Beatrice; You did say something about that pin a long time ago but as I did not know how to answer you I said nothing. But since you pushed me to the wall I will have to say or do something.

(1) please excuse me for forcing such a horror of a thing on you and (2) please throw it into the middle of the lake as sir Bedivere did the sword of Arthur . . .

Tell me truly do you wish the head or horns of that goat for by my old agreement they are yours measuring twenty nine inches and smelling twenty nine times worse than they should. Still say the word and I will afflict them on you smell and all.

[He was coming east a little early to be sure of getting to West Point in time; expected to be there] about the twenty fifth so that I may see you just for a little while . . . would you mind writing to me at the Touraine in Boston and telling me whether you will be at home and if I may come to see you.

Give my love to every one.

Before he departed for the east, he purchased a small notebook in which to keep a record of events and some of his thoughts. "Lake Vineyard, Aug 1905," he began. "If found return either to Cadet Geo. S. Patton Jr. United States Military Academy West Point N. Y. or Mr. G. S. Patton San Gabriel, Los Angeles Co., California $5.00 Reward will be paied to any person finding this book if he returns it. G. S. Patton Jr."

The first entry was: "Do your damdest always."

He would write in this notebook until he graduated. He would include in its pages military principles of one sort or another, aphorisms, remarks and phrases he treasured, lectures to himself, a few addresses, and several martial poems. For example, he listed "5 principles of Strategy 1. Cut line of communications 2. Cause enemy to form front to flank 3. Operate on internal lines 4. Seperate bodies of enemy and fight in Detail 5. Direct attack"

He recorded: "Genius is an immense capacity for taking pains." And he told himself: "Always do more than is required of you."

Letter, GSP, Jr. (Hotel Manhattan, New York), to his father, August 28, 1905

Dear Papa. I am here on the edge of the pit and . . . I will take the plunge at 11:15 with all the rest of them [referring to the train from New York to West Point].

[He had a perfect time in Beverly, Massachusetts with the Ayers.] That Beat. is certainly the best thing in her line in the world and I swallowed her hook to a swivle (as one says of a fish) I guess that I am a fool to have such a case at such an early age but? what would you. I will never see an other such and damn that God forsaken Debora [at Catalina].

[Describes sailing with Beatrice when the wind was blowing hard.] And though B. knew the danger better than I did she never got the least frightened . . .

I am not feeling as bad as I expected about returning to West Point and am going to work . . .

I had a peach of a time at home which after the rottin way in which I fell down the first time I had a chance to do any thing for my self is better than I deserved . . .

P.S. Have Charley Parker pack that goat head and pay him. I will tell you next letter where to have it sent.

Letter, GSP, Jr., to Beatrice, September 1, 1905

To forestall the excuse that I did not invite you to any particular hop I here by ask you to every dance to be given at West Point from now until I graduate and ask only that you will let me know three or four days in advance so that I may make out your card.

My new room mates are very nice fellows and we get on well for I lived with one before and the other is very young and obeys me well . . .

It seemed very funny the first night at parade not to have any one tell me to get my shoulders back . . . If I am not the meanest corp. in the world when I do become one it will be a wonder for I will then have been a private three years.

Letter, GSP, Jr., to his father, September 10, 1905

. . . all is well. Lessons are not hard infact they are so easy that I find difficulty in studying enough. Still I have done pretty well . . . that coaching was of great use.

. . . think that I shall do all right and get the first section [in mathematics] though there are some hellish smart and well educated men here I am sorry to say . . .

I am very well and having a pretty easy time.

This was borne out in his class and conduct report for the month of September. Among 155 members, he stood 17 in mathematics, 60 in English, and 2 in drill regulations. He had received 9 demerits.

The most exciting thing that happened to him was going out for football. He made the third team, playing left end. But his fervent desire to make good led him to reckless behavior on the field, and before long he had dislocated or broken — probably both — his right arm and was unable to play.

Letter, GSP, Jr., to Beatrice, October 23, 1905
I know that unless I am found [flunked out] or killed I shall make this team before I graduate. This is of course between our selves. Excuse me for saying it but I know it and must tell some one.
[He enclosed a poem:]

> Oh! here's to the snarl of the striving steel,
> When eye met eye on the foughten field.
> And the life went out with the entering steel,
> In the days when war was war.

> And here's to the men who fought and strove,
> And parried and hacked and thrust and clove.
> Who fought for honor and fought for love
> In the days when war was war.

"This is worthless," he added, "but you asked for it."
On the same date, apparently feeling somewhat depressed, he informed his father, "I went to see the com. [Commandant of Cadets, Lieutenant Colonel Howze] to night on a very fragile excuse merely to let him know that I still lived and was glad to see that he knew me."
At the end of October, George stood 14 in mathematics, 37 in English, 1 in drill regulations. He had been penalized 1 demerit that month.

Letter, GSP, Jr., to his father, November 5, 1905
Dear Papa; Another week [h]as winged its silent way into the unrecoverable past carrying with it oppertunities that never shall return.
And still I live and am content to be a member of the second section [in mathematics].
Don't be alarmed. I have been trying to write blank vers for the Howitzer [the school magazine]. And have not succeeded . . .
I have not gotten out of the hospital so that perhaps there is more excuse for my stupidity than would otherwise be the case . . .
Here is some blank (or blanked) verse [describing the stages in the life of a cadet]

his early mind perverted by untruthful literature
He sees a picture of war glorified . . .
And knows not blood is pain and glory but a bubble . . .

In the first place this is not connected and in the second it is I fear not poetry . . . I am not going to turn it in but thought that you might like to see it. Please tell me what it is and what you think of it.

With lots of love your devoted son

He was probably unhappy with the sentiment expressed in the poem, preferring to believe that war was glorious and glory more than a bubble. But he was uncomfortable.

Far more satisfactory was the sentiment he put into his notebook: "What then of death? is not the taps of death but first call to the reveille of eternal life."

Thoughts of his approaching birthday probably produced: "We live in deeds not years." And again: "You can be what *you* will to be."

For some reason, the following struck him as being significant, or perhaps merely interesting: "A Saxon can die without a murmur. A Frenchman can die laughing. But only a Norseman can laugh as he kills."

Letter, GSP, Jr., to his mother, November 11, 1905

Dear Mama: I am twenty and still alive . . . a peach of a birthday. B. came up friday and we walked around . . . [went to the football game and ate lots of candy, went to the hop Saturday night, then went to Beatrice's hotel after the dance] and ate a lot of cake. It must have been pretty rich for I did not sleep over an hour that night and had a head ake for several days but now am all right . . . Truely one is in a bad way to be 20 and as hard hit [over Beatrice] as I am.

It was probably during this visit that Beatrice pleased him enormously by saying, "You are one of the few people in the world who can be courteous without being idiotic." He recorded it in his notebook, identifying the source as "B."

He was by then out of the hospital and back to duty, which he found extremely easy. Elected manager of the plebe football team of Companies A and F, scheduled to play the rest of the plebe class on Thanksgiving, he was busy coaching. His arm was weak and stiff; it would never be as straight as it had been before his football accident but it would be, he was assured, every bit as strong.

Letter, GSP, Jr., to his father, November 20, 1905
I found my wrist watch so dont need a new one . . . I weigh 160 pounds stripped. Well we have a fire-drill now which I must attend so good by . . . Your loving 20 year old son

At the end of November, graded in relation to the 152 members of the fourth class, he stood 19 in mathematics, 27 in English, and 1 in drill regulations; he had received 4 demerits.

He attended the Army-Navy football game, met Aunt Nannie and Nita there, saw Beatrice and her sister Katharine. The President was there. He sat on the Navy side during the first half, then at half time crossed the field to the Army side. Four men of each class at West Point had been chosen to escort the President, and George was one of those selected. "It is a pretty big thing to be an escort to a president," he wrote to his father.

He was helping his roommates in their studies, but they would probably have to take the examinations "as they are awful goats apparently hopeless. I have helped them as much as I could but it is a bad job and I get so excited that I throw books and things around. I fear that I could never teach."

Letter, GSP, Jr., to his father, December 24, 1905
This is the third Christmas away from home and still am I cadet Private . . . but perhaps it is for the last time. I certainly hope it is for this perpetual Pleabism is hard on a patrician like me and getting pretty wearisome . . . I am all right and getting fatter every day. I got a fine pair of brushes from the Ayres (my 4th pair) . . . I also got a letter from Miss Dunn the girl I had up here. It was only a Christmas card but it showed what a terror I am. Truely I must be watchful.

Letter, GSP, Jr., to Beatrice, January 1906
Dear Beatrice It certainly is fine of you asking me to a dance but as usual the regulations of this place make it necessary for me to refuse. It is things of this sort that make this place so hard. It allowes no pleasures in its self and at the same time keeps us from the possibility

of enjoyment out side. I am realy just dying to accept but I can't. I
know that I should have answered sooner so that you might have
time to ask some one else but we have been having a unusually hard
time lately so that I simply could not write. That is not exactly so
either. I wrote part of a letter but it was so bad and I said some
things that sounded funny so I burned it.

What you said about things not worth failing for were not worth
trying was fine. I had never thought of it in that way and [it] encouraged me a lot. But I am afraid you are wrong in thinking that I
cannot realy fail in any thing for I am pretty stupid and lazy . . .

[But] I will be an upper class man some day.

Helping him to become an upper classman, he was certain, were the
observations he placed in his notebook:

In a cavalry fight the side which has the last reserve must win.
Leo.

It is better to live in the lime light a year than in the wings for
ever.

Fame never yet found a man who waited to be found.

When next at Cat. [Catalina Island] go around the south coast on
foot and see how little one can live on.

Rules of behavior he thought useful were:

. . . 2. Do every thing possible to attract attention . . . 4. Always
be very neat and when you get any new clothes let every one know it.
5. Do with all the snap and power you possess what ever you do. 6.
When ordered to do a thing carry out the spirit as well as the letter.
Do all you *can* not only all you *have* to do.

He also recorded a remark by Beatrice: "Dont argue with a man. If
you cant convince him lick him. If you cant lick him keep still. B."

Letter, GSP, Jr., to his father, January 6, 1906

I guess that I am naturally stupid for though I have studied hard
last week I made a poor mark in both French and English darn it. I
am a goat and had just as well learn to be content with my lot
though I never shall but will like the snake keep on kicking til the
sun goes down for I hate to be a goat even though at times I seem to
incline towards it . . .

I grow weary of the rear rank and for a person of my temperament turn-back year is a lot worse than Plebe. I don't know why unless it is the restraint one is forced to exercise over ones conduct. That is you don't have to but still I feel that I should. Still I am not very popular not because there is any thing the matter except that I am "Too damed military." That is I am better than they are. Now no one is more unjust than he who feels him self an inferior but dam them let them keep on. Some day I will show and make them feel how infernally inferior they are.

In his notebook he wrote: "No sacrefice is too great if by it you can attain an end. Let people talk and be damed. You do what leads to your ambition and when you get the power remember those who laughed."

Letter, GSP, Jr., to Beatrice, January 21, 1906
Think of it. In four years I and the corps go to Washington . . . and if all goes well I shall be one of the luckey ones who walks in front and carries a sword . . . But unless I exhibit a little more interest in lessons I shall get turned back again which would be too bad.

By the end of January, his class had been reduced to 145 members. He stood 30 in mathematics and 37 in French. He had 4 demerits for the month.

Letter, GSP, Jr., to his father, March 3, 1906
. . . those March makes [cadet promotions] should be here soon but I am not very much excited for if one misses first captain and adjutant there is little choice in what follows . . . graduation will not be until the 14 [of June] so I will only get 75 days of furlough. Still I will make those last as long as possible. Because the next time I get off I will be saddeled with a commission and the imposing look of second lieutenant and will be supposed to be grown and a finished product of a modern fighting machine.

Letter, GSP, Jr., to his father, March 11, 1906
Dear Papa: — We have had one week of March general reviews and I am sorry to say I did not do very well on them. I did well enough to hold my section but not as I had hoped to go up. I made 20. out of 24. Of course I may be able to do better but I doubt it for I got up

every morning at half past four and cannot do much more than that. There is as I have often said no use in my trying to be high ranking in my studies. I havent got the grey matter. Perhaps I am not stupid and I may be a very efficient soldier but my brain is poor. I fear I will never be a general though I expect I can charge a battery [of artillery] with the next man. You know I have always fancied my self a coward but from a few things which I have noticed lately I begin to think I am not. Of course I have enough sense to calculate chances but I do not let my inclinations interfere with me when I have decided to do a thing. Don't worry I have been in no fights though I have called some blufs . . .

I begin to think that perhaps I am one of the most popular turnbacks here. But this thing of being constantly a plebe is pretty waring on a man for every good thing one does one gets no credit for. They say he ought to know it he is a damed turn-back where if one makes a mistake they say oh God how stupid he has been here a year and should know better.

Letter, GSP, Jr., to his father, March 24, 1906

. . . it looks rather foolish for a person who has always had the military crave to say it. I dont believe the army is the place for a soldier.

We see lots of them here and they are so narrow that while they can drill a company they could not for their lives drill a battalion. Now don't think that I don't like the army for . . . it is the only place I would be worth a darn. But either I must get into an other army and fight or else wait on til the trampled worm [the United States] turnes into an avenging dragon . . . This sounds funny from a person who has never yet done any thing but God willing I can and given the chance I will carve my name on some thing biger than a section room bench.

. . . It is a funny thing. B told me they were going to Cuba but did not send any address so I did not write when today I got a letter from K. [her sister] about ten words long and with their address written large at the end. This is the second time K. has been very use ful. I don't know whether it is coinsidence or not.

I am as glad as you are that it will not be long until I see you.

At the end of March he stood 34 in mathematics, 43 in French, 4 in drill regulations; he had received 1 demerit.

Letter, GSP, Jr., to his father, April 16, 1906

. . . since I have either killed or been killed [in sham battles] over every squair foot of West point the novelty of the fights some what wearies me.

Letter, GSP, Jr., to his father, April 23, 1906

Is not San Francisco having a bad time for what we hear. It must be completely gone and I suppose you have a lot of indigent relatives coming *South* [to San Gabriel]. Send me a paper telling about the fire [and great earthquake].

. . . I have been out practising running and am doing very well except that I cant start.

. . . every body is talking corps. Whether I will get one or not does not bother me but I do want first. Every body else thinks I will but I don't think I will. I have wanted one so long that I think I shall die when I get it but perhaps not.

. . . All the family in fact seems to be having good luck lately and I hope it continues. We are such superior people that we deserve to be successful and we at present are.

At the end of April, he stood 32 in mathematics, 49 in French, 3 in drill regulations; he had escaped demerits.

Letter, GSP, Jr., to his father, May 13, 1906

. . . laying aside sower grapes I think that I have not lost much by being turned back besides it was probably destined. At least to the small extent to which I am able to read Providence it seems so.

I will not possibly be able to come out above thirty in every thing. For this I am sorry but I do not believe I have the ability to be any higher than that in studies. I have tried hard and am content at least as much so as I can ever be when I do not stand 1 . . . I got a new blouse and dress coat so I will be as always the spoonies [best-dressed] man in my class even if I do have to spend an hour pressing my trousers . . .

I am quite well and stupid. Your devoted son

Letter, GSP, Jr., to his father, May 21, 1906

Tomorrow we begin the general review that last year got me by a tenth [of a point] . . .

What ever stand I get and what ever Corp. I get I shall at least soon be through being a plebe thank God.

Letter, GSP, Jr., to his father, May 29, 1906

I am very well and a little thin. I will write mama now and tell her what I have written you or better I will enclose this letter to her.

When the promotions were announced on June 13, George learned that he had been named second corporal. That meant that only one man in his class had been judged more military in appearance and conduct than he. Later, George would write in his notebook: "I got second corporal June 13 1906 but perhaps the price was over high."

He passed his academic subjects and advanced to the next year of his studies, becoming thereby an upper classman. As a third-classman, he was assigned to duty at the summer camp, where the newly entering men, the plebes, were welcomed and shaped into cadets who at least would begin to look and act like West Pointers.

Letter, GSP, Jr., to Beatrice, July 9, 1906

Dear Beatrice. The Plebes are here at last but sad to say they do not afford me much amusement as I had hoped. At first I hated to get after them and felt like a bruit when ever I "crawled" (got after) them but soon I began to feel angry when ever I saw a Plebe and have been mad for a bout three days and that is not a very pleasing condition of mind . . .

All the cadets you and K. met are missing you very much. Realy I had never thought West Point could be so nice before. But while you all were here it was great.

I told an officer here the other day that I knew a girl who had gone up the side of Crows Nest to the top and back again in an after noon and he would scarcely believe me. You are certainly great to do a thing like that . . .

[Visited people across the river the other day and] their received the greatest blow of my life. A young lady by (courtesy) and actually she is over forty nine beat me a set of tennis. It was a great shock but fortunately I was too mad for words. My last words to Papa [who attended the graduation exercises] were remember B's goat so I fancy you will soon have the nasty beast with his wood land fragrance. Please give my love to every one.

Letter, GSP, Jr., to his mother, July or August, 1906

Dear Mama: — Here I am officer of the day again sitting in the guard tent with my sword by my side waiting for mid night so that I may turn out the guard and inspect it. Truely it is funny how circumstances make a man. If I were at home I should be as young as ever but now I am so damed dignified that I seem twenty years older. I marched the batallion to dinner to day as Greble [first corporal] was on guard and last night at parade gave at last the command "Forward guide center march." Which ever since I first saw Ragland do at the VMI I have longed to do. Some people say that I have made the spooniest looking O.D. of my class. I hope so. It may help to hold down my place in September. But whether that may be or not I know this that I am the only man in my class who can march them and keep them in hand. It is true that they don't like me because of it but never the less when I get out in front of them the foolish ness stops . . .

    With lots of love your devoted son, George S. Patton
                    Cadet Corp
                    Commanding Co. "F"
                    Officer of the Day

Letter, GSP, Jr., to Beatrice, August 19, 1906

Dear Beatrice — Realy I am not half as vicious a person as you think. I have never had a duel and never want to have because if one is cought the results are too serious besides one can have just as much satisfaction in an ordinary fight. Of these I have had two . . .

During the absence of the first class last week he [Greble] was first captain and I was second. Mr. Godfrey was adjutant. Both Mr. Greble and Mr. Godfrey did very well . . . when he [Greble] was on guard . . . I was first captain . . . It was a lot of fun to command a company and once a battalion. I was also officer of the day twice . . . I believe that I reported more men [for deficiencies in dress and conduct] than any other officer of the Day this summer.

Tomorrow we are going on a six day practise march which I expect will be pretty good fun though very dirty. I fancy Mr. Greble is good enough to hold his place but I am trying my best to be at least good enough to keep my own.

He was a holy terror to the plebes that summer, a god of wrath who reported them without mercy for the slightest infraction of dress, discipline, or regulation. He even went so far as to record in his notebook some guides for "skinning," that is, things to look for when inspecting the

plebes. Many years later, Patton wrote beside these entries: "Such sentiments are unworthy of a man and a soldier. I never acted on them or
similar ones. They are left in this book to show what a fool a boy of
twenty is."

Letter, GSP, Jr., to Beatrice, August 28, 1906

Now I must say some thing that will probably make you think that
I am no good. The makes were read out to night and I went [from
second] to six. Why I don't know unless I was too d—— military.
For I certainly am the only man who can march this class.

It certainly was the biggest shock I have had for a long time for I
have tried hard to be a good soldier. Please don't think me too worth
less for I will be adjutant yet. I would not have mentioned all this
foolish ness but you are one of the few people who know the difference between one corp and an other.

His reduction in rank led him to write the following thoughts into his
notebook:

Never trust a person who has or thinks he has a cause to dislike
you. He will surely stick you in the back.

I think that there must be Destiny.

. . . if one has done ones best to prepare one will certainly succeed.

I hope and pray that *what ever* it cost I shall gane my desire.

Ambition is the projection of that which a man knows he may
become.

Letter, GSP, Jr., to his father, September 23, 1906

I have not been doing at all well in foot ball. That is in the results
I have gotten for I have not been in a single practice game with the
first team still I have managed to get pretty well bruised up and have
been so stiff that I could scarcely bend over enough to put on my
shoes . . . The picture [enclosed] is one of me as o.D. inspecting for
confinements. Then man in the tent is answering his name. Don't
let Aunt Nannie send this to B for the man in the tent is in his
underclothes (The usual uniform worn in camp.) I did not know
that the picture was being taken hence do not look very fierce . . .

I will write that letter [to Mr. Gerberding] as soon as possible.

Tell him that I did not know his address so had to send his letter
to you to forward.

I will send an other envelope just stuck together at the end addressed to him care of you. After you have corrected the letter you
can put it in there and forward it. So Mr. G will never know you
have seen it.

*Letter, GSP, Jr., to E.O. Gerberding (Hueneme, California), Septem-
ber 23, 1906*

I was so fortunate as to obtain a standing of twenty five out of a
class of a hundred and twenty men. While in the military line I am
the sixth highest ranking cadet officer in my class . . .

Hoping that I have not wearied you with these details and thanking both you and Senator Bard for your kind interest.

At the end of September 1906, he stood, in a class of 124 members, 40 in
mathematics, 110 in French, 56 in drawing. He had accumulated 7 demerits during the month. He had also written into his notebook, "Daring
is wisdom it is the highest part of war. Napier."

Letter, GSP, Jr., to his father, October 7, 1906

I have only been in two practice [football] games this year; some
way I seem to have lost my confidence and play in a sort of listless
way. I can't get back into my last years spirit to save me though I
shall make a develish try this week. The food we get at the training
table is great almost worth playing for alone . . . I hope nita has a
nice coming out Party and that she raizes hell in society a lot better
than I do in athletics.

Letters, GSP, Jr., to Beatrice, October 29, 1906

I can be absent from here any four days from the 23 of December
until the 31 that is I must be back here before 9:30 p.m. on the latter
date. So please ask your mother to tell me at what time during the
above period I would be the least trouble.

He dropped considerably in his academic subjects during October, for
at the close of the month he stood 56 in mathematics, 111 in French, and
67 in drawing. Demerits totaled 4.

Sometime that fall he started another notebook, this one devoted to
military thoughts. Identifying its contents some years later, Patton wrote
on the flyleaf: "This is the notebook kept by George S. Patton, Jr. While

a cadet at the usma. Many of the ideas are good many bad. It shows however interest in the profession of arms. G S Patton Jr."

Representative entries were:

Dummy intrenchments seem excelent devices In order to prevent the enemies artillery fire from doing much harm persuade him to believe he has put your batteries out of action by slowing [and] discontinuing your fire then when the opposing infantry advances disclose your dumy trenches and wate for the favorable opportunity to strike with your artillery. It might be possible to so confuse the enemy as to begin the counter attack at once.

Never make preparation for a retreat go into action confident of victory or at least determined not to live to conduct a retreat . . .

Do not forget the old Norman device of a feigned retreat.

The Scotch-English wars in the 14th century are not very instructive and often misleading for in many cases a *passive* defence proved effective on many occasions (not owing to its own merits which were and ever shall be O) but to the profound ignorance and carelessness of the enemy. And also the falty combination offensive strategy and tactics.

One of the chief reasons that the French and Spanish failed is that they never comprehended the true function of cavalry. Namely that it should always strike from behind.

Tactics is stratigy in minature and the essence of both is speed.

Letter, GSP, Jr., to his father, November 11, 1906

Dear Papa: Having reached the uncertain dignity and useless prerogatives of 21 I give it as my fiexed opinion that one should not be a voter until he is thirty and only then if he shows remarkable intelligence.

. . . if at 42 I have as little to cause me self respect as I now have at 21 I had better say with Hector "gape earth and swallow me." For certainly If I cannot succeed to learn french make the foot ball team or be first corp how that can I do when I have to attain ends for which I have eaven less ability.

George's class had 123 members at the end of November, and George stood 57 in mathematics, 107 in French, and 55 in drawing; he had received 2 demerits.

Letter, GSP, Jr., to his father, December 14, 1906

Dear Papa: — Mama was up here to day and I was delighted to see
her we had a nice day . . .

If I had come here to get a free education how woefully would I
have been dissapointed for what with my own and you all transcon-
tinental vageries I must cost a lot. Are you bank ruped or
not. . . .

I am feeling fine I had those two teeth pulled Friday and so am
perfect again except that I ate to much canday to day.

His standing at the end of December was substantially the same, but he
had received no demerits, apparently because he was especially careful of
his behavior, not wishing to jeopardize his four-day vacation with the
Ayers.

Letter, GSP, Jr., to Beatrice, January 11, 1907

. . . as soon as you do vote I hope you . . . vote for the Army
Appropriation Bill. I don't know just what it is for but it sounds
very military.

. . . I have recently evolved a thoery which is of great comfort to
me. Namely I think that people who are not musical are usually not
good at languages because their ear is so constructed that the fine
differences of sounds do not affect them hence they cannot pro-
nounce.

At the end of January, the third class numbered only 114 members.
George was 70 in mathematics, 99 in Spanish, 33 in drawing. He had
received 1 demerit.

Letter, GSP, Jr., to Beatrice, February 3, 1907

[Asks her to thank her mother for asking him to stop with the
Ayers for a few days in June.] I would just love to visit you all but
dont believe it would be quite square to Papa and Mama . . . the
hop is on the 21 of February. Could not you come Please.

Letter, GSP, Jr., to his father, February 3, 1907

I have been working to beat hell lately . . . for if I can go up a
little in March I may yet get *Seargent Major* which is the only job I
would like very very much. Nita says you are working too hard for
heavens sake sell every damed thing and quit.

Letter, GSP, Jr., to his father, February 10, 1907

Dear Papa. Harris, C. T. the first Captain is going in the Coast artillery and he is thinking of applying for San Diego he asked me the other day what it was like and I told him all I knew and a lot that I guessed and ended by saying I would write and find out about it.

Now the make over [promotions] comes the first of March and his recomendation is all powerful so it is as you see very needful for me to know the following facts as long before March as possible . . . [Do soldiers stay at Fort Rosecrans? how far is the fort from San Diego? does one walk or ride from the fort to town? are there any theaters in San Diego? how many hours ride is it from there to Los Angeles?] Of course I dont give a dam for Harris but I do give a lot for his recomendation . . .

I am feeling very well. Dont forget to find out those things and do so right away. Your politic son

Letter, GSP, Jr., to his mother, February 17, 1907

I am either a Philosopher or a fool perhaps both for I realy dont mind this place much infact I have been at this job nearly four years that I cant imagine any thing else . . . had I stayed at V.M.I. I would be a second lieut in the army this sommer and probably too young to be much good . . . Dont forget to look up that sandiego business *at once.*

Letter, GSP, Jr., to Beatrice, February 17, 1907

I added greatly to my popularity yesterday by putting a man on the area [that is, reporting him for an infraction of the rules and for punishment] but I only did it because I thought it was my duty and not because I wanted to for I was a great friend of the fellow.

At the end of February, he stood 50 in mathematics, 108 in Spanish, 27 in drawing; he had received 4 demerits.

Writing to Aunt Nannie some time that spring, he said he had bought a self-heating gas iron for pressing "great creases in my trousers," and he seemed to be spending a great deal of time ironing his clothes. He sold his tuxedo to a classmate named Fletcher for $15, and would Aunt Nannie send the suit — "my suit and not Pa's" — to Fletcher's aunt in New Jersey; she was to send it express collect, for he had sold the suit cheaply and therefore Fletcher had to pay the express charges; "also take all the trade marks that show it is ready made out of it I think there is one in the inside pocket on either the right or the left side . . ." He asked for five pairs of white duck pants exactly like the pair he would send her. "You see," he explained, "I must get a high ranking corp and to do it I must have lots of white trousers. The Commandant is such a fool that he will only let me have ten pair so I must get at least five more pair. . . . I went to a lecture on balloons by a french man last night it was in french . . . and I understood most of it to my great surprise."

In March, he was promoted from sixth to second corporal.

Letter, GSP, Jr., to his father, March 17, 1907

I cannot account for my sudden rise from six to two of course I skinned [reported infractions] a lot and braced my self . . . more than any one in the class . . . With any sort of luck now I should get either Sergeant Major or senior 1st Sgt. in June on[e] of which puts me in line for 1st Captain the other for adjutant

Still I must not count my chickens too soon. And owing to that very cheerful disposition inherited from you I have been worrying now for fear of loosing 2nd as much as I did before for fear of not gaining it . . .

With lots of love your devoted son 2nd Corp Patton, G. S.

At the end of April 1907, among the 112 members of the third class, George stood 65 in mathematics, 102 in Spanish, 50 in English, and 42 in drawing; he had received 7 demerits during the month.

Four compositions he wrote during the spring of 1907 indicated some of his thoughts. Describing graduation parade at the Military Academy, he expressed deep feelings of loyalty to West Point and its traditions. Depicting "The Hills," probably the Pasadena Mountains from which could be seen the sea, he made clear his fascination for the beauty of the land and nature. An essay entitled "The Necessity of a Good Library at West Point" concluded with: "we are sorry to say that there are comparatively few men in the corps who realize the importance of military study and military history which is, as Napoleon says, the only school of war." A book report on *Henry Esmond* ended with "the marriage of this most lovely and purest of women to this most noble and generous of men."

He passed all his subjects that year and moved into the second class. On the day of his departure for summer vacation in California, he was named cadet sergeant major.

CHAPTER 7

West Point: Adjutant

"How can a man fail if he places every thing subordinate to success? . . . I must do some thing."

GSP, Jr., "My Father," 1927

When I came home on furlough [in the summer of 1907] we bought a White Streak Buick and drove quite a lot, limiting ourselves to 20 miles an hour. Once we went up to Altadena to see Uncle Glassell who was dying in a T.B. sanitarium, there supported by Papa. I remember that when we went to select the car we hesitated a long time as to whether or not we should buy so complicated a machine as a four cylinder one; many favored two cylinders. That was but twenty years ago.

It was during this summer that for the only time in my life so far as I know I hurt Papa's feelings. Nita and I were going to a dance at the Wesley Clarks and I insisted on wearing Papa's opera hat with a tuxedo. We are at the Car station in front of our place on Huntington Road when Papa caught up with us with my straw hat and said the silk one was ridiculous and that just the day before he had seen Mr. Huntington wearing a straw with a tuxedo. I said that Papa did nothing but copy Mr. H. which was not true and hurt his feelings. I wore the straw.

Letter, GSP, Jr., to Beatrice, July 6, 1907

I had forgotten so many people [on Catalina Island] that it was hard to present people properly still I tried . . . I do love very much the old brown hills and the cactus. I almost felt as if I could get out of the coach and kiss them but did not go quite that far.

Beatrice asked him to spend as much time with the Ayers as he possibly could at the end of the summer before returning to West Point, and he stayed with the family the last ten days of August.

Letter, GSP, Jr. (from Avalon, Pride's Crossing, Massachusetts), to his father, August 20, 1907

Dear Papa; I got to Chicago on time after a rather bad trip for it was so hot and dusty that I got hay fever and had as usual lots of fun with my eyes and nose . . .

Mrs. Ayer met me at the station in Boston but as my train there was late I fear I gave her some bother.

Their place here is lovely almost more beautiful than it is possible to imagine. It is right on the Shore. B is here and I have no doubt at all which is the only girl I ever *loved*. She is a *peach* and I am a fool but in earnest.

This is before breakfast and I have just completed a bath in process of which I got a pound of dirt out of my hair . . .

Letter, GSP, Jr., to Beatrice, September 3, 1907

[Referring to flowers he sent to her and to her mother] I am also afraid that the ones I sent your mother were not very pretty but as I was in a great rush and the man said that they were nice I sent them.

Foot-ball has not, I am sorry to say begun yet so I have not found my self so to speak but hope I shall. People usually do if they work hard enough and play straight . . .

Mechanics is the most miserable thing I have ever struck for though I have studied the same lesson three times over I can't find out what it is about.

Around this time he wrote in his notebook: "Characteristics of a cavalry leader 1. Indomitable courage 2. Quick perception of right moment to attack 3. Capacity of inspiring confidence in troops." He added an admonition to himself: "Always work like Hell at all things and all times."

Letter, GSP, Jr., to Beatrice, mid-September 1907

. . . practice [football] has been killing but I am all right as far as nerve goes. It is funny I have changed entirely and realy enjoy getting hurt though aside from a small kick in the head I am not much the worse for the first weeks work. Of course I may not make good at first but realy I think that I will get in some games . . . if I don't it is because I am not phisically able for I am doing my best and I will win. Realy how can a man fail if he places every thing subordinate to success?

I wish you were a coach for some how you seem to be able to make me try harder sort of give me extra will power . . .

Letter, GSP, Jr., to his father, October 1907

A lot of Cadets have told me that I dropped from 2 to six [corporal last year] because I was too military and the Cadet officers thought I was sort of reflecting on them. How ever that may be I am certain that I am the best officer in my class and that there is not an other man who can controle it when marching by its self except me. Besides there is many a change between now and first class June so I have not given up being Adjutant yet though at first I felt pretty bad.

The game with Franklin Marshall College was the closest Patton ever came to playing varsity football. Toward the end of the contest the coach sent him onto the field as a substitute. After he reported to the referee but before the teams could get off a single play, the final whistle sounded, ending the game.

He told his father he had no time to read or to do anything except study and play football.

On the day after his twenty-second birthday, he confessed to Beatrice that he would not accompany the football team to Philadelphia for the game with Navy.

However I shall continue to practice until the end in the hope of learning some thing and perhaps of helping ever so little to beat the Navy . . .

I once swore that I would never ask you to another game unless I was on the team but that has proved to be impossible so as I can see no use in cutting off my nose no matter how little I like my face please come.

GSP, Jr., Notebook, November 27, 1907

George Patton you have seen what the enthusiasm of men can mean for things done. As God lives you must of your self merit and obtain such applause by your own efforts and remember that though at times of quiet this may not seem worth much yet at the last it is the only thing and to obtain it life and happiness are small sacrifices. You have done your damdest and failed now you must do your damdest and win. Remember this is what you live for. Oh you must! You have got to do some thing! Never stop until you have gained the top or a grave.

His standings in his class, reduced to 107 members, continued to be about the same. He stood between 68 and 77 in philosophy, between 91 and 105 in chemistry, between 65 and 86 in drawing. He accumulated a total of 8 demerits, a small number.

His father was coming east around Christmas time, and he would travel to West Point. George was "awfully glad . . . The Ayers have asked you and me to dinner Christmas day . . . and of course we will have to go."

Beatrice had an operation shortly after the turn of the year, probably for appendicitis, and George wrote a very short note asking her to check the appropriate box on the page — was she well, fair, or still sick? — and return it to him so he could have some news of her.

GSP, Jr., Notebook, spring 1908

I had the honor of assisting at a small dance given by Miss Tillman. Mrs. Greble said "Mr. Patton you will be a Major General yet, you are always helping doing something in the very front row." A good point George keep there.

Cadet promotions were to be announced in mid-February, and George was in a fever of excitement. There were, he wrote his father, "lots of rumors about 'makes' . . . any extra prayers will be thankefully welcomed. I may require them." Then in an utter irrelevancy, "I must admit I can't 'hit the booze' in the way a future second Lieut of Cavalry should."

Letter, GSP, Jr., to his father, February 5, 1908

I had a dream that I was adjutant and I was having a fine time then next night I dreamed I was found [failed out of West Point] and I was having a hell of a time. Every body was pointing their fingers at me and calling me stupid. I was so scared that I woke up . . .

There is no use talking the only thing I am good at is military. I can't to save my life care about studies and even if I did care about them I have not got the head for them. I can not sit down and study because I like to as some of these fools do.

Letter, GSP, Jr., to Beatrice, February 1908

I fancy I am queer but I would like to find one thing if it were only peeling potatoes that I could do better than any one else in the world. It is awful to see other people do not only some things but all things better than you do . . . there is always some one who is better in at least one thing and . . . I am not even an expert potato peeler.

The long-awaited order announced the appointment of Cadets Greble, Philoon, Simpson, Stearns, Harrington, and Delano as captains in command of the companies; and named Patton lieutenant and adjutant of the cadet battalion.

He wrote Beatrice at once, a short letter of four lines: "I got it thanks to you and have been worked to death ever since . . ."

Letter, GSP, Jr., to Beatrice, February 1908

Dear Beatrice, I have just come back from a Class meeting which as senior member I was obliged to call . . . no sooner had I called the meeting to order and proposed two men one for Editor and the other for Manager of our Howitzer [the year book] than I saw that every one was satisfied so put it to acclamation and the whole thing was over in a minute . . .

I had a little fun the other day at a lecture in Electricity. The Prof. had an induction coil with a twelve inch spark and one of the men asked if it would kill him if it passed through a mans hand or arm. The Prof invited him to try it and the man refused. I hardly liked to see the class so easily scared so after the lecture I went down and asked if I could try it for I realy was curious to see how it would feel. At first he did not want me to do it but at last he allowed me and it hardly hurt at all though my arm is still a little stiff. He did not like at all having his bluff called through.

Please don't think I am trying to pose as a brave youth. I am not. I knew that if it was really strong enough to kill the professor would not allow me to try and if it were not it would only burn for a second.

His letters to his father fell off in number as he wrote regularly to Beatrice. Under her expert probing, which was probably unconscious, he thought seriously about himself, his aims, and his ambitions. She chided him about using "I" so frequently in his letters, but it had little effect.

He was self-centered and visualized the world as an extension of himself.

Beatrice also noticed his habit of depreciating himself, of running himself down, and she admonished him gently, accusing him of fishing for compliments. It was true that he wanted reassurance and reinforcement, for he usually felt inadequate, but for the first time he seemed to begin at least to be aware of his insecurity.

Yet his appointment as adjutant gave him a new self-confidence. He had worked hard and everything had turned out well, just as he had always believed. He had attained his long-sought though hardly hoped-for prize. This seemed to give him a maturity lacking earlier, an inner conviction that he had been right all along. All he had to do to succeed was to continue as he always had. The secret was simply to strive mightily all the time.

If he had not gained that objective of being named adjutant, if he had received a lesser cadet appointment, would he have considered all his other desired goals as being beyond his reach? He might have come to accept his limitations, to renounce his wildest dreams, to be satisfied with smaller distinctions. He might, in short, have become more realistic, consequently better adjusted, and finally less strongly motivated.

The class of 1909, Patton's class, presented a "Washington's Birthday Ride for the Friends of the Cadet Corps," members of the local and larger community who supported the Academy and its activities. A large audience was present, the Academy band played martial music, and selected cadets took part in a horse show that had eleven events. George competed in the high jump with eight other cadets.

Letter, GSP, Jr., to Beatrice, February 22, 1908

Dear Beatrice; Thanks for your congratulations [on his being appointed adjutant]. I appreciate them a lot. Do you remember long ago when we rode out to the "Farm." I said I would like to be adjutant but feared I never would be and you said I would.

Since then I decided to get it and thanks to you have so they are realy your chevrons . . . The inclosed order . . . is the first one I published and I am rather proud of it. You probably think me a fool for being so pleased with my self but realy I am not so teribly stuck up for when you come down to it I have only beaten about a hundred men and that is not so very much. I wish it were more lots more . . .

[The Washington's Birthday ride that morning went well, but] my horse got foolish and I had a beastly time in getting him over the 4 ft. six mark but finally by great energy of spurring I did.

Four of us succeeded in clearing four feet eight and could have gone higher but they made us stop. Each man had a nigger soldier to hold his horse. My nigger was named Lee he was the blackest thing you can imagine but a very good orderly . . .

I shall not smoke. It is bad for the teeth and any way I dont like it for when ever you have one less habit or vice than other men you have just that much the advantage and in life particularly in the army every inch counts.

You see I have decided to stay in the army. If there is a war I will be all right. That I know. If there is not a war which God forbid I am no worse off than I would be in any other profession for aside from the army I am not of any use . . . I have convictions founded on nothing but which are a lot to me.

GSP, Jr., Notebook, spring 1908

Remember that you have placed all on war. Therefore you must never fail. Hence if you attack and you must never do any thing else put in every man and win or mark the high tide of your charge with your body. The world has no use for a defeated soldier and nothing too good for a victor.

What ever may happen what ever be the temptation to slump into a cit. [civilian] remember that you are a soldier and ever seek command. If you die not a soldier and having had a chance to be one I pray God to dam you George Patton

Never Never Never stop being ambitious. You have but one life. Live it to the full of glory and be willing to pay.

Letter, GSP, Jr., to Beatrice, March 1908

Dear Beatrice, I was realy a fool at the furlough dinner but did it from an entirely scientific desire to see what it was like and will never do it again for it was horrid. Any way to make sure I here by promise that I will never drink not even Beer. I think it is a good thing to promise to do or not do a thing because then you can't go back on it which if you only say you wont you may at times get around it or excuse your self . . .

[Had a good time fencing with the New York "Turnverine," a German fencing club from New York, using broadsword; George registered ten touches against one of their professionals while receiving only two.] of course I think he was out of practice still I was glad to beat him. Please pardon my boasting but . . . I would so like to be good with the sword.

There are two chief reasons why I prefer the cavalry. First because . . . a junior officer has a great many more chances of independent command in time of war than in the artillery and because I think that though as you say cavalry as such is out of date yet cavalry as mounted infantry is the arm of the future and I am fool enough to think that I am one of those who may teach the world its value in that line. Now this is a rash thing to say and if twenty years from now with no war and no promotion some one should say "I thought *you* were going to teach the world"? why it would hurt. But if there were no dreamers I honestly think there would be little advance and even dreams may, no must come true if a man gives his life for what he believes. Of course it is hard for any one particularly for me who have never done much to give reasons why he believes in my self but foolish as it seems I do believe in my self. I know that if there is a war "which God grant" I will make a name or at worst an end. And after all to gamble on a war is no worse than to risk a rise in stocks, and often more sure.

Perhaps . . . it is only the folly of a boy dreamer who has so long lived in a world of imaginary battles that they only seem real and every thing else unreal. But even so is it not better for a person to stick to the profession he has always thought about than for him to do something for which he has no particular desire or capacity and I certainly have none for any thing but the army. I have thought about it so long that all the other parts of ambition are dead.

The great danger in the army is that since now it is so stagnant that one is in danger of drifting not swimming and if once a young person starts to drift to busy him self with little details which seem of much moment though they are not he is lost.

The other reason of the two mentioned several chapters back [why he preferred the cavalry] is that I will hardly come out high enough [in his class standings to choose anything else].

Letter, GSP, Jr., to Beatrice, March 23, 1908

You say if I take a way heredity, and love of excitement and desire of reputation will I like the army life? . . . if you take away those three things what is left in life? If there is any thing to live for except those three things you have taken away as worthless all I have ever dreamed of . . . My field of view may, no must be small but realy tell me what else is there, for in justice to my self I ought to know.

And think in any occupation under heaven what would there be in it if you took away the desire of success which being translated means fame or more baldly glory.

. . . a man who does not make a name for him self in the army is a failure . . .

I know that it is a hard unpleasant life with lots of unfairness and lots of unplesant places where every one is against every one else, where people of small narrow spirits are taken and placed over you. I know that to a fool of my nature it is not going to be easy or plesant but I will take it all and more if I can for just one day command even a single regiment and win even a single fight . . .

I am not on the fencing team in the way you probably understand the word. I am not one of those who hopps about and tries to poke an enlarged hat pin into his opponent but I am on the broad sword team. In fact I am its papa having been trying to get up one for a long time and I hope having at last succeeded.

He was very busy that spring. His studies, his duties as adjutant, and his activities in track, polo, horsemanship, and the broad sword gave him little leisure time. What also consumed much of his time was his habit of changing his uniform, he told Beatrice, fifteen times a day in order to be clean and neat always. If Congress passed a bill to increase the number of officers in the Army by 600, there was a chance that his class would graduate in December 1908 instead of in June 1909. He wondered where he would be stationed after graduation, still a year away — in the Philippines perhaps, "I hope in China or Japan."

He confided to Beatrice, "I always feel that people only believe half what I say." Which was probably why he was prone to exaggeration.

He told his father that a new field gun, "the damdest contrivance for killing you can amigane," had a range of 6700 yards, fired a shell at a velocity of 2200 feet a second, and could get off 5 rounds per minute; with the gun in front of the house "you could aim at Alhambra and hit a man in Pasadena." He was sending a pair of trousers home, he informed Mr. Patton, and he wanted his father to take them to the tailor and have the tailor make several pairs precisely according to the model; the tailor was to "follow pattern exactly no matter how much it hurts his artistic soal." A postscript demanded: "Send some stamps."

Letter, GSP, Jr., to Beatrice, April 1908

Speaking of hats . . . foolishly I got a plume some two inches taller than regulation and . . . I have to tack around the Tacks [Tactical Officers] in truly feminine fashion . . . [California] is not so nice there are too many people electric cars and houses. California was never intended to be any thing but a ranch and City life spoils it at least for me . . . I suppose I should study but every week I hate to do it more.

Letter, GSP, Jr., to Beatrice, April 1908

things get rather monotonous here at times One can scarcely be thrilled by going to Parade with four or at most five people to watch you.

Letter, GSP, Jr., to Beatrice, April 26, 1908

As for my views on "war" as discussed by Mr. Ruskin I am inclined to think that inspite of his perfectly beautiful language and felicity of expression he knew absolutely nothing about his subject.

That is his ideas were entirely ideal and as such impossible . . . to me war is as much or more of an art than sculpture. It is really a very beautiful intelectual contest. The "butchers bill" part so to speak is to war what the physical exertion of using a hammer is to the sculptor: besides just think that in all the thousands of years during which man has been killing man there are just seven men who ever have risen above vulgar murder just seven who by scientific methods and uniform success have raised them selves to a place far above the heads of any other men that have ever lived. There are lots of great poets lots of great artists every land has one or more but there are only seven men who's greatness has made them to be recognized not by one land or one language but by all peoples and all tongues. Now I don't expect (I do hope) to be of their glorious company but it seems to me more worth while to be of their guild than to belong to any other. Of course failure in this walk of life is without conseleation [consolation]. It is awful in its perfection of obliteration. But I would rather risk this life in its entirety than by not risking not getting anything. I guess I am a F. [fool] perhaps over trained call it that in charity . . .

I am first Lt. at cavalry drill and it is lots of fun realy fine you must be here for the June ride. I am about the worst in it "No Fishing" [for compliments] partly from natural stupidity but partly from the fact that I cant practice toomuch for fear of being stiff in running as riding stunts is very hard on the knees.

The activities scheduled for the annual inspection — little more than a ceremonial visit — by the Board of Visitors in June included riding, track and field events, and a baseball game. Patton was to ride and to run both.

Letter, GSP, Jr., to Beatrice, May 1, 1908
I fear that by trying to both ride and run I shall do badly in both for at the riding hall one gets so lamed up that running is hard . . .

I am getting popular at least by some whim of fortune I was *elected* to read the Declaration of Independence in July. It is not much of a job but as I had not tried for it I was a little pleased to have even that given to me by my class. The Com. was quite funny about it. He said he heard I was chosen and then coughed a lot and finaly said, "Mr. Patton — Try not to — well dont be too military when you read it."

I have been bothered about that last letter. Perhaps I said things which though true sound rather strange. But I am rather strange too I fear.

GSP, Jr., Notebook, spring 1908
You may have made one mistake but it was due to the only noble impulse you ever had.

Letter, GSP, Jr., to Beatrice, May 17, 1908
Dear Beatrice, One of the most perfect days (as far as weather goes) that you can imagine is just dropping to sleep while the air as if fearing to wake her is so soft and balmy that it seems a crime to shut it out by walls of stone.

When assembly or call to quarters sounded the harsh notes of the drum so at variance with the quiet lovliness of Nature seemed almost symbolic of violent war compared with tranquil peace. Like the cruel clang of some heavy door shutting out beauty and quietness and imagination from the lives of those who seek ambition even at the cannon's mouth.

Letter, GSP, Jr., to Beatrice, May 22, 1908
[Had a dream and saw clearly] a man with foalded arms at the foot of my bead [bed] looking at me. He seemed to be gray and his head was sort of like the head of an Egyptian Mummy . . . It was

not in the least bothered by my sitting up but took his time and finally vanished and left the open door. Strange to say I was not very much frightened . . . I had not been reading or thinking of Egypt. Perhaps he was me as I was 4000 years ago.

At the Fifteenth Annual Field Day held at West Point on June 9, 1908, Patton won the 220-yard hurdle race, which he ran in 25 4/5 seconds, breaking the previous school record of 27 2/5 seconds. He also won the 120-yard hurdles and placed second in the 220-yard dash.

Mr. and Mrs. Patton, Aunt Nannie, and Nita came to the Academy early in July. They heard George read the Declaration of Independence at the Fourth of July exercises. Then, while George stayed at West Point with his class to welcome and train the incoming plebes at the summer encampment and to become somewhat proficient in the use of weapons, the Patton family went off to England, France, and Italy on the Grand Tour.

The Pattons were by this time quite well-to-do and probably rich. The trip to Europe was a manifestation of this relatively recent status gained by turning landholdings into cash. In addition, Mr. and Mrs. Patton were talking of building a new house — which had prompted George to ask somewhat excitedly and incoherently, "Where would you put it?"

Mr. Patton had been in business for himself — in land development and sales, wine making, investing in oil fields, and the like. He was also associated with the Bannings in various ventures — for example, he held one-seventh ownership of the Catalina Island Company, while three Bannings owned the remaining parts.

In the early years of the twentieth century, Mr. Patton worked ever more closely with H. E. Huntington, and they formed a rather impressive number of corporations dealing with matters connected to the more basic problem of transforming raw acreage into housing subdivisions. They were active in lobbying the state and the county to open roads, while they themselves extended power and light, trolley and rail transportation, water, and other amenities to land they were opening up and selling.

While the Pattons were away during the summer of 1908, E. T. Cook, secretary of the Huntington Land and Improvement Company of Los Angeles, was looking after the business details and also attending to some of Mr. Patton's personal affairs. In a letter that reached Mr. Patton at

West Point shortly before he departed for Europe, Mr. Cook assured him that everything was "in beautiful shape, and you could never have left your ranch at a better time, or the business of the office in better condition, than at present."

Mr. Cook then went on to review the latest occurrences for Mr. Patton's information. Mr. Huntington had called in a large portion of the balance due the San Gabriel Wine Company from the Dolgeville Land Company and the directors of the former corporation were therefore meeting soon to levy an assessment against the stock of the latter corporation. A letter had come from the attorney handling the estate of an Englishman who had owned some stock in the San Gabriel Wine Company. The attorney had, in Mr. Cook's words, inquired into the valuation of the stock. At the suggestion of Mr. Huntington, Mr. Cook had written a very careful letter intimating that Mr. Huntington might be willing to purchase the stock held by the estate. As for the San Gabriel River Improvement Company, it was in perfectly good condition.

Cook then listed the balances on hand in the various companies in which Mr. Patton had an interest. Huntington Land and Improvement Company, $21,404.31; Los Angeles Land Company, $3159.98; Pacific Electric Land Company, $560.79; San Marino Land Company, $47.13; Dolgeville Land Company, $1909.14; San Gabriel Wine Company, $1323.48; San Gabriel Valley Water Company, $619.38; Newport Beach Company, $36.51; Redondo Improvement Company, $2306.41; Huntington-Redondo Company, $65.10; San Bernardino Inter-Urban Railway Company, $171.43.

A movement had been organized, Cook continued, to create interest in and clamor for good roads in California. This group was sure to secure passage of a state bond issue at the end of the month — "and we will have funds then provided for the extension of many miles of fine boulevards" where Mr. Patton was developing and selling land. Mr. Huntington was building a new house and buying palm trees and rare shrubs. The Redondo Water Company was in the process of being organized. The earnings of the Pacific Electric and Los Angeles Railway companies had temporarily fallen off.

Finally, Mr. Cook had paid some of Mr. Patton's small personal bills, club dues and the like. Mr. Patton could therefore travel in Europe with an easy mind, without the slightest worry about business matters.

At West Point, George was practicing on the rifle range. "I made 'marksman' [the lowest qualified category]," he wrote Beatrice, "and tomorrow have to try for 'Sharp Shooter.' If it is a good day I think I shall make it but if it is blowing very very hard in different directions perhaps I shall not."

Letter, GSP, Jr., to Beatrice, July 1908

[Eight cadets were dismissed from West Point for hazing plebes.] Those cadets who got it were in general no worse than any others but were unfortunate in being found out. The hazing they were doing and that was being done [by others] was not of a bad sort and hurt no body not even the Plebes. Infact lots of them require just such treatment to make them wake up and find them selves . . . There are regulations which say that what they did is hazing so that . . . they only received the regulation punishment . . . and in a way it is good for the corps that it happened for it has broken up the notion that a first class man is the greatest thing on earth and that he can't be found [dismissed]. An idea which though very satisfactory in its self is not very efficient in promoting good order etc.

I was fortunate to make sharp shooter and am now trying for "expert rifelman" the highest grade of all. Perhaps I can make it too. At least it is not impossible and so far in practice I have the highest score though that does not count for much in the record shoot . . .

Mr. Nelly is now head coach [of the football team] and has put me at end again and told me he wanted me to make good. Lord I hope I can. I have been practising as much as I can and have improved a lot on getting forward passes which have always been a bother to me . . .

A little boy told his mother that he could not see any difference between church and a base ball game for at one they said stand up for the Lord and at the other they said for God's sake sit down.

Letter, GSP, Jr., to Aunt Nannie, July 1908

[Hoping to get expert rifleman] it will do me a lot of good on military efficiency if I can get it. Besides I would like it for its own sake . . . The polo team I am on . . . has not been beaten yet and has never played a period with out scoring.

Letter, GSP, Jr., to Beatrice, July 31, 1908

I did make "Expert Rifle Man" which is the best you can get [and after qualifying as Expert for three consecutive years, he could try for Distinguished Marksman] . . . We have been making maps lately at the scale of three inches to the mile. You have no idea how small it is. You can put all W.P. on a half dollar and have room left over too but it is quite interesting and very instructive for it is just the sort of work a man has to do in war particularly in the cavalry . . . Which do you think is the better branch the Infantry or the Cavalry. I cant decide at all. A lot of people have been talking infantry at me.

Letter, GSP, Jr., to Beatrice, August 13, 1908

[Took a very pretty ride to look over some ground where a sham battle was to take place. Described the hills back of Highland Falls, apple trees, blackberry bushes, ruined houses, and stone walls in poetic terms. The apples] were so green that only the horses and I ate them.

We are going to have a polo game with the officers this after noon. I play [number] two on the cadet Team. We will have four horses each and it will be fine if we win.

[Sunday morning the class was going to Fort Wright on Fisher's Island off the New York shore to spend a week] shooting big guns and getting sun burned.

Letter, GSP, Jr., to Beatrice, August 20, 1908

We had realy a very nice time at Fort Wright and I got fat so you will hardly know me unless I shrink this week.

I will go over to the hotel and look for you as soon as I get back [from a practice march to be held] on the 29.

Beatrice came to West Point for the weekend, accompanied by Miss Rosalind Wood, her cousin — the daughter of Beatrice's half sister — who would later become Countess Guardabassi and who would see George in Paris during World War I.

At the beginning of the following week, the Commandant of Cadets made some startling changes in the military standings of the first class, Patton's class. Now the captains were to be, in order, Cadets Baehr, Philoon, Delano, R. D. Smith, Stearns, and Harrington; Patton was to remain as lieutenant and adjutant; lieutenant and quartermaster was to be Greble, formerly the First Captain; lieutenants were to be Donaldson, Marks, Simpson, Sage, Johnson, Caher, Godfrey, McGree, Fuller, Rumbough, Briscoe, Brice, Eichelberger, Gage, Milling, Purdon, Everts, and Ahern.

George was elated.

Letter, GSP, Jr., to Beatrice, September 1, 1908

I was not skinned I was not busted and you were here and I had the best time I had enjoyed since July [when Beatrice had been at West Point too]. The new makes were a great surprise to every body particularly the new first Captain. As far as looks go he is not much being short and awkward. As far as culture goes he is worse being a German from Chicago but he is efficient and a good man at heart a man who, though I would not give you a dance with, is still very much a man and a clean one at that.

I was very mad over the way some people treated him. They sneared in his very face which only made me more noisy in my congratulations. Mr. Greble acted rather well but it hurt him a lot to be dropped.

Sunday morning [before the announcement of the new makes] the Com sent for me and told me the new makes and said some very foolish yet very nice things about me. I went about inflated to the bursting point all day.

Foot ball starts tomorrow and it is now or never oh God grant that it be now.

Letter, GSP, Jr., to Aunt Nannie, September 1908

[The new makes were surprising; Baehr, an acting First Sergeant, moved all the way up to First Captain; Greble was dropped from captain to quartermaster; Simpson was reduced from captain to lieutenant.] But I stayed on and there is no longer any doubt who is who. I am *it*. The Com. called me over and told me all sorts of things which I do not see fit to write but at least while he is here I am the man behind the throne.

I am sorry for Mr. Greble. It hurt him very much.

Letter, GSP, Jr., to Beatrice, September 9, 1908

If you realy want to know what the Com was foolish enough to say I think it would go better in conversation than in print realy it was not much . . .

[Football practice started, and George was playing end and

center.] Realy it is awful to see men worse than you think your self put in a head of you. I wish you were here all the season for some how I work harder when you are around. Should I fail to do some thing please cuss me out once in a while will you I must do some thing [in life].

Letter, GSP, Jr., to his mother, September 13, 1908

I am awfully glad Aunt Nannie got those [military] books for I wanted them and I think that they are very good books and this practice march has more than ever convinced me of the value of book knowledge of war. It is the whole show and there are surprisingly few men who seem to realize its importance.

Beatrice insisted that she wanted to know what the Commandant of Cadets had told him to make him "inflated to the bursting point," and she finally ordered him to tell her, sweetening her ultimatum by sending him a photograph of herself.

Letter, GSP, Jr., to Beatrice, September 18, 1908

[Thanks for the photograph, which he prizes] it being as you know the first and only picture you ever honored me with . . .

. . . the Com. sent for me and having told me to stand "at ease" informed me that he was going to remake a lot of men and would I please give him my honest opinion (that sort of a please is an order). He then said a lot of rot about me to the effect that I was the only man who did my duty in the class (which is not so). Also he asked me who to make first Capt. We did not agree on that and he then said would you like it. I said NO! He said "I did not think you wanted it besides I want you as Adjutant but I wanted your opinion. But if Mr. Baehr is no good we will have to make you [First Captain]." Mr. Baehr is good thank the Lord. He then asked me who to make Lieutenants and made four out of the five I named. This I realy do consider a compliment to my judgement. There was some more stuff that I have forgotten.

Now I have obeyed orders [from Beatrice] and feel like a silly person to say so much about my self.

Realy B. you must never tell any body either now or here after because they would not understand. Please remember.

Now to a state secret also entre nous. We are in one H—— of a fix for foot ball men . . . I am not kicking but I fear they will make me play center not because I can't play end but because there are absolutely no centers none what ever . . .

The first scrimage is next Saturday.

As yet I am not nervous.

Letter, GSP, Jr., to Beatrice, September 29, 1908

. . . all I ever wanted chevrons for was to impress the people I liked. We had a very hard practice monday and I did my self proud until the last down when I broke the small bone of my left arm. I am rather put out over it (so is the bone) as I was going in the game Saturday also as it has kept me awake . . . Still the doctor says I will be out in five weeks and that would give me four weeks more of this my last season; I have already devised a brace so hope to get in again. . . .

I would rather that you say nothing to any body about that little accident to my flipper. Realy it can't be helped and it might worry them. You are tuffened so I can tell you.

Letter, GSP, Jr., to Beatrice, October 2, 1908

The coaches are going a good deal for me trying to get me out of this —— place but Dr. Gandy is a stiff necked old fool and my spirit sinks from week to week. I would take another year to play on that team realy I would and you know I have been here over long already. I am going to change my name for I dont like the "Smith" part of it and as with out that I am not a Jr. I shall drop that too.

What do you think of the notion? It will be particularly useful here as it saves time in signing my name.

My but it is hard to decide between the white [infantry] and the yellow [cavalry]. There are so many considerations each way I stay awake during many hours drifting first one way then another . . . There seems to be a nicer class of people in the cavalry than in the Infantry but in time of war the infantry is best and the promotion faster. Again the drills in the cavalry are more plesant and it takes about 13 years to be a first Lieutenant while in the Infantry the drills are slow and a first Lieutenant comes in seven years with prospects of being more rapid. Oh! it is hard to decide.

Letter, GSP, Jr., to Beatrice, October 15, 1908

. . . these fool Dr's insist that I am still sick, asses that they are. I have been trying for the last week to get them to take a large quan-

tity of cement which they call a cast, off my arm but they refuse to do
it D—— them . . .

I have lost all interest in West Point and every thing else. What is
the good of being at all if one cannot be what one wants to be?

And when I graduate and become a second Lieutenant of infantry
or cavalry ranked by a lot of hounds and with no prospects of war or
any thing else why Hang it all any way.

Letter, GSP, Jr., to Beatrice, November 11, 1908

I am growing old inside while to all external appearances I am as
big a fool as ever. Yet the voice inside says, "You are twenty three
years old [today] other men at your age have been men you are a
school boy. Before long they will be playing taps over you and how
will you answer the question "What have you done?" Answer nothing.

Now the worst part is that these wise reflections do not bother me
at all. I go on living for the next breakfast . . .

The question of branch is very hard indeed. Not that I should not
like either but which is best where is there the most opportunity or
where the least sameness I am having a most hellish time trying to
decide realy a HELLISH time . . .

We are going to New York tomorrow to the horse show and I expect to have a stupid time . . .

I shall not break training or promises either. Nothing but soda
water shall pass my mouth.

Letter, GSP, Jr., to his father, November 1908

I went down to see Capt. Summerall to day and asked him about
things in general. He said that he would advise me as a choice between cavalry and infantry to take the cavalry and he gave a lot of
good reasons. Infact he was very nice about it.

We went to the New York horse show last night and it was the
bummest thing I ever saw. Nothing was good but the horses. The
riding was horrible. There were no people of note there and infact
the attendance was very small and no enthusiasm was shown . . .
Capt. Henry conducted the expidition and I think I got my quill to
work on him [meaning George was very attentive and flattering to
Henry]. At least I did my darndest and I usually succeed. Tell
Mama not to worry. I won't fall in love with Kate [a student at
Vassar] until B busts me then I would be a fool not to. [There are]

40 000 000 reason [meaning that Kate's family or Kate herself was worth $40,000,000].

I have been having a great slump in studies lately but hope to stop soon or I will get the infantry any way [traditionally, those at the academic bottom of the graduating class became infantry officers] . . .

My increased age does not affect me very heavily. I am still an ass.

Letter, GSP, Jr., to Beatrice, November 1908

[He was wearing an arm brace and hoping to start football practice the next day on the scrub team, but would be playing left half back]. They never will put me where I ought to be but what is the difference if only I get in the mixup and help beat the navy . . . realy I hate to graduate and leave this place for though it is hard it has a power that no other place would have had in my case; that of making me less of a child and more of a half man and of showing me that there is no such thing as the great "they say" that fantom which has scared so many people out of doing what they knew to be best . . .

Promotion is not the only reason for taking or not taking the Cavalry. Realy it is a most complex question in which inclination makes war on reason and glamor blinds me to advantages.

. . . Papa has no objection to my changing my name and it's so much easier to write and Smith such a name.

Letter, GSP, Jr., to Beatrice, November 25, 1908

[Playing full back in practice; talking of graduating from West Point and getting out into life] No matter how hopeful a person is it is not possible to dive into black water with out wondering what sort of devil fish and sharks inhabit it. Not that I fear them but that I am curious . . .

If I could only do the things that don't show with as much ambition as I try to do the things that show I might in many years ammount to some thing but I am as weak as water in such matters . . .

. . . it is that slackness at the middle distance which looses the race of life . . . I know that to run a hundred [yard dash] you must say to your self the next step will be faster must be faster and as it is but a short distance you can drive your self and win but in a twenty five year race it takes a lot to keep going faster. Some times I fear that it takes a lot more than I have got but God grant that I may be mistaken . . .

I am on guard and having just skinned a lot of people feel rather mad. It is strange but this guard business always makes me mad.

I called on Capt. Sommerall last week . . . and we talked . . . the business of being a soldier and realy I look on it in just the same way that I would look on law or potatoes. There is realy very little difference except that mine is more respectable being older [as a profession]. He (Capt. Sommerall) said that in his opinion Cavalry was a better branch than infantry that there was more to do and that therefore a man was likely to be happier. As to promotion it was undoubtedly slow but that in any case promotion in peace was not worth any thing and that a man though a second lieutenant ranked where his ability placed him . . . And that in time of war they began to look for any body no matter what his rank so long as he would win. That is so long as he was good in his profession. This means that a man may work a long long time and not be noticed . . .

But I went into this thing with my eyes open perhaps wider than many. I don't want pleasure I want success. I would rather work a hundred years to win one battle than play a thousand . . .

Oh what an ass I am.

CHAPTER 8

West Point: Graduation

"I have got . . . to be great . . . It is in war alone that I am fitted to do any thing of importance."

GSP, Jr., "My Father," 1927

The winter before I graduated Papa was at West Point and I had a long talk with him in the libruary. I said that I was in love with Beatrice but was afraid to propose. Papa encouraged me to do so, I did, only to be accepted.

Letter, GSP, Jr., to Mr. Ayer, January 3, 1909

My dear Mr. Ayer: I am writing to thank you for my splendid Xmas [spent with the Ayer family in Massachusetts] and to explain myself.

I have loved Beatrice ever since the summer in California but as I am not very old and have never done anything I have never until the thirtieth of December told her so. I then decided that it was my duty to speak as it was perhaps the last chance I would have before going I know not where.

I could not have done it here at West Point in June as she would be my guest. I did not do it at the Farm while walking or driving as it would have been taking advantage of the privilidge of being with her. I therefore told her at your house in Boston which was as near neutral ground as I could get.

I know sir that my profession is one of slow and in cases uncertain rise, that the lives of those connected with it are not easy. For some reasons therefore I could have wished that I had chosen another course. But after examining all the possible ones for which I might have any ability I believe that I am only capable of being a soldier.

Bearing those things in mind I told Beatrice that I loved her, but I asked nothing in return.

That I may do some thing which shall make her think me not too unworthy is all I hope for.

I trust sir that you understand my position and that you will forgive any unusual presumption which I have shown.

Thank you ever so much for all the kindness you have shown me ever since I first met you.

I am very sincerely and respectfully yours.

George Patton

Letter, Mr. Ayer to GSP, Jr., January 1909

My dear George, Your frank letter of the 3rd deserved an earlier reply, but absence in New York, and pressure of important matters, since my return, have prevented.

It is no wonder to me that you, and I may say Beatrice, have felt a growing admiration for each other, and I admire the delicate manner in which you have treated the matter.

Beatrice has a pretty well developed, mature, mind of her own, and can speak for herself.

Referring to your profession I believe that it is narrowing in tendency.

A man in the army must develop mainly in one direction, always feel unsettled — That his location and home life are subject to the dictation and possible freak of another whom he may despise or even hate.

A man like you should be independent of such control — His own master — Free to act and develop in the open world. I would compare the military man to a tree grown in the forest — as against one in the field with plenty of room to spread!

You must pardon my assumption in commenting upon an occupation known to be most respectable, and earnestly sought and won with great labor, and this without suggesting a better one, but I do it from the point of a free man — always at liberty to go and come — governed only by surrounding conditions, and my own judgment . . .

. . . I believe that the qualities of a good soldier — and let me add the training will help a man to win whatever calling he may choose

With affectionate regards I am

Yours very Sincerely —

Letter, GSP, Jr., to Beatrice, January 6, 1909

Dear Beatrice: At last the letter came and though it took me some hours to get up courage enough to read it, it was the nicest finest most generous letter I ever hope to get. Your father is a King and a great one.

. . . I have loved you a long time but as I have said with all honesty I did not think you would ever like me very much because you are so much to good for me. Therefore I fixed my life so to speak in such a way as to best do something worthy of you . . . I had intended to stay in the army and to resign and join the first foreign nation which might have a war. For it is in war alone that I am fitted to do any thing of importance. I could have had plenty of employment and some honor and have been ready for our war, the one of my dreams which will come.

But since I found out that you don't hate me that is perhaps changed . . .

Therefore I must look for something else perhaps for the army in peace is worse than "dry rot." I will have to prepare for the war but get out of the army after I have done a year about. That is if I can find any place less dead that I can get into. If not I will stay in the army and try to pull wires for special detail. All this for love of you. The "all" I just used is in derision of the little I can do to be good enough for you . . .

. . . after I read the turkey letter [acknowledging how Beatrice felt about him] I sat with out moving for an hour and then went out and ran around the hills like a loon.

Good night and try to make me think properly.

George.

Letter, GSP, Jr., to his father, January 10, 1909

Dear Papa: You were right last Christmas . . . you then said I was having puppy love. I must be having the mange now but it feels the same. B said she had been keeping her heart down so long that it was like a cold storage turkey when it first got loose . . . Gosh I have the queerest feelings. I am actually afraid to see B for fear of doing things. She did not want me to propose though because she said that she had me too much at her mercy here and hoped I would wait until I had gotten out and seen other girls so that she would catch [me] fairly . . . For the same reason I have not made any exact propositions. That is I made her stop answering what I said. Undoubtedly I am in the hell of a fix [in love] yet this did not prevent me from going up to Vassar with Kate and falling in love with her for the entire afternoon. Yet if you put the $40 000 000 [of Kate's] against the B. I fear that I would take the B ass that I am when with the money I could be a general in no time.

Letter, GSP, Jr., to his parents, January 17, 1909

Dear Papa and Mama. Of all the many fine letters you have written me the one I got yesterday was the finest. Thank you ever so much. The

Ayers are allright. I wrote Mr. Ayer and he wrote me a long letter I must admit that not much of it refered to B directly but all of it indirectly by asking me why on earth I wanted to stay in the army. It is strange those people cant understand ambition except to get rich and actually I dont believe they give much of a dam about that even. All they want to do is to live happily until they die. Now if I should live that way I would die all through life . . .

She saw my letter to her father in which I stated what I had done and the reason I had done it and she said it was the "most manly kiddiest dearest letter in the world."

Now for some serious talk. All my life I have done every thing I could to be a soldier for I feel inside that it is my job and that war will come though at present prospects I am very blue. When however I proposed to Beatrice I did something from instinct and against reason. At least it seems unlogical because she does not like war, because she is not as rich as another girl "Kate" who would I think have married me and because a soldier should not marry. This because money seems an excellent tool, not for my own use, but to buy success and if I were unmarried I could get more things by paying attention to daughters of prominent people if necessary marrying one of them. Now these things are not nice but they are logical and I had carefully planned to climb the ladder and I had a pretty clear field. But when I see B. all logic goes to hell . . . Realy I have no strength of character. I know what is right but I think of Beat and straight way stop all sane mental manoeuvers and fall down and worship her and enjoy doing it better than any thing else in the world. Am I an ass or just human. Would an embrionic great man have acted as I did or do I show my self a *mess*. God knows I am worried to death. I have got to, do you understand got to be great it is no foolish child dream it is me as I ever will be. I am different from other men my age. All they want to do is to live happily and die old. I would be willing to live in torture, die tomorrow if for one day I could be realy great. Yet with all this I have stepped aside from my course and could not no would not help it, inconsistent fool that I am.

. . . Would I in justice to my self do right to stay in the army during long years of peace and by so doing become pot bound and with out ambition. Could I do better by resigning in a year or so and trying to do something as a citizen [civilian] while waiting for a chance to do somewhat as a soldier. That is could I be safe in relinquishing the certainty of average military success in peace, say by efficient work which I can do and retire as a brigadier or to quit the army and try some thing which would permit me to get into politics. Of course what I say is exceeding general and unspecific for in the first place I could do but few things as a cit. Second I would do even fewer for I don't want to become local. I must stay national, that is in the harder yet wider field. Do you see what I mean and do you think me a unusually brainless fool? . . . There is inside me a burning something that makes me want to do . . . I wake up at night in a cold sweat imagining that I have lived and done nothing. Perhaps all people have it but I dont believe they do. Perhaps I am crazy. There is no use concealing things from you for you might help and ought to know. I want to be a dictator or a President. No small ambition for a goat yet why not some one has to be why not me. At least I think a man can not do wrong to try for the most. If you look always up you are not apt to go down. Now it is so important I start right yet so hard oh so hard to know just what is right. Oh god could I but see a head ten years. But enough of this. I don't believe after all that had I been intended to do things which Beatrice would stop that I would have been allowed to meet her for it would have been too cruel. She got the idea that I thought she wanted me to resign on her account so she said, "A woman who hampers a man at the beginning of his career is a hateful abomination, and he always thinks so sooner or later. So you had best not consider me at all in making your decision. The family might not thank me for telling you this but I think it . . . A girl might just ruin a man's life by upsetting it at the beginning. You can decide better if you consider your self as one instead of as two. You must decide alone and then I will go with you *any* where." How is that? Realy she could not be such a bother could she?

I am writing an answer to Mr. Ayer's letter and in it I explain as far as possible my rather unexplanable views and suggest the possibility that I may resign [from the Army] some day this with the object he wants me to and therefore if he thinks I might he might get me a good thing. At least he has a lot of influence and it is a possibility not to be thrown away. You see I dont commit myself. I just let fall a hint and wait development . . .

[Has a high average in drill regulations] but it is tactics and the stuff I have always loved so I dont deserve much credit . . .

Your devoted much perplexed ass of a son

George Patton

Letter, GSP, Jr., to Beatrice, January 17, 1909
Dearest Beaty . . . before every thing else I am a soldier and what ever I do as a citizen will be to help me as a soldier . . . But one thing I must

clear up in your mind though it hurt you. I am *not* a *patriot*. The only thing I care for are you and my self, my self in that I may be worthy of you. I would just as gladly fight for any country against any country, except this one. I say this because I am what you should know me. Perhaps I am no worse than others only more honest but if I were worse I could not help it . . . I may loose ambition and become a cleark and sit by a fire and be what the world calls happy but God forbid. I may be crazy but if with sanity comes contentment with the middle of life may I never be sane. I don't fear failure I only fear a slowing up of the engine which is pounding on the in side saying up — up — some one must be on top why not you.

Darling you cant know what that which I have just said cost me . . .

. . . Please love me inspite of my folly but don't love me by reason of ignorance of it. You see the chance of my doing what I wish is so small that I will be very likely to be dissapointed and being so dissapointed it might revert to others who I love so I must tell them.

I am glad your father thinks it all right for me to stay in the army . . . he thought I could get on out side well too. But my hopes and views are so insane that I don't think he understands them; no one does, not even you, and Lord knows I bother you seven days in the week with them — poor B.

. . . I begin to think I was a fool to tell you all I did at first in this letter but I would rather make you made [mad] now than dissapoint you later.

Letter, GSP, Jr., to Mr. Ayer, January 18, 1909

My dear Mr. Ayer. You seem to be for ever doing things for me and I never doing any thing for you. I am grateful but wish I could give more substantial proof.

The reason I have not answered sooner is that I wanted to devote proper time . . . to my reply and dont get much except on Saturday and Sunday.

With reference to the profession of a soldier; I think I appreciate most of its draw backs. As you say it is very narrowing, but don't you think that a man of only very ordinary capacity in order to succeed against great competition must be narrow. That is have only one motive.

I have had no experience but from what I have read of successful men they seem to be of the one idea sort.

It is hard to answer inteligibly the question of "Why I want to be a soldier." For my own satisfaction I have tried to give my self reasons but have never found any logical ones. I only feel it inside. It is as natural for me to be a soldier as it is to breathe and would be as hard to give up all thought of it as it would be to stop breathing.

But being a soldier, and being a member of the army in time of peace, are two different things. I would only accept the latter as a means to the former. As you say sir peace service is narrowing tedius, perhaps unplesant, and above all distructive of initiative which is the one quality necessary to a successful soldier.

Therefore it is my intention if possible to resign after serving a year or so first. This service is necessary to learn the ground work and detail which are necessary in every business. Of course I can not say when I will resign for two reasons: first I would have to find some thing to do which my special training would enable me to do. Second I have got to find some thing which offers more advantages than the army. For special details [in the Army] may be gotten by hard work and political influence which offer some chance for independent action.

As you say, my resignation would not effect my desire to accomplish military success, for in any war . . . nearly our entire army will be volunteer and malitia [militia] and a retired army officer could I think get higher command as a malitia man than as a regular. Higher command gives freedom of action and freedom of action opens the road to success or failure in war . . . besides should I never resign I can always live in the Army . . .

I have expressed my self as well and clearly as I can, as far as I can see. If I have ommited any thing you would wish to know I hope you will tell me and I will answer if I can. I hope I have not bothered you with this letter but thought you had a right to know my views. Thanking you again for your kind interest I am Very devotidely your's George Patton.

GSP, Jr., Notebook, January 20, 1909

Napoleon never niglected a detail. When he could not win over a man he made it at least appear to others that he had done so. Nothing is too small to do to win.

Letter, GSP, Jr., to Beatrice, January 27, 1909

Dearest Beatrice . . . I suppose I am pretty variable but just now I have shifted back and fear that the army is the only place for me. I have tried hard for your sake as you don't like it to think of another profession but it is like pulling hair. I don't know or care about other things . . . This will shock you but the other things don't seem worthy some how. I don't want to make money and that is all success in business amounts to in the last aspect.

I might go out of the service if I had a startling chance but to go out and just start business for its own sake I don't believe I could. As far as will goes I could but it would be self murder. I might if you wanted it but I would be no good to you I fear. The chief difficulty you have is in realizing that the army is a profession just like any thing else yet it is and please try and think of it as one. I don't want to boast but the chances seem to point to my being some thing in the army out of it nothing. Dear don't bother about it. I am only trying to think visibly as it were. But Im not at all decided. Dont be bothered please.

GSP, Jr., Notebook, January 1909

Should a man get married he must be just as careful to keep his wifes love as he was to get it. That is he should always be spoony and make love to her so she will continue to like him for it would make her most sad if he said as it were "Now I have got you I will take a rest." Don't do that ever.

Letter, GSP, Jr., to his father, January 31, 1909

Dear Papa, I read and appreciated your fine letter. And it agrees exactly in most points with what I had concluded so having you say it renders me more happy in my decision.

B was here all day and I had the time of my life. So did she and I can say this without boasting she is fool enough to be crazy about me.

. . . the poor kid is in the hell of a fix. She wants to marry me right away but can't on account of thinking it wrong to leave her father who is pretty old [Mr. Ayer was eighty-seven]. That is the reason she does not want to be thought engaged for fear that it would have to last too long a time, until he dies to be brutil and exact. Of course she did not say that. She . . . was lamenting her inability to cook and take care of a house and not spend too much money . . . I have had letters from boath of them [Mr. and Mrs. Ayer] and neither of them object to me at all. In fact they are a lot more warm than you all would be over a suitor of Nita's. But though they don't say it is just as clear as day that they dont understand the army business at all. It is inconceavable to them that a man can have no desire to gain [money] and can wish to kill a fellow being by any such coarse method as shooting. They prefer starvation I suppose or other "trust" and trusty methods.

. . . She [Beatrice] is all right. I think if I was a bar keeper she would say that it was an enobling job poor little fool girl . . .

Any how it is settled that I go in the army and I told her so. It will be harder telling Mr Ayer. So far though I have been doing it steadily for years he won't believe me yet . . .

With lots of love your devoted and decided son. George Patton

GSP, Jr., Notebook, February 1909

When you have thoughtfully chosen a course stick to it as if it were the only one and don't bother about other courses. Papa.

Letter, GSP, Jr., to Mr. Ayer, February 3, 1909

My dear Mr. Ayer. Please pardon my slowness of reply but questions of moment cannot be too rapidly disposed of.

You know, I hope, of the great admiration I have for you and of the high reguard in which I hold your wisdom and experience. So in trying to decide what my immediate future shall be I have considered carefully the advice you have been kind enough to give me; and have *come to a decision.* I am some what *young* to be talking about having decided any thing yet in this case decision is imperative as any thing started with vascilation had better not be started.

Now no matter how logical a man may be in trying to dicide on his course he must of necessity be guided in a great measure by that unexplained force called instinct. I have combatted this force as much as I think is safe but find that it still impells me to the army as my primary, to the civil only as my secondary, occupation and not the reverse.

As you say to succeed in business a man should start young. Therefore as I believe the army to be my first business I must learn it well and at once.

. . . I am aware of what may almost be called presumption, on my part, in following my own untried judgement in opposition to the honest opinion of many people of vastly more experience than I possess. But in the army I am sure of my self and I like it, while in other walks of life I have no assurance nor enough experience to say whether I like them or not. Also being young I still believe that I can succeed in any vocation where will and hard work are necessary to success. Yet even great success in an occupation not to ones liking would be less valuable than a smaller success in a congenial occupation.

. . . Hence I am going in the army as if I intendid to stay in it always and make what reputation I can so that should I remain I may do well and should I find occasion to resign I will be thought a man of capacity.

I regret that my resolution may not in all respects accord with your judgement nor perhaps with that of Beatrice. Yet as I am acting in good faith and to the best of my ability what I do cannot be very wrong.

I hope you will not think me visionary or brainless for I am not so intentionally.

Thank you again for your great kindness and consideration towards me believe me

    Devotedly yours George Patton.

Letter, Mr. Ayer to GSP, Jr., February 9, 1909

My dear George, — On returning from New York I find your favor of the 3rd inst . . .

You state very fully and clearly your position and decision, upon which I have very little comment to make. Your high position in your profession (as it comes to me) shows that you have a taste for it and that you have devoted yourself to the business, which makes it natural that you should want to continue and reap the benefits; or at least, continue long enough to see a little further into the future and to enable you to guess at the possibilities.

    Very sincerely yours,

Letter, GSP, Jr., to Beatrice, February 16, 1909

Dearest Beat . . . Sometimes I get violent with my self in defence of my profession which to me seems very good. It is the oldest and at one time was the only business that was proper. Why then should it be degraded by the products of its own exertions. Only because long peace has blinded people to its value. When danger comes it at once assumes its old proportions and is all. Nothing else counts. I dare say that for every man remembered for acts of peace there are fifteen made immortal by war and since in my mind all life is a struggle to perpetuate your name war is naturally my choice. It is true that there is nothing particularly heroic in drilling a troop yet is there any thing very elevating in an office chair . . . Realy I cannot see where any business holds out at its start attractions which over shadow mine nor chances better if as good.

There are very few people who start life with all they want where every thing is to their taste. Friends houses worldly goods etc. nor do I think that they would amount to much if they were so situated. It is hard for me but vastly harder for you to appreciate this for both of us have had all we want and more than was good for us. We have been fortunate too in seeing those we loved often well provided for at the start.

The vast majority of people die with out one tenth the comforts you commanded at birth. Nor do I think were I a civilian that I could offer you as much as I can in the army and this is distinctly not much . . . I have decided that it is not right to go around and continually apologize for ones profession when one is proud of it and knows it and would not be otherwise if he could. This thought was brought home to me the other day by some army women who were lamenting their sad state. I could not but think that they were probably very much better off than they would be had they married civilians. It was quite true that their houses were not of the best but that cast discredit on the government not on them and besides there was no rent and every four years or oftener they change. It is true that families get seperated but when they are together they see lots more of each other. And though they have to live in queer places and have a right to kick at that part of it I am not so affected as Lord deliver me from all cities (unless you are there) any way.

Beat I love you very much and I can't tell it to you at all yet some how I think you know it and I love to hope you do.

Darling girl good night

George.

GSP, Jr., Notebook, early 1909

Do not regard what you do as only a preparation for doing the same thing more fully or better at some later time. Nothing is ever done twice. There is but one time to do a thing that is the first the last . . . There is no next time. This is of special application to war. There is but one time to win a battle or a campaign. It must be won the first time . . . In making an attack make only one and carry it through to the last house holder. Make the men who have gained ground lay down and hold it. What folly to let them fall back to take part in a fresh assault when to gain what they have given up you have to make a new assault to that point. Remember Frederick the Great how he said to his faultering men "Come on men do you want to live for ever?"

I believe that in order for a man to become a great soldier . . . it is necessary for him to be so thoroughly conversant with all sorts of military possibilities that when ever an occasion arises he has at hand with out effort on his part a parallel.

To attain this end I think that it is necessary for a man to begin to read military history in its earliest and hence crudest form and to follow it down in natural sequence permitting his mind to grow with his subject until he can grasp with out effort the most abstruce question of the science of war because he is already permiated with all its elements.

Letter, GSP, Jr., to Beatrice, February 18, 1909

Dearling Beatrice: You are a dear but just a little foolish for I am not worth much. There have been Adjutants [at West Point] every year so realy I am not extraordinary nor efficient . . .

. . . there is a sort of feeling that is caused by masses of people. I can't explain it but it thrills and moves me wonderfully. I have it when there are crowds at Parade or other places and it is great.

Letter, GSP, Jr., to Beatrice, February 21, 1909

Beatrice dear . . . Realy all joking aside I don't expect ever to be sixty not that it is old but simply that I would prefer to wear out from hard work before then. Nor do I care for a home and friends and peace and a regular order of life. I would like to fight up to the top and then go off the edge and rest in a better at least quieter place than earth.

And if a man makes a success in the Army . . . To do his duty and be retired bah! Now what I have said is not horrid but if I go early you will too if we love each other enough and we do.

Letter, GSP, Jr., to Beatrice, March 10, 1909

We fenced off the broad-sword champion ship to day and I am not it. Mr. Pullen beat me and unfortunately . . . I lost out. I am pretty poor in athletics . . .

I used to fancy that I was [King] Arthur come back from the Island-vally of Avilion . . . I realy used to be quite sure I was. There was an old iron stick or bolt in a wall near the wood house and I used to pull at the thing quite sure it was Excalibur. But it was not. At least it is still there. I have never pulled it out. I had best stop this foolish talk.

Letter, GSP, Jr., to Beatrice, March 21, 1909

[Describes a tug of war.] I thought I had broken some thing in side but could not ask any one for if some thing had been broken they would not have let me pull the next time. It was pretty hard to pull the second heat when I was expecting all my inside to rip but they did not and this morning I went to the hospital and found that it was only a muscle pulled out of place a little. It is all right now only a little stiff. It only shows what a coward a man is to always think he is killed when he is not even hurt. I got an awfully nice sweater with an A on it . . . My but I wish that I had gotten my A in foot ball. If I only had I would think that I was pretty good but as it is I am not much of an athlete.

I lunched with Capt. [Guy] Henry to day . . . Breeding tells in men just as in horses and he is a corker realy I have never met a more charming man. While off duty he is very friendly. On duty he is strictness its self. You ought to see him ride realy it is wonderful . . . [Henry graduated in 1898 and went to Cuba, where five of his classmates died, three shot, two of fever]. But Capt. Henry got neither bullet nor bug and was made 1st Lieutenant . . .

I have a notion . . . that usually, not always, the great things only appear large when we have past them. When they are at hand they are apparently only of small size like other usual things and people do them without knowing it.

Just as with a general the almost superhuman knowledge he is supposed to possess exists only in the mind of his biographer while the general while alive made lots of errors but had enough strength of character to carry through his ideals so to speak. Napoleon at Jena made three mistakes in two days and won the battle. What an ass I am to quote history to you. Pardon me but I like it and put it down with out thinking.

Letter, GSP, Jr., to Beatrice, March 25, 1909

Dearest Beatrice It has been raining all day so there was no drill and having nothing to do I read for about four hours until I could hardly see then went for a walk with my self and thought of you . . . just a little rain and enough wind to shake the trees while the leaves under foot made no sound at all . . . not a sound with low gray clouds hurrying over the circle of leafless trees and the rain hitting the surface of the water with just a faint metalic sound. The whole place was like a church . . .

I know you have a temper but all people worth being called people have so don't bother. Still I would like to know what you could get mad at your father and mother about. They are such sort of unmadable people . . .

. . . when I write I let a lot of improperly spelled words run all over the page and say what ever they happen to fancy and often not at all what I want them to. You are a long suffering dear to stand such things but I will just be ——— if I can make either my letters or my writing improve . . .

This thing of graduating is mighty strange . . . If there is not a war the starting pistol may never sound and if it sounds I may be beaten . . . What I [would] not give to see a little a head but perhaps it is better that I can't. I wish I was a foolish nature that can laugh and not think. Not that my thinking does any good but I do spend a lot of valuable time and to little purpose.

Letter, GSP, Jr., to Beatrice, March 26, 1909

[Referring to his assignment upon graduation] I do wish they would just order me some place and not give me any choice at all. People can usually stand things they have to do and it saves a lot of bother which is often useless any way.

Letter, GSP, Jr., to Beatrice, March 27, 1909

[The Pattons were building a new house.] I will never be there much so let it pass.

Letter, GSP, Jr., to Beatrice, March 29, 1909

I dont fit but get fits in cities if I live in them . . . I may never do any thing in the army to justify the apparent sacrafice of staying in it but at least there I can hope and else where, not matter what I should manage to do, else where it would be with out soul so to speak.

Beat that sounds as though I thought more of my self than of you but I dont dearest can't you understand? please do.

Another of the little dears that bother me is the fear that you no matter how willing you would be to be bothered could not stand army life.

Enclosed in this letter was the program for the laying of the cornerstone of a new chapel at West Point. He wrote on the program that there was a place set aside to bury "celebrated graduates I hope I make it as a sort of P.G. [post graduate]."

Letter, GSP, Jr., to Beatrice, April 4, 1909

It does seem funny though when you have always thought about being at last a real soldier to be one at last. When you have rehearsed every detail many many times you can hardly realize that the pistol you get is for men not goats. It seems as if you were only getting it to practice with not to realy use.

I think that this same notion of every thing being a practice game for some future contest is very common in connection with every thing we do and as wrong as it is common. Every thing is a "final heat." There are no practices nor . . . do we ever do twice any thing.

. . . Every thing I do from now on will and must have a most direct bearing on what I eventually am or am not . . .

As you said once it would be so much easier if there were but some great things to do but there is not only small things that are often neglected by over sight yet when viewed in retrospect they are mountain high. Like one little tenth [of a point] I did not get in math four years ago next month. That one mark the simple mark of a pen may have entirely changed the course of things who can say.

Letter, GSP, Jr., to his father, April 5, 1909

I have been thinking quite a little on other [cavalry] regiments. The 15th as you know is stationed part at Meyer [Fort Myer, Virginia, near] Washington, D.C. and part at Sheriden [Fort Sheridan, Illinois, near] Chicago. I would like very well to get to Washington for several reasons. Namely that I think I am about as well fitted for society as most graduates. At least I seem to make pretty good impressions here. This may be due to big head or to the fact that I am adjutant but I ascribe it more to the fact that I was well raised and that I try.

Now if I have any capacity in this line I might do somewhat at Washington and get a boot lick on people of note. At least it would be more fun than there is probably to be found at Des Moines Iowa where the 1st is going. But I fear there are no vacancies at Meyer . . . I don't much fancy that place [San Francisco] . . . I think that it is simply a question of suiting my self for Beatrice would not like any of them and any way I don't see any present prospect of marrying here [and staying on at West Point].

It seems ridiculous that I should have fallen in love with a girl so completely useless as a wife for an army officer and there is no use avoiding that fact she has not one redeeming feature for a wife aside from the fact that I am madly in love with her and she is a d—— sight worse in love with me.

Letter, GSP, Jr., to Beatrice, April 6, 1909

The path that I seem intended to follow is not one that any one else will enjoy particularly you who are not by nature intended for such a life being too grand and bright and well educated. A woman to like the army ought to be narrow minded not over bright and half educated and that is the truth how ever gloomy it may sound. If I ever get to what I want you will like it and perhaps forget the mud of the road . . . But if I don't get there mud mud mud and finally a six foot hole in the same old mud.

Letter, GSP, Jr., to Beatrice, April 7, 1909

I have been reading a german Translation on Tactics to night and it is a most saddening work for to be a good soldier one has to know so much and they seem to know it all and I know so little. How can I ever learn enough to fight with them yet I must. It is an awful job to learn so much and then be cheered in the task by perpetual talk of "brotherly love" "Infernal peace" etc. But worth it all if only I can succeed.

Letter, GSP, Jr., to Beatrice, April 9, 1909

I have not heard from my sister Anne other wise nita for a most hellish long time nor to be honest written for a longer . . . She is a good sort that nita and likes me quite a lot. I wish I knew of a man I thought was good enough for her. There are not many such.

Letter, GSP, Jr., to his father April 11 (?), 1909

Some times I fear that I have such an easy life that I will never amount to any thing. Yet there is apparently no good to be had by foregoing the pleasures that come along.

Letter, GSP, Jr., to his father, April 25, 1909

[After graduation] I think I will have to stay for a while [with the Ayers] at Pride's for various reasons.

Mr Taft has the house at Beverly Point where the Ayer's were three years ago. It is about two hundred yards from Prides. I might meet the President and eventually get to Washington.

How sanguine youth is.

Letter, GSP, Jr., to his father, May 2, 1909

There is no use arguing about it. The best thing for a boy or girl is to send them away from home. The V.M.I. was the best thing that ever happened to me. I hate to think what would have happened to me had I come here right from home.

I never felt less like graduating than at this moment . . . Yet it is high time in some ways that I was leaving . . . I don't take the interest in things I used to and that is bad. It soon degenerates into indiference or is apt to. I am awfully anxious to see you for many reasons.

I am very well but getting thinner than ever.

Letter, GSP, Jr., to his father, May 9, 1909

Mama and Nita got here yesterday afternoon and we had a nice talk . . . I gave Ma a few of B's letters to read so that she might get some idea of the "status quo." I think she got the idea. We [his class] are going down to Gettysburg tomorrow night and will be there two days visiting the scene of the death of the Confederacy for such it was. Then we return and after making one trip to Sandy Hook for the day stay here until the end which is not far off. Rowe asked me to be best man at his wedding which is on the 12th of June I guess I will as it takes only half a day. And I think it well to do all things which come in ones way.

Letter, GSP, Jr. (from The Eagle Hotel, Gettysburg), to Beatrice, May 11, 1909

. . . the vast city of the dead that stretches all around.

Vast only in the intensity of death not in the size of the area for that is rather dissapointing in its lack of size. Nor are the features clearly marked as one is lead to expect from reading and the map . . . There are no high hills. Even Round Top is but a bump . . .

The trenches are still easily seen and their grass grown flower strewn slopes agree ill with the bloody purpose for which they were designed and used.

Nature covers up the scars of earth far better than those of men.

There is to me strange fascination in looking at the scenes of the awful struggles which raged over this country. A fascination and a regret. I would like to have been there too.

This evening after supper I walked down alone to the scene of the last and fiercest struggle on Cemetary hill. To get in a proper frame of mind I wandered through the cemetery and let the spirits of the dead thousands laid there in ordered rows sink deep into me. Then just as the son sank hind South Mountains I walked down to the scene of Pickett's great charge and seated on a rock just where Olmstead and two of my great uncles died I watched the wonder of the day go out.

The sunset painted a dull red the fields over which the terrible advance was made and I could almost see them coming growing fewer and fewer while around and beyond me stood calmly the very cannon that had so punished them. There were some quail calling in the trees near by and it seemed strange that they could do it where man had known his greatest and his last emotions. It was very wonderful and no one came to bother me. I drank it in until I was quite happy. A strange pleasure yet a very real one.

I think that it takes an evening like that to make one understand what men will do in battle. It was a wonderful yet a very foolish battle.

Letter, GSP, Jr., to his father, May 16, 1909

[Only two more weeks of studying.] It is the end of a long and not unhappy period. A period which has seen great changes in me. In fact all that is left of the boy who entered here . . . are the aspirations. The rest is changed completely so perhaps the one that is here was also present then in the same way that the gold in the coin is the same as the gold in the nugget yet how different. And I think that the stamp mill hits only a little harder than West Point hit me. Thank God it did. If at the end of the next period which may be the last I can say as I can now that I have all I came for how wonderfully fortunate I will be. It is true that I got the things in not quite the way I dreamed but I got them and am content.

Letter, GSP, Jr., to Beatrice, May 23, 1909

I hope that after I get out of here I shall find plenty to do for so many officers get in to that awful habit of being always busy and not doing any thing . . . Now it is right to be for ever busy but one should do some thing. I am going to try . . . to read war for a certain number of hours each day and hope to have time to read other things too, also for society if there is any and for athletics. It is better I think to attempt more than one can do . . . than to do much less than one can . . .

I have about decided to go in the 1st Cavalry if I can get it as by all accounts it seems to have the nicest people in it both men and women and is the oldest regiment in the army having been the first Dragoons in the Revolution. It is however quite possible that some skunk may rank me out of it . . .

If my foot will ever get well I think that I can do something in the races . . . What ever happens I will now as ever enter with the hope of making the other people run like hell to beat me.

Letter, GSP, Jr., to Beatrice, June 3, 1909

How scared I was that [first] day [at West Point]. How earnest in my desire to succeed. I failed a little and did not succeed much eventually either but I did my best as I found it. At least I have tried to do that always.

Graduation exercises for the class of 1909 were held on June 11. Patton was number 46 of the 103 graduates, "arranged according to general merit."

Others who were to attain high military positions in World War II were John C. H. Lee, ranked 12 (he would command the Services of Supply and be Eisenhower's Deputy Commander of the European theater); Jacob L. Devers, 39 (characterized by the cadets as "I suppose we are all of us a little lazy, except those who are a good deal so," he would command the 6th Army Group in Europe); Robert Eichelberger, ranked 68 (he would command the Eighth Army in the Pacific); Stanley Rumbough, 70 (he would be a member of Eisenhower's staff); Edwin Forrest Harding, 74 (he would command a division in the Pacific); and William H. Simpson, 101 (he would command the Ninth Army in Europe.

After the sun broke through a heavy layer of clouds, the day was bright and somewhat hot. Secretary of War Jacob McGavock Dickinson, appointed by President Taft three months earlier, was the principal guest. He was met upon his arrival that morning by a cavalry detachment and was greeted by a seventeen-gun salute when he reached the Superintendent's quarters. The cadet corps paraded for him.

In his commencement address, the Secretary stressed the need for the cadets to dedicate their lives to the nation, whether they remained in the service or became civilians. He reviewed the history of West Point, remarking the absence of West Pointers in the War of 1812, which was badly fought, and, in contrast, the many West Point graduates who served in the War with Mexico and in the Civil War, both of which were well fought.

General Horace Porter, a graduate of the class of 1860, also spoke, stressing the need for efficiency among the officers of the U.S. Army and Navy.

GSP, Jr., "My Father," 1927

In the spring of 1909, the year I graduated, Papa was on the board of visitors [to the Military Academy]. General Marshall of the engineers weighing three hundred pounds was also on it. At the graduation exercises the Board sat on the stage in Cullum Hall but Papa was no where to be seen until General Marshall rose to present the diploma to his nephew . . . and disclosed Papa sitting behind him.

After the exercises Capt Morton F. Smith (Willie Pickels) [as nicknamed by the cadets] the officer in charge sent for me as I was hurrying to get out of uniform and told me to read off the new list of Makes. I think that up to my time at least I was the only cadet adjutant to function after he had graduated. While I was reading the list, Capt Smith saw Papa and told [him] "You need have no worry over the future of your boy. He always does more than is asked of him." Papa was pleased and told me this. With some exceptions I have always lived up to the idea.

After dinner that evening, the newly commissioned second lieutenants traveled to New York for the class banquet at the Hotel Astor.

GSP, Jr., "My Father," 1927

The day after graduation Papa Mama and I went to Tiffany and they bought me a watch. It was a stop watch repeater priced at $600.00 but we got it for $350.00 because it was thicker than the then style.

I carried it in Mexico and France. It keeps perfect time and is a great watch. Aunt Nannie bought me the chain to go with it. B gave me the locket.

After the purchase of the watch, he returned, presumably, to West Point to act as best man at his friend's wedding.

. . .

His classmates regarded George Patton with some ambivalent emotions. They accepted him generally with affection and admiration for his sincerity, candor, and fairness. They smiled in condescension over his naïve earnestness and enthusiasm. They believed that he tried too hard, had too much spirit, and they were uncomfortable with his obsessive concern with future glory, which he could not resist confessing from time to time.

He had no close friends.

According to his class *Furlough Book,* his nicknames were Georgie and Quill. In the special West Point slang, to quill meant to skin needlessly, and to skin meant to report someone for an offense. Patton's fondest pipe dream, the *Furlough Book* reported, was "to get back [to the Academy], so as to be near that dear skin book." He was therefore known as a "quilloid," one who demanded an impossible sort of perfection, who admitted no human frailty, and who had no hesitation to report those who failed to live up to the strictest interpretation of the rules of the game. More charitable was the characterization in the *Furlough Book:* "He stands erect, right martial in his air,/His form and movements." They all knew he was hard on himself too.

He was labeled "spoony," excessively neat in dress and impeccable in appearance, which was a compliment. He was also judged a "bootlick," one who was addicted to the practice of currying favor with his superiors in order to have bootlick or pull, which was anything but complimentary.

The 1909 *Howitzer,* the Academy yearbook, mentioned Patton as being "faultlessly attired, as usual." It noted his sensitivity: "We believe that George's heart, despite its armored exterior, has a big soft spot inside . . ." It made a permanent record of his inability to punctuate his sentences correctly by citing "the order that Patton unblushingly published [as adjutant], 'No matches will be left in the pockets of clothing sent to the laundry as they may take fire by order of Lieut.-Colonel Howze.' " It remarked his football career: "Two broken arms bear witness to his zeal, as well as his misfortune, on the football field."

Listed as "Georgie" in the *Howitzer,* Patton had been corporal, sergeant major, and adjutant. He was an Expert Rifleman. He had won his Army "A" for having broken a school record in the track and field events of 1908. He had been on the football squad for four years. He had participated in broadsword competitions. He had entered the tennis doubles tournament and was eliminated in the first round of play.

He had been a member of the Kappa Alpha (Southern) fraternity at the Virginia Military Institute, as had Walter Robertson at the University of Oklahoma, and John S. Wood at the University of Arkansas, both of the class of 1912 at West Point. Robertson would command the 2d Infantry Division and Wood the 4th Armored Division in Europe during World War II.

The class of 1910 included Oscar Griswold and John Millikin, both of whom would be corps commanders. In the class of 1911 were Paul Baade and Ira Wyche, who would command divisions. In the class of 1912, in addition to Robertson and Wood, were Gilbert Cook, Willis P. Crittenberger, and Wade Haislip, who would be corps commanders, Terry Allen, Raymond Barton, and William Weaver, division commanders, Millard Harmon, an important U.S. Army Air Forces commander in the Pacific, Robert Littlejohn, Quartermaster General in the European theater, and Franklin Sibert, operations officer of the 12th Army Group.

The Superintendent of the Academy was Colonel Hugh L. Scott, later U.S. Army Chief of Staff. Commandant of Cadets was Lieutenant Colonel Robert L. Howze, who would command a regiment in Mexico and a division in France. Among the senior instructors were Captains Charles P. Summerall, later U.S. Army Chief of Staff, and Guy V. Henry, later

Chief of Cavalry. First Lieutenant Pelham D. Glassford of the class of 1904, an instructor in drawing, would be the Chief of Police in Washington, D.C., at the time of the Bonus March in 1932. Second Lieutenant Joseph W. Stilwell of the class of 1904, an instructor in languages and also a football coach who looked after the second team, the scrubs, on which Patton played, would be the U.S. theater commander in China and Burma during World War II and Chief of Staff to the Generalissimo, Chiang Kai-shek.

How could the instructors at a provincial college like West Point, which specialized in the honor code and in rather rigid behavior, have begun to prepare the cadets for their ultimate responsibilities of directing the U.S. Army in the largest war in history? How could the few and restricted courses at the Academy, the parochial outlook, and the narrow teaching have started young men on their way to conspicuous success 35 years later?

The answer remains to a large degree a mystery. What West Point inculcated was devotion to duty, honor, and country. It stimulated a love of order and the habit of obedience, which were symbolized by the gray and somewhat gloomy walls on the bank of the Hudson. It inspired a lasting affection for the spirit and the traditions which, everyone believed, had enabled Americans to subdue a raw continent and build a great nation. The precepts and the ethic of that relatively innocent age must have been enough.

Together with the other members of his class who were now newly commissioned second lieutenants, young Patton had three months of furlough and freedom before reporting to his first assignment as an officer. He would go to the 15th Cavalry at Fort Sheridan, Illinois.

GSP, Jr., "My Father," 1927

I do not recall that Papa ever visited me at Fort Sheridan, my first station, but he stopped there on his way west after graduation and saw F. C. Marshall my first captain. I stayed behind for a few weeks with the Ayers.

After I entered the army I saw much less of Papa though [as George remembered, not entirely accurately] I wrote home to either him or Mama every week of my life both at school and in the army. Papa was most keenly interested in all I did and used to urge me to be more restrained in my conversation which was and is apt to become over emphatic when I am excited by the sound of my own voice.

It was not the sound of his voice that excited him in the summer of 1909. It was the opportunity to continue on a larger field of battle his quest for achievement and fame, which, he was convinced, lay just ahead in the near future.

IV

Young Officer

"you cant fill an empty heart with chairs"

CHAPTER 9

Fort Sheridan

"God but I wish there would be a war."

THAT MR. PATTON STOPPED at Fort Sheridan on his way home after graduation in order to have a word with his son's first commander was a mark of affectionate and thoughtful kindness. What he said to Captain Francis C. Marshall on that occasion — probably nothing more than to ask him in a most indirect manner to look after George — was no doubt unnecessary, for Marshall had been stationed at West Point during most of young Patton's schooling, and he knew at least some of his strengths and weaknesses.

Patton was at San Gabriel and Catalina Island until August 25, when he traveled east to visit the Ayers at Pride's Crossing. He wrote on July 31 to inform the Adjutant, 15th Cavalry, of his whereabouts, and he misaddressed the letter. It was an understandable *gaffe,* for the regiment was split three ways, with one part of it at Fort Leavenworth, another at Fort Sheridan, and the third at Fort Myer, Virginia.

Somehow, Captain Marshall received the letter. He returned it with a note: "Dear Mr. Patton, This is all right except that the Adjutant is at Fort Myer, Va. I believe I'd rewrite it — Yours, etc." Then, apparently remembering the pleasant visit he had had with George's father, he added, "Hope you're having a splendid time — Regards to your family."

Patton obeyed: "Sir: I have the honor to inform you that owing to a mistake of my own, I [mis]directed the letter . . ." Which showed a commendable willingness to accept responsibility for error.

He wrote to ask about the quarters available to him at Fort Sheridan, and Major J. B. McDonald, the squadron commander, replied. A bachelor officer was assigned two rooms and a bath. A new officer could bring side or center table, bed, comfortable chairs, pictures, portières, rugs; or he could buy them in Chicago. The post quartermaster furnished "a nice mahogany round dining table six table chairs two arm chairs and a desk, all very neat and serviceable." Bachelors messed in the building where their quarters and the officers club were located. They paid about $1.10 per day for fairly good meals.

Spending a carefree summer, Patton did a great deal of fishing. Using a six-ounce rod, he told Beatrice, he landed a 34-pound yellowtail after a fight of two and a half hours; it was only the ninth fish over 30 pounds recorded as having been taken on such light tackle. He also went to a dance where "we all knew one another. It was fine except that you were not here."

He wrote to ask Mrs. Ayer, whom he adored, whether he might come to visit and concluded his letter: "I do not send my love only remind you that you have it and my gratitude as well. Most devotedly George."

Letter, GSP, Jr. (from Avalon, Pride's Crossing), to his father, September 3, 1909
  B. met me and we went up the coast about seventy miles in the machine [automobile] and met K. [Beatrice's sister] and some others. We came back by moonlight and reached here at four o'clock in the morning. I went to bed and did not get up until eleven o'clock. My trunks arrived before I did and were in good condition. My new clothes came and are perfect beauties. Every one admires them and they fit well.

He had awakened that morning to a brass band playing on the terrace and serenading Katharine on her birthday. There was a big party at breakfast. He made a speech, congratulated K, and presented her with a big bunch of balloons. It was all very chic and sophisticated. He had watched a race between large German and American sailing yachts. That evening the Woods, neighbors of the Ayers, were giving a dinner and dance to which all were going. On Monday he was to serve as a crew member on Mr. Wood's boat in a race. Everything was exciting and lots of fun.

Then he had a sobering thought. "But inspite of all this gaiety," he assured his parents, "I had a better time at home. Infact I could not have had a finer time any where or ever. It was ideal. I did hate to go."

A few days later he informed Aunt Nannie that he was having trouble with his hay fever and was sneezing a great deal, "but it is so old a story to

me that it does not bother me much." He was looking forward to reporting to Fort Sheridan, which he called his fourth plebe year — after one at
VMI and two at West Point. "I do hope that I make out all right. I
suppose I shall for I usually do."

Letter, Beatrice to Aunt Nannie, September 11, 1909
   I have just come back from seeing Georgie off for Chicago. He
certainly did look handsome — you are right, "beautiful" is the word
— and we have had the happiest visit . . . You and Aunt Ruth
[Mrs. Patton] and Uncle George [Mr. Patton] know — don't you?
— how I appreciate your having spared him to us; we have been so
happy.

The first letter he sent from Fort Sheridan was to Beatrice:

September 13
   The Marshalls are very nice and have made it easy for me. I met
Rumbough [a classmate] at the station and we came up together
yesterday evening. We were a little scared but things went on well.
The first thing he did was to congratulate me on my supposed marriage . . . and O'Brien [Class of] '08 did the same when I met him.
It seems that some paper had a full account of it. I suppose coming
events cast their shadows before but what a long shadow. Some times
it scares me.
   My rooms are on the third floor and pretty bad. There are two of
them large empty and very dirty. Save for one mahoginy desk rather
a pretty on[e] and an iron bed there is no furniture.
   They [the rooms] should have been cleaned but for unknown reasons my striker [an enlisted man who served as his personal servant,
did his laundry, kept his clothes and quarters clean] has not showed
up perhaps he died.

He had been awakened that morning by his first Army reveille. After
dressing he accompanied Captain Marshall to the Troop K barracks. He
drank a cup of coffee in the Troop K mess hall, then inspected the kitchen
— no doubt Marshall inspected the kitchen, in the process instructing
Patton by example how to do so. He returned to his quarters for breakfast. He went to the target range, but only to observe, for he had as yet
not been assigned to all his duties. While he was there, his orderly reported to him with two horses. He sent his orderly to pick up his trunks

at the railroad station. Later that morning Patton worked in the company office, helping to sort papers. After lunch he went to the stables. "To night all three of us [new officers] are to dine with our Major Mc-Donnald a very nice man with a large family."

He expected to go out in the morning to exercise with the troop. He had a horse that was neither good nor bad, a saddle, and an orderly who, in conformance with the practice of addressing officers in the third person, called him "the lieutenant" — would the lieutenant like him to do thus and so, would the lieutenant be so good, and so on. The weather was hot, he had "hay fever to beat hell," and he could go to Chicago any time during any afternoon and return on the midnight train. But since he had duty at the stables at four-fifteen every afternoon, he would not be going to town very often.

Letter, GSP, Jr., to his father, September 20, 1909

"K" Troop is having target practice now so I will be able to try for expert again yet with doubtfull success for I am not shooting as well as I could wish . . . When they shoot record for Marksman and sharpshooter I go down in the target pit and superintend the marking as being an expert. I don't have to shoot record on the lower courses. I have also to go to the stables at four fifteen in the afternoon It consists in walking around and watching the men groom horses and correcting them too. As yet I don't see fit to do that . . .

I certainly am glad that I got into Capt. Marshall's troop as he teaches me things that the other two [new officers] never hear about from their troop commanders . . .

Col. Pitcher of the 27th Inft [Infantry] who commands the post has every one bluffed to death . . .

Most of the people here are nice, not very nice, yet nice. About the class that as cits. would have a small house and a "hired girl" and think they were raising hell. The Marshalls seem the best of the bunch and are very nice to me. There is also a bunch here that are not even decent. They belong to what is called the sin of 1898 [that is] to the crowd that got in [to the Army] from the malitia [after the Spanish-American War], they are pretty fierce but only number eight to ten [on the post]. Rumbough and I have been to two plays. The Co-ed and Going Some both fine . . .

My hay fever is much better and except for a slight cold I feel fine.

His first tour of duty at the guardhouse shocked him somewhat, he told Beatrice. A total of 120 military convicts imprisoned for crimes ranging from drunkenness to attempted desertion

> filed past me with their arms folded. One or two had irons on and one was lame and on crutches where he had been shot trying to escape . . . [The majority] seem under twenty five . . . It is to me a very sad sight . . .
>
> None of them had very bad faces though they were awfully ignorant looking and lord how they "stunk." That is the word, no other would do at all . . .

He was surprised by the ignorance of the enlisted men, most of whom had a poor command of English, expressed themselves haltingly, used big words improperly, and spoke with incorrect pronunciations.

> Yet they try hard all of them or at least I think so and are very respectful . . . They never question what you tell them nor do they seem to mind being cussed. I have never done it but I have seen others especially the sergeants and they never mind or don't show it . . .
>
> So far I am head man in my troop firing but as I have to shoot again in the morning with out sleep [because of the guard duty] I may loose out.

Despite his pessimism, he qualified again as Expert Rifleman.

Letter, GSP, Jr., to Beatrice, October 1, 1909
> At last I had time to get some furnature . . . the Gov. gives a mahoginy desk a chair and a book case to each bachelor . . . I thought it best to get my stuff of the same wood. I got a bureau and a sort of tall thing a little larger than the sort known as shaving stand yet just the right hight for that use. They are in dark mahogany of what the man called Colonial Patern with nice big leggs that will not break off. Also I got a big table of the same wood with two drawers in it, it was to my mind awfully pretty and quite expensive. Last I got a big chair with a place that pulls out to rest your feet on. It has a bump that fills up the hollow in ones back and is very comfortable. It is also mahoginy. I also got two rugs one pretty big and the other smaller as I have four small ones now that will be plenty. I think

that after I get some covers for the table and desk and some brass
corners for a blotter that I will look quite well . . .

Oh! yes I also got a lamp some thing like the one in the Library
at [the Ayer house in] prides [Crossing] for the big table. I think a
sort of shaded lamp like that lends refinement to a room . . .

You know what the [Cadet] Corps was. Well the army seems like
that only the coating of nice ones [nice people] is thinner.

God but I wish there would be a war. Until there is I see no hope
of my ever needing to buy any more furnature for you cant fill an
empty heart with chairs.

George.

He started a letter to Beatrice on Sunday but could not complete it
until the following evening. "I am very sorry dear that this was not written last night but I was too busy." The reason, he confessed, he was having a good time on a practice march. Captain Marshall had given Patton
command of a small advance patrol working ahead of the main body of
men as though in the face of the enemy. He had eight wagons, had made
his way by map, was responsible for selecting camp sites, fixing camp, and
setting out picket lines.

I was struck with the difference between regulars and cadets.
While cadets are better in ranks and about not talking etc they are
away behind in obidience out of ranks and in doing real work such as
making camp. These men work hard and fast and when you call
them come at a run.

We had our meals at our tents eating the same stuff the men do.
Our strikers waited on us.

He spent part of the day helping to pitch 22 tents for higher ranking
officers who were coming out to visit and inspect the troops.

They certainly have an easy time particularly the officers of high
rank like general Grant. Some day I will have a big tent and a re-
frigerator and a stove and a trunk and a lot of men cussing me for
having so much bagage.

Letter, GSP, Jr., to Beatrice, October 14, 1909
Mr. Cooke [an officer in Troop K] is an awfully nice fellow . . .

To day he and I laied out the polo field. I was surprised to find that I remembered how to use a transit so all that hot yearling Engineering was not for nothing.

To day I called at a house [each new officer on post was expected to call, but if no one was home, he could leave his card] and to my disgust was forced to go in there. I met some of the people who positively make me ill when I think of the effect they would have on — a girl I know [Beatrice].

In the course of conversation one so called lady placed her hand in a very obvious place and said "Ah said I cant eat 'sech' stuff as that it gives me cramps, awful cramps." Later she and the wife of a Lt. Colonel had a lengthy argument over the relative merits of various sorts of beere. And when I left — glad to go — they were saying that servants should not get over twenty dollars a month. No wonder their houses look like they do. Do you know that most of them Captains Majors and Colonels even have only one servant and a striker.

I would not have the nerve to live like that even if I could. Yet the Marshalls have three [servants] and a striker and seem to have more ready money and dress better than any of them and not only have they nothing but their pay but they give twenty five dollars a month to charity. That is pretty good for a Captain.

On Saturdays, George continued, he went to football games, for Mr. Cooke was nice enough to take his place at the stables, and George diagrammed the good plays and sent them to the coach at West Point.

A dance or hop was scheduled on post, but was then canceled.

I will have to call on and condole with poor Miss Bishop the daughter of she of the cramps and tell her the daughter that I can't take her to the hop. She is too nire for such a mother.

Letter, GSP, Jr., to Beatrice, October 21, 1909

[Beatrice was visiting Natural Bridge in Virginia only a short distance from V.M.I.] The N.B. Hotel was the first place I ever wore a uniform in public. It was when I was a rat and Col. Marr took Mama and me over there one Sunday. I remember I had two dishes of ice cream. As it was the first time I had eaten [ice cream] since I entered the Institute it seemed very good to me. There were some girls on the porch and when they saw a cadet in the carriage they became interested until I got out and with a look of disgust one of them said "Oh its only a rat" and then I first saw the necessity of chevrons . . .

You will notice under the bridge the place where G. Washington (Cousin George) carved his name. It is the highest of all.

My cousin Mercer Patton is Professor of Languages at the V.M.I. Should you go there you will find him dirty but very nice. At least he was.

I am taking a girl Miss Bishop to the theater so must dress. Why in hell is her name bishop [and not Beatrice].

Good night and forgive me [for so short a letter or for taking Miss Bishop to the theater, perhaps both].

He had a good time on Halloween. He was invited to the Marshalls', who had a costume and a mask for him. With horns and tin pans, he, the Marshalls, Miss Page, her brother, and Miss Bishop called at every house on the post, and if they were let in they danced around and "raised the duce generally." It was an old Army custom. Having made their rounds, they returned for supper. Rumbough was with another party, but he and Miss Cooke both sprained their ankles and had to quit the group.

The following evening Patton had supper with Lieutenant and Mrs. Cathro, who were "nice people," meaning a gentleman and a lady.

He wrote Aunt Nannie:

I ordered a very nice over coat. At first the man wanted to charge me $90 for it but I told him I would not pay over sixty. He said he would make it for $65 so I took it. I think it will be very pretty.

Writing to Beatrice who was near Lexington, Virginia, he said he hoped she liked it there.

I did and I was never lonely there. Some way it seemed so full of people . . . most of them dead ones [meaning uninteresting] yet I liked it. For in spite of their very many faults the cadets there [at V.M.I.] are more gentlemen than any place I have been or seen. And most of them there [were] third generation [at the school] some fourth. In my time you could find the name of almost two thirds [of the] corps either on the monument or on the pictures in the library . . . [Lexington was] quite a nice old place and so absolutely out of date.

He had, he continued, just returned from town, where he had purchased a new rifle and whip and had ordered a coat. He had also run into Mr. Cooke who, Patton was shocked to discover, was quite drunk. "I am sorry for him as he is such a fine fellow."

At times the greatness of my boldness in daring to tell you that I loved you strikes me with over powering force. I don't see how I ever did it for I am nothing have nothing and have neither prospect nor possibility of either becoming some one or of obtaining some thing. And it seems horribly wicked to have caused such a wonderful girl as you to love such a fool . . . Dreams happy dreams that melt like fog before the sun of reality . . .

I bought a little rifle and go out shooting quite often. It is good practice for the course next year and I will need all the practice I can get [to qualify as Expert] for they have changed the regulations so that it is said to be impossible to make expert. Still I can but try.

One afternoon Patton came out of the Post Exchange and heard a band playing in the distance. Since it seemed about time for the retreat ceremony, he thought the music must be "The Star-Spangled Banner." He therefore stood at attention. Several soldiers near him did the same thing. The wind then drowned the music, so he continued walking, only to hear the band again. Once more he stopped. The soldiers near him halted also. Beginning to think that it was a mighty long retreat parade, he looked around and saw a funeral procession. "An ear for music is a great thing," he wrote Beatrice, "and think of how often I have been to parade."

Letter, GSP, Jr., to Aunt Nannie, November 25, 1909
I am going to a dinner in highland park [a suburb of Chicago] this afternoon and to a cotillion there in the evening to another dance Friday and the theater Saturday so by Sunday morning I will be willing to sleep. [It was very cold, with snow on the ground, and this] certainly has a bad effect on shooting. I made a total miss at one range so did not shoot any more as I was not required to.

Patton had Thanksgiving dinner at the mess, which was "fierce," quite different from that at West Point. "The stuff on the table is not silver and not always clean and the service is punk . . . I am the only man who dresses for dinner regularly and one of the few who wears a white collar and cuffs with my service clothes."

He wrote to his father in December: "This is one hell of a day it started with a rain turned into snow and ended up with a blizzard and is freezing hard. I went to church this morning and also to Communion at Lake Forrest." Captain Banning, who was passing through Chicago, had spent Wednesday afternoon with him and on Thursday had asked him to dinner and to see *The Virginian* at the theater. The first big dance on the post was to be held Friday, with the officers going in full dress and to supper afterward. He was escorting Miss Page. There was also a Miss Fessenden, who "seems quite devoted to me and bothers me by continually inviting me down. I have to go to night and it is too stormy to be pleasant." His new suit pleased him; he was going to get a silk hat — "I will look great and hope I get a chance to use it." He was the best pistol shot at Fort Sheridan. He was good with the rifle too. The day before he had made fifteen successive bull's eyes so "I may get a gold medal yet." He asked his father to send him a subscription to *Life* magazine. "I must dress now and go to supper with Dot. Fessenden. She is very pretty and a debutant so a fool. Beat says they all are."

Shortly thereafter, Patton qualified as Expert Revolver Shot.

He told Aunt Nannie that he had dinner in Lake Forest with Mr. Russel, vice president of the "Elivator Trust," who had one of the most beautiful houses he had ever seen. Nothing in the dining room, parlor, and hall, according to Mr. Russel, was less than one hundred years old, and many pieces were much older. The electric light fixtures were of old bronze or wrought iron. Next to the Ayer home, he remarked, perhaps out of loyalty, the Russels had the best place he knew.

"It must be good taste," he wrote his father, "for the gate to Mr. Russels place cost $30,000 and does not look like much either. It is made of two urns about eight feet high he stole in Greece."

The Russels, he informed Aunt Nannie, had a daughter of fourteen or fifteen "who entertained me vastly though she utterly refused to sit down." She was too young to eat with the guests, had dinner upstairs, "and I saw her no more but I shall pay my party call on saturday and may see her again."

He dined at Lieutenant Segall's and at Lieutenant Friese's, both meals in honor of "some girls of doubtful antiquity" who were visiting on post.

There was a Charity Ball on Wednesday that officers were expected to attend in uniform; he took Miss Smith of Highland Park.

Letter, GSP, Jr., to his father, December 20, 1909
[Miss Bishop had a birthday party to which he had gone. Later, when he made some calls in Lake Forest, he learned about a rumor that was circulating to the effect that he and Miss Bishop had eloped.] She is a nice girl and rather pretty and very useful. I have taken her to a lot of plays. More than Beat. would care to hear about . . . You ought to see me in my silk hat and stick with an artistic slouch. I can't blame Miss Bishop for loving me and I fear she does a little.

Patton's extensive social life at Fort Sheridan, which was close to the wealthy suburbs of Chicago, was normal for young Army officers. Yet the dances and balls and dinners he attended never interfered with his real purpose, his serious endeavor to learn his profession.

On December 13, he related to Beatrice an incident that foreshadowed an occurrence 33 years later in Sicily, where as a three-star general in command of an Army, he almost brought his military career to an abrupt end by slapping several shell-shocked soldiers in the hospital.

This afternoon I found a horse not tied and after looking up the man at the other end of the stable I cussed him and then told him to run down and tie the horse and then run back. This makes the other men laugh at him and so is an excellent punishment.

The man did not understand me or thought he would dead beat so he started to walk fast. I got mad and yelled "Run dam you Run." He did but then I got to thinking that it was an insult I had put on him so I called him up before the men who had heard me swear and begged his pardon.

It sounds easy to write about but was one of the hardest things I ever did I think but I am glad I did it now that it is done.

Had he shouted "Run damn it run," he would have thought no more of it. But it was the "damn you" that was unforgivable and required an apology. In 1943, Patton would again apologize to those he had slapped and to those who had heard about it. He would again find it difficult to do so.

. . .

That month he wrote to Mr. Ayer to explain his plans for his life's work. It was a rather equivocal statement. While he made clear his devotion to the military, he implied that he might eventually be attracted to civil life.

Letter, Mr. Ayer to GSP, Jr., December 24, 1909

My dear George. Your letter . . . is very clear and comprehensive.

Your ambition I admire. Your "plan of life" is all right if you can have a command for a year in Gods Country — not in the Philippeens.

Fighting malaria is not war.

After all, as the civil life is what finally you fall back upon for an indefinite period the question may occur to you whether this first year will not be worth more to you in that than in any command you can get. That is a question no one can decide for you. You too can best judge how much opportunity a year's command will give you to investigate and decide upon another occupation. Always keeping in mind that the younger a man starts in business the easier it is for him and the better his chance for success.

In regard to speaking to Beatrice; there are times in ones life when one feels impelled to speak and to follow that impulse, which comes after long thought, is natural and generaly wise.

Hoping you will pardon the above suggestions, I am, Sincerelly yours, F. Ayer.

Patton spent the Christmas holidays with the Ayers. He and Beatrice seriously discussed marriage.

Shortly after his return to Fort Sheridan, he asked his father about his own financial condition. Mr. Patton responded at once. George was surprised.

Letter, GSP, Jr., to his father, January 17, 1910

I had no notion I was so wealthy and with half of what you say I would have think that I would have plenty. The great difficulty will be getting quarters but I trust that will work out all right . . .

As I told you that B. for reasons if any best known to her self will not say definitely that she will marry me then but as she has no objections or appears to have none to my telling her family I fancy she will not object to their decision and I am pretty darned sure I know what they will be [say].

She certainly is an awful ass but then I suppose it is hard to blame a person for clinging on to present happiness and being slightly scared at changing it for any other even though it may be better for it might be worse. I think that the only thing that scares her is the thought of leaving her family not of leaving her wealth for she does not care a dam about that. Any way she has got to or never leave them for I would look like an ass hanging around much longer.

I have been down to Grand Opera three times already and really like it though I don't understand a hell of a lot about it. I have seen Aunt N. three times she is very comfortably fixed at the Virginia an exceeding fashionable place and cheap too. It is only a few blocks from where Adelaide lives and is near the North Western depot and in seven minutes of all the shops and theaters. Still if she were going to be here for a long time I think that the Moraine in H[ighland] Park would be better as it is nearer here. This will be particularly so when the weather opens up a little so that I can ride down there which at present is impossible for the ice . . .

The Marshalls left this morning. I saw them off and gave Mrs. M. some flowers which pleased her. I have learned these (Ayers) and graces well of late [a nice pun].

In some ways I think Mr. Cooke is a better troop Commander than capt Marshall for being mentally smaller he attends more to detail. I also have more to do which is a great blessing for I have been too idle for comfort. He and I have taken up a course of military study too for the afternoons of four days a week which ought to be interesting and useful both.

Captain Marshall departed on a temporary detail. He would return in May and again take command of the troop. Sometime in June, he wrote the first efficiency report on Patton as an officer. Marshall commended Patton's attention to duty, his professional zeal, general bearing, military appearance, and intelligence and judgment in instructing, drilling, and handling enlisted men — all of which he rated "good." He thought that Patton had a peculiar fitness to serve as an instructor of tactics at the Military Academy or at a service school. "He has availed himself fully of his opportunities for improvement, is qualified for his position, and should be intrusted with important duties." In the event of war, Marshall believed, he would be best suited for duty with troops. He was

a young officer of especial promise. He is the most enthusiastic soldier of my acquaintance and misses no chance to improve. I am con-

vinced that as he develops he will be an especially valuable officer. I
have watched him from the time he entered the Military Academy,
and know him to be efficient, loyal and capable.

No one could have wished for a better report.

On January 23, 1910, Patton was on guard duty and counting the prisoners at the time of the retreat ceremony when a corporal rushed in and
said that Sentinel #4 had called "The Guard!" a signal used in extreme
cases of riot, murder, and the like. He wrote Beatrice:

> I grabbed my sabre and hat and ran for post No. 4. I think that
> rapidity was the only military virtue in the movement for the only
> command I gave was "get out here quick." When we got to the place
> — The Q.M. [quartermaster] store house — I still looking for mur-
> der surrounded the house and then climed in by a broken window.
> The smoke in there was terrible so that we could not breathe and
> some one squirted me in the back with a fire extinguisher.

It turned out that spontaneous combustion in a pile of oil-soaked cotton rags had set some shelves on fire. A sergeant had seen the smoke at the
same time as the sentinel who had given the alarm and was already putting out the flames.

> It was one of the few occasions where stupidity is right. What
> number four should have yelled was "Fire No. 4." in which case I
> with out looking further in the matter would have fired the cannon
> and given the alarm so that twelve hundred men would have assem-
> bled at a fire the size of a match.
> Luckily when I did find it was a fire I decided to look before leap-
> ing and so saved trouble.
> Any way we all had a nice little run and I a cut finger so it did
> some good . . .
> [The prisoners in the post stockade] Poor ducks I feel sorry for
> them. It is hard to have the ignorance or folly of a few days result in
> the erasure of two or three years from ones life yet there is no other
> way. People must not have the folly or they must take the prison.
> And there are too many deserters. Five thousand last year in the
> best paied army on earth . . .
> Well the prisoners are inspected and unfortunatly I did not have
> your cold in my nose lord what a human smell . . .

The common soldier certainly is a beau for they are giving a dance to night — they do each Saturday and women are thicker on the post than is the snow . . . Some of the girls who come up are not bad looking nor do I see any reason to think them bad at all in spite of popular opinion. The soldier is an average young man and there is no reason why his friends should not be average young women.

[Aunt Nannie was leaving Chicago. The Grand Opera had departed. He regretted the illness of Beatrice's grandmother, but he was sorry for Beatrice and her mother] not for Mrs. Banning [the grandmother]. She is an example of why I would love to get killed all at once. Though I hope to do it at such a late date that it will be immaterial to you whether black is becoming or not so don't be angry with me and say I want to leave you. For . . . if I go first I will come [back] at once and kill you so as to have company.

Writing to Beatrice on February 20 of his quarters on post,

words fail to describe the perfect horror of its looks . . . This darling is what you are willing to exchange for Adam furnature and marble halls. No wonder I love you beyond words . . . there are no worse quarters hence any thing would be an improvement.

He had asked Major McDonald for leave and learned that he could have time off from his duties whenever he wished. Therefore, if they married in the latter part of June, they would get to Fort Sheridan near the end of July. That would give them a month together on post before he would have to leave with the troops on maneuvers. "When we love each other as we do then we can be happy any where. I wonder is it so. Oh God grant that it be so!"

Letter, GSP, Jr., to Aunt Nannie, mid-February 1910
We were all inoculated with typhoid fever bugs. Many were quite ill but it did not halt me in the least. I guess I am tough or some thing . . .

We don't start on the Manoeuvers until September first so it sort of nocks hell out of certain plans. Whether this will precipitate or delay the great event is as yet not known.

Letter, GSP, Jr., to Beatrice, February 28, 1910
If you marry [me] in June — please do . . .

[He had to put a man in the guardhouse for not doing what he was told, and he had to prefer charges against a prisoner for not obeying a sergeant.] I hate to do it but it is necessary not so much for its effect on the men them selves as for the effect on others. And any way to do right one has to divest ones self of the personal feelings and do with a man as you would with a stick. For if you let your self think of his sadness, his repentance, his misery etc you would be in a constant state of torment and no justice would be done.

And the same feeling must I think be applied to the losses of war. Not a hundred souls but a hundred units should be counted . . .

[Now he had to] examine a hundred and fifty four pair of unclean feet and then wander out beneath the darkened moon and hunt up sentinels. Who says officers don't work.

Letter, GSP, Jr., to Aunt Nannie (traveling in Europe, to Gibraltar and Rome), March 1, 1910

You sound like you were having a fine time but don't spend too much money.

And especially not on [field] glasses for me. But if you do get them get also a case to go with them. The case ought to be russet leather but really it makes little matter.

There is a strong reason to think that B will get married in the first part of June . . .

Where we will live is yet veiled in obscurity but the best way to find out is to plunge . . .

As soon as any definite plan is reached I will promptly let you know by wire if necessary.

Letter, GSP, Jr., to Beatrice, March 2, 1910

[West Point to him is] a holy place and I can never think of it with out reverence and affection

. . . I never did a thing [there] with out calculating its effect on you. I even skinned less than I wanted to because I thought that if I got too unpopular you would not have so nice a time [at the dances and during visits].

Beaty we must go back some day for it is almost home to me . . .

Truly for so fierce a warrior I have a damned mild expression.

Letter, GSP, Jr., to his mother, March 6, 1910

I have a black eye . . . that I got Tuesday. My horse bucked a round and got me off once because I think my cap which was held on by an elastic over the back of my head got over my face and I could not see. I lit on my hand and knee and got on at once. He bucked a lot more and finally reared and fell but I stayed on and stood accross him as soon as I got my leg out from under him. When he got up I was in the saddle and leaned forward as he got up first with his front feet. But when he started to get up behind he threw his head and got me on the eye brow so that it cut it about half an inch. I did not know it was cut until I saw the blood running down my sleeve but I hated to pay any attention to it so kep on drilling for about twenty minutes with out even wiping my face. I certainly looked like a stuck pig when I finally went up to the troop [headquarters to have the cut looked after]. I taught the non com school and went to my own school before I had it fixed though I did wash my face first. Then the doctor fixed it and it is fine but the blood began to settle in my eye lids . . . I hated to be thrown but think that my subsiquent bearing gave a sufficient evidence of "sang froir" [sang-froid]. At least the other day when the surgeon was sticking the needle into my arm to put in the last batch of pus [for inoculation against tetanus infection] and I was joking about it he said he wished he had my nerve. Though I am inclined to think that it is really lack of them [nerves]. And a determination to be frigid. It is a good thing . . . for naturally I am not over bold and am inclined to show emotion — a most un military trait.

If Patton's performance at West Point — his recklessness on the football field, his track and broadsword activities, his faultless attire — marked the beginning of the Patton legend among his peers, his behavior on the bucking horse at Fort Sheridan started the legend among enlisted men. Who among the witnesses of the incident could have failed to be impressed by the young lieutenant who stoically carried out his duties even though he was bleeding like a stuck pig? The story must have run through the enlisted barracks in a flash, gaining increasingly lurid details as it proceeded.

Continuing his letter to his mother, Patton wrote:

I just got a telegram from B. which said. "Pa and Ma willing for June if you are rejoice." Being thus importuned? I accepted her. She is going to announce it after she visits you when you get here . . . I wrote Mr. Ayer at once on getting the wire. The house question is a great embarasment for though I am very sure we will have one none are at present vacant. Yet putting things off would not help things would it? it would not . . . I fear that it will be sort of hard on her but I do hope I can make her happy. Perhaps I can for I certainly like her enough to do my damdest.

I am a mess officer now and it would have amused you to see me down among the whole[sale] groceries getting prices and looking wise at samples but I know more than I thought.

Letter, Beatrice to Aunt Nannie, March 7, 1910

Aunt Nannie darling — By the time you get this, our engagement will be announced! Things have been moving very quickly for the last few days, so that I haven't had time to tell you before. But isn't it joyous?

We hope to be married in June if Georgie can get leave; and will cable you as soon as we can tell you anything definite.

Hastily & lovingly — B

Letter, Mr. Ayer to GSP, Jr., March 7, 1910

My dear George, I thank you for your letter and [financial] statement, the latter of which I return herewith.

Am sorry that you have hesitated to write me or that you should have had any misgivings about doing so. Also sorry that Beatrice should have had any hesitancy about speaking to me freely on any subject pertaining to herself or her interests. I have always endeavored to cultivate the most confidential relations with my children and to make them feel free to confide in me and consult me on all matters. I invite you to the same confidential relations and freedom of intercourse.

You know how Beatrice lights our lives, and how dearly we all love her.

Our beloved younger children, so full of promise, will always remember Beatrice, who brought happiness, as a shining example, who strained every nerve to do her best, to be the light of our home, to be the moving spirit for the good of all, to improve every gift, and never to withhold from father, mother, sister, or brother the constant expression of her love and devotion. She has no discounts, no minus traits — Is all to the good. She has made us all happy — always, and we hope she will always be a joy to you, as she always has been to us. Of course, we feel that half the house will be gone when our Beatrice goes, and we confide her to you with our love and fullest confidence. Her frequent return to us we shall look for with longing.

Will you keep this ever in mind?

I know that your accomodations are not what you would have them in private life, but think Beatrice enjoys roughing it to some extent, as all good soldiers and sailors must; and you know she is a pretty good sailor.

I did not know that you had such a fine nest egg in your property. I would not sell the land.

It has been my custom when my children have married and left our home to give them a monthly income, and shall do the same to Beatrice and the younger ones. This is without regard to their circumstances and for reasons which I will explain later.

I am hoping to take Beatrice to Chicago, and if so, will, of course see you, but it is not certain. I admire your firmness of purpose in sticking to the army until more strongly tempted by another occupation, and with every good wish for your early and steady advancement, I am Sincerely your friend, F. Ayer.

Letter, GSP, Jr., to Aunt Nannie, March 8, 1910

B wrote me that her mother and father had consented and then wired me that she had announced it so I did like wise and my popularity has fallen a pace as a result.

Truly 'tis sad to think that they but loved me for my marriage ability yet I am not suffering over much though I do hate to tell Kate and Caroline for even *if* they did not like me, I liked them and a lot too so hate to state that all is ended. It seems so needlessly rough. Yet must be . . .

B wants to go to Europe for a wedding trip so I suppose if I can get leave I will go. I would like to too.

Letter, GSP, Jr., to Beatrice, March 23, 1910

Darling Beatrice: Capt. Marshall is a corker. He certainly is nice to me and I like him ever so much. He has written to Capt. Bowley [the regimental adjutant] on his own account asking a five weeks leave for me as a personal favor. You see officially I have no right to any leave [and] custom of the service allows only twenty five days [to be married] and the rest is charity and pull. But I ought to get it . . .

Letter, GSP, Jr., to his father, April 1, 1910

[The wedding was set for Thursday, May 26, but because no trans-
atlantic liners sailed on Fridays, they would have to stay in New York
that day, which Beatrice disliked. She might change the wedding
date. He was not sure his leave would be approved. He had asked
for 35 days] all I dared ask for. If I fail to get this I will put in
another and then get you to write [Major General Fred C.] Ainsworth [the all-powerful Adjutant General in Washington] . . .

This formation of matrimony at a thousand miles from the leading
lady is a thing very difficult to stage.

I hope you do go into politics again it would be a shame for you
not to go to Washington. You have never had a chance to show what
a heller you are so please do it now.

A few days later, learning that his request for leave had been approved
from May 25 to June 30, he booked passage across the Atlantic for Beatrice and himself. The only thing still lacking was a house for them on
the post.

He was spending a lot of money, he told his father. He was "nigotiat-
ing" for a horse in Virginia, and he was trying to buy two polo ponies.
He asked that a $250 check on his savings account be deposited in the
Highland Park State Bank, "that is if you think I can afford it, it seems to
me I can." In conclusion, he advised his father to *"Go into Politics."* He
genuinely believed in his father's abilities as a politician and no doubt he
figured that having a father prominent in politics, particularly at the national level, would hardly be disadvantageous to his own military career.

George informed Aunt Nannie of the wedding date and that Mama
and Nita were staying at the Moraine Hotel in Chicago. Beatrice was
getting clothes in New York — "she has pretty good taste in most things.
Except husbands. I am very well and not as disconserted as one might
imagine."

In two letters to Beatrice on April 7, he expressed surprise over receiving congratulations by mail from some of the West Point classmates upon
his approaching marriage. "I had no idea that any or many of my class
mates would take the trouble to write me." He also revealed his concern
about having Beatrice's mother, who was accompanying Beatrice to Chicago, see the Army at close range, for she was hardly conversant with
Army customs and might find fault. "But on thinking it over I have
decided that it is as well for her to see the worst and the best at once." Yet

he expected some trouble. "I know for I had the same row with mama and she does not see it well yet. You can't buy rank on a post." He was referring to his inability to get a house, for houses were assigned on the basis of rank, and he was but a lowly second lieutenant.

In a very short letter to his father, he said that Mr. and Mrs. Ayer and Beatrice were in Chicago. Looking after them, plus playing polo and riding, was keeping him, he said, "jumping." Nita and Mama were there too. He was sorry his father was unable to be with them, but he was glad that Mr. Patton had decided to re-enter politics, had his eye on a seat in the U.S. Senate, and was attending a political convention in California. "With much love," George concluded, "and best wishes for the convention. *And keep it up.*"

Mr. and Mrs. Ayer were delighted with Fort Sheridan, which looked "exceptionally nice just now," and were extremely pleasant and affable. After they returned to Boston, Mrs. McDonald gave a reception for Mrs. Patton, Nita, and Beatrice, and most of the people on the post attended — "it must have been very hard on B.," he told his father,

> but she did very well. Really I think that she will be ever so much more efficient than I Had dared to hope. She made such a hit with the Q.M. [Quartermaster] that I think our chance of getting a house went up a number of points.

He and Beatrice were going to stay in Boston on their wedding night, go to New York on the noon train next day, spend that night aboard the *Deutschland,* and sail for England at 9 A.M., Saturday, May 28. "After that Heaven alone can say what will happen."

Mama had been talking of getting them an automobile as a wedding present, but he was against it — "you both have done entirely too much for me and I do not think that you can afford to do this so please dont consider it at all." He hoped his father, "having both brains and presence," was doing well politically and would get to the Senate.

Several days later he wrote to tell his father he was glad Mr. Patton was staying on in California in order to promote his chance to be nominated for the election to the U.S. Senate.

> I am very well and having a nice time though the nearness of my fate gets a little alarming at times. Twenty five days . . . I am absolutely at sea as to where in Hell I will live when I get back but the

only thing to do is to trust to God and good luck . . . With much love and best wishes for the senate.

Mr. Patton wrote to Beatrice on April 25, while sitting alone in his office looking out over the patio — the "dingle dangle," he called it — and across the countryside. "In my memory I saw the little white headed kid who was 'Georgie' — at the end of the walk . . . [whom he] surrenders without fear or misgiving — his only 'little boy' to your loving keeping 'for always.' " He was sorry he had been unable to be "with you and my dear ones in Chicago," but he was "looking a little into politics & may find myself rather busy if events move along as they now appear." Yet he hoped to get away from California in a week or two and spend a fortnight in Boston before "the joyful day — when I shall find another daughter."

On the same day George told Beatrice — "if you go on crying at all times you will hurt your looks so stop."

He wrote in great excitement on May 12 to tell Beatrice that "Allerdice's house" on post had been assigned to him. He drew a map of Fort Sheridan to show its location.

> The Osbornes who have half of it are 1st Lts and very nice and I hope will not borrow much. It is much nearer the stables so is nicer for me and in all ways is fine.

Letter, GSP, Jr., to Beatrice, May 16, 1910

We certainly are getting some fine presents. It is nice to think that People like us so much. I hope they are right in liking me. I know they are loving you . . . You want the walls just off white do you not . . . I think it is much better to get married young than to wait until we are older for things are so much more real to us and so splendid. Beaty we must amount to some thing.

His father arrived in Chicago, his nomination by the Democratic Party for the seat in the Senate still not settled. After several days of visiting with his son, he and Mrs. Patton — Nita had probably accompanied Beatrice home — departed for Boston to get ready for the wedding.

George was busy on the target range and trying to organize a polo game.

On Sunday, May 22, he wrote Beatrice his last letter before their marriage. She was, he said, "the inspiration for a weak and cowardly nature." He was speaking of himself, of course. "Small hills seen against the sky line of an unknown horizon assume the size of mountains through uncertainty and lack of comparison. And I have always so wanted to win that I have ever feared lest I might loose . . . May our love be never less than now. And our ambition as fortunate and great as our love. Amen. George."

CHAPTER 10

Marriage and Fort Sheridan

*"There may be no war. God forbid such an eventuality how-
ever."*

THE WEDDING was a grand occasion. All the Boston newspapers covered
the festivities at great length and in great detail.

Unfortunately, Mrs. Patton was ill. Unable to travel, she remained in
her room at the Hotel Touraine in Boston.

At the wedding breakfast, Patton later remembered, his father "made a
great toast to her which was so fine that every one cried."

A special train left North Station in Boston at two-fifteen, carrying ele-
gant ladies and gentlemen, most of them Boston society folk, others from
New York, Washington, D.C., Virginia, Minnesota, and California. At
Beverly Farms, where the train stopped, carriages waited to drive the
guests to St. John's Episcopal Church.

It was a lovely Gothic church in miniature, and its chancel was pro-
fusely decorated with spring blooms, masses of white flowers and greenery.
An organist played, and at three-thirty sounded the opening chords of
Wagner's wedding march.

The bride, described as "quite a beauty" — "fair and slight," wore the
dress her mother had been married in 25 years earlier, a cream-colored
embroidered satin gown with clusters of fresh orange blossoms and a court
train. Her veil of tulle was fastened with orange blossoms. She carried a
prayer book instead of a bouquet.

Her younger sister Katharine, a schoolgirl in New York, was her maid
of honor. Anne Wilson Patton of San Gabriel, Katharine Ruth Banning
of Los Angeles, and Rosalind Wood and Helen Longyear of Boston were
the bridesmaids. All wore ecru lingerie frocks richly trimmed with lace
and insertion over satin. Their "novel" hats were trimmed with blue
satin ribbons and small wreaths of pink moss roses and forget-me-nots —

"very smart and Parisian in effect." They carried small 1830 bouquets of lilies of the valley, which they held demurely at the waist when they posed for the photographer.

The best man was Frederick Ayer, Jr. The ushers, all in dress uniform, were Lieutenant George Patton Brown, U.S. Navy, a cousin of the groom, and Lieutenants James A. Brice, Francis G. Delano, Philip S. Gage, and Stanley S. Rumbough of the Army.

Dr. George A. Gordon of the Old South Church in Boston performed the ceremony. He was assisted by Rev. Eugene Huiguin, the rector of St. John's, who added a bold touch of color by wearing over his black academic gown the scarlet hood of his Oxford University degree. The choir-boys of St. Peter's Church in Beverly sang nuptial hymns.

As the bride and groom turned to leave the altar and the organist began to play Mendelssohn's wedding march, the ushers drew their sabers and formed an arch. When the newly married couple had walked through, the ushers sheathed their sabers and escorted the bridesmaids from the chancel.

Carriages took the bridal party and guests to a reception at the Ayer home at Pride's Crossing, "one of the most beautiful and extensive of any on that fashionable shore." The house was decorated with garlands of laurel, rambler roses, and palms, and the proceedings were "crowned with perfect weather, making the reception at the superb estate, Avalon, almost entirely al fresco."

The "only shadow," as one newspaper reported, was Mrs. Patton's absence.

Mr. and Mrs. Ayer received at the entrance of their spacious living room, which, together with the library on one side and the dining room on the other, covered the entire floor of "the beautiful country seat."

Mrs. Ayer wore a gown "the perfect taste of which was as conspicuous as its beauty." It was of palest blue satin, so pale as to be almost gray, with brocade trimmed with venetian point lace and silver embroidery, and veiled with chiffon of the same tone. She wore a white hat with white plumes, no jewels except a single string of pearls and a pendant.

Mr. Patton and his sister-in-law, a radiant Aunt Nannie, stood with the Ayers. Miss Wilson was gowned in mauve embroidered chiffon over changeable silk and wore a large hat of mauve tulle with white plumes.

A full orchestra played on the terrace overlooking the sea. There was dancing in the library. The bride cut the wedding cake with her husband's sword. Then followed Army cheers and "The Star-Spangled Banner."

Carriages transported the guests to the special train, which left Pride's Crossing at six fifty-three for Boston.

Lieutenant and Mrs. Patton left for New York and a month's honeymoon in Europe. They found their bridal suite on the *Deutschland* filled with flowers and other bon voyage remembrances from their friends and relatives.

Patton carried a black leather notebook with him, intending to keep a diary. Entitled "My Trip Abroad," it received very few notations. According to the entries, George and Beatrice landed at Plymouth and visited the town. They drove in a motor car over excellent roads to Tintagel, Cornwall, where they spent three days. The hotel was fine and the castle fun. They read about King Arthur — "The people talk of him as if he were still here." They drove in a double team to Bude, where they had lunch and changed horses. They passed through Kilkhampton, where they looked at the old and interesting church and saw the grave of Sir Bevil Grenvil, his helmet, and his "goanlettes." They reached Clovelly. They took the boat to Biddeford. And there the writing ceased.

After spending some time in London, they returned home. Docking in New York, they took the 10 A.M. train to Boston. They reached the Ayer residence to find no one there except Mr. Ayer, who was riding his horse. He was surprised to see them.

Letter, GSP, Jr., to Aunt Nannie, June 27, 1910

All our presents were boxed for us and every thing possible has been done. Now the real opening chores of being married begin. I hope I make good at it. I think I will. B is all that I thought her and a little more which is sufficient praise for any one. I hope Pa is doing well in politics. Gosh I hope he gets to the senate. I have not heard one word from any one for over a month so for God sake write.

He soon learned that Mr. Patton had failed to obtain his party's backing for the election that fall.

The young couple reached Fort Sheridan on June 29 and moved into the "Allerdice house." On the following day, Patton resumed his military duties. Troop K participated in a tournament at Grant Park, Chicago, during the first two weeks of July, but there was ample time for him and Beatrice to be together. They spent a happy month.

On July 29, George left for Sparta, Wisconsin, where extensive maneuvers were to be held during August. He was in charge of transporting the animals by train, and the last view Beatrice had of him was as he supervised the loading of the mules.

She had wanted to accompany him to Sparta, but Captain Marshall and everyone else discouraged her from going. The troops were to be first at Camp Robinson, then at Camp Bruce E. McCoy, and both were seven or eight miles from the village. George would be able to spend only a few hours with her once a week. No other ladies from the post would be there.

So on the same day that George left Sheridan on the horse train, she departed and, with her sister Kay, who had been visiting the newlyweds, returned to Avalon, Pride's Crossing.

"During our short housekeeping experience together," she told Aunt Nannie, "he has added to his other accomplishments that of champion furniture polisher, varnish-and-painter, cook, plumber, carpenter, gardener, and heavy chaperone. He will be a piano-tuner next."

After unloading the animals at their destination, Patton rejoined his troop, which had also traveled to the encampment by train.

"Dearest Little Bug," he wrote Beatrice on August 2, there were neither people nor houses around the camp, the village of Sparta was eight miles away over a road eight inches deep in dust, and it was better for her to be at Avalon. "Quite a number of my class mates are around here but none that I care about except Miner who I have not yet seen."

"Behold a letter from the dead," he wrote on August 11, "or so I was for about an hour this morning until I found Colonel Bishop the chief umpire and by his word was restored to life." The occasion was a mock battle, during which he led a patrol of eight mounted men, covered his unit's flank, put some "enemy" artillery out of action, sneaked away from "enemy" infantry to keep from being captured, saw an opposing patrol of four or five men, which he charged but hit a wire fence, charged again when two troops or companies struck his patrol in the flank, ran, but found another troop in front and two closing in from the rear, "so we were fixed all right."

He was having lots of fun at the summer games that brought together cavalry, infantry, and artillery units of both the Regular Army and, as he called them, the "malitia."

Yet he found time to read, and he informed Beatrice that he had almost finished the second of the several military books they had bought in London,

> so feel quite learned. But Clausewitz is about as hard reading as any thing can well be and is as full of notes of equal abstruceness as a dog is of fleas. The war to day was of little interest. I got lost but so did the umpire and as I found myself before he did I won out.

In a letter to Aunt Nannie he described the maneuvers as problems against an imaginary enemy. "One is going along a road when the um-pier says 'about fifty men are firing at you from that hill' you at once at-tack some times with success some times with out but always with great heat." Chasing a band of nonexistent guerrillas and locating them in a field, troops launched a saber charge "which literly cut to pieces the imaginary enemy; it was thrilling. I was not in it as I had the rear guard. I heard an old sergeant say that he had been through three wars but this beat them all."

He was thinking of applying to go to the Cavalry School at Fort Riley, Kansas, but an officer named "Stevenson was turned down at Riley on account of being married so I guess that nocks me too. Well it might be worse. I guess you learn little towards being a general there but I would like to go all the same." He talked of getting a job as military attaché and said he would prefer a large country. "Tell Papa if he hears of any [such jobs] running loose to get it [for me]. I would like Brazil or Ar-genteen, or some such dump as that and in the interim will struggle along at Sheridan."

Major Sturgis, the adjutant, sent for Patton and asked him to investi-gate alleged depredations by troops on an adjacent farm. "He spoke of the kindness your family had showed his mother," he wrote to Beatrice,

> and asked me to dinner tomorrow night so I fancy I will see the general at close range and also that I may take note how to do — or not to do when I am as he is. When? Yet there is probably not a shadow of doubt that even with out a war I will be a general — if in such an event [meaning, if no war came] I should stick it out. Just

how I don't know but I do know that I am more efficient than most of them.

Troop K left the maneuver area on August 31 and on horseback and with wagons marched through Ontario, Viola, Richland Center, Clyde near Loon Rock, Mineral Point, Darlington, Browntown — all in Wisconsin — on the way to Sheridan.

Darlington was Captain Marshall's hometown, and when Troop K passed through, he received an ovation from the townspeople. Houses were decked with flags, Patton wrote Beatrice, and the firemen's band was

playing to beat hell. It is a small old town that people never leave and where they all know and respect one another. There is no servant class, none are rich none poor all happy. A great thing for a nation to have such towns full of honest narrow minded men.

Patton reported on sick call the first three days of September because of trouble with his eyes. The doctor diagnosed "conjunctivitis, acute, traumatic, due to foreign body in cornea" — no doubt from the dust raised by the horses and mules.

The troop was on the road for two weeks, reaching Fort Sheridan on September 15.

Beatrice returned to the post soon afterward with news for George. As she informed Aunt Nannie on October 2, "It is so lovely to think that *both* my families are glad of God's little present to us!" She was learning to sew, for she wanted to do underthings for the baby — "I can't aspire to the dresses" — and her fingers were sore.

Letter, GSP, Jr., to Aunt Nannie, October 22, 1910
[Had been in the field for four days.] K troop was supposed to capture a bridge eight miles out. We dodged around all after noon — I was commanding the troop as Captain M[arshall] was an umpire — and bothered "I" troop so much that they reported us to be two troops. At about seven we took the bridge then we had to go into camp in the dark and rain in a strange place but we managed it . . . I am having lots of fun this fall. If I could only play polo too it would be great but I can't. I have not the time at the right time of

day. I am translating a french article for the General Staff. At least
B is and I do the copying. I may be famous yet thanks to her. I mean
other wise than as being her husband.

A few days later he learned that he was to take temporary command of
the machine gun platoon during the absence on leave of its normal commander. He was not "highly delighted" because it was a rather poor outfit. Beatrice thought that leading it for a while would be good experience
for him, and she was right.

"He is also developing a double chin *in spite* of my bum housekeeping!" Beatrice wrote Aunt Nannie, thanking her for sending "Georgie's
baby picture," which "is enthroned on my bureau and it is indeed beautiful . . . Georgie is busy heaving coal on the furnace — that is his great
occupation nowadays."

Patton commanded the machine gun platoon during November and
December. Not only did he shape up the unit, thereby impressing his
superiors with his capability as a commander of troops; he also learned
how to fire, deploy, and use machine guns, all of which was valuable
knowledge.

In a "Small Accounts Book," Beatrice and George managed to keep a
reasonable record of their household and personal expenditures, but only
for four months. They were both impatient with the notations. Since a
strict budget was unnecessary — they were hardly living on his army pay
of nearly $170 per month — the bookkeeping was useless and a waste of
time.

Mr. Ayer was taken ill around Thanksgiving, and instead of having the
Ayer family come to Chicago for the holiday, Beatrice went to Boston.
Patton had several bachelors in for dinner, and they gorged themselves
on a meal that Beatrice had prepared for six people. Mr. Ayer was quite
well again after a few days.

The Pattons in California finally completed moving into the new house
that Mr. Patton had had built.

George went to the horse show in Chicago twice and was captivated. "I
am going to get a horse and enter it next year," he told Aunt Nannie, as
"it is a fine advertisement for a man [in the Army]. Mr. Chaffee [Adna
R. Chaffee, Military Academy, class of 1904] has been doing wonders in
it . . . I got Pa's letter with the check all right."

He and Beatrice owned an automobile. After going to the auto show in Chicago, he wrote his father, "I think that the car I should have gotten is a Stevens-Dourly for at $1750. one gets a bigger show for the money than I did." He went into a long discussion of various automobiles, demonstrating an obvious familiarity with them and their advantages and disadvantages, and concluded: "The six [cylinder] is with out doubt mechanically better than the four."

This marked the beginning of his considerable interest in and knowledge of motorcars and would lead him eventually to the tanks.

Mrs. Ayer and Aunt Nannie arrived at Fort Sheridan in February to look after Beatrice, who was sick in bed with a cold.

A piece of legislation proposing an increase in the number of Army officers was introduced in Congress about this time, and Patton reported to his father: "It is thought here that the 612 bill will sure pass. It would be good for me if it did, but a good that is universal is of little personal benefit."

Several days later, he wrote:

There seems a chance of the extra officers bill going through but I think the principal of legislation to help promotion by an increase [in the number of officers] is wrong. It should be gained by elimination or a larger army. The other is a weak policy of those afraid to hurt the feelings of the influential vagabonds that should be eliminated.

He informed Mr. Patton that he had bought some stocks on Mr. Ayer's recommendation — Atcheson, U.S. Rubber, American Telephone and Telegraph; they gave him an income of about 175 dollars per year, over 5.5 percent, which he thought "not bad."

As Beatrice's time approached in March, Mr. and Mrs. Ayer arrived, bringing a nurse. "Mrs. Ayer certainly has been just as fine as possible," George wrote Aunt Nannie. "I am very fond of her."

The baby, Beatrice Smith Patton, later renamed Beatrice Ayer Patton, was born that month. George informed Aunt Nannie that "B and the baby are very well. B comes down to meals now and the baby is out in its carriage. I was very sorry to have Mrs. Ayer go as she was very nice indeed but she had to go to her family."

A few days later, he wrote Aunt Nannie in great excitement about the prospect of war with Mexico. He admitted that "there may be no war. God forbid such an eventuality however." Yet he was depressed, perhaps because the baby demanded much of Beatrice's attention. "I hear very little from home," he told Aunt Nannie, "and what I do hear is not worth hearing so what the hell is the use any how."

Letter, GSP, Jr., to Aunt Nannie, March 22, 1911

The accursed infant has black hair is very ugly and is said by some dastardly people to slightly resemble me which it does not, since it is ugly. B is very well indeed and all things are fine . . .

We traded our auto for a bigger one that holds four or five people . . . It is a very handsome machine indeed and easy to look after too. We made a pretty good trade on the old one . . .

The Mexican trouble seems dormant for the moment but even should all present hostilities close it is not for long. We will cross the border yet. I feel sure of it.

He would, of course, be absolutely right.

Letter, GSP, Jr., to his father, April 12, 1911

[Mama, Nita, and Aunt Nannie had arrived for a visit and] they all thought Smith a very remarkable child . . .

An order came the other day stating that all horses belonging to officers could be entered in four races one at Richmond one at Baltimore one at N.Y. and one at Saratoga N.Y. One race at each place to be a flat race and the other for the hurdles. I don't know yet that I will go but if I do it will be from the middle of May to the tenth of June or there abouts. As the horses will be transported free and as I will be also it ought to be a nice trip even if I get beaten and I hope I don't.

I wrote Col Garrard of the 15th and asked him whether or not I could get to [Fort] Riley [to go to school] this year. He said I could not. As I have to finish three years commissioned service . . . It is up to me to hunt a job unless I want to go to the Islands [the Philippines]. There seems to me to be but two jobs open to me. Namely a Tack [tactical officer] at West Point or an Attache some where . . . It seems to me that South America is the most important place except Mexico where one can go as we will with out doubt some day own it.

There is at present no attache in Belgium but I think Mr. Lodge and Mr. Flint and Mr. Culverson might make it apparent that there should be one there. [These men were prominent in politics in Washington and friends of either the Pattons or the Ayers.]

Mama said some thing about your going to Washington next winter. Should you [do so] I think there would be no difficulty in getting me transfered there. For great is civil influence on the army. I should like to be there a winter for it has ever seemed to me nearer God than else where and the place where all people with aspirations should attempt to dwell. Besides asside from me it would give you some thing to think of and to do which would be fine especially if you could sell enough land not to need to bother [to work].

I wish you could think over these things and don't forget that you know Dr. Ainsworth [Adjutant General of the Army], and that he who knocks it shall be opened unto. The trouble is that we hate so to knock. Yet why?

I am very well. Your devoted son

Letter, GSP, Jr., to his father, April 17, 1911

To day all of us except B and Smith went to church and we picked B up later and took her to dinner at the Moraine. It is the first time she has been out at all to a meal. She looked fine and did not get too tired . . .

The new auto is fine. I am glad I got it.

Letter, GSP, Jr., to his father, April 23, 1911

I got a dividend of $10 for telephone the other day and felt oppulent. I wish I saw the chance of a war. I get horribly bored doing nothing at all. Yet the day of the great business man is over too. I wonder what is coming . . .

[A baseball game on post.] We won. I played though I know absolutely nothing of the game.

Captain Marshall departed Fort Sheridan toward the end of May on detail to Fort Leavenworth, Kansas, and in his absence Patton took command of Troop K. To be entrusted with the command of a troop was a mark of great confidence in his judgment, balance, and military knowledge. No doubt his work as commander of the machine gun platoon had been outstanding.

No doubt too, his stature in the eyes of the enlisted men was high, particularly since he had continued to drill them even though severely cut above the eye by the butting of his horse's head.

Even more important, he had impressed not only Captain Marshall but all his superior officers with his enthusiasm, zeal, and competence.

Being troop commander was a marvelous experience for Patton. Second lieutenants usually waited years to assume command of a company. Even though the job was temporary — he would hold it until an officer of higher rank arrived on post to claim the prerogative — Patton retained command for almost four months.

He should have been, and probably was, exhilarated by the task. Yet strangely enough, he never mentioned his command of the troop in his letters, never discussed his problems or his satisfactions as a company commander. Perhaps he was, as he had frequently admitted in earlier correspondence, addicted to living in the future instead of in the present.

In any event, he was interested mainly in securing a transfer from Sheridan — out of the country as a military attaché or, preferably, to Washington. The chief reason was his desire to avoid being sent to the Philippines, a normal tour of duty for young cavalry officers. There seemed little point in going. Aguinaldo had capitulated, the insurrection was at an end, the islands were quiet. Army officers had made reputations there, but 1911 was too late. Why go all the way across the Pacific Ocean simply for garrison duty?

There were probably other reasons why he wished to escape from Sheridan. Chicago was distant from Boston. The houses where he had been more than welcome as a bachelor were no longer open to him. He felt isolated at a post where there were neither important officers nor significant activities. He believed he had absorbed all that he could possibly expect to learn there, even to the extent of coping with the direction of a cavalry troop.

Better opportunities existed elsewhere, and, as always, he had his view fixed firmly on the future.

Meanwhile, to find relief from the oppressive summer heat, Beatrice and the baby went to Pride's Crossing.

Letter, GSP, Jr., to Aunt Nannie, July 2, 1911

B writes that the Baby is well and has gained nearly a pound. I suppose that is fine . . .

We had a polo match Saturday and I won a cup a foot high. It is very pretty. I wish you could see it. As I have to make my bed on the porch I will say good night.

Letter, GSP, Jr., to Beatrice, July 2, 1911

Darling One: You are one fierce woman. What in H do you mean by "Doing what I like best to do — reading." I would rather a damed sight look at some thing else than book and you know what it is too. It looks like a skunk . . .

I am inclosing a letter from Capt. Marshall . . . Saumur [the French cavalry school] is of course the Nirvana of Riley so that could one get there direct it would be so much gained . . .

I wrote Capt M. saying that should you think favorably of it I would try for it [Saumur] and then I told him that I knew Gen Ainsworth the Adjutant Gen. And that your father would work the Mass. people for me and that papa would try to fix it in California and in Texas. I said "there are the weapons now please show me how to use them."

Rhodes that Capt M speaks of is the personal aid of Gen Wood so is quite influential. He is the man who was chiefly active in getting the present detail for the Capt.

I was glad to get the letter from Capt M. broaching the subject for it gave me a chance to inquire how to use influence. So that if nothing else comes of it we will at least know more on that important point than we do at present.

Enclosed Letter, Marshall to GSP, Jr., June 26, 1911

My dear Patton: . . . Captain Andrews says that it is the present purpose of the War Department not to send anyone to the Military Academy from the cavalry who has not been to Saumur, so if you lose [command of] the troop I would advise you to work your rabbit's foot good and hard and get sent there. There's no use putting it off, either. If you can get your friends interested you will have no difficulty.

Let me know what you decide, and I will write Rhodes a letter about it, so that when your name comes up he will be able to tell General Wood a few things that could scarcely appear in your application. Don't make the application until you let me know what preliminary steps you have taken.

. . . Give my love to Mrs. Patton — thank you both for your attentions to Mrs. Marshall.

Cordially yours,

Letter, Beatrice to Aunt Nannie, July 11, 1911

Georgie is getting pretty lonesome, so I am planning to go west just as soon as I dare to; I couldn't take Smithy in this heat, although I have not told him that. I am just hoping for it to let up . . . for I don't want to make him jealous — dear soul.

Letter, GSP, Jr., to Aunt Nannie, July 22, 1911

B Gets back to day and I shall be darned glad to see her. I thought the little devil would never come back . . .

I have been translating some French for the General Staff. It is not very hard but I am curious for B's revision of it. I may find some startling changes in my ideas.

Last night I went to a dance at the Naval Station at Lake Bluff.

Letter, Beatrice (from Fort Sheridan) to "Darling Aunt Nannie," around July 25, 1911

[George has slight touch of hay fever.] We are having all the Marshalls and Pages to dinner — and you know what *that* is in this house.

Letter, Beatrice to Aunt Nannie, September 11, 1911

We are much excited over our possible transfer. There does not seem any immediate — I was about to say danger — but you never *can* tell. How happy we shall all be together in W[ashington, D.C.] this winter, if we do! G. thinks we can get leave about Oct. 1st but does not want to apply for it until he is sure. But we are all impatient. Our new 1st lieut. [who would take command of Troop K] is here and is awfully nice — just a few years older than G. — G. is on an examining board for the admission of 19 new 2nd lieuts. (cits) [meaning, coming directly from civilian life] last week & this week & we have breakfast every morning at 6:30. The early [morning] is glorious (after one is up!) His hay fever has almost left him and he looks fine. Now I must practise for the rehearsal this P.M. of my musical debut here tomorrow — a reading with music.

Letter, GSP, Jr., to Aunt Nannie, September 18, 1911

I think it quite probable that I will get my transfer to [Fort] Myer as Maj. Horton [who is] K's suitor is doing all he can in Washington and he is quite influential. Of course say nothing as to his help.

I have been so uncertain as to leave etc. that I have not gotten up my foot ball team yet but will in November I hope.

I have been very busy all week getting up the examination papers of sixteen candidates for second lieutenants . . .

They were a very poor lot and if that is the best way we can get up second lieutenants I think we had best omit them completely

I think I told you that I had my horses in the horse show at lake forest.

He, Beatrice, and the baby spent the month of October at San Gabriel with the Pattons in their new house.

Letter, GSP, Jr., to his father, November 12, 1911

[Has been busy] with this nasty French. Now however we are all but through [with the article] and will have it off by Tuesday. I think it is a good translation . . .

Hunting is great fun and sort of grows on you, you never know what is coming next and all the surroundings are very attractive too . . .

[He and Beatrice went to Chicago by auto to see the famous Scottish comedian Harry Lauder. Started back at 11 P.M., and it was sleeting, blowing, and freezing hard.] That we got here with out accident is a wonder. We each drank a whole glass of jin and never felt it . . .

I feel sure that I will hear from the transfer this week and think that it will be favorably acted on. I shall hate very much to leave but think that W. is really a better scene of activities though perhaps not so pleasant.

He enclosed a carbon copy of an article he had translated from the journal *La France Militaire*. Entitled "The Danger of Morocco," it described French military successes in North Africa but warned that the French were winning because the Moroccans had no artillery. What was especially dangerous was the widespread belief among French military figures that their techniques in Morocco would work everywhere. They were being lulled into overconfidence, for how to fight successfully in Europe and overcome the resistance of a strong and modern foe would require forces, tactics, and weapons far different from those used against poorly armed and poorly organized North Africans.

The article was, it turned out, rather prophetic, and it was perhaps this quality that had made Patton select it for translation.

• • •

During the autumn of 1910 and the following winter and spring, as Beatrice became less active during her pregnancy, then busy with the baby, Patton had been somewhat disoriented, even bored. Marriage restricted him. The increasingly bad weather precluded many outdoor activities. His duties on post were now somewhat routine. He was at a loss to know what to do with his off-duty time.

He tried unsuccessfully to develop an interest in the stock market. He sought to keep track of his money on a regular basis, but keeping up the "Small Accounts Book" was too much trouble and filled no practical need.

He therefore turned to writing, learned to use the typewriter, and found to his astonishment that he enjoyed the work and could produce interesting and useful papers. Aside from his translations of articles in French military journals, which he did with the help of Beatrice, who was fluent in French, he wrote several military disquisitions and practiced putting his thoughts on paper.

Probably the first paper he turned out was a practical and detailed "Saddle Drill" for his cavalry troop. Shortly thereafter, probably for his own amusement, for it remained incomplete, he wrote a treatise entitled "National Defense."

National Defense! What a charming [picture] to the mind of the unenlightened does it not conjure up. — Fertile fields far from the clamor of war, Sunny cities and smiling towns, the tranquility of whose infernal uproar of commerce is not disturbed by the alarming roar of cannon.

An apt phrase too in the mouths of those glib panderers of their nations interest, the politicians, who use the hard-worked epithet as a means of diverting revenues from their proper course of helping National eminence by increasing National strength, to the more complacent object of lining the pockets of unprincipled lobbyists . . .

"TO ARMS!!" The cry rings from the flannel mouth and inflamed of ten thousand orators. "Resist the invader! Raise a volunteer army! Defend our 'Hearths.'" And while raising this army, have our polite adversary wait like the French Guards at Blenhime until we fire the first volley? What? They do not wait! we are set upon, attacked before Gen. Jones, ex-editor of the Windtown Bladder has had time to learn how to make a latrine. Our gallant but insufficient regular forces defeated or rather annihilated; our untrained levies, capable only of passive resistance, turned or forced out of position after position. Our cities taken, our capitol stormed and not for the first time on account of untrained defenders . . . plenty of oratory, plenty of courage, plenty of blood, but no cannon, no wagon trains, no organization, no cohesion, and the result: Capitulation . . .

. . . would it not be cheaper to take a few boxing lessons than to spend a month in the hospital? . . .

All nations of any consequence except ourselves and England have vast standing armies. Preparation for war with them is not a matter of months and weeks, but of days and hours. When they strike it is all or nothing. Blow follows blow with the rapidity of thought. Attack, push forward, attack again until the end. And what have we to oppose to such an onslought? An army? Yes and for its size excellent but . . .

The words "Attack, push forward, attack again until the end," uttered even in written form with such ardor, were to become a George Patton trademark.

Another theme he would sound continuously throughout his military career appeared in a paper he wrote about the same time, late in 1910 or early in 1911.

we children of a mechanical age are interested in and impressed by machines to such an extent that we forget that no machine is better than its operator . . .

Many years later, after World War II, the U.S. Army, in an age of increasing mechanization, automation, and gadgetry, would transcribe this thought into the motto that what was important was not the gun but the man behind the gun.

The remainder of this paper by Patton wandered into several dead-end byways. But one paragraph expressed his thinking about war and gave evidence of his growing familiarity with military writers and historians, also to become a George Patton trademark.

From the beginning has our gifted species expended vast amounts of time and ingenuity in a largely futile attempt to devise safe methods of war; means of killing with out being killed for as Ardant du

Picq [a 19th century French officer and writer on military subjects who was killed in the war with Prussia in 1870–71] puts it "Man ingages in battle for the purpose of gaining victory not for the purpose of fighting." Nor have our efforts been wholy futile for despite the bellowings of sob sisters asto the extremination of the race the fact remains that in each war since recorded history began the proportional losses both to the soldiers and the civilians have steadily decreased.

He was not yet the polished writer he would become, but he was in the process of evolving a personal style of his own. He was learning to organize his thoughts on paper, to question dogma, to look behind the immediate meaning of statements, regulations, and fixed beliefs.

His ability to write would be a distinct asset in Washington, D.C., where he was transferred in December 1911.

He reported to Fort Myer, Virginia, on December 3, and his life and military development entered a wholly new phase, the real beginning of his rise to fame.

CHAPTER 11

Fort Myer, Stockholm, and Saumur

"All the big men were there."

WASHINGTON was a relatively small town, endowed, as one wag said, with the virtues of southern efficiency and northern charm. It had little commerce, trade, or manufacturing, for its prime business was politics. It had yet to emerge from the nineteenth century, for its location between Virginia and Maryland gave it distinct overtones of the plantation. It was dominated by no indigenous aristocracy but rather a transient one founded on wealth or government, and for these souls life was slow and easy, friendly and filled with partying. It was also infested by the newly rich who came to be seen and by pushers who came to make their fortunes.

Everyone of any prominence knew everyone else, and Army officers automatically belonged to the best circles of society. They mingled freely and often with members of Congress and the Cabinet. On New Year's Day it was their practice to call at the White House and pay their respects to the President and his family. All Academy graduates belonged to the Army-Navy Club, where friends and benefactors could be suitably entertained.

Fort Myer, just west of Washington and across the Potomac, was a short distance from town. On land that had once belonged to George Washington — who bequeathed it to his stepson, whose daughter married Robert E. Lee — it was a showplace. Situated on a hill and adjacent to the Custis-Lee mansion and the Arlington Cemetery, it overlooked on one side the Potomac, Georgetown, and the broad mall leading to the Capitol, on the other, rolling and sparsely inhabited countryside.

A cavalry station, Fort Myer featured officers from the best families in the nation, probably the finest horsemanship in the Army, and the most exciting polo games in the area. It furnished the personnel and trappings for impressive military funerals.

Its officers served as escorts for kings and presidents and their daughters and nieces at occasions of ceremony and state. They danced in the halls of foreign embassies and hunted on the estates of landed gentry. They attended balls in the attractive suburb of Chevy Chase, Maryland, visited the homes of the fashionable in Fairfax, Culpeper, and Warrenton, Virginia, and occasionally spent weekends in Baltimore and New York.

They knew and were familiar with the influential people of official Washington — the Secretary of War and his immediate assistants, the Army Chief of Staff (who resided at Fort Myer) and the other officers of high rank who staffed the War Department and ran the Army, the members of the congressional military committees who recommended the appropriations, and all the others who held position and wielded power.

Despite its sleepy appearance, its many unpaved, muddy, and rutted streets, its provincial character, Washington was an exciting place for a young man on the make to be, particularly one who had the material means to make a splash, the family connections to stay afloat, and the personal qualities to be in the swim. It was, as Patton had said, "nearer God," the center of his world, where the decisions were made and where, in the interest of advancing his prospects, he could exercise his fatal charm on those who counted and who made the decisions.

Letter, GSP, Jr. (Fort Myer), to Beatrice, December 11, 1911

The trunks get here in a few minutes and then we will get things straightened out a little I hope . . . [Can do little until the furniture arrives.] Hannah [the maid] is very much delighted with the house and says it is better than 395 [Commonwealth Avenue, the Ayer residence].

The bath room is all white tile both floor and walls half way up and there seems an abundance of hot water which comes up quickly.

The front room which I have chosen for you is smaller than the middle one but nicer. The baby is going in the back room as it has more windows . . .

I lunched to day with the Summeralls [whom he had known at West Point] and had a fine time. They are very nice and want you to stay with them when you come [if the Patton house was not yet ready for occupancy]. People work much harder here than at Sheridan and it is all together more military. I dined with Mr. Wood [probably the neighbor of the Ayers at Pride's Crossing], Maj. Horton [Katharine Ayer's suitor, as Patton had called him, who had been helpful in arranging his transfer to Washington] and the presidents sergean[t] at the Metropolitan Club last night. All the big men were there and it was most interesting.

Try and get your mother father and K to come also Nannie and Nita. We would have a roaring time.

He was assigned to Troop A, 15th Cavalry, and Captain Julian R. Lindsey, the troop commander, rated his military performance as "excellent" in his attention to duty, professional zeal, bearing, and appearance, "very good" in his general efficiency.

It was a fine rating for those days when the Army was small and officers judged their subordinates strictly. Words still had their original meaning. Many years later exaggeration in efficiency reports would become normal, "excellent" would come to be regarded as mediocre and "satisfactory" the equivalent of poor.

Despite the attractions of the good life in town, Patton was taking his soldiering seriously.

Granted a two-day leave, he spent Christmas in Boston with Beatrice and the Ayers.

Letter, GSP, Jr., to "Dearest Ellie" [Beatrice's mother], January 1912

Smith as you know got here safely and already has many admirers. . . . [His dog Flipper, a bloodhound, was there too. It was 15 minutes downtown by automobile, 40 minutes or more by streetcar, depending on the connections.]

The dress B got for a Xmas present is a beauty. She wore it to the chevy chase ball Saturday and was the prettiest person there.

We were going to the Charity ball tonight but unfortunately I went on guard so we can't go but we are going again tomorrow . . .

I truly hope you and Mr. Ayer and K will come down and see us. It would be fine and we want you. I will behave better.

With love. George.

Letter, GSP, Jr., to his father, January 8, 1912

Dear Papa: I have been quite anxious to hear from you as to your [political] success in N.Y. but so far have been dissapointed.

I hope you are doing as well as you did here. Certainly no one could ask more.

We went to a reception and met Senator Works. He impresses me as a sort of a weak man trying to give the appearance of unusual sagacity but at least he seemed quite anxious to see you again. I should think that you had best come back here before going home and see that every thing is working smoothly. You can get people started writing in California [in your behalf] just by writing them [from here] and asking them to do so . . .

With much love and hopes for success

Patton had owned the best horses at Fort Sheridan, but he soon discovered that this was not the case at Fort Myer. Taking two days of leave in January, he traveled to Lexington, Kentucky, and to Front Royal, Virginia, to buy horses and upgrade his stable. He purchased a full thoroughbred with a pedigree in Lexington, found nothing to his liking in Front Royal.

"I still continue to like Washington," he wrote his father late in January. "We have a chaufer [because] every one else had either one or a driver and we could not keep up [without one]."

In February he prepared for instructional purposes a treatise entitled "Principles of Scouting." Designed for Troop A, it consisted of 42 maxims in the manner of Napoleon — very much like the perorations he had written to himself in his various notebooks. His principles were practical as well as imaginative. For example, the last piece of advice read: "If you have used a fire [to cook a meal or to keep warm while campaigning in the field] move away to sleep [for] the enemy may have located it."

In March he was transferred from Troop A and appointed squadron quartermaster, or supply officer at Fort Myer. The change was probably made in order to relieve him of his duties with troops, thus enabling him to practice with and play on the Fort Myer polo team. It also allowed him time to participate in steeplechase racing at nearby courses.

In conformance with proper military practice, upon the occasion of Patton's transfer, Captain Lindsey rated him. Lindsey wrote virtually the same appreciation as before, evaluating Patton "excellent" in his attention to duty, professional zeal, general bearing, and military appearance, "very good in intelligence and judgment, and in instructing, drilling, and handling enlisted men."

. . .

Patton had hardly mastered the duties of his new job as quartermaster when he learned that he was being considered for a most interesting detail. The Fifth Olympic Games were to be held that summer in Stockholm, Sweden, and he was being talked about as the Army's representative in the Modern Pentathlon. Intended to test the fitness of the man at arms, the pentathlon consisted of five events: (1) shooting a pistol at 25 meters, (2) swimming a distance of 300 meters, (3) fencing with the dueling sword, (4) riding a steeplechase of 5000 meters, and (5) running a cross-country foot race of 4000 meters. The final score was determined by the sum of the standings in each match, and the man with the lowest number of points was declared the winner.

The competition seemed made to order for Patton. He was an Expert Pistol Shot, he had done long-distance swimming as a young man at Catalina, he had been an enthusiastic swordsman at West Point, he was an outstanding horseman, and he had been a runner in the track meets at West Point. In good physical condition, extremely likable and anxious to please, handsome in his soldierly appearance, he would be an excellent representative of the model American Army officer and would make a favorable impression abroad. Furthermore, he was in Washington, where decisions of this sort were made. Finally, he could be spared from his duties as quartermaster, which could be handled satisfactorily by an experienced, intelligent, and senior noncommissioned officer.

Learning on May 10 that the preliminary decision had been made in his favor, he started training at once, for there was very little time to prepare for the competition. He went on a diet, confining his meals to hearty foods of no special sort, drinking hardly any liquids, and abstaining from alcohol and tobacco. Since he had not run for two years and had not swum for three, he concentrated on these activities, practicing daily. He also fired the pistol every day on the range. He fenced three times a week and entered the National Championship tournament in New York that spring. Because he had taken part in Army steeplechase racing and because he played polo, he thought it unnecessary to brush up on his riding.

It was probably around this time that he made two entries in a miscellaneous notebook he kept between 1909 and 1919, a ledger filled with undated instructions to himself on a variety of matters. Putting down some ideas for "steeple Chasing," he wrote craftily: "In finishing it is generally better to be on the side away from the judge." He also advised himself on "How to get thin . . . Do not eat. Bread, cake, potatoes, rice, cream, milk, butter, fat, sweets, stews, minces, puddings, pastry, salt meat, salt fish or any thing containing sugar or starch."

Letter, GSP, Jr., to Aunt Nannie, early June 1912
 I think I have a pretty good chance of going both on the sword and saber team and on the Pentathelm team . . .
 It used to be the great event and for it was given the Savril Crown. It is mentioned in the Victor of Salamis. There are very few men who can do all the above things so I might do well.

The pentathlon, an important competition in the Hellenic games, had originally consisted of throwing the discus, doing the standing broad jump, throwing the javelin, running about a mile, and wrestling, all designed to test the military abilities of the soldier. Baron Pierre de Coubertin of France, who was instrumental in reviving the Olympics in 1896 as a means of promoting worldwide amity through sports, had transformed the pentathlon in order to reflect more accurately the physical prowess and military virtues of the modern soldier.

Although international games had been held every four years since 1896, they were relatively small affairs. It was only at Stockholm in 1912 that the prestige of the Olympic meetings was firmly established. Jim Thorpe, the great Indian athlete from Carlisle, would dominate the track and field events that year and capture the imagination and plaudits of the world.

It was in these proceedings that Patton would take part. On June 4, he was directed to sail on the *Finland,* leaving New York ten days later.

Apparently as a practice run or tune-up for the steeplechase in Stockholm, he took part in a race less than a week before he sailed for Europe.

Letter, GSP, Jr., to Beatrice, June 9, 1912
 Dearest B. Rumbough and Tate both got afraid of their horses or rather their wives and wired me they could not ride so I took the midnight Frieday and went to N.Y. and rode yesterday . . . [the longest course he had ever done — 2½ miles with nineteen jumps 4'6" high. Greble set] a hell of a pace . . . I got 4th (there were only four entries) Gray fields [his horse] never rode a worse race. He smashed into every hurdle on the second round. I fear he was all out of condition.

Accompanied by Beatrice, Mr. and Mrs. Patton, and Nita, Patton boarded the *Finland,* which carried most of the American competitors. On the following day, while at sea, the teams began to work out. Patton practiced with nearly all. He would later acknowledge the kindness, encouragement, and assistance offered him by various coaches and managers.

His schedule of training started at 6 A.M., when he ran two miles on deck with the cross-country team. From 10 A.M. to noon, he practiced with the pistol team. From 3 to 5 P.M., he worked with the fencing team. Later in the afternoon, he was with the swimming team — in a canvas tank, 20 by 8 feet in size, 4 feet deep, where a swimmer was roped to a ship's bolt and swam against the rope, remaining in one place in the water but getting a great deal of exercise. "It is much more distressing than ordinary swimming," Patton later remarked, "and we had to cut down the length of time we worked."

If he had abstained from alcohol during his training at Fort Myer, he relaxed at least once during the ocean voyage, for he was billed $4.25 for wine delivered to his stateroom.

The ship docked at Antwerp, and the Pattons went sight-seeing in the city before proceeding to Brussels, where they spent the night. They reached Stockholm on June 29.

From then until July 5, Patton trained every day, giving special attention to running and swimming. In a practice pistol shoot on July 4, he made 197 of a possible 200 points, "which I am informed," he said later, "was one point better than the record."

"We had a fine time together [in Stockholm]," Patton later wrote. "Papa went with me to all the Practices and he and the rest of the family were present at the competitions."

On July 6, the day before the competition started, he did nothing, which, he later admitted, was a mistake. He should have partaken of at least some light exercise. His lack of physical exertion and the fact that there was only one hour of darkness that night, plus his nervousness, made it difficult for him to sleep.

The Modern Pentathlon opened on July 7, with 42 competitors actually starting of 68 originally entered. Three Americans had intended to participate, but the two others, both civilians, had dropped out.

At 9 A.M., the pistol shooting commenced. Each contestant had two sighting or practice shots, then 20 rounds, fired in braces of five, that counted. Patton's two sighting shots were tens, the highest score. Down to business, he first scored 3 tens, 1 nine, 1 eight; he next scored 3 tens and — surprisingly, even inexplicably — 2 complete misses; he then registered 2 tens, 2 nines, 1 eight; and finally 3 tens, 1 nine, 1 seven. "This missing of the target, a thing I had done but once in all my practice," he later explained, "made me come out 21 out of 42."

Some have suggested that his bullets passed through holes previously made in the bull's-eye and therefore did not register, which was entirely plausible.

At 11 A.M., July 8, the swimming took place in a tank 100 meters long; two turns were necessary. Six men swam simultaneously and were timed. Of the 37 who competed, Patton ended in sixth place.

That afternoon the contestants were shown over the cross-country steeplechase course. They were allowed simply to see the jumps, their locations and the nature of the obstacles, but were permitted to make no written notes.

At 8 A.M., July 9, the fencing started. By then, only 29 competitors remained, the others having dropped out. The matches were held on the asphalt courts of the Royal Tennis Club, where the footing was excellent. Each bout was for three touches. The weapon was the dueling sword, which weighed 1¼ to 1½ pounds, was 2 inches in circumference at the hilt and tapered to the point, and had a bell guard 5 inches in diameter. "It is the rapier of history and the ancestor of all swords," Patton remarked, adding gratuitously, "The curved saber is a hybrid, being a cross between the rapier and the scimitar and having the good qualities of neither."

Every competitor fenced every other opponent, and the one having the least number of touches won. The fencing lasted two whole days and was a great strain on all. Patton was third. "I was fortunate enough to give the French victor the only defeat he had."

The cross-country steeplechase started at 11 A.M. on July 11, with riders starting singly at five-minute intervals over a course marked by flags through woods, over rocks, and down hills. About 25 jumps were designated, but about 50 minor obstacles, such as small ditches, fences with a ditch beyond, and double ditches, were unmarked. Two Swedish riders and Patton were judged to have turned in perfect performances, but since Patton was third in timing, he received third place.

A few days later, the cross-country foot runners, wearing regulation uniforms, made a striking picture as they lined up in front of the royal boxes in the stadium and waited to be sent off separately at one-minute intervals. Each man ran a third of a lap around the track, then left the stadium, went over the hills behind it, dashed over sheer rock, plowed through a heavy forest, splashed through a swamp six inches deep in mud, and finished in the stadium in front of the royal boxes. The contestants had been prohibited from seeing the course beforehand, and the course itself was marked only an hour before the race.

The starters were three Swedes, three British, three Russians, two French, two Danes, one Austrian, and, according to the Los Angeles *Examiner,*

our own Lieut. George S. Patton Jr. This tall, slim, fair man took the regulation sprinter's start and undoubtedly took too much out of himself in the early going. He appeared well spent when he re-entered the stadium, and though he had a lead of fifty yards over Asbinik of Sweden, he could not keep it. In the last fifty yards Lieut. Patton stopped almost to a walk as the Swede brushed by, and when the American finished he dropped into a faint.

As Patton remembered it fifteen years later:

In the 4000 meter cross country race Mike Murphy the trainer gave me some hop before the start. I fainted after finishing the race and was out for several hours. Once I came to but could not move or open my eyes and felt them give me a shot of more hop. I feared that it would be an overdose and kill me. Then I heard papa say in a calm voice. "Will the boy live?" and Murphy reply "I think he will but cant tell."

He had finished in third place.

The English edition of a Swedish newspaper complimented Patton's "fine cross-country running," which was "a particularly fine performance . . . to run such a fine race over our strange and difficult country. It exhausted him completely and he fell immediately after having passed the post. The Swedes all finished fit as fiddles."

His final place in the pentathlon was Number 5. "My standing," he wrote in his official report after returning home, "of 6 swimming, 3 fencing, 3 riding, 3 running, was seven less than that of any other competitor in those four events . . . but my standing of 21 in shooting ruined my average."

He made neither complaint nor excuse, commenting only that

the high spirit of sportsmanship and generosity manifested through-out speaks volumes for the character of the officers of the present day. There was not a single incident of a protest or any unsportsmanlike quibbling or fighting for points which I regret to say marred some of the other civilian competitions at the Olympic Games. Each man did his best and took what fortune sent like a true soldier, and at the end we all felt more like good friends and comrades than rivals in a severe competition, yet this spirit of friendship in no manner detracted from the zeal with which all strove for success.

Lieutenant Colonel Frederick S. Foltz, the senior officer in charge of the Army representatives, wrote in his report to the Adjutant General on July 26, 1912:

[Patton] made a most excellent showing and but for the misfor-tune of nervousness at the time when the revolver score was shot, he might have been the winner. He deserves great credit for the enthu-siastic and exhaustive way in which he prepared himself for this very difficult, all round competition. At the end of the cross-country run he fell insensible, after crossing the line, but sustained no serious injury.

Foltz corroborated Patton's report, saying that Patton stood fifth over-all in the event, with Sweden winning the first four places. Of the 42 competitors starting, an Austrian and an Englishman were civilians; the others were officers representing England, France, Austria, Russia, Sweden, Norway, Denmark, and, of course, the United States. Patton, Foltz added, had given the fencing champion of the French Army the only defeat he had suffered.

If the War Department sent a team to Berlin for the 1916 Olympics, Patton suggested, elimination tournaments at least nine months before the games would insure the best qualified athletes. This was the method the Swedes had used, and they had run away with the prizes.

The Stockholm Olympics ended on July 17. Ten days later, the King of Sweden conferred on Patton and the other contestants his commemorative medal, which was worn, his Grand Marshal explained in the citation, like any other military decoration. Not until May 1928 would the Congress authorize and the President approve the wearing of the medal by the American participants.

• • •

GSP, Jr., "My Father," 1927

After the games we had a good time around Stockholm and then went to Germany where we visited Berlin, Dresden and Nurenburg.

The first night we were in Berlin we had peaches floating in white wine for dessert. They were in tall glasses and kept bobbing up and down. Once we went to a restaurant where the floor was of ice and there was fancy skating during the meal. In Dresden while on a walk Papa and I bought Mama the twisted stem green champagne glasses she uses now.

In Nurenburg Beatrice and Papa used to eat donkey meat sausages and drink beer in little restaurants.

But he was thinking primarily of other matters. He wanted to perfect himself in fencing. To that end, he had inquired of all the fencers he had met in Stockholm who was considered the best master in Europe. The consensus named Monsieur l'Adjutant — a military rank somewhere between the grades of warrant officer and sergeant major — Cléry, Master of Arms and instructor of fencing at the Cavalry School in Saumur, France, the professional champion of Europe in the foil, the dueling sword, and the saber.

Deciding that the opportunity was too good to miss, he and Beatrice — in the latter part of July, while his father, mother, and sister toured Europe — traveled to Saumur, the "Nirvana," he had called it, of all American cavalrymen. They stayed at the Hotel Budan, which had central heating, electricity, and a telephone.

Every day — for about ten days or two weeks — until they had to leave to board their ship on August 10 for their return home, Patton took private lessons from Cléry in the dueling sword and the saber, paying more attention to the latter.

Interested in the fencing for his own benefit, he also learned how Cléry instructed his students. Writing in his notebook, he inscribed Cléry's methods and techniques as well as his own impressions. "Remember," he said in one entry, "in the proper guard you look under your saber."

Patton undoubtedly improved his performance as a fencer. But what was more valuable was his appreciation of Cléry's teaching style, which was different from that used in the U.S. Army — "and, in my opinion," Patton would report to the Adjutant General in September,

far better. It minimizes effort and is safer. I have fenced a great deal with the saber . . . so I believe my opinion is based on knowledge, not on a desire for something new. The French use the point far more than we do for reasons I will presently state . . .

The whole French system of mounted saber fencing is concentrated in the word: "Attack!"

The recruit is taught little or no fencing mounted but he has the one idea to reach his adversary with the point hammered into him constantly and he spends much time running at dummies mounted.

It is argued that America being a country of axmen the edge comes more natural but from what I saw and was told the French recruit wants to use the edge just as much as ours do but it is drilled out of them and "La pointe . . . toujours la pointe" is put in its place.

The above position [as described] gives the advantage of reaching the enemy at least a yard sooner than ours does, of presenting during the approach about one third the human target, and of instilling the desire to speed up and hit hard.

The general advantages for the use of the point mounted or dismounted are the following [He listed five well organized and lucid advantages, then wrote a short but authoritative description of how the curved sword had developed.]

For these reasons the French, English and Swedes and I believe most other nations are adopting straight swords or sabers.

The new French saber is straight with a blade 37 inches long and 1⅛ inches wide at the hilt. It has a cutting edge the whole length and is an ideal cutting weapon, being at the same time perfectly adapted for pointing which is indeed its first purpose.

This interest in and knowledge of swordsmanship Patton would turn to great advantage in the development of his career.

CHAPTER 12

Fort Myer

"What I am doing looks like play to you but in my business it is the best sort of advertising."

WHEN THE PATTONS RETURNED from Europe, Beatrice visited her parents at Pride's Crossing and George went directly to Washington and Fort Myer. He found it somewhat difficult to get settled, discovered some irritating conditions, learned what had transpired during his absence, and was gratified to be welcomed home as a hero by some of the really important people in his life.

Letter, GSP, Jr., to Beatrice, August 23, 1912
Dearest Beat. You are $96.88 over drawn. I told the bank to take $1000 out of your savings account and place it to your drawing account . . .

I cannot find in your check book any sign that you ever paid for those tires. I think you must have been mistaken . . .

Letter, GSP, Jr., to "Dearest Beatrice," August 24, 1912
I got here so late that I had to get an extra days leave to cover my absence.

No troops are here so the post is very quiet.

Mr. Tate was acting Adjutant and after I had reported I said how is your wife and could have been nocked over with a string when he answered she is dead . . .

Tate feels terribly. Some think he is going crazy, I do not.

I am going to the [firing] range in the morning to stay I do not know how long.

The house is in fine shape. Every thing is very clean and in good order. Marshall is an excellent cook.

Last night Gen Wood [the Army Chief of Staff] asked me to dinner. The Secretary [of War] was also there. They were both very nice. I went riding with the general this morning . . .

I have a slight touch of H.F. [hay fever].

[Adna] Chaffee is staying with me. Hurry up and pay the bills as I can't trade at a lot of the stores until you do. There is a bill here of $124 for auto tires. I thought you said you had paid it? Find out and let me know at once, as they have sent out three bills.

Late in August, Patton drove to Baltimore, where he rode his horse Roman Wing in a flat race. He was in the lead for the first mile and a quarter, but then no more finish was left in his horse, and he came in far behind the winner. "I had on my new boots and a silk uniform I had made and with the saddle was only 167 [pounds]." He started back from Baltimore at 5 A.M. in a downpour of rain and was nearly to Washington when his car became stuck on a hill, then skidded into the ditch. The car was at such a tilt that the gasoline would not run to the carburetor. He had to hire a team of horses to pull him out, and it cost him four dollars. He had bought a new horse, a black one, for $500. Would Beatrice sell his horse Grayfields stabled at Pride's Crossing.

Letter, GSP, Jr. (Edsall Target Camp, Alexandria, Virginia), to Beatrice, August 29, 1912

Darling Beat, You are so sweet, But you are not much hell on writing. I have had only two letters from you so far . . .

Capt Lindsey has just retired lamenting about the loneliness of his bed? as usual.

Last night I was not here so flipper [his bloodhound] stepped on my bed and used the pillow so I fear it may not be lonely enough.

All the houses at Myer are full of flees. I went down staires the other day in my bare feet and each foot got six flees on it.

Letter, GSP, Jr., to Beatrice, September 1, 1912

. . . the deluge is certain to come and the clouds of it are already darkening the sky. It is every where the effort of the inefficient to pull down the great . . . People who have money had best enjoy it for they may not have it long. The many headed beast called the "people" is howling for food . . . it will get it and then stupid with gorging will be chained as before.

I hope I help make that chain.

Letter, GSP, Jr., to Beatrice, September 2, 1912

[Bought and paid for Gus Strause, a race horse, and also a polo pony ordered before leaving for Sweden; also paid for the tires. This] leaves me pretty near broke.

Your finances are perfectly ridiculous. To put all your money at practically no interest and so tied up that it takes an act of god to get it is pretty foolish . . . Besides some four hundred that I have already paid exclusive of horses there is at least that much left to pay. I don't see how you could have let so many bills run from April or May the way you did. I think you had better let me run your bills here after or you will go to prison . . .

Inspite of your lack of brains I love you more all the time and miss you even here where I am very busy. I love you.

A few days later he drove to Timonium, about twelve miles beyond Baltimore, to the races at the state fair grounds, where a big crowd of about 1500 people had assembled. The track was less than one-half mile around, so the racers had to go around so often to make the distance that he lost count. The jumps were the worst he had ever seen, being boarded too near the top. The turns were so sharp that he could not hold Gus Strause, his horse, to them. But it was a fine race, the fastest he had been in, and the first three finishing were not a length apart. He came in third.

Letter, GSP, Jr., to Beatrice, September 7, 1912

I am one of the three who are supposed to be sure of [making] the Fort Myer [polo] team. The other two are Johnston and Graham so I am in good company . . .

I really like Capt. Lindsey very much. When you get onto him he is fine. Maj Rhodes is fine also . . .

The more I see of target practice the less I think of it. Our great trouble is that men do not do what they are told. They think too much! This talk about the independence of the American soldier will cost a lot of lives. If we would teach them to obey we would do much better than teaching them to shoot . . . Col Foltz speaks well of me in his report [on the Olympic Games]. I have to write one also. You will have to help.

That Major Charles D. Rhodes was "fine" — meaning that he liked Patton — was important. Intelligent, urbane, and extremely capable,

Rhodes, as a captain in 1911, had traveled secretly in Mexico on a confidential mission to gather information for the War Department on the political turmoil in that country. He was now the principal aide to the Chief of Staff and to a large extent regulated and controlled the access of officers, particularly those of junior grade, to General Leonard Wood.

Letter, Beatrice to Aunt Nannie, September 7, 1912

[Georgie] is at the range & very well & suffering much less than usual from his hay fever. He is very busy & enjoying his work immensely.

Letter, GSP, Jr., to Beatrice, September 8, 1912

Darling Beat. Yesterday as I told you I raced at Timonium and won. I beat the rest by about six lengths and never touched Roman Wing with the whip or spur.

I held him last for a mile and ate dirt by the peck, then I began to crawl up and at the quarter simply let him go and he went by the rest like they were tied to a tree.

. . . I got a hundred dollars and a silver plate, very nice.

As far as I know it is the first time the engineers [the elite corps in the Army] have ever been beaten in a flat race.

Papa is here for the day and we came to the [Army-Navy] club for lunch.

The club is in the new building now and there is a fine ladies annex so you can use it.

Mama is coming down for a day or so before she goes to Boston.

Where is Hannah?

Have you paid Marshall?

I would but as usual am broke. I think that we run our finances rather badly like we did not trust each other. I think it would be better to put our money in one bunch and each draw on it. Then when you were away I could pay the bills and also keep you from letting them run six months. Besides that is what your father said we should do . . .

The longer I am away from you the more I feel how much I love you but please don't use absence as a means of increasing my affection.

Except for hay fever I am very well. Love to all

Letter, GSP, Jr., to Mr. Ayer, September 14, 1912

[In reply to a letter from Mr. Ayer] I quite understand that I am working my self pretty hard but it is not done in a thoughtless way nor with out good reason. If you had not done more work than other people when you were my age you would not be now what you are.

Of course I quite understand that what I am doing looks like play to you but in my business it is the best sort of advertising. It makes people talk and that is a sign they are noticing. And you know that the notice of others has been the start of many successful men. Especially in politics and politics is what I am after, only I am not approaching by way of the lecture platform.

From the way things are running and the number of "Probes" [investigations resulting from the muckraking] that are flurishing it seems clear that the "People" are on horse back and that things are going to happen. It is my ambition to be around when they fall of[f] the horse.

Letter, GSP, Jr., to Aunt Nannie, September 1912

[Had] a three day leave in Boston and saw Smith. She is quite grown up and really intelligent, can walk and talk a little.

[Sold the gray horse to Fred Ayer for $650 and bought two new horses with the money, so now has seven horses. Won a race at Timonium, Maryland, on Roman Wing and got a nice piece of silver but only $100 in the purse.]

They do a lot of talk about [war with] Mexico but there is little in it and I think nothing will come until after [the elections in] November.

Letter, GSP, Jr., to Beatrice, September 18, 1912

[The men of Troop A wanted him to coach their football team.] I think I will though I will hardly have time to play my self.

Letter, Beatrice to Aunt Nannie, September 20, 1912

Georgie will be showing some horses on Long Island . . . I am leaving here for Myer on the 1st, as Georgie is back from the range now. He is very busy & well and happy, he says.

Letter, GSP, Jr., to his father, September 22, 1912

The other night Flip [his bloodhound] went for a trip and a soldier found him down in the red light district of Washington.

Every body is busting them selves to winn the two races at Laurel Md. on the seventh and ninth [of October]. One is for $1000 the other for $700 which is a flat race of one mile on a mile track. I hope I get it . . .

I had dinner last night at Chevy Chase with two Major Generals a Major and a Captain last night so feel that I am going some though they have probably forgotten me by now.

Letter, GSP, Jr., to Beatrice, September 23, 1912

Dearest B. I hope you are editing that length[y] report [on the Olympic Games and the fencing with Cléry] I sent you. It probably needed it. I am going to have a professional copy it so you need not bother about the spelling.

Letter, GSP, Jr., to Beatrice, September 27, 1912

Dearest B. I got my report off just now. It made twelve pages of typewriting and took me most of the day to do. I made five carbon copies.

Letter, GSP, Jr., to Beatrice, September 28, 1912

I have gone back to my job with Captain Smither and am rather glad of it as I have actually had nothing to do at all and it grows tiresome.

As I don't have to be at the office until nine I get a chance to ride in the morning and have breakfast about eight.

Col. Garrard [commanding officer of the 15th Cavalry] is quite pleased with my report and so is Captain Elting. They want me to inlarge the Saber part of it into an article for the Cavalry Journal.

And I am going to do it. I hope it makes a hit I think it will. They are almost certain to adopt my sword blade as the new regulation so I may get some prominence yet I hope so.

Letter, GSP, Jr., to his father, October 28, 1912

[Went to New York to race, rode Rumbough's mare] She did very well but I was to heavy for her and came in last. There is great excitement here now about quarters. I fear we may loose this house but hope not . . . I came very near being made M.F.H. [master of the fox hunt] of the rock creek hunt but I did not quite land it. Gordon Johnston did.

On November 6, he was admitted to membership in the exclusive Metropolitan Club of Washington, where, he had noted earlier, "all the big men were." He would retain his membership until the end of 1932. Perhaps by then, although the club remained known for the high social standing of its members, its attraction for men of high military rank had declined.

Letter, GSP, Jr., to his father, December 2, 1912

[Bea and he went to the Army-Navy football game; Army lost. A fox hunt Thanksgiving day] and got very wet riding through the snow covered trees. We lost both hounds and the fox in the woods . . .

Col. Thompson [President of the American Olympic Committee] of the Finland [the ship they had taken to the Games] gave a hunt breakfast afterwards which we all attended.

With all the various horses I own I had to ride a government horse but he did well . . .

The result of this law removing so many officers will send a lot of them here and I may loose my house. I *hope* not, but one can never tell . . .

I do hope you get busy and pull some thing out of this Democratic wave [of popularity and victory] . . . . But there are a lot of people trying to do the same thing so you have got to "DO IT NOW!" I hope you do. Smith is quite well and always speaks of her self as a "perfect charmer."

· · ·

On December 14, Patton was placed on detached service for duty with the Office of the Chief of Staff. Perhaps General Leonard Wood asked for him. On occasion Patton acted as an aide to Wood and to the Secretary of War, Henry L. Stimson. More frequently, his tasks were those of a staff officer, looking up information, writing studies, and answering letters to Wood and more general inquiries to the War Department. On December 17, for example, in reply to Representative John Q. Tilson's request for historical incidents of troops going into battle without training, Patton referred the congressman to Emory Upton's *Military Policy of the United States,* a remarkably influential book, and cited several specific page numbers. To Representative Julius Kahn on December 20, with respect to their conversation about the possibility of Patton's assignment as military attaché to Sweden, he regretted that the Army War College had already selected someone else.

It was a propitious time to be associated with General Wood, who had been Chief of Staff since 1910. With the active support of Secretary of

War Stimson, who had assumed the office in 1911, Wood broke the enormous power of General Fred Ainsworth, the Adjutant General who, with the help of conservative members of Congress, sought to block the implementation of the General Staff system instituted by Elihu Root in 1903. Wood and Stimson, the latter a disciple of Root, forced Ainsworth to resign in 1912, thereby establishing without question the Chief of Staff as the top military officer in the Army and enhancing the prestige of the corps of General Staff officers.

Although Patton's detail conferred upon him no status as a General Staff officer, it brought him in contact with men who were judged the most intelligent, advanced, and articulate — the intellectuals, the "comers." He would learn much from them. Especially useful was his acquaintance, which would blossom into friendship, with Secretary Stimson.

Sometime during Patton's tour, Major Rhodes asked him to prepare an informal study on the war then taking place in the Balkans. Patton's effort undoubtedly pleased him.

The paper, entitled "Notes on the Balkan Campaign, to Include the First Peace Negotiations," displayed Patton's usual erudition, thoroughness, and imagination. "Balkans," he wrote, "means mountain gulches, and both the character of the people and the conduct of the war seems inseparably connected with the sinister aspect of some dark, rocky chasm." The mountainous territory occupied by Rumania, Bulgaria, Servia, and Montenegro had, since the third century, served as a gateway for invaders of Europe, including Goths, Huns, Tartars, and Turks.

After describing the plans and opening operations of the current conflict, Patton, in a typical statement, wrote: "Thus far the plan worked well, but only thus far." Discussing the tactics of the campaign, he pointed out that the converging attack launched by one of the opponents at first sight seemed to violate the principle of interior versus exterior lines. Yet the error was more apparent than real. "So far as I can recall, the only other instance of exterior lines being better than interior is the case of the Peninsula war where the strategical conditions are very similar."

In the course of developing his thought, he referred perfectly naturally, without ostentation or pretension, to Epaminondas in the fourth century B.C., to Frederick the Great's "oblique attack," to the battle of Lule Burgas as an example of combining frontal attack with a turning movement and fire action with bayonet combat at night. In the end, he cited the importance of artillery by emphasizing that shrapnel accounted for 37 percent of the casualties sustained in the Balkan wars.

It was a first-rate staff paper and no doubt exactly what Rhodes wanted.

Patton also prepared an essay for Colonel Greeley, probably a member of the General Staff, on why racing and polo playing by Army officers were advantageous to the Army. Among the benefits he cited were the improvement of cavalrymen, the amelioration of training, the stimulus to the better breeding of horses, and, most important, the fact that influential people were spectators of these sports.

Letter, GSP, Jr., to Aunt Nannie, December 23, 1912

Mexico seems to be waking up again and they are doing a lot here that does not appear in the papers. We all think here that intervention will be necessary just as soon as Mr. Wilson [the newly-elected President] gets in. Nothing but taking them [Mexico] can shut them up and the sooner we do it the easier it will be.

I sit on my but[t] so much that I have great fear lest I get too fat so I am not eating much if any lunch and getting up early each morning to go riding . . .

When is nita coming? I hope it will be soon and that we have a house when she gets here.

Colonel Joseph Garrard, the regimental commander of the 15th Cavalry, rated Patton's attention to duty and appearance "excellent," his ability to handle enlisted men "very good." With more age and experience, Garrard wrote, Patton would do very well as a member of the General Staff corps. He had availed himself of opportunities for improvement and could be entrusted with important duties. A soldierly officer, he had given more than the usual attention to athletics — riding, swimming, running, shooting, fencing, and the like.

Meanwhile, because of the Democratic victory in the elections of 1912, Mr. Patton was trying to obtain an appointive job for himself in the Wilson administration, hopefully in the War Department.

Letter, Frederick Ayer (New York Yacht Club, 37 West 44th Street) to Mr. Patton (staying with his son at Fort Myer), January 2, 1913

This morning I had an interview with Mr. [William G.] McAdoo [vice chairman of the Democratic National Committee and soon to be appointed Secretary of the Treasury] who was pleased to talk about the Wilson administration.

He was modest enough to say that he did not expect to be called upon to fill a Cabinet position. I found that his mind was dwelling more on the Treasury position than on the War [Department].

He admitted that the great demands on the War Department in the coming administration would require the very best ability in the country, and was greatly pleased that you and I should have thought of his name in connection with it, and should have taken the trouble to mention it to him.

He remembered you, and that you had had lunch with him — I told him that in the event of his taking that position you would make him an able second; and showed him the importance of having a man from the Pacific Coast in the Department.

Mr. McAdoo is very accessible to men for business interviews, and you should have no difficulty in approaching him. His address is No. 30 Church Street —

Hoping that you will press the matter to a favorable termination, I am, Very truly yours,

Letter, Mrs. Ayer (Fort Myer) to Mrs. Patton (Lake Vineyard, San Gabriel, California), January 5, 1913

My dear Friend.

G. B. & K are all at Chevy Chase, at lunch . . .

B & G are gaying it, He in splendid form.

I see the love gifts from you everywhere, and your picture with book in hand, is ever queening it in their living room —

Well you know what I think of you — God sent you to this world to bless — I'm glad I'm in your world

Letter, GSP, Jr., to Aunt Nannie, January 7, 1913

Dear Aunt Nannie: I have just finished writing an article for the Army & Navy Journal which will come out this coming Friday. It is about the Sabre and I hope it does some good in educating these mutts to get over thinking they are all occupied in a carpet beating contest every time they get hold of a sworde.

Mr. Ayer and Fred went home last Monday but K and Ellie [Mrs. Ayer] are still with us . . .

I succeeded in getting Pa to go to the Gotham [Hotel in New York

City] in order to give him a more imposing address when he sends in his card . . .

The poor man who is typeing my article is having the devils own time making it out. He ought to have more imagination.

Letter, Mr. Ayer (Boston) to Mr. Patton, January 11, 1913

[Since departing Washington, he has been watching the appointments of the new administration. He believed two essential things insured success — ability and persistent push on the part of the applicant. He defined push as bringing to bear the influence of one's friends together with the active management of that influence.]

. . . I am very anxious that you should secure the appointment you want, for the reasons that I think you and your family would enjoy life in Washington for a few years, that your abilities in an official position would be of great service to our country, that your moral influence is greatly needed there, and that it would be a great help and comfort to George and his family to have you and yours there.

With every good wish for your success, I am Sincerely yours,

The *Army and Navy Journal,* a newspaper influential both socially and professionally and read religiously by officers and their wives, carried an article on January 7 headed "U. S. Army to Have Old French Swords." The Army staff, the paper reported, was about to select a straight sword for the cavalry, and it was to be molded after the sabers of Napoleon. Lieutenant Patton had bought in Paris a French sword used at the battle of Waterloo, and it was on display at the Army staff headquarters.

Four days later, the *Journal* printed a long article entitled "Use of the Point in Sword Play." It was an anonymous piece — there was no mention of Patton — and it opened with the words: "An officer at the War Department who has given the subject a great deal of earnest thought says:" The entire remainder of the article was a quotation from this officer. Anyone who was cognizant of cavalry affairs and swords knew that Patton was the author.

The article was learned and authoritative. In it Patton talked about the oriental invention of the curved sword, which was designed to cut through protective clothing and turbans; discussed the effect of gunpowder on armored cavalry; referred to the swordplay of the Moors; described the claymore of the highlanders and the campilan of the Moros, "two of the deadliest cutting weapons known and both straight"; and stressed the need to use the saber as a thrusting weapon.

Some officers, he wrote, advocated using the saber as a cutting or hacking weapon, saying that this was a more natural employment of the arm, but Patton rebutted this argument as follows:

> when a recruit is first handed a rifle he jerks the trigger and closes his eyes. Yet we never see this apparently natural method of firing advocated as effective. Why, then should the initial incorrect use of the saber be of permanent advantage?

The article was well done. It displayed erudition and logic. It did his career no harm at all.

Patton continued, meanwhile, to write letters in the Office of the Chief of Staff. Directed to ask the Army Relief Society to help the daughter of a former captain who was ill, he wrote on January 6:

> General Wood recommends that you look into this matter and give it your careful consideration. Anything that you can do in the case will be appreciated by him.

A few days later, he cleared up by mail a misunderstanding on the part of Representative George Curry with respect to a sergeant's discharge from the Army after court-martial.

He wrote to the Military Academy and to the Army Service School at Leavenworth about the Peruvian military attaché who wanted to take a course at either institution. To the former: "I doubt if such an arrangement will be possible, but in order to comply with his wishes I am writing you this letter embodying his idea." To the latter: "Hoping you will pardon any trouble I am putting you to."

He informed Major General James B. Aleshire, the Quartermaster General, that General Wood was referring to him a clergyman who was seeking "condemned" tents no longer useful to the Army but suitable for his "Boys Brigade."

To Captain G. C. Martin at the Maryland Agricultural College on January 25: "Pursuant to our conversation the other day, I showed the letters you handed me to General Wood," who was pleased by Martin's idea — which was in line with Wood's feelings about "preparedness," a subject he was already advocating. According to Patton, Wood hoped that Martin would persuade the college to adopt universal military training among the students. It would be good for the general discipline at the college, help develop the students' physiques, make them better citizens, and provide a reservoir of men who could more readily be trained as soldiers at small per capita cost in the event of a large foreign war. "General Wood wishes me to thank you for bringing this matter to him."

When Wood asked Patton whether the Military Academy would take part in the Intercollegiate Fencing Tournament, Patton wrote to find out, explaining that the general was deeply interested in fencing and was thinking of adopting a new straight saber for the cavalry. Patton himself was interested in learning what course was being offered in saber instruction. "The General has not asked about this yet, but he is likely to, and I would like to be in a position to answer him." Which was exactly what a staff officer was supposed to do — keep a step ahead of his boss. "Please regard this as a purely personal letter of interest on my part," he concluded, "and not an attempt to butt in the Academy affairs." He was learning well.

To a civilian in Brooklyn, New York, he wrote, "I am directed by General Wood to express to you his appreciation of the interest evinced by your letter of February 9th." Army Regulations, he explained, required dismounted officers in the field to carry the pistol and not the sword. The War Department from time to time considered the advisability of arming officers with a light rifle, but believed that an officer carrying a rifle would pay more attention to personal combat than to the welfare of his men.

He was getting on so well with General Wood and the general's assistants that he hoped to get a job as aide-de-camp to the major general commanding the Cavalry Division if he was transferred from Fort Myer — "but that is not to be told," he warned Aunt Nannie.

Letter, GSP, Jr., to Aunt Nannie, January 27, 1913

There came very near being a serious uprising in Mexico on the twentieth [of January] but the cold and rain stopped them. Now we expect nothing until June or July . . .

I hope Pa is getting on the job. He has only about three weeks before he will have to start back and he ought to get all finished up before that time.

I don't know how long I shall hold this job but I will not kick when I loose it as it is too confining to suit me.

We are all going to three receptions to day so you see we are still at it.

He was also "still at it" on the job, studying the British Cavalry *Sword and Saber Notes* of 1911 and the French Cavalry *Drill Regulations* of the same year. Both stressed the thrust with the point rather than the hack with the edge of the sword. Patton had no hesitation about making this known around the War Department. He went so far as to translate portions of the French regulations for circulation among cavalry officers and quoted with special glee: "In the melee . . . the troopers single out their adversaries, seeking especially the Officers. They attack with the point, shouting 'Thrust, Thrust.' "

Patton's activity had some effect, probably a great deal, on a decision reached formally by General Wood on February 24, when he dispatched a memorandum to the Chief of Ordnance. Wood informed the Ordnance Department that the Secretary of War ordered the manufacture of 20,000 cavalry sabers exactly like the model accompanying the memo. The new model saber for the cavalry was designed according to Patton's specifications. It was quite a coup for the young officer.

On March 4, he rode in the Inaugural Parade as an aide to General Wood.

As an indication of his professional and social prominence, the *Army and Navy Journal* on March 12 carried no less than five items in that single issue about the Pattons. A photograph showed Mrs. G. S. Patton, Jr., serving at the punch table at a reception. A notation indicated that Mr. G. S. Patton of Los Angeles was the guest of his son. A paragraph reported that Lieutenant and Mrs. Patton gave a "small but delightful dinner" at the Chevy Chase Club. An item noted that Mrs. G. S. Patton entertained at luncheon her husband's classmate, Lieutenant Simpson, and his wife. Several lines reported that Miss Anita Patton, a guest of her brother, had departed for home in Los Angeles.

Letter, Beatrice to Aunt Nannie, March 20, 1913

Georgie certainly has done fine work since he has been in the War Dept. He is a great kid . . . G. has said so much about his charmed life that I half believe in it sometimes. We are all fine here, but were terribly disappointed about Uncle George [who had failed to get an appointment in the Wilson administration] and that you did not all come East.

On March 22, Patton was relieved from temporary duty in the Office of the Chief of Staff and reassigned to his proper station, Fort Myer.

Letter, Major General Leonard Wood, Chief of Staff, to Lieut. G. S. Patton, 15th Cavalry, Fort Myer, Va., March 22, 1913

Sir: On your relief from duty in the office of the Chief of Staff, I wish to express to you my appreciation of the satisfactory manner in which you have discharged the duties assigned to you. Very respectfully,

In those days of measured praise, a letter of appreciation was a significant token. General Wood was the first Army Chief of Staff whom Patton would work for and would come to know. There would be others, and all would be devoted to him and do their best to promote his interests.

He had hardly rejoined his unit for troop duty when he was directed to perform another function. As Beatrice told Aunt Nannie, "Georgie has gone to Springfield [Massachusetts] and won't be back till Sunday. He was sent for to approve the new sword."

At the Springfield Armory on detached service for three days, he made certain that the sabers being manufactured fitted his designated specifications.

A letter from Colonel Rogers Birnie, Acting Chief of Ordnance, to the Adjutant General on April 2 made a formal record of his appreciation for Patton's assistance in determining and selecting the new model sword for cavalry use. Patton's skill and experience as a swordsman, Birnie said, had been invaluable to the Ordnance Department.

A good deal of Patton's reputation as a connoisseur of the sword stemmed from an article appearing in the March issue of the *Cavalry Journal*, a quasi-official publication that was the leading professional magazine of the Cavalry branch. Patton had expanded his *Army and Navy Journal* piece into a full-scale thesis on the employment of the saber. He wrote:

At first sight it seems rather curious that, though the saber has been a component part of the cavalry equipment ever since the beginning,

its use and form has never been given much thoughtful consideration.

Yet on second thought, he continued, this was not so strange. The only
target practice troops used to engage in was simply firing their muskets.

It was through the personal interest and excellence of individual
officers and men that attention to [real] target practice was first introduced . . . and at first they were met by obstructionists and the
cry of "let well enough alone." They persisted, however, and as people began to see the results they accomplished they ceased to hinder,
and rapid and wonderful progress both in the rifle and in the manner of its use have followed.

It now seems that the turn of the bayonet and saber has arrived, or
at least is starting to arrive.

The bayonet and saber were essential weapons for the cavalry. But
since the introduction of these arms into military units, there had been
controversy between the advocates of the edge and of the point. "Beginning with the 11th Century, from which time accounts are fairly consecutive," scale armor, later chain armor, made the point obsolete, whereas a
violent blow from the edge could cripple a soldier without cutting his
armor. When German mercenaries in the Italian wars wore plate armor,
Italian troops returned to the point in order to thrust through the joints.
Then the bullet "put the armor out of business."

Some light cavalry wearing no armor developed, for example, Cossacks,
Poles, and Turkish unarmored horse. They inherited from the Arabs the
curved scimitar. This Oriental weapon was originally designed to cut
through defensive clothing made of wool wadding. But the curve reduced
the efficiency of the point, and fighting became a matter of hacking, and
defenders parried with a light shield.

The present saber of our Cavalry is almost the last survival of the
incorrect application of the mechanics of the scimetar. [It is not a
good cutting or pointing weapon.] . . . Yet it is clung to as fondly
as was the inaccurated Civil War musket and the .45 Springfield with
its mule-like kick.

The tenacity evinced for the retention of an illogical weapon [in
the U.S. Cavalry] seems without basis in history, while from the same
source [history] we find numerous tributes to the value of the point.

In support of this statement, he cited Verdi du Vernois, the English in the Peninsular War, French dragoons, Marshal Saxe, and Napoleon at the battle of Wagram.

All recruits, he said, had a tendency to use the sword as a club. The French Army was already training soldiers to overcome this deficiency, and Patton thought that it was time for the U.S. Army to start doing the same. Unfortunately, many American officers believed that troops should continue to use the edge rather than the point because that was the natural way to handle the weapon.

The child starts locomotion by crawling, but on this account do we discourage walking? The recruit flinches and blinks on first firing a gun, but he is certainly not encouraged to continue this practice. Why, then, should the ignorant swinging about of a sword be indicative of its proper use? . . .

In the melee which follows a [mounted] charge, there is no objection to using the edge, for the horses will be going at less speed and things will probably open up. At least, there will be no rank formation and a man can chop away as ineffectually as he likes, though here, too, the point would be more deadly. In the pursuit there is little choice between the edge and the point, though it might be a little easier on the horses to strike a man when he is several feet ahead then to be forced to ride almost abreast of him to deal a cut . . .

As to the question of recovering his sword thrust into an opponent . . . when a man has been run through he is going to be pretty limp and will probably fall from his horse, clearing the weapon for you . . .

Finally, many of our possible opponents are using the long straight sword and the point in the charge, and to come against this with our present sabers and position of charge would be suicidal.

Marked by lucidity in argument and exposition, the article showed knowledge of military history and the ability to draw lessons applicable to the solution of current problems.

•   •   •

On April 5, while riding in a steeplechase, Patton fell from his horse and sustained scalp injuries on the top and back part of his skull. The medical report called it "lacerated wound of scalp, 1 inch in fronto-parietal region slight; lacerated wound region occiput, 1¼ inches, slight." He was lucky. He spent two days at home sick in quarters.

Letter, Beatrice to Aunt Nannie, April 10, 1913, continued April 14, 1913

[Went to Congress and heard President Wilson read his Message. He was very impressive] never saw W. look so pleasant — actually smiling. [George took off much weight without trouble, mainly by a meat diet supplemented with spinach and bran muffins. He is in good condition.]

I called on the cabinet yesterday — all very nice. Mrs. Lane said Uncle G. [Mr. Patton] was an awful man not to have called before he did; she tried to get him to dinner but he had gone!

Mrs. Lane's husband was Franklin K. Lane, who had just been appointed Secretary of the Interior and would remain in that post through both of Wilson's terms. A lawyer from San Francisco who had been the unsuccessful Democratic candidate for governor in 1902 and for mayor in 1903 and who later was chairman of the Interstate Commerce Commission, he gave Wilson's cabinet the West Coast representation that Mr. Patton had hoped to impart.

Letter, Beatrice to Aunt Nannie, April 29, 1913

Yesterday, today and tomorrow is horse show at Myer, and . . . all the High Mugs . . . are coming to it . . .

I did not write you about Georgie's accident because I didn't want to worry you. It never occurred to me that such a slight one would come out in the [Army and Navy] Journal . . . he is O.K. now . . .

G. and I went to Ringling's circus last night. It was fine and the best part of it was to see G. laughing at the clowns like all the other kids. I took a lot of post babies to the parade in the morning, and we had such fun!

Letter, GSP, Jr., to Aunt Nannie, May 5, 1913

We have been having a very busy time here lately. The Fort Myer Horse Show was last week and I was connected with it; we had three races for soldiers which I ran. They were quite a success.

I won second place in a potatoe race for which I got a nice riding crop. I have about eight already so I am well fixed.

Spy my best pony got his eye hit at polo the other day and almost lost it! I held an ice pack on him for two hours. He is better now . . .

I am going on leave for two days in the morning to stay in a stable at Pimlico [race park in Baltimore] and see how to train horses. It is a good thing to take advantage of oppertunities . . .

I was judge Advocate [in a court-martial] the other day and must write up the case to night. I am glad pa liked the article in the Cavalry Journal.

I thought it rather good my self.

Letter, GSP, Jr., to his father, May 19, 1913

Dear Papa: I hope by the time this reaches you that we will have declared war with Japan, but I suppose with our natural ambition to apoligize for living we will have let them dictate to us what we should do.

This fellow [William Jennings] Bryan is truly a fit secretary of state for a country whos noble ambition is to be the punching bag of the world . . .

Our races at Benning's [in Washington, D.C.] come off this week starting Thursday. I ride in eight of them I hope but of course may not as horses do go bad so easily . . .

We got an express notice to night that the wine had come. And we will get it in the morning. Thank you ever so much.

We are all well. I hope you get [elected] governor

The Washington Riding and Hunt Club of Bennings, D.C., held a three-day racing meet late in May. On the first day, Patton rode in the second race, a two-mile event, and came in fourth. In the sixth race, a flat course over a distance of one mile and 70 yards, he finished second. On the following day, Patton won the steeplechase over a course about 2½ miles long. In the fifth race, for the Army and Navy Cup, he was fourth. On the third day, he took fourth place in the seventh race, the Federal Handicap Steeplechase over a course 2½ miles long.

Letter, GSP, Jr., to Beatrice (at Pride's Crossing), June 3, 1913

Memorial day I passed a little church out in the hills and there were some old ladies three or four decorating two old graves with out even head stones with wild daisies. I suppose they were as sweet to the dead as the costly flowers heaped by unthinking hands at arlingon. Who can say.

We have the last game of the polo tournament tomorrow I hope we win.

If I can work it I will come to boston the night of the eleventh. Ask Fred [her brother] to tell me the best road to drive and how far it is.

On June 9, the third day of a meet sponsored by the Piping Rock Racing Association in Locust Valley, Long Island, he won the second race, a two-mile steeplechase.

Letter, GSP, Jr. (Hotel Astor, New York), to Beatrice, June 10, 1913

Dearest B. I wish you could have been with us yesterday. We had a great time.

The Polo Game was wonderful. I had never dreamed that either man or ponies could be so fine. It was beyond words . . .

It [the race in which he rode] was exactly the same sort of race I rode at Bennings. I went to the front at the second jump and staied there winning by about a hundred yards.

At Belmont Park, Long Island, he raced on June 11 in the Belmont Military Handicap, a flat race of one mile, and came in second.

An article in the Boston *Transcript* of June 12, headed "Amateurs in the Saddle. Army Day at Belmont Park has Three Events for Gentlemen Riders," described the Army race as follows:

after a thrilling final struggle for more than a quarter of a mile Lieutenant C. K. Rockwell of the Corps of Engineers got his mount, Kinnelon, to the finishing line a head in advance of Gilbert, owned and ridden by Lieutenant George S. Patton of the Fifteenth Cavalry. Highland Chief, the property of Captain William Mitchell of the 15th Cavalry, who was in the saddle, finished third.

He raced again on June 13 at Belmont Park, finishing third in the Military Steeplechase.

When the Inspector General of the Army made a formal visit to the cavalry squadron stationed at Fort Myer on June 22, Patton wrote to Beatrice:

[I] took [the troops on] the Russian ride [a test for proficiency]

. . . at Seven [A.M.] then we pitched a camp and later had squadron drill. Then about five I went down and played polo with Col. Allen and a pick up lot from town . . .

I would make no plans about Gettysburg yet. I may never get there. Col. Allen said as soon as Gen Wood returned [to Washington] I would be ordered to France. That is hardly possible but I may get the order next week. Col Allen told Graham the same thing about me. I think we will be gone about two months.

Letter, GSP, Jr. (New City Hotel, Frederick, Maryland), to Beatrice, June 25, 1913

I have been absolutely too busy to write.

[On his way to Gettysburg, Pa.] To day we past a field and saw a monument in it. We found it was to commemorate a regiment destroyed by gen Early in his raid on Washington [during the Civil War]. My grandfather commanded the advance guard on that raid, it was a pretty place for a fight.

I ought to hear about my detail [overseas] any day. If I get it I doubt if we get time to pack up. I think they will let us hold quarters until we get back though of this I am not sure. I know they want me to go quick if I go.

Please pardon my not writing sooner. I could not.

I love you. George.

Letter, GSP, Jr. (from Gettysburg), to Beatrice, July 1, 1913

No news yet. I just wrote Capt Mitchell to stir things a little.

Yesterday we were out all morning doing park policeman work and in the afternoon I distributed some 7900 blankets to Vets. [who were celebrating the 50th anniversary of the battle of Gettysburg.]

They are a disgusting bunch dirty and old and of the people who "God loves."

One old hound has been beating a drum ever since he got here.

Two others have a small cannon which they fire as often as possible.

As one of my men said yesterday the best of them were only damed malitia men and did not no [know] much.

Letter, Beatrice to Aunt Nannie, July 7, 1913

Poor Georgie got the order Thursday & got here [Fort Myer] too late to do anything about passages that day & the offices everywhere

were closed [for the Fourth of July holiday] from the night of the 3d
till today! He went to N.Y. at midnight last night and today at 2 I
got a wire which I repeated to you at once . . .

What fun it will be to have you and Aunt Nelli in France with us!
We expect to be at Saumur all the time, I think, and while it isn't an
exciting place you will love it.

A bientot! Your B

P.S. G. hasn't told me our bankers but I will let you know at once
as soon as I know.

Letter, War Department Adjutant General thru Commanding General Eastern Department to Lieut. G. S. Patton, June 25, 1913, subject: Authority to go to France

1. [The Secretary of War] . . . authorizes you to proceed to
France for the purpose of perfecting yourself in swordsmanship. You
should so adjust your time as to be able to arrive at Fort Riley, Kansas by October 1.

2. The Secretary directs that you be informed that it is understood
that in conformity with your suggestion no expense to the Government will be incurred on your visit abroad.

1st Indorsement, Headquarters Eastern Department thru Commanding Officer, Fort Myer, Virginia, to Lieut. G. S. Patton, June 27, 1913

[Noted and forwarded.]

2nd Indorsement, Headquarters 15th Cavalry, Fort Myer, Virginia, to Lieut. G. S. Patton, June 28, 1913

[Noted and transmitted.]

The letter order was the culmination of a campaign engineered and
executed by Patton. He had for some time discussed and promoted with
his friends, colleagues, and superiors at Fort Myer and at the War Department the idea of introducing a course in swordsmanship. The obvious
place for a course of this sort was the Mounted Service School at Fort
Riley, Kansas, which would in 1920 be renamed the Cavalry School.

His published articles on the saber and his work in designing the new-
model saber had provided substance not only to the idea but also to the
notion that he should be the one to conduct the course.

Having secured informal agreement and approval of his project, Patton drafted an appropriate paragraph on swordsmanship and this was inserted into a rather routine letter dispatched on May 7 by the War Department to the Mounted Service School on the grooming of horses, changes in equipment, and the like.

Then Patton wrote a draft letter for the consideration of the commandant of the Mounted Service School. If the commandant saw merit in the proposal, he would, after making whatever changes he wished in Patton's draft, sign the letter and forward it as his own recommendation for the approval of the War Department. The proper officers in the War Department were, of course, alerted. Since they already favored the plan, they would take immediate final action and approve the commandant's suggestion.

Alerted by the letter of May 7 and no doubt advised informally by the grapevine that the War Department was aware of the proposal and was ready to move on his recommendation, the commandant signed the letter. It read as follows:

Letter, The Commandant, Mounted Service School, Fort Riley, Kansas, to the War Department Adjutant General, June 18, 1913, subject: Swordsmanship

Reference Letter 2035528, AGO, May 7, 1913 . . .

To make a good swordsman, requires time. To make a capable instructor requires a great deal of time. The schedule at this School requires hard work, and the time is fully occupied. It is realized that the introduction of a course of instruction in swordsmanship at this School would be of the greatest benefit to the Mounted Service . . .

[After consulting graduates of the French School at Saumur now stationed at this post, after thought and discussion, the Commandant recommends]

1. That a Master of Swordsmanship be ordered to report for duty at the School about September 20, 1913 . . . [Also that a noncommissioned officer from each regiment in the continental United States be ordered to report for a six-months course in swordsmanship.]

3. That the Senior Instructor of Equitation in making out his program of instruction for the Company and Field Officers' Classes for the ensuing year, arrange for as much instruction daily [in swordsmanship] as is deemed practicable without detriment to the course in equitation . . .

6. By requiring the instructors in equitation and officers detailed for the second year's course to take daily instruction from the Master of Swordsmanship, it is believed that in a few years, there will be quite a number of capable instructors in the Mounted Service.

Signed: J. A. Gaston, Colonel of Cavalry [Commandant]

1st Indorsement, Headquarters Fort Riley, Kansas, to the Adjutant General, June 18, 1913

Recommend approval.

Signed: J. A. Gaston, Colonel of Cavalry, Commanding [**Fort Riley**]

2nd Indorsement, War Department Adjutant General's Office to the Chief of Staff, June 23, 1913

Note: The above in general seems good. Col. Allen

Master of the Sword or Swordmaster preferable to Master of Swordsmanship. H. T. S.

3rd Indorsement, WD AGO to Commanding Officer, Fort Riley, Kansas, July 7, 1913

The essence of the recommendation made herein is approved. Lieutenant Patton has been directed to proceed to Paris for the purpose of perfecting himself for duty as Master of the Sword at the Mounted Service School.

By order of the Secretary of War: A. F. Ladd, Adjutant General.

4th Indorsement, Mounted Service School, Fort Riley, Kansas, to the Adjutant General, July 10, 1913

Information is requested as to the probable date of the arrival of Lieutenant Patton for duty as Master of the Sword, and whether or not the specially qualified non-commissioned officers recommended to be sent here for instruction (See (b) Par. 3) will be ordered here. If these N.C. Officers are ordered here, the date of their arrival should be about ten days later than that of Lieut. Patton so as to give him time to perfect his [teaching] plans.

6th Indorsement, WD AGO to CO, Fort Riley, Kansas, July 17, 1913

[Lieutenant Patton's orders required him to return to Washington, D.C., on or about 1 October. No further action would be taken on this matter until he returned.]

The importance of this development was threefold. First, it enabled Patton to spend a summer at Saumur studying the use of the sword and saber, which would make him the leading expert in the U.S. Army. Second, it would allow him to attend classes as a student at the Mounted Service School, which was a prerequisite for advancement and promotion. Third, it would confer upon him the distinction of being the first officer in the U.S. Army to hold the title Master of the Sword.

Master of the Sword. It had a fine sound about it.

The whole thing was not a bad deal at all. He was, it appeared, a far better politician than his father. As he had told Mr. Ayer, he had been busy advertising himself. He had made "people talk" about him. It was all paying off.

CHAPTER 13

Saumur and Fort Riley: Master
of the Sword

"I hope it means war and a good big one."

WHILE HE AND BEATRICE crossed the Atlantic in July 1913 on their way to Saumur, Patton amused himself by writing into a notebook some "Facts, dates, and incidents of my life which I hope will be of interest to posterity but which I fear will not." He was then twenty-seven years old.

The Pattons arrived in Paris on the evening of July 14, "just too late for that [traditional Bastille Day] review." They remained in the city several days because Patton had to call on the American military attaché at the Embassy and because they had to await the arrival of their automobile, which was coming by a slower ship at a cost of $300 round trip.

On Friday evening they boarded the overnight train for Cherbourg. It took them all day Saturday to get their car unloaded, uncrated, and registered. At 6:10 P.M. they left Cherbourg and drove 52 miles to St. Lô, which they reached at 7:20. "The roads were fine with no dust."

They spent several days in St. Lô, discovering lots of "real [antique] furnature . . . all real." Beatrice bought a Henry IV chest for $60 and a very old chair for $75.

Then they drove leisurely to Saumur, 140-odd miles away, stopping to look at interesting châteaus and churches and to have long and pleasant lunches and dinners in the bocage country. He found the trip "a pretty but not an interesting drive . . . the hedges are lovely."

Patton would remember the countryside very well thirty-one years later, in the summer of 1944, when the hedges were not so lovely for the American troops who fought across those fields.

Arrived at Saumur toward the end of July, they stayed again at the Hôtel Budan. When he wrote to his father a few days later, Patton had already fenced twice and did quite well but it is hard work. The hotel is much nicer than last year and there is [now] a bath tub. I think we will be here until September. We will sail [home] some time in the latter part [of the month] I think . . .

I hope I make a success of this Riley business and get a really good school [going] and good system [operating]. I don't know how long I will be kept at Riley. I could be there over two years. Whenever I leave [Riley] I will go to the [Philippine] Islands. Except for the distance they are not so bad now I fancy but they are so d— far away . . .

The only way you can keep me from going there is to get up a war so do it . . . your foolish free trade has ruined the country and made it too poore to fight.

On August 15, Assumption Day, many French parents made an all-day pilgrimage to a nearby church to have their small children blessed. Beatrice described her impressions to Aunt Nannie:

George and I went over this afternoon, but he certainly does hate the masses! [Not the religious services but the people.] I couldn't get him to stay, so he left me in high dudgeon — "no decent French woman would want to stay here alone to watch all these — fleabitten, ignorant people." I couldn't tear myself away for over an hour — hundreds of round, red-faced peasants in curious caps . . . with round red babies of every age, going up to be blessed; and being rewarded with doughnuts & wine afterward! . . . I returned home to find George patting himself on the back for having been so broad-minded in letting me stay.

They did lots of driving, visiting Blois, Amboise, and other beautiful places in the château country of the Loire. They now expected to sail for home some time before September 15. Patton purchased a new-type saddle and sent it as a gift to General Wood, remarking that it might be an excellent model for campaign purposes.

Despite the motor trips, which made him familiar with the terrain and roadnet of the area, a priceless asset in 1944, Patton worked hard with Cléry, now promoted to Adjutant Chef. He learned not only how to be a better swordsman but also how to transmit his knowledge to students. He and Cléry became fast friends, and in the process Patton learned to speak French passably well.

Beatrice was working too. Patton kept her busy translating lectures on fencing, some designed for delivery to officers, others to noncoms.

In mid-August Lieutenant Hassler of the French Army, an instructor in swordsmanship at a service school located at Joinville-le-Pont, came to Saumur for several days to supplement Cléry's instruction. All three had a fine time as they fenced, talked, and argued.

Returning to his home station, Hassler wrote a letter to Patton, calling him "Mon cher Camarade." He told Patton how pleased he was to have made Patton's acquaintance, to have worked with him, and to have enjoyed his company. He concluded:

> You must demonstrate and explain to your pupils the ways, tactic, and mechanism of the different actions of fencing. It is to you, too, to have the glorious task of teaching them the beauty and love of arms. I know it will be easy for you, for even in the short time I knew you I felt that you were a master.

The sentiment may have been Gallic, but it was, no doubt, sincere.

This letter reached the Pattons only after they had returned home. Beatrice received it in Massachusetts, where she was staying temporarily, and she translated the French into English by writing between the type-written lines, then sent it to her husband at Fort Riley. "What a *splendid* letter," she added. "You ought to keep it. You may want to show it sometime."

The 29th of August was Patton's last day with Cléry. Visibly moved, Cléry presented Patton with a formal photograph of himself attired in fencing costume. A short man with the inevitable French mustache of that time, he had posed stiffly for the picture holding his dueling sword and mask and wearing a white shirt buttoned at the neck and baggy white trousers that seemed much too long for him. He had inscribed the words: "À mon meilleur élève [to my best pupil], le Lieutenant Patton. Saumur France 1913."

Cléry also wrote that day to a firm in Paris that sold fencing equipment. He ordered for Patton 50 champion vests in three sizes, 25 pairs of swords, 50 leather masks, and 50 sword blades. These items, Cléry specified, were to be ready by September 4, when Patton would be in Paris on his way home. He would stop by the establishment and direct their shipment to the United States.

Leaving Saumur on August 30, the Pattons drove into Brittany to the south shore. They visited the beautiful city of Vannes, saw the numerous prehistoric stones, the dolmens and menhirs, at Carnac, and traveled down the charming Quiberon peninsula. After looking at the large and silent stones spaced like sentinels on the Quiberon plateau, they crossed Brittany to St. Malo and Mont St. Michel. Heading into Normandy, they drove to Caen, then to Le Havre, where they shipped their car home.

All these places would figure in the fighting in 1944.

He and Beatrice took the train from Le Havre to Paris and spent a few days there. Patton made sure that the fencing equipment Cléry had ordered for him was in good condition and in the correct amounts and gave instructions to send it to Fort Riley.

On September 10 they sailed from Cherbourg on the *Majestic*. They landed at New York on the 17th and went directly to Fort Myer, where they packed their household goods for shipment. Beatrice then went to Pride's Crossing while Patton traveled to Fort Riley to prepare his course in swordsmanship and to enter the First Year Course of study at the Mounted Service School.

When their furniture arrived in Kansas, Beatrice and the baby would go west and rejoin him.

At Fort Myer, Colonel Garrard, who commanded the 15th Cavalry, judged Patton "excellent" and "very good" in all categories. More service, he wrote, would make Patton suitable for assignment to the General Staff Corps. He was markedly fitted for recruiting, college, and militia duty. He had a good working knowledge of the French language. He was particularly proficient in horsemanship and fencing. During several short periods, Garrard noted, he had worked directly under the personal directions of the Army Chief of Staff.

Letter, GSP, Jr. (from Fort Riley), to Beatrice, around September 25, 1913

I have not done much to day except get a house . . . It is fully as ugly as the one at Sheridan but a little larger. Though it has no attic.

The rooms are finished in yellow pine like sheridan and it is not allowed to paint it. The walls are very light brown and in very excellent condition. The floors are not bad.

There are four rooms on the second floor one of which must be used by a servant as there is no other. There is a second W.C. in the basement but only one bath tub and that very small.

Still as the colonels daughter used to live in it it is as good as may bee [had] and much better than three rooms at the [officers] club.

The house is high off the ground so that it might be possible to fix up a room in the cellar but I am doubtful of this. So unless you can get some one to work for us and sleep in the town which is near by I don't see just how you can fix it.

I hired a colored woman to come and clean it. It is the dirtiest thing you ever saw though clean dirt only dust.

So far I have found out nothing of what I am to do but I am going to see Capt [Guy V.] Henry this evening.

It has been very cold all day and I have had little bother from Hay fever.

Letter, GSP, Jr., to Beatrice, September 29, 1913

I have been working on my course and have it pretty well planned now. I have to give a lecture Wednesday the day we start. I have been varnishing the floors and doors of the house and it looks better though it is terribly small. I think if you are to survive this place at all you will have to ride horse back as there is not another thing to do. There is not even a place to go to in an automobile.

Tate says that fort Riley must have been selected by a hermit who thought he was quite alone when he got here. It is on a sort of a hill and always reminds me of the ocean as the sky meets the horizon with out a single sign of a mountain. There was a fox hunt to day but I had no horse and could not go.

The M.F.H. is going to keep Flip [Patton's dog] in the pack.

Letter, GSP, Jr., to Beatrice, late September 1913

[He hired two women to clean the house. He painted a floor. He was having the entire back hall turned into a large closet with shelves and with a rod for clothes] it will be very roomy . . .

There are a lot of colored ladies around anxious for jobs as cooks or maids.

I had a nice talk with Capt Henry. He is very enthusiastic and much better to deal with than I had hoped. He is strong for the mounted fencing part and will I feel sure be a great help.

The Commandant has asked for two sergeants and a private to

assist me permanently. And I hope to get them. There is a nice swimming pool here and it is quite clean. It is in the Gym. You had better bring your bathing suit.

You have no idea of how deserted this post is. It is out in the plains all by itself with nothing near it.

Mrs. Henry wanted to be remembered to you.

Letter, GSP, Jr., to Beatrice, October 2, 1913

I am sorry you are so sorry about the house but you can't imagine it worse than it is. I have painted all the floors and have painted the wood in our room white and varnished the wood in the other rooms. Did I tell you there is *no* laundry in it . . .

I had shelves built in the kitchen and also some six feet high and twelve feet long in the back hall.

The cellar will not do for a room. It will be entirely full of trunks and furnature.

The town is only ten minutes on the [street] car and they run every half an hour, the station is about five minutes from the house . . .

I had my first lesson to day and I think I got on fairly well. All the men paid good attention and did well even Captain Thomas who calls me "George."

He [Captain Thomas] will not sleep in his house for fear of raising scandel because he has a maid with him, his wife is not here.

Captain Henry has been ordered to the Islands in January. It is too bad. He is fine and backing me for all he is worth. We have a damed fool Government to send him away.

Love to all. I love you and miss you but don't want you to come until every thing is all right here.

You certainly have to give up a lot on my account.

Letter, GSP, Jr., to Beatrice, early October 1913

There is nothing to do here Sundays as far as I have been able to see. It is very much like Sheridan with Highland Park missing.

Of course it will be better when we are settled.

Barnett got here last night Mrs. B. has rented a place with a stable for 15 horses and a house with twenty rooms. She must intend running quite a dump . . . They may be trying out the country life stunt with the idea of getting out of the Army . . .

You will certainly have to ride here or you will go crazy entirely.

Our house was built in 1881 and I think has never since been cleaned. I cleaned the cellar to day and it was fearful.

Letter, GSP, Jr. to Beatrice, October 10, 1913

I don't get a minute until after 3:30 . . .

[There is] a reasonable chance that we get a better house. [It would be Chaffee's, which had two servants' rooms and a den downstairs. Colonel Gaston, the school Commandant, had recommended that the house go to Patton, but Colonel Millard, the post commander, thought that an officer named Van Deusen ought to have it because he belonged to the 13th Cavalry, which was stationed permanently on the post] but I hope we have the better pull.

[Starting next week, he would be riding from 8 to 12, fencing from 1 to 3:30 daily.] Also I will have Wooltex [his horse] to exercise so you will have to ride or never see me at all.

The only other person on the post who ownes an auto is the vetenareon and his is [only] a Ford. I think I will start a buss line, and put Smith [the baby] on as conductor.

People roller skate a lot here so if you have any [skates] you had better bring them unless you have other plans . . .

[He and Tate were going to Kansas City to get the other Patton automobile, which had been shipped and had now arrived. They would drive 135 miles] over average bad roads.

[His hay fever usually bothered him until about 10 A.M., when his nose dried.] I have a very black striker [servant] named Duncan who cleaned the front lawn of the few remaining blades of grass it once boasted. Compared to Myer or Sheridan this post is very down at the heels. All the lawns are dead and full of bald spots . . .

P.S. I think I would open an account in a Boston bank and put the $6970 etc there in your name. We have a thousand here and this is a small bank.

Letter, GSP, Jr., to Beatrice, October 13, 1913

. . . we got the Chaffee house with two large servants rooms. Two bath tubs and W.C's and a laundry tub. Also a guest room and a little den on the first floor back of the dining room. [He had moved their belongings over to the new house that day. Kane and Hannah, a married couple hired by Beatrice and sent to Fort Riley, would get busy straightening up the things in the morning.] . . . They seem very good and on the job so far.

Some one told me that this house was the hottest one on the post but I hope we shan't have to stay here in the summer time.

Letter, GSP, Jr., to Beatrice, October 14, 1913

We had a big day to day. Three men were thrown [from their horses] . . . These are the first to have been thrown this year so every one is delighted not to be in danger of being the first.

[He had three classes in fencing, one of 14 students, one of 5 students, and one of 13. The large] bunches are the regular class. The other bunch is the second year men or assistant instructors. In November I will also have the field officers [those above the rank of captain]. As yet none of our equipment from France [the items he had ordered through Cléry] has come so we have to get on with make shirts which is pretty hard but can't be helped.

Letter, GSP, Jr., to Beatrice, October 15, 1913

The colonel has been over to see the fencing every day lately and has ordered the field officers class to take it beginning November 1st.

I have heard from out side sources that all [my students] are much interested but to keep them so is the hardest job I ever tried and I certainly am tired at night.

Letter, GSP, Jr., to his father, October 16, 1913

This is the most strictly army place I have ever been in and also the most strictly business. We start at eight o'clock and get through at three thirty which is more work than I have ever done in the army . . .

Tate and I went up to Kansas city to get the machine and we had a hell of a time. The oil plug on the machine he was driving jorlted out so all the oil ran out. He is not an expert so drove it dry until it stuck. We were about five miles out of Topeka so I started back to get oil and had gone about a mile when a man on a motor cycle fell off just in front of me and I had to turn out or run over him. I turned into a mud hole where I went in up to the hubbs. It took four hours and all the inhabitants of Kansas to get me out. There was only two quarts of oil in Topeka which was not enough so we toed the little car thirtymiles which is a hell of a job. Then it got dark so we left it at a village and went on. We got lost in the woods and I hit a stump and bent the front axel of the big car. We had quite a day.

Colonel Foltz wrote to him from Washington, D.C., saying that he was just about to get a letter off to Patton "when I received your interesting letter." Glad to hear of the successful start of the classes in swordsmanship and pleased that Colonel Gaston, the school commandant, was interested and helping, Foltz said that the Cavalry Board wanted Patton to prepare new regulations pertaining to the sword. Since Patton had already suggested that he do so, "they are very glad to hear that the idea is acceptable to you." The Board wanted, as soon as possible, drill regulations suitable for recruits, volunteer units, and militia, somewhat later, a manual of the sword in the form of a separate pamphlet like the manual of equitation. As guides, Foltz sent along the French and English Drill Regulations.

I think the board can help to push that [the manual] into print also. Please show this to Captain Henry and tell him that I was about to write to him in the same vein . . . but as I see he is coming east on leave I will wait and talk it over with him. . . .

The cavalry seems to be in a blue funk about possible loss of promotion and reduction in strength. They are going around Washington with their tails between their legs, like whipped curs. I fear that this attitude is having a bad effect on the War Department. The Infantry and artillery are very cocky and talking about increase, and in view of the situation on the Mexican border [where the bulk of the cavalry units had patrolled in 1911 from the mouth of the Rio Grande to San Diego, a distance of 1700 miles, and now again in 1913] I see no reason why we should not hold our heads up too.

Mrs. Folz joins me in kindest remembrance of yourself and Mrs. Patton.

With best wishes for your success, I remain, Sincerely yours,

Letter, GSP, Jr., to Aunt Nannie, October 22, 1913

[His horses arrived today, he secured part of a good stable for them, and discovered that Kane was very good with horses.] Horses or something of the sort are absolutely necessary here as there is nothing else to do at all . . .

The house is entirely settled now and every thing running very smoothly and will until something happins.

Both machines are broken down but as Swan [his chauffeur-mechanic] got here to night I hope they will be operating soon again

I think it is going to be hard to find enough for him to do but on the other hand to get any where he must be used as I have no time to act as driver.

There are quite a few fort parties here with a dance every two weeks and moving pictures Sunday so there is not a great deal of material for a letter.

Beatrice and the baby arrived toward the end of October, having traveled by train to Kansas City, then taking the day coach. Mrs. Patton and Nita visited briefly in November before going on to New York. He and Beatrice were hoping to go to California for Christmas. The vacation was supposed to start on December 24, but he planned to leave on the 20th, "if I can work it."

Letter, GSP, Jr., to his father, November 27, 1913

Before I go [home for Christmas] I have got to write the drill regulations for the new Cavalry Sword as the new regulations will be published about the first of the year.

The treasury Department is still fondly clinging to the Fencing equipment I had shipped over. They certainly are a bunch of fools. Infact any one connected with Mr. Wilson is to start with more or less of a fool. He is doing just what one would expect of a creature who represents an ideal rather than a personality.

Letter, GSP, Jr., to his father, December 8, 1913

Nothing here to write about. [The fencing equipment from France finally arrived.]

I think I am doing fairly well on the regular course [as a student]. I am also writing part of the new cavalry drill regulations and am assistant editor on a book. We will get home I think about the twenty third at least I hope so.

The book to which Patton referred was a pamphlet entitled "Army Racing and Records for 1913." A sixteen-page typed manuscript, it listed the races throughout the country in which military officers had competed and gave the results, including the owners, riders, and horses. Its purpose was to promote Army participation in racing and in polo matches in order to give the mounted service, the cavalry, a better public image and bring its members into closer contact with influential civilians.

Patton contributed the introduction, although it was unsigned. He opened with a tribute: Thanks to the encouragement of the Army Chief of Staff and the officers of the War Department, thanks to the courtesy of the National Steeplechase and Hunt Association and the stewards of all the meetings, the year 1913 was the best for Army racing ever recorded. He stated his thesis: Military races were the equal of polo matches in usefulness to the mounted service. Finally, he discussed the advantages accruing to the officers who participated in racing, to the cavalry, and to the Army at large:

Pluck, determination, quick eye to see and will to take a fleeting chance, a firm seat, confidence, and above all an increased interest and knowledge of the horse; all these are instilled by racing.

We talk a great deal about bold riding, and, outside the club, do very little of it, chiefly because at many posts we are fined if we get off the roads. When we go out with our troops to jump, we caution the men to go quietly, not to rush, and this is all very well and will be our most frequent method of procedure. But occasions will arise when we must surmount obstacles in a hurry, a very great hurry perhaps, in some neck or nothing dash. Then our quiet practise must be abandoned. Then the man who knows nothing of the capabilities of a horse going at full speed is lost.

It is at such times that we will appreciate the superior ability of men who, at the drop of the flag, have dashed as one man with clashing irons at quarter speed at the first hedge, who have risen to it together and stood the bobble when a bad jump tore down half the brush. The men who have had the eye and nerve to pull a racing horse side wise while in the air to avoid a fallen leader or who having fallen have remounted and ridden home with a broken arm. Those who have gone at the last liverpool of a three mile race using whip and heel on a spent horse, and who, by a last supreme effort of nerve and will, have kept him straight and in the lead until the race was won. These are bold riders, and will reap the reward. For, even should an event requiring such ability never arise, the training a man's nerve gets, the confidence it gives him in his horse, are worth the effort . . .

[Furthermore] army races have done more to popularize army equitation with the masses of the people than all the horse shows and polo games put together. This is a bold statement but I believe a little reflection will show its justice.

Horse shows and polo are notoriously society events, and at both, the seats are expensive and limited, and the crowds select and comparatively small. At races the seats are ample, the crowds large, and if not select, at least very representative of the American voter — the man who makes or breaks us.

At Belmont Park last spring I twice saw crowds of ten thousand people (mostly men) rise, take off their hats and cheer wildly when the army riders paraded before a race . . . Wherever we have raced, we have been the drawing card and have had fine support . . .

Many people who have never raced or owned a thoroughbred or any other good horse, will tell you racing spoils a horse and that any way thoroughbreds can't be used for drill. Such statements are the result of ignorance, or of rumors of some mythical horse owned long ago by some friend whom they can't quite remember . . . The last three years I have owned six thoroughbred horses, all of which I have raced, and five of which I have used at drills with perfect comfort.

In the last Inaugural parade I rode a race horse who had been out of training only four months, and had never before had a double bridle on. I happened to be an aide and rode him all day long through all sorts of crowds and music with no trouble . . .

Another very important benefit derived from racing is an increased insight into the care of the horse.

Ninety-nine officers out of a hundred have no conception of the care civilians devote to the feeding and exercising of good horses.

Of course in the service we cannot do all that they do, but we could do a great many things that they do, which, through ignorance, we neglect. I do not make this statement unadvisedly, for I have twice taken leaves and worked in racing stables under good trainers . . .

There is a belief in some quarters that army officers who race amass large fortunes by the purses or by betting. I regret deeply to say that this is not the case. Within my knowledge, no officer owning his own horses has ever come out even. What has been done has been for sport, not gain.

Patton, Beatrice, and the baby went to California for Christmas.

Colonel Gaston, the Mounted School commandant, evaluated Patton as "excellent." Patton, he said, was an expert swordsman and an excellent instructor. In the event of war, he was best suited for duty with troops or as an aide to a general officer.

Letter, General Leonard Wood to GSP, Jr., February 2, 1914
I have been trying out the new saddle, and find it very satisfactory.

I wrote you sometime ago thanking you for your kind thought in this matter. As far as I can see, this saddle is an excellent type for campaign purposes.

Write me and let me know how you are getting on with your work.

With kindest regards to Mrs. Patton and yourself.

Very sincerely,

Letter, Lieutenant Colonel Frederick S. Foltz (Washington) to GSP, Jr., March 23, 1914

My dear Patton: The Chief of Staff has just signed this and it goes at once to the printer to be rushed so as to appear at the same time as the Cavalry Service Regs [regulations] — same size and bound uniformly with it — promised to be ready in about a month.

This copy is for you to keep.

My congratulations on your good work. . . .

The Point fencing [meaning, stressing the thrust] should not be broadened until this [idea] sinks in, say in about 6 months, so that the cuties who say the Point requires fencing skill [on the part of the soldiers] will have no handle for their objections.

Regards to Mrs. Patton

Yours in haste. Foltz

The typed copy of the brochure sent by Foltz was to be printed by the War Department, Office of the Chief of Staff, and entitled "Sword Exercise, 1914." It was sent to the printer with a letter of transmittal:

The following Sword Exercise prepared by Second Lieutenant George S. Patton, Jr., 15th Cavalry, Master of the Sword, at the Mounted Service School, and revised by the Cavalry Board, is approved and issued for the information and government of the Regular Army and the Organized Militia of the United States. By order of the Secretary of War: Leonard Wood, Major General, Chief of Staff.

Containing sections on nomenclature, drills for dismounted instruction, and drills for mounted instruction, the Sword Exercise was thorough, detailed, and logically organized in the sequence of steps laid out to train men how to use the saber in warfare.

Letter, GSP, Jr., to his father, April 19, 1914

Dear Papa: We have been quite interested all day over [the incident at Vera Cruz] Mexico and have just heard over the phone that Huerta has refused to salute so mr. Wilson is up a stump. The betting is ten to one on Wall St. that Mr. W. will back down and even at that they can get no takers. It will be interesting to see how he will crawl. If he should not I hope it means war and a good big one. I certainly should like to try one and see how I make out at it.

If the war is to be short there will be no chance for a man of my rank to make any reputation as a leader of men but it might afford an oppertunity to make a personal record on which to base something in the future. Such a personal reputation can be gotten better with regulars than with the malatia.

But should the war last a long time and attain any proportions a man with a reputation for personal ability ought to get a good volunteer or malatia command. Hence should I succeed in becoming notorious you must try to get me a place as a major at least of state cavalry as I think infantry will not have so good a chance in Mexico as mounted troops. If not in California then else where but with mounted troops.

Mr. Ayer will do all he can if you will tell him how to pull and for what objective. So will Mr. Wood. Now it is quite important to remember this for some body will get good places and why not me?

Washington is the place to realy find out what is what and where the new regiments will go and you ought to be there and on the job and don't be modest. My name will sound just as old to a man who has not seen me as any other name and as a matter of fact I will have twice the ability.

It is quite important to find out where the regiment is to go as it would be very unglorious to command a regiment guarding a railroad.

Of course in all probability we will make up as peaceful as possible yet on the other hand we may not in which latter case I might have no chance to write you another long letter.

We are all well and having a fairly good time and the weather is delightful.

With much love to all and hoping that we wake in [the morning at] war.

Your devoted son

Despite his hope, Patton was involved on the following morning in completing a report. The Chief of Ordnance had advised the Adjutant General of some adverse reactions on the fencing equipment furnished the infantry and cavalry. He submitted a long list of dissatisfactions, deficiencies, and difficulties, concluding:

It is recommended that the question of a suitable fencing equipment for infantry be submitted to the School of Musketry at Fort Sill, Oklahoma, and of a suitable fencing equipment for cavalry be submitted to the Mounted Service School at Fort Riley, and that, in addition, these schools be required to submit rules which will prevent the improper use and unnecessary breakage of the fencing bayonets and blades during instructions in fencing.

After several indorsements, the Chief of Staff ordered the Chief of Ordnance to send sixteen sets of fencing equipment each to Forts Sill and Riley for the purpose of testing the equipment, and he directed the commandant of each school to inform him of the results of the tests.

The sixteen sets of equipment sent to Fort Riley were passed down the chain of command to the Master of the Sword, Lieutenant Patton, who received them on February 10. On April 20, Patton turned in his report.

The equipment, he wrote, had been "thoroughly tried and experimented with," and following were the results and his recommendations. The single stick with wicker basket guard, apparently a simulated saber, was too light and broke very easily; it was unserviceable and dangerous. The wooden fencing saber was strong and lasted, but the guard was too small and the blade so stiff that using the point, especially when mounted, made serious accidents likely — one officer experimenting with it broke a rib; it was too heavy for dismounted point fencing and the balance was poor — the men became tired before they had time to absorb the instruction. The mask was excellent — but the adoption of a lighter saber, which he recommended, would make the mask unnecessarily heavy and expensive; furthermore, the mesh would be too large. The glove was good, but was overpadded and too stiff. The plastron was much too heavy and cumbersome and gave insufficient protection at the throat; hot and uncomfortable, it was unserviceable mostly because "it stimulates in the man [wearing it] a desire of sticking too hard."

He recommended a new sword and described its specifications — "the idea that metal blades are dangerous is incorrect. I have seen them used here, at West Point, and in France and have never seen an accident." He sent along a model and explained that it would facilitate instruction because soldiers could work with it for longer periods of time without muscular fatigue.

He attached to his report a new mask, lighter than the one then being issued as regulation equipment. "I have personally used such a mask in daily fencing since July, 1913, and it is still good."

He sent a jacket, which gave ample protection and was more comfortable than the plastron then in use.

After making several other comments and suggestions, he concluded:

> The most important part of the equipment recommended is the saber.
>
> It is respectfully recommended that if any models of the above equipment is made, some sets be sent here for experiment before large quantities are manufactured.

A lucid and sensible report showing authoritative knowledge of the subject, sincere thought, and hard application to the problem at hand, it was up to Patton's usual high-caliber performance.

When Colonel Gaston, the commandant, was reassigned to another post in May, he rated Patton's performance as "excellent" and recommended him for duty with troops. He also sent a letter to the War Department Adjutant General to commend Patton's work. Patton, he wrote,

> has been in charge [of swordsmanship] and has shown great zeal and proficiency in his work. With the exception of one non-commissioned officer detailed to assist, Lieutenant Patton has been alone.

Captain Henry R. Richmond, the senior instructor in equitation who served very much in the capacity of dean of the faculty, mentioned Patton favorably in his annual report to the commandant:

> The course in Swordsmanship was introduced this year and carried on with much energy and enthusiasm by Lieut Geo S. Patton, the instructor. The results were most satisfactory.

Graduated from the First Year Course at the Mounted Service School on May 8, 1914, Patton was certified as proficient in equitation and horse training, hippology (including forage), and horseshoeing. His instructors found him qualified for assignment as an instructor in equitation for special classes of enlisted men and, when necessary, of officers. They were unable to judge him in swordsmanship, for he was the first Master of the Sword at the school.

Patton was hoping to be selected to attend the Second Year Course at the Mounted Service School and, of course, to continue as Master of the Sword.

Letter, GSP, Jr., to his father, May 17, 1914

Wooltex [his horse] got a straw in his throat and nearly choked to death but got sufficiently over it to run away with me yesterday but he did not go far . . .

[No polo yet on post, but he was looking forward to playing, for he was getting too fat.]

I suppose that the only way to start a war is to kill Bryan [the Secretary of State] and no one thinks enough of him to do that. Still I think we are getting near it from day to day and personally would just as soon wait until after the end of this school [meaning, the end of the Second Year Course].

Letter, GSP, Jr., to Major C. D. Rhodes, 15th Cavalry, Commandant-designate of the Mounted Service School, June 1, 1914

[The grades in swordsmanship that Patton was assigning his students who had successfully completed his course, he suggested, should for now] pertain only to the use of the saber mounted. As that is the really essential thing. Had we more time and a number of better instructors it would also be useful to consider gymnastic fencing dismounted. However, we are dealing with what actually exists.

The last sentence, in various forms, would always characterize his military thinking.

Letter, GSP, Jr., to General Hugh L. Scott, War Department, Washington, D.C., spring 1914

Sir: In writing this personal letter I fully realize that I run a grave risk of overstepping the bounds of military decorum.

I trust however, that you will excuse any presumption on my part on the grounds that I am personally, perfectly disinterested in the matter.

While out hunting with various farmers of this district and from conversations I have had with civilians of Junction City . . . there is quite a movement on foot here to try to have the government to dispose of the Sandy Hill Flats of the reservation to private individuals at about $100 per acre. I am told that much of this land could be resold by them at $200 or more per acre.

The people reported as desirous of getting this land from the government, base their claim on the fact that owing to the destruction of the bridge across the Kansas river in 1912, the troops of this garrison do not use this part of the reservation and have not since 1912, and hence can get along without it.

The fact that the Flats have not been used since 1912 is true, but they could be used during most of the year, for the ford is shallow. Also, much valuable hay is grown there and used by the government, and by putting about two miles of fence along the river bank they could be converted into excellent pastures. Add to this their value as a reviewing ground for the garrison, as Polo Fields and as Race Courses, it seems to me that their loss would be very deplorable.

I am quite sure you have been stationed here and are familiar with the ground, but on the small chance that you have not, I inclose a photograph I had made and a map of the Flats. The area of the Flats is about 1500 acres.

I know that this matter is none of my business and that it is probably being watched by the proper department. My only excuse for bothering you with the matter in this personal letter, is the fact that I take great interest in things that belong to the army and hate to see civilians get them.

Very respectfully

The reason he was writing to Scott was that Wood had terminated his tour of duty as Chief of Staff and was succeeded by General Wotherspoon, whom Patton did not know. He could claim some acquaintance with Scott, who had been the Superintendent at West Point, who was then serving as Deputy Chief of Staff, and who would, in November, replace Wotherspoon as Chief of Staff.

Letter, Scott to GSP, Jr., July 13, 1914
My dear Mr. Patton: I received your letter about the Fort Riley reservation some time ago and forget whether I replied to it or not.

Anyway, I gave instructions to watch that matter and not to let any part of the Fort Riley reservation get away from us.

I thank you very much for your writing to me on the subject.

With kind remembrances to yourself and to Mrs. Patton, I am always,

Sincerely yours,

That summer, the American Committee for the Sixth Olympiad, to be held at Berlin in 1916, convened at the New York Athletic Club, acted on a recommendation by Colonel Robert M. Thompson of Washington, D.C., and unanimously elected Patton a member of the committee. Patton replied gratefully: "I have the honor to acknowledge with many thanks the honor done me . . . I shall be glad to receive any instructions you may have to send me."

On July 17, he was formally notified that he was being detailed "as an additional member of the Second Year Class in addition to your other duties as Instructor in Swordsmanship." He would be one of ten students, captains and lieutenants, to take the Second Year Course for company officers.

This meant that his work as a student and as an instructor had been judged first-rate. Being retained for the second year was a distinct vote of confidence, a compliment, and an assurance that his superiors regarded him as worthy of eventual advancement and promotion.

CHAPTER 14

Fort Riley: Second Year

"There is but one International Law — the best army . . .
Some day I will make them all know me."

WHILE BEATRICE AND THE BABY fled to Massachusetts to escape the heat of
the Kansas summer in 1914, Patton worked in the target pits at the firing
range, was on guard duty, and did considerable hunting. One Tuesday
after supervising the pits until noon, he and Dr. Mills, probably the post
veterinarian, departed for Columbia, Missouri, to purchase some horses.
They drove 135 miles by nine o'clock that evening and stopped for dinner at a Harvey hotel,

> but they would not let me into the first [class] dining room . . . be-
> cause I had on an O.D. shirt [the normal duty uniform] . . . I told
> them that I would have them prosicuted under the law for discrimi-
> nation against the uniform and then they could not do enough [for
> us]. The head waiter served us and went out and escorted us to the
> machine.

They spent the night at a run-down hotel along the way and reached
Columbia the next day. Patton bought a mare for $400. He and Mills
left immediately, starting for home at four-thirty in the afternoon and
driving until eleven o'clock. They "slepped on the grass until three
[A.M.] when the mosquitoes woke us." They arrived at Fort Riley at nine-
ten in the morning, having driven 530 miles in 26 hours,

> with darned little sleep. The last sixty miles I was so weak and stiff
> in the shoulders that Dr. Mills had to help me make most of the turns
> and my hands are still swollen up like I had been stung.

After breakfast, he tended to some business on post, had a good lunch at home, and wrote to Beatrice. Later that afternoon he was going to the regular Thursday hunt. "Then I am going to take a good sleep."

He was on leave at the Ayer residence in Massachusetts when the drama that Sarajevo had triggered earlier that summer reached its climax. On August 3, the day that Germany declared war on France and started its invasion through Belgium and Luxembourg, Patton wrote to General Leonard Wood, now Commanding General of the Eastern Department with headquarters at Governors Island, New York:

Sir: From reports it seems that at last a war of good size has broken out and that France will be in it.

I have always wanted to have the experience of actual combat, not as an observer but as a participant because in the latter capacity I believe I can get knowledge which will be of great military value. It is only by doing things others have not done that one can advance.

Hence, I would like to get a years leave on some pretext and go to France and take part in this war.

I know officers and several French rigiments who would take me as an extra man if I would pay all expenses. I arranged this last year as I thought then that war with Germany was probable.

Therefore if I can get the leave I can manage the rest. Of course with the understanding that I will never apply to the United States for help if I get in trouble or captured.

I can turn over the Swordsmanship at Riley to an officer who did well under me last year and will continue my method.

As my family does not rely on me for support I would only be risking my self.

Please do not think this plan a spontaneous folly. I have contemplated it for years.

I would not bother you except that I am encouraged by the interest you have already taken in me and because I value your opinion above that of any one . . .

If you think any thing of my plan I can come to New York in one day to see you. Trusting you will reply to me, I am, Very respectfully,

Letter, Wood to GSP, Jr., August 6, 1914

My dear Mr. Patton: Yours of the 3d received. Don't think of attempting anything of the kind, at present. If you can get a leave, all right; but go to look on. We don't want to waste youngsters of your sort in the service of foreign nations unless they need you more than appears to be the case now. Stick to the present job and go ahead . . .

Of course, I know how you feel, but there is nothing to be done. I also am required to look on with patience, but I hope to get over at some later time.

With kind regards, Very sincerely,

Captain Richmond, Acting Commandant at Fort Riley, rated Patton "excellent" in all military qualities and added that he was "a very zealous and ambitious young officer."

Mr. Patton visited Pride's Crossing that month, and he accompanied his son back to Fort Riley, planning to stay several weeks.

Letter, Mr. Patton to Beatrice, September 22, 1914

Georgie is fine — really as well as I ever saw him. His gain in weight of 15 pounds has helped him. He had a fine welcome from every body — Major Rhodes and Capt. Richmond both seemed emotionally glad to see him.

Letter, Beatrice to Mr. Patton, September 25, 1914

You don't know what a comfort it is to me to have you with Georgie! . . . He loves you so much that you can keep him in order better than anyone else in the world.

GSP, Jr., "My Father," 1927

When ever he [Mr. Patton] visited me at an army post it did me a lot of good as his intelligence, character and learning impressed favorably the better class of officers whom he met. He never criticised any of my activities, including football, polo and steeplechasing and was proud of my successes at them . . .

While I was at Fort Riley . . . we used to have pleasant gallops over the Prairie. Papa rode Roman Wing and liked him. Later I gave Wing to Papa.

Letter, GSP, Jr., to his father, November 12, 1914

I certainly am ageing . . . I fixed twenty-seven as the age when I should be a brigadier and now I am twenty nine and not a first Lieutenant. Yet things are going on well here and I am doing well both in the second year [meaning as a student] and as an instructor. But I will be glad to leave as it is very tedious work . . .

I went to the old riding hall to day with the baby and an air gun to shoot pigeons. I killed one and pulled its head off. The baby retrieved both body and head and took them to Beatrice. She [the baby] covered her self with blood and announced that if I had let her she could have pulled its head off her self. She seems to be a natural hunter and tip toed around the hall pointing out birds . . .

I must work on a fencing manual.

Letter, GSP, Jr., to his mother, November 14, 1914
Sold Wooltex I only got six hundred for him which hardly pays expenses but it at least stops further expenditure.

Sometime that fall, in response to a request from the Cavalry Board, Patton prescribed a test as the basis for awarding the swordsman's badge. A candidate wishing recognition for proficiency had to ride a designated course, cover the first 75 yards at a charging gallop, the rest at a maneuvering gallop, in the process attacking dummies, jumping hurdles, all the while displaying prowess with the saber.

The War Department accepted his criteria "in order to secure uniformity throughout the Cavalry in awarding the swordsman's badge."

The Pattons went to California for the Christmas holidays.

Letter, GSP, Jr., to Aunt Nannie, January 17, 1915
I was so impressed with the beautiful condition of the machines at home that I worked on mine all Saturday and Sunday. I took it all to pieces and am now having a hell of a time getting it together again. It is quite a job and so cold that you have to warm the tools before you can handle them. Still it is very instructive and I am glad I did it . . .

Gen. Scott was here Thursday and we had quite a show for him. He asked me to especially remember him to Pa . . .

My business inability is being over taxed trying to figure out the income tax and not go to jail. I guess that no one ever had so much money and knew so little about it as I do. It's something fearful.

Tell pa to read The War of the Trenches and the War of the Marshes in the last Worlds Book. They will give him a shock.

Major Rhodes judged Patton's military performance to be "excellent," found in him a peculiar fitness for college and recruiting duty, as well as the post of military attaché, and thought him especially qualified for duty in war with troops. He would make an excellent aide-de-camp and was physically adept for all assignments. His energy, horsemanship, and aptitude for field service were "excellent"; his swordsmanship was "most excellent"; he was ready for promotion. Rhodes added:

Lieutenant Patton though lacking experience with troops, is a most promising young officer of high ideals, devotion to duty, and marked industry. He is somewhat impulsive and intolerant of the opinions of others, and needs a period of severe duty with troops to counter-balance his protracted duty away from troops and to round out his efficiency as an all around officer.

Letter, GSP, Jr., to his father, January 26, 1915
Dear Papa: I am very sorry to hear about [the illness of] Grandpa [Smith] and hope he either recoveres completely or does not completely.

I bought two mares and a yearling colt Saturday . . .

Letter, GSP, Jr., to Aunt Nannie, January 31, 1915
B and I have been out to three parties this week so are still quite gay . . .

I did not get any money from Cataline [Island] for December. I don't need it but think Pa had better ask about it as the letter [containing the check] may have gotten lost.

Early in February, Mrs. Patton and Nita came to Fort Riley to take Beatrice to California, where she would await the birth of her second child. The baby, Smith, or Beatrice as she would be called, remained with her father.

Letter, GSP, Jr., to Beatrice, February 11, 1915
My stay at Emporia [Kansas, after seeing Beatrice off for California] was not so bad as last time. I got my hair cut, went to the Drug Store and the movies. I got home a little after eight.

You were fine not to cry.

Letter, GSP, Jr., to his father, February 11, 1915

Dear Papa: I have just read your letter about Grandpa. He was a great mind wasted and I am sorry. I was very fond of him and wish I could have seen more of him. He did not have the military mind in its highest development because he was swayed by ideas of right or wrong rather than those of policy. Still he was probably more noble for his fault. Also the education of law hampered him . . .

I hope that B, Ma, and nita arrived safely and that B is not too tired. She is a brave woman and I hope she will have no trouble.

You must tell the doctor that if there is the least question between her life and that of the child the child must go.

This is probably an unnecessary caution but I insist on it. If he will not subscribe to it get another doctor who will.

Letter, GSP, Jr., to Beatrice, March 1, 1915

. . . now that it is over successfully I am very glad from a selfish point of view that I was not there . . .

The message came about 2 A.M. and Kane woke me scared to death. I think he felt sure you had died. Hannah telephoned all the post . . . I have steared clear of her all day for fear she would embarass me.

You had better have it named out there where you can get more advice. All I know is that I don't like the sound of either Ruth or Ellen. You might call it Beatrice Second like a race horse. I certainly like the sound of that name the best of any.

I love you with all my heart and hope you have not suffered or are not suffering more than necessary.

Beatrice named the baby Ruth Ellen.

Patton sent his father a copy of a lecture, probably on the sad state of the American military establishment, given by Captain LeRoy Eltinge at the Army's school at Fort Leavenworth. It was, Patton thought, one of the best and most logical presentations he had seen. He was enclosing it because he thought it "might give you valuable data for your political campaign."

Mr. Patton was again thinking seriously of politics, and his son gave him some advice. The Allies, he said, were widely publicizing a book written in 1912 by German General Friedrich von Bernhardi. They were doing so to point out an example of ruthless German political ambition. Bernhardi had noted that it was impossible for a nation to surpass an enemy nation in every detail. For that reason, a nation had to select a single detail of great importance and excel in that. The lesson, Patton pointed out, was applicable to human beings, and he advised his father to follow this principle in his political campaign.

From the nature of California it appears to me that by voicing a strong logical advocacy of proper and consistant military preperation you might gain much ground. This would be easy for you as it is already more or less your opinion.

I think Mr. Garrison [Secretary of War] deserved to fail in his military legislation because he did not support the scheme of the general staff. What he advocated was excellent but not consistent. It diverged from policy.

If you use the data of the [enclosed] lecture do not quote Capt. Eltinge by name as this so called president of ours might object.

. . . Be sure to run for the Senate. Also fix the grass for my horses.

Letter, GSP, Jr., to Beatrice, March 9, 1915

Keep after Pa about running for the senate. He should and I think would be there — if successful — during a most exciting time for if we don't fight some body in a year or so I shall miss my guess . . .

War now will not be gained by a highly educated "bottom" but by a well developed "top." [He was referring to the high command.] I wish . . . I could transfer the two years here into two at Leavenworth [the next school up the military ladder of education — what he meant was that he wished he could have already graduated from Leavenworth, which would qualify him for a senior assignment in case of war.]

Letter, GSP, Jr., to Beatrice, March 10, 1915

I shot two hounds to day . . . both no good and too old. They did not suffer a bit. I have just ordered two new ones from Kentucky which will be my last contribution to this pack.

I must stop now and write some more on my fencing.

Letter, GSP, Jr., to Beatrice, March 19, 1915

The baby had a fine birthday and got altogether too many presents. People ought to stop sending them to her. She is getting spoiled all to pieces and soon will be in my condition and have nothing to wish for . . .

I finished my sword Diary just now and am glad to get it off my chest.

What he called his sword diary was a manual of instruction. Illustrated heavily by photographs showing the correct positions, both mounted and dismounted, of how to wield the saber — Patton, immaculately dressed, was the model — it was a solid and detailed work. The Mounted Service School sent it to the printer so that it could be widely disseminated as a guide to instructors everywhere in the cavalry.

Published on June 1 as *The Diary of the Instructor in Swordsmanship* and signed at the end by Patton, "Instructor in Fencing" — a much more modest title than Master of the Sword, the manual described the course Patton had given. Its purpose, he explained, was to create "vigorous, offensive, thrusting fighters." The saber used tactically was an offensive weapon and "not for individual defense . . . The men [being instructed] must be impressed with the idea that the proper defense is a transfixed opponent."

It must always be remembered that the point must be the dominant idea in teaching its use . . .

This dairy [sic] is not intended to supplant the Saber Exercise 1914 [which he had written], but [is meant] simply as a system of applying the teaching therein laid down and of bringing into notice special points which experience has shown required emphasizing . . .

. . . the instructor [Patton] desires to disavow any pretense to the writing of a work on fencing or to the expounding of anything original.

. . . it is neither the desire nor the object of the course here to teach fencing for its own sake or to make individual champions.

. . . [we] use fencing as an adjunct to teaching the use of the point when fighting mounted with the regulation saber.

In other words, the course was designed to teach students a few parries and attacks that they, as instructors, could pass on to others. It followed closely, he stated candidly, the lessons and methods of M. L'Adjutant

Cléry, Maître d'Armes at the Cavalry School, Saumur, who taught non-commissioned officers each summer to become assistant squadron instructors in France.

Significant comments by Patton were:

A man who does not admit touches should be tried [by court-martial] or in some other way to have his sensibilities awakened . . .

Do not develop the skin of an elephant and be unable to feel touches. Always admit the least touch. When you find a man who will not, only fence with him before a judge . . .

Fencing is an art, of which the best elements perish when put on paper . . .

To repeat, this diary was compiled at the request of student officers who wanted something on which to base the instruction of the men of their troops. This instruction . . . has for its object to develop by means of the gymnastic game of fencing, the desire and ability to thrust and thrust accurately in battle.

Early in April, he wrote to Beatrice to tell her that the first real polo game had taken place. His team lost because of Adair, who "has no more head than a chicken and will not stay in place."

Letter, GSP, Jr., to Beatrice, April 8, 1915
I wrote you last Saturday that Sylvia Green [his horse] stepped in a hole and fell but neglected to add that she rolled on me and that in getting up she kicked me in the head with her hind foot and cut quite a hole in which I had five stitches taken.

It was a glancing blow and not her fault. She was simply trying to get up. It did not nock me out as I rode back about two miles to the kennels and got the ambulance there. It did not even give me a head ache so don't get worried about it.

. . . it was just like the cut I got in Washington and did not hurt a bit.

When I get less hair than I now have I will look just like a German duelist.

The doctor called the injury a lacerated wound through the skin and the periosteum, four centimeters long, in the left lateral parietal region of the skull. It was more serious than "the cut I got in Washington." He reported on sick call for treatment for nine consecutive days.

Letter, GSP, Jr., to Beatrice, April 16, 1915

Poor little Hindenberg just will never win his derby. He died to night at eight o'clock of blood poison. We kept him alive all day with sherry and eggs but it was no use he was too weak. He was a brave little fellow and whinnied to me a minute before he went back to the horse Heaven from which he came only fifteen days ago. I felt very sad over it for he was my first horse child . . .

We left him with Rose [the mare] and she was licking him when I left her but [she] will forget him in a day or so. Such is the nature of horses . . .

Pray for the repose of little Hindenberg.

After going rabbit hunting on Sunday morning, he read for nearly twelve hours. Then he worked on and wrote up the solutions to two tactical problems, probably a student requirement. "I am ashamed to admit," he wrote to Beatrice, "that they [the tactical problems] are the first ones I have done since early in 1912." Changing the subject abruptly, he said that according to rumors, the 15th Cavalry was leaving for the Philippines in October. "I got only two months leave though I had asked for four but if we have to go to the islands I can get two more."

Letter, GSP, Jr., to his father, April 30, 1915

Riley is beautiful now as green as France.

Early in May, the War Department published a list of ten second lieutenants, including Patton, who were eligible for promotion and who were to be examined for their general proficiency as soon as practicable after July 1.

Letter, GSP, Jr., to his father, May 16, 1915

Dear Papa: Your letters confirm me in a theory, which I have long entertained, that soldiers should not be allowed to study law.

Law is based on long usage by which the weak have sought to protect them selves against the strong by the amassing of precedents. Hence to them every thing new is illegal.

One can picture the impatient anger of some hairry cave man the first time he saw a companion wounded by the lance of a more inventive lake dweller in stead of in the orthodox fashion of crushing the skull.

The Knight felt the same thing about the use of [gun] powder and so on yet here we see [President Wilson] the head of a nation of fools protesting against the [German] use of the sub-marine. Because — God bless us — there is no president. He feels as agrieved as the French Knights did at Crecy when the arrows killed them with out letting them strike back.

The right of "visit and search" worked well enough when a wooden vessel was brought up by a similar one. And a prize crew was put on.

But how in the name of reason could a submarine visit the Lusitania when one shot from one of her hundred ports would have sent the submarine down?

Such a clame is utter folly and no mind unless it were trammeled by "Law" would entertain it.

Such reasoning would preclude progress.

As to the loss of life. Any one but a woman can see that the loss of life is a question of indifference to Germany. In the abstract what is it to her? All must die a day sooner [or later] what is the difference.

It is ridiculous to attribute to a great nation waring for what she thinks she needs the foolish prudishness about blood shed peculiarly suitable to an ex school teacher [Wilson]. Who dares more over to say that one can be "Too proud to fight." In any other country or age that pride has always been called another name.

Another view of the case which is very pertinent and hence not mentioned in any of our fool papers, is the fact that the Lusitania carried $2 000 000.00 dollars worth of cartridges. Each cartridge costs 3 cents so you get 6 666 666.66 cartridges which at a liberal estimate would wound 6 666 german soldiers who are certainly worth more than 1000 civilians many of whom would have died any way from the diseases of child hood.

This is the German side.

For as I think that we ought to declare war if Germany failes as she should to pay heed to our foolish talk.

If Wilson had as much blood in him as the liver of a louse is commonly thought to contain he would do this. Because he could by it very cheaply show the need of an army with out the danger of an invasion. And by the time Germany beats the allies we will have time if we start now to get an army.

As for your notion that I am probably less informed on the war than you are I doubt it. Since to begin with I can make my observations unhandicaped by either devotion to Wilson or a knowledge of law.

There is but one International Law — the best army.

Letter, Master of the Sword to the Commandant, Mounted Service School, thru Senior Instructor, June 1, 1915, subject: Standing in fencing and swordsmanship

I have the honor to submit the following list of the proficiency of the second year and first year classes in the Expert Saber test.

[He listed 9 second-year students, 25 first-year students. After explaining in a very serious disquisition the system he had used to determine each man's standing, he listed those who had passed swordsmanship in the order of their proficiency.]

Neither Lt Cullum nor Lieut Stewart have half completed the course. It is recommended that they not be graduated in fencing and that such notation appear on their diplomas.

Early in June, Mrs. Ayer informed Patton that she had heard the "News that you must go to Philippines." She was hardly enchanted.

The Mounted Service School published a booklet entitled *Graduation Rides, 1915,* showing a three-day exercise to display the proficiency of horsemen who had completed the prescribed courses. The book consisted mainly of photographs of officers and a few noncommissioned officers on horseback in the process of jumping various kinds of obstacles, all with excellent riding form. One photo captioned "Lieutenant G. S. Patton, The M.F.H., Fort Riley Hunt Club" showed him wearing his hunting outfit with cap, jacket, white trousers, and boots — all very smart.

As a graduate of the Second Year Course, he was judged proficient in equitation and the care of the horse, suitable as an instructor in equitation, qualified for any detail requiring exceptional knowledge of equitation or horse training. He was, in short, "a good general horseman."

In his annual report, Captain Richmond remarked:

> The course in Swordsmanship has been carried on with much vigor and enthusiasm by 2d Lieutenant G. S. Patton, 15th Cavalry, Master of the Sword; and the class has attained a degree of proficiency that ought to render them very useful in fencing and in mounted work with the sword, upon their return to their regiments.

Major Rhodes, commenting on Patton's performance, observed:

Lieutenant Patton is a young officer of high ideals, conscientious devotion to duty, and marked industry. His work in building up a high standard of swordsmanship at the Mounted Service School and in the Army, merits the highest praise. His usefulness as an officer is somewhat impaired by impulsive intolerance *at times* of restraint by superiors, although his intentions are always of the highest character. He should be encouraged to practice self-restraint.

Graduation took place on June 17, and three days later, he and Beatrice and the babies were in Massachusetts. Patton had been granted a special leave of eleven days to look for a job that would keep him from going to the Philippines with his regiment. He left immediately for Washington.

Letter, GSP, Jr. (The New Willard Hotel, Washington, D.C.), to Beatrice (Pride's Crossing), June 21, 1915

I got here about five. I came here so I could get my clothes pressed at once and not have to send them out as I would have [had to do] at the club.

I called on the Summeralls and Mitchells and found them both out.

I hope to do better in the morning.

I certainly like Washington. Even its whiskey smell at the theater charms me and I was gratified that the nigger door keeper at the Club knew me. No one else did. Some day I will make them all know me.

He spent about a week in Washington, then returned to Massachusetts to start a regular leave of absence of two and a half months. He needed a long vacation, for his second year at Fort Riley had been especially grueling.

Letter, Beatrice to Aunt Nannie, July 1, 1915

Georgie is here since Sunday . . . He hasn't ascertained any more about our future . . . but he is having a rest at any rate. He sleeps till about 9:30 every morning! Dear soul, I am so happy when we are together, and now he will very soon be gone. But I would not keep him here for the world . . .

G. went to see [the movie] "The Clansman" . . . and said it was

finer than anything he had ever seen. He took me yesterday and has
been reading the book all day. Certainly, it is a marvelous thing, but
the war part made me sick and I dreamt about it all night. I can't
stand war pictures!

In July, Patton learned informally what would appear formally in War
Department Special Orders later that month. The 15th Cavalry was indeed going to the Philippines. But Patton was being transferred to the
8th Cavalry, which was stationed at Fort Bliss, El Paso, Texas.

He had somehow worked it. There was no point, he felt, in going to
the Philippines. The islands were quiet, distant from the United States,
and on the wrong side of the globe. The action, the excitement, the war
were in Europe. Not much was happening at El Paso, but at least he
would be at the border, close to Mexico, where revolutionary upheaval
had kept that country in turmoil since 1911. War with Mexico, he was
certain, was destined, and at El Paso he would be in the wings and ready
to move on stage.

The post commander of Fort Bliss was Brigadier General John J. Pershing.

CHAPTER 15

Fort Bliss and the Border

"I would not miss this for the world . . . I like this sort of work a lot . . . Tickled to death at the chance of a fight."

UPON NEWS of Patton's transfer to Texas, he and Beatrice left the babies at Pride's Crossing and returned to Fort Riley. After packing their things and arranging to ship their eleven horses to San Gabriel, they started driving to California. They traveled 114 miles in five hours the first day, 138 miles in nine and a half hours the second. The next morning they made 85 miles and stopped for lunch in Burlington, Colorado, at the Hotel Montezuma, where Patton wrote to his father. He gave explicit directions on how to feed his animals, exercise them, and look after them. "I shipped the horses to you collect as I did not know what it would cost so please pay it for me."

The incident made a good story twelve years later:

GSP, Jr., "My Father," 1927
   I shipped Papa nine horses, three hounds, an automobile and my household goods and sent him a wire . . . saying that he was to pay the freight. He thought this a great joke and used to tell about it at the California Club . . .
   He and the family met us at San Bernardino. We were so dirty that we had lunch at the station restaurant instead of at the hotel.
   While home . . . I had a new body built for my Loco[mobile] . . .
   When I left for El Paso at the end of my leave I left papa a stallion and three mares; we then had plenty of pasture. These horses multiplied and were a great nuisance to Papa but he never complained.
   When pasture got scarce he had to send them to a place in the hills near Duarte. About 1922 I sold them all for a loss.

Patton and Beatrice traveled by train to El Paso, and Beatrice continued on to Pride's Crossing.

After getting a room on the post and having his trunks brought up
from the railroad, Patton could find no one to tell him what was expected
of him.

Letter, GSP, Jr., to Beatrice, September 16, 1915

I hung around and called on the Johnsons and Capt. Going and
Chap[lain] Brander and Cooke and Surles. At last at five the adjutant Capt. Morris appeared. He is a most casual person and said that
there was nothing for me to do but hang around until the 8th [Cav-
alry] gets here about the 25th, so I am hanging. He also told me
that I would be examined [for promotion] to day. That rather
frightened me so I went to Col. Koheler [Herman J. Koehler] and he
advised me to wire for a delay which I did . . . I dined with
maj[or] Langhorne who is president of the [promotion] board
which is luckey as he likes me and I him.

I have studied all day and Capt. Oliver has lent me his troop to
drill in the morning. Barnett is going to help me.

I am staying with capt. Kirkpatrick. He has a house and a cook,
and it is very nice. I will stay with him until I go to the border . . .

I love you more all the time. George

My hay fever *is gone.*

Letter, GSP, Jr., to Beatrice, September 18, 1915

I got my exam put off until Oct. 20 so I have sufficient time to get
ready for it. This is fortunate as Capt. Hickock is on the board and is
a "High Brow" and very strict.

Maj. Marshall [his former troop commander at Fort Sheridan]
came yesterday and I saw him. He is corking. [He was leaving for
the Philippines and would command the regiment en route to its
destination] . . .

This post is not much to look at, the officers houses are small and
not well made and the stables are of wood but new as are the quarters.

So far I have had no duty to do and don't expect any until the end
of next week.

Letter, GSP, Jr., to Beatrice, September 19, 1915

The party [at the officers club] was a great sight. Most of the

women were painted [wore cosmetics] and their clothes were of fash-
ions never seen before. Probably Paris translated to Texas.

There is nothing doing on the post all the 15th [Cavalry] non
coms are going to the islands and all the 8th [Cavalry] are coming
back so everyone is packing . . . [glad he has no duties] as it gives
me more time to study. . . .

Mr. Eltinge is helping me with map drawing [for the promotion
exam].

Letter, GSP, Jr., to his father, September 20, 1915

[This is] not a bad place but quite new looking. Most of the
buildings have been erected within the year. And the U.S. certainly
got stung on them too. They are poorly made. The stables are of
wood and are regular fire traps.

I will have nothing to do until the end of this week so can study a
lot and I certainly need to as I have two Leavenworthers [graduates
of the very highly thought of General Service School, later renamed
the Command and General Staff College at Fort Leavenworth, Kan-
sas] on my board and they are great on speck [details]. Still I usually hold my own in that.

I have been out twice helping Maj. Langhorne train polo ponies. I
have a method in this as he is president of the board and I like it [the
work] too . . . I would prefer not to stay as there is fine hunting on
the border and nothing of interest here except some bum society and
little of that, and the polo will be inferior as most of the men are
beginners.

Col. Morgan has it in for me on account of the saber letter I wrote
him but [he] will be relieved the 24th so I don't care much what he
thinks. Lt. Col. Koehler is a great supporter of mine and so is Maj.
Langhorne. As luck would have it Maj. Marshall is staying with
Capt. Hickock the second member of my board and I called and
quoted history to him to show what a hell of a soldier I was. I hope it
had the results desired. Any how Maj. M. will blow my horn . . .

The officers quarters are in one long line facing a similar line of
barracks accross the parade [ground] with the stables behind the
barracks. So for a big post it is quite compact. There are no trees at
all. We are about a mile from the border but cant see the river as the
post is on a mesa which extends back of the stables to mountains 30
miles away perfect[ly] flat no trees. The town is behind the officers'
quarters.

Hurry them up on my machine.

Letter, GSP, Jr., to Beatrice, September 20, 1915

. . . very poor polo game to day . . . I am much the best player here which is a comfort though it does not mean much . . .

Col. Koehler is very friendly and so is Col Johnston. Both send their regards to you.

I can't send any kisses as we had onions for dinner. I love you.

Letter, GSP, Jr., to Beatrice, September 23, 1915

Things here are very quiet and un war like . . .

I am getting on well with my studies and hope to pass a good exam, though there is a lot of stuff to learn.

The colonel commanding the 8th Cavalry, eight officers, and all the noncoms arrived at Fort Bliss. Patton played in a "nice polo game." Colonel Morgan was "quite nice after all and I felt sorry for him loosing his command" because of the arrival of the new colonel. "I have done nothing at all except study."

When the 15th Cavalry departed, Patton went to see the noncoms off — "they were a fine looking lot of men realy inspiring," he wrote Beatrice. "They had the band and the regimental colors and the Standard and the guidons." He was deeply affected. He gave the sergeants of Troop K, his old command, "a box of nice cigars."

Patton was assigned to Troop D of the 8th Cavalry. Captain Barnhardt was the commander and First Lieutenant Daniel D. Tompkins was second in command. Since both had yet to arrive, Patton took temporary command of the troop.

Letter, GSP, Jr., to Beatrice, September 26, 1915

My 1st Sergeant [the senior noncommissioned officer in the troop] seems good as do most of the non-coms . . . I took the troop out yesterday and it seemed strange to command one again. It rained and we all got wet. Maj. Langhorne is commanding the squadron.

The new Col. Taylor [the regimental commander] seems nice. He is fat and has a mustash like Col Bishop but he is clean. The Adjt. [Adjutant] Capt Gadsom is very fine looking, an Englishman.

Letter, GSP, Jr., to Beatrice, September 28, 1915

. . . my rule in "D" Troop will not be for long [Tompkins was expected to arrive soon] still I have at least gotten them [the men] to groom and feed [the horses] in the proper way which is something.

Letter, GSP, Jr., to Beatrice, September 30, 1915

They have just finished a regimental review my troop was on guard [duty] so I was an interested spectator.

It was a fine sight all with sabers drawn and all my sabers [the ones he had designed]. It gives you a thrill and my eyes filled with tears . . .

The nearest similar feeling I can remember is on the occasion of certain very noisy Opera music.

It is the call of ones ancestors and the glory of combat. It seems to me that at the head of a regiment of cavalry any thing would be possible . . .

Pa writes that the machine will be finished Nov. 1st but it probably wont.

Letter, GSP, Jr., to Beatrice, October 2, 1915

Mr. Tompkins is a very nice man and very much of a gentleman.

Letter, GSP, Jr., to Beatrice, October 8, 1915

We go out in the field on Tuesday to relieve part of the 13th Cavalry. A & D Troops go to Siera Blanca Texas about ninety miles from here. It is up high about five thousand feet and in a grass country. The climate is better than here being less dusty.

There will probably be some detached posts out from Siera Blanca and I may get one of them [as an independent command, which would please him] . . .

I will probably come back here . . . to be examined [for promotion] which will take several days.

Letter, GSP, Jr., to Beatrice, October 10, 1915

I went down town and got a fine lantern and a coffee pot and an alcohol lamp yesterday. The lantern is the best I have seen and gives a good clear light. It also packs in a tin box so will be easy to put in the bedding roll.

In addition to his duties with Troop D, Patton was appointed squadron adjutant, serving directly under Major Langhorne, the squadron commander.

The threat of being transferred to the Philippines was still hanging over him, but he learned that he would not be sent there until he was promoted and until a vacancy opened there for a first lieutenant. It was a "safe guess that we won't go before February at the earliest."

Letter, GSP, Jr., to Beatrice, October 10, 1915
We play a match polo game . . . on Monday I will be Captain [of my team].

Captain Barnhardt was named regimental quartermaster, and Tompkins took command of Troop D.

Letter, GSP, Jr., to Beatrice, October 13, 1915
I have been busy as a bird dog all day as I am [squadron] Q.M. as well as adjutant and know nothing whatever about it. Still it is good practice so I don't mind if it were not for this d——— exam. I should like it very well as it keeps me busy but just now I am a little too busy. I think that my board will be changed and that I will be examined at Siera Blanca by Maj. L. Goster and Tompkins which ought to make it easier. Still I want to know all I can and think that I will do well. I hope so any way.

The squadron departed Fort Bliss, marched for three days, and reached "a place called Finlay. It is one house and a station in the middle of a desert." He had ridden with the wagons because a sergeant had killed a mule by pushing the animals too hard. "Maj. L. [Langhorne] is very nice to serve with and every one is contented."

It took the troops another day to get to Sierra Blanca, which was connected by rail to El Paso; the main line of the Southern Pacific passed nearby.

Letter, GSP, Jr., to Beatrice, October 20, 1915
This is the funniest place I have ever been. It is supposed to be very tough and at least half the men wear boots and spurs and carry guns.

I met a Mr. Dave Allison yesterday. He was a very quiet looking old man with a sweet face and white hair. He is the most noted gun man here in Texas and just at present is marshall.

He alone killed all the Orasco outfit [a notorious local bandit gang] five of them about a month ago and he kills several mexicans each month.

He shot Orasco and his four men each in the head at sixty yards.

He seemed much taken with me and is going hunting with me.

Another noted man I met is Mr. English who is hired fighter for the T.O. ranch across the border. He is about sixty and has two grown daughters. Cow girls who are very dashing ladies. He is the only American who can bluff the bandits over the river and he does. Each of these men gets about $100 a month for risking their lives daily.

There are seven Love brothers who own the whole country and are supposed to be worth millions. They own the town and all work either in their ranches or in the store. To look at them they would appear like laborers. But all seem very nice . . . I think I will get on with them well as I usually do with that sort of people.

There are not over twenty houses in the town and one saloon. Yesterday a ranger jokingly threatened to shoot me for not taking a drink with him so after I refused I bought him a bottle of beer and drank one my self. Don't get worried. He was only trying to be hospitable according to his view and had not the least intention of being rough.

We have a three room house and a stable and a garage so are very comfortable.

I would not miss this for the world. I guess there are few places like it left.

I will be examined [for promotion] here by Maj. L., Capt. Ray and Mr. Tompkins so it is a sure thing.

We have two out posts about 30 miles from here and sixty miles apart one at Loves Ranch and one at Calduan. There is no wagon road to the latter place. It is in the mountains, so is this [Sierra Blanca]. It is 4500 feet up.

Peace strength of our army is 80,000 besides 10,000 Phillippine scouts and constabulary.

The President can raise it to 100,000 exclusive of Scouts etc at any time. To go beyond that requires an act of Congress.

There are supposed to be 200,000 militia but there are only about half that number [in the entire country] and they are not worth a damn.

He and Tompkins made a three-day trip, riding 100 miles, to inspect the outposts.

Letter, GSP, Jr., to Beatrice, October 26, 1915
We had a fine trip and got back yesterday evening at four
The first day we rode about twenty miles through the mountains

and camped at an outpost on the river. I got some excellent shooting. I took a soldier with me and we got 20 quail and two rabbits in about an hour and a half. We could have gotten many more but only shot them in passing while we hunted ducks, which we did not find.

The Rio Grande is very narrow and shallow at that point not over thirty yards wide with heavy bushes on both banks. And many ponds on our side.

That night we slept on the ground taking off only our boots. It was quite cold but we were comfortable.

In the morning we hunted some more duck but got none and saw only two who got up out of range.

The map showed a good road along the river to Hot Springs about thirty miles. We started at ten with two men and a pack horse and rode until five thirty before we reached H.S. which was only two houses. The distance was fifty miles instead of thirty and there was no road at all only the worst cow trail you ever saw. Miles and miles of loose stone with high mountains to the north and the river south. We passed many deserted ranches that is hutts for Americans can't live there or if they do they don't live long. A party of four was safe but I think one man could hardly get through with out being shot at. We hoped they would shoot at us but saw no one at all but one mexican in a hut. One place we found a camp with two guns and a pistol resting on a tree. We got some water there and at Hot S. found the owner an American. He is probably a cattle runner so the Mexicans leave him alone.

It is the most desolate country you ever saw. Rocks and these thorny bushes.

At H.S. a man gave us some beans and coffee which we were glad to get but there was nothing for the horses so we pushed on to Loves Ranch where we had an outpost. The man said ten miles but it was over twenty. The road which was good lead through the mountains and we had a fine moon. It was very pretty and wild. We made camp at ten thirty having been in the saddle eleven and a half hours exclusive of halts and having gone seventy miles. I rode sylvia [Green] all the way and she was shying at sticks as we made camp.

There are some cow boys at Loves Ranch who have invited me to visit them and hunt deer. They say you can shoot them with a pistol.

From Love's here was thirty miles which we made in four hours and a quarter. . . .

Grandfather Patton,
circa 1860

Grandmother Wilson,
circa 1865

Grandfather Wilson,
circa 1860

Father and mother,
circa 1884

George S. Patton, Jr., 1892

The family home, Lake Vineyard, 1898

Aunt Nannie

Family dinner, 1900. Seated: Aunt Susie, Mr. Patton,
George Jr., Nita, Mrs. Patton

Father and son, 1901

Cadet George S. Patton, Jr., VMI, 1903

Nita, 1905

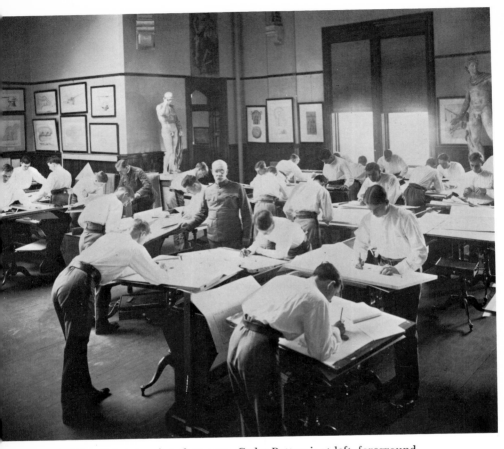

West Point drawing class, 1907. Cadet Patton is at left, foreground

Cadet Patton, Adjutant, 1909

Cadet Patton, West Point
graduation, June 1909

Beatrice Patton and her father, wedding day, 1910

Coming up I made the darndest shot with a pistol you ever saw   I hit a jack rabbit running at about fifteen yards while riding at a trot. My reputation as a gun man is made. . . . don't worry about me. No troops have ever been shot at and lots of them have taken the ride I spoke of. I love you.

Patton was examined in the subjects of cavalry drill regulations, field service regulations, and applied tactics. He passed and was certified as qualified for promotion.

At noon, October 29, he received a telegram ordering him to guard the railroad at Hot Springs or Hot Wells, Texas, while Mexican forces belonging to General Carranza moved over it.

I started at 3:20 P.M. and got here at 6:30. 23 miles. I have ten men and 30 miles of R.R. to guard. But really I think that there will be nothing to guard on this part of the line. Any way I will soon know as the first train comes past at 5 and it is now two.

There is a pump [bath] house an alledged hotel and a store here. I take my meals at the hotel.

Guarding the railroad to permit Carranza forces passage through American territory was but the latest development growing out of the tangled web of Mexican affairs.

The revolution of 1910 overthrew Porfirio Díaz, who had ruled as dictator for more than 30 years, and Francisco I. Madero became president in 1911. But the stability that Díaz had ruthlessly imposed by force and terror dissolved as various groups, motivated by social reform or simple banditry, competed for power. To prevent incursions by Mexican bands of one sort or another into the United States, American troops were stationed along the border.

In 1913, Victoriano Huerta deposed Madero, arrested him, and was widely thought responsible for his subsequent death. President Wilson denied Huerta's provisional government U.S. recognition, and relations between the countries worsened. Incidents at Tampico and Vera Cruz provoked American military units to shell Vera Cruz, to land troops there by force in April 1914, and to occupy the city.

In the same month, as expectations of war grew, General Pershing received orders to move the 8th Brigade, which he commanded, from the

Presidio in San Francisco to Fort Bliss, Texas, there to be ready for an invasion to the south.

Huerta resigned the presidency in July and went into exile in Europe. The American troops withdrew from Vera Cruz in November, and their commander, General Frederick Funston, became head of the Southern Department with headquarters at San Antonio.

The departure of Huerta brought to prominence several regional leaders. Among them were Pascual Orozco, who drew his power fom the area south and west of the capital, Venustiano Carranza, who operated in the northeastern portion of Mexico, and Francisco "Pancho" Villa, who had his base in the states of Chihuahua and Sonora. As these factions sought to establish a central government, Mexico was overrun by endemic disorder, lawlessness, and violence.

To protect American life and property from Mexican violation, Funston received more infantry, cavalry, and artillery forces for deployment along the border. Meanwhile, Pershing remained at Fort Bliss. Realizing that his presence at El Paso would be more permanent than he had originally believed, he was on the point of moving his family from San Francisco when, on August 25, 1915, a tragic fire destroyed his house and killed his wife and three daughters. Only his young son Warren was saved.

The United States government, at first sympathetic to Villa, gradually turned toward Carranza, and on October 15, 1915, Wilson gave de facto recognition to his government. When Villa learned that Carranza had received permission to use American railroads to transport his troops, he became bitterly anti-American.

Letter, GSP, Jr., to Beatrice, October 30, 1915

This is the greatest side show you ever saw. Yesterday a circus came through followed during the afternoon by two trains of Mexicans.

The first train had the damdest bunch of ancient carriages on it you ever dreamed of. Most of them of the vintage of 1850.

There were also several good french autos. One car had an armored gun on it.

The second bunch started through about 4 A.M. I had to get up at 2:30 and ride down to a bridge. I sent some men the other way also at the same time.

I had only three privates with me and it was cold as could be.

When we got near the bridge it was so cold we dismounted to lead [the horses]. One man was 200 yards a head then my self and one man then one 100 yards behind. The object being that if we were jumped some one would be clear to carry the news or act as a reinforcement.

The bridge is in a sort of wash on a curve. As I neared it the man in front galloped back and said he heard mexicans on the bridge. So I mounted the men and trotted to it with our pistols out.

I could see no one so when about 20 yards from the bridge as near as I could get on account of the fence I called "Who is there." A voice which to me sounded foreign said "Friend" and at the same moment six heads with rifles stuck over the bank. Strange to say I did not think of running but wondered if I could get one before I was gotten. I called what are you doing here and to my surprise and delight they answered patrol 13 Cav.

They should not have been there as I was covering the bridge.

The rest of them [13th Cavalry troops sent out to relieve Patton and his men] came by to night so when you get this I will be at Sierra Blanca . . .

P.S. About half the mexican troops are in the words of McCauley, "Ancient men on crutches and women great with child."

All the Mexicans traveling on the railroad guarded by Patton passed safely. At least one quarter of them were women and children. Most of the women were young girls, and those in the officers' cars were quite pretty. The Mexican soldiers had had nothing to eat for three days because their quartermaster, who had received 75 cents per soldier per day to buy food, had "eloped with the whole [sum]."

Patton had been up for two days and nights, but it was interesting duty even though the weather was cold. The Mexican horses were "the thinest thing you ever saw."

Letter, GSP, Jr., to Beatrice, November 1, 1915

. . . one very dirty and fairly pretty girl on the last train told me that she would come and live with me if I would feed her as the mexicans gave her no food. I had to refuse.

It may be fine to die with ones boots on but it is very hard on the feet to sleep with them on which is what I have been doing up to last night.

The Maj. and I gave a dance to the two Mallard girls last night. Their father owns a whole mountain range.

Letter, GSP, Jr., to Aunt Nannie, November 1, 1915

There were several interesting people [at Hot Wells].

One man had hair to his shoulders. He was a good shot. We had some [shooting] matches. I beat him with the rifle and he got me with the pistol.

Another man was a panther hunter and told many strange adventures which others said were true.

He was very dark and commented on it. Saying "Dam it a fellow took me for a Mex and I had to shoot him three times before he believed I was white." This impressed me very much and I assured him that he was the whitest man I ever had seen.

This place is very high and healthy and we have fine quail hunting so I like it.

Tompkins had an attack of dysentery he had contracted in the Philippines, and he went to the hospital at Fort Bliss, leaving Patton in command of the troop "and doing every thing else still am not very busy." He was planning to ride 30 miles to the Love Brothers' ranch for four days to hunt deer, bobcats, and wild pigs, "so I have a regular arsenal with me."

He spent a week visiting an outpost of twelve men near the Love ranch.

Letter, GSP, Jr., to Mr. Ayer, November 11, 1915

. . . about two o'clock we saw two men on horseback and thinking they were bandits we ambushed them only to find that it was an old rancher and his son.

The next day I started for Quin's ranch which is fifty two miles over the mountains. One place the trail is very bad and it took us two hours and a half to go five miles.

A corporal was a head of me going up a very sharp grade when all at once he simply fell off his horse and grabbed his rifle. I asked him what was the trouble and he said a bullet had just missed him. I went up and he said there it goes again. This time I heard it also and once more — it was an eagle screaming at us!

We camped that night at a ranch which was a mad house. The owner Mr. Merivale wanted us to sleep in the house but it was too much inhabited so we slept out in the dust. There is no grass in that place. We cooked our own meals of potato, bacon, and coffee. We had had a hard march so were hungry.

Mr. M. was a great character and the most profane man I ever heard. His particular aversion was Mr. Wilson. He would recount all the wrongs he had suffered from Wilson's mismanagement on the border then he would puff on his pipe and at last say with the deepest feeling God Damn the Dirty S—— B——. I have never heard one say a thing with so much emphasis.

We left there in the morning and went through a place called Pilarres which used to be the home of bandits but our men made them move over the river and the place is in ruins.

Quinn's is a log house up in the high mountains . . . they are the most desolate places you ever saw but sun rise next day was fine except that there were very many skunks very obvious to the nose.

That day we rode forty miles back to a place called Boski Bonito where the Morris Packing Co. has a ranch over the river in Mexico. The ranch is 80 by 75 miles [in size] and very fine. We stopped just over the river from it. The people were just recrossing as the Mexicans had had them driven out for a year.

You never saw so many guns. All sorts of them. I fixed a broken one and they could not do enough for me so I sent my men on to camp 14 miles [away] and stayed all night and went hunting with an old trapper next day. We killed a fox and a bob cat. I have the skins.

. . . just before we got to Boski I came over a high mountain and saw just over the river a column of dust about four miles long. It looked just like that raised by cavalry. I thought that it must be [Pancho] Villa's army so left the trail and went down to the river to see. Giving careful orders to my men just what to do if we were fired on so that at least one would get away to give warning, we then advanced and found that it was a lot of cattle!

I got back here yesterday and will go out again Monday for five days. It is surprising how soft the ground gets [for sleeping] when you are tired.

I like this sort of work a lot.

Two days later he was in El Paso for a brief visit.

Letter, GSP, Jr., to Beatrice, November 13, 1915
[Spent most of the day at the gun store] got a new rifle and a knife

and two pretty carved leather holsters. Also a shooting coat for $15
. . . As Capt. Kirk[patrick]s house is closed I have been staying
here [at the Hotel Paso del Norte] and ordering [full] course dinners which I eat in lonely grandure like I used to do at [Fort] Sheridan . . .

I am going out on the river Monday noon and will be gone until
Saturday but after duck this time or Mexican Lion.

Since he could get no leave at Christmas, Beatrice decided to spend the
holidays in Texas.

Letter, GSP, Jr., to Beatrice, November 16, 1915
Maj Langhorne said I could have three days in El Paso when you
come through so that will be fine. Mrs. Broadhurst wants you to stay
with her but of course you can't as she has but one room.

The Delnorte is not a very wonderful hotel though it is not bad.

Letter, GSP, Jr. (at Sierra Blanca), to Beatrice, November 23, 1915
I am counting the days until you get here . . .

. . . on account of pay day a number of men got drunk. Two were
very drunk at the Saloon and I tried to get them to camp. One tried
to hit me but did not. After I got them to camp I went back to see
how the thing had happened [how they had got so drunk]. As I
started for camp I heard shots and met the two men coming back [to
town] one with a pistol. He was crazy drunk and did not recognize
me but as I was the only one between him and town so I started to
stop him and was pretty close and very scared when the 1st Sgt. ran
up and grabbed him from behind so I had nothing to do.

I killed 18 ducks the other day and had a fine time.

Langhorne's father fell ill, and the major took leave and went to Washington for a month. Captain Rhea and Lieutenants Tompkins and Foster went to Fort Bliss for Thanksgiving. That left Patton commanding
Troop D. Since he was senior to Lieutenant Raborg who remained at
Sierra Blanca in command of Troop A, Patton was the commanding
officer of the post.

Letter, GSP, Jr., to his father, November 24, 1915
About six a clock I got a wire from El Paso from some D[amn]
F[ool] that 200 mexicans were going to rade this place. I don't be-

lieve it at all but have had the men put their guns beside their beds and told them where to form in case of an alarm.

I wish they would come. I have about a hundred men or more and could give them a nice welcome. But it is a baseless rumor as there is nothing here to rade.

I have the Majors Chineese servant so am quite comfortable and can sleep late in the morning . . .

I ordered a new uniform . . . the other day as I don't know when I will go to the P.[hilippine] I.[slands] . . .

Well if this is the eve of battle it is not at all interesting nor so exciting as a polo game.

Despite Patton's nonchalance, when he received the telegram that Chico Cano, a noted bandit, was on his way to raid Sierra Blanca, even though he did not believe it, he called Raborg and the two first sergeants to him and ordered that all men were to sleep with their rifles beside them; they were to assemble, in case of alarm, at the first sergeants' tents. "I hoped that Mr. Cano would come," he wrote his father, "for he would have never got back."

He was going to bed at 11 P.M., when three telegrams arrived. One, signed by Pershing, repeated the warning about Cano. The other two instructed Patton to capture or drive back into Mexico about 80 Carranza men who, near Calduan, had been pushed across the Rio Grande into the United States by Pancho Villa.

Patton at once dispatched three patrols to find out what had happened — one to Finlay, another to Calduan, and the third to Fort Quitman. At 5 A.M., he sent Raborg and Troop A to Fort Quitman with the same mission. "I wanted to go but could not in view of Gen Pershings wire about Cano."

The patrols and Raborg's troop returned to Sierra Blanca on Thanksgiving afternoon, November 25, and reported to Patton what they had learned. On the basis of that information, Patton immediately sent a message.

Letter, GSP, Jr., to Commanding Officer [Colonel Rivers], West Texas Cavalry Patrol District, November 25, 1915, subject: Mexicans near Calduan

. . . [an Indian] said to be trustworthy [told a patrol] that a party of Carranza men about 80 strong crossed the river into Mexico on the night of November 23. This crossing was made some where near Fort Quitman. On the morning of the 24th they were attacked by about 200 Villa troops and retired into U.S. territory leaving seven dead among whom was their leader.

When they managed to get to this side they moved west up the river. The fact of this move . . . is corroborated by a cow boy who saw what he judged to be 50 Mexicans . . . near Finlae the afternoon of the same day (Nov. 24) . . . a mexican at Calduan . . . [said] that he had seen Gen Villa commanding the men on the other side. Lt. Raborg investigated this report and found it not at all substantiated . . .

It does not seem likely to me that this band of Carranza men were organized on this side for in the vacinity of their place of crossing there is no place where eighty horses could get water except at the river and we patrol that. I think it more likely that they are a part of the force of Carranza troops who Capt Dean reports camped opposite [Fort] Hancock.

This supposition is strengthened by the fact that they retreated that way.

I have a patrol out now near [Fort] Quitman.

Letter, GSP, Jr., to his father, November 27, 1915

You may imagine that I did not sleep much the rest of that night [of November 25] for the wind was blowing tuns of dust and I had on every thing but my spurs and pistol.

Next day, had Raborg and his wife and the doctor to dinner and then read until about eleven when going to the depot to mail my report I got a wire from Col. Rivers . . . Saying he had information that there were 80 Carranza soldiers camped on our side of the river near Fort Quitman and to capture them or drive them across. Ending [his message] "act with vigor." I went back and told the 1st Sgt of D troop that we would start at 4 A.M. which would put us at Quitman just at dawn. To do this the men had to get up at 2:30 as they think they have to eat breakfast. I told him to get me up at 3:30 as I prefer sleep to food. I ordered them to take a feed of oats and some sandwiches with them.

I went to bed and decided that to act with vigor meant to attack first and ask questions next. So I decided that if possible I would make a saber charge on the [enemy] camp. I thought I had a medal of honor sewed up and laid awake planning my report until one A.M.

when much to my disgust Capt. Rhea and Mr. Tompkins came and I had to get up and explain the situation to them. Though Tompkins has disentary he decided to go and being a d—— f—— he dicided to leave the sabers [home]. I went to bed about 1:30 and slept well until 3:30. There was a fine moon when we started and the men were in great spirits. They were tickled to death at the chance of a fight.

I took a patrol of ten men by way of Calduan to meet Tompkins at Quitman. I gave orders to fire at any armed man they met. We got to Calduan just at dawn and to Quitman an hour later having gone 32 miles in four and a half hours over trails. We met nothing. There was nothing to meet.

It was just another false rumor. We hunted around Quitman for a while and found 14 Mexicans working on some dug outs whom we were sure were Carranza soldiers but there was no way to prove it though we violated law by searching the house for arms.

When we got to Finlae Tompkins gave out and I brought the troop in. The last 17 miles was awful. The dust was so thick that you could not see the fence at the side of the road.

All the horses stood the trip well enough. We were in the saddle eleven hours and covered between 60 and seventy miles . . . I had a good sleep and feel fine.

Shortly after Thanksgiving, Beatrice started from Massachusetts to visit her husband in Texas.

Letter, GSP, Jr., to Mrs. Ayer, November 28, 1915
[Told about the exciting Thanksgiving] I was pretty tired not having had more than two hours sleep in two nights.

We were all disgusted at not finding the Mexicans. It was fine to see how pleased the men were at the prospect of a fight. I think they would have done well. I had great hopes of seeing how my sabers would work but better luck next time . . .

I will be there [El Paso] to meet her [Beatrice].

At the end of the year, Tompkins rated Patton's service as "excellent" and "very good." Patton was "an excellent field soldier." He was fitted for promotion. He was "a very energetic and capable officer, showing much interest in his profession."

Beatrice stayed with her husband during December and most of January. When she decided that El Paso was a suitable place for her and the babies to live, Patton requested quarters on the post.

Letter, GSP, Jr. (from Sierra Blanca), to Aunt Nannie, January 10, 1916

B and I went on a duck hunt to the river. We rode the 26 miles then hunted all afternoon and slept in the open then hunted till two next day and came on in. We got thirteen fine duck most of them Mallard and B killed two of them besides a quail and a pluver so she had a fine time though she did not like the cooking so did not eat much . . .

We have only about a week more to do out here and think that we will get quite a large house at [Fort] Bliss. This is fine news as we feared that we would draw only a two room one.

We are now enjoying our weekly dust storm so things are pretty bad.

Soon after Beatrice departed for Massachusetts, Patton came down with acute respiratory influenza and entered the hospital at Fort Bliss. When he was discharged, he remained at El Paso, for his troop had come in from the field. A day or two later, Mr. Patton, who had been ill, came from California to spend a few weeks with his son.

Letter, GSP, Jr., to Beatrice, January 29, 1916

I had fever 104 for a day or so and lost lots of weight which was very satisfactory for I was too fat . . .

Pa is here and feels much better.

Patton was assigned a good house at Fort Bliss, and his furniture arrived at the end of January. Helped by his father and his striker, he moved into his house and started unpacking. Since it was impossible to find a Chinese servant, he wired Mrs. Ayer and asked her to send a maid named Julia. Until her arrival, father and son hired the wife of a soldier to keep the house clean for $17 per month; wash was extra.

Letter, GSP, Jr., to Beatrice, January 31, 1916

The Adventure magazine has not accepted my story so I shall try some other probably the Wide World Magazine.

The story he referred to was probably very much like a piece he wrote around this time about Willie, an American who was fighting in the French Army. Realizing during an attack that he had lost his identification tag and fearing that Helen, the girl he loved back home, would not even know it if he died, Willie started running back to his lines. In the course of his flight he was fired on by some Germans. He became cold as ice, lost his dread, faced the enemy, and killed them all. Curious to see the dead soldiers, he entered the enemy trench. One man was still alive, and Willie turned him over and looked into "the dying face of his mothers buttler Ernst." At that moment, several Germans captured Willie. They executed him because they believed he had been murdering the wounded. The letter telling about poor Willie's death arrived in his hometown on the day "she [Helen] married young Ainsworth."

Early in February, Mr. Patton left El Paso for home and Beatrice and the children arrived. Julia came somewhat later and was, consequently, of little help in getting the house clean.

Letter, GSP, Jr., to his father, February 17, 1916

Beatrice did not think much of the cleaning ability of our find [the soldier's wife] but after nearly making her self sick she has at last got the house into what she considers [good] shape and it is really quite nice.

With the family settled into a nice house on post, life was pleasant. He and Beatrice looked forward to a long stay at El Paso, where the hunting was fine and the polo passable.

But Patton hardly forgot the war in Europe. To remind General Wood that he was still available for more exciting service, he dropped the general a line and discussed a new notion, the idea of turning cavalrymen into mounted infantrymen, that was being talked about and that he disliked.

Letter, Wood (Headquarters Eastern Department, Governors Island, New York) to GSP, Jr., March 3, 1916

My dear Mr. Patton: Yours of the 27th received. You are quite right as to the mounted infantry proposition. This is impressed on me every day. It will be a long step backward if we revert to the old drill regulations. However, there is no use in being discouraged. It is one of those things we have got to keep at until we put it over. The instruction you gave at Riley is very valuable and will eventually count. With kind regards to you both, Sincerely yours,

• • •

Nita came to visit the Pattons, and though she was rather restricted in her activities because the wind was blowing hard every day, she met Pershing in the course of the social functions on post and felt herself attracted to him. He seemed to like her company and conversation. He was fifty-five and a widower. She was not yet twenty-nine and unmarried.

Tompkins would soon rate Patton: "He cooperates energetically and loyally with others. General estimate: A very energetic, and capable officer."

Major C. D. Rhodes, formerly commandant at Fort Riley, now president of the Cavalry Equipment Board in Washington, wrote to inform Patton that the Board was considering making some changes in the model 1913 saber that Patton had designed. Before doing so, the Board was interested in Patton's opinions. What, specifically, were Patton's views on the following questions?

Replying the same day, Patton copied the questions in order and took six typed single-spaced pages to give his answers.

Was the saber too heavy? Or if the same weight were kept, could it be better distributed? The saber weighed two ounces more than the latest French saber, about the same as the Swedish saber, and one ounce less than the English saber used in the line regiments; the English Guards used a much heavier weapon. "From the above it would appear that the present saber is not too heavy." The distribution of weight "was very carefully arranged to give the maximum effect to the charge with the point and to the lunge . . . In this particular the present saber is the superior of any existing weapon in the hands of foreign nations." It felt awkward to the inexperienced and perhaps also to those who were used to the old saber.

Its length? It was one and one-fifth inches shorter than the French saber and one-half inch longer than that used by the British — "about the average of well-instructed armies."

Since, in the event of war, sabers would be used by Regular and Volunteer recruits who would be non-experts, would it be better to give the saber a slight curve for cutting? Curving the blade did not improve the ability to cut, and this was supported by the facts of history, which he cited at great length — writing of chain and plate armor, the Scottish highlanders, the English revolution and Cromwell, Rupert, the dragoons of Charles XII, and Peter the Great. He was unalterably opposed to curving the blade, for "the curve is sufficient to interfere greatly with the use of the point."

Could the hilt be improved? No, it provided balance.

Would the current saber be the best all-around weapon for an army of Volunteer cavalry sent into the field after perhaps only six months of training? Yes, and he based his claim on the "universal practice of all nations except Russia and Japan. I believe that their retention of the cutting weapon is due to oriental tradition."

After going on at some length on the proper way of using the saber and why, he concluded: Since other nations

adopt our ideas in shooting it seems only reasonable that we profit by their work with the saber.

I appreciate very much the honor you have done me in permitting me to express my views. I feel very earnestly on this subject which I have examined and studied ever since I was sixteen. If there is any point I could further explain I will consider it a great privilege if you will allow me to come to Rock Island on leave at my own expense at any time and for any period you may designate.

Letter, GSP, Jr., to his father, March 8, 1916

[The Cavalry Equipment Board was thinking of changing back to the curved saber] so I am very much excited and will probably have to go to Rock Island Arsenal to convince them what D[amned] F[ool]'s they are. Still I shall enjoy the trip as any absence from this place is welcome. . . .

What are you doing about the senate. You ought to run as I think there is much fear that Wilson will be reelected.

As it turned out, Patton was not about to go to the Rock Island Arsenal. The day after he wrote that letter, Pancho Villa and a band of several hundred men raided Columbus, New Mexico, shot up the town, and killed seventeen Americans.

The stage was set for the Punitive Expedition into Mexico under Pershing. Patton was about to emerge from the wings.

V

Mexico

"This may be the start of a very interesting period."

CHAPTER 16

Chasing Villa

"I have at last succeeded in getting into a fight."

Letter, GSP, Jr., to his father, March 12, 1916

Dear Papa: Well at last it seems that we are about to go over the line [the Mexican border]. In fact unless something very strange occurs it is sure we will. It is the general opinion here that this movement will mean war and not simply a punitative trip, because as the rumor got out the Carranza troops opposite here started digging trenches and on thursday night had machine guns placed to sweep the camps of the 16th and 6th Inft. camped in the city [El Paso]. Also a band of these same patriots [Carranzistas] tried to stop Maj. Tompkins on his return from chasing Villa [south of Columbus into Mexico].

Personally I hope that they [Carranza and his government] break with us before we cross [the border] as if they don't we would have to leave them [the Carranzistas] in our rear which in the event of trouble would be very awkward.

Things are being conducted with great secrecy but it is thought that our force will consist at the start of about nine regiments of Cavalry, 7500 men and one regiment of mounted artillery. This force will be divided in two or possibly three columns.

The troops will go at peace strength of 75 men [each] which is better as it removes the necessity of taking about 30 recruits.

So far the only orders we have are to be ready. The men are not even required to stay on the post. There is a grape vine rumor that we start Wednesday or Thursday but this has no foundation in fact.

I think that we will have much more of a party than many think as Villas men at Columbus fought well and the country [in Mexico] is very bad for regular [U.S.] troops. There are no roads and no maps and no water for the first 100 miles. If we can induce him [Villa] to fight it will be all right but if he breaks up [his band into small groups and fights a guerrilla war] it will be bad, especially if we have Carrenza on our rear.

They can't beat us but they will kill a lot of us. Not me though.

If it turns out to be a long war there ought to be volunteer regiments later so if I do well keep an eye out and get me a job. As I told you when you were here I think it would be a mistake to enter the Vol. at first but if one had a reputation in the regulars a high commission could be gotten later but it ought to be a regiment with enough pull to get over the line and not simply to stay on the border.

It occurs to me that if Japan is after us now is her time as no one on earth can help us. So this may be the start of a very interesting period.

Since writing the foregoing I have discovered that . . . we [the 8th Cavalry] are not going but will sit here and watch the rest go past us. It is hell to be so near a fine fight and not get in it . . . so I went to General Pershing and asked him to make me as an aid[e]. He said he would if he could so I still have hopes. Of course the rest of us will go sooner or later but I would like to be in the first outfit and not tag along after all the fun is over.

There should be a law killing fat colonels on sight [the colonel commanding the 8th Cavalry, his regiment, was fat].

Now don't let this chance of my going to Mexico detur you from running for the senate. In fact if there is a war your presence in Washington would be more useful to me than at any other time. Another point is that if we are at war Mr. Wilson is almost sure to be reelected so your chances are vastly improved. So do something and do it at once.

You must declair your self and you must do it quickly otherwise it will be too late.

On that day, he started a journal of his activities.*

According to his diary, on March 12, Patton "was worried all day for fear the 8th Cav would not go to Mexico." He knew that Pershing was a

---

* A year later, after the dissolution of the expeditionary force, General Pershing, who knew that Patton had kept a diary, asked to borrow it to refresh his memory of the events and their sequence. Patton had the diary typed for the General, but he judiciously edited it, omitting certain details, expanding and explaining others as his own memory was roused, improving the English, spelling, and style. I have here used the original, supplementing it with additional facts mentioned in the revised version.

stickler for physical conditioning, and he feared that his own regimental commander would be judged unfit for extended and difficult field service.

Patton was Officer of the Day. It was a rotating position, usually for 24 hours, assumed according to roster by all the officers on post — except the high-ranking commanders and certain others who were excused because of the nature or importance of their regular duties. The OD, as he was called, was in charge of routine matters, keeping order, welcoming visitors, making sure that ceremonies were held on time, and the like.

He was sitting on the porch of the headquarters building after lunch, smoking his pipe, when he learned that his regiment would definitely not go to Mexico. He immediately went to his regimental adjutant, Captain Barnhardt, who had formerly and briefly been his troop commander, and "asked him to recommend me to Gen Pershing as aid[e]." Learning that Major John L. Hines would be the adjutant general of Pershing's expeditionary force, Patton went to him and asked the same thing. He repeated his request to Lieutenant Martin C. Shallenberger, one of Pershing's two regular aides.

Later that afternoon, while he was in the OD's office, he was called by Pershing, who said he had learned that Patton wanted to go with him. Patton emphatically affirmed this, and the general said he would take him if he could.

"I called [on him] after supper that night and said I was good with [newspaper] correspondents."

On the morning of March 13, "General P called up at 8:30 to say I could go as aid on the condition that I be relieved later for Lt. [James L.] Collins who had been his aid before" and who was absent but would join later.

"This was all right as it took me any way." All he needed was an opportunity to show how hard he could work, how devoted he could be, how indispensable he could become. And this, of course, is what happened. He proved himself useful in a number of capacities — as aide to the general, as his assistant on inspection trips, as his confidant on recreational horseback rides taken for exercise, as message bearer, as headquarters commandant who looked after the mess, the motor vehicles, the horses, the escort troops, the guards, and the clerks, and as a general factotum, eager, willing, and anxious to do what was asked and more. He was also extremely engaging and likable. Boyish and enthusiastic, he was always very respectful and loyal to his superiors and to all officers of superior rank. His endurance and stamina, his uncomplaining nature, and his desire to do more than was required won Pershing's affection and that of all his staff members.

On that day, March 13, the headquarters of Pershing's 8th Brigade published General Orders 7, which detached Patton from the 8th Cavalry for service as aide-de-camp. Several days later, Punitive Expedition Headquarters issued Special Orders 2, relieving him from this duty. But by this time, he had proved his value, and he remained simply as a member of the headquarters, still on detached service from his regiment.

Eight years later, Patton recalled in a speech entitled "Personal Glimpses of General Pershing" why he was selected to accompany the expedition:

> I was Officer of the Day . . . and learned by grapevine methods and good eyesight that a Punitive Expedition was in progress of formation, gleaning at the same time the knowledge that my regiment was not to form part of it. Being, however, determined to participate, I got permission to speak to the General and asked him to take me to Mexico in any capacity. He replied "Every one wants to go; why should I favor you?" "Because" I answered, "I want to go more than any one else." This modest reply failed to get any answer except a curt "That will do."
>
> Fortune in the form of an alleged wire tapper, whom I apprehended, favored me so that I saw him again and renewed my request, with similar results. Undiscouraged I then went home and packed my bedding roll and saddle. At 5 o'clock next morning the telephone rang and on answering it the General's voice inquired, "Lieut. Patton, how long will it take you to get ready?" When he heard that I was ready he exclaimed "I'll be G.—— D.—— You are appointed Aide."
>
> It was three years before I learned from him why he took me. It seems that in '98 Lieut. Pershing was an instructor at West Point. The policy was that no instructors should go to the war. Lieut. Pershing used every normal means to secure an exception and finally went A.W.O.L. to Washington where, by a line of talk similar to the one I employed on him in 1916, he secured the detail to Cuba.

When she learned that Patton was to go with Pershing, "B acted fine and did not cry or any thing."

Patton obtained authority to take his striker and his horse, then

had lunch at 11:30 A.M. went to attend to loading of Hq's horses at
12:15. Helped Maj. Hines in office coading telegrams till 5:30. Then
the Gen, Nita, B, Maj. Hines and my self Rode to the train in my
machine. Lt. Shallenberger went ahead to decoy the newspapermen
away so they would not bother the General, and we could board the
train unseen. I got the Gen a little lunch on the train . . . Got to
Columbus [N.M.] at 10:30 after leaving the train about a mile from
town and finding the staff [who reported to Pershing] . . . I went
back and unloaded the Generals baggage then waited around until 5
A.M. to get the Hdqs horses off. Went to bed.

Diary

March 14: worked all day organizing the Expedition, receiving reports, and dodging newspaper men . . . Gen P and I rode around
camp at 5 P.M. All was in pretty good order.

March 15: Selected what part of the baggage was to go. Each officer
only allowed bedding roll . . .

We had three wall tents, two conical wall tents, and three
wagons . . .

At noon Gen P told me to take two Fords and 7 Sig.[nal] Corps
men and go to Los Cienegos [to] get the Telefunken [radio] set
there and take it to Col. Dodd . . . at Culbersons Ranch . . .
started at 12:05 PM. Reached Cienigos 100 miles at 4:30 PM . . .
Reached Culberson's Ranch at 7 P.M. delivered order to him. At 9
PM as the Gen had not appeared I suggested to Col Dodd that he
wire and see if the Gen had started. We could not get them [on the
radio] so we sent a car.

March 16: orders from Gen for Dodd to start . . . [did so] at 1:15
A.M. Gen P . . . and some others arrived at [Culberson's Ranch] 2
am. We started . . . at 2:45 am. We crossed the line [into Mexico]
at 3:16 am . . . [made 52 miles] and some Mexicans cooked us a
good dinner. The Gen loaned me a saddle blanket to replace one
that someone stole from me while we were eating. I stole another one
for him.

March 17: got to Cases Grandes (or Tres Alamos) 58 miles . . .
just north of Colonia Dublan [a Mormon community] . . . Got to
bed 11 P.M. very tired. Slept well. My horse fell on me this day but

did not hurt me much. Broke electric light [flashlight]. . . . Lost 2 mules and 8 horses [on the march].

March 18: Moved entire command to river. Fine camp. Plenty of water. Took [bought] hay and corn from Mormons. Set up wireless and got Columbus . . . Gen P planned campaign that night under large tree near river. Had only 1 flashlight for map . . . Had dinner with Mormon Bishop Call. Fine man good dinner. Had bath.

March 19: moved Hdqs to group of big trees across the river . . . arranged for arrival of Aero Sqdn at Colonia Dublan. Shallenberger and Collins arrived with four machines at 10 AM — 1 Buick, 1 Dodge, and 2 Fords . . . [At Pershing's order] put one correspondent in arrest for sending message with out authority. Rearranged duties of aides.

The aides decided what each would do as his primary task. Shallenberger would look after the headquarters personnel, Collins would handle the general's personal chores, Patton would be in charge of the orderlies, guides, loaders, and, in addition, serve as assistant to the Intelligence Officer.

Pershing's staff was extremely small, and as a consequence the three aides were extremely busy. Colonel De Rosey C. Cabell was chief of staff; in 1919, he would be a major general commanding the Southern Department. Major Hines was adjutant general; he would command a division, then a corps in France during World War I, and would later succeed Pershing as U.S. Army Chief of Staff. Major James A. Ryan was the intelligence officer. Captain W. B. Burtt was Colonel Cabell's assistant; he would be a general officer in World War I.

A photograph in the San Francisco *Chronicle* of April 12, printing the "First Pictures from the Front Passed by Army Censor," showed eight officers "somewhere in Mexico" standing in front of tents, wearing field uniforms and campaign hats. Pershing in the center was flanked on one side by Colonel L. G. Berry, listed as supply officer, Cabell, and Shallenberger; on the other by Hines, listed as the censor, Major J. B. Clayton, the chief medical officer, and Burtt. In the rear, as befitted a young man, was Patton. The uniforms were anything but uniform. Cabell, a short stocky man with white mustache, wore a sheepskin coat, Berry a sweater. Pershing had on a blouse buttoned to the chin. The others were in khaki

ARIZONA

NEW MEXICO

Columbus

El Paso

Douglas

Culberson Ranch

Finlay

Sierra Blanca

Hot Wells

TEXAS

Colonia Dublan

Casas Grande

SONORA

CHIHUAHUA

Rio Grande

Namiquipa

Santo Tomas

Bachinivia

Rubio

Guerrero

Santa Ysabel

Sativo

COAHUILA

Parral

Providencia

SINALOA

DURANGO

Tepahuanes

Area of
Punitive Expedition, 1916

+++++ Railroads

0   50   100   200

MILES

SKB

shirts open at the neck — all except Patton, who was wearing a tie, the only one in the group.

Diary

March 20: aeroplanes arrived in morning . . . great trouble landing on account of the altitude of 4000 feet.

March 22: nothing but duty around camp till night when I went to [R.R. station] . . . to get Gen. Garcia and his two aides . . . talked to him all the way up [to camp]. He was well dressed in O.D. cut like French [uniform. He had a] pearl mounted pistol. Gen G had dinner with Gen P and scratched himself all the time.

March 24: I volunteered to go by Auto to Col Dodd. He [Pershing] told me to get ready. Then decided to go with me. Finally his staff dissuaded him . . . Woke . . . to find Gen. telling Maj Ryan and I to get ready to go with him to Namiquipa. Took three autos one Guide and four guards . . . Lt [John] Lucas gave us dinner in dug out. Gen had only 1 blanket and slept in Auto. Lucas, Maj. R and I combined our blankets and slept on oats. Very cold. All I took off was my field glasses.

March 31: Reached Providencia at 7 A.M. [bringing order from General Pershing] . . . I had a discussion with the maj. For the way he interpreted the order did not comply with the [General's] plan. I told him I would take responsibility for moving in the way which I thought the order intended. He acquiesced. Searched mountains and all dwellings in area . . . It got cold sleeted snowed, hailed and finally rained. We all suffered much. Reached San G.[eronimo] at 4:30 having riden at a walk for 16 hours with one hour rest. Still very cold. Gen. approved what I had done. Took a big drink and went to bed 11 P.M. Slept well. Awoke at 6 covered with snow.

April 1: Gen sent me to Namiquipa with dispatches in an auto giving as complete an account as possible of Dod[d]'s fight at Guerrero . . . On the way I inspected a hacienda where every one was drunk. One old lady had Smallpox. I took one man [with me] because he had on soldiers shoes. On way to town he told me he lived in Namiquipa and that his children had Small Pox. They did, so I let him go.

Letter, GSP, Jr., to Aunt Nannie, April 2, 1916

[At altitude of 7500, cold with snow and sleet.] Day before yesterday I was with a column hunting Villa. We rode from 11:20 PM till

4:30 P.M. with a halt of only one hour but found no body. We are now at a big hacienda but it is all ruined by various bandits. There are wild duck on the lake near by who are very tame. The hard riding we are doing is killing lots of our horses. So far I have ridden very little so my horses are all right. We get plenty to eat but nothing else to amuse us.

Diary

April 3: I left in auto at 1 P.M. to take message [to] Col Dodd at Santo Tomas. Had six punctures but unable to find Colonel. Got in to camp very cold about 11 P.M.

GSP, Jr., "Personal Glimpses of General Pershing," 1924

From March until the end of May he [Pershing] slept on the ground without a tent, doubling up with one of his Aides for the additional warmth secured by the two blankets, but no frost or snow prevented his daily shave so that by personal example he prevented the morale destroying growth of facial herbage which hard campaigns so frequently produce . . .

During our first stay at [Colonia] Dublan . . . the General made frequent motor . . . trips to our advanced detachments 30 to 50 miles in the front and never carried anything except one blanket and his toilet articles.

When he moved forward to a place called San Geronimo Ranch, the American Punitive Expedition Headquarters consisted of the General, Colonel J. Ryan . . . myself, a stenographer, a cook, 3 drivers, and 4 soldiers. For days at a time there were no other troops within miles. The office consisted of a box in front of the Dodge car which now carried the General and whose headlight formed his only reading lamp. Shortly after the battle of Guerrero I was sent to find General Dodd and failed to locate him. Two days later it was requisite to send orders to the 11th Cavalry located somewhere . . . to the south of us. Almost a needle in a haystack. As I started the General shook me warmly by the hand saying "Be careful, there are lots of Villiastas." Then still holding my hand he said "But remember, Patton, if you don't deliver that message don't come back." It was delivered!

Early in April Patton wrote and dispatched a number of messages, all dictated or ordered by Pershing, to the columns pursuing Villa and to his immediate superior, General Funston. Patton was proud of this duty and carefully saved many of the communications he wrote on the pads of U.S. Army Field Messages.

Letter, GSP, Jr., to his father, April 6, 1916

I had a most exciting ride the other night. I went 26 miles through the mountains at night with two men. We expected to be jumped and once hid from some six horse wagons whom we thought were Mexicans, I did not know where the troops I was hunting were but I finally found them by the reflection of their [camp] fires on a cloud.

On the way back I saw a flock of wild Turkey but could not shoot at them as I did not want to advertise my presence.

I crossed the continental divide at about 8000 feet and it was very cold. But hot by day. I have never been so dirty in my life but hope to get a bath some day.

The general is fine and a great soldier full of energy. I think he likes me almost too much for I have volunteered to take several messages which he has refused to let me do for fear of my getting hurt.

I am very well and most interested.

Patton came to know the war correspondents traveling with the headquarters — Floyd P. Gibbons, who would be a prominent reporter in World War I, where he would lose an eye, and later an internationally known journalist; Frank B. Elser of the New York *Times;* R. Dunn of the New York *Tribune;* and Blakesley of the Associated Press. Their acquaintance did him no harm.

A New York *Tribune* story in April by an unnamed correspondent presented a reporter's conversation with Patton as follows:

Then I told my intention to his [Pershing's] athletic young aid — a victor in the last Olympic games, by the way.

"Remember, if you go up there," he said with military frankness and duplicity, "I don't know it. And it's at your own risk."

Patton learned much from Pershing, his procedures, habits, and methods. He also became familiar with the tactical use of the primitive airplanes and motor vehicles of the expedition.

Diary

April 10: 3 planes scouted 700 square miles. Scouting failed to find either our men or the enemy.

April 11: Gen P, Maj R, Capt Kromer, Capt. [William O.] Reed myself with 6 dodge cars one truck left . . . for Sativo at 10 A.M. We had with us 23 rifles [to guard the General]. At San Ysabel we found the road impassable so made a Detour . . . found 2 planes about 3 miles from Sateva with pilots hiding in bushes. Trucks of aero squadron with 18 [men] of 6th Inf as Guards got in at 10:45. They were fired on 18 miles out. About 150 shots were exchanged. No one was hit. One man got a bullet through his hat. Lt. Davis in command of guards driving last dodge in column bumped truck when firing started and broke radiator. Dodge and one side car motorcycle abandoned.

April 13: Capt. Reed, Lt Winters with 15 men and two trucks left to investigate shooting and salvage cars . . . returned with car and cycle. Both had been burned, Used parts of car for extras [spare parts].

April 15: It was clear that Maj Tompkins had been attacked by Carransa troops. Full report was handed to correspondents. We all left camp at 10:04 in 8 autos. We had 30 rifles . . . We past Santa Ysabel just at dark where a Ford broke down. We feared being shot up.

April 16: Gen came here to get a wire to Columbus because wireless and airplanes were too unreliable. Gen had had no sleep for two nights but worked all day. I had a bath.

April 20: Fine day. Nothing to do. I trapped chipmunk.

April 21: I inspected horses for Gen.

April 22: I wrote memo for Gen on feeding of horses.

April 22 (Revised Version): Gen P published a memorandum relating to the feeding of the horses.

GSP, Jr., "Personal Glimpses of General Pershing," 1924

The evening of the Par[r]al fight (of which we then knew nothing) the General decided to move to a place called Satavo, 480 miles south of the border. We knew that the 11th Cavalry, a Squadron of the 13th, and another of the 10th were in that direction, but could get no reports. The move was for the purpose of getting closer to them and of gaining touch by means of airplanes which were to fly to, and join us in the morning.

The trip was made in three open cars and our force all told was 15 men with 9 rifles. The country to be traversed consisted of 90 miles of unmapped and semi-hostile mountain and desert. Night came on, when suddenly the headlights of the leading car in which I rode as guide showed an armed Mexican, balking our way, while in the bushes on either side a veritable army seemed to lurk. The leading car stopped while, according to previously issued orders, the second car with the General, came up on its right; the third car on the right of the second, thus sandwiching the General's car between the other two. The eight soldiers sprang out and took their allotted places to cover all avenues of attack. With halting Spanish and beating heart, I rushed forward to solve the problem, always most difficult, as to the friendliness or hostility of the Mexicans. I had just prejudiced my hope of eternal salvation by a valuable description of ourselves as the advance guard of an automobile regiment when the General appeared at my side and frustrated my efforts at deception by declaring himself to be General Pershing, and demanding Why in H—— these people dared to stop him. For a moment I had visions of a second Mountain Meadow massacre with ourselves in the role of victims, but the commanding presence of the General and his utter disregard of danger over-awed the Mexicans and we went on, though personally it was more than a mile before I ceased feeling bullets entering my back. Two hours later a convoy of three trucks with airplane spare parts and gas was attacked by these same Mexicans. The incident respires the statement attributed to Ceaser that "Fortune favors the bold."

Letter, GSP, Jr., to his father, April 25, 1916
[President] Wilson ought to take iron or something to stiffen his back . . . we have helped the army and especially the cavalry by this trip [meaning that the Punitive Expedition had strengthened the Army image in the eyes of the public] . . .
Please don't put off the Senate affair too long if you have even an even chance of winning.

Diary
April 27: Gen staied in camp. Very hot and dusty wind storm. Gen and I went for a ride about camp and to inspect forage.

Letter, GSP, Jr., to his father, April 28, 1916
We have been very idle ever since reaching here and it is most

tiresome sitting out on a bluff over a river in the sun and dust. We can't go to town because they shoot at us now and then and the gen. does not want to start any thing unless he can finish it . . .

[Fine game country, with ducks, deer, bear, wild turkey] also wild Mexicans so if you go out hunting you are very apt to be hunted . . .

Intervention in this country would be the most futile thing in the world. We must take it or leave it. If we leave it ruine total and complete will follow . . . If we take the country we could settle it and these people [here] would be happier and better off. . . .

It looks to me as if T.R. [Theodore Roosevelt] would get the Presidency. How will that affect you. Don't stop trying.

Diary

May 2: Troop C [Lieut] Swift and I went to San Megel [Miguel] . . . At a ranch 6 miles north of San Megel we took a man [who was] the uncle of [Julio] Cardenes [a Villista]. Surrounded San M[and] found wife and baby of Cordenes. Allowed no one to leave. Camped near house [waiting for Cardenes to come] . . . Tried to get information out of uncle. Failed.

Letter, GSP, Jr., to his father, May 1916

I got permission to go out with the 13th Cavalry to hunt for Mr. Julio Cardenes. We captured his uncle and wife and baby. The uncle was a very brave man and nearly died before he would tell me any thing.

Diary

May 3: Left camp at 2:55 A.M. Walked and lead to foot of mountains. Got there about 4:30. Halted for day light. Found Swift was missing. Sent three men back to find him and went ahead. Cut many trails but none fresh. Found big Villa camp with corrals etc. Swift had not yet showed up. Decided to water and feed. Killed a steer. Swift came. Heard two shots in hills. I took four men to investigate Spillsbury [Lemuel Spilsbury, a Mormon guide] went to find trail. When I got back at 9 AM Lt Rogers 13 Cav was there ordering us back to Rubio. Reached Rubio at 12 n[oon]. Took bath.

May 6: Part of 13 Cav [moved to another location] . . . Their [old] camp [site] was dirty so I [rode after them and] caught them . . . and one troop came back to clean up.

A week later, the highlight of Patton's service in Mexico took place.

Diary

May 14: Gen sent me with three autos and ten men 6 inf [and] Howerdal and Lunt [guides] to secure corn. I was to pay 4 P[esos] per hectaires of corn delivered [to camp at Lake] Itascate. Went to a ranch at Coyote, Rubio, Salsito, secured 250 hectaires of corn. Decided to go to San Migel and see if I could find Julio Cardenes. Did so and killed him and two of his men, a Captain named Isadore Lopez and an orderly Juan Garza. Saw 40 or 50 mounted men approaching at a gallop so left. Got five [ammunition] belts three rifles one pistol two sabres two saddles. Fight started about 1230 PM lasted till 12:45.

Letter, GSP, Jr., to Beatrice, May 14, 1916

As you have probably seen by the papers, I have at last succeeded in getting into a fight. The Gen. sent me with three autos ten infantry soldiers and two guides, to get some corn in the vicinity of Rubio, which is 20 miles from here . . . I have always expected to be scared [in a fight] but was not nor was I excited. I was afraid they would get away. I never heard a bullet but some say that you do not at such close range. I wondered a little at first that I was not hit, they were so close.

Pershing authorized what would later be called a public or press release — information to be used by the newspapers.

Telegram, Pershing (Lake Itascate, Mexico) to Major William R. Sample (Columbus, N.M.), May 15, 1916

Lieutenant Patton with small detachment was sent to Rubio, twenty miles east of here, yesterday to search for corn. Upon arrival at adjoining ranch he was fired upon by Julio Cardenas, Villista captain. Latter and two companions were killed by Patton's detachment which suffered no casualties.

Letter, GSP, Jr., to his father, May 15, 1916

Dear Papa: At last I succeeded in getting into a fight. I went out yesterday to buy corn and as I got near to San Miguel where I had been before hunting for Julio Cardenes I decided to combine business with pleasure and see if I could get him . . . I was much less scared than I had thought I would be, in fact all that worried me was the fear they would get away.

I am very well. With much love your devoted son George S. Patton
Jr

Run for the *Senate*.

Letter, GSP, Jr., to Aunt Nannie, May 17, 1916

I was in great luck to be in it [the fight] also not to get hit at all.
Three of them [were] shooting at me about 15 yds off. I kept wondering why they did not hit me. The guns seemed pointed right at
me.

I did not get made [angry] as one is supposed to do but was worried for fear they would get away.

People have been teasing me about not using the saber on them.

The Gen. calls me his bandit and is very complimentary. But as a
matter of fact it was pure luck or fate.

I have a fine silver mounted saddle I got from Cardenes after he
was dead. It will look well in Pa's office. I also have his sword.

Patton wrote several full accounts of the Rubio affair. His letters to
Beatrice and to his father (written in the first person) and his official
report (in the third person) were all substantially the same. So was a
letter (written in the third person) he sent in January 1928 to an officer
who had asked for his account. And so was a newspaper story by Elser,
who spoke with Patton immediately after the event.

As reconstructed from these narratives, this is what happened.

After securing corn at Coyote and at Rubio, Patton noticed at Rubio
50 or 60 men who, though unarmed, were "a bad lot. One of my guides
Holmdahl, an ex Villa soldier, recognized a number of old friends among
them. Rubio is about 10 miles south of San Miguel, and it was at this
place that Palmer Swift and I so nearly caught Julio Cordenas so I decided to go and see if I could get him."

He and Swift twelve days earlier had searched the ranches of Saltillo
and San Miguelito, four and ten miles, respectively, north of Rubio. Patton knew that Cárdenas' uncle was at the former place, his wife at the
latter. Perhaps Cárdenas was visiting one or the other.

"Having as just staited searched these ranches he knew their arrangements completely." Both were quite similar in location and construction.
The houses were about 200 yards east of the road running north from
Rubio. Each was "fairly large" and built of wings formed into a rough

square about a central courtyard. The main entrance, an arched gateway, faced eastward, looking toward a stream flowing parallel with the road. West of the road was a mountain range. If Villistas or bandits were surprised at either house, they would try to escape, no doubt, into these hills. They would have to cross the road to do so.

A horseman could emerge from the interior court only through the main gate facing east, but a man could jump from any of several windows high on the western wall of the house.

As soon as Patton and his men were out of Rubio, he stopped and explained what he planned to do. He had ten soldiers and two civilian scouts named E. L. Holmdahl and Heaton Lunt. He had three cars, two driven by civilian chauffeurs, the third by a soldier. They were altogether a party of fifteen, and they traveled five to a car.

Patton rode in the leading automobile, driven by Leonard Hudnall of El Paso, who was to speed up as soon as he came within sight of the ranch, pass the house, and halt just north of it. The driver and Holmdahl would remain in the car while Patton, Lunt, and a soldier ran across the northern end of the hacienda. The second car, driven by the soldier, and the third, by Bill Walker of Arizona, were to stop just south of the house. Three men from each of these cars were to race across the southern face of the ranch. That would leave six men in the cars to cover the road, and the northern, western, and southern sides of the house. The other nine would meet on the eastern side and search the place.

They carried out this plan at Saltillo but found only Cárdenas' uncle, who agreed to furnish some corn at Patton's offering price. Something in the behavior of the uncle led Patton to believe that Cárdenas might be home.

The party proceeded toward San Miguelito, some six miles away. "About a mile and a half south of the house the ground is lower than the house. And one cannot be seen [from the house] until topping this rise, as soon as I came over this therefore, I made my car go at full speed." While the car was approaching the house and racing past it, Patton saw three old men and a boy skinning a cow in the front yard east of the house. "One of these ran to the house and at once returned and went on with his work."

When his car stopped just beyond the northwestern corner of the ranch, Patton "jumped out and carrying my rifle in my left hand hurried" along the northern edge of the house. "Lunt who was unarmed came with me, a little behind, I rounded the [northeastern] corner and walked about half way to the gate" — "the big arched door, leading to the patio."

The two other cars had stopped near the southeastern corner of the ranch, and six men rushed along the southern face of the building. Because they were unfamiliar with the outbuildings and corrals, they took longer than Patton to get to the eastern side.

"When I was about 15 yards from the [main] gate three armed men dashed out on horseback." They carried rifles and pistols. Seeing Patton, they wheeled to the right toward the southeastern corner.

"So schooled was I not to shoot, that I merely drew my pistol and waited to see what would happen and if they were Carrencistas." Pershing's orders prohibited Americans from firing against Mexicans until their hostile identity was certain. "Not sure who they were" — "as I thought they might be carranza men" — "Lt Patton ordored them to halt but they kept on until they saw the [my] men coming from the southe."

"When they got to the corner they saw my men coming that way and turned back" — "and galloped at Lunt and Lt. Patton firing" — "all three shot at me, one bullet threw gravel on me. I fired back with my new pistol, five times" — "the range was about twenty yards."

He did not know it then but two of his shots struck home — one hitting a man in the right arm, breaking it, the other entering the belly of his horse.

"Then my men came around the corner and started to shoot, as I was in their line of fire I told Lunt to come back around the corner, as the men were apt to hit us, moreover I did not know who was in the house, and there were a lot of windows only a few feet from our right side, just as I got around the corner three bullets hit it [the corner] about seven feet from the ground, and put adobe" — "dobe dust" — "all over me."

As a result, he did not see the man and the horse his bullets had struck turn into the arched gateway and reenter the interior court.

"I reloaded my pistol." Holmdahl and the civilian driver Hudnall, having heard the shooting, had come running, and they joined Patton, Lunt, and the soldier who had trailed Lunt and had now come up.

"I started back [around the corner] when I saw a man on a horse come right in front of me, I started to shoot at him but remembered that Dave Allison had always said to shoot at the horse of an escaping man and I did so and broke the horses hip, he fell on his rider."

"Impelled by misplaced notions of chivalry," he wrote in 1928, "Lieutenant Patton did not fire on the Mexican who was down until he had disentangled himself and rose to fire."

"As he got up Holmdahl, two soldiers and I all fired and as it was only about ten yards, we all hit him, he crumpled up. I saw another man about 100 yds off, I shot three times at him with my rifle four or five others fired also and he went down. Two [of my] men went to him and yelled

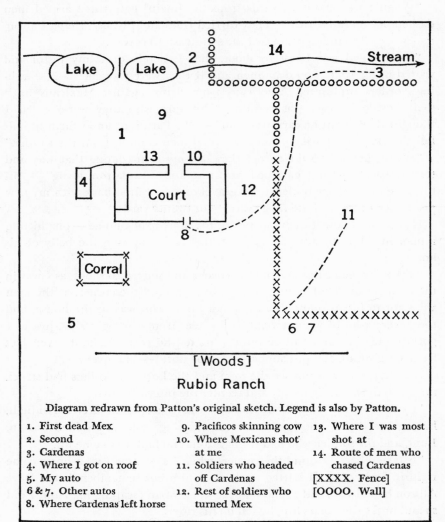

Rubio Ranch

Diagram redrawn from Patton's original sketch. Legend is also by Patton.

1. First dead Mex	9. Pacificos skinning cow	13. Where I was most
2. Second	10. Where Mexicans shot	shot at
3. Cardenas	at me	14. Route of men who
4. Where I got on roof	11. Soldiers who headed	chased Cardenas
5. My auto	off Cardenas	[XXXX. Fence]
6 & 7. Other autos	12. Rest of soldiers who	[OOOO. Wall]
8. Where Cardenas left horse	turned Mex	

that another man was running along the wall, about three hundred yds south. I told them to get him and sent two others around to head him off, soon I saw one of them aim [at the running man] and fire, shake his head fire again hold up one finger and grin; it was remarkable how cool they were."

The man on the wall was the one who had been hit by one of Patton's bullets at the beginning of the fight and who had turned his wounded horse into the courtyard. He had reentered the house and had jumped from a window. He "was running down the wall when he was dropped."

When he fell, "Holmdahl started to go up to him and" the man "held up his left hand in surrender, but when H was 20 feet from him he raised his pistol and shot at H but fortunately missed him and H blew out his brains."

Before he was killed, although he had a broken arm and two bullets through his right lung, he had fired at the Americans about "30 times."

"As it was thought that Cardenas had a band of thirty five men it was feared that the rest might still be in the court yard . . . as the flat roof had a parapet I was afraid they would climb up there and shoot us. I hated to climb up but hated worse not to."

While Holmdahl and a soldier covered the front gate and two soldiers watched the roof, Patton had two men place a dead tree against the wall of the house and hold it while he went up. As he stepped on the dirt roof, he broke through and fell to his armpits. He extricated himself.

"I could see no one but knew from my previous visit that there were a lot of rooms inside and that if I jumped in [to the court] I could be hit from cover, so I got down. Now all this time there had been four men out in front skinning a cow, they never looked at us at all."

"It speaks well for the discipline of the men that these four Mexicans skinning the cow had been at their task the whole time. Not a man [American] fired at them or bothered them in any way. It now was necessary to search the house."

"I called them [the four Mexicans] and took" Lunt and two "soldiers and we each got behind a Mex and went in . . . through the archway . . . we searched all the rooms, and following a blood trail, we found a horse in one of the rooms with a silver saddle and a saber."

"Nothing [else] was found in the house except some women and old men" — "among whom was [were] the wife, mother and baby of Cardenes." Those inside the house remained silent while the Americans searched the house. No one so much as spoke a word.

"The three dead men were not identified but each of the four Mexicans [was questioned] separately and [the bodies] proved to be Col. [Julio] Cardanes, Capt. [Isador] Lopez, and Pvt [Juan] Garza. To further verify them they were placed on the cars for transportation to [Headquarters at] Lake Itascate. Cardanes was the man first shot . . . by Lt. Patton and later killed by Holmdal when he attempted to escape by jumping from a window."

"We took the saddles guns sabers etc, and put the corpses on the hoods of the machines, and were just about to start when we saw about 40 men coming toward us at a gallop, about 1000 yds away. The men [Patton's men] were a little nervous but stood. We had [yet] to get Cardenas body [in the distance] and at that time some shots were fired."

"As no one [at headquarters] knew that the machines had gone to San Miguelito and as a shot in the gas tanks to the rear of the cars would put them out of action it was thought better not to wait . . . We withdrew gracefully."

"As we had to pass through [the village of] Rubio again [on our way back to camp]" — "after passing Saltillo" — "I had a man cut the telephone wires so they" — "The Mexicans, some fifty in number who had been there" — "could not be warned and lay for us."

When the cars passed through Rubio, the inhabitants were much excited by the sight of the dead. But there was no trouble.

"The fight started at twelve o'clock noon. Camp was reached at four."

"We got home with out accident. The Gen let me keep the silver mounted saddle and saber of Cardenes."

Letter, GSP, Jr., to Beatrice, May 17, 1916
[Just killed two snakes outside his tent, and everyone was teasing him because he used his pistol instead of his saber to kill them] but it simply goes to show that an officer should be able to use all arms, for being on foot I could not have used a saber. The Gen has been very complimentary telling some officers that I did more in half a day than the 13 Cav. did in a week. He calls me the "Bandit" . . . You are probably wondering if my conscience hurts me for killing a man. It does not. I feel about it just as I did when I got my sword fish, surprised at my luck. From the latest news we may stay here some

time. I hope not as it is very stupid unless we have war. Mr. Elser N.Y. Times wrote a good article about me. He thinks that it is published to day.

Written on May 16, Elser's story went by truck train to Columbus, New Mexico, where it was telegraphed to New York. It appeared on May 23, headlined: "Cardenas' Family Saw Him Die at Bay — Shot Four Times, Villa Captain — Dramatic Fight at Ranch — Lieut. Patton and Ten Men Killed Three Bandits — Peons Kept on Skinning a Beef."

The newspaperman called the incident "one of the prettiest fights of the campaign." Admitting that three dead Villistas were not many, even in this guerrilla campaign, Elser labeled the action a new type of combat. Patton and his men had fought from automobiles, they had leaped directly from cars to fight, and no American, to his knowledge, had ever done that before.

Elser was right, of course. Patton had initiated motorized warfare in the U.S. Army. It was ironic that a cavalryman should have first employed the motor vehicle that would make the horse obsolete in warfare. But it was also fitting, for, as Patton would argue later, the motor vehicle simply appropriated and assumed the characteristic mobility of the horse — and a cavalryman could make use of this asset better than anyone else.

The report by Elser was a fast-moving story that gave a good picture of the event. He made Patton a hero, quoting him, "As Patton put it to me, Cardenas had nerve even if he was a Mexican."

Elser also raised the question without ever stating it explicitly: How could Cárdenas, "even if he was [only] a Mexican," be killed in the virtual presence of his wife, mother, and baby without provoking from Patton the slightest allusion to their probable thoughts and emotions?

Perhaps Patton dared not even so much as entertain the idea for fear it would betray his deep and well-hidden sensibilities.

If he had been asked, he probably would have answered: Because it was a military action against the enemy. Because it was a fair fight in the open and according to the code of the West. Anything else was extraneous to the event.

The Rubio action created a minor and short-lived sensation in the United States. There had been no real news about Pershing's Punitive Expedition, no real results, no glorious triumph — only accounts of col-

umns endlessly marching through difficult country, of soldiers enduring
hardships, of the General and his staff inspecting this or that unit. The
public was bored, almost as much as the soldiers engaged. The skirmish
at Parral had been exciting; but it was a small conflict and a month old.
Suddenly the Rubio exploit appeared in the press, and it thrilled newspaper readers who could identify with a young and attractive hero. Although Patton hardly became a household institution, his name was reported across the nation.

The Pasadena *Star-News* secured the information from Pershing's press
telegram and placed the story on the top right of page 1: "George S.
Patton Shoots Villista Outlaw Captain — Pasadena Officer with General
Pershing in Mexico Engages in Lively Brush with Bandits Today at
Rubio Ranch."

Damon Runyon wrote an inaccurate account for the Los Angeles *Examiner*, which added that Patton had gone to Stockholm in 1912 "as the
sole U.S. Army representative, and defeated the best swordsmen of
France in the fencing contests. After spending some time at the French
army school, Saumur, he was assigned to General Leonard Wood's staff
and designed the new saber which is now in use in the U.S. cavalry."

Another newspaper featured the fact that "Bandits Killed at Rubio
Ranch Wore Military Outfits Stolen at Columbus." Cárdenas and his
companions, according to this account, had been wearing olive drab trousers of American military cut, carried army blankets stenciled "13 Cav,"
and had apparently participated in the Columbus raid. Where this information came from remained unsaid.

A Boston newspaper on May 25 showed a photograph of Patton standing in front of his tent looking pensively into the distance. He was wearing a campaign hat, smoking a pipe, wearing a tie, and looked very thin
and rather mature. He resembled Pershing somewhat. The caption read
that he was "Aid" to General Pershing, married to the daughter of Frederick Ayer, a rider in military races at the Brookline Country Club and
elsewhere, and a participant in the Olympic games. The story contained
the line, "They sprang directly from their cars into the fight, putting the
encounter in a class by itself." He added that Cárdenas' wife, daughter,
and mother had witnessed the entire event.

As late as June 15, a magazine featured a photograph of Patton, who
was acclaimed as having fought Mexicans from an automobile, and whose

killing of Cárdenas was second in importance only to the death of Candelario Cervantes, a prominent Villista leader shot a few days later.

Letter, Frederick Ayer (from his office, Boston) to "My dear Son & Daughter," May 31, 1916

Yesterday we were reading and enjoying the various newspaper accounts of George's scrap at the ranch, when his typewritten letter without address or signature came. . . . Of course the letter took the place of the newspapers, and was read with the most intense interest. I am trying to think of words to express my feelings and admiration of your courage and bravery, and our joy that you came away alive.

Congratulations and the whole list of ordinary expressions used in such cases do not cover the case and I am obliged to give it up, and say "It is good to be alive."

"Somewhere in Mexico," the boredom was stifling.

Diary

May 15: Staied around camp all day . . . Plaied horseshoes with Cabell, Kromer, and Collins.

May 16: I had a chil and went to bed early.

May 18: I did absolutely nothing but take a bath.

May 19: Terrible wind all day. No one did anything.

Occasionally there was a prospect of excitement.

Diary

May 22: [I went to] San Geronimo to get four men 13th Cav for my section [at Headquarters]. Saw Mexican with gun on horse but he looked so powerful we did not chase him. We should have.

Diary

May 22 (Revised Version): I saw a mexican with a gun ride off from the mountain and at first I decided to kill him, but later I thought he might possibly be innocent and I let him go. I believe however that I should have shot him [meaning, he probably would have turned out to be a Villista].

Usually the duties were routine.

Diary

May 26: Nothing doing. Had talk with Maj Howze on equipment also longer argument over saber.

May 27: Started new mess for correspondents because too many in Gen's mess.

May 31: Cav Board met. Called several witnesses. I was one.

He had yet to learn that he had been promoted to first lieutenant on May 23.

The days in June dragged. It was hot, there was nothing to do. He wrote an article for the *Cavalry Journal*. He went hunting and saw a deer. He went duck hunting. He helped move the camp two miles from its former site.

Letter, Beatrice (Fort Bliss) to her mother, June 5, 1916

Darling Ma . . . This new army bill will make a tremendous difference in all our arrangements. Georgie is a 1st Lieut. now (since May 23d) and on July 1st there won't be a single 2nd Lieut. in the army. All the West Pointers graduating this month will be made 1st Lieuts. at once and the new 2nd Lieuts. will have to come in from civil life & the [enlisted] ranks. Georgie will be a captain in 2 years at the outside now. Ordinarily he would get his Captaincy in from 10 to 12 years. The Manchu list [officers could serve no more than four years in any six-year period on staff duty, nor could they serve in Washington, D.C., indefinitely] & foreign service roster have also been suspended so we don't know *where* we are! And G. will have all his foreign service behind him now when he comes back — *So,* we may stay here indefinitely. No one can tell how all this new increase [in officers] is going to work out. But it will be fine to have one's captaincy so soon. The Col. is very complimentary & says he wants to keep us in the reg't & I think they all would, as G. is so able. I think, if we are to stay in the U.S.A. at all I would rather be here myself, as the cavalry will probably be on or near the border for some time & this is undoubtedly the best border station.

I went to market this A.M. & think of this. They had: Red cherries, black cherries, raspberries, blackberries, strawberries, watermelons, canteloupes, nutmegs (melons), pineapples, cocanuts, loganberries, dewberries, black figs, apples, oranges, grapefruits, limes, lemons, plums, peaches — and vegetables accordingly. This is certainly a fine place to keep house in.

The War Department regularized his administrative status by transferring him from the 8th Cavalry, which was not part of the Punitive Expedition, to the 10th Cavalry, a regiment made up of colored soldiers who were present in Mexico. This paper change had no effect on his duties.

On June 13, Patton secured permission to accompany a troop that was going out to look for a noted Villista, Pedro Lujan. Patton spent three days in the saddle with Captain Frederick G. Turner's Troop M of the 13th Cavalry, helped surround a house near Tepehuanes, and assisted in Lujan's capture. This was exciting work. Field operations, he noted, were far more satisfactory than hanging around a headquarters, even in the company of high-ranking officers.

Letter, GSP, Jr., to his father, June 15, 1916

[Out the last three days chasing Pedro Lujan.] I planned the surprise and tried to work up a fight. We surrounded the hacienda and a hill back of it with a dismounted line and the eight of us galloped up to the door but nothing doing. They would not shoot. If they had we would have murdered them. It had all the elements of good tactics but the shooting.

With the nomination of [Charles Evans] Hughes [by the Republican Party for the Presidency] it looks to me as if your chances had come up a lot. [Governor Hiram] Johnston [Johnson of California] won't do much and so far as I can remember the Republicans won't have a strong man. I hope *you* win.

I have been assigned to the 10 Cav but after July there will be a general shake up and I am trying to get to [Fort] Myer or Monterey [California] as I think that these 3 months here [in Mexico] will keep me from [being sent to] the Islands as there will be a lot of new 1st Lts with none at all [no foreign service]. If I do go to the Islands I will try for Hawaii as from there I can get back for the next war with Mexico if the present one ever ends.

I am very well and having a stupid time.

Colonel H. J. Slocum, who commanded the 13th Cavalry, congratulated Patton and the others for their good work in capturing the Mexican outlaw Pedro Lujan, a prominent Villista leader, and Slocum's letter of appreciation went into Patton's official file. But there was no publicity, no notoriety as in the case of Cárdenas.

Pancho Villa had disappeared, his bands had melted into the mountains or departed Chihuahua, and the pursuit phase of the Punitive Expedition came to an end.

CHAPTER 17

Punitive Expedition

"It will not take many of us to beat the Mexicans in battle but it will take a lot to cover the lines so that those who fight may also eat."

PATTON kept a notebook and inscribed in it messages dictated by Pershing, miscellaneous thoughts, and regulations to be posted or announced. For example, an officer posting a letter in the mailbox at Headquarters was to observe the rules of censorship and, to certify his compliance with them, place his name on the envelope; a soldier was to show his unsealed letter to his company commander, who was to read it and initial the envelope if the contents conformed with regulations. The only acceptable heading on letters was "Somewhere in Mexico." No military information was to be disclosed, including the dispositions of troops, their movements, and the names of organizations. There was to be no conjecture on plans. "No crytocism will be allowed." No stamp was needed. The words "Soldier Mail" in the upper right hand corner were sufficient, plus the signature or initials of the certifying officer and his "tytle." All guides, reporters, messages, and other civilian members of the command were to pass their letters, with envelopes open and stamped, to Major Ryan or Lieutenant Patton, who would give or withhold approval.

Patton also made notes, studies, and reports for the staff — for example, on the grass and other forage to be found in Chihuahua.

All this, the routine of camp life and administration, was part of soldiering too.

Letter, GSP, Jr., to Mr. Ayer, June 27, 1916
I think that war now is the best for two reasons. First it is inevitable hence the sooner the better. Second it will surely give us a better army for I doubt if over half of the militia muster in and even they will be too few.

This [Mexico] is a big country and very difficult to operate in. There are no rodes at all just tracks over the plains and mountains. There is very little water and most of the cattle are dead so there will be no way to live off the country.

It will not take many of us to beat the Mexicans in battle but it will take a lot to cover the lines [of communication] so that those who fight may also eat.

You have no idea of the utter degredation of the inhabitants . . . One must be a fool in deed to think that people half savage and wholy ignorant will ever form a republic. It is a joke. A despot is all they know or want. So when they lost Diez they set up bandit kings who were worse tirants than he [Porfirio Díaz] ever dreamed of being . . .

I have written Beatrice that if we go to war she ought to go to you. It will last six months at the least. If I am wounded she could get to the border before I could and if I am killed — which I shant be — she would be better at home [in Massachusetts].

Of course I miss her terribly because the longer I am married to her the more I love her. She is so wonderful and always new.

A field day on June 29 temporarily broke the monotony. Patton took part in a jumping contest for officers on horseback. There was another "very amusing" field day on July 4.

Diary
July 4: Got letter offering to make me major or Col Volunteer Inft [Infantry regiment].

July 5: Bad wind all day. Had stomach ache.

The pain in his stomach was probably related to some extent to his indecision with respect to the offer of a commission in the Volunteers. By the following day, he had made up his mind. He wrote two letters, one to R. F. McReynolds, the other to his father.

He thanked McReynolds, a former Army captain who was the Collector of Internal Revenue at Los Angeles, for the honor proposed. He would consider it a great privilege to serve as a field grade officer in a regiment raised in his home area. But since the law required the War Department to approve a Volunteer commission for a Regular officer, he would have to comply with this procedure to accept "your very complimentary offer."

Patton's letter was rather vacillating, but his main purpose was to keep the prospect open. Skipping captain and jumping to major after being a first lieutenant little more than a month was attractive. But he hated to leave the Regular Army, the cavalry, and General Pershing. Besides, he wanted no part of commanding an infantry unit that might be stationed to guard a railroad or detailed to protect a rear-area installation.

He sent his father a copy of his letter to McReynolds and explained that his reply was "complimentary" to McReynolds and did "not involve me in using political influence which is against the law." He had "talked it over with Capt. Burt[t]," and they were both thinking of asking the Adjutant General to put them on the list of officers desiring increased Volunteer rank. Patton hesitated to do so because his letter to the Adjutant General would have to go through Pershing for his approval. Pershing might not feel that it was "playing the game on my part to ask for such a job after he was good enough to bring me down here." Furthermore, he doubted that infantry would ever do much fighting in Mexico, which was suitable rather for cavalry operations. "If I want you to go to Washington," he wrote — in order to exert political influence on certain people, he left unsaid — "I will wire you through B. as you suggest."

He added:

> From present indications I doubt very much if war will break out right now. What Mr. Wilson is doing I can't see but it certainly looks as if he would not fight. A man who is supported by people like Governor Glenn with his speech placing a premium on dishonor is not going to win even in unspeakable America.

Diary

July 8: Gen P went for horse exercise with me in morning. We rode about eight miles and killed rattle snake.

July 9: killed a snake at horse exercise.

July 10: killed rattlesnake at horse exercise.

Having kept track of snakes, he next monitored for a week or so the arrival of supplies by railroad and by truck convoy.

Letter, GSP, Jr., to his father, July 12, 1916

We are all rapidly going crazy from lack of occupation and there is no help in sight . . . big prize fight to night and we are all going. It will pass the time at least.

I would like to go to hell so that I might be able to shovel a few extra coals on that unspeakable ass Wilson. How you can support him is beyond me and if he is reelected the American *People* are worse than even I imagine . . .

After talking with the Gen I decided not to make an application for volunteer rank. But this will not prevent [Mc]Reynolds from asking for me. I am also offered the job of Capt. and Adjutant of the West Texas Cavalry. So you see I am quite popular. Don't tell Reynolds that.

Letter, GSP, Jr., to his father, July 20, 1916

Dear Senator: I am glad you decided to run and hope you win but even if you don't you will have made a good fight and ought to get some job if as seems probable that creature Wilson wins.

Don't go at it in any half way but whoop it up and tell them all sorts of lies. Especially how much Wilson helped the army — which he has not — still it ought to sound well.

Tell them that Japan is swarming with Japanese [and] that Japanese have made an accurate survey accross america along the line of the S.P. [Southern Pacific] . . . They [the Japanese] have also surveyed the country in Mexico . . . [in short, tell them anything that will win votes].

I now begin to think that we will be here till November . . . it is very tiresome and hard on every one. The flies are getting bad too.

Diary

July 23: Discussed the saber with the General. He does not think much of it.

July 24: Tenth Cavalry gave dinner celebrating 58th year. Preceded by ceremonies showing all fights regiment has been in . . . Quite impressive ceremony. Ceremonies staged by Major [Charles] Young [colored officer, West Point graduate, highly respected by all] who refused to sit down at the table [with the white officers] on the pretext that he was not feeling well. [This was a mark of consideration on Young's part, for he was well aware of the discomfort he would provoke among some officers of southern origin.]

July 29: Maj Cavana told me he had danced with B [at Fort Bliss].

Letter, GSP, Jr., to Beatrice, July 29, 1916

I inclose to [two] disgusting poems I have composed. Tear them up.

Letter, GSP, Jr., to Beatrice, July 30, 1916

Collins is going to Columbus in the morning to meet Gen [Tasker] Bliss [Acting Chief of Staff, who was making an inspection trip of the troops along the border and in Mexico] . . . I wish I were going. If it had been Gen Wood instead of General P. I think he would have sent me as Collins' wife is now in California. I could kill Collins with pleasure for being so lucky. In fact I think that he worked it to go in my place. It was Shallenbergers turn or mine as Collins has been once already. If he did it he is a dirty skunk. I rather think he is any way, but such is life.

On rereading those poems I am sorry I sent them to you, you will think me nasty but at the time I thought them very clever.

I saw Maj. Cavanaugh who said he had a dance with you about a week ago and that you were looking fine. I wish I had been he.

Actually, Pershing sent Collins to Columbus because Collins had a bad tooth and needed to see the dentist. Patton's remarks about Collins, who would be a major general in World War II, were only his extreme disappointment showing. They were good friends.

When General Bliss completed his inspection tour and was ready to return to Columbus, New Mexico, Pershing detailed Patton as Bliss's escort.

Diary

August 6: started north at 7 A.M. with Gen Bliss, Maj Noland and [Major Fox] Conner, one Studebacker one Ford two dodges. Reached Columbus at 7 P.M. Beatrice met me. Saw Gen Bliss to his car.

Shallenberger wired instructions from Pershing. Patton was to make sure that Pershing's mare, left with Captain Ben Lear, and that his son Warren's Shetland pony, left with Sergeant Alexander, were all right; he was to pick up a sack with saddle equipment left by Collins in the baggage room at Columbus; he was to bring back two cases of White Rock charged water.

Diary

August 9: Got new Studebacker for Gen. got cigars [for] Maj Hines.

August 10: started 7 A.M. with eight guards. Three cars, two dodges, one Stu. Got into mud at Vado Fusiles. Heavy rain at Corraletos. Had to push cars for some distance. Got in at 8:30 P.M. Reported to Gen P. Found new camera waiting for me.

August 14: Shallenberger Mr. Boyd and I went hunting in Parajo mountains. We rode 13 hours but saw nothing.

August 18: Field meet. I was one of judges and also won shooting event pistol — Big boxing meet at night.

August 19: Gen P [guides] Barker [and] Boyd and I went hunting antelope east of Camp. The Gen got one shot at about 400 yards. We rode part way back and got into an auto leaving horses. After a little it stuck in the mud so the Gen, Barker, and I started to walk. We did four miles in 50 minutes the General setting the pace. Hardest walking ever did. Barker and I were stiff for several days. Getting back I found Sim [his horse] badly cut in a barbed wire fence.

August 21: Gen P. reviewed entire command at 8:30 A.M. It took 50 minutes for review to pass at a walk.

Pershing decided to inspect the troops in Mexico, and he formed a special team for that purpose. He and Collins would examine the men for general appearance. Colonel Cress and Captain Reed would look at their personal equipment. Colonel Cabell and Patton would go over the horses and their equipment, checking the condition of the animals and their shoeing. "I am glad to have something to do," Patton noted in his diary.

For a week the inspection team traveled to the units and examined them.

Diary

August 27: Inspected regiment at 1 PM not very good. Especially wagon train. Few men had underclothes and no attempt to get them.

August 29: Gen inspected camp and . . . wagon trains. I helped Col Cress condemn horses and inspect the hospital . . . Lunched on road and inspected Co I 24 Inf at Charcos. It was in excellent condition . . . we met a patrol 13 Cav looking for two escaped prisoners. These had held up a Chinaman and taken all his provisions out of wagon . . . The sky was black when we reached the town [Colonia Dublan]. The streets were a foot deep in water. Trying to cross flood, flooded carbureator with water and were stuck so the truck towed us in. I had to walk ahead in order to find the bridges, water over top. I fixed up a report of my inspections and handed them in.

On the last day of August, Pershing, some of his staff members, several civilian clerks, a few reporters and photographers, and Patton left camp for Columbus, New Mexico, and a few days of vacation. They reached town on the following afternoon, and Beatrice and Nita were there to meet them.

Diary

September 2: in afternoon Gen P, Nita, Col and Mrs. Farnsworth, B and I went to Palmas for a ride.

September 3: B., Nita, and Mrs. Collins, Collins, and self . . . dined with Gen. P.

September 4: Gen., Nita, Collins and wife went in auto to see Aviation field. I was sick and stayed home with B.

Letter, GSP, Jr. (from Colonia Dublan), to his father, September 7, 1916

I am sorry you have to fight Johnston [Hiram Johnson] but never the less feel sure of your ultimate success [in the election] for you will have a big Republican backing.

Try to get them to come out for you and split the [Republican] party. You ought to do it. Also don't hesitate at rough stuff with Johnston. He will probably sling mud. If he does you sling rocks. In fact I would start it as you have more on him than he can have on you.

Go after his private life. That will get the Sufferage vote. *Remember* this is no practice game but the whole show the *finals*. You can go to bed for a month after November 7th [Election Day] but till then keep moving and never assume you have a vote. Go after each and every vote as if it were the only one you had. You must win. All your life has been a preparation for this so you *must* land it.

You are not polite enough to people in general. Treat each one as if he was an army officer you were friendly to on my account.

Get a lot of cigars and give them to people and ask about the children and the crops.

It is perfectly possible to be for every policy under heaven to the man who is interested in that policy . . .

I hope you will win and I know you will.

Patton took a two-day hunting trip with Major Hines, two guides, and two soldiers. They spent the night in a deserted house, "where we all walked guard. The rats ate Maj Hines hat cord and some parts of the saddles . . . While I was sitting on the floor a large centipede ran out from between my legs." The hunters killed two antelope, eight rattle-snakes, one centipede, and four tarantulas.

Beatrice went to California in September to help in Mr. Patton's campaign. "Write me fully," her husband instructed, "how Pa is getting on and what you think his chances are I do hope they are good."

Letter, GSP, Jr., to Beatrice, September 15, 1916

I wish Pa was out of politics so I could say what I think about Wilson.

Letter, GSP, Jr., to Beatrice, September 18, 1916

[General A. L. Mills died recently] so I guess Gen P will be a major General. I hope so. He ought to be. He's all the time talking about Miss Anne [Patton's sister]. Nita may rank us yet.

Letter, GSP, Jr., to his father, September 20, 1916

. . . make the fight of the time and stay to the end.

If Johnson gets T.R. to come out and stump for him why don't you get Wilson. Try it any way. He can't but refuse and it would bring you to his notice.

My own views on Wilson are not fit to print so I will keep them to my self. But Hughes [the Republican candidate for President] is equally poor so realy there is no choice . . .

The Carranzistas fear to chase Villa for fear their men will desert. And they would.

Intervention will be useless. We must Take the country and keep it.

Keep fighting and win.

Letter, GSP, Jr., to Beatrice, September 24, 1916
Nothing to report. Even the wind did not blow today.

Letter, GSP, Jr., to Beatrice, September 25, 1916
[Pershing was promoted and had a reception] with leamonaid for a refreshment.

Letter, GSP, Jr., to Beatrice, September 27, 1916
. . . more to do lately as the general goes to manuvers every morning and I have been helping on a map in the afternoon as I know the country around here better than any one else . . .

[John] Lucas and I are trying to start polo and have sent for mallets, balls etc. It will be something to do.

Letter, GSP, Jr., to his father, September 28, 1916
[Glad] you are advertising your self more and Wilson less . . . He has not the soul of a louse nor the mind of a worm. Or the back bone of a jelly fish.

This alledged preparadness is a lie. We have no army and will never have until we have universal *service* not [universal] training . . . Still I would vote for him rather than Hughes who I think is even worse.

Don't stay home long but keep working and talking. You are in the fight of your life. Now use the last reserve to win.

Letter, GSP, Jr., to Beatrice, September 28, 1916
[Glad] that Pa has come out for him self and not for Wilson only. It would be fine if he could carry the state instead of Wilson. But however he wins it is all right if it only gets him elected.

Letter, GSP, Jr., to Beatrice, September 29, 1916
[At maneuvers that morning, a fine cavalry charge would have succeeded except that the commander] started to charge then seeing a ditch his ground sqiril instincts got the better of him and he tried to dismount and the others hit him before he could. It just shows that even in open country a charge will work.

Even Gen. P had to admit it and got quite excited and yelled around a lot.

Collins is still away [in Columbus] with his tooth. I wish I had one like it.

As a major general, Pershing was allowed to have three aides instead of two. Patton hoped that Pershing would make him the third, for he wanted badly to wear the aide's insignia. "Perhaps he is waiting," Patton wrote wistfully to Beatrice, "till he gets his [formal letter of] comission [promotion]."

Although Pershing would sometimes refer to Patton as his aide, he would never formally assign Patton to that duty.

On the evening of October 2, Patton was working in his tent on a musketry paper when his lamp burned him badly about the face and hand and set his tent on fire. He put out the flames and went to the hospital, where he spent, he admitted, a "Pretty bad night." He was cheered that General Pershing and all the other officers on the staff came to see him as soon as they learned of his accident.

He was in pain for several days, then "got fever and felt pretty badly. All officers very kind. They visited me every day from the time I was burned." He listed in his diary all who had called.

The doctors called it severe first degree burns of the entire face and the dorsum or upper surface of the right hand.

He felt better on October 7, well enough to write to Beatrice.

Darling Beat: You are indeed fortunate in not being able to kiss me right now. My face looks like an old after-birth of a Mexican cow on which had been smeared several very much decomposed eggs. I have a large and flatulent double chin and jawls like the tipical Wall St. Magninate. Also both ears are red and inflamed and I have no hair nor eyebrows nor eye lashes. No I have nothing catching. I simply set my self on fire with the above distressing results. All this happened on the second [of October] and I have been back at my own tent for the last two days. So don't get excited. Also it will leave no scar.

I came back from the movies and having some work to do I pumped up my lamp and lit it. It did not burn well so I started pumping again while it was lit. There was too much gasoline in it so when I stopped pumping a lot of gasoline flew out of the hole instead of air and caught fire. As it came it hit me in the face and got in my hair. I ran out side and put my self out. Then came back and put out the lamp and the tent. Then I reported to Gen. P. that I was burned and went to the hospital. The first persons I met were dentists who only announced that fact and told me to hunt for a surgeon. Then I found Maj. Dr. Baker who was very nice but every thing he tried to get for my face was "just out" like a cheap hash house so at last he put vasaline on it. It was hurting like hell by then. Gen. P. and all the staff and Mr. Lucas of the 13th came to see me that night and repeated their visits daily. The Gen. and Shallenberger and Collins coming two or three times each [day]. Marchant and West and Col Tompkins and Mr. Blunt also came. I was much touched by their interest as I probably would not have visited them. Also my corporal and Cook came over. . . .

I realy did not suffer too much the first night and got to sleep for short periods after about 2 A.M.

Next day they put on a saturated solution of Bi Carbonate of Soda and wet it every half hour all day. It was fine. I slept all night. They repeated that next day and night then yesterday they started bandaging with Zinc oxide. And to-day took the bandage off but will put it back to night so I will not stick to my pillow.

The first couple of days I had to eat through a tube but now can eat almost any thing solid. I ate rost beef potatoes, green pees, coffee and pudding for lunch.

My eyes were not hurt at all and I can read which is a great comfort. The Dr says I will be all pealed off in five more days. He says it was just like very severe sun burn and will make no scars except perhaps on my right cheek a little one.

I wrote you this long letter to keep you from being worried. I also had a couple of pictures taken which I will send you . . .

I love you with all my heart and would have hated worst to have been blinded because I could not have seen you.

Beatrice had apparently asked whether he could get a leave of absence to help his father campaign. He replied that he would be unable to depart Mexico until the Punitive Expedition was withdrawn, and "when that will be God knows!" Even if he could get some time off to go to California, "I don't think it would do any good as I look so funny in my present hairless state that I would frighten people away. I am getting on pretty well and will grow a new skin in a week or so I hope."

Diary

October 8: Capt Reed advised sick leave.

Granted sick leave on October 9 for 15 days, Patton traveled on a truck train with Captain Graham and Dr. Darby — who "were very nice to me" — and reached Columbus on the afternoon of the 10th. Beatrice met him, and they took the train to California.

Several California newspapers remarked his arrival on sick leave. The Los Angeles *Examiner* headlined a story "Rubio Hero Here, Injured — Pershing's Aide Returns," and carried a photograph of him bandaged about the face and hand. He was quoted as saying that he would like to stay in California until after the election, but would not ask for an extension of his leave for that reason.

Letter, Pershing to GSP, Jr., October 16, 1916

Dear Patton: I hope you are rapidly recovering from your accident and that your personal appearance has improved. At the same time no doubt you are enjoying the visit with your family.

Apropos of your discussions with your father on the Mexican situation, do not be too insistent upon your own personal views. You must remember that when we enter the army we do so with the full knowledge that our first duty is toward our government, entirely regardless of our own views under any given circumstances. We are at liberty to express our personal views only when called upon to do so or else confidentially to our friends, but always confidentially and with the complete understanding that they are in no sense to govern our actions.

The real purpose of this letter is to tell you that, in addition to the new bridle which you were kind enough to present to me, I have purchased the Saumur saddle you ordered for Captain Johnson. I am now in the market to buy a horse in keeping with such an outfit. I wish you would keep your eye open for anything in that part of the country that might suit me.

Everything is moving along here about the same as when you left. Please give my regards to Mrs. Patton and your sister, and tell Mrs. Patton that I cannot thank her too much for the sleeping bag, which is now in constant use. But I must hold you to your promise to obtain for me the cost of this bag so that I may remit.

With best regards, I remain, Yours hastily,

Without Patton's knowledge, Dr. LeMoyne Wills of Los Angeles telegraphed Pershing, then wrote, to say that he was dressing Patton's burns every day, that his face was healing well but his ears were slower to respond to treatment. He advised an extension of leave.

Without Dr. Wills's knowledge, Patton telegraphed and wrote Pershing the same information.

Pershing answered Patton on October 24 to extend his leave. "I am sincerely delighted," Pershing added, "to hear that your father has such an excellent chance of winning out. Personally, I never had any use for Johnson and sincerely hope the republicans turn in and beat him."

In an exceptionally nice gesture, Pershing also wrote to Dr. Mills, thanking him for the news of "my aide" Patton. "I am sure," Pershing continued, "that he would not remain away one moment longer than his leave, unless he thought it necessary. I have already granted two weeks extension of his leave and hope this will suffice, as his services are important and I need him right along."

Patton was then unaware of his having been "mentioned in dispatches," a high honor. Pershing on October 7 had submitted a report of his operations to Funston, and in it said:

> The activities of Colonel Cardenas, an important member of Villa's Staff, had stirred up Rubio and vicinity and our troops had made several unsuccessful attempts to capture him. On May 14, Lieutenant G. S. Patton, 8th Cavalry, of my staff, with a small detachment was sent to that section in automobiles to purchase corn. Upon reaching San Miguel Ranch near Rubio, several Villistas ran out, firing upon the detachment as they went. Lieutenant Patton and one of our men opened fire in return, killing three of the Villistas, one of whom proved to be Col Cardenas.

GSP, Jr., "My Father," 1927

In October 1916 I came home on sick leave to recover from a burn. Papa was in the midst of his senatorial campaign and campaign for Wilson. I accompanied him on a trip to the Imperial Valley and was with him at the California Club the night the returns came in defeating him. He never flinched and took it with a smile. Papa's efforts carried California for Wilson and secured the latters reelection. On the strength of this I tried to get Papa to push himself for secretary of war, but he was too high souled to be a good advocate for him self and lost out. This was a great calamity as he would have made a magnificent secretary. My love for Wilson was not heightened by his failure to reward the man to whom he owed so much.

Hiram Johnson, a Republican, who defeated Mr. Patton, had been elected governor of California in 1910 and re-elected in 1914. One of the founders of the Progressive Party and its vice-presidential nominee in 1912 — Theodore Roosevelt was the presidential candidate that year — Johnson was a reformer who shattered the domination of the railroad men in state politics and who brought the railroads under strict state supervision. A superb and forceful politician, he won the election to the U. S. Senate in 1916 primarily because he rode the crest of the muckraking, anti-corruption wave that swept a host of mayors and governors into office. Assured of a seat in the Senate, Johnson resigned as governor.

Mr. Patton, closely connected with the Huntingtons and allied with the big business of land development, seemed suspiciously standpat in local politics and was, besides, a colorless campaigner. Despite the bitter fight between Republicans and Progressives in California, Patton was unable to capitalize on the split and was badly defeated.

On the evening of Election Day, the early returns indicated that Hughes had won the presidency. When the California votes were counted, the totals gave the thirteen electoral votes of the state to Wilson. Had the Republicans carried California, Hughes would have triumphed, 277 electoral votes to Wilson's 254. With California, Wilson stood 267 to 264 for Hughes.

Patton always believed that his father had won the state and the election for Wilson, while losing himself. But a more realistic appreciation indicated that Wilson had carried the state and the election without Mr. Patton's help.

Beatrice and Patton departed Los Angeles and reached Columbus, New Mexico, on November 9. No truck train was scheduled to leave for the south, so they went on to El Paso and stayed in a hotel there. On the following morning, they visited the post and their house. That afternoon they returned to Columbus.

Diary
November 11: Birthday. Did not get up till 11 AM as there was no truck train. Had nice day with Beat.

He departed on the 12th, reached camp on the 13th.

Diary

November 13: all glad to see me. Capt Reeds room was fixed up nice for me. Horses fine.

November 14: Staied home all day. Ear better but not all well. Went back to Gen P's mess. Found I was on pistol board with Maj. Lindsley, Capt Latrobe, Lts. Groninger, Hickam, Clark, and myself.

Letter, GSP, Jr., to Beatrice, November 14, 1916

. . . every one was glad to see me and the Gen was deeply interested in polatics. They were all delighted with their presents . . .

. . . keep on making him [Pa] work now not later [for a political appointment].

Letter, GSP, Jr., to his father, November 14, 1916

After the fight you made there is certainly no one man entitled to the gratitude of Wilson than you and you ought to get something *good* but you will not get a thing unless you go after it at once as there are few places and many who think themselves deserving.

I was awfully sorry that Johnson beat you but it may all be for the best and will be if you get some post that is more important than senator.

It would be a crime for you to settle down and fold your hands after the fight you have made. And in fact would not be just to the thousands who supported you. The only way you can show them that you were worthy of their support is to keep on and get something worth while. Besides if you stopped now you would get sick.

This place is as usual colder but the flies are all dead.

Before his accident with the lamp, Patton had written to General Leonard Wood about his action at Rubio, and shortly after his return to Pershing's headquarters he found Wood's reply. The general had written from Plattsburg, New York, where he was stressing Civilian Training Camps as a means of national preparedness for war. His letter seemed not terribly relevant to Patton's concerns.

Letter, Wood to GSP, Jr., October 7, 1916

Yours of September 24th reached me last night. I read of your little fight [with Cárdenas]. It was well handled.

Don't let the mounted infantry get control of the cavalry. Cavalry has never been more in demand in history than it is on the western front at the present time and the French and English are carefully building up their cavalry forces on the western front and expect to have a tremendous demand for it as soon as the final break up begins. Work such as you are in and the work we have done in this country during the past 50 years is not cavalry work in the sense of cavalry work in war and our people have mixed up mounted police and similar work with the real work of mounted troops in war.

Sincerely yours

Patton was hardly grateful for Wood's depreciation of Pershing's cavalry campaigns.

Diary

November 15: Shot on pistol board in PM. Gen told me to write article on instructions the troops had received also to get pictures.

Letter, GSP, Jr., to Beatrice, November 15, 1916

. . . the general has asked me to write an article which he will be sponser for about the proper training of cavalry. Since there are a lot of supposed good cavalry men here I am quite elated over it. He must think I have some brains after all. I am also official photographer of the expedition and so am realy busy.

I hope Pa is on the job with some life.

Diary

November 16: Went out riding with Gen in morning. Sat on pistol board in PM. Started article in evening.

Letter, GSP, Jr., to Beatrice, November 16, 1916

I had no idea Pa was beaten so badly but hope he gets a job any way . . .

Even Gen. P. thinks now that we may come out [of Mexico]. I hope we do and that that damned Villa keeps quiet till we do . . .

Collins and I are very busy over some musketry problems.

Diary

November 17: Got my right ear out of the bandage. Did not shoot [on Pistol Board] as Dr. thought ear too sensative.

Letter, GSP, Jr., to Beatrice, November 17, 1916

You will be surprised at the article I have written for the Gen. It sounds very mounted infantryish until you get to the end but it is true that as we will have to fight as infantry in Mexico . . . we had just as well know the game too . . .

We still have hopes of getting out [of Mexico] and Gen P aludes to it all the while.

Diary

November 18: Gen Scriven signal corps flew down by Aeroplane. He was so stiff that when he tried to get out of the aeroplane he could not move and had to be lifted. He did not come out at retreat so Gen. P. went in and got him.

Letter, GSP, Jr., to Beatrice, November 18, 1916

Gen Scriven Chief signal officer of the Army came down by aeroplane this morning when he got here he was so scared he could not move and had to be lifted out of the machine. He has been reviving him self on whiskey all day.

Menu, General Pershing's Mess, Sunday, November 19, 1916

Oyster stew, celeries and ripe olives, roast turkey and dressing, cranberry sauce, banana fritters with creamsauce, mashed potatoes, string beans, lettuce with mayonnaise, apple pie and cheese, assorted fruit, coffee, tea, milk, distilled water.

Diary

November 20: I went out early to show Col Winn 24 Infantry where to go to start problem — deployment of attacking force and attack. Then I watched from good place on hill with field glasses. Later joined Gen.

Patton knew where Pershing wanted the maneuver of exercise to start, so he indicated the place to the infantry, then went to the top of a big hill and watched the show. Four regiments of cavalry, a battery of artillery, and twenty machine guns made the sham attack. The day was perfectly clear, and he could see everything and with his glasses every detail. Colonel Tompkins, the cavalry commander, won the mock battle by making a flank march and putting the whole 7th Cavalry behind the infantry.

Letter, GSP, Jr., to Beatrice, November 20, 1916

Just before he [Tompkins] appeared a historic thing happened.
At chancelorsville [during the Civil War] the first news [Union]
Gen. Howard had of [Stonewall] Jacksons flank march was the appearance of deer and other animals driven in by the advancing
troops.

Just before the seventh [Cavalry] came in sight two big deer a
buck and a doe rushed by with in twenty five yards of where Gen. P.
and I stood. . . . and jumped right over a skirmish line laying down.
It was the prettiest thing I ever saw in Mexico.

Tell Pa to write Col Horn and that Prof. Buttler [probably Nicho-
las Murray Butler of Columbia University] and strike while the iron
is hot. Get after him.

Letter, GSP, Jr., to Beatrice, November 21, 1916

Mr. Ivers one of the twelve apostles of the Mormon church took
dinner with us yesterday. He is a very interesting and educated man
and is the one who lead the migration to Mexico and founded the
colony [here]. He made a speach to the soldiers which was fine. It
seems strange that such a smart man could be a leader in such a fool
religion. But such is the case . . .

Tell Nita to send Gen. P. the [book] Lions of the Lord he would
like it.

Diary

November 24: Machine Gun attack problem in afternoon. Tried
advancing for 100 yards firing pistol 14 times at run. Did not like
idea of letting men halt when they have to put in new clip [of am-
munition]. Because believe [they] would never advance again.

November 26: Discussed cavalry with Gen P. He said I was very
broad Cavalry man. Quite a compliment from him.

November 26 (Revised Version): Discussed cavalry with Gen P.
who seemed to think my ideas were alright.

Letter, GSP, Jr., to Beatrice, November 26, 1916

Darling Beat: Gen P. and I were going over my article to night and
I mentioned the fact that though I was crazy over the saber I saw
some good in the rifle too. He said "Why of course you are one of the

broadest and best Cavalry men I know." The more I see of the man the better my opinion of his brains becomes.

Letter, GSP, Jr., to Beatrice, November 28, 1916

I got a check for $2.50 from the Cavalry Journal for my article on the saber. I returned the check as I will not take money for defending the saber. It would be sacrelidge.

In the same letter, he said that Beatrice's brother Fred advised selling the four shares of Calumet and Hecla and the twenty shares of steel stock he owned, for the sale would bring a profit of about 2000 dollars.

There may have been no connection between this and his return of the $2.50 to the *Cavalry Journal.*

Letter, GSP, Jr., to Beatrice, November 28, 1916

I am coming to the belief that it is possible to charge with it [the pistol]. If this proves true it would be a great help against the lance for the saber alone is rather inferior to the lance.

Letter, GSP, Jr., to Beatrice, November 29, 1916

Just one year ago I was sitting up at Sierra Blanca waiting for Senor Chico Conjo to attack me and here I am still at it. I certainly have not seen much of you since and miss you more all the time.

Letter, GSP, Jr., to Beatrice, December 1, 1916

I had a little spat with the Gen. about the saber. In his quotation on page ten he had written, "Perfect control of the horse and expert use of the pistol." I said by leaving out saber you imply it is useless. He said well I don't like it but don't want to start an argument. I said well why not put in "and saber." He said no I can't do that. I immediately picked up the papers and said very good sir but went out slowly. Just as I left he called out put in or saber. I did as it was what I had expected. To day he said well you got your way didn't you. I said why no sir not at all, and we both laughed. I also got the pistol board to indorse the saber.

CHAPTER 18

Somewhere in Mexico

"To Hell with the People!"

GSP, Jr., "Personal Glimpses of General Pershing," 1924

The weary months of "watchful waiting" [in Mexico] . . . had little waiting so far as we were concerned. Under the personal supervision of the General every unit went through a complete course in range and combat firing, marches, maneuvers, entrenching, and combating exercises with ball ammunition. Every horse and man was fit; weaklings had gone; baggage was still at the minimum, and discipline was perfect. When I speak of supervision I do not mean that nebulous staff control so frequently connected with the work. By constant study General Pershing knew to the minutest detail each of the subjects in which he demanded practice, and by his physical presence and personal example and explanation, insured himself that they were correctly carried out.

The article that Patton worked on under Pershing's supervision was completed on December 1. Entitled "Cavalry Work of the Punitive Expedition," it appeared under Patton's name in the *Cavalry Journal* of January 1917. It was an important article and attracted widespread attention throughout the Army. Professional soldiers, particularly those who had not been to Mexico, were curious to learn not only about Pershing and his methods but also about the operations of the largest American force assembled since the Civil War.

The nature of the country and of the campaign against an elusive guerrilla force had placed the operational burden on the cavalry. Unlike the war on the Western Front in Europe, where immobile infantry and artillery formations fought long, drawn-out battles of attrition, the action in Mexico was characterized by broad cavalry sweeps, reconnaissance missions, and scouting. How had Pershing, himself a cavalryman, directed his force and what had he gained from the experience?

Readers of Patton's article would discover little about the operations. They would instead be treated to a discourse on training. They would comprehend how hard a taskmaster Pershing was. And they would see an early, if not the earliest, example of progressive training, a course of instruction that went step by step, starting with individual practice to attain proficiency in a skill, and continuing through exercises by small units to maneuvers by large formations composed of the combined arms. It would become the standard method of preparing troops for combat.

Patton's opening was eye-catching:

"Cavalry can fight anywhere except at sea and only the fact that the horse is not web-footed restricts its prowess even there." The limitation of a field library prevents an exact quotation but something like the above is the goal toward which American Cavalry has ever aspired.

He went on to show in detail how Pershing's comprehensive training program brought his force of four cavalry regiments, one infantry regiment, and his artillery units — all camped in the midst of hundreds of square miles of varied terrain unrestricted for movement — to peak fitness, efficiency, and effectiveness.

According to Pershing, quoted by Patton:

The Cavalry Service Regulations say that "mounted action is the principal method of fighting of cavalry." By adopting that view and inserting it in the drill book, the cavalry has done itself irreparable harm . . . [It] creates the impression that cavalry is no longer to be considered for dismounted work . . . I do not subscribe to any such narrow conception of the role of cavalry. If our cavalry is to be limited to mounted work, then it has failed to profit by the lessons of the civil war. For open warfare, under modern conditions, it is more necessary than ever to have troops that are able to move rapidly from one place to another over any kind of country and arrive at the point of action fit for a fight. In addition to the important functions of reconnoitering and screening and the dashing sphere of mounted combat, the cavalry must know how to fight on foot. Perfect control of the horse and expert use of the pistol [and at Patton's insistence]

or saber are demanded for successful mounted attack, while thorough
training in rifle firing and mastery of the principles of fire tactics are
equally essential in the dismounted fight.

In other words, the cavalry had to be ready to perform both missions.
It had to be as good as the best infantry in the world and at the same
time to excel the mounted work of any cavalry.

This was, Patton concluded, in what had already become his rather
typical style,

> our ideal. To be able to fight anywhere, any time, and to do it better
> than our opponent. So that should the Fates and Mars call on us to
> meet the thundering squadrons of a civilized foe, we may charge
> them with as headlong an ardor as ever animated the troops of Seid-
> litz or Murat; or, if we are required to hold the foe in play while our
> citizens arm, we may do so as well as did the men of Forrest or De-
> Witt; or, if we are called on to pursue an enemy, as cruel and elusive
> as the cayote, we may be able to dislodge him from his mountain
> fastnesses with our perfected fire attack, to saber and pistol him as he
> flees vainly seeking fresh cover.

Some readers may have smiled at these inflated words. But no one
could help being struck by the sincerity of the message.

To some extent, the article had the additional virtue of enhancing Pershing's image as a tough military man.

Patton always regarded the operations of the advance guard as a specialty of his, and he submitted a paper to Pershing on the deficiencies he
had remarked during the training exercises. After defining the duties of
the advance guard — the major function was to insure the safe and uninterrupted march of the main body of troops — Patton insisted that the
point or advance guard be pushed farther ahead of the main body than
was the normal practice, that it desist from cautious and timid operations,
that it send informational reports promptly instead of numerous negative
reports, that it refrain from establishing unnecessary connecting files and
other unwarranted formations. In support of his contentions, he cited
relevant paragraphs from the *Cavalry Service Regulations,* the *Infantry
Drill Regulations,* the *Field Service Regulations,* and a Fort Leavenworth
publication on minor tactics.

The "lack of distance," he wrote,

is one of our chief faults . . . we frequently see points and advance parties leaping from their horses at the simple mention of a hostile patrol. This is playing the enemies game; they should go on mounted and see something . . . Patrols cannot gain information of the enemy in time for it to be of any value unless they get out far enough to see and report in time. Distance again. Nor can they prevent his [the enemy's] seeing unless they push him [the enemy] back. Offensive not defensive tactics . . . The normal advance guard like the normal attack should not exist [meaning that every formation and every action should be tailored to meet the specific situation at hand].

In conclusion:

Cavalry must use its mobility to gain early information so it can assume the offensive well informed and not poke along like Infantry must until it bumps its nose. It should remember that the enemy is just as ignormant of its whereabouts as it is of him.

These remarks indicated well the aggressive and offensive-minded attitude he personified and, in addition, showed his familiarity with regulations pertinent to tactics.

Letter, GSP, Jr., to Beatrice, December 3, 1916
Collins and I dined with the 13th Cav. this evening. They have a nice regimental mess hall and tin dishes. It was very plesant, afterwards we sat around a big fire place and talked shop. It is quite obvious that the effect of so many troops together has in making men take their profession more seriously.

Letter, GSP, Jr., to Beatrice, December 5, 1916
I have been reading the Book of Morman and it is the darndest rot I have ever run into.

Letter, GSP, Jr., to Beatrice, December 8, 1916
It is very cold to night and water has been freezing in the shade all day. The poor horses will suffer I fear . . .
Don't loose the [my] poems as I have no more copies.

Letter, GSP, Jr., to Beatrice, December 9, 1916
[Wrote a] very gastly poem this evening [on the typewriter] but as

I put the carbon paper in rong I can't send you a copy until tomorrow.

Letter, GSP, Jr., to Beatrice, December 11, 1916

[Polo today; played number 4 position and made 2 goals] Quite unusual for [number] four but was due to the heavy dust which prevented ones seeing the ball so they would all ride over [the ball] then I would come up and score.

Letter, GSP, Jr., to Beatrice, December 13, 1916

[Played polo and won, very exciting.] lost three quarters [of a goal] on fouls by my self . . . several people said I played the best game of the crowd but it is so dusty that it is not much fun . . .

The troops here are realy in fine shape and the best trained we have ever had. Gen. P. is certainly a fine leader and tireless worker.

Letter, Joseph R. Anderson, Historiographer of the V.M.I., Lee, Goochland County, Virginia, to GSP, Jr., December 13, 1916

My dear George: I feel that I must address you thus for the love I bear your father . . .

I have watched your very brilliant career, my dear fellow with the keenest interest and rejoiced that another of your glowing name had become distinguished. That was a "narrow call" you had with those devils in Mexico.

I am distressed that your father was defeated in his candidacy for the Senate but suppose it was a very difficult thing to "buck against" that seasoned politician Governor Johnson . . .

. . . you may not be a full graduate of the old V.M.I. [but] you are one of her most cherished *alumni* . . .

Letter, GSP, Jr., to Beatrice, December 14, 1916

I don't want any present if I am still in Mexico at Christmas. And the only thing I could send you would be something I picked out of a catalogue which would not be nice so I will not send you any thing.

Send some cards to people for us both.

I want to give Gen. P. a present. If there are any shaving sets for Durham Duplex raizors. That is a set with brush soap raizor and blades. Get one and send it to me for him. Marked J.J.P. Get me a pipe in a case for Schallenberger and a whip for Collins. If you see some little things for Maj. Hines, Capt. Viner, Capt. Campanole

Maj. Walton, Col. C. get them but very trifling affairs as they will not give me any thing and might feel badly.

Letter, GSP, Jr., to Beatrice, December 17, 1916

We rather think that Carranza wants us to stay for a while as our presence keeps Villa out of this part of Chihuahua. . . .

There is no use in Ma's asking Gen. P. out for Christmas as he could not possibly leave here while he is in command.

Letter, GSP, Jr., to Beatrice, December 19, 1916

This will probably get to you the day before Christmas and I wish that I could come with it but I can't. Last Christmas was not much but we were together and I enjoyed it for I fear I am still and ever will be jealous even of B Jr. and R. E. [Ruth Ellen] Still I had hoped to be with you this year. If we were doing any good here I would not mind but to just sit and see things go to hell . . . is not very pleasant.

But please don't worry about me and get gray hair I don't like it. You are too pretty to be gray. . . . you ought to ride a little or you will loose your figure also you ought to exercise regularly which you don't do. . . .

[There was to be a big Christmas tree for all the soldiers, with a present for each sent by the Red Cross.] I gave the Hdqs detachment $20 for a Xmas dinner.

Letter, GSP, Jr., to Beatrice, December 20, 1916

Darling Beat: It is just about a year since we had that wind storm at Sierra Blanca and you cried and wished I would resign [from the Army]. It has been awful here for the last two days. I have never seen such dust. And it made me wish I was out of it. If I could only be sure of the future I would get out. That is if I was sure that I would never be above the average army officer I would for I don't like the dirt and all except as a means to fame. If I knew that I would never be famous I would settle down and raise horses and have a good time. It is a great gamble to spoil your and my own happiness for the hope of greatness. I wish I was less ambitious, then too some times I think that I am not ambitious at all only a dreamer. That I don't realy do my damdest even when I think I do.

This job I now have is not good as I have not enough to do and get lazy.

Well this is not much of a Christmas letter. I hope you have a nice time and stay young.

A large Christmas box from home reached Patton on December 22, but he was waiting for the holiday to open it. He hoped it contained books. There was a motion picture show every night, but not much else to do. He was in charge of a sports program for the enlisted men on Christmas morning, and he was planning a burro race, greased pig contest, relay race, shoe race, and football game.

Letter, GSP, Jr., to Beatrice, December 23, 1916
We had a holiday to day but it don't mean much as there is nothing to do any way and nothing to Holiday with.

A terrible wind storm came up on Christmas day and blew dust everywhere all day long. It was impossible to face into the wind and breathe, impossible to see beyond ten feet. The wind threw down nearly all the tents and tore them to bits. It knocked over the adobe storehouses and unroofed most of the other buildings. Patton saved his own roof by putting nails in the floor and tying the rafters to them. Even then the roof jumped up and down. More than half an inch of dust lay on the floor. There was no Christmas dinner because the storm blew away the kitchens and all the turkeys and pies. The poor horses suffered. The Christmas celebration was postponed.

Letter, GSP, Jr., to Beatrice, December 25, 1916
All my presents were fine. The phonograph is realy wonderful and Gen. P. came in and we had a concert . . .
The Gen. told me to night that he would probably go to Columbus about the middle of January and would take me. He is going to invite Nita too. Get her to accept as then he will surely take me.

Letter, GSP, Jr., to his father, December 30, 1916
Only in epochs where the state is dominent has men advanced. Individualism is the theory of decay . . .
Individual man has habitually failed to run himself for himself. He must be run. Germany has the only true idea. The few must run the many for the latters good. To Hell with the people!
Asto your jocular assertion, that the central powers are on the

point of ruin, even the after effects of Christmas cannot justify such a belief. The allies are on the point of rupture and another year of war will see their shadow policy an utter failure . . .

I hope that the oranges [in California] are all o.k.

With best wishes for a happy new year in Washington. . . .

P.S. Please get me a medium sized Spanish-English Dictionary. And a couple of simple Spanish stories like Nick Carter or Robinson Cruso.

Letter, GSP, Jr., to Beatrice, December 30, 1916

There is very little to do just now and time passes slowly. I certainly am sick of this but so is every one else so there is no use growling.

Pershing rated Patton "an efficient young officer, very enthusiastic in his work. Has served at my headquarters during the entire period of the expedition and his services have been most satisfactory." From Pershing, whose sole criterion was efficiency, this was high praise.

Letter, GSP, Jr., to Beatrice, January 1, 1917

[City Troop Philadelphia Polo team came to play and] we selected a team to play them. I was on the team but at [number] three which I can't play [well]. We had a practice game with a second team this morning and they beat us with the result that Anderson got put on in my place. At first they were going to put me on at four but finally decided to let Erwin stay at that place. I think this is a mistake as I am a better four than he so I hope that they will be beaten.

Beatrice had sent Pershing Christmas letters that the children, Beatrice Jr. and Ruth Ellen, had dictated to her. She had added a note from herself: "Merrie Christmas dear General John!"

Letter, GSP, Jr., to Beatrice, January 4, 1917

Your book which came with the pistol is fine. I have several other books which Maj. Eltinge sent me on war so am well supplied . . .

P.S. The Gen was much tickled with B's letter and then he seemed to think of his dead children and his eyes filled with tears. GSP

Pershing replied to the letters from the children by writing to little

Beatrice on January 7, ending his letter: "With love to you and your little sister and your Aunt Nita and your Mama."

Letter, GSP, Jr., to Beatrice, January 6, 1917
[Bullfighting] is quite an interesting sport though a little hard on the bulls. Still I should like to see a real good one.

In a small notebook marked Dublan, Mexico, January 1917, Patton described how Pershing carried out an inspection on January 8. The general had first issued a memo order to say that the troops would shortly be inspected in appearance, equipment, arms, mounts, transportation, drill, maneuver, fire tactics, horsemanship, signaling, estimation of distances, first aid, scouting, marching, herding animals, patrolling, entrenching, night operations, physical training, bayonet fencing, saber work, napping, packing. Then the general went over the inspection program, assigned special inspectors to various subjects, and prescribed the system of marking and grading the units.

Nothing is too minute to escape him. A button a shirt not fastened a loose spur . . . Every arm is inspected intensly and so far as possible personally by Gen. Pershing. It is this personal care which gets the results and only this *personal* care will.

Letter, GSP, Jr., to Beatrice, January 9, 1917
When this reaches you you will have had a birthday and I shall not have been there. I am very sorry both for your having a birthday and also for my absence. I hate to get old and also for you to get old. It is true you look just as young as you did when I went to West Point but I hate to have us out of the twenties. Since we have lost a year of each other it almost seems that we should not age.

Letter, GSP, Jr., to Beatrice, January 10, 1917
We worked from eight thirty to twelve thirty and from two to five inspecting to day. It is very tedious work but gets the results. I had to open all the horses mouths in four regiments of cavalry which is some job. It is realy surprising that in nearly three thousand horses you hardly find any who make any trouble about opening their mouths. In the morning we will inspect the infantry and artillery which will be an easier job for me as there are fewer horses.

The 10th Cav. [the regiment of colored soldiers] had the best equipments and altogether put up the best show. You never saw any thing like their stony gaze when at attention. I asked one why he had a certain strap on his bridle he replied "I don't know sar it is de regulation." It was not [regulation] but I let it go at that as he was so sure of it.

There is no better way of learning what is required than by participating in these inspections. I have learned more useful soldiering while in Mexico than all the rest of my service put together. But it has been at a high price being away from you so long.

Letter, GSP, Jr., to Beatrice, January 11, 1917

[Will have to work 8 hours in the morning on the horsemanship test.] I got it up so have to run it . . .

Lots of men desert all the time now. It shows how desperate they are for desertion here is ten years [prison] . . .

I am getting fat at a disgusting rate but hope to reduce soon.

Pershing's plans to go to Columbus in mid-January were dissipated by the arrival of General Funston, who came on an inspection trip.

"Gen. P. says to tell you," Patton wrote to Beatrice on January 14, "that we will not get to Columbus until between the twenty fifth and thirtieth. I doubt if we get there even then. He said to also tell Nita of the dates." He had been ordered to take the examination for promotion to captain on March 1, but no action would probably be taken until July 1 at the earliest. "I am glad you got the roses" he had sent for her birthday. And in the same old self-depreciating manner of his, "they were not much but the best I could do from here."

Pershing put on a review for Funston, who then inspected the camp, later departed with Pershing for the south.

There was much excitement, and rumors were flying. Everyone took Funston's trip as the final inspection before the Punitive Expedition was pulled out of Mexico. According to some, Funston already had orders designating the destinations of the various units but would show the orders to no one. Everyone wildly speculated where his unit would be sent once gone from Mexico.

Letter, GSP, Jr., to Beatrice, January 15, 1917

Collins swears that the eleventh [Cavalry] will go to El Paso. I wrote Gen. [Hugh L.] Scott a personal letter asking if he could transfer me to it . . . If Pa goes to Washington I will get him to go see Gen Scott also . . .

Gen. Funston has a medal of honor but he is afraid of a horse. Coming in from the review his horse figited a little and he squealed just like a puppie.

Letter, GSP, Jr., to Beatrice, January 16, 1917

There is absolutely nothing to write about. And I have one of my worthless streaks on when I don't seem to do or care to do any thing. I guess I have been here too long.

He was not too "worthless" on the following day to reply to a memorandum that had stirred his indignation.

2nd Indorsement from 1st Lieutenant G. S. Patton, 10 Cavalry, Dublan, Mexico, to Commandant, Mounted Service School, Fort Riley, Kansas, January 17, 1917

. . . I beg leave to submit the following statement.

With reference to certin troop commanders who favor the introduction of cuts and parries, the following seems pertinant.

Each point, lunge and the charge saber taught in the Saber Manual 1914 is also a complete parry for any cut or thrust delivered from the direction of attack. This being the case it is clearly better to use the lunges now taught which are also parries than it would be to use simple negative parries. Since this latter . . . does not threaten the enemy in any way [it] simply raises his morale.

The fact that all the attacks taught are also parries is a fact which is not understood by the vast majority of officers whose only knowledge of fencing comes from reading the manual not from practising it . . .

The complicated passive parries were invented by the various teachers for the use of duelists where the contestants fought uninterrupted. In the melee such will not be the case. Meetings between combatants will be brief and to gain success they must be bloody for the enemy. A soldier who goes about defending himself is doing no good to the tactical issue and will soon be killed. Since he injures no one he will be set upon by several at once and be dispatched.

. . . In the Charge in Ninetynine cases out of a hundred the initial impact will decide the day. Offensive, mordant troopers imbued with the fierce desire to destroy the enemy by always attacking him will break troops who having been over educated in selfdefense will enter the fight more desirous of escaping alive by the use of parries than of remaining victorious surrounded by slain opponents.

It is for the purpose of developing this idea of attack that in the present manual so much time is devoted to running at dummies and so little to combats between men . . .

In the charge the point will always beat the edge. It gets there first . . .

[After citing Xerxes, the Turks, Charles Martel, Crusaders, the Highland Claymore] I respectfully suggest that the present manual be continued in force till after the close of the war in Europe when it in company with most other manuals may have to undergo changes to conform to the lessons there to be learned . . .

Letter, GSP, Jr., to Beatrice, January 18, 1917

Some damned fools are trying to get cuts put in the saber manual so I wrote an indorsement . . . I hope they all die. Ignorance is more profound on the saber than on any thing else yet every ass has an idea.

I also inclose a very bum poem to give you something to read as there is no other news.

Letter, GSP, Jr., to Beatrice, January 20, 1917

It looks as if we were about to come out [of Mexico]. Every one is packing and rushing about. I am going to a bull fight.

Letter, GSP, Jr., to Beatrice, January 20, 1917

If you divest your self of the foolish sentiment of the bulls feelings it is a fine sight and takes a lot of nerve.

Three days later he wrote to say there was nothing definite but he had a feeling they were ready to come out. Beatrice, he suggested, better make arrangements to get a room at Columbus in the big hotel or at the feed store.

Two days still later, he expected the headquarters to be in Columbus on February 4. If Nita was coming to Columbus with Beatrice, Beatrice had to get two rooms.

In accordance with Pershing's instructions, Patton observed a series of pistol charges made by the four regiments of Cavalry and then wrote a detailed report "respectfully offer[ing] the following criticism." In a charge, whether made with lance, saber, or pistol, the horse was the chief weapon and the determination to close with the enemy was the chief factor in success. Therefore, the charge had to strike the enemy at maximum speed. "Had any of the troops which pulled up to fire been opposed by a real enemy, they would have been ridden down as happened to the Austrians at Luthen. A bullet fired into a charging horse at ten yards will not stop him unless he is struck in the brain." Ground scouts and combat patrols were not well used. Forming the charge line too soon was a common mistake, and not taking the gallop early enough was a usual error. "During . . . the charges . . . the guides seemed more intent on cautioning the men not to go fast and not to shoot any one than on the gait and direction."

This was, obviously, deplorable. What he wanted were mordant troopers in reckless charge motivated by the desire to destroy the enemy.

Toward the end of January, orders arrived for the Punitive Expedition to leave Mexico. At the same time, the War Department prescribed the stations where the units were to go. Patton's regiment, the 10th Cavalry, was directed to Nogales. That meant moving from El Paso, losing the house at Fort Bliss, and, worst of all, quitting Pershing.

Letter, GSP, Jr.. to Beatrice, January 28, 1917

I also got a letter from Gen Scott saying he could not transfer me. So I felt very blue expecting to have to ride in with the 10th. I went to the General and asked him if he would give me a leave so I could go to El Paso and pack. He said that it was his intention to take me there with him if he could as he said he did not want to "loose me."

So I guess we will get to our house a little while anyway . . . if I get to be a Captain in July I will have a fine chance of getting to a decent regiment. So cheer up.

Gen P. and I went out to see the refugees to day. There were over a hundred wagons of them [leaving because the American troops were departing]. It was the most pathetic sight I ever saw. Women and children and old men and young men with all they had in rickety old wagons. Leaving a country where neither life or virtue is respected . . .

One family was all mounted on burros. One old man limped after the thinest cow and calf you ever saw. All he had. It was very cold and they were shaking. Then in the midst two wagons full of painted whores under a guard . . .

I expect that all the Carranzistas will follow us out.

All the mormons are leaving too and they had better.

Letter, GSP, Jr., to Aunt Nannie, January 29, 1917

Beatrice has probably told you that I am sure of getting transferred to the seventh cavalry which will be in El Paso . . .

We have been busting up houses all day. We do it a funny way simply pull the roof off and then back a truck against the wall. It pushes them over as nice as you please.

He was sure of going to the 7th Cavalry because Lieutenant Menoher of that regiment had asked Patton whether he wanted to exchange transfers. Menoher wished government quarters, which were available in Nogales, for he could not afford to rent quarters on the open market in El Paso. Patton agreed at once, and both lieutenants sent a wire off immediately to the proper authorities. Therefore, whether he stayed with Pershing or not, he would get to El Paso. The 7th Cavalry, he said, was not a very good regiment but at least it had some nice people in it.

Letter, GSP, Jr., to Beatrice, January 29, 1917

This is the last letter I shall write you from Mexico. I have learned a lot about my profession and a lot how much I love you. The first was necessary the second was not.

VI

France

"The idea that any[one] but a trained soldier can conduct war is absurd. . . . the job I now have is too easy . . . one must work for success."

CHAPTER 19

El Paso to Paris

"I think that people are being entertained too much."

PERSHING'S PUNITIVE EXPEDITION withdrew from Mexico early in February of 1917, and the headquarters and certain units returned to El Paso to a tumultuous civic and personal welcome.

"The arrival of Gen. Pershing, George & the army," Mr. Ayer wrote his daughter Beatrice, "was an occasion of a lifetime & your description of them is most picturesque & entertaining."

On February 1, Patton was formally transferred to the 7th Cavalry, stationed at El Paso, but he remained on duty with Pershing's headquarters, continuing as acting aide. When the Punitive Expedition was dissolved on February 14, Patton stayed on, serving in the same capacity.

General Funston died on February 19, and a few days later, Pershing was transferred to San Antonio to succeed him in command of the Southern Department.

On his departure from Fort Bliss, Pershing rated Patton's efficiency and gave him good marks — excellent in his general military proficiency and "most satisfactory" in his specific duties.

To Patton's disappointment, Pershing referred to him not as his aide but only as having been in charge of — not even in command of — the mounted detachment of the headquarters.

Joining his regiment, Patton was assigned to the 1st Squadron, which was stationed at Camp Stewart, near Fort Bliss. On February 27, he was placed in command of Troop A.

It was a choice assignment, particularly for a first lieutenant, for normally a captain commanded a troop. But Patton was eligible for promotion, and in March, after a period of intensive study, he took and passed the examinations to qualify for the advancement in grade.

His squadron commander, Major Edmund M. Leary, when reassigned to another position within the regiment in mid-March, judged Patton's performance and noted that he was "progressive, active, zealous, and an excellent troop commander."

Meanwhile, the friendship between Pershing and the Patton family had grown enormously during the past year and a half. While Pershing was still at El Paso, when he learned that Mr. Patton was in Washington and staying at the Metropolitan Club as a guest of his son, he telegraphed to invite Mr. Patton to a small luncheon in his honor when he passed through on his way home to California. The death of Funston and Pershing's move to San Antonio necessitated canceling the luncheon. A subsequent exchange of correspondence culminated in an invitation extended by Mr. Patton for the general to visit the family in California. Pershing accepted. The Pattons, especially Nita, were delighted.

Shortly before starting for California, Pershing sent Patton an official piece of mail he had received from the Cavalry Board, which Colonel Rhodes headed, and asked Patton to let Pershing know what he thought of the matter.

Letter, GSP, Jr. (El Paso), to Pershing (Fort Sam Houston, San Antonio), March 20, 1917

When I first got your letter with the inclosed communication from Col. Rhodes I was in the midst of my examination for promotion and since an opinion on equipment from one who had failed to pass his examination would have been of little value I defered writing until I was safely finished.

Rhodes had queried Pershing for his comments on a new-model saddle that the cavalry was thinking of adopting, and Patton was extremely flattered that Pershing had solicited his opinion. It meant that Pershing valued his judgment, still considered him an unofficial member of his staff, and regarded him as an excellent horseman.

The remarks that Patton forwarded to Pershing as a draft reply to Rhodes or as a staff study were detailed, clear, and expert. He wrote with authority on the bearing surface of the horse's back, the pommel arch, the shape of the withers, the splay of the bars, the problems of flat-backed horses, the rear tips of the bars, the side bars, the padding, the saddle flap or skirt, and the stirrups.

I strongly favor carrying the rifle on the back as it is much better for the horse and the man always has it with him. Lazy people will object and raise all sorts of spurious arguments against it. One of these which recently came to my attention is that the rifle, when carried on the back, will catch when riding in brush. Such brush however will not be encountered in more than one out of every thousand miles marched . . . It would be just as foolish to condemn carrying the rifle on the back for such a cause as it would be to require every soldier to habitually wear a life preserver in order to escape drowning at a Galveston flood once every fifty years . . .

[The lariat is] an utterly useless weight.

He ended his letter on the usual self-depreciating note: "Thank you for letting me see the report. I trust that this long reply has not bored you."

Not long afterward, the *Cavalry Journal* published in its April issue an extract of the memorandum Patton had sent Rhodes from Mexico on the saber. Patton had then been enraged to learn that the Cavalry Board was considering changing both the saber that he had designed and the manual he had written, and he had defended his creations with such great gusto that he convinced the Board he was right.

The article in the *Journal,* entitled "The Present Saber — It's [sic] Form and the Use for which it was Designed," was introduced by an editorial note:

In addition to criticisms as to the balance of the present saber, many officers have favored a slight curve in the blade . . . In explanation of the omission of these features from the Manual, Lieut. Patton, who wrote the Manual and who is well known as one of the foremost authorities on fencing in the army, has prepared the following memorandum for the Commandant, Mounted Service School, which has been forwarded to the War Department as representing the views of the School. — Editor.

This was, of course, a great victory for Patton over the advocates of the curved blade and the saber cut rather than the thrust with the point of the straight weapon.

The article stressed military history turned to Patton's purposes:

When Cyrus the Great first invented "shock tactics" (500 B.C.) he gave his men short pikes, pointing weapons, though for hundreds of years they had used cutting swords dismounted.

It featured Patton's observations, among them that he knew only two examples of men cut by a saber in battle, a soldier in the Civil War, and a soldier in China. In both cases, the skull turned the edge of the sword, and only a flesh wound resulted. If the point had been used, the men would have been run through.

His conclusion was temperate and sound:

> I am of the opinion that the present manual should be continued in force till after the close of the war in Europe, when it, in company with most other manuals, may have to undergo changes to conform to the lessons there to be learned.

After spending a week with the Pattons in California, Pershing stopped at El Paso on his return to San Antonio. He took George and Beatrice to dinner and gave them news of the family. They discussed the World War and the nearness of American involvement. It was a pleasant evening, and on the following morning the Pattons took him to his train and saw him off.

"It must have been quite exciting," Patton wrote to Aunt Nannie that day, April 1, "while he [Pershing] was there."

It must have been particularly exciting for Nita.

All was about to change, not only for Nita and Pershing, but also for all Americans. On April 6, the United States declared war on Germany.

Patton had anticipated this by several days. He had already started proceedings to obtain a commission as a field grade officer — major or lieutenant colonel — in the Volunteer forces he was sure would be raised for the war. The first requirement was to secure letters of recommendation, and he had three.

Major Leary, his former squadron commander, had written:

> Lieutenant Patton is energetic, an enthusiastic horseman and zealous in the performance of duty. I believe that he would make good as a Field Officer of Volunteer Cavalry.

Brigadier General Eben Swift, the post commander at Fort Bliss, said:

> I believe that Lieutenant Patton would make a good Major of Cavalry in any volunteer force that may be raised.

Pershing remarked:

Lieutenant Patton is a capable, energetic officer, and would perform the duties of a field officer of volunteers with credit to himself and to the government.

Letter, GSP, Jr. (3915 Mountain Avenue, El Paso), to Pershing, April 11, 1917

Mrs. Pattons father [Mr. Ayer] has pneumonia and the doctor advises that we come east so I have asked Gen. Swift for a months leave to take effect about the fifteenth as it will take me that long to get my accounts [as troop commander] cleared. We had hoped to come by way of San Antonio [to see Pershing] but as it would take us twenty four hours longer we cannot spare the extra time this trip.

I am very sorry to give up [command of] my troop as I was doing well with it and had the horses in fine shape.

As the Seventh [Cavalry] is now full of captains I doubt if I get my promotion in it and if I do not I shall try to get some regiment nearer Boston so Mrs Patton can be near her parents. That is if she has any after this attack.

I expect to mail you the diary [of the Punitive Expedition] in two days. I wish it were better but even as it is it is quite a help to the memory.

I have just had a letter from Nita. She talks in a most warlike way and speaks of fighting in Flanders as if it were a thing assured.

Telegram, Pershing to GSP, Jr., April 14, 1917

Letter received. Sorry to hear of illness mentioned. Wire me your address east.

Patton's leave was approved, and he and his family departed for Massachusetts.

A few days later, Captain Charles H. Boice, commander of the 1st Squadron, 7th Cavalry, evaluated Patton's military performance. According to Boice, Patton was "An efficient young officer with exemplary habits."

Letter, GSP, Jr. (Pride's Crossing), to Pershing, April 23, 1917

Dear Gen Pershing. The inclosed diary is not so good as I could wish because I had no time to typewrite it my self and so had to read it into a dictaphone and when the man wrote it he made a great many mistakes. I have another copy which I will correct and send you. As you know the rather exciting circumstances under which I left El Paso I hope you will not think too badly of me for sending you this. It was not completed when I left and had to follow me here hence the delay in its reaching you.

When we got here we found Mr. Ayer had just regained consciousness but he was terribly weak and being over ninety it is still very doubtful if he recoveres. Mrs. Ayer is also in bed with two nurses and My sister in law Miss Ayer is trying to get married. Beatrice is adding to the general jollity by being also in bed sick so I am having as you may guess a very gay time and my disposition is in a fair way to be spoiled.

All the people here are war mad and every one I know is either becoming a reserve officer or explaining why he cant. It looks to me as if we were going to have Too many reserve officers many of whom are meer children.

My business affairs are progressing very well but I expect that the new taxes will hit every one pretty hard. I wish that they would exempt officers?

If I can possibly get away from this combined Hospital and matrimonial establishment I am going to Washington for a day and see if I cant get into some regiment near here as when Miss Ayer is married Beatrice will have to be here as her parents are too sick to be left alone. Of course if we go to France it will be all right as in that case she cant be with me any way and could stay here as well as any where else.

This is a very stupid and personal letter and the machine [typewriter] is out of order. Please excuse all the defects.

Very respectfully,

Mr. Patton wrote his son a letter on the last day of April, but when he reread it, he found it so depressing that he decided not to mail it. It was petulant and full of complaints. For Mr. Patton was sick over the declaration of war. He had supported Wilson's policy of neutrality, and he was disturbed and distressed because he believed that the country had been pushed into the world conflict. Just the day before, on April 29, Congress passed the Draft Act providing for Selective Service, and although amendments and conferences would hold up final passage until May 18, its enactment into law was a foregone conclusion.

In addition to his general malaise and low spirits, Mr. Patton had been unwell since returning home from Washington in February. He had then refused several appointments offered him, for he was unwilling to take what he considered to be a second-class job, and those were the only opportunities available at the time. Aunt Nannie was leaving for New York on the following day, and Mama, Nita, and he were going next Friday. En route, they would stop over in San Antonio and visit with General Pershing for two days.

Mr. Patton was thinking of returning home to California from San Antonio, but if he went on to New York, he would spend a few days in Washington. Perhaps the war had created some new positions suitable for him. He was quite dissatisfied with conditions, vaguely pessimistic about everything, and needed to talk with George and be cheered up.

Mr. Patton thought that the war would continue at least another year unless an internal revolution broke out in Germany. It seemed foolish to him for the United States to send a military force to Europe. But he felt that Theodore Roosevelt's fiery speeches and the inflamed reports in the press would compel the government to do so. "I hate to think of your going [overseas]," he wrote, "but I would hate you to be passed over if you want to go."

His son wanted badly to go. And he was in Washington trying to discover what the War Department had in mind for him or, if possible, to find a good job for himself, one that would get him to the front in a hurry. The draft act ruled out Volunteer forces. There would be, instead, a National Army composed of conscripted recruits to be trained by Regulars. Though he had no aversion to training recruits, he hoped to be where the real action was.

It was difficult to learn much about his future. Washington was in tumult as a horde of job-seekers and others descended on the capital in search of profit, in one form or another, to be gained from the war.

Avidly interested in what was going on in Europe, Patton attended a lecture given by an English officer. Afterward, Patton talked with him at the Metropolitan Club until midnight.

As for his own prospects, he wrote Beatrice on May 3,

I know no more about my self than I did last night except that Capt. [Malin] Craig said they were holding me up as J.J.P. [Pershing] wanted me so I wired Shalenberger to find out if he did.

I went up to fort Myer and Col. Glascoe said not to ask Mrs.

[Hugh] Scott so I did not. Capt. Haight almost got me a Mess Officer for 2500 reserve officers but I ducked it as it does not appear much of a job to me . . . I will have to stay here till I learn something.

Pershing had indeed asked that Patton be held for future assignment to him. A telegram from the Army Chief of Staff, General Scott, on May 2, informed Pershing that he was to form at once a division composed of four regiments of infantry and one of artillery, and he was to train it for shipment overseas. At that point, Pershing designated a list of officers he wished to have in his headquarters, and Patton was among those he selected.

Three days later, Pershing replied to Patton's letter of April 23 by telegram to Pride's Crossing. In view of the illness in the Ayer family, Pershing said, he had no objection to Patton's seeking to be detailed to a training camp in the east. But he suggested rather cryptically that Patton consider the possibility of more important service elsewhere. He sent his best wishes to Patton and Beatrice and hoped that Mr. Ayer was feeling better.

Pershing also telegraphed Mr. Patton in California. He said he was happy that the Patton family was planning to be in San Antonio, and he hoped they could remain several days.

The visit in San Antonio was cut short. Pershing was suddenly ordered to Washington. All left together and traveled to the capital.

In Washington on the evening of May 9, Pershing made several calls on the following morning. He talked with Scott, then with the Secretary of War, Newton D. Baker. Pershing learned that not only was he to organize and train a division but he was to take it to Europe as the first American contingent to join the Allied forces. Several days later he received word of increased responsibilities. He had been selected to command all the American forces that were to be sent to Europe. He would be the Commander in Chief of the American Expeditionary Force.

Meanwhile, alerted by Malin Craig's information early in May that Pershing had asked for him, perhaps in receipt of a telegram from Shallenberger that Pershing wanted him, warned by Pershing himself vaguely of more important duties awaiting him elsewhere, and probably troubled by an intangible presentiment that it would be a mistake to return to Texas, Patton left Washington, went back to Pride's Crossing, and wired

El Paso for an extension of his leave of absence, which was to expire on May 15. His request, probably made on the ground of continuing illness in the Ayer family, was granted.

On May 15, although he was unaware of the action and would remain ignorant of the fact for some time, Patton was promoted to captain.

On the following day, the War Department Adjutant General telephoned the headquarters of the Southern Department in San Antonio — Pershing's command — and directed the commanding general — Pershing, who was, of course, absent in Washington — to order Lieutenant Patton to Washington for duty with the Adjutant General's Office. Patton was to be detailed to Front Royal, Virginia, on temporary duty for the purpose of purchasing horses for the Army.

Pershing had other ideas in mind for Patton. When he learned from his staff in El Paso of Patton's imminent assignment to Front Royal, he had the order rescinded. In its stead, he had the Adjutant General send a telegram to Pride's Crossing ordering Patton to report to Pershing in Washington.

Upon receipt of that telegram, Patton started a diary.*

Diary

May 18 (Friday): I had been riding at Mr. Rice's in Topsfield, Mass., and when I returned to Prides I found a wire from the Adjutant General to proceed to Washington at once and report to Gen Pershing. I telephoned Papa at Washington. He could say nothing definate over the phone but said to come at once and to bring Beatrice. Caught the 12:30 A.M. train after driving to Boston with Kay Ayer and Keith Merrill (whom Katharine would marry) in our new machine.

May 19 (Saturday): reached New York 7 A.M., went to Penn Station for train to Washington. At station read in paper that Gen P was to precede troops to France. Reached Washington 2 P.M. Papa met us and said I would have to start almost at once. I told Beatrice to wire El Paso and have Williams bring all my outfit, then went to War Department and reported. Capt. Nelson Margetts, Pershing's aide, told me to get some uniforms at once as we were leaving Wed-

* I have paraphrased the Diary entries for the most part (although I have tried to keep the flavor of Patton's language, spelling, and punctuation) I have quoted certain passages, directly; these are designated by quotation marks.

nesday. Got a uniform started (meaning, tailor-made) at Keen's and borrowed one for time being from Capt. E. S. Hughes. Went to hotel and saw Mama and Nita.

May 20 (Sunday): went to Fort Myer at 9 A.M. and inspected 30 men who had been selected as Headquarters orderlies; found them in good shape "and gave them what instructions I could." Papa, Mama, Beatrice, and I went to St. John's at 4 P.M. for church service.

So that was what he was going to do as a member of Pershing's staff. He had the rather menial task of looking after the orderlies.

He cared not at all. He would have taken any job. The important thing was to be going to France with Pershing, to be part of the initial American forces sent overseas, to be in the war at the very beginning.

Whatever his status, whatever his role in the headquarters, he was sure he would prove to be just as useful to Pershing in France as he had been in Mexico.

· · ·

In May 1917, he was in his thirty-second year of age, stood 6 feet 1 inch in height, and weighed 165 pounds. Very slim and very erect, he had a distinctly youthful appearance. He was starting to lose his reddish-blond hair. His light-complexioned face was boyish and unlined when in repose but fierce and awesome when he scowled.

According to a card he filled out to list his qualifications and proficiencies, he had a special knowledge of navigation to a limited degree; he had a special acquaintance with gasoline engines; he had a special competence in athletics; he was an expert fencer and swordsman; he was a specialist in horsemanship; he spoke and translated French and Spanish fairly well, read French well, and read Spanish to some extent.

Diary

May 21 (Monday): to office in the morning and worked till 3:30, then to Fort Myer and carefully inspected the equipment of the men; all in good shape. He listed the men's names.

May 22 (Tuesday): Gen P and all staff busy organizing and getting things clear.

May 23 (Wednesday): Papa, Beatrice, and I had dinner with Senator Phelan and Secretary and Mrs. Lane.

May 24 (Thursday): Williams and all my stuff arrived. Gen P told me to design a uniform for field clerks; no time to get a new one made, so adopted the regular OD uniform and campaign hat but without the braid cord showing branch of service.

May 25: "Nothing."

May 26: Mama gave B some orchids and me a gardenia. Had the Fox Conners, Senator Phelan, a major and a lady from San Francisco to dinner. Got transportation tickets and found that neither Collins (Pershing's longtime aide) nor Margetts had secured travel order for Sergeant Lanckton, the General's orderly and cook. "I was much upset for fear the general would find it out. Col. J. S. Tracey AG. fixed it up for me and was very nice about it."

Photograph with caption from unidentified newspaper, May or June, 1917
Miss Anita W. Patton, daughter of George S. Patton, a Los Angeles lawyer, is to be the bride of Gen. Pershing after the war, according to rumor. The Patton and Pershing families have been friends for years. Mr. Patton and his daughter gave a large dinner in Washington for Gen. Pershing before his departure for France.

Diary
May 27 (Sunday): Left for New York at 11 A.M. on Baltimore and Ohio Railroad with my detachment and 10 engineer soldiers; reached New York 4 P.M.; marched the men to ferry and took them to Governors Island where met General J. Franklin Bell (a former Army Chief of Staff who had succeeded Leonard Wood in command of the Eastern Department) and Tillson (probably Bell's aide). "To be sure that none of the men left I put them under guard and went up to the [Hotel] Walcott [where] all the family were very dolerous."

According to Patton's imperfect recollections ten years later, this was what he said happened.

GSP, Jr., "My Father," 1927
When I got my orders for France, Papa, Mama and Nita were on their way east and came to Washington to see me. I had no uniforms so Papa arranged through his friends to have my striker Williams

rushed from El Paso to Washington with my clothes. While at Washington Papa introduced me to Secretary Lane who told him: "That boy of yours is all wool and a yard wide or I am no judge." This pleased him a lot.

The whole family and Beatrice went to New York with me on the train which carried the Headquarters Officers and soldiers of the first [contingent of the] AEF. Aunt Nannie was in New York and we all spent two nights at the hotel.

The morning we left, Papa went with me to the Governors Island ferry where he told me good by with a smile.

Diary

May 28 (Monday): up at 6 A.M., said goodbye, "much tears," Pa went with me to the ferry. I stayed there till 10:30 directing people where to go and seeing to the placing of the baggage. It rained hard. At 10:30 Gen P arrived with Collins and we all went to the Department Headquarters at Governors Island. Everyone got on tender named the *Thomas Patten* at 12 noon; the boat started but was called back for mail, then went to Graves End Bay and lay around waiting for the steamer. Issued transportation tickets to both men and officers while waiting. When the *Baltic* arrived, tried to board on the weather side, but the easterly wind was too rough. Finally, all got on at 3 P.M.; fortunately I had caused the men to be fed at the Island. I drew Cabin 95 with Mr. Lewis, a 1st Lieut., Reserve aviator. "I had 38 orderlies. 10 Engineers. 10 Chauffeurs. 7 Signal Corps [enlisted men]. Total 65 enlisted plus 2 Medical Corps." We left the harbor in a heavy fog.

According to Pershing's figures, his party consisted of 60 officers and 128 War Department clerks, civilian employees, and enlisted men.

In his diary, Patton listed all the officers with Pershing and their branches and assignments — general staff, adjutant general, quartermaster corps, and the like. Under "Line" officers were Captains Hugh A. Drum and G. S. Patton, Jr., who had no specific staff duties. All the officers would later form themselves into the "Baltic Society" and meet once a year to commemorate their crossing with Pershing to Europe.

Diary

May 29 (Tuesday): heavy fog, nothing to do but get our sea

legs; officers assigned to instructors for work in French 2 hours daily; boat has about 100 trucks and several "tanks" with out the armor. Boat would be a fine prize for a U-boat.

May 30: I gave the men some drill this morning and started French classes among chauffers, all speak it and 2 signal sergeants are college men, one of whom instructed French at College of New York. Heavy fog.

Some of the officers began to work on staff studies. Everyone was inoculated against typhoid.

GSP, Jr., "Personal Glimpses of General Pershing," 1924
The second day out all officers were divided into sections for the study of French. The more fluent and the interpreters acting as instructors; the General himself coming regularly in the lessons.

Letter, GSP, Jr., to Beatrice, June 1, 1917
I have worked over five hours a day on French ever since we started and am one of the best on the boat which does not speak well for the others.

Diary
June 2: Concert in evening and $315 collected for war orphans.

June 3: Got civilian clothes for all members of the staff, borrowing from the civilian clerks for the enlisted men. So if they were torpedoed and forced to take to the lifeboats, the Germans would be less likely to shell boats full of civilians. Doctors lectured on venereal disease, quite prevalent in France. "Every one jokes about the U-Boats but we would all like to see a convoy show up. Some are quite nearvous and sleep in their clothes. The temperature of the sea which has been 52 F is now 60 which will be a comfort if we have to get in it. There was church to day but I did not go."

June 4: reduced speed in order to make rendezvous with convoy; boat drill.

Letter, GSP, Jr., to Beatrice, June 4, 1917
. . . if I only was a little better on [French] verbs I would be all right.

Diary

June 6: "When we got up this morning every one was more cheerful for on either side of our bow were two Destroyers [the *Tucker* and the *Rowan*] Of course they could not absolutely prevent our being shot at but they could prevent the shelling of the boats which is a comfort. It would be rather an experience to be torpedoed but one would not enjoy being shelled later."

June 7: sighted land at 8 P.M.

Letter, GSP, Jr., to Beatrice, June 7, 1917

I have not done so well in French for the last two days but can read it fluently almost as fast as english.

Letter, GSP, Jr., to Mr. Ayer, June 7, 1917

When I left you I had no idea that I was going to France, and when I did find out I could not tell you . . .

We have had a fine trip so far and as we are now in sight of land we might be justified in saying that it was over.

H.M.S. *Baltic,* carrying Pershing and his party of officers, enlisted men, and civilians, 188 in all, docked at Liverpool on the morning of June 8. The Lord Mayor of Liverpool, Rear Admiral Stileman, and Lieutenant General Sir William Pitcairn Campbell — the latter a blimp of a man who made Pershing look positively anemic — came aboard to welcome the Americans. The group gathered on the deck of the ship, and the regimental band of the Royal Welsh Fusiliers, the guard of honor, played "The Star-Spangled Banner" and "God Save the King" while everyone stood at the salute.

Pershing and his staff took a special train to London. At Euston Station they were welcomed by the U. S. Ambassador, Walter Hines Page; the Secretary of State for War, Lord Derby; the Commander in Chief of the British Home Forces, Viscount French; American Admiral Sims, already cooperating with the British naval authorities; Lord Brooke, who was to be attached to Pershing's staff as liaison officer; and others. Pershing was driven to the Savoy Hotel.

Diary

June 8 (Friday): Liverpool. Docked 9 A.M. Disembarked 10 A.M. All baggage passed without inspection. 10:30, started for London.

Reached Euston Station 3:30 . . . My 67 men were directed to go to London Tower for quarters, and I was to stay with them. Took Capt. Paddock with me. British Captain Collins of the Honorable Artillery Company met us at station and took us to Tower. There formed into a column and preceded by the band of the HAC, went under Byward Tower and around the White Tower. 1st Battalion, HAC lined the walks and cheered us. It was very thrilling. Saluted colonel, then men fell out. Assigned to quarters. I reported to Col. Treffry. Had tea and supper at 6:45 P.M. 10 P.M. the Picket Officer (the Sentry Officer or Officer of the Day) asked if I wanted to see the ceremony of the keys. Did so. The impressive ceremony had been performed the same way for over 500 years.

GSP, Jr., "Personal Glimpses of General Pershing," 1924

I commanded the Headquarters Troop, AEF, then consisting of 46 enlisted men. We were quartered in the Tower of London attached to a battalion of the Honorable Artillery Company, and by them treated in every way as friends and brothers. Our entry into that historic fortress; marking as it did the only occasion on which foreign troops have ever marched through that venerable portal save in the guise of prisoners, was impressive in the extreme. The stability of the British race was impressed on me when one evening after dinner their Officer of the Day, called "Picket Officer," asked me "if I wished to take the keys." Presuming that it was some sort of drink I at once assented, but was soon disillusioned. We proceeded with due solemnity to the vicinity of the guardhouse, where we saw the guard lined up under an ancient colonade with No. 1 sentinal stalking up and down before them. Presently a lantern appeared approaching the guardhouse. No. 1 challenged "Halt! Who comes there?" to which the lantern replied "The Keys." No. 1 answered "Whose keys?" The lantern replied "King George's keys." To which No. 1 exclaimed "God bless King George." The guard then presented [arms], and the Officer of the Day called "Amen." No 1 then called "Advance keys, all's well." So the incident ended. On inquiry I discovered that this same ceremony of locking the Tower at 10 o'clock and placing the keys in the guardhouse had been in effect since the time of Henry II, nearly 1000 years.

Diary

June 9 (Saturday): Breakfast with officers at Tower 10 A.M.; got orders to report to Gen. Reached Hotel Savoy and found he had

gone to call on King George. With others went to the American
Embassy. Met Mr. Page, the Ambassador. Then returned to hotel
where met Colonels Summerall (who had been sent to England to
study British battlefield methods), Baker, and others. Gen. P, My
Lord Guy Brooke, oldest son of Earl of Warwick, Collins, and I went
to lunch at a club founded by Edward VII. Met Major Dodd and
Chief of British Flying Corps (Hugh Trenchard). After lunch, Gen
Pershing, Lord Brooke, Collins, and I went to call on the Duke of
Connaught. We stood up all the time, except the Gen. whom the
duke asked to sit down. Then Lord Brooke and I went around and
left cards on a lot of people — the Prime Minister, the Secretary of
State for War (whom we met), the Commanding General of the London district, and others. Went to palace where I signed in Kings
Book. Also at Duke of Connaught's, then Lord Brooke took me for
tea to White's, the oldest club in the world. Lord Brooke a fine man;
a brigadier recovering from shell wound which smashed his left hand
and went through both hips and belly; kept him in bed 16 weeks.
Lieuts. Skinner and Cartwright of the Honorable Artillery Corps
took us to club for dinner; had cocktails and champaigne, then to a
play, where Lord Brooke and Gen P were also. After theater, to
coffee and in two blocks, I was stopped 20 times by women of the
street. Because I was registered in at the Tower, I was asked to have
whiskey and soda at 10 A.M. Tuesday and be shown the whole Tower.

    June 10 (Sunday): Hotel Savoy for lunch. Gilbert Miller, son of
Henry Miller, the actor, took me to drive in the afternoon to Maiden
Head on Thames. Met Mrs. Leslie Carter and had tea with several
actresses and the Duke of Manchester — "he was not well dressed but
very nice and asked me to come up and fish at his place if I got
wounded." Country was beautiful and everyone acted as though
there was no war.

    June 11 (Monday): to Black Heath to see HAC recruits in train-
ing. Threw some Mills grenades and fired rifle. Theater in evening.

    June 12: Taken through Tower by Lieut. Skinner. Packed trunks
in afternoon. That night HAC mess gave us dinner, Lieut. Frechet
of French aviation my guest. After dinner, Lieut. Cartwright, the
Mess President, proposed the King's health. Then Col. Treffry

toasted us saying that HAC would take pride in our success and look upon us as adopted children and hoped we would far outshine the H.A.C. I responded saying in substance, among other things, "My sincere hope is that we your adopted children shall be able to equal your noble record for to excell it were impossible." There was much cheering. There were other ceremonies and a special dinner for the noncommissioned officers. Returned to officers mess and "though I tried to persuade the officers to go to bed they insisted on sitting up to see us off at 4:30 A.M."

Letter, GSP, Jr., to his father, June 15, 1917

Being English the name artillery corps does not mean anything, as they are an infantry regiment belonging to the Guards Brigade. The reception they gave us in the Tower of London was worth the trip. The officers took us in and treated us like more than brothers, we could not spend a cent. The HAC is a VERY smart regiment even now, the privates have to pay 12 dollars a year for the privelege of being killed in it . . .

I do not send you these [written copies of the speeches and toasts, enclosed] as master pieces of oratory but as spontaneous effusions. They are not bad, and received much applause partly due no doubt to liberal potations.

For everyone in Pershing's party, the days spent in London were pleasantly exciting. The British were very kind. There were banquets and receptions, as well as conferences and exchanges of viewpoints with military authorities.

Diary

June 13 (Wednesday): left Charing Cross 5:30 A.M.; took boat and landed. While waiting to start for Paris at 11:40, saw first signs of war, several train loads of British wounded; they did not look very happy. Paris, 6 P.M. Marshal Joffre and others met us. Gen P to Hotel Crillon with some of personal staff; rest of staff either to the Hotel Continental or to the Hotel Meurice. Men went to Pepiniere barracks, Boulevard Malesherbes. All the way from the station, the Gare du Nord, the streets were full of people who shouted and threw flowers. Went to military club for dinner; Gen P to embassy.

They landed at Boulogne and were met by a detachment of French infantrymen recently arrived from the trenches and still wearing their battle uniforms. René Besnard, Undersecretary of State for War; General Pelletier, chief of the French staff attached to Pershing's headquarters; General Dumas, commanding the Region of the North, all welcomed the Americans. They were driven through Boulogne, where great crowds cheered them, then took a special train to Paris.

At the Gare du Nord, French troops lined the platforms. Military bands played "The Star-Spangled Banner" and the "Marseillaise." Marshal Joffre, Messieurs Viviani and Painlevé, Generals Foch and Dubail, Ambassador Sharp, and others were there to greet the Americans.

French soldiers patrolled the route from the station to the Hôtel Crillon, where Pershing established his headquarters temporarily. The streets were full of Parisians waving American flags and crying "Vive l'Amérique!"

Diary

June 14: Gen P and most of the staff went to Les Invalides where he was allowed to kiss Napoleon's sword and was invested with the Grand Cross of the Legion of Honor. All staff except Gen P had lunch at Circle Militaire at noon. 3 PM went to see the airplanes; 400 of them and wonderful. Lewis, Capt. Reed, and I had dinner. Then to theater with Lewis. Capt R. went chasing girls. With success.

Letter, GSP, Jr. (Hotel Continental, 3 rue Castiglione), to Beatrice, June 14, 1917

I have never before known what flying was. It is impossible to imagine the perfection which these people have attained . . .

The French people are really awfully glad to see us and do every thing they can to help us out.

Pershing visited the Chamber of Deputies, and when he entered the diplomatic box, the legislators spontaneously stood and cheered him. Enthusiastic visitors in the galleries violated tradition by joining in the applause. Pershing bowed.

He and Joffre stood together, bareheaded, on the balcony of the Military Club, symbolizing to the teeming crowd in the Place de l'Opéra the Franco-American military alliance.

Diary

June 16 (Saturday): Have an office at 29 rue Constantine. Have 1 noncommissioned officer and 3 privates on guard at Gen P's, 6 privates on guard at the office. Went to the theater.

June 17: Office open all day but not doing much. "I think that people are being entertained too much and that it would be better to prohibit officers going out more than twice a week . . . Went to bed at twelve which is the earliest I have been to bed."

This was no way to fight a war.

CHAPTER 20

Paris to Chaumont

"I am worked to death."

According to General Orders 1 of the Headquarters, American Expeditionary Force, Margetts, Collins, and Shallenberger were Pershing's aides, Major James G. Harbord was chief of staff, Major Hines was the assistant adjutant general, Major Fox Conner was an assistant inspector general, and Major Samuel D. Rockenbach was an assistant quartermaster. Captain Drum and Lieutenant (as he was still being carried) Patton were shown as "attached," meaning they still had no specific duties on the staff.

Letter, GSP, Jr., to Beatrice, June 18, 1917
Personally I have not got a great deal to do.

Patton was actually functioning as the commander of the headquarters troops, the enlisted men working at the various staff offices. His major duties concerned the guards, chauffeurs, and mechanics.

Diary
June 18 (Monday): "Capt. Reed and I had talk on vageries of human affairs. And the lack of ability of all members of the staff except our selves."

June 19: "Got 3 Cadillacks and one Packard in shape." Placed 2 orderlies at 120 rue Haussmann at the Medical, Ordnance, Field Artillery, and Signal offices. Now has 4 men on guard at Gen P's, 3 men and 2 motorcyclists on guard at 29 rue Constantine, plus 2 who are there all the time; 1 man and 1 motorcycle man at 127 rue Haussmann. 1 man charge of quarters. "I expect before this row is over that there will be a battalion or perhaps a regiment on this job. We started a prophylactic station at the Barracks."

Letter, GSP, Jr., to Beatrice, June 19, 1917

We started to wear the English officers belt to day with the cross piece. It is very pretty but costs a lot . . . One has to wear the belt all the [time] here as other wise they don't know that you are an officer. My job just now is fixing a way to account for autos. I spent all the afternoon talking french to a captain out at a big auto Park. I was surprised how well I got on. I can say any thing I want to quite fast and they get my drift at once as is evinced by the fact that they answered all my questions off the bat.

Beatrice wanted to come to France, and Patton advised her not to start before August.

Diary

June 20: "Col. McCarthy and I called on Col. Gerard the chief of the automobile service of France and arranged for the marking of our cars. Col. McC. does not know how to handle the French.

"At 4 I went to the big reserve park of autos at a place called Boulogne just out side Paris. Here I examined the method of accounting for French cars. They now use a card index system copies of which I got."

June 21: "Marking of autos was turned over to Capt. Liebman U.S. R.[eserve] Q.M.C. I did nothing of interest."

He was obviously piqued to be deprived of this job.

About this time, Pershing or more probably his chief of staff, Harbord, asked Patton to look into the establishment of a Military Police system, not only for Paris but elsewhere in France where American troops would be stationed, and also to see how prisoners taken in battle were handled. Patton conferred with the Assistant Provost Marshal of the British Service on duty in Paris, then reported as follows:

Men selected as Military Police or MPs had to be characterized, above all, by a sense of self-control. Policemen in peacetime tended to wink at certain crimes in order to prevent repression among the population that only led to higher criminal rates. But in wartime, "all crime must be detected in its insipience and rigorously suppressed."

The main duties of MPs in large towns were the control of "drunkardness" and the checking of soldiers' passes. They were also charged with the task of insuring that soldiers in public places were dressed neatly and wearing the proper uniform. MPs had the authority to arrest soldiers and to report officers who were judged delinquent in their behavior or dress.

In the zone of the armies behind the front, MPs regulated traffic and moved prisoners of war to the rear. In the division areas, the normal assignment of 30 MPs per division was insufficient. Other soldiers had to be detailed as MPs, usually about 200 per division. Front-line troops built wire cages in the support trenches, that is, the rearmost trenches, where 200 captured enemy soldiers could be held temporarily. Prisoners were commonly sent to the rear in groups of 150.

Diary

June 22: "In afternoon Col. [Billy] Mitchell asked me if I wanted to go out to the Flying grounds with him and Fly. When we got there he arranged for me to go up in a Farman Biplane . . . I had always thought it would frighten me but it did not. One feels perfectly safe and the machine seems as steady as a church. The entire country spreads out like a map beneath and it is fine.

"We did not go up very high only 3600 feet but it did not seem that."

Letter, Pershing to Beatrice Patton, June 23, 1917

My dear Beatrice . . . I appreciate your letter very much, especially what you say about my little boy and about Anne. Wasn't it rather odd that we should sail away on the anniversary of your wedding? I have no doubt it is a very good omen. George is looking well and is quite as busy as the rest of us.

The Los Angeles *Graphic* featured a story entitled "George S. Patton, Jr., Soldier, Diplomat, Poet," and the reporter wrote: "I'll miss my guess considerably if Capt. George S. Patton, Jr. doesn't make a fine soldier, if he has half a chance."

Diary

June 23 (Saturday): "one of the machines ran over a French man and broke his collar bone. I called on the Prefect of Police of the district and after giving him a cigarette and a ride he assured me that the victim was a robber an assin [assassin] and that my man [the driver] was a poor victim. In fact for two cigarettes he would have jailed the poor chap [who was run over]. Politeness pays especially in France."

Went to the Femina Theater, Champs Elysees, saw light opera.

Maurice Chevalier was there, home recovering from wounds; he was in a German prison for 26 months.

"The French are very hard hit for men. And the last 'victories'? must have cost terribly. We had three cooks all over 47 who had to go to the front last night."

Patton was then in charge of the headquarters motor pool, the vehicles used for official business. His job was much like his previous duties with respect to the mounted detachment of the Punitive Expedition in Mexico. Late in June he was busy having a small American flag and a number painted on each car, truck, and motorcycle.

Diary

June 24 (Sunday): went to tea at the Carl Boyds', whom they had met at Saumur in 1913.

"later went to see Gen P. As he was alone I staied with him till ten thirty going with out supper. We had a most interesting conversation. Among other things he told me that during the week ending 23 the U. Boats had gotten over 400,000 tons of shipping. At that rate they would get over a twelfth of the worlds shipping in a month.

"He said that unless it could be stopped we would never get over 500,000 men to France. He also told me that the French were very shaky and that things were not so bright as they were painted.

"We talked of anne [Nita]. He felt terribly but thought it best that she should not come [to Europe]. I thought the same and told him so."

Letter, GSP, Jr., to Beatrice, June 24, 1917

[Busy last few days but work was] unreal not at all like Columbus N.M. before we went to Mexico. The fighting is apparently at a stand off. At least so we hear as so far none of us have been there.

I had a talk with J. [John Pershing] to day about Nita. He does not think she should come over and I am inclined to agree with him. He has too much on his hands and it would make a bad impression just at present.

He does not favor any one's coming so if I were you I would write a very sweet letter about only coming to Saumur so as to be near etc etc. Make it juicy. Of course don't mention me.

Letter, GSP, Jr., to Beatrice, June 25, 1917

[To Boyds' for tea yesterday.] Mrs. Chuichill was there and is

most charming . . . Billie Mitchell took me home later and then I
had a talk for several hours with Nita's suitor. We mulled over the
past and talked of the future.

It will be absolutely wrong for them to get married now or for her
to make her proposed trip. Be sure not to encourage her in any way.

It certainly is the most intense case I have ever seen.

Diary

June 26: Col Graves (who would later head the American troops
sent to Russia during the revolution) and several other American
officers arrived. Had supper at Ambassadors with (Captain John G.)
Quekemeyer who had been to the British front for three days. Sent a
courier to St. Nazaire where our first division has landed.

Quekemeyer, a member of a group of officers sent to France by the War
Department to study matters of organization and equipment, worked
closely with Pershing's G–3 Section. He would make himself quite useful
around the headquarters and would eventually become an aide of Pershing's. He told Patton, who wrote it to Beatrice, that "the horrors" of
the front were "rather over stated."

Pershing had moved into a fine house at 73 rue de Varenne owned by a
wealthy American. It was the most beautiful place Patton had ever seen,
with a wonderful garden right in the heart of Paris.

André de Coppet, who was an interpreter, Waldo Reed of the American ambulance corps, and Patton took an apartment at 40 rue d'Artois,
one block up the Champs-Elysées from the Grand Palais and three blocks
over. It had a parlor, two baths, dining room, kitchen, and three bed-
rooms on the first floor.

Diary

June 29: moved into my apartment; have everything but linen and
rent that. Have a maid who cooks breakfast and cleans up.

Letter, GSP, Jr., to Beatrice, June 29, 1917

The auto driving in Paris is worse than ever. There are no rules at
all and most of the drivers are foreign as there are no French men left
to drive . . .

[Not much to do but] if I were not here I would be a raving
lunatic by now . . . One thing is sure. With my present job I am
bound to live long even if I am not happy.

Diary

June 30: "Maj. Frank McCoy reported yesterday and spent a day of pernicious activity as assistant Chief of Staff. Among other things he enaugurated a bureau of information with me at the Head of it. He assured me that the ideal man for the place would be the hall boy at a club or lacking him I would do."

July 1: "nothing mutch."

Eleven years later, Patton related what might well have been an apocryphal story.

GSP, Jr., "Tanks Past and Future," February 27, 1928

One hot July day in 1917 I was drowsing over the desk of the Concierge at GHQ [General Headquarters] in Paris (at that time I was holding this high office on the staff). Suddenly my slumbers were disturbed by an orderly who told me to report to the Operations Officer. There a certain Major . . . [Fox Conner] introduced me to a French Officer and directed me to listen to his story and report my conclusions. This Frenchman was a Tank enthusiast who regaled me for several hours with lurid tales of the value of his pet hobby as a certain means of winning the war. In the report I submitted . . . I said, couching my remarks in the euphemistic jargon appropriate to official correspondence, that the Frenchman was crazy and the Tank not worth a damn.

On July 3, he wrote Beatrice that he was keeping busy but had a rotten job. "I only don't resign it because I think I will get a better one some day."

He cabled to tell her to come to Europe whenever she was ready.

Diary

July 3: 2d Battalion, 16th Infantry arrived from St. Nazaire to take part in celebrating the Fourth of July. Lunch at Cercle Militaire with Maj. De Georges of the 4th Zouaves. Mrs. Thayer of Boston and Paris and her daughter Alice Countess de Montgomery called on Gen P this morning. "The festive Alice is very nice. I got her two tickets for Les Invalides tomorrow."

July 4: Band of the Guard Republican awoke Gen P at 8:30 at his house; at 9:30 to the Invalides and great show. "Place de la Concord & Rue Rivoli the women often broke into the ranks [of the marching

American units] and hugged and kissed the men. I was sitting in my
machine at the end of Rue Constantine watching."

July 5: "I bought a packard five passinger 1917 [car] and traded it
for the one B. had given the Gen. It cost 25 000 F."

Letter, GSP, Jr., to Beatrice, July 6, 1917

When we got our car over here I found another new Packard five
seater one of the last new cars in France so I bought it and then
traided it for ours so I have ours again for my self. I had to pay $4200
for the car on account of the high freight rates.

The bill of sale for the Packard Twin-Six — a twelve-cylinder motor —
actually came to $4386, payable by U.S. check in dollar funds at the rate
of exchange that day — 5 francs 70 equaling one dollar.

He wrote Beatrice on July 7 that he had been to dinner then to the
Grand-Guignol with the Countess de Montgomery and her sister, the
Countess d'Affrey Daudet.

Diary

July 7 (Saturday): 3:20 P.M., Col. Harbord told me to go with
Queck [Quekemeyer] and learn road to Sir Douglas Haig's headquarters. Left at 4:10 P.M.: reached there 9:50. Had supper, started
back 11:05 over same road. Returned 6:30 A.M. For more than 10
miles on return trip passed artillery moving north. Difference in appearance between British, Australian, and Canadian troops favorable
to British, very marked.

His trip through part of France, he wrote Beatrice, was lovely. France
was "just like a great lawn." There were no signs of war, except for a few
villages that had been shelled. Beatrice could start for Europe any time
— through Cuba to Spain, then by railroad to Paris. He was working
from 8:30 A.M. till seven or eight at night, but he took a couple of hours
off for lunch because everyone else did it, and there was no way of doing
business then.

Diary

July 8: Gen P had conference of all officers and decided on several
points on policy of instruction. I had tea with Countess de Montgomery. Quek and I dinner.

July 13: Gen Sibert and staff came today; met Col Coe and Capt (George C.) Marshall of his staff. "Had a terribly annoying day. Every one wanted a car and there were no cars to give."

The fact that he had his own car, which he drove between his billet and his office, probably caused some resentment among senior officers who did not know he owned the automobile. They undoubtedly wondered how a junior officer could have transportation when they could not, and they figured that he was using a headquarters vehicle since he was in charge of assigning the cars.

Diary

July 14: up at 5 A.M. (for the Bastille Day celebration) and with Quekemeyer and Maj and Mrs Desgeorges went to seats in tribune. 8 A.M. President of France came in open carriage and was cheered a little but there were open murmurs because Joffre was not with him.

The parade, he wrote Beatrice, was splendid. The French authorities decorated no less than 260 regimental colors. About 30,000 troops marched. The scene was impressive because everyone watching "knew he was looking at men who had been through the test. I did not see ten officers with out a wound chevron and many of them were beardless boys." Beatrice, he added, could start for Europe any time she wished.

Letter, GSP, Jr., to Beatrice, July 16, 1917

Darling Beat: I got your wire asking me to get Gen. P. to give his consent. He can't do it because it was on his advice that the order [prohibiting wives from coming to France] was issued. You see the British had to send back 60 000 women who came over with the Canadians.

Now the only thing to do is to put pressure to work on the secretary of state so you can come. Not as a nurse but straight out. I know it can be done for the reason that Mrs. Bertie McCormick of Chicago is here also Mrs. Ester Johnson of N.Y. Also Mrs. E. B. Krumbhaar of Philadelphia whose husband is a Red Cross Doctor. Maj. Delaney told me that this woman got pasports after the law prohibiting them was passed.

I am sure that with Freddie and Mr. Car and Senator Phelan and John Ropes and Hiram Johnson and Lodge and Pa and every one else the thing can be done. The sooner you do it however the better as the restrictions will probably get more and more severe.

I disapprove your coming as a red cross nurse for there is no telling but we would be so far apart we could never meet . . . You might get Mr. Cabot who is getting up a unit in Boston to bring you as secretary. I think Chil. knows him. He could bring you and you could be discharged on landing. It is perfectly clear that you should not be here and be tied down to a nursing job. It is very hard work . . . There is not the *least* doubt that with proper influence you can get pasports. Use the influence. Nita ought not come. Must not. Try to get busy at once.

As a suggestion the [Boston] Transcript might send you as an accredited correspondent at a nominal salary.

Remember you must come and you must *not* come as a *nurse*.

Letter, GSP, Jr., to Beatrice, July 17, 1917

I have just wired you as follows. "John can do nothing. Do not come as nurse. Sure authority for trip can be had by use all influence . . ."

The Gen. can do nothing as it was on his recommendation that the ruling was made. If I asked him he could only refuse so I am not going to ask him as that would only complicate matters when you eventually get here.

I talked with Maj. Robert Bacon who was at one time Secretary of State and has more recently been Ambasador to France. He assures me that by the use of influence any thing can be gotten out of the State Department. He also agrees . . . that you should *not* come as a nurse. The condition would be bad and what is worse you would almost surely be some place where I could not see you.

. . . If Pa. gets a diplomatic job you could come either as his secretary or his interpreter and he could leave you when he went home. Still I am certain that by the use of Phelan, Lodge, Mr. Carr, Col. House etc etc you can swing a regular pasport and that is what you ought to try to do.

Or you could come as Paris correspondent for the Transcript.

I am so sorry that it is giving you a lot of trouble but I am sure you can get it some way.

Letter, GSP, Jr., to Beatrice, July 18, 1917

I wish you had come right after I did for then you would have had no trouble [getting a passport] but of course the stories we heard in

America were so exagerated that it did not seem the right thing to
do . . .

I have been leaving the kissing marks off [my letters] for fear that
they might be misinterpreted [by the censors] as cipher but you
know I mean them anyway.

Major McCormick told Patton that his wife came over to France because she had an independent mission.

Beatrice cabled Patton to try to get her a job in the American ambulance corps. He saw some people there, but received only vague replies to
his inquiries.

Letter, GSP, Jr., to Beatrice, July 19, 1917
You will not get a letter from me for a few days as John and I are
going some where on a little trip. It promises to be most interesting
but probably I will not be able to describe it to you . . .

[He was fencing an hour each morning for exercise.] Fenced with
the man this morning and after 10 minutes he said "You have taught
fencing." I asked why, and he said "Because you have all the faults
of a teacher, you have the habit of letting your self be touched."

. . .

At 7 A.M., July 20, Pershing, accompanied by Colonel Alvord and Patton,
together with Pershing's strikers Lanckton and Moline and drivers San-
tine and Jennings, departed Paris to visit Field Marshal Sir Douglas
Haig's headquarters at Mons-en-Pevele. They met a host of people —
Haig himself, his aides Major Sir Philip Sassoon and Captain Stracher;
Adjutant General Fawke who was an old friend of Pershing's; General
Peyton, the military secretary; Colonel Fletcher, his assistant; General
Hugh Trenchard, head of aviation; General Birch of the Royal Artillery;
General Kiggell, chief of staff; General Butler, his deputy; General Har-
wood; Lieutenant Colonel Whitehead; Lieutenant Sacre; Quartermaster
General Maxwell; General Lord Lovat, the chief forester.

There were ceremonies and guards of honor. But there were serious
discussions too — on how best to organize a field headquarters, how to
establish a logistical structure, and other like matters.

Pershing was billeted with Haig at the marshal's house, Alvord with
Fletcher, "I with my self in nice house near by. Dined with marshal at
7:45."

On the following day, Pershing and his party visited Haig's General
Staff offices and talked about training and specialists' schools. They drove
to the Second Army headquarters, then to the X Corps.

"Returned to G.H.Q. for Dinner at 8 P.M. Gen. Charteris was there. I
sat on Marshal Haigh [Haig]'s right. talked to him about saber. He believes in it and in cavalry."

Escorted by General Trenchard, they saw the airdrome shops, the cap-
tive balloons, and the "parishoots." At lunch Trenchard explained his
theories of surprise attack. At the intelligence section, Charteris described
how "nearly every thing is reduced to diagrams. Among other things he
keeps track of some 3 hun. thousand suspects. He has also information of
6000 Belgian suspects behind the German lines."

Leaving Haig's headquarters, they proceeded to the Fifth Army, where
they learned how maps were made in the field and visited the camouflage
school. They spent the night at Montreuil, where Pershing discussed matters pertaining to military construction, transportation, docks, canals, and
railroads.

They started for Paris at 11:30, July 24, and reached the city at 6 P.M.

*Letter, GSP, Jr., to Mrs. C. G. Rice (of Turner Hill, a neighbor of
the Ayers at Pride's Crossing), July 24, 1917*
I have just returned from a most interesting trip where I saw the
working of over a million men from the inside. It is stupendous and
fine. The more one sees of war the better it is. Of course there are a
few deaths but all of us must "pay the piper" sooner or later and the
party is worth the cost of admission.

The aviators do the most wonderful things in the quietest way. I
met one chap just twenty three who had gotten fifteen Germans.

Also any one who thinks that cavalry is a thing of the past is mistaken.

We are working from eight A.M. to nine P.M. so time gets by pretty
fast. At present we have a stupid time and are most distressingly safe
but we will get in the row long before it is over. There will be at
least a year and a half more. So you ought to have a lot of new horses
before I have a chance to hunt again.

Letter, GSP, Jr., to Beatrice, July 24, 1917
I had a great trip and sat next to Marshal Haigh once. We talked
of the saber and he is more of a charger than I am and was very nice

to me. He is a fine looking man and used to be in the cavalry. He plays polo and hunts.

One of his aides Sir Phillip Sassoon is a great fisherman and we had a fine time. I went to five lunches and four dinners and never sat next to less than a Brigadier General, usually a major General. They are mostly quite young, and most friendly. The commander of one of the armies, Gen. Gough walked round with his hand on my shoulder for some time and when I looked at his shoulder strap [and saw his rank] I nearly fainted.

We saw all sorts of interesting things . . . I wish I could tell you all the things I saw but I can't.

Every thing in the world is used by a modern army including moving picture films. I saw it all from the in side. The idea that any but a trained soldier can conduct war is absurd.

On July 26, when General Peyton March, Colonel Hines, Majors Nolan, Conger, and Westervelt, Captain Collins, and Lieutenants Swing and Rinehart, departed for an instructional visit to the British General Headquarters, "I acted as aid for Gen. P. also took Col Hines place."

Letter, GSP, Jr., to Beatrice, July 29, 1917

I am a sort of "Pooh-Bah" and do everything no one else does. The chief difficulty comes in making seven cars do the work of twenty. My chauffeurs are fine and work 15 hours a day with out a whimper especially one Sgt. Brain [Braine — Patton's assistant and motor pool sergeant] who is almost a super man.

The reserve officers we have so far are a mess and as there are a lot of them in the Q.M. it is a great nuisance. They ought never make them higher than lieutenants. The majors are insufferable.

Maj. Frederick Palmer is a thorn in the flesh. He thinks that the war is run for the newspaper men and he keeps stealing cars from me.

This war is very serious and far from over but the fear of the G[er-man]s coming through is I believe over.

Letter, GSP, Jr., to Beatrice, July 29, 1917

I am worked to death. Collins and Margetts have both been away as well as Col Hines so I have been Aide [and] Adjutant General and in charge of autos all at the same time. It has been fierce. Besides we have had a lot of accidents running over people etc which take a lot of time to settle. I am going on a trip with J. P. Monday to be gone three days. We will see our own troops . . .

There is a recommendation in for the Headquarters troop [which he was more or less in charge of] to be 400 men and 70 autos with six officers. If I get that it would be pretty good [meaning, he would be promoted] but I would rather be "au trenche" [in the trenches].

Diary

July 31 (Tuesday): Gen. P, Col Harbord, Col de Chambrun, and I left office at 2:50 in Hotchkiss and Packard to St. Dizier. We passed for miles along scene of battle of the Marne, the road marking almost exactly last French line of battle. Many graves along road. "Where hospitals were, large squair inclosures full of crosses. Just north of the road is where Napoleon fought first half of campaign of 1814. Reached St. Dizier at 8 P.M. Pershing and Harbord at hotel, Chambrun and I bilited with private family."

August 1: left St. Dizier 8:10 AM, to Vittel and Grand Hotel, where good supper. Inspected American troops and were disappointed. Men did not look smart, officers were lazy, troops lacked equipment and training, were listless.

August 2: through Neufchateau to Chaumont, lunch at Hotel de France. Left 3 PM by way of Troyes, reached Paris 10 PM.

August 4: lunch and dinner with K, Beatrice's sister, and her husband, Keith, who was with the State Department in London.

Letter, GSP, Jr., to Beatrice, August 7, 1917

Lots of women come over here on all sorts of alledged jobs and make a go of it. But being at Pride's you are sort of out of the run of things.

We are working long hours but apparently not doing much though of course we are but it is like a rat chewing an oak tree because there is so much to do.

Letter, GSP, Jr., to Beatrice, August 8, 1917

Things seem to be in a very bad way about your coming over. Mrs. Connor, wife of Col. W. D. Connor of Engineers, whom we knew in Washington, tried to come and Col Connor got wire from War Department they would recall him if she came.

Don't think that I am having a roaring time and not thinking of you for it is not so. Paris is a stupid place with out [you] just as heaven would be under the same conditions.

Letter, GSP, Jr., to Beatrice, August 10, 1917

J.P. asked me to lunch, why I don't know, Marechal Joffre, Gen Dubail and one other general was there also. J.P., Gen Blatchford, Gen Biddle and the staff. After lunch we all walked in the garden . . .

I also fenced this morning with Mr. Heidt [probably James Hazen Hyde] who is a rich american. We fenced in his garden and after wards his valet gave me a bath and dressed me. I could have done a better job alone but of course had to submit . . .

I am still waiting to hear from Spain about you. I am terribly worried over your getting over. It seems a hard thing to do.

Col. Harbord the Chief of staff seems to have taken a great shine to me. Capt. Reed says that it is J.P. delicacy reguarding Nita which keeps him from making me [his] aid. I wish he were not so d——delicate. When we go to the country I am to live at his [Pershing's] house.

Letter, GSP, Jr., to Beatrice, August 11, 1917

To my great delight eleven more automobiles came in to day and now I can look the world on the face on the subject of transportation. It certainly has been hard sledding trying to keep people con†ented. The only good thing has been that I have been backed up in any thing I said by the Chief of Staff and the Adjutant General. An old colonel came roaring in this morning and went to see the Adjutant General because he had no car. Pretty soon he went slinking out and no one even asked me a thing.

Letter, Beatrice (Maymont, Mayworth, North Carolina) to Aunt Nannie, August 16, 1917

You have heard by this time how the War Dept. turned me down. [Mr. Cramer came up to Washington to help if possible, brought Stuart, his son, a West Point graduate and veteran of the Punitive Expedition, with him, then both kidnapped her and brought her there to recover.] This disappointment was so unexpected & cruel [she had stateroom booked, letter of credit, and had given away all the clothes she didn't need for the trip.] And poor Georgie — with

his little apartment for us two, in Paris. I wouldn't care so much if I
didn't know how he is feeling. And I tried so hard to go. Well — I
will try to behave and fill my place here as well as I can, so help me
God. This is a hard time for all of us.

Patton wired Beatrice that the Munroe job, whatever it was, was the
best he could do. But he feared they would both be disappointed because
he saw a letter from Mrs. Connor to her husband, saying that though she
had a good job in Paris with the YMCA, her request for a passport was
turned down by the War Department.

Letter, GSP, Jr., to Beatrice, August 17, 1917
   I am quite hopeless of your getting over for a while yet and am
feeling particularly low . . .
   Baird, Quekemeyer and my self have formed a club . . . to be a
member you must be a cavalry man who never rides and who never
goes with in fourteen miles of the trenches. I inclose the song of the
society [written] by my self.

Mr. Patton wrote Pershing and discussed the support of the war and of
Pershing by the American people. He added, "Nita has been very busy
with the Red Cross and other work — in fact has over worked."

Letter, Pershing to Mr. Patton, August 17, 1917
   It is gratifying to know that the people are behind the Administration, because that is the only way that will bring us success . . .
There is a great need for the utmost and strongest cohesion among
our people, to back up the President in this war; and this foolish talk
of slaughtering troops in Europe, and all that sort of thing, is only
the work of German agents . . . The time has now arrived for
united action without discussion, and it is almost a crime for any
American now to begin discussing whether the nation should continue this war or not. We are in it, and we must fight it out to the
end, as this is the only way we can secure the peace which we all most
earnestly desire. I deplore very much the inconsiderate talk of
thoughtless and, I will say, unpatriotic people. It angers me very
much.
   . . . George is eager to get to the front when the time comes, and I
shall of course give him his chance.

Nita writes me the general news, but I should be very pleased to hear more from other members of the family.

With affectionate wishes, I remain as always, Yours very sincerely,

Letter, GSP, Jr., to Beatrice, August 20, 1917

I keep hoping that in some way you will manage to get here.

We have rented a very nice house at the place we are going and things ought to be much nicer there. I certainly have too much savage in me to enjoy living in a large city. This is the longest time I have ever spent right in one and I can't say I think much of it. When one can go to the play [theater] every night it is not so thrilling as when you can only go every year or so . . .

[He knows many officers there] all of whom I have served [with] before. We have certainly always been lucky in being with real people. It is a big thing for me. I can't see for the life of me where I am going to do much in this war personally but my luck will hold I suppose and I will run into something. I wish it would be you.

Letter, GSP, Jr., to Beatrice, August 22, 1917

All sorts of people are being promoted . . . I don't think they will get down to making me a major but they will before the end of the war so that will be fine. You had better send me some gold leaves [major's insignia] . . .

I fenced with Mr. Hyde again and this time he had two valets to dress me. It was awful but as I was not in a hurry I let them do their worst. They steal my suspenders every time which is a bore.

Letter, GSP, Jr., to Beatrice, August 24, 1917

Dearling Beatrice: Poor Beat and poor me also. I got your letter . . . and felt very much cheered up then to day I got a letter from William Wood written from Washington in which he speaks of your being in tears and of how dissapointed you were. Poor Beat! I feel as badly for your sorrow as for my own dissapointment . . .

Cheer up lots of times we have thought things would turn out badly and it was realy been for the best. I admit that at this moment I fail to see any good which will come out of not seeing you but one can always hope.

Beat I love you with all my heart. And I am so sorry.

Letter, GSP, Jr., to Mr. Ayer, August 26, 1917

My particular job consists in knowing a little about the job of every one else. In getting pasports from the French and English. In running the Soldiers about two hundred [of them]. In seeing that all the twenty seven automobiles go even though there is nothing to make them go with and in doing every thing else which no one wants to do. It is what might be called a "stinking" job but at least it is devoid of monotony, which after all is a great thing and so far I have made a go of it.

To look at Paris one would never know that it was at war. All the people seem gay and spend a large part of their time being run over by our automobiles or else running over us.

The men here at Headquarters are a fine lot all except my self being picked men of known ability . . .

I have been fencing every day and making a success of it. If I go broke, or rather if you do, I can always teach fencing.

Letter, GSP, Jr., to Beatrice, August 26, 1917

[Soon moving to a small city not far from the front.] I am to live and mess with John which is fine as it insures meeting a lot of interesting people and as we have a fine cook we ought to do very nicely.

Letter, GSP, Jr., to Beatrice, August 27, 1917

Chil. said you were bothered about my getting killed. Don't. I am a lot safer here than I usually am at home because I don't play polo or race or jump or do any other interesting thing.

We will not be in any active service for months and months perhaps a year so the only danger we run is natural death. And the climate is healthy.

Letter, GSP, Jr., to Beatrice, August 29, 1917

[Have been separated since their marriage 2 years and 3½ months. After figuring out] the above gloomy facts Col. Eltinge came in and asked me to dinner. During the meal he mentioned you and asked if you were coming. I said no. He said it can be done for Mrs. Conger has just come.

I inclose the method of procedure in type and have sent a duplicate to Pa . . . I think that this is the best idea possible and if [Colonel] House [President Wilson's closest associate] or [Secretary] Lane wont do it perhaps Mrs. Gen. Scott would or your family must know some body who could do the trick. It must be done by word of mouth not by letter.

Enclosure (paraphrased): Mrs. Conger, wife of Major Conger on duty at Pershing's headquarters, was refused a passport to come to France. At the request of her brother, who is secretary to Mr. Mac-Adoo, the latter asked the President whether she could join her husband. The President agreed and directed Secretary Lansing to issue the passport. Mr. Wilson was indebted more to Pa. Feels sure that Col. House would put matter before the President. Following excellent reasons why Beatrice should be allowed to come to France: 1) We were separated 11 months when I was in Mexico; 2) Beatrice speaks and writes French like a native because she was educated in France, and she would be a great help to me — also Mrs. Robert Munroe had promised her a position in the Red Cross here; 3) B and her family have given more than $40,000 to the Red Cross and should have some consideration; 4) Unlike most Army women, B is very rich so there is no possibility of her becoming a burden on the government. To work, the proposition had to be put to the President in a personal way, and he was sure that Col. House or Sec. Lane could and would do it. Thinks passport for B and little B could be secured, but if the latter threatened to jeopardize the proceedings, forget her. Don't let Pa jeopardize his chances of getting a political appointment. And cite the precedent of Mrs. Conger.

He had obtained a fine folding bath and a portable shower so if their house in the country, to which they were moving, lacked some of the modern comforts, "I will at least keep clean. Col Fox Conner and I are going together in my car. It is painted O.D. and is number 41. It looks much better than it did before."

Diary

August 31: "Worked all day fixing for move to Chaumont. Assigned cars so that each officer could ride to Chaumont. Went to bed late."

September 1 (Saturday): Up at 4:30 to see Headquarters Troop start; left with 34 motor cycles and side cars. Checked property at 27 and 31 rue Constantine and left 10:55 in my car with Col Fox Conner. Stopped for lunch about 30 miles out of Paris. About 70 miles from Paris, valve spring on No. 1 cylinder right side went out. Worked for an hour hunting trouble, then went on with 11 cylinders. Just as got into Chaumont, left rear tire got puncture; changed tire and reached house 4:30 P.M. Col. Alvord, Maj. Bacon, and Capt Shallenberger already there. I took small room on third floor.

Telegram, Beatrice to Mr. Patton, September 1, 1917

Have business position and it will be all right to visit Katharine [in London] if I dont go elsewhere. Have ascertained this will not hurt George. Leave last of month. Will not try any funny business. Have written confidential [letter to you].

When Beatrice learned that she could go to England without hurting her husband's position in France, she worked out a deal with the E. T. Slattery Company, a big shop in Boston. On the basis that she was hired as a buyer of gloves, gowns, blouses, lingerie, infants' wear, and leather goods in London for the store at a salary of $2500 a year, she could secure a passport good for three months. Beatrice planned to refund her salary, for Slattery's real agent in London would make the actual purchases.

This was what she wrote Mr. Patton in her "confidential" letter. She said she had informed George and asked him not to tell "John" and not to ask for leave. Willy Horton, a friend of theirs on duty in Washington, had asked the Secretary of War whether an officer's wife could go to England on a business trip and had received an evasive answer. But the important point, she informed Mr. Patton, was that no officer's wife must set foot in France or in the war zone, and England was not in the war zone. The earliest Beatrice could sail was the twenty second of October on the *Saxonia.* "I hope I have your blessing."

Letter, GSP, Jr., to Beatrice, September 2, 1917

[Everything in confusion.] Hundreds of clearks rushing about and officers shouting for a place to stay we could do nothing so let them yell . . .

[Living in a house built 1914.] The fellow who built it must have got rich suddenly for the furnature is in the damdest taste you ever saw. All gilt and bras[s] but quite new. The man wanted to be thought a sport so he bought all sorts of game heads which are growling at one every where. There is a huge crocodile fifteen feet long with gaping jaws who appears ready to spring on you when you enter the front hall. In Collins room two eagles are about to pounce on the bed while a wild boar threatens you when you eat . . .

A year ago to day I was at Columbus and you and I and Nita and J went to Palomas. Things have moved rapidly since have they not?

He liked Chaumont, which he described as a town on a high hill with rivers on each side and a pretty canal. The countryside was mountainous and covered with forests. Recreation consisted of a movie twice a week. Paris was five hours away by car.

Diary

September 2 (Sunday): "great mess every one bossing and no one to boss. Fooled around all day trying to get right. Arranged to store cars at Riding hall Artillery Post." Rode on horse with Margetts along canal; pretty.

September 3: "Things cooled down a little." Changed room to second floor, better. Arranged for chauffeurs to mess at hospital.

Telegram, Beatrice to Mr. Patton, September 3, 1917

Of course I will regard your wishes. If you change your mind when you get my letter please wire as I will lose my ship if I wait till I get yours. Am only going to Katharine [in London] and would not try even that if it would hurt George. Much love

Diary

September 4: "Felt lazy after lunch but got over it."

Life in Chaumont, Patton wrote his father, was unexciting, but that condition was better for work because there was nothing else to do. The headquarters offices were in an old barrack built around a court with only one gate, so it was easy to establish a guard. He had a telephone and a desk and everything was convenient. He was living and eating at the general's house, which was only 300 yards from his office. His room overlooked a pretty garden and a park.

every thing is booming except the war which is certainly a stupid affair. We hope it will be more interesting when we start fighting.

Did you ever get any offer of a job in Washington and if so what was it.

Letter, GSP, Jr., to Beatrice, September 4, 1917

The town . . . is hardly large enough to accommodate all the people in it and we will be crowded to death if the staff gets any larger.

Diary

September 5 (Wednesday): "Gen. P. and Capt. Boyd arrived at 4 P.M. I had a guard of honor of 16 men at the house but they came to the office. Gen. P. looked tired but seemed pleased with conditions. Col. Harbord had a bad cold. I gave him some asperin."

September 6: Gen P, Col Harbord, Collins, Boyd, Shallenberger, and I left 6 A.M. for review at Grandcourt. Petain and French President there. Returned for lunch.

He wrote Beatrice that the war would hardly be over even by 1919. The Russians were doing nothing. One Frenchman asked another how far the Russians retreated today; reply, 14 kilometers, and will retreat the same tomorrow. How do you know? That is as far as a tired German can walk.

I am Provo Martial [Provost Marshal] of this town for the time [being] and yesterday had to arrest a man for carrying a woman down the street in an inverted position. She was very angry when we arrested the man and [he] said he was only playing.

Margetts was, Patton wrote, "kicked off" the staff as Pershing's aide, and Patton was disappointed when Pershing selected Boyd rather than Patton to replace him. "I don't see why as J. goes out of his way to be nice to me."

Most of the clerks brought over were commissioned as reserve officers, and he believed that everyone would get at least one promotion out of the war.

The town where he lived, he wrote Aunt Nannie, used to be in the corner of Burgundy and Lorraine and some other duchy, "and they all used to take turns capturing it." Then the English took it once or twice and finally the treaty of 1814 was signed there. "If you are a good historian you know what it is but don't tell any one. The Germans might hear and would bomb us."

He liked it better than Paris, for he was "too much of a savage for city life and it bores me to death." He was reading "The Three Muskateers" in French, and his French was pretty good. "I think the secret is that I have no scruples and go ahead while a student . . . is always trying to remember rules of grammar. I know none so don't bother."

At present at one post there are 50 doctors and 300 nurses and 5 patients. At another there are fifteen vetrinarions and three horses.

This is not J's fault but is all done at home.

There is a big american hospital here and a lot of nurses whose only function seems to be to be sweethearts for doctors.

Kay wrote Patton from London that she was expecting Beatrice in October.

Patton had to drill all the civilian clerks because they all wore uniforms, and the French were unable to tell them apart from the soldiers. Therefore it was necessary that the clerks play the part. "I hope I can get them into shape. John is much on his ear about them . . . It is funny I never expect to have any thing to do but always find a lot."

Diary

September 7: engaged laundress in morning; drilled 160 clerks in evening. "They did not like it much but it is necessary as they look like soldiers and must act like them." Shallenberger became Provost Marshal of Chaumont, Collins was attached to the General Staff, Boyd was still Pershing's aide, "and I am nothing but hired flunkey. I shall be glad to get back to the line [with troops] again and will try to do so in the spring."

September 8 (Saturday): "Inspection at 8 A.M. Nice day."

Telegram, Mr. Patton to Beatrice, September 8, 1917

Letter received. Am still firmly convinced your plan wrong and very dangerous. I beg you will at least put whole matter including my letter before George and await his decision. You have ample time before Saxonia [sails].

Letter, Beatrice to Mr. Patton, September 9, 1917

Please don't think I am just silly, wanting or willing to jeopardize G's career; if that were the case I would have sailed for France on this same job, Sept. 8th, yesterday . . .

I don't want to get G. into trouble, but he wants me to go and I am certainly going if there is any way I can do it that will be safe for him.

Letter, GSP, Jr., to Beatrice, September 10, 1917

This is a very historic town as the treaty of 1814 was signed here which sent Napoleon to Elba. If you have a dictionary that might let you know where we are. Don't tell if you find out . . .

J told me the other day that he wished he could have Nita over but he could see no way of doing it. I told him not to try. It would ruin him and as I am one of the rats it would get me too.

Telegram, Beatrice to Mr. Patton, September 13, 1917

Letter from George says impossible has been done very recently for another woman. He has sent you method and procedure. Please wire me on receipt his letter what you think can be done. Much love.

Beatrice amplified her thoughts in a letter to Mr. Patton. She thought "Mrs. Gen Scott would be of no use as she probably has axes of her own to grind." The only other person Beatrice knew who might be able to put the matter personally to Colonel House was John Hays Hammond, whose family was a neighbor of the Ayers. Secretary Lane was awfully nice to Beatrice when she was in Washington, but she could not ask him to go to the President for her, and he probably would not do it if she asked. Could Mr. Patton do anything? "I don't want you to jeopardize your own chances any more than Georgie does and if you can't, perhaps I might try Mr. Hammond if I found out he & House are friendly."

Patton wrote his father that Headquarters Company was getting bigger all the time. He was supposed to have 458 men, but he actually had about 150, with four officers, including himself. He had a lot to do, or rather a lot of things that took a long time doing "for when you go to see some Colonel or General you usually have to wait half an hour to get in a word."

it does seem an injustice to keep army women, who are the only ones who have any right to be here, home and let every one else in the world come . . .

I guess that the old army even as I knew it is dead and if we ever have peace, which personally I doubt, it will be more like the German army. We are very strict on discipline and we must be. It is discipline which has made Germany the terror she is . . .

A man has so many chances to shirk in a charge that only iron discipline which prevents a man ever thinking of disobeying will get them over the top.

Lots of men are shot by their officers in each attack. If they hang back a second they get it. No questions are asked.

The Germans have some of the smartest ideas . . . There is talk of a ray of light which will kill at 30 yards and the Germans are not the ones who have it either.

Don't mention the above.

Letter, GSP, Jr., to Beatrice, September 13, 1917

. . . the lady who caused all the trouble about coming over here . . . you remember her in Washington . . . she is chiefly noted for having worn dinner dresses which would have permitted her to nurse a baby at any time with out unbuttoning any thing . . . You certainly had a great lot of pull working and I am astonished that it failed.

I feel terribly over your disappointment and hope that it did not make you sick or give you gray hairs . . .

My clearks whom I drill daily are much improved and salute very well . . .

There are all sorts of generals here with nothing to command . . . I think commanding nothing is about all a lot of them are good for . . .

[Heard a Marine singing about a boat in a high sea; the chorus of the song went] Roll, roll, you son of a bitch; the more you roll the less you pitch; pitch, pitch, god dam your soul; the more you pitch the less you roll.

Truly the author was an optimist.

Letter, GSP, Jr. to Beatrice, September 14, 1917

You know how long long long ago when we were second lieuts we used to want to be post Adjutant. Well now I am . . . The Post Commander is Maj. Robert Bacon Q.M.C. USR, and he does not know much so I am C.O. also or nearly so. Like all things which one wants it usually becomes dust on the getting so now I can think of about one million things I would rather be.

I am Post Adjutant, in addition to commanding the Headquarters Company of 250 men and a motor car company of 90 machines. I am also in charge of Passes and anti air craft defenses and any other little thing that people think about giving me. You know how I hate to telephone. Well I live at the end of one now . . . [A Reserve captain, a Regular first lieutenant, and a Regular second lieutenant were serving under him] so I feel quite an old soldier . . .

[John had his birthday yesterday] And I drank to his next [birthday] being in Berlin. But I fear he will be older than that before he visits the forbiden city.

Diary
    September 15: Sgt Braine and I to Paris to settle up auto bills.

The Paris firm of Gaston, Williams and Wigmore, with offices at 5 rue
Daunou (later to be the location of Harry's Bar, a famous landmark for
American tourists), 14 rue Roger-Bacon, and 5 rue Newton (in Passy),
apparently operated as a procurement agency for the U. S. Army on the
French market. It owned a garage and offices at the Roger-Bacon address,
which it rented to the U. S. Army for 550 francs (about $150) per month,
and it furnished materials and labor, tools and rags. It repaired vehicles,
and sold gasoline, oil, paint, tires, and spare parts. All bills were submitted at cost, plus 15 percent for profit. For example, when the automobiles then belonging to the headquarters were painted khaki color — 1
Rolls-Royce, 1 Hotchkiss, 1 De Dion, 2 Renaults, 1 Mercedes, 17 Cadil-
lacs, 15 Fords, and 4 Peugeots — the cost of the paint and the labor,
including overtime for nights and Sundays, came to 2790 francs.

Assisted by Sergeant Braine, Patton checked the bills, and when he was
satisfied that they were correct, he authorized payment. Patton also received and acted on reports of accidents involving headquarters drivers.

"I got well sunburned to day," he informed Beatrice soon after returning to Chaumont, "as I drove down with out my hat in order to develop
my hair."

Letter, GSP, Jr., to Beatrice, September 19, 1917
    The end of another busy day. I ride from eight to 9. I inspect
barracks & kitchens from 9 to ten. Attend to various jobs in my capacity as adjutant from 10 to 12:30. Eat lunch from 12:30 to 1:30.
Do a thousand and one things from 1:30 to seven. Drill the clearks
from 7 to 7:30. Eat dinner from 7:45 to 8:30. Read the 3 Muskateers
from 8:30 to 10:30 and so to bed . . . I have a rubber bath [tub]
and take a bath every morning.

John has gone to Paris for a few days but things go on as usual for
me though some of the others rest a bit when he is not here to poke
them up.

A lot more promotions came over the wire to day . . .

All my class mates in the Field Artillery are Majors. But I am a
long way from one.

There is a lot of talk about "Tanks" here now and I am interested as I can see no future to my present job. The casualties in the Tanks is high that is lots of them get smashed but the people in them are pretty safe as safe as we can be in this war. It will be a long long time yet before we have any [tanks] so don't get worried. We will see each other and talk it over before I will even have a chance to apply. I love you too much to try to get killed but also too much to be willing to sit on my tail and do nothing.

CHAPTER 21

Chaumont

*"I would give a lot to have you consol me and tell me that **I**
amounted to a lot even when I know I don't."*

Letter, GSP, Jr., to Beatrice, September 20, 1917
. . . my time is very fully occupied so it passes rapidly . . .

The Germans shoot a gas which makes people vomit and when
they take off the masks to spit they shoot the deadly gas at them. It is
a smart idea is it not?

Don't tell this. Though it is probably in the papers.

Letter, GSP, Jr., to Beatrice, September 22, 1917
[Curious to know what] you are up to in England [meaning, what
was Beatrice's scheme for getting to England? No leaves were
granted there, but he might be sent to London] . . . as I have a
great drag with the Chief of Staff [Harbord] and with the Adjutant
General as well as with J.

I am now number 113 on the list of captains of Cavalry [eligible
for promotion] . . . It is certainly an outrage the way they are making [promoting] majors and even Colonels out of the 3 months training men and leaving men with 9 years training captains. I don't see
what they think they are doing . . .

The English made a big attack yesterday which seems to have been
successful but one can't tell for four or five days as the Germans don't
hold hard but make terrible counter attacks afterwards.

Today is Saturday and I had the usual inspections. All my men
are in fine shape and only two so far have gotten the disease d'amour
which is a good showing.

Letter, GSP, Jr., to Beatrice, September 23, 1917
I feel sure J. would let me go to England if you get there. I asked

Collins and he said he thought he would. He could probably find some reason for my going there on duty.

Col. Campbell the leading bayonet instructor of the British army lectured here to day and his chief point was physocoligy [psychology] of war. His words were almost verbatim what I used to say at [Fort] Riley and for saying which people thought me brutal.

Letter, GSP, Jr., to Beatrice, September 24, 1917

K. told Mrs. Pardon whom she met in London that you were coming so Mrs. Pardon at once wrote to John and John asked me if I knew it.

He said "Surely Beatrice would not come after all the orders are against it." I said there were none against England. This surprised him but he bore it well and changed the subject. I wrote K. to keep her mouth shut.

Secretary Lane told Mr. Patton that he thought there was real danger of hurting young Patton if Beatrice went to London. Great pressures were being exerted in Washington to obtain exceptions to rules. Lane knew of no one who had profited by desiring that an exception be made for him.

In a letter to his father, Patton said he still thought it was best to go directly to the President to get Bea over. He expected "J" to be very mad, but J would do nothing, and the war was going to last so long that Patton could risk a little displeasure at the start. He saw no prospect of getting into the fighting where success lay. A school of bayonet instruction was about to be started, "and I am thinking of trying for head of that. It is exactly like what I did at Riley."

I think he [Pershing] works the staff too hard. Sunday is just like any other day and if this war is to last three years more as we think that will be more than men can stand. It is true the British staff works all day and every day but a Britisher never works very hard. He is less intense than we are so stands it better.

Letter, GSP, Jr., to Beatrice, September 25, 1917

[Thinks Pa is unduly excited, for] even if the secretary [of War] ordered me home J. would not let me go . . . When J finds out that you are here, if he does and if you make it, he will be awfully angry

but it will wear off in time. I have as you know a rather unfair
advantage over J. which I have never used but I could in that particular case . . .

[If the Russians quit the war, the Germans can bring 3 divisions to
the Western Front for every division the Americans can.] They
can't . . . break this [defensive] line but they can give us hell when
we start to break theirs. Of course we will break them. This talk of
attrition is all rot. We are going through no matter what cost.

Letter, GSP, Jr., to Beatrice, September 27, 1917

. . . curious to see how you are progressing with your hellish design. I suppose the idea of taking the bull (Wilson) by the horns
scared Pa to death.

This war would be a lot more interesting if we could have some
fighting but as it is this everlasting getting ready gets tiresome and I
fear we will be at it a long time yet before we do any killing.

To day is sunday but the only way one knows it is by seeing the
callender.

Letter, GSP, Jr., to Mr. Ayer, October 1, 1917

We run railroads and build them. Build docks, charter ships,
houses, hotels, factories. We buy coal wood, movable houses. Horses,
Automobiles. Aeroplanes. Clothes. Move troops. Make telegraph
lines and almost every other sort of human occupation.

We have a hell of a time finding office space for all our clearks and
officers. Each day we think that the town will not hold another man
then ten more come and we tuck them in.

Letter, GSP, Jr., to Beatrice, October 2, 1917

I am darned sick of my job. It is just like commanding a troop,
being Adjutant and Q.M. and Ordinance officer all at the same time
and being expected to enjoy ones self doing it. I would trade jobs
with almost any one for any thing.

Diary

no date: "Some time about the end of September Col. Eltinge
asked me if I wanted to be a Tank officer. I said yes and also talked
the matter over with Col. McCoy who advised me to write a letter
asking that in the event of Tanks being organized that my name be
considered. I did so."

Letter, GSP, Jr., to Commander in Chief, AEF, thru Headquarters Commandant, AEF, October 3, 1917, subject: Command in the Tank Service

I understand that there is to be a new service of "Tanks" organized and request that my name be considered for a command in that service. I think my self qualified for this service for the following reasons. The duty of "tanks" and more especially of "Light Tanks" is analagous to the duty performed by cavalry in normal wars. I am a cavalryman. I have commanded a Machine Gun Troop and know something of the mechanism of machine guns. I have always had a Troop which shot well so think that I am a good instructor in fire. It is stated that accurate fire is very necessary to good use of tanks. I have run Gas Engines since 1917 and have used and repaired Gas Automobiles since 1905. I speak and read French better than 95% of American Officers so could get information from the French Direct. I have also been to school in France and have always gotten on well with frenchmen. I believe that I have quick judgement and that I am willing to take chances. Also I have always believed in getting close to the enemy and have taught this for two years at the Mounted Service School where I had success in arousing the aggressive spirit in the students. I believe that I am the only American who has ever made an attack in a motor vehicle. This request is not made because I dislike my present duty or am desirous of evading it but because I believe when we get "Tanks" I would be able to do good service in them.

Indorsement: Forwarded, Approved. I consider Capt. Patton unusually well equipped & fitted in every way for the command — [signed] Robert Bacon, Headquarters Commandant.

Letter, GSP, Jr., to Beatrice, October 5, 1917

[Blanchard Scott was in Paris with the Red Cross in a canteen job] which is not what I would want for you. It is a sort of bar maid position. The best thing for you would be Historian or some such thing . . .

If you don't get over here try not to worry too much and get gray hair. I don't like them. I put tonic on my head every day and take exercises so as to keep my youthful apperance.

Letter, GSP, Jr., to Beatrice, October 5, 1917

[Went to a dance given by nurses at the hospital.] I have never seen such a lot of horrors in my life . . . and they dance like tons of brick. I don't think I shall go again. It is too much work with people out of ones own class who are not dressed up.

He moved the headquarters troop into some new portable huts called Adrian barracks. Each held 50 men. They were better than tents. He wished the troops had had them on the border and in Mexico.

Letter, GSP, Jr., to Beatrice, October 8, 1917
J. was delighted with the telegram Mrs. Ayer sent him [on his promotion]. He got quite a lot [of telegrams]. He certainly has been going some. A little over a year ago he was only a Brigadier General and now he has gone clear through the top and there is nothing more he can get or do except to prove he is worthy of what he has.

I certainly don't see any stars in prospect for me but one can always try. Some times I think I don't try as hard as I ought but probably I do . . .

I would give a lot to have you consol me and tell me that I amounted to a lot even when I know I don't.

Letter, GSP, Jr., to Beatrice, October 9, 1917
You certainly are a peach and very pluckie. The way you are acting is fine. Of course we are both more dissapointed than we can say at not being together but things with us have always turned out for the best and perhaps this will too. In fact I am sure it will. It must. We have both always done our duty as we saw it to the best of our ability and God or Fate never forgets that. Your letter has made me more happy than I can tell you for I was dreadfully worried for fear the dissapointment would make you sick and sickness would make you old. You are a peach and I am sure that we will get together sooner than either of us think. There is nothing however in the story that J. is going home. He is not.

Speaking of fate. I was very low in my mind yesterday. There seemed no future to my job and I was disgusted with the daily grind. Last night we had a promotion party for the Gen. and all the officers were there. After the show the Gen called me and said he was about to recommend some promotions in the national army [the wartime component] and would I like to be a major of cavalry or any other branch or staff department. He told me to think it over and tell him frankly what I wanted and he would try to see that I got it.

As I have said the only chance for a man of my age is to command troops. For such staff jobs as I could get would not amount to much. Where as if I commanded an infantry battalion of a thousand men or a Tank battalion of twenty Tanks it would be something worth while and with luck I might go a long way.

A major of infantry is not in any particular danger. It is the lieutenants who catch hell. The Tanks are yet in an unsettled state but they may have a great future. I have consulted Col Malone and am waiting for Col Eltinge to get home to talk to him. I will write you what I decide.

Letter, GSP, Jr., to Beatrice, October 10, 1917

Gen. P. has made a great impression on the English and also on the French. I think it is largely due to his looks for he certainly has the military air.

Letter, Beatrice to Mr. Patton, October 11, 1917

. . . if John would be angry about my going there [to England] he would not be likely to get G. over there to see me on either business or leave. I think G. overestimates his drag with J. I have told him so . . .

I have written G. that I will do just what he says about England after he's read your letters.

On October 17, Patton entered the hospital sick. He had what was diagnosed at first as "cholangitis, acute, catarrhal," later changed to "jaundice catarrhal." He referred to his illness as "jaundice."

Diary

November 3 (Saturday): "About October 10 I began to feel badly and get yellow and when Marshall Joffre dined with us October 14 I felt very ill indeed. I went to the Hospital (No. 15 Roosfelt Unit) On October 17 and was put in the room with Col Lox Conner who had been operated on for a stoppage of the bowls on September 14? I talked Tank with him and decided to try to become a Major of Infantry. Next night October 18 Col Eltinge came and said Gen McAndrew wanted to start a Tank school at Langres on November 15 and would I take it. Inspite of my resolution to the contrary I said yes. But I kept discussing it pro and con with Col F. Conner and again decided on Infantry . . . I left the Hospital Sat. Nov. 3." A major under charges for immoral conduct killed himself "and as he had a family he did a good thing."

Letter, GSP, Jr., to Beatrice, October 19, 1917

I am in the same room with Col Fox Conner who is getting over an operation. When he was coming out of the ether he yelled out. "I know what pane is for I have had three children and you bet your life I am not going to have any more!"

On October 20, Pershing sent a message to the War Department Adjutant General recommending that Patton, who was especially able for duty as a field officer with troops, be transferred to the National Army as a Major of Infantry.

Letter, GSP, Jr., to Aunt Nannie, October 21, 1917

Collins, Shallenberger, and Boyd are all full Colonels as aides to J. It looks funnie to see them around with eagles on their shoulders. Still I am glad they have them and their families all need the money.

Letter, GSP, Jr., to Beatrice, October 26, 1917

. . . you had better send me some Major Leaves. One pair because Col. Conner has a lot he will give me when I need them. I am counting my chickens before they are hatched but I feel sure of being a major very soon.

Letter, GSP, Jr., to Beatrice, October 28, 1917

. . . if I had been in Pa's place I could have made it [a passport for Beatrice to come overseas]. His legal training gives him a too great respect for law. The real thing about law is knowing when to break it not always to obey it . . .

Thanks for sending the candy from S. S. Pierce but tell them to stop the tobacco as now we get plenty here and any how I have quit smoking for the war . . .

I think you are right about my pull with John and it is for that reason [too] that I am going to get away from him and stand on my own feet. Then if I can't make a go of it why it is my fault. Besides if he and N. do [get married] every one will say I rode up on the [gravy] train and I don't want that.

Letter, GSP, Jr., to his father, November 1, 1917

I rather expect to be a temporary [National Army] major soon and if I get it I will go either to the infantry or "the tanks." The job I now have is too easy . . . one must work for success.

GSP, Jr., "Personal Glimpses of General Pershing," 1924

Arriving in France General Pershing was so occupied that I saw him only at meals and occasionally when I accompanied him on visits of inspection, such as that to the British front in July 1917.

There never was a man more worked upon by all the arts of flattery and persuasion than was he during those early months, yet it effected him not a bit. No adulation could persuade him to countenance the placing of American men in French and British units. It is to his iron resolution to form an American Army that we owe the great heritage of a victorious America, victorious in her own right, and by her own means. But for him her man power would have been bled white to fill the depleted ranks of allied units, where their valor would have been unmarked and their achievements unheralded.

To those who have known General Pershing only by his pictures or by an occasional distant view, he appears as a grave, austere man of fine presence, but cold and almost frigid in his loneliness. Just so it is with Mount Washington. Viewed from afar it rises in cold and isolated majesty; in, but not of, our universe. It takes the more intimate personal knowledge of a ramble on its craggy sides to discover the warmth, beauty and latent grandeur of its very self. All great men suffer from this fact. Of American Generals, none has suffered more than General Pershing because none have commanded such hosts or risen so high.

In his office or on his inspections an unnatural severity, most unlike and distasteful to him, seemed of necessity to invest him, but in his quarters he was no whit changed from the man of Mexico. Displacing worry by marvelous control of the will, he laughed and talked of casual, simple things interluding from time to time his conversation by some incisive question of momentous decision.

No matter how late he worked, and he usually did work well into the night, he always took a violent (no other word describes it) walk for half an hour before retiring. In the morning he took 20 minutes setting up exercises before breakfast. In his mess, no wine was served for the benefit of an occasional French visitor. His smoking was confined to one or two cigarettes after dinner.

The immense responsibilities of his position were impotent to remove his human interest. In October 1917 two of his junior staff officers were in the hospital while he was at St. Nazaire inspecting, yet each day he had a telephone report of their condition sent him.

Diary

November 4: "Saw Col [Paul B.] Malone who said my name had gone to general for detail to T[ank] School. Talked to Maj. Bacon and Shallenberger who advised tanks. I did not sleep a bit that night and decided to try the Tanks as it aperes the way to high command if I make a go of it."

November 5: 12 Congressmen came to visit. "They were a lousy lot." Pershing was back from Paris after seeing Lloyd George on the Italian collapse.

Beatrice wrote to Pershing on November 6. She addressed him as "Dear John," then explained why it was no longer "Dear General John." It was because, among other things, he was almost her brother and also he had her little girls' picture on his desk. She then explained how she had tried to get to England and had decided against it in order to keep from hurting George's career. She hoped that the Pattons would come from California to Massachusetts so that Nita could get out of her war work for a while; she was overworked. "Georgie tells me that he may leave your staff when he gets his promotion. I am sorry, for I like to think of you as a sort of comfort to one another."

Letter, GSP, Jr., to his father, November 6, 1917

I believe that with my usual luck I have again fallen on my feet. It is so apparently a thing of destiny that I thought I would discribe it. To begin with Col LeRoy Eltinge my old troop commander is here on the general staff and is in charge of T[anks]. While Col Paul B. Malone an old friend of mine since [Fort] Sheridan is head of the training section. Col E. asked me some time ago if I was interested in T. and I said yes but then I got to thinking that I would rather command a battalion of infantry. Then I got sick. When I was pretty sick Col E. came to see me and said that Col Malone was going to start the T. school and asked me if I would take the job as head of it. Though I had decided not to. I said I would. So my name is in and [I] will start in before I am thirty two.

Here is the sporting side of it. There will be a hundred Majors of infantry but only one of Light T. The T are only used in attacks so all the rest of the time you are comfortable. Of course there is about a fifty percent chance that they wont work at all but if they do they will work like hell.

Here is the golden dream. 1st. I will run the school 2. Then they will organize a battalion. I will command it 3. Then if I make good and the T. do and the war lasts I will get the first regiment. 4. With the same "IF" as before they will make a brigade and I will get the star [of a brigadier general].

On the other hand if I commanded a battalion [of infantry] it might be in reserve in an emergency and some one else get the credit. Also the T. will be a great drawing card in the papers and illustrated magazines. The casualties in the tanks is about 25% but in the crews only about 7½% which is much lower than the Dough boys. Also in the tanks you are not apt to be wounded. You either get blown to bitts by a direct hit or you are not touched.

I have a hunch that my Mexican Auto Battle was the fore runner of this. Who can say?

The only thing holding me up now is Gen P who has not consented. I am going to see him to night and put it over . . .

P.S. Don't talk about T. it is a secret.

Diary

November 6: "Gen Petain and his staff came to dinner with us. He is not very fiery looking and is not like a Frenchman."

Letter, GSP, Jr., to Beatrice, November 7, 1917

Gen Petain was here and we were all on our toes. He is not so impressive a man to look at as one would think but he is very large being as tall as J.J.P. he dresses with Napoleonic simplicity wearing no medals and just three little stars on his sleave to show that he is a Major Gen. For though he is the boss of all he is only a Major General. That is all they have in the French Army except Marshall.

I think it is rather unfair as he has so much responsibility he ought to be paid for it at least.

His aid is a cavalry man and a nice chap. We all had to talk French to keep up with them.

Diary

November 8 (Thursday): Col Malone wanted me to start Tank School at once but I got him to hold off because I wanted to go hunting Sunday.

GSP, Jr., "Tanks Past and Future," February 27, 1928

One day while I was in the hospital at Chaumont recovering from an attack of excessive fish-eating . . . an officer who had once been my troop commander came to my fevered couch and said: "Patton, we want to start a Tank School, to get anything out of tanks one must be reckless and take risks, I think you are the sort of darned fool who will do it." I accepted the offer and the next day received an order to proceed to Langres and organize and establish the First American Tank Center . . . my striker, two horses and an automobile should accompany me . . . In March, 1919, there were some four hundred tanks and five thousand men at that center.

Letter, GSP, Jr., to Beatrice, November 9, 1917

What do you think of me. I am detailed in charge of the School for Light Tanks. To begin with I will have to go to the French Tank school for two weeks then to the Factory for a week then start the school at a Town about twenty miles from here.

The proposition is this. I am doing no good here, that is to my self. The best I could get in the line would be a Battalion of infantry. There will be hundreds of such battalions and my chances of exceptional distinction would be divided by just the number of Battalions. By starting the Tank School I am sure of getting command of the 1st Battalion of tanks. At first there will be only one battalion. If I and the tanks make good I will get the first regiment and if the war lasts the 1st Brigade. The gamble is this. The light tank is a new invention and may not work at all. If it does not I can still go to an infantry Battalion and would only have lost my time.

Another thing the Tanks are only in during an attack. The rest of the time they are safe and comfortable while the poor Dough Boy gets gassed all the time.

Col. Eltinge is head of all tanks Heavy & Light and he will put me forward as much as he can. Col. P. B. Malone is head of the schools and he will do his best for me. These two and Col Davis and Col McCoy and Shallenberger and Col Drum advised me to try it. Gen Harbord and Col Fox Conner advised not. As they said it was a gamble while infantry is sure. All said I was right in getting out of here.

I did not do this in a hurry. I thought about it for over a month and the night I decided I did not sleep at all . . .

J.J.P. talked to me a long time last night and asked me to write you the following.

It appears to him from Nitas letters that she is very much alive to the responsibilities she will one day assume and that her nature has grown largely. She tells him that she feels tied too much to her mothers apron strings. This being the case he would like her to visit you for six months as you have a wonderful influence on her etc.

I think that he has told her to go to see you if you ask her. It seems to me that she might be a comfort to you and certainly she would not be a bother as she gets on well with your family and the kidds. You might coach her on maternity? Of course if you think that you are too much bothered to have her don't do it for J. but I should think it would be nice for you.

I did not mention the tanks much before as I feared it might not come out but if it works I have pulled one of the biggest coups of my life so far. If it don't I will not have lost much for all the schools are at the town I am going to and I will be able to take some courses at the staff college.

Diary

November 10: Order for tanks approved by GHQ AEF General Order 153, Paragraph 37.

On that day, GHQ formally asked the chief of the attached French Military Mission for permission to send Captain George S. Patton, Jr., Cavalry, and Lieutenant Elgin Braine, 6th Field Artillery, to visit suitable French tank installations for the purposes of studying and familiarizing themselves with tanks.

Elgin Braine, twenty-eight years old, was a Reserve officer with the artillery in the 1st Infantry Division. When he suddenly received orders to report to Captain Patton in connection with tank matters, he was mystified. A trained technician, perhaps even a mechanical engineer, he knew something, probably a great deal, about motors, blueprints, and other details of industrial engineering, but nothing about tanks.

A rather reserved person who had been born in Ridgewood, New Jersey, and whose home was in New York City, he would prove to be an invaluable and loyal assistant to Patton on the production end of the tank program.

Braine would later write: "Being the first member of the Tank Corps, although not a volunteer, I have had at all times a great personal interest [in it]." He was mistaken about being the first member assigned to the tanks. That distinction belonged to Patton.

On the day before he was thirty-two years old, Patton wrote to Beatrice and noted that it would be the third successive birthday of his they were separated.

> I have not seemed to get any older for the last ten years but just how long we can keep up fooling time is hard to say. I hate to get old away from you. It will be sixteen years next July since I decided to marry you and we have only been together about five years out of that time. Hard luck God Damn.

He was to go to a French school for tanks near Paris for two weeks, then to a tank factory in Paris for one week. He would actually have only one tank until sometime in the summer. "So don't picture me dashing to battle in them. There will be none in which to dash."

The idea of a tank had originated in the mind of British Lieutenant Colonel Ernest D. Swinton late in 1914, when he saw a small American-made caterpillar tractor in France. He recommended that tractors be armored, that is protected, and armed, that is with guns, for use in combat. Winston S. Churchill, First Lord of the Admiralty, heard of the notion, liked it, and gave it strong support. As a consequence, the Royal Navy sponsored experiments and tests of a "land ship" during 1915. This background of tank development led to the usage of naval terms to designate parts of the tank — hatch, hull, bow, and ports. When some early models were shipped to France for combat testing, they were carried on ships' manifests, for the purpose of deceiving the enemy, as water tanks en route to Russia. From that stemmed their name as tanks.

They first appeared on the front in the Somme area on September 15, 1916, when the British employed 49 thirty-ton Mark I tanks in combat. The French, having independently developed a lighter tank, first used tanks in battle on April 16, 1917. The distinction between heavy tanks, British type, and light tanks, French model, was retained.

The American Military Mission in Paris, established as a fact-gathering agency long before the United States entry into the war, noted and reported the experiments with these interesting new weapons. The Chief of the Army War College in Washington, functioning in his capacity as the principal War Department planner for operations, became aware of tanks and directed the Military Mission to submit a detailed report on the latest British and French tank technology and tactical ideas. This report was assembled and sent to Washington in May 1917. To it were attached rather full notes gathered by Major Frank Parker, liaison officer at GHQ of the French Armies of the North and Northeast, on how the French employed tanks.

Soon after Pershing reached Paris, he saw the report of the Military Mission and was impressed. In June he appointed several committees to look into tank warfare, and a few staff members visited the French and British fronts to study equipment, organization, and tactical planning. Although the early employment of tanks was marked by numerous mechanical failures, Pershing decided that heavy tanks in the British style and light tanks in the French mode would both be useful components of the American Expeditionary Force.

The French St. Chamond and Schneider tanks, the first ones developed, seemed to be less than adequate in battle, but a board of American officers appointed to examine a new and promising model called the Renault was satisfied that the Renault had a better potential and would be suitable for American operations.

Apprised of Pershing's decision to have American tanks, the AEF Chief of Ordnance asked him to determine the number that would be needed in France. Pershing delegated this task and other tank matters to Colonel Eltinge, a member of his staff. Late in September, when Pershing approved plans for an overseas army of 20 combat divisions, Eltinge suggested that between 375 and 600 heavy tanks and between 1200 and 1500 light tanks would be required. Pershing accepted these figures and requested the War Department to procure them in the United States and furnish them to him.

The heavy tank to be produced in America was a 43.5-ton Mark VIII patterned very closely on the British model — with an eleven-man crew, a maximum speed of 6.5 miles per hour, and an operational range without refueling of 50 miles. The American-built 6½-ton light tank was to be a copy of the Renault — with a two-man crew, a maximum speed of 5.5 miles per hour, and an operational range of 30 miles.

To collect additional information on the design and production of tanks, the Chief of Ordnance in Washington detailed, in October 1917, Major James A. Draine to look into the French experience and Major Herbert Alden to report on the British. These officers submitted a report early in November. When an Inter-Allied Tank Commission was formed to coordinate tank production, Draine became the American member.

It soon was apparent that tank production in the United States would be delayed beyond reasonable expectation. Actually, American tank manufacture would start only in the summer of 1918, when the Ford Motor Company developed and began to build a small and wholly American three-ton tank.

In order to obtain tanks more quickly for the American forces, the American member of the Supreme War Council, with Pershing's approval, secured permission from the War Department early in December 1917, to enter into an agreement with the British and French governments for the joint production of heavy and light tanks. The competing demands of aircraft and other new requirements forced by the Ludendorff offensive in March 1918 would dislocate this program.

Meanwhile, in the fall of 1917, Pershing decided that the tank force of the AEF would consist of five heavy battalions (the number was later doubled) and 20 light tank battalions, all to be directed by a tank officer at Headquarters, AEF.

It was the light tank battalions that Patton hoped eventually to command. But first he would have to find out how tanks worked, how they were run and kept in repair, and how the French and British trained tankers and employed them in battle.

No one in the American Expeditionary Force had sufficient knowledge in these matters to qualify as a tank expert.

Letter, GSP, Jr., to Beatrice, November 12, 1917

J. is getting more and more weak on the subject of N. so I think he would let me go [to England on leave if Beatrice managed to get to London] . . . Ask Nita to come and see you. It would do her good.

Letter, GSP, Jr., to Beatrice, November 15, 1917

I got a sweater to day presented to each of the first 100 Americans in France. It is not so good as the vest you sent me.

Stuart Cramer wrote me that there was much talk of J and N in Town Topics.

While awaiting the permission of the French authorities to visit tank installations, Patton managed to keep busy. He addressed a memo to the

Commander in Chief, AEF, on "Military Appearance and Saluting" and observed that some officers compared unfavorably with many enlisted men and field clerks in military courtesy and dress. Patton frequently had to correct lieutenants and captains for failing to salute or for saluting in a slovenly manner, usually with only one or two fingers. He felt that it was discouraging for a soldier to turn out a snappy salute and have an officer acknowledge it with a casual wave of the hand. Many officers, even some Regulars, failed to dress neatly. They wore unpressed uniforms, unpolished belts, muddy boots and leggings, and tarnished brass work. Patton suggested that a circular be published directing all officers to correct this negligence.

He himself, he admitted in his diary, was doing a lot of disciplining "around here; cussed out a lot of captains and majors for not saluting."

A few days later, in another memorandum he suggested that the wearing of insignia on raincoats, always more or less a personal matter, be standardized; that each soldier be required to carry a clothes brush and a shoe brush so he could look clean even in bad weather; that officers be encouraged to dress for dinner; that each man be provided with a razor to be shown at full pack inspections; and that hair be clipped short to minimize exposure to head lice.

Appointed a member of a board looking into the uniform worn in France, he recommended abandoning the campaign hat in favor of a small folding cap similar to that worn in the French Army. He suggested that it be of simple design without buttons; that it be of olive drab color and piped along the top of the earflaps with the color of the wearer's branch of service; that officers pin their insignia of rank in the center of the front of the cap; that officers be allowed to wear their current service cap on certain occasions, for example, when not actually commanding troops in formation who were wearing another form of head covering.

Strict military discipline and courtesy, neatness and standardization of dress were already fetishes — or trademarks — of Patton.

Curious to see Langres, where the AEF was establishing its school center and where the tank school would be located, he drove there and met several officers who showed him around. Langres was a pleasant and pretty walled town with streets that were narrow but clean. Patton ascertained that it was founded by Marcus Aurelius, that a Roman gate was still part of the wall, and that the drawbridges were still operable.

A letter on November 16 to the Commander in Chief, AEF, from General Ragueneau, Chief of the French Military Mission to the American Army, authorized Captain Patton and Lieutenant Braine to visit the Center of Artillery Attack Instruction at Chamlieu near Compiègne — actually the tank center — and also the Renault factory at Billancourt, just outside Paris. They could go immediately and spend from eight to fifteen days, as they wished, at Chamlieu. They were then to pass through the Ministry of Armament in Paris, Department of Automobile Service — Materials Section, to get a letter permitting a visit to the Renault factory.

Patton arranged to turn over his headquarters troop to a new commander, and Pershing promised to inspect the final formation of Patton's men.

A Troop Order published by Patton on November 17 pleased Pershing immensely. In it Patton wrote that upon relinquishing command, he wished to recapitulate, for the benefit of the more recently joined members, the enviable record which the troop had thus far made. Organized on May 23, 1917, landing in England on June 8, and quartered in the Tower of London, the men demonstrated exemplary conduct and appearance. Reaching Paris on June 18, the first Regulars to arrive in France, and welcomed with open arms, the men again behaved with dignity and restraint. Their dress and bearing established a splendid opinion of American soldiers among the French people. There had been only two trials by court-martial and one case of venereal disease. During the six months of the organization's history, no superior officer, so far as Patton was aware, had ever found fault with the troop. "Such a record," Patton concluded with pride — and to stimulate unit morale — "is hard to surpass and the Troop Commander takes great pleasure in reciting it and desires in leaving to urge on the troop the necessity of ever living up to their proud beginning."

For Patton's official file, Pershing noted that Patton had commanded the AEF Headquarters Troop, that he had performed his duties "very efficiently," and that he was best fitted for service with troops or tanks.

Diary

November 18 (Sunday): I inspected troop at 7:30 A.M. to see that all was OK; threw out for kitchen police and fatigue duty 6 men who had dirty uniforms. Gen inspected at 9:30 — 110 men in ranks. Gen

made speech and complimented men and also me; a nice ending for
interesting but hard job. Shallenberger and I left for Paris at 11:30.
Lunched on way and got in at 4:30. "Saw a lot of reserve officers
slouching around."

Letter, GSP, Jr., to Beatrice, November 18, 1917
There is a recommendation in to have the Chief of Tanks a colonel
and the assistant chiefs (light & heavy) Lt. Colonels so I may be Lt
Col. Patton yet.

CHAPTER 22

Chamlieu

"The job I have tentatively possessed my self of is huge for every thing must be created and there is nothing to start with nothing but me that is. Some times I wonder if I can do all there is to do but I suppose I can. I always have so far."

THE OVERRIDING TACTICAL PROBLEM for both sides on the Western Front was how to break through the opposing trenches. To reach the hostile trenches, troops had to cross no-man's-land. Under the bullets and shells of enemy machine guns and artillery pieces, they had to cut the barbed wire in no-man's-land, then come into physical contact with and eliminate the hostile soldiers entrenched in a series of defensive lines.

The standard method of getting soldiers across to the enemy trenches was by protracted artillery bombardment, usually lasting several days. The shells cut the wire, knocked out machine guns, and rained down on the entrenched enemy troops. When the defenses were deemed sufficiently destroyed, the attacking soldiers assaulted, that is, they left the relative safety of their own trenches, went "over the top," and swarmed across.

Invariably, some barbed wire, some machine guns, some defenses remained intact. Furthermore, having alerted by the artillery preparatory bombardment, the enemy launched his own counter-barrage fires and usually moved reserve units into position behind the front to strengthen the sector being threatened.

Those who were charging across the relatively open ground were exposed to the defensive fires, suffered losses, and met enemy troops who were strengthened by the reinforcement of reserves. Attacks were costly, and advances were measured in yards.

One solution to the problem was to launch a surprise attack. This was virtually impossible to accomplish because of elaborate precautionary measures, such as alarms, bells hung on the wire, and most of all, the almost constant sorties by small patrols to give warning of the approach of enemy troops.

Surprise could be gained by the use of gas or chemical warfare, but this had disadvantages. One's own troops were unable to enter contaminated areas. Wearing masks restricted the attacking soldiers.

Another solution to overcome the static or stationary warfare of the trenches was to restore mobility to the battlefield by means of tanks. They could cross no-man's-land in relative safety and destroy the enemy trench system.

While Patton was at the French tank training center at Chamlieu in the forest of Compiègne, the battle of Cambrai took place. The British massed tanks in combat for the first time and showed that the new weapon, if employed with surprise, could get troops across no-man's-land without incurring a high rate of losses.

At dawn of November 20, without a preliminary bombardment by artillery pieces, more than 300 British tanks advanced on a six-mile stretch of the front near Cambrai and led five infantry divisions in assault against the Hindenburg Line, called by the Germans the Siegfried Position. By noontime, the tanks had broken through the trenches of that strongly fortified defensive sector and penetrated the enemy lines to a depth of four miles. They shattered the two German divisions holding the position, took 4000 prisoners and more than 100 guns against a loss of 4000 British casualties.

This brilliant success, economical in blood when compared to other offensives, gained more ground in a shorter period of time than any other attack since the stabilization of the trench system along the Western Front.

Although the British were unable to exploit the breakthrough of the initial assault and take advantage of its momentum, Cambrai marked the first employment of successful tank tactics in war. The absence of preparatory artillery fires had gained surprise, and the massing of tanks in the assault had demonstrated that mobility could be restored to the battlefield. No-man's-land could be crossed and the opposing trenches destroyed

The immediate effect and the lasting value of Cambrai were to vindicate the tanks at a time when many military authorities had lost faith in them.

Diary

November 19 (Monday): Left Paris. Reported to Gen. Garrard, French Army, and was sent to Chamlieu. "Saw some Renault tanks. They seem fine. [Was] given a very nice room and an orderly."

Letter, GSP, Jr., to Beatrice, November 20, 1917

[My orderly is] very attentave and calls me either lieutenant or general as the humor takes him.

Far more important, Patton drove a tank — a Renault *char d'assaut,* as the French called it, and crossed trenches in it. It was easy to operate, particularly if one knew how to drive an automobile, and was surprisingly comfortable. It was a little higher than a man if one measured to the top of the turret and about as long as a touring car. The driver sat in front and the gunner stood in the turret.

The tank was noisy. It went about as fast as a man could run. It could turn like lightning. It could rear up like a horse and stand on its head.

The only trouble was, it was difficult to see from inside it. The driver had three small slits to look through. The man in the turret had a little better visibility, but not much.

Patton found it a funny sensation to hit small trees and watch them go down. Standing in the turret he fired the gun while the tank was motionless and while it was moving.

He was immensely pleased. In the evening he examined the workings of the machine, and he asked so many questions that his instructors had to send for an expert mechanic to answer and explain.

He was especially impressed by the fourteen French officers with whom he messed at Chamlieu. They were from all the arms — that is, from the infantry, cavalry, and artillery. All were under thirty, and all had been decorated for bravery in combat. They argued continually, but in good humor, over the battles they had been in and over the exploits of their regiments. And they joked — when an infantryman said that his regiment had been in mud to the knees for three days of fighting, another said that his had been up to the armpits for a week, and a third said that his had been in the mud for so long that when they came out of the trenches they found that their clothes had rotted away below the belt.

His orderly, he discovered, was a sergeant named Count Everest de Pas; "he holds my coat and then asks me to dine with him in Paris."

During the first week that Patton stayed at Chamlieu, which was a training school for French officers newly assigned to tanks, he drove tanks, fired tank guns, worked on tactical problems, observed a maneuver, inspected the repair shops, visited the tank park, and had long discussions on how best to employ tanks in combat.

On Saturday afternoon he took the train to Paris, visited friends, saw General Pershing for a moment, went to the theater, and ran into a classmate, a non-flying aviator already a lieutenant colonel, who said that two of their classmates had been promoted to full colonels. Patton returned to Chamlieu Sunday night without knowing that Pershing, on November 23, had cabled the War Department Adjutant General to recommend his promotion to major.

Lieutenant Braine joined him at Chamlieu on Tuesday for the second week, which Patton found even more interesting. He watched a maneuver and liked the way the tanks "crawled in a most impersonal manner." He lunched and dined with General J. E. Estienne, the commander of all French tanks, and talked tanks with him during those meals. He observed how tanks crossed trenches and how drivers and gunners were tested for proficiency. He translated lesson plans, saw tanks chained in couples to cross very wide and very deep trenches, drove a tank up and down very steep banks (and "did it well," he noted).

He also noticed what he considered to be a shocking example of French bureaucracy. To make a few small changes desired by the tankers in the design of the tank, a board representing the Ministers of Munitions, Construction, and Inventory, plus Louis Renault, the manufacturer, came first to Chamlieu, where they argued at length over every point.

On Thursday he went to Compiègne, where he called on Colonel Frank Parker and obtained some champagne for the mess at Chamlieu. On Friday evening, his last at Chamlieu, "Gave mess champaigne and made speach, in French."

Letter, GSP, Jr., to Beatrice, November 26, 1917

Since the English success the other day [at Cambrai] lots of people have suddenly discovered that in the tanks they have always had faith and now express a desire to accept the command of them but fortunately I beat them to it by about four days . . .

. . . the job I have tentatively possessed my self of is huge for every

thing must be created and there is nothing to start with nothing but
me that is.

Some times I wonder if I can do all there is to do but I suppose I
can. I always have so far.

This was a sober assessment both of his extreme good fortune in the
matter of timing his assignment to the tanks and of the immense and
unprecedented task he had been given and now had responsibility for
executing — the creation from nothing of an American tank force, capable and aggressive in combat.

Leaving Chamlieu on Saturday, December 1, he lunched at Compiègne
with Colonel Parker, who had recommended that tanks be part of the
American forces. They drove toward Cambrai to Albert, in the process
crossing earlier battlefields of the Somme. At Albert, they talked about
the Cambrai action with the chief of staff of the British Tank Corps —
Colonel J. F. C. Fuller, the brains of the tanks, who was largely responsible for originating tank doctrine, the methods of employing tanks in
battle. Patton secured what he called some interesting data.

Riding to Paris with Parker in an automobile, he saw a company of
English infantry going into the line; "they were very young looking and
the lieutenants were children."

Between Amiens and Paris, "I had my usual yearly accident," he later
wrote Beatrice. The car ran into a closed railroad gate, "and I carelessly
put my head through the front window and cut an artery on my left
temple and cut a hole at the point of the jaw on the right side about an
inch long and deep." He bled freely, but Parker wrapped his head in a
towel and drove him to the American hospital at Neuilly, where a doctor
closed his cut with five stitches.

In Paris, he arranged to visit the Renault works and saw Pershing
briefly. He and Braine spent Monday at the Renault factory, where he
"got much data" on design and construction and where Braine found
himself more at ease. In the course of their visit, Patton and Braine suggested four minor improvements in the tank, which the French later
adopted. One was a bulkhead to separate the gun room from the engine
so the crew would be less liable to be burned to death; another was for a
self-starter.

Patton and Braine then returned to Chaumont and reported orally on the results of their trip to Colonel Eltinge, who was temporarily in charge of tank matters for the AEF.

Before he could get to work on a written report of his observations at Chamlieu and Billancourt, Patton was pressed into temporary service as an acting aide to Pershing. He met at tea and chatted with Colonel E. M. House, the President's personal assistant, and also Lord Northcliffe, who was accompanying House. He escorted several important visitors, including a Congressman, around Chaumont and showed them the AEF schools at Langres.

He finally managed to get back to tanks, and all day long on Friday, helped by Braine, Patton worked on his report.

Letter, GSP, Jr., to Beatrice, December 5, 1917

. . . this battle of Cambrai shows what they [tanks] can do and with small loss at that. I have a very long report to make out on them as no one knows any thing about the subject except me. I am certainly in on the ground floor. If they are a success I may have the chance I have always been looking for.

Letter, GSP, Jr., to Beatrice, December 7, 1917

I go riding every morning with Gen Harbord [Pershing's Chief of Staff] at 7 A.M. It is almost dark but the only time he gets. I like him and do it so he will like me.

Letter, GSP, Jr., to Beatrice, December 7, 1917

. . . the war is not over nor even decided and . . . its final outcome depends on U.S. and on us only . . .

We are all cheerful and confident but well assured that we will have to fight hard to win but that we will do it and win. J. has grown with responsibility and is a wonderful man and strange to say [despite his long hours and many activities] in fine health . . .

My stitches came out this morning and I am as well as ever.

I have been working every possible moment on my report and think that it will be a good one. At least I hope so as on its reception depends my future and that of the tanks.

Diary

December 8: Maj Drum, Col Eltinge, Lt. Braine, and I talked tanks.

Letter, GSP, Jr., to Beatrice, December 9, 1917

Yesterday Col R[ockenbach] and I worked from nine a.m. to 10 p.m. on our organization with only half an hour for lunch.

I got ten officers started in yesterday. They belong to me but are getting special courses in machine gun and small cannon at other schools. I wont have any Tanks before the first of February but will fill in the time teaching maping as we must know it.

Diary

December 10: dictated report and worked on Table of Organization. Gen Harbord proposed Col Rockenbach, Lee, Johnston, Shelly McKuskie as Chief of Tanks at AEF headquarters. "I did not oppose Rockenbach though I dislike him."

Patton's Memo to the Chief of the Tank Service — a position soon to be filled by Rockenbach — was dated December 12. Its subject was "Light Tanks." A 58-page report, typed double spaced, it was fluent, authoritative, thoughtful, well organized, and to the point. Patton had absorbed a tremendous amount of information about tanks, and he presented it with his customary thoroughness and verve. In later years when Patton was arranging his files, he wrote in pencil across the top, "This paper was and is the Basis of the U. S. Tank Corps. I think it is the best Technical Paper I ever wrote. GSP Jr." It was, in fact, the rock upon which the American tank effort in France was established.

Pursuant to verbal instructions, the report read, Patton, later joined by Braine, visited the tank center of the French Army and the Renault factory for orientation. Patton's chief impression of the Renault works was that the

French are experiencing great difficulty in having the manufacturer collaborate with the fighting end of the Tank Service. The manufacturer continues to make tanks containing faults to which his attention has been drawn by the people using them . . . [who] fail to remonstrate with sufficient vehemence and continue to accept imperfect materiel.

This was a clear warning to those at the AEF headquarters who would be responsible for the procurement of tanks, and it underscored Patton's perception of difficulties to arise in the future.

The report had four attachments, which described the mechanical structure of the tank, the organization of tank units, the tactics of tank forces, and methods of instruction and drill.

In the first attachment, he defined the tank. It was an armored self-propelled vehicle "which must be able to deliver a predetermined fire power on the field of battle at the time it is required." To do so, it had to fulfill three principal conditions: overcome all obstacles of terrain; give maximum protection to its operators and its motor power plant; and be armed. It had to be easy to manufacture in quantity. Its weight had to be proportionate to and in consonance with its motor and traction potential. It could not be too heavy to allow of its transportation to training or battle areas by rail or by motor truck.

A tank shielded its crew only against a direct hit from a small-arms bullet, that is, a round fired by a rifle or machine gun. Protection against a larger projectile fired by a cannon would require armor so thick that the weight of the tank would become prohibitive. Therefore, safety from larger caliber weapons had to come from the tank's mobility — its ability to move and maneuver — and from its near invisibility, because of its comparatively small size. Both of these factors reduced its vulnerability as a target for enemy guns. The weight of its own guns and ammunition was negligible.

The French Renault light tank had no wheels directly on the ground but was supported and propelled by two endless-chain tracks, one on each side. Each track worked on a side frame called a longeron. A track ran on two wheels, one propelling the track by means of the motor, the other keeping it in tension and aiding the return of the track. Traction was obtained by forcing the lower part of the track into the ground by the weight of the machine, and this weight was supported by rollers on the back of the lower part of the track. Axles of these rollers were fixed to two rockers called front and rear chariots placed inside the lower frame of the longeron.

Patton described in detail the mechanical parts and their functions — gasoline tanks, magneto, carburetor, radiator, clutch, universal joints, gears, and other features. The turret could turn 360 degrees — full circle — by means of two handles located inside. The engine, the standard four-cylinder monobloc L-head motor used in the small Renault truck, generated 18 horsepower. The tank weighed 5 tons; its top speed was 7 kilometers and 800 meters, or about 10 miles, per hour. It could climb no slope greater than a 45-degree gradient unless the soil was especially good for traction.

"Hence a tank is essentially an armored tower rolling upon tracks of its own laying."

Probably depending to a large extent on Braine's knowledge, Patton then became quite technical, exposing certain relationships of weight and power by means of equations and formulas. He also indicated certain improvements recommended by the Chamlieu Tank Center, explaining in each case the justification for the change — a self-starter (the current system of cranking on the inside was all right as long as the tank was level, but if the tank stalled on a steep incline, the crank handle was either on the floor or against the ceiling), a hand accelerator, a speaking tube for gunner and driver, leather helmets for the crew, a more easily adjustable fan belt, a better method to grease the clutch bearings, improved headlights and taillights, and so on. The eye slits needed to be raised about one and a half inches because Americans were generally taller than Frenchmen.

In the second part of his paper, Patton took up the organization of tank units. A platoon, he recommended, should consist of one tank with a 3-inch gun, two tanks with 6-pounder guns, and two tanks with machine guns — a total of 5 tanks and 15 men.

A company should have three platoons and a company headquarters. The latter should consist of two officers, a first sergeant, supply sergeant, mess sergeant, signal sergeant, company clerk, ten drivers, twenty privates, one mechanic, two motorcyclists, ten chauffeurs, and three cooks — a total of 2 officers and 51 men, with an additional tank equipped for signals, a tank for the company commander, eight tanks for support, training, and reserve, five trucks for ammunition, two trucks for gasoline and oil, one truck with trailer for baggage, one kitchen truck with trailer, one automobile, and two motorcycles. A company would thus have, all told, 5 officers and 96 men, 25 tanks and 12 vehicles.

A battalion should have three companies, plus a battalion headquarters and a repair unit. Headquarters personnel would include a major in command, two lieutenants [adjutant and quartermaster), and so on. A battalion would then consist of a total of 18 officers and 331 men, 77 tanks and 42 vehicles. Patton suggested placing all the supply trucks at the battalion headquarters in order to provide flexibility. He thought it would be better to assemble the twelve mechanics of the three companies from time to time at the battalion level to facilitate large repair jobs.

In addition to the battalion repair unit, a large repair shop had to be established at some permanent or semipermanent center, where badly damaged tanks and vehicles could be sent, where motors in need of thorough overhaul could be shipped. He believed that this would work better than the French system, which had repair units functioning at company, battalion, and rear echelons.

As for moving tanks to combat or training areas, Patton suggested an attached carrier company — either of 77 trucks, each capable of pulling a tank by trailer or carrying it loaded; or of 27 specially built, heavier and larger trucks, each capable of carrying one tank and of pulling a second by trailer. He discussed the pros and cons of each method — for example, the larger carriers would be limited to traveling on the best roads only — and finally recommended that a combination of both types of vehicle might be practical. He pointed out that absolute mobility would have to be weighed against cost and tonnage factors.

Patton then listed the material to be carried by each tank and truck — the tools, spare parts, and so on.

The third and tactical section of Patton's report opened with a historical account. "The evolution of the tank as a weapon of war," he wrote, "may be said to have started with the cessation of open warfare on the Western Front." After the battle of the Marne in 1914, the Germans entrenched themselves, having but one line of trenches at first. Soon they had several lines, and these were strengthened by wire entanglements and machine guns. "While thus the passive and active power of defense increased, the man power of the assailants diminished and it became necessary to augment with machinery the loss of flesh." The first method tried was massed artillery, but even an intense bombardment left some barbed wire uncut and some machine guns unsilenced. The price of attack was still too high. Then, "Strange to say the French and British, acting independently, struck on very similar solutions at almost the same time, that is, the spring of 1915."

The French, instigated by General Estienne, thought of reducing manpower losses by carrying men to the hostile lines in bullet-proof machines, which could cross shell holes and broken ground to reach their destination. Discovering the American Holt tractor, the French adopted its mechanism almost exactly and covered the chassis with an armored box.

The plan was to construct a very large number of such machines and by using them in a surprise attack along the entire line to have these modern "Trojan Horses" disgorge their contents of infantry within the German trenches. Unfortunately for the success of their plan the English made their first tank attack when the French building program was not yet completed. This premature action, as the French see it, on the part of the English removed the essential element of surprise from the French plan.

The English had looked for a fighting machine capable not only of cutting the barbed wire but also of destroying by its fire the remnants of resistance left after bombardment — and "so far it has done some excellent work." This British idea compelled the French to change their troop-carrying machines — which many years later would be called personnel carriers — into attack machines.

But the French tanks were not wholly satisfactory, for they lacked sufficient power and climbing ability. Since the French had built so many tanks, however, they decided to give their older tanks, somewhat superficially modified, a trial before producing a newer version.

The employment in battle of the two original types of French tank — the Schneider, with a weight of 16 tons, a 40-horsepower motor, a short 3-inch gun and two machine guns, a crew of one officer and five men; and the St. Chamond, 22 tons, an electric-drive 60-horsepower motor, one long 3-inch gun and four machine guns, a crew of one officer and seven men — quickly proved their relative inefficiency. Both were underpowered for working among shell holes, and both required the infantry to prepare trench crossings for them before the assault.

The French then determined to construct a new machine purely for fighting, and the result was the Renault light tank. Although the French had produced less than 50 of these new and improved tanks by December 1917, they expected to have a large number available for action in the spring of 1918.

What were the problems and results of employing light tanks in combat?

On April 16, 1917, the French at Jovincourt used 80 tanks on a front of 8000 yards. They attached the tanks to the attacking infantry and placed them directly under the infantry commander who "knew nothing of tanks nor their power and hence directed that they all deploy in one line without supports [supporting elements]." The artillery and aviation commanders were equally unused to working with tanks, and as a consequence the former failed to support them with fire and the latter failed to report their positions after the battle started. The infantrymen, who knew little about tanks, were detailed to work with them during a very dark night just before the attack, and they had little idea of how to perform their functions and thus remained too far behind the machines. "They [the infantry] behaved very gallantly but to little avail." The tankers themselves were inexperienced, and they failed to define operational sectors clearly; many tanks became lost. Because drivers were insufficiently trained, many tanks stalled unnecessarily and made no contribution to the attack.

Despite these handicaps, eight tanks under Captain Goubernaud, the current Chief of the Light Tanks, gained their objective, the fourth German trench, 800 meters from the starting point of the attack. At the objective, because the tanks had no smoke bombs to blind the enemy and thus secure cover long enough to maneuver and attack, a single German gun put six tanks out of action and brought the operation to a halt.

The signal success of this one group [of eight tanks] in gaining its objective is due to the fact that it was the only one which had an exact sector assigned and it was the only one in which the drivers had made a careful study of the map. Both of these facts are very significant.

On May 5, 1917, having studied and corrected the errors of the previous tank action, the French attacked at Laffoux with 20 tanks. The assault was a complete success. No tanks were lost.

The French launched another attack at Laffoux between August 21 and 23, this time with 100 tanks. They gave the same attention to detail, and again the attack was completely successful — all the tanks reached their objectives. "It must be admitted, however, that the artillery preparation was so heavy that there was little for them [the tanks] to do."

Patton remarked that the tank fire had been quite inaccurate in all these engagements. This indicated that far more attention had to be paid to instruction in target practice.

The British attack at Cambrai in November proved the combat effectiveness of tanks. Although bad management of the railroads bringing the tanks to the front made it necessary to spend 72 hours to assemble the tanks for combat, "still the attack was a surprise." Consequently, there was no German counter-barrage. Whereas during the sixteen-day artillery preparation and counter-barrage preceding the battle of Ypres the British infantry had lost 10,000 casualties before zero hour, the British took no prior casualties from counter-barrage fires at Cambrai. The offensive progressed successfully until hostile artillery found the range against the tanks "with disastrous results."

Wherever the tanks went the infantry met with success, except where the tanks got ahead of the infantry. In these cases losses to the latter resulted as the tanks overlooked concealed guns. The wire was cut by the tanks and the infantry crossed firm ground. Had the wire been cut by artillery barrage the ground would have been so torn up as to be almost as much of an obstacle as the original wire. Also the fact that the ground was not torn up made it possible to bring forward field guns and cavalry through the holes in the wire without difficulty. Another point is that French villages in the hostile area were not destroyed by the preparatory bombardment. To have cut the wire by artillery bombardment as it was cut by the tanks would have required in the neighborhood of two million rounds at a cost of twenty-five million dollars. This cost was greater than the cost of the total four hundred tanks engaged. Had the heavy British tanks been followed by an equal number of light tanks to mop up after them and to push past them and exploit their success better results would undoubtedly have been obtained . . .

The proper conception of the light tank is as a heavily armored infantry soldier, with equal activity and greater destructive and resistant powers. The light tank is in no sense artillery nor an independent arm but simply a form of specialist who aids the infantry to victory — the expulsion of the enemy from his position. If resistance is broken and the line pierced the tank must and will assume the role of pursuit cavalry and "ride the enemy to death." The ever present chance of this last role is the chief reason for the deployment [of tanks] in depth and the maintenance of a [tank] reserve.

To aid the infantry, Patton postulated, the tanks must: 1) facilitate infantry advance by cutting wires ahead of the infantry; 2) prevent hostile infantry from manning the trench parapet when the preparatory barrage lifted; 3) prohibit machine guns and trench cannon from attacking the infantry; 4) help mop up, neutralizing strongpoints and blockhouses by masking them with fire and smoke bombs; 5) guard against counterattack by patrolling; 6) push on at own initiative beyond the final objective — but only after infantry consolidated that position — in order to seek every opportunity for pursuit. "At this phase the support and possibly the reserve should join the leading tanks."

"Deployment in depth is as necessary to them as to any other attacking troops." To have tanks act in accord with infantry, "to which they are attached," sectors must be carefully defined. "If possible the company commander and each chief of platoon should be allowed to see from an aeroplane the exact ground over which he is to attack." The company commander of tanks must supervise "and personally inspect these maps and routes and himself calculate accurately the time required for the platoons to go from the position of readiness to the attacking position." Tanks should arrive at the line of departure just before zero hour, "thereby avoiding loss incident to remaining stationary under hostile bombardment."

> Mobility is a most essential feature in all arms and is the chief place where the light tank has an advantage over the heavy. The latter must always be moved by rail while the light tanks can be moved by autotruck and by trailer . . . To get the full value from light tanks they must have maximum mobility . . .
>
> The best defense against any and all . . . methods of attack is constant movement and watchfulness and a supply of smoke bombs to mask a tank suddenly attacked by a small cannon.

In the last part of the report, Patton discussed how the Americans could obtain a sufficient number of trained personnel to operate tanks. He recommended a plan "for the quick production of [tank] personnel" by means of a tank center and a school of instruction for each type of tank, light and heavy. The officer in charge of each school should also command the tank center "of that variety," meaning the light or the heavy tanks.

On the assumption that sufficient tanks would become available at once, he suggested training men by units. That is, send to the tank center enough officers and men to fill one company, plus one or two instructors.

After all the officers and noncoms and as many privates as possible took a full four-week course of instruction, they would instruct the remainder of the men in the company, plus some from a second company arriving at the school at the beginning of the fifth week. At the end of two months, two proficient companies could instruct two more companies, perhaps as many as four companies, and at the end of three months, six companies or two battalions would be trained.

"The advantages claimed for this system are that it turns out complete units and that it gives to the newly trained personnel a chance to put into practice at once the principles they have learned." During a total of four months of instruction, officers and men would, furthermore, become used to each other's methods of operation.

On the assumption that a limited number of tanks would become available at once and an increasing number only later, Patton suggested making the instructors the future unit commanders and sending to the school as many officers and noncoms, in a two-to-one proportion, as the school could handle. Six men could be taught on a single tank each day, and three fourths of all the available tanks would always be ready for active service if needed. If no further tanks were available, the graduates of the tank school could be sent to machine gun or small cannon school.

This system was less effective, in Patton's opinion, because it trained instructors rather than units.

He recommended that men be selected for the Tank Service from among those who had mechanical experience, who had driven automobiles or motorcycles — it was easy for experienced drivers to know, for example, when to change gears or when the motor needed maintenance. Blacksmiths, foundry hands, gasfitters, and plumbers would also be needed.

There should be at least one regular officer per company to enforce discipline, as it is a well-known fact that working with machines has a very disastrous effect upon discipline. It seems to run out of men as the oil soaks into them.

After detailing the subjects to be learned during a four-week course of instruction — how to shift gears, apply brakes, accelerate, shift gears blindfolded, drive on level ground, and so on, plus lectures on the general theory of gas engines, including lubrication, as well as the practice of firing and cleaning weapons — Patton warned: "This course will not fit men to enter combat the instant of graduation, as the question of maps, information and camouflage has not been touched." These were better taught in the companies. The course he outlined was for the average intelligent person without previous knowledge of tanks or motors. For persons who were better qualified in engines and the like, three weeks would be enough, plus a fourth week for map-reading and other essential military subjects.

He suggested certain drills, pointing out that commands were transmitted by signal, by visual means, by touch, by voice, and by example. Normal intervals between tanks in column were 40 yards; lateral distances 10 yards.

Letter, GSP, Jr., to Beatrice, December 12, 1917
[Finished report this morning and waiting to have it typed] and observe the result . . .

[Col. Rockenbach is to be Chief of Tanks — of both lights and heavies] and I expect to hold my job as chief of the light ones . . .

[Things are more expensive and he spends more than his pay now] but of course I don't acconomize as there is no use in it.

The day after he finished his report, he visited Gondrecourt, where the AEF correspondence schools were located, saw a Stokes mortar and a six-pound gun, which he found interesting, and went to Langres, where he spent some time at the AEF staff college. He "fooled around all day" on December 14, probably suffering mixed emotions about his report, pride in his conception and concern over its reception.

Letter, GSP, Jr., to Beatrice, December 14, 1917
All that [he included in his report] had to be worked out to fulfill all conceivable conditions. Even a list of tools and spare parts down to and including extra wire and string [plus numbers and ranks of officers and men] . . . All that and nothing to base it on but a general knowledge of soldiering. Honestly I think not many men could have combined the exact mechanical knowledge with the general Tactical and organizational knowledge to do it. But I think I did a good job. Infact I surprised my self and hope others will think as well of it as I do . . .

I hope I can make a success of this business but starting with nothing is hard. After we get a little nucleus it will go easier. Now I feel helpless and almost beaten but I will make a go of it or bust Rockenbach or no. I wish you were here to sympathize and correct spelling for me. I miss you in all I do or think. We are so united that I don't function well alone.

Letter, GSP, Jr., to Aunt Nannie, December 14, 1917

I am the only one who came on the Baltic in the first bunch [with Pershing] who has not been promoted but mine will come some day and probably quite shortly.

I worked up a pretty good report on tanks. It was interesting as it was original. I had to decide on the number of men officers autos Trucks, screw drivers and in fact every thing down to extra bals of string but I think it is a good organization. The proof is in the eating and we are getting ready for dinner.

Letter, GSP, Jr., to Beatrice, December 14, 1917

I am sort of like a Rat with out a tail just now running tanks when there are none. I don't know where to go or what to do yet feel that I should be doing something fast and furious.

The discipline among even the militia Divisions over here is fine. You never saw so much saluting and general neatness.

Letter, GSP, Jr., to Beatrice, December 15, 1917

Tomorrow I start on my way again. All alone to go to a new place and organize the Light Tank service. I feel unusually small in self esteem. I have been so long a small but important cog in a machine. A cog with its position [so] well assured by great ones just at hand that it is hard to go off and be the last word all by myself. But just that feeling of lack of support and the desire for it shows that it is time to go else I will become only a staff officer useful but lacking in initiative. One sees many such but they don't get farther. Actually I am in quite a "Funk" for there is nothing but me to do it all. Starting the Fencing school was a similar experience but vastly smaller and then too I had a model to copy. Here it is all original and all to be concieved and accomplished. The most cheering thing is that Gen. Harbord, Col. Eltinge and Col. Malone all seem confident I can do it. I wish I were as sanguine. I am sure I will do it but just at this moment I don't see how. I will have to grow and grow a lot. But I *will.*

Here is my chance. If I fail it will be only my fault. I won't even have you to pick on. That ought to cheer you and insure my doing my best . . .

I had no leave in prospect when I wired you nor did I have this Tank job. Now all thought of leave is out of the question so don't think of coming [to England] till you are absolutely strong [after her minor operation] and have been strong for some time. Then if you get here God who has always helped me inspite of lack of merit will fix it so I shall see you.

Diary

December 15 (Saturday): Decided to go to Langres and start Tank School. "This is [my] last day as staff officer. Now I rise or fall on my own. 'God judge the right.' "

CHAPTER 23

Langres

"I am shamefully safe and comfortable . . . Heres Hoping I make Good."

Diary

December 16 (Sunday): Left Chaumont at 3 P.M. with Lieut. De Coppet; reached Langres 4 P.M.; found no one in at the school headquarters; got room at hotel.

While Patton went to Langres, Braine traveled to Paris, reported to Lieutenant Colonel Draine, the Chief Ordnance Officer for Tanks, and helped draw up a tank procurement program. Braine then conferred in London with Lieutenant Colonel Alden, who would soon return to the United States. Braine acquainted him with the progress being made in light tanks and gave him a list of 21 suggested changes to be made on the Renault tank to be manufactured in America.

Patton, meanwhile, was trying to get his tank school started.

Diary

December 17: Looked around school in morning. Went out to find location for my school in P.M. Visited machine gun school. Talked with Col. J. H. Parker "who insisted on calling me major."

December 18: Went to see various special schools and talked with Engineers about combining my school with theirs.

December 19: Closed deal for house; hired cook and waitress; wrote some recommendations for school; very hard to get things started "but they marche a little."

Letter, GSP, Jr., to Beatrice, December 18, 1917

This is certainly hard to get started in. I have been fooling around two days and have not got a thing going yet but I am getting oriented and like learning a language I may eventually discover that I know what I am doing.

I rented a house to day with three bed rooms a dining room a kitchen a garage and stable all furnished with sheets and silver ware for 200 Francs a month but I guess the few small arrangements which the man spoke of will amount to four or five hundred more. Still it will be worth it for one must be comfortable and the hotel is fierce just like an ice box full of cabage and dead fish . . .

My house has a big court yard with lodges at the gate also a garden full of snow. The front hall is of stone and very handsome but cold. I am going to get a cook and a maid in the morning. Shallenberger and Lt. De Coppet will live with me. I guess that the cook will soak us but it is the war.

This town has a wall around it and a mote and is Galo-Roman. Infact some Roman Engineer Beat the Germans here in 339 A.D. The wall only dates from 1617 so it is not interesting but very pretty.

Letter, GSP, Jr., to Beatrice, December 19, 1917

If I go about as a bachelor long enough I ought to make a model husband. To day I hired a cook and a maid. First I went to the police and got a list of names then I went to the houses [where they lived]. At the first house I found two who said that they were respectively a cook and a maid so I said you are hired how much do I pay you? They fixed a less amount than I had thought they would so I was much relieved. I then told them that Williams [his striker] was Tres forte avec les femmes [very good with the ladies] and that if they allowed his advances I would fire them. They said Entendre [Entendu, Agreed] so tomorrow I am going to escort them around and tell them to get busy and warm the place. But not like a maid at another officers house tried to do it for me when I was out with John Rogers. I said that the room was cold and to warm it she replied "Alor Je va couche avec vous. I said mais non Je suis tro vieu. Je voudrai du feu [she replied "Then I shall sleep with you." I said but no I am too old I would like a fire made] and the incident was closed.

The light question is hard here as there is little oil and no gas or electricity still we manage some way . . .

Williams and the horses got here to night and though it was a long cold ride they seemed quite all right.

I am going to train my cook to do it a la Americane and not bring on one potato then one bean and so on as they do here . . .

Sometimes I feel most depressed **over ever** getting a school started.

If I ever get the staff I know I can deliver the goods but just as at
[Fort] Riley before the swords came it is a hell of a job. Fortunately
I have no students so far.

As I am having a great argument on the war with a lot of people
who don't know what they are talking about I must stop to devote
my entire attention to it.

I love you with all my heart.

Letter, GSP, Jr., to Beatrice, December 20, 1917

Another day has gone and yet no tank school is going. I am getting
nearvous very much so feeling that I am lazy and worthless and yet
not seeing how to procede. I hate the feeling. Perhaps if I had more
brains I would see something to do but the roads are so slipperly that
one can not even explor the d—— country.

Well cheer up here is a bum poem I wrote . . .

Having been on a staff where some one else does your thinking is
quite plesant but bad for ones originality. I feel just [like] a poison
ivy with the trelace [trellis] removed but may be I shall get some
back bone.

It is one of the few times I ever felt I lacked it but I seem to or
maybe it is just the situation. But it is most unpleasant any way . . .

Don't loose my poems. They may be priceless some day and I
never keep copies.

He moved into his house, known as the Hotel of the Countess d'Aulan.
Someone informed him that the house was originally built by a very
famous soldier killed in battle. Picturing a hero of the Marne, Patton
asked where the man had died. In the Second Crusade, he learned. Built
around 1300, the house was full of funny little rooms and stairs leading
nowhere.

"I bought a ham and some bacon and milk and things to day," he wrote
Beatrice. "It took my mind off not getting along with the school."

Letter, GSP, Jr., to Aunt Nannie, December 22, 1917

I pay only 45 [dollars] a month for it [my house] which is nothing
. . . don't worry about me. I am shamefully safe and comfortable.

His first meal in the house was the best he had had since leaving Paris;
it was "served all at once and not one vegetable at a time as is the French
custom." He told Beatrice about having met General Vasili Gourko of the
Russian Army at General Pershing's sometime earlier. Gourko had com-

manded cavalry against the Japanese, and in this war in turn a division, corps, and army. In 1917, he was acting chief of staff of the Russian army, then was dismissed by Kerensky. His *Memories and Impressions of War and Revolution in Russia* would appear in English in 1918.

. . . now he is with out even a striker it was sad to see a soldier who had lived his life for a profession turned out at the end with nothing to fight for. I felt very sorry for him. Still he did not ask for sympathy or imply a need of it but talked in a most interesting and impersonal way in perfect english.

Letter, GSP, Jr., to Beatrice, December 23, 1917
. . . my reason for getting off the staff was that for a man of my age and experience it is a cemetary of ambition. I would have been simply an office boy. Even had I accepted an offer from Gen. Brewster the inspector General to work as his assistant it would have led no where. Besides I am conscientiously opposed to it. I have always talked blood and murder and am looked on as an advocate of close up fighting. I could never look my self in the face if I was a staff officer and comparatively safe. The men who get on the staffs now will stay on them and see other men from the line pass and beat them.

The Tanks were I truly believe a great oppertunity for me. I ought to be one of the high ranking men one of the two or three at the top. I am fitted for it as I have imagination and daring and exceptional mechanical knowledge. I believe Tanks will be much more important than aviation and the man on the ground floor will reap the benefit.

It would not have been right either to J. or myself to have hung on any longer [at GHQ AEF] besides I was loosing my independence of thought and a little more of it would have made a nothing of me.

Had I gone in the infantry I would have had one of hundreds of battalions and might have been in reserve on the day of the big fight. Spending the rest of my time like a rat in a wet trench. In the tanks one is always in the attacks and the rest of the time one is safe and comfortable. One will always be in the hedlines in the Tanks while twice the heroism in the infantry will be covered by "nothing to report."

As to danger it is less in the Tanks than in the infantry because while the Tanks catch it worse while they are at it they have not the daily losses in trenches when nothing is going on.

The whole Tank program is in a mess now as about three departments are trying to run it but Col Rockenbach will I hope straiten that out if he does nothing else. I guess he does not care a whole lot for me but my theory that if you do your best no one can hurt you will be put to the proof. Here are a couple of bum poems written at Champlieu last month. They don't amount to much except the ideas are not bad.

They may amuse you especially the spelling. I hope so.

On December 24, Patton drove to Chaumont to see Rockenbach and they had a "very satisfactory talk. He seemed more sensible than usual."

Colonel Samuel Dickerson Rockenbach was formally appointed Chief of the Tank Corps, AEF, on December 22 and thereby became Patton's immediate boss. He was sixteen years older than Patton and a stolid and somewhat pompous man with little sense of humor. Even-tempered, with a tendency to be fixed and narrow in his opinions and preconceptions, he was capable of hard work. Having served in Cuba in the early 1890s, in the Santiago campaign during the Spanish-American War, in the Philippines, where he became Chief of the Philippine Scouts, and along the Mexican border, he was a mature officer who knew staff procedures at a large headquarters. He would counterbalance and steady the somewhat impulsive Patton.

Neither liked the other at first, but they quickly established and developed an ability to work and get along together. Starting from their common family roots in the state of Virginia — Rockenbach was born in Lynchburg — and from their attachment to the Virginia Military Institute, from which Rockenbach graduated in 1889, they discovered that their strengths of personality and character were complementary.

Although they never became warm and close friends, they learned to cooperate in the interests of the war effort and their own personal ambitions. They had to, for each depended on the other for success in the common venture and for consequent career advancement. Whatever each did reflected on the other. The tanks provided a big opportunity for both men, and neither wanted to spoil his chances for achievement.

Eventually, Rockenbach came to admire Patton and was one of his strongest supporters. Patton, on the other hand, would always remain somewhat uncomfortable with Rockenbach.

As Chief of the Tank Corps and a member of the AEF headquarters staff, Rockenbach functioned in the dual capacity of command and staff — in much the same way, for example, as an Engineer officer sometimes acted both as a commander of Engineer troops and as Engineer adviser to the overall commander. Rockenbach had general supervisory authority, and more, over all tank activities in the field, including Patton's tank school. He was also Pershing's principal staff adviser on all tank matters in France and England.

Actually, Rockenbach was primarily concerned with organization, administration, and equipment, whereas Patton was involved in tactical training. Rockenbach would expedite the procurement and shipment of tank matériel, supplies, and personnel, whereas Patton (as would the commander of the American heavy tanks) would actively lead the tank troops and units in training and, as he hoped, in battle. Rockenbach would support Patton, but only as long as Patton's handling of his responsibilities satisfied Rockenbach. And except for routine business, all that Patton did required Rockenbach's approval.

As Rockenbach later explained his duties, the Office of the Chief of the Tank Corps functioned as a staff section to work with the AEF General Staff on all matters of tank planning, including personnel, equipment, and supply; as a directorate for designing machines and training programs; and as a general headquarters — to command tank organizations unattached to field armies, to furnish staff support for field armies directing tank units in the field, and to supervise tank centers engaged in training tankers.

Rockenbach would also be the American representative on a new Inter-Allied Tank Committee to be formed in April 1918. Consisting of the chiefs of the French, British, Italian, and American tank corps, the Committee would meet at Versailles on the first day of each month to keep abreast of mechanical and tactical improvements and to coordinate the production, shipment, and distribution of tanks.

All of Rockenbach's tasks required tact and push. And Rockenbach, with Patton's loyal support — despite an occasional reservation expressed privately — would make a go of his job.*

* The organization and training of American tank components would take place in 1918 in France (light tank units), in England (heavy tanks), and in the United States (both types). Early in 1918, the War Department would authorize the AEF a strength of 14,827 tank officers and men, including those in France and England; and a total

After his "very satisfactory talk" with Rockenbach at Chaumont, Patton saw Braine, who had just returned from England. He took Braine to Langres, where they had dinner together and talked shop until late.

On Christmas Day, he stayed in bed until eight, had breakfast and a bath, and drove out to visit and dine with a friend who was instructing at the trench mortar school. Of the forty officers present, only four were Regulars, and Patton marveled at that proportion.

After driving to Chaumont in a blizzard that afternoon, Patton dined again, with Pershing, Harbord, Boyd, Collins, Shallenberger, Major Bacon, and Paddock. Pershing gave him a cigarette holder, Bacon a box of Corona cigars, and Collins a purse. "We all drank to being Together Christmas 1918."

Letter, GSP, Jr., to Beatrice, December 25, 1917
I dreamed about you last night. You were walking down a station platform in a rain coat looking fat and complacent like a chip-munk . . . I wish you were here because the room is cold and for other reasons . . .
Col. Rockenbach was given the Tanks instead of Col Elting and I have only got Acting Charge of the Light Tanks but feel sure I will get it actually unless I pass out.

Patton and Braine reconnoitered for land that would be suitable for the tank school. They found and looked over some ground near Bourg and decided that it was exactly what they needed for a school, tank park, and maneuver ground. In a heavy snowstorm, they drove to Chaumont, talked with Rockenbach, and recommended its requisition from the French.

Before Rockenbach came to a decision, he wanted to see the sort of ground the French were using. What had they found adequate for tank training? On the following day, therefore, although it was still snowing, he, Patton, and Braine traveled to Martigny-les-Bains, where a French tank park and center were located.

---

of 16,660 in the United States. There would be no direct relationship between the Tank Corps of the AEF and the Tank Service (later renamed the Tank Corps) at home until after the war. In the same manner as Rockenbach was the Chief Tank Officer of the AEF, Colonel Ira C. Welborn would serve at the War Department level and supervise the activities in the United States. His principal training area was Camp Colt, Pennsylvania, which would be commanded for almost seven months in 1918 by Captain, Major, then Lieutenant Colonel Dwight D. Eisenhower.

Satisfied with their inspection, they returned to Langres — the snow was still falling — and Patton gave Rockenbach his room. He and Braine stayed at the Hôtel de l'Europe.

It had been a wearing day. They had talked business almost constantly, and Patton had done much of the talking.

In the morning, the three officers went over the site tentatively chosen by Patton and Braine, and Rockenbach approved it. At Bourg, about five miles south of Langres on the road to Dijon, the land was in the Bois d'Amour, a rising piece of ground crowned by a wood and flanked by two good roads and a railroad. Bourg and the nearby villages of St. Geosmes and Brennes, as well as Langres, were conveniently close for billets.

Letter, GSP, Jr., to Beatrice, December 29, 1917
  We had a cold time as it was snowing hard all the while and we were in an open car. Still it was worth it as I got Rockenbach to my way of thinking and today heard him get off all my stuff as his own but I don't care if I get it through.

  I had also picked out a piece of land for the school and to day we got it approved. An old Roman road runs along one side of it. We will build a lot of temporary barracks there and get going to some extent at least by the end of the month . . .

  Col. R. and I are going up to the big Tank place of the French [at Chamlieu] . . . and then on to the British place so I ought to have a most interesting week . . .

  You have to have a lot of ground to work tanks on as you must have trenches and shell holes and hills and woods and all sorts of things. The place we have it is very suitable and I only hope we can get it.

Rockenbach and Braine returned to Chaumont, where Rockenbach would start the high-level actions to obtain the land and Braine would try to secure buildings for billets, offices, and classrooms.

Patton went to see the headquarters commandant in Langres and requested that the land be made available to the Tank Corps.

Going back to the site, "I examined land in P.M. on horseback and liked it still more." On Sunday he made some plans for the tank camp. That afternoon, unable to stay away, "Went over the ground again."

Letter, GSP, Jr., to Beatrice, December 30, 1917
  It is funny how things we think little of eventually help us. I never

could see the use in making maps but there is no map of my Tank place so I am going out and make one in the morning. As it will have to be done in a foot or so of snow I don't look forward to it with very much pleasure.

In that connection I got hold of my book on fencing and some one said "How much waisted effort." Well there was but perhaps it will be useful to me some time I may be an optimist but it seems to me that all the things I have ever done have come in useful except fishing and that is at least useful as a great pleasure.

He completed his map of the tank camp and judged it quite good. He wrote and dispatched a letter complaining that American soldiers and officers in and around Langres were not saluting properly. He closed his diary for the year by noting, "I hope and think that by this time next year we will be nearer Berlin."

Starting his diary for 1918 in a new notebook, he headed it "George S. Patton, Jr., Captain Cavalry, Director, Army Tank School, Langres; 2 rue Pierre Durand; house built at end of 1200 AD."

On New Year's Day, he drove to Chaumont in the afternoon and together with Rockenbach took the train to Paris, where they checked into the Hôtel Meurice. Leaving the Gare du Nord next morning, they arrived at Crépe-en-Valois. After lunch with General Estienne, they went to the Chamlieu tank camp. That evening they observed some Schneider tanks in a night maneuver. The exercise was less than successful because of the snow, which clogged gear sprockets and broke gear teeth. They returned to General Estienne's office, where "he gave us all his theory of attack which in essence is absolute association with infantry especially for small tank."

The trip was actually for Rockenbach's benefit. He was learning about the employment of tanks, and Patton, who knew the French tank officers at Chamlieu, was along to act as a sort of aide, to facilitate the introductions, to translate and explain what Rockenbach was seeing and hearing, and also to make sure that Rockenbach got everything "right" — that is, Patton's way.

They returned to the Chamlieu camp the following day and watched tanks crossing trenches and being pushed out of shell holes. "Col. Rockenbach took a ride. I drove." They listened to a lecture on the use of small tanks in battle, lunched with General Estienne, went to

Compiègne, where they took the train to Amiens. After an early departure next day, they reached the British tank corps headquarters at Bernecourt.

General Hugh Elles, already a legendary figure because he had led the Cambrai attack, was at breakfast, and Rockenbach and Patton joined him, Colonel Fuller (his chief of staff), Captain Stewart (aide), and Lieutenant Colonel Searle (supply officer), and "talked over objects [of tank fighting]. Col. S. took us over shops." Then Elles briefed them on the battle of Cambrai, and Serle delivered a long lecture on maintenance procedures and the importance of spare parts. "All were very nice and hospitable."

Rockenbach and Patton visited the British tank drivers' school near Arras, and Patton was somewhat critical of the establishment: "Too much idea of schools not enough [of] soldiering."

Returned to Paris and the Hôtel Meurice, Patton lunched with the Boyds on Sunday, read a book, went to the Casino de Paris, where he saw Gaby des Lys, and described for Beatrice his

interesting and useful trip for in it we learned all there was to be found on Tanks and I think I made quite a favorable impression personally. Gen. Ellis who commands the British Tanks is not much older than I am and is a very fine looking man. He is a real major [meaning, his Regular Army rank] and temporary Brigadier . . . it is funny how the English always detract from them selves.

After Rockenbach left for Chaumont on Monday, Patton had some designs made up for a Tank Corps brassard and collar ornament, looked into the matter of securing boots for tankers, bought a gold bracelet for Beatrice, and took the train to Chaumont. He was met by Braine, who had been busy securing offices, renting houses, hiring servants, and attending to other housekeeping duties.

Tuesday, "Rocky and I" — indicating a new and closer relationship, the result of their trip together — "worked on organization all day and till 10 at night. He approved my plans."

Ten lieutenants made available by the Coast Artillery Corps for service with the tanks arrived in Chaumont. Braine took them to Langres, where five would attend the machine gun school, the others the 37-mm. gun school.

While Rockenbach and Patton continued to work on organizational plans and have long discussions, Braine sent word from Langres that the French had refused to make available the ground they wanted for their tank center.

Completing his work with Rockenbach, Patton obtained from the AEF Adjutant General the names of eleven more Coast Artillery lieutenants who were unassigned and requested their assignment to the tanks.

He left for Langres after removing all his things from Pershing's house "as I think it too much like hanging on to live there now."

The first thing he did at Langres was to examine a new piece of ground, probably discovered by Braine, perhaps recommended by the French, as a possible alternative location for the tank school. Patton found it completely unsuitable. "Went to see French Col about it and told him he was a fool in a polite way. He did not like it."

Letter, GSP, Jr., to Beatrice, January 10, 1918

Dear Beat: I got here for lunch in a heavy snow and had to go out to look over some ground at once as the French refused to let us use the ground we had picked. They are the d—— fools. You would think we were doing them a hell of a favor to fight for them. I got mad and told the French Col. that if he would do a little more to help he might get on better and that the reason the war was lasting so long was that they were too afraid of civilians. He did not like it much. And said any way if I got the ground I wanted I could not shoot on it. I said if he would give me the ground I would attend to that, for I fully intend to shoot French or no French. That shocked him terribly, but I will get the ground or bust now.

There is an awful lot of detail to attend to. Tomorrow I have to put in a list of every monkey wrench screw driver bolt pistol and cartridge for my tanks. It will be rather a job I think but I know what I want so hope to get it . . .

P.S. Here is a nasty story. You will like it. A wife once woke up in the night and said to her husband, "John if that is your elbow sticking in my back turn over, if it is not I will."

After talking with General McAndrew, director of all the schools at Langres, who probably counseled Patton to be sure that the new site being offered was altogether inappropriate, he re-examined the new piece of ground. He still disliked the place, and "Wrote renewed request for [original] Land."

He sent Beatrice a telegram on her birthday and also a gold identification bracelet with her name on it "like I wear. They are all the go here . . . Of course one wears the old lead [and regulation] one under neath."

He and Braine worked for two days on lists of spare parts for the tanks; "it takes an awful lot of stuff to kill a German."

Up until after midnight reading Mark Twain, he wished he and Beatrice "were together to day but then I wish that every day so it makes no difference."

Patton drove to Chaumont Sunday afternoon for discussions with Rockenbach. He returned quite late that night because of the snow on the road.

Letter, GSP, Jr., to Aunt Nannie, January 14, 1918
I have now 18 officers under me in the school but they are going to various special schools so I have little bother with them. We ought, however to get started about the first of February at least I hope so.

On Monday he worked on a paper to requisition spare parts and replacements.

Letter, GSP, Jr., to Beatrice, January 14, 1918
[The requisition] was rather an affair as you can judge by the fact that the stuff asked for will cost over twenty million [dollars] that is if we get as many tanks as we hope for.

We requisitioned for battalion complete with motor trucks, Tanks, repair unit and autos and motor cycles. One must specify every extra bolt and socket fire extinguisher and piece of rubber. Lt. Braine was responsible for most of the details though I did my share. It is a big job and I feel sure that tanks in some form will play a part in all future wars. They are in idea simply a heavy armored infantry soldier. At least that is the theory of operation of the light tanks. The heavy are a little different. My fear is that the fighting will be over before we get any [tanks] or enough for if too few they will not ackomplish their mission.

Very sadly he concluded he would have to discharge two of his newly commissioned officers, both former noncoms with long service, one having had more than twenty years in the Army, the other fourteen. They were not doing well and would be reduced to their former enlisted grades. When Patton told them, "they broke down and cried like babies. To see old strong men cry is not pleasant but there was nothing to do. War is not run on sentiment."

I am getting a hell of a reputation for a skunk. When officers don't salute me I stop them and make them do it. I also reported a reserve lieutenant for profanity. I expect some of them [reserve officers] would like to poison me. I will have to eat [only] eggs like Louis XI.

The requisition was typed and completed on Tuesday morning, and Patton carried it personally to Rockenbach in Chaumont that afternoon. It took him three hours to get there because the roads were so slippery.

The next morning, Patton carefully went over the requisition with Lieutenant Crosby, Rockenbach's new adjutant, in order to make sure that all was clearly listed and understood. There were 24 pages of detailed tables showing the material requirements, plus spare parts, for a battalion of light tanks and a battalion repair unit, including, for example, the number of screws and bolts needed. "The spare parts called for in 'C' are based," Patton warned, "on a generous estimate and after we get large repair shops established we will be able to reduce it materially. But in order to make the first battalion function all the spares called for are necessary."

The requisition having been delivered, it would now be up to Rockenbach to get what was required.

After talking with an officer in the land requisition section of the AEF headquarters about the ground he wanted at Bourg, Patton drove home. He called on a French colonel in Langres who turned out to be "most accommodating." He visited the acting commandant of the Army schools and arranged for the use of target ranges by the tankers.

Letter, GSP, Jr., to Beatrice, January 16, 1918
We are more or less held up now by the French who seem to put every obstacle in the way of our getting the ground we want for Tank centers. I am going down in a few minutes to see the French Mission and see what I can do. You would think they were doing us a great favor to let us fight in their d—— country.

Braine had been busy at Langres. He secured office space, arranged for tank personnel to take some of the regular courses offered at the Army schools, worked up a course in mechanics, and obtained a dilapidated and consequently surplus Atlas truck and some tools from the quartermaster people so that the tankers could take the vehicle apart and rebuild it to get a better idea of what made it go.

Letter, GSP, Jr., to Beatrice, January 17, 1918
[He had 19 officers and would have the first two companies of men as soon as he could get the French to give him the land he wanted.] It is hard as any thing to get things started but they are coming along pretty well. I will have an office in the morning and so by degrees I grow . . .
[He had to deliver a lecture on tanks at the Army school next week; he wished he had a tank to use as illustration; there was nothing written on the small tanks except what he himself had done.] There are as many fighting tanks in a company as I was years old when I first met you if you know how old I was.

Diary
January 17: "My eleven new [Coast Artillery] officers reported. A fair lot but not fine." Appointed Lieut. T. C. Brown adjutant and ordered him to set up office.

The French Mission promised him he could have at least part of the ground he wanted. But that good news was somewhat spoiled when he had an argument with a Reserve lieutenant, the same one he had reported for profanity, who was trying to run Patton out of his house.

He went to Chaumont to see Rockenbach off for England, where he would inspect organizational activities designed to get American heavy-tank unit training under way.

"Everything for the tanks looks fine," Patton noted. He meant his own. He visited Colonel Fox Conner to make certain that GHQ AEF would approve the land for his tank school.

He consulted with the French on target ranges and after much talk got all he wanted, including the tank ground. In great exuberance, he took Collins, who had come for a visit, out to see the place where the tank center would be located.

Letter, GSP, Jr., to Mr. Ayer, January 20, 1918

Dear Mr. Ayer: [thanks him for the check of $500 as a Christmas present to Beatrice and him] . . . It was the nicest present I could get because it takes up so little room yet fills so many gaps . . .

I will tell you a funny thing. In November I got a letter from you saying that war was so wasteful of life and that some means ought to be devised of reducing the killing. At that very moment I was talking with Col. Conner about whether I should go into the Tank service. Your letter decided me and next morning I asked for the Tanks. They save life as two men in a tank are as good as ten out of one.

I am having an interesting and difficult time organizing them as every thing is new and there is no precident to go on. I have to originate every thing. I had even to design a trailer to carry them so they, the Light ones, are or will be all mine. Unless I do so badly that some one else gets the job. I trust this will not be the case . . .

Distance [from the United States] makes Gen. Pershings job infinitely hard but he is doing it and there is no one else who could. He is a very great man and getting greater all the time.

Mr. Ayer was touched by this letter. Several years later Beatrice wrote on it, "This was found in Father's wallet, which he always carried, by Mother, after his death." Quite obviously, he had great affection for his son-in-law who was so very different from him in make-up, temperament, and interests.

Letter, GSP, Jr., to Beatrice, January 20, 1918

I am feeling much more cheerful . . . as I have definately gotten the ground I wanted for the tank school. That is a large step in advance for now all I need is the one essencial for Tanks namely Tanks.

I hope to get these shortly but things dont turn out here much on schedule . . .

I have just gotten a new pair of very nice boots at a very high cost but one must look well in order to hold peoples attention.

He took Colonel Drum to see the tank center site Monday morning, for Drum would recommend approval to Colonel Conner. Then he worked in his office on a lecture he was to deliver to senior officers — generals and colonels — on Wednesday. While he was there, General Sample called to apologize for the conduct of the Reserve lieutenant who had tried to run him out of his house.

Letter, GSP, Jr., to Beatrice, January 21, 1918

I got into my office to day for the first time and am having a hard time getting all the officers I have here kept busy while waiting for the arrival of the tanks. It is a long job but I am not the only one who is having a hard time. I got quite a compliment from Gen. Mc-Andrew, Commandant of the Army Schools. He told Col. Drum that I was taking hold better than any man he had. All I can say is that the rest must be pretty poor for I certainly have not done much to be proud of so far.

I don't feel that I am doing my best some way. I never do. If I ever do feel that I am earning my pay I may realy begin to get some where. I sort of wish I had gotten a battalion of infantry then I could have seen some results where as it is all so far in the future that one can't see it but in the minds eye.

Undoubtedly this is a hell of a world, still I am perhaps feeling low as I have a soar throat but it is not very bad and I am taking asperin.

On Tuesday, Patton typed his notes for the lecture, went to Chaumont, and "found all gone to hell. Coordination section had disapproved land and held up buildings. I got it smoothed out again but Gen. Williams told me that we could get no tanks from the French. I talked over trailer business with him" — the use of truck trailers to move tanks from one sector of the front to another — "and he seemed much interested."

Patton delivered his lecture on tanks on Wednesday morning. It was an interesting talk, well thought out, clear, and colloquial. He said that an operation planned for tanks and infantry had to observe two limitations — for the infantry, the physical endurance of men; for the tanks, the obstacles in the terrain. It was futile to attack where the ground rendered tanks impotent. It was equally futile to expect infantrymen to follow tanks at a speed or for a distance that would tax their endurance.

For Tanks in common with all other auxilary arms are but a means of aiding infantry — on whom the fate of battle ever rests — to drive their bayonets into the bellies of the enemy . . .

. . . liaison between the tanks and infantry must be of the closest. It must be worked out in the most minute detail for so complex is its nature that hazy ideas or ill digested plans will become abortive or ruinous in the excitement of the close fighting where the cooperation must be put into practice.

To insure this mutual understanding, the cooperation must be

more than a mere matter of rutine. Tank and inft. officers must associate and by conversation at mess and else where interchange ideas
and so become thouroughly conversant with all the difficulties which
beset their respective arms. A failure to do this has — in my opinion
— been the cause of much waste in time, money, and blood [in previous British and French attacks].

In order to syncranise effort in an attack inft. and tank commanders must know definately and collectively

the objective of an attack, the direction of attack, the attack formations,
the plan of organizing and holding the objective when secured, what the
neighboring units are doing, "to whom and where to send reports."

He then explained the essential element: the infantry needed to know
about tanks and their capabilities. He went on to dissect the nature of
battle:

Two of the determining factors in war are weapons and movement.
Movement naturally seperates its self into two parts. Approach and
attack. In the approach movement is paramount to weapons. In the
attack weapons assert them selves to allow movement by killing.

He concluded by describing, in schematic terms, an attack on a trench
system and an attack against a defended farm.

Among those present and listening to him were General McAndrew,
head of the Army schools at Langres, Colonel J. McC. Palmer, close to
Pershing, Colonel Fiebeger, a former professor of engineering at West
Point, two generals he could not identify, and six colonels — altogether
fifteen senior officers. "I . . . got away with it all right," he informed
Beatrice.

I am feeling very low over the Tanks again to day. Every thing
seems to be getting in the way and no one can tell when we will ever
get any tanks. I am disgusted with the whole business.

I am within eleven [on the list] of being [promoted to] a temporary Major U.S. so ought to get it pretty soon.

Letter, GSP, Jr., to Beatrice, January 24, 1918
The Tank business is absolutely at a stand still but ought to either
die or get well by Monday. I have done every thing I can for the
present.

We have gotten a new house and will move in on Saturday. It is not so good as this one yet not bad and there is more room in it.

Letter, GSP, Jr., to Beatrice, January 25, 1918

Unless I get some Tanks soon I will go crazy for I have done nothing of any use since november and it is getting on my nerves.

I cussed a reserve officer for saluting me with his hands in his pockets to day and he said that he demanded to be treated like an officer. I almost hit him but compromised by taking him to the General [probably McAndrew] who cussed him good. Some of these new officers are the end of the limit. I bet the Tank Corps will have discipline if nothing else.

The trouble is that most of the regular officers do not do their part either by way of example or correction. We have a long way to go to make an army.

Moving into his new house, he found the same Reserve lieutenant trying to run him out of that one. The problem no doubt was that this officer had responsibility for assigning billets in Langres, and Patton's rank of captain was hardly sufficient to warrant his having so large a place.

A welcome distraction occurred when two French officers came from their tank center at Martigny-les-Bains to look over his tank ground. They found it quite good.

He occupied himself on Sunday with paper work. He put in a recommendation that an officer be tried by court-martial or be reprimanded for losing some secret papers. He wrote an order on neatness and saluting in the Tank Service. "Got no news of tanks."

Letter, GSP, Jr., to Beatrice, January 27, 1918

I just put in my first set of charges against an officer. He lost some secret papers I gave him to study. He is only a kid so I am sorry for him but one can't run a war on sentiment . . .

I fear that it will be a long long time before we do any fighting with the Tanks. Indeed the war may end too soon for them. If it does I shall regret that I did not go into the infantry. Still I am pretty luckey so hope to fight from a tank yet.

My writing seems to be getting worse and worse. Can you still read it.

Headquarters Army Tank School, Memorandum No. 1, January 27, 1918

1. The Chief of the Tank Service is desirous that all members of the Tank Service shall be models in respect to soldierly appearance and deportment.

2. To carry out these wishes all officers on duty at the Tank School will provide themselves with necessary leather and brass polish together with suitable brushes to keep their shoes and leggins or boots polished; also their belts polished and the buckles and other metal work on there belts brightly shined.

By using gasoline, or other cleaning material, they will be sure that their uniforms are free from spots or stains.

3. Officers and men will shave daily and will see that their hair is kept short. Not clipped but kept cut short so that they look like soldiers and not like poets.

4. The officers on duty with the Tank School have been cautioned as to exactness and smartness in saluting officers and men, and in the payment of other military and social courtesies which are founded on customs of the service and gentlemanly deportment. They are again reminded of those instructions and they will carry them out.

5. All officers in charge of Platoons, or other units, will be responsible for the appearance and deportment of their men and the officer will be held responsible for the appearance of his men.

6. There is a wide spread and regretable habit in our service of ducking the head to meet the hand in rendering a salute. This will not be tolerated.

In rendering salutes the head will be held erect and the eyes turned in the direction of the person saluted, whether officer or soldier. The hand rendering the salute will move smartly both to and from the headdress or the forehead if uncovered.

G. S. Patton, Jr.
Captain of Cavalry
Director Army Tank School.

Letter, GSP, Jr., to Beatrice, January 28, 1918

I am going up to Headquarters [in Chaumont] this P.M. as Col Rockey is back [from England] and I want to see him even if he dont want to see me.

Diary

January 28 (Monday): "Went to Chaumont to see Col. Rockenbach. He talked a lot and said nothing."

January 29: "Got R. to send Braine to U.S. It was hard but finally he took the hook like a fish."

Letter, GSP, Jr., to Beatrice, January 30, 1918

We had a fine demonstration of an attack yesterday using all sorts of guns and rifles. It was very well done and most instructive. We have one every two weeks. I hope to have some Tanks in the next one if possible. Also yesterday we at last got the land question for the Tank center settled so may be able to begin work in earnest in a few days.

I also got permission to send Lt. Braine to the states to suprentend the building of the Tanks which is now in progress so I did a pretty good days work.

Col. R. is the most contrary old cuss I ever worked with. As soon as you suggest any thing he opposes but after about an hours argument comes round and proposes the same thing him self. So in the long run I get my way, but at a great waste of breath.

It is good discipline however for me for I have to keep my temper. At the end of each argument I feel completely done up. I guess he does too. Still he is trying to have me made a Lieutenant Colonel so I ought not be too hard on him.

In a formal letter, Patton respectfully suggested that Rockenbach give Braine written authority to 1) supervise certain points in the construction of light tanks, trucks, and trailers in the United States, and 2) communicate directly with Rockenbach by telegram in case of difficulty or doubt — instead of going through military channels. He thought that Braine should pay special attention to the design of a tractor truck with trailer, either two- or four-wheeled, whichever was more practical. He believed that all tractor trucks produced should be uniform, capable of carrying tanks or other baggage and supplies, low hung, equipped with solid rubber tires if possible in order to reduce road strains, and able to be loaded while uncoupled. Although a revised War Department specification sheet mentioned the existence of seven-and-a-half-ton trucks that seemed suitable, he wished Braine to seek a lighter vehicle. Braine, Patton thought, should foster experiments to develop better forks, armorplate tracks, lubricants, engines, ammunition racks, turrets, and interchangeable parts. For example, if the gearbox was changed in later tank models, it should be made to fit earlier models. Braine was to guard against increasing the total weight of the tank. He was also to seek im-

provements in the leather helmet and steel splinter mask worn by crewmen. Finally, Patton admonished — in words that were to become,
whatever the context, standard with him for the remainder of his career
— "a fairly good tank or trailer here is worth more than a perfect one in
America."

Diary
   January 31: "Lt. Braine left for Paris [and the United States] to
day. I was sorry to see him go. He is the most reliable man I have yet
met and has plenty of sense."

Letter, GSP, Jr., to Beatrice, January 31, 1918
   You ask how I know so much [about] machinery I think I am
more or less of a mechanical genius for I simply know by looking at
an engine all about it. In fact the French adopted some of my ideas
of change on their Tanks. It was a greater surprise to me than to any
one else but so it is.
   Lt. Braine who has been working with me is going to America soon
and if he goes to Washington which is probable you might be able to
see him. He is a little deaf so you will have to speak loud . . .
   I am sending him to supervise the construction of some special features which he and I invented. These should make the American
Tanks much more mobile than any thing that has thus far appeared.
   The whole thing now is infernally slow and up hill work but I
keep hoping to get over the crest some day soon and start coasting.
Right now however it is not at all easy in fact the reverse. Still every
one else is having the same trouble so we have no monopily on
gloom.

Pershing had said something nice about Patton in a letter to Nita, and
she sent the extract to Beatrice, who forwarded it to her husband. Patton
copied it into his diary: "George has left me to teach tanks at school for
such. I miss him very much he's such a fine fire eater. But there's one
thing about him he believes in that way and would do all he says if he got
a chance. He has had a fine company at Headquarters and it will be hard
to replace him."
   To which Patton added: "Heres Hoping I make Good. G."

CHAPTER 24

Langres to Bourg

*"I am the absolute boss and it seems strange at first not to have
to ask any one any thing at all."*

ON FEBRUARY 1, Patton conducted the first close-order drill of tank men
in the history of the U. S. Army. That afternoon he started working on
tank drill regulations.

Letter, GSP, Jr., to Beatrice, February 2, 1918
We have been having some most interesting lectures on special
subjects and all of them go to show what a complex war we are in
and how much we have to learn. It seems more and more certain to
me that we cannot punch a hole [through the German defenses] with
out tanks. There are too many instruments of death in the way but I
believe that Tanks well backed up will do the job. I hope the war
lasts long enough for us to try our hand.
The tanks have attracted a lot of good men and I get requests from
them to transfer nearly daily.

According to a cable received from the War Department, 100 American-
built Renaults would arrive in France in April, 300 would be delivered in
May, and 600 would come every month thereafter. It would turn out to
be a wholly overoptimistic assessment of American tank production.
Patton traveled to Chaumont and had a long talk with Rockenbach,
who authorized him to select two General Staff officers from the Staff
School at Langres to help Patton run his organization. Rockenbach also
said he was recommending Patton for promotion to lieutenant colonel.
As Patton explained, "I have not sufficient rank [as a captain] to get proper
subordinates. He told me that I was to organize the 1st Tank center and
see to biliting arrangements for 12 companies [of] light tanks he had asked
for."

Carrying out Rockenbach's instructions, he called on the appropriate offices at Langres about securing billeting areas for the tankmen who would be coming to the tank school and made tentative plans for organizing the staff of the 1st Tank Center.

He wrote Beatrice that if everything worked out well, he would have 1400 men under him by May. Rockenbach wanted him to go to England to take a course at a school there, but Patton would try to put this off until Beatrice, who had been ill, was strong enough to visit her sister in London. He was elated by Rockenbach's formal recommendation for his promotion, for this meant — if the War Department complied — that he would have sufficient rank to command the first two battalions of light tanks.

Attending a meeting at the Army Staff School, where assignments of graduates were arranged, he asked for two officers by name. The chiefs of staff of all the divisions and of the I Corps were present for the same purpose, and their appearance disturbed him. "They were not an impressive lot, yet there are none better available."

Letter, GSP, Jr., to Beatrice, February 5, 1918
We have done about all we can organizing till we get some machines. I have been trying with some success not to fall into the habit of doing every thing my self but of directing others to do it and seeing that they do. Still one has a natural tendency to try to pull all the strings one self. My only crytocism of J. [Pershing] is that he is over prone to do that. It is a great mistake.

Rockenbach telephoned to say he was having trouble getting tanks from the French. He directed Patton to go to Paris and see what he could do.

In Paris for two days, he secured a promise that the French would deliver several tanks to him by the middle of March, these to be used for training at the center. He extracted the pledge, no doubt, by sheer persistence coupled with charm, the latter enhanced by his highly original yet completely fluent use of the French language. He characterized his accomplishment as quite a feat, for he had given up hope, he said in some exaggeration, of ever getting any tanks at all.

Letter, GSP, Jr., to Beatrice, February 8, 1918
I bought my self some more leather junk [in Paris]. A saddle store

has a hellish fascination for me as you know and I always buy something . . .

Asto my staying in the Tanks after the war I doubt it because it is a specialty. And specialists don't get supreme command. Besides we will have another war in Mexico and Tanks would be useless there so I will be back in the Cavalry. At least that is my present notion . . .

I want you to be the same age when I get back as when I left. Also die your hair for I don't like gray hair at all.

He was drawing up tables of organization and equipment for quartermaster and ordnance supplies of tank companies when Rockenbach telephoned and told him he would soon have to go to Blois to select men for the first light tank company.

Letter, GSP, Jr., to Beatrice, February 11, 1918

Don't send me any more sweaters this year as I have six. Gen. P. has twelve and 14 pairs of heavy socks. I was at the house last night and counted them.

Former Secretary of War [Henry L.] Stimson is going to join my mess and live in the house . . . Mr. S. is now a Lt. Colonel . . .

This is a soldiers war not a staff officers [war] for as all the attacks are frontal there is little strategy possible only a vast mass of detail to arrange like a cleark. If we or when we break through things will be different but first we must make the hole with the Tanks.

With four of his lieutenants — Borland, Hebert, Sweeny, and Winters — Patton tramped all over the site of his tank camp. He instructed his junior officers on how to unload the tanks if they arrived while he was away at Blois. He showed them what he wanted done to prepare the land for tank exercises. He made some notes to instruct his adjutant. He wrote the following letter to an old friend with whom he had served in Mexico.

My dear Col Burt. Sir: I respectfully call your attention to the fact that I am about to procede in a most unmilitary manner. My excuse for so doing is that I desire if possible to get some results and my experience, limited as it is, leads me to the belief that "Channels" are not built according to the mathematical axium "That a straight line is the shortest distance between two points."

Between the Langres-Dijon road and the Bois-sur-Marne, Foret Du Mont woods there is a tract of ground one and a half Kil. long extending north from the Cross Roads at Burg. It is my intention to use this ground for Battle Practice with the Light Tanks. There are three lines of trenches crossing this ground. In Tank operations it is most important to correct maps with Aeroplane Photographs. I have heard that Col. Alexander, Intelligence section, G.S. has asked to have some pictures taken near Langres. If possible I would like some pictures of this ground taken at the same time . . . so that I can use them to instruct officers in conjunction with a map I now have . . .

If I am wrong in assuming that the Air Service takes these pictures or if a more formal request is necessary will you please inform me.

Very respectfully.

Letter, GSP, Jr., to Beatrice, February 12, 1918

It is hard to get out of the habit of doing every thing my self but absolutely necessary and it is the sign of efficiency or lack of it in an officer. Those who can only do them selves are not much good as human power is limited while those who can make others do have the world to pick from.

The trouble is that my officers have all been N.C.O's and lack initiative. Still they do what they are told and that is something.

His travel orders having arrived, he went to Chaumont and left for Blois. His train was delayed, and he was two hours late when he reached St. Aignan-Noyers, the headquarters of the 41st Replacement Division, which served as a manpower pool and furnished men to fill ranks and positions in other units. Discovering that Lieutenant Colonel F. B. Hennessy had gone ahead with the selection of men and had already gathered what appeared to be a fine group, he accompanied Hennessy to Montrichard and inspected another group; these men pleased him too.

He obtained an automobile to drive to St. Aignan-Noyers and the train, but the car skidded off the road and was damaged. He walked five kilometers to town, missed his train, and slept on a stretcher in the hotel lobby. He managed to send a telegram to his adjutant:

Two hundred men should arrive Friday morning. They will have equipment C with three blankets. Draw one hundred extra blankets two field ranges [stoves] and two march kits [for] cooking. Get permission to use stjoemes [the nearby village of St. Geomes] for temporary billets if Burg [Bourg] not available.

Taking the train to Saumur — like Langres, Saumur was a great AEF school center, but for artillerymen — he found many old friends "all were dilighted to see me." He rode to Tours, dined at the Hôtel de l'Universe, boarded the Army special train that evening, and arrived at Chaumont in the early afternoon. He reported to Rockenbach the results of his trip.

From Rockenbach he received a copy of Tank Corps AEF General Orders 2, dated February 14, which assigned Patton formally to command the 1st Light Tank Center.

Rockenbach accompanied him to Langres that evening and left after supper. Both were elated by the way things were working out.

On Saturday, Patton completed the arrangements for the proper reception of his new men.

Letter, GSP, Jr., to Beatrice, February 16, 1918

I have two hundred men coming to day for the first two companies I hope that they are good men . . .

I also got the inclosed order [assigning him to command the tank center] yesterday. A center is two or more battalions.

Col. Fox Conner got wounded last week. They were inspecting and came to a part of the trench full of water. They climed out on the top and ran along to avoid the water when just as they were jumping in again a shell blew up and cut Col C's nose and throat. He is all right again and will get a wound badge which is nice.

About this time, several buildings began to appear on his camp site. The former Coast Artillery officers assigned to him, plus a few infantry officers who had also joined, had been constructing workshops, getting water piped in, and preparing barracks. Patton had secured, by proper and legal means, some lumber with which to build a tank shed. In addition, he later wrote:

[six buildings mysteriously] sprang up in the night like mushrooms and they looked strangely like French barracks . . . freely daubed with serial numbers . . . each number backed with large obtrusive U.S. A still closer examination would have revealed places where other numbers had been removed with a plane. But why be inquisitive.

Major Farman of his West Point class came for a visit on Sunday morning. He was two places above Patton on the promotion list, but he said that Patton had been promoted to Major on December 15. This was hardly official notice,

> but after much debate [with himself] I decided to put on my [major's] leaves and now I am wearing them. I feel sort of like a thief but that does not bother me at all as there are so many militia majors around here that one must have leaves to keep ones self respect.

Soon after Patton put on his new insignia, a soldier addressed him as "Lieutenant" — "which proves that I am still not 'old' looking."

"Inspite of my increased rank," he wrote Beatrice, "I still love you."

Actually, his date of rank as major was January 26, but the War Department order announcing the promotion would be issued only on March 11 and arrive in France still later.

That Sunday, February 17, the men of his first two companies reached Langres. Patton was at the railroad station to meet them. He marched them to St. Geosmes and to temporary billets in a tent camp — "195 men all told good lot." Most of them, including one officer who accompanied them, had volunteered for the tanks.

As though he had not enough to do, Patton received a telegram from Braine in Paris. Braine expected to leave Thursday for the United States, and before he departed he wanted to talk with Patton — "will need help to carry out your plans." Patton was too busy to attend to Braine, who, he probably figured, had enough ability to make his own way and do all that was expected of him.

Letter, GSP, Jr., to Beatrice, February 18, 1918

> My two companies arrived here yesterday and I have them Bileted in a Town near here. They are very well fixed and my officers are good and efficient. When the men got in they found a hot dinner waiting for them, and a nice latrine all dug.
>
> I think all the villagers thought we were digging for gold as they came out and watched the operation.
>
> The sgt. Mjr. [sergeant major — the highest enlisted man] is part owner of Mark Cross [Stores — Fred Murphy] and a graduate of Yale. Twenty other men are from big colleges. Quite forty owned their own machines inclusing a couple of Pierce-Arrows. They are really a very fine bunch of men much above the ordinary. All drafted men.
>
> I must stop now. I love you.

He inspected the billets, arranged for medical support, and ordered lumber for more buildings.

GHQ AEF issued provisional drill regulations for the light tank service with an acknowledgment that they had been prepared by Lieutenant Colonel George S. Patton, Jr., who was still, so far as anyone knew officially, a captain. In pencil, written a dozen or so years afterward, he noted: "This was wholy original with me. GSP Jr."

Drills or exercises on foot, Patton specified, were to follow generally the instructions in the Infantry *Drill Regulations*. Machine drills on foot were to accustom the men to signals and to the proper intervals and distance between tanks. Commands were to be given by signs, visual or touch, by sounds, voice or Klaxon (horn), and by the example of leaders. For instance, touch signals between crew members: to turn, the gunner in the turret pressed the right or left shoulder of the driver, who turned in that direction as long as the pressure lasted; to go faster, repeated pats on the back of the driver's neck; to halt, pressure on the top of the driver's head; forward from halt, the same as faster; backward, the same as halt followed by several pats on top of the head. "By Claxton. One long blast means attention. Other signals," it was candidly admitted, "not worked out."

He designated drills by platoon and by company and drew diagrams to show how the tanks were to move. It was all quite typically Patton, detailed and thorough.

Patton was at the camp at 8 A.M. on Tuesday, February 19. He gave the men a talk on discipline and behavior. He had an officer lecture them on camouflage. He himself went to the gas course that afternoon. In the evening he sent Rockenbach a list of proposed ranks for tank officers.

"Things are looking better for us now in the Tanks," he wrote Beatrice.

The gas course was a great bore, particularly since his thoughts were with his troops at the tank center. One type of mask made him look like a member of the Ku Klux Klan, another like an incubator baby —

a most unplesant disguise in which to fight . . . Each form of specialist like the gas men or the aviators or the artillery or the Tanks talk as if theirs was the one useful weapon and that if there were but enough of that sort the war would end. As a matter of fact it is the dough boy in the end who does the trick.

When he wore his mask in a chamber full of tear gas, along with everyone else taking the course, he found to his surprise that the "resperator absolutely nutrilizes gas."

On February 22 he moved his two companies, now named Companies A and B, to Bourg and their permanent billets. He inspected the old quarters they had occupied at St. Geosmes and found them clean. He heard that a tank had arrived and became terribly excited before learning that it was only a mistake due to his adjutant's imperfect understanding of the French language. After telephoning Rockenbach and requesting several vehicles for his tank center, he received — that afternoon, which was quick work on Rockenbach's part — a Dodge sedan, a motorcycle, and a truck.

Letter, GSP, Jr., to Aunt Nannie, February 22, 1918

I have my battalion in a town of my own near here and am very independent. Tanks are Army Troops so we are not bothered by little superiors which is a great help.

My town is the dirtiest place in the world full of cows and chickens but it has a fine view being on the edge of a cliff over a long and beautiful vally.

We had a rumor to day that our first tank had arrived but it proved only the result of bad French. The station agent said one was going to arrive which we knew already.

Letter, GSP, Jr., to Beatrice, February 22, 1918

We moved down [to Bourg, about 5 miles south of Langres] and got settled. It is a nice little town full of manure and smells but we are the only troop in it so are not bothered, every thing is quite well fixed. I rented a room for a soldiers Club at 7 F[rancs] a week and they ought to be quite comfortable. I am the absolute boss and it seems strange at first not to have to ask any one any thing at all.

I can see how hard it must be for officers who have been subordinates longer than I to ever do any thing for them selves.

It is a good experience. I also inspected my old town to see that things were done right. The men did well. Every thing was neatly put away and cleaned. I have a Q.M. who is a good one and does lots on his own initiative. We will start drills monday and will spend tomorrow removing the manure to a degree.

Just as I got through an officer rushed up shouting that a tank was

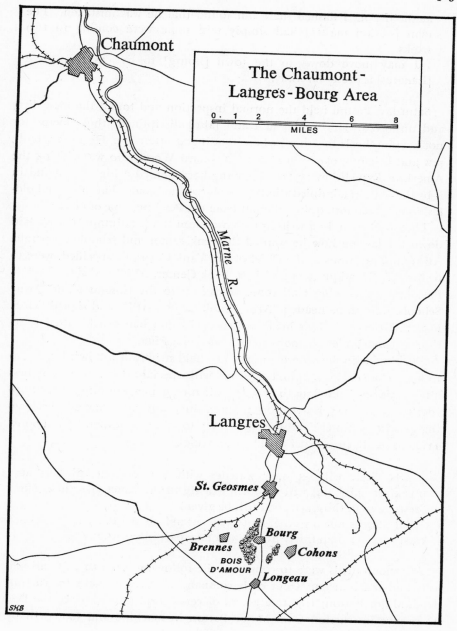

Chaumont

The Chaumont-
Langres-Bourg Area

0   1   2   4   6   8
MILES

Marne R.

Langres

St. Geosmes

Bourg

Brennes

Cohons

BOIS
D'AMOUR

Longeau

SKB

at the depot. I dashed there but found that he was mistaken. The man [station master] had simply said some were coming in two weeks.

I may move down to the town [Bourg] to live as this place [Langres] is pretty far away.

Saturday, Patton held the normal inspection and found the men dirty and unshaved. He "raised hell and [also] disciplined [the] Doctor for not keeping heels together" when standing at attention. He took a bath, saw and briefly spoke with General Leonard Wood who was visiting the American Expeditionary Force (having been denied a high command in it by the Wilson administration) and who seemed somewhat puffy and old-fashioned, even lost, quite different from the Pershing type of officer.

That afternoon, in a written memorandum to his adjutant, Patton laid down the law on how he wanted the tank center and school to operate. All communications to the Chief of the Tank Corps, he specified, were to be headed "Headquarters 1st Light Tank Center, AEF" and signed "G. S. Patton, Commanding"; all communications to the Commandant, Army Schools, were to be headed "Army Tank School, AEF" and signed "G. S. Patton, Director." This made a nice distinction between his dual functions as commander of troops and director of a school.

Morning drills, he ordered, were to be held strictly as follows: from 8:20 to 8:30, close order drill and saluting, with special attention to exactness and precision; from 8:35 to 9:25, calisthenics, games, running, and jumping; 10:05 to 10:35, instruction in guard duty, military courtesy, challenging, posting sentinels, and the like; 10:45 to 11:15, foot drill by platoons; 11:20 to recall, close order drill by companies.

All officers will set their watches with that of the Adjutant at breakfast daily and will conform exactly to the times specified. No "rests" except those specified will be given.

All officers not on other duty will attend all drills . . . [All officers] younger than thirty five [would take part in calisthenics].

Afternoon drills were to consist of the following: 1:00 to 1:45, all officers and ten noncoms from each company to receive pistol instruction from Major Patton; 1:50 to 2:30, all officers except the Officer of the Day to receive instruction from Major Patton in machine and foot drill by platoon and company; 2:50 to 4:00, classes in the theory and operation of gasoline engines.

The men were to be occupied during the afternoon by what was known as company fatigue, that is, duties in housekeeping, the maintenance of property and grounds, and the like; they were also to perform what Patton called town fatigue, that is, keeping the village of Bourg clean and neat.

Morning reports were to be turned in to the adjutant every evening before taps was sounded. Company commanders were to inspect personally the billets of their men at least once every day. Officers were to leave camp only after reporting at the adjutant's office their time of departure, destination, and expected time of return.

Letter, GSP, Jr., to Beatrice, February 23, 1918

I think it will keep them fairly on the go for a while till we get the tanks. It is absolutely necessary to do so as there is nothing else to amuse them and as they live in stables and lofts so can hardly be said to have much home life if any.

I have always thought and still more strongly think that our chief fault as an army has been that of taking things too easily. When the days get longer I can work them more which will be a help to them.

You ought to see me brace when they can look at me. And already it has so I fancy given them a better carriage.

The officers have a nice mess and one well located so things ought to go well.

I was issued a truck, a motor cycle, and an auto yesterday so shall have to hoof it less but still fear that I will unduely develop my legs and hence not look so well in boots . . .

I make the chauffeurs wash their machines after the last trip each night no matter what the hour. This I got from the english . . .

Gen. Wood was here to day and looks quite well. He was most cordial and asked after you.

Riding ten miles on Miss Green [his horse] daily has improved her disposition and my health vastly.

I also had the pleasure of militerizing my doctor. To day he was talking to me with his heels apart but will not offend in the future.

Letter, GSP, Jr., to Mr. Ayer, February 24, 1918

I have two companies of Tank Soldiers here. About seventy percent of them are drafted men and of an exceptionally high class. Three sergeants are Yale graduates and many other colleges are represented. It is a pleasure to work with them because they are so quick to learn.

If we have only luck getting material we should have two battalions ready to fight by June. That does not mean that we will fight but that we may.

Letter, GSP, Jr., to Beatrice, February 24, 1918

Madame La Baronne Pig and Sheep which is her name [an inaccurate approximation of Madame de Vaux de la Porquière, a distinguished French family with whom he would be friends for the rest of his life] has asked me to tea at her chateau which is in my town. Her husband is a colonel in the French Army and she is quite nice and safely old.

(Maj) Stanley Rumbough is here at the school also Farman. They are both to mess with me.

Letter, GSP, Jr., to Beatrice, February 25, 1918

I am getting all sorts of applications for officers in the tank corps and they are a good lot young and full of pep. But we will need a lot to keep things going.

I have got them [my men] pretty well to heel as I am very mean with them every once in a while.

Letter, GSP, Jr., to Beatrice, February 26, 1918

I ate dinner at the officers mess [in Bourg] and had just the [same] effect Col Pitcher [the commanding officer] used to have at the mess at [Fort] Sheridan. It was most amusing. They all ate hurridly and went out. They have a very nice mess and a good cook.

Through some mistake the Motor Transport Service . . . issued me two autos. I told them that I only had asked for one but they said I must take both which I have done.

The poor Dr. is so scared of me that he giggles when I speak to him and is almost incoherent. It is quite amusing. If I ever get to be an "old general" I fear that B Jr. & R.E. [his daughters] will have a fiew suitors. Or perhaps many for "bootlick."

The man I have for a Q.M. is certainly good (Lt. Borland) but I can't say so much for my adjutant. He rushes around a lot but does little work so far as I can judge.

I am getting to talk to you about my Battalion as much as you used to talk about the children. As I objected to that I will stop this.

I started pistol practice again to day and found I needed it. So I shall devote more time to it here after. It might come in handy as in Mexico. I hope I get another close up like that. I rather think that they are rare in this war.

Letter, GSP, Jr., to Beatrice, February 27, 1918

When this war is over I am going to insist on using a single bed for *both* of us at the same time. There is perhaps more than one reason for this, but the only one which the censor and modisty will allow me to mention is that I am tired of being cold and especially of getting into a large and empty bed full of cold sheets. Hence you will have to go to bed first.

You see we have only enough wood for one fire in the house and that is in the parlor. So when I go to bed my room is like a vault and the bed like a shroud. Besides a large double French bed, just like the one we had at Saumur, is not sociable.

Letter, GSP, Jr., to Kay Merrill [Beatrice's sister in London], February 27, 1918

At last after all the reserve officers in the world have been promoted they have made us majors. So I am very grave . . .

I have a battalion of Soldiers (Tankers) under me now but as yet no tanks. Still I have hopes . . .

I am pretty busy and quite well but still too d—— safe.

Diary

February 28: "Went to drill. Found B. Co. not out on account of rain. Got them out."

Patton expanded the provisional drill regulations for tanks into a larger "Tank Drill and Training Manual (Proposed)." Chapter I, the introduction, was pure Patton:

Success in battle presupposes the destruction of the enemy. This is brought about by killing and wounding his men so as to reduce his strength and destroy his morale. The above happy results may only be looked for when the training has been intelligent and thorough, so that the men are educated in what to do and have the discipline to do it.

Commanding officers are responsible for the proper training and discipline of their units . . .

Simple movements, elastic formations and iron discipline are the essentials to success in battle.

The drill regulations are furnished as a guide . . .

In interpreting the regulations the spirit is to be sought. Quibbeling over minutiae is a demonstration of failure to grasp the spirit.

Diary

March 1(Friday): It snowed. Got hut from Gen Shipton. Unloaded lumber for shops. "R[ockenbach] sent me a scheme to train 116 off. and 1638 men in no time. Worked out [an improved] scheme."

Letter, GSP, Jr., to Beatrice, March 1, 1918

I just got an order to train 40 Companies in no time with nothing and it has put me to it to find means. I finally got a scheme for training 32 Companies in a fair sort of way but my temper is shot to hell as a result. For fear of showing it I will stop. I love you.

He wrote a memo to Rockenbach and suggested altering the program of having 400 tanks and 40 companies by June 30 to one of having 400 tanks but only 28 companies. The reason was a problem that was hardly specific for tanks alone but was a universal difficulty whenever shipments of equipment — any kind — and of men were made, particularly overseas. The process of requisitioning a specified amount of men and matériel for delivery to a certain place by a certain time was in and of itself simple. But the execution was infinitely complex. To gather together an entire and balanced kit or package, consisting of different parts coming from different places, then to load it and ship it, and finally to check it upon arrival comprised an operation that was a nightmare. Success demanded an extremely high level of organizational and logistical competence.

Patton's memo was very clear and to the point.

Memo, GSP, Jr., to Rockenbach, March 2, 1918

The shipment of Tanks is absolutely dependent on the space allotted by the shipping board. Hence we must have a definate promise from them in the case of each shipment, otherwise we would get more men than we could possibly use and whose space could be better utelised by infantry.

There should be an officer of the Tank corps with rank and experience on duty in the U.S. as your representative to coordinate the shipment of both men and Tanks for the reason that the elements of Tank units are handled by three different departments. The Ordnance, the Q.M. and the Adjutant General. Now if tanks were held up by the shipping board the Adjutant General [who assigned personnel] would not know it and the men would come and be in the way.

It is a well established military principle that men should travle with their units. This is particularly true with a new unit like Tanks. You know what happened in the case of our trucks. Bodies landed in one place. Chassis another and both were useless. No spare parts came at all. Tanks would be in even worse case. A Q.M. told to ship them would not know what comprised a unit and would send off what he had on hand with the result that he would get incomplete tanks or that the spare parts would get sent to some truck park.

To obviate this your representative should coordinate the shipments of men and tanks and an officer of the unit should have a list of the shipment so that he could supervise the loading and have a complete list of all prepared. Then he and his men could see that the stuff was collected on debarcation.

To my mind the foregoing are absolutely prerequisite to success. The men must be shipped with regard to the tanks . . .

I take the liberty of repeating that the men should syncranise in quantity [numbers] and time [of arrival] with the tanks.

The expanded training program would work because billets available in Bourg and in the neighboring communities of Noidant and Cohons could accommodate 51 officers and 1645 men. But he would need several prefabricated huts, each of which housed 17 officers; he strongly recommended sending Lieutenant Robinson and Sergeant Major Murphy to the replacement division to select new men for the tank center and school.

Diary
March 2: Took memo and went to Chaumont to see Col R about training. Recommended that Tanks have a representative in U.S. R. said no.

Somewhat depressed, Patton was pleased to be invited by Pershing's aide Boyd on Sunday to go on a short trip with the general that afternoon. Patton accepted, not only because he always enjoyed being with Pershing but also because he felt that a change in routine would do him good.

He accompanied Pershing to the headquarters — near Toul — of the 1st U. S. Infantry Division, which was occupying a quiet front-line sector under the French. Pershing wanted to compliment the division on its recent repulse of a German raid. He discovered that Premier Georges Clemenceau, who made it a practice to visit units at the front every Sunday, had come also to congratulate the American division. Clemenceau, characterized by Patton as "quite an active little chap and nice to meet," was enthusiastic over the conduct of the American troops.

Learning that there was to be a "show" that night, Pershing decided to stay. General Summerall, the division commander who knew Patton since his West Point days, promised Patton he could watch the action from an advance OP — observation post. But when Pershing saw Patton getting a helmet, he said, "Where in hell are you going?" Patton had to tell him, and Pershing forbade it. So Colonel Purrington took Patton up the road to General Duncan's brigade, a safer place.

The barrage was to start at 1 A.M. with 90 guns, and Patton stayed up to see it. The shoot started exactly on the designated second, and in three minutes the Germans came back with their own artillery fire. The regiments were supposed to attack at 1:20, but the infantry was unable to get started, and the preparatory shelling was halted. The German guns continued for almost twenty minutes. Then all was quiet. Everyone went to bed around 2:30.

Somehow Patton found time to write to Beatrice about an imagined slight on the part of his sister.

> I think you and nita and all got much excited over nothing. I feel sure that J's sentiments are as always but what you all don't know is the pressure he is under over here . . . He is still fond of me . . . am sorry I made Nita angry.

Pershing and his party left the 1st Division that morning, and Patton went on to Langres. That afternoon he was at Chaumont where, with Rockenbach, he took the train for Paris. They boarded the train for Boulogne.

Patton managed to write to Beatrice.

J. was most contrite over Nita. Neither of us imagined that she would be hurt and we are both sorry. There are no doubts that he feels the same as ever only more so and he said he wished they had married. Of course don't tell him I said so.

Rockenbach and Patton were going to England to consult with the British on tank training, to visit the British tank training area at Wareham, and to make preliminary arrangements for the reception of a battalion of American heavy tankers.

In London Patton met several interesting people at his sister-in-law's, accepted an invitation from Mrs. Leverton Harris, wife of a deputy secretary in the Ministry of the Blockade, to see *Faust*, and enjoyed the opera, which was sung in English.

He and Rockenbach spent nearly a week in England. They examined a new tank model — "I argued in favor of four speeds, but was ruled an ass. Time will show. Also think there are too many guns." They looked at new tanks in production, visited tank schools, observed machine gun practice, watched tank guns firing at the target range, saw antiaircraft guns in operation, and inspected the site of what would be the American heavy tank area.

Letter, GSP, Jr. (Langres), to Beatrice, March 12, 1918

I feel pretty tired and dirty [after the trip]. We have a stupendus job and little time and none of my officers are worth a damn. I have to instruct all of them in every thing under heaven except infantry drill and I have to check them up at that. I have to teach maping, Visual training, Aiming, gas Engines, signaling, reconnaissance, Intelligence, and some other things that I cant recall. I send them out to teach classes and have to watch them for mistakes. I hope to get Viner [whom he had known in Mexico] soon and that will be a help but so far I have gone on alone to the detrement of my temper.

I am going to bed early to night and will feel better in the morning.

Rockenbach wrote to Hennessy at the replacement division to whom he was "greatly obliged . . . for your continued interest in the Tank Corps . . . The prospects in the Tank Corps are, I believe, better than anywhere else, considered from every point of view." The tank center needed officers with knowledge of mechanics and experience as commanders. Would Hennessy please try to find and send five majors, who could look forward to promotion to lieutenant colonel "when tried out and found effective"; 34 captains, who would have a good chance of promotion to major; a large number of first lieutenants — the best 119 would be promoted after trial; and quite a few second lieutenants — 249 would eventually win promotion.

On impulse, Rockenbach drove to Bourg. He inspected the tank center and was extremely impressed with what he saw.

Letter, GSP, Jr., to Beatrice, March 13, 1918

I am sorry I stired up such a mess over Nita. It was well ment but shows that with out your advice I am apt to make mistakes of judgment . . .

I got a fine letter from Mr. Ayer in which he said he took great pride in my efforts. It delights me to have him think so and I hope I justify his confidence.

When I realize that I am with out question a very superior soldier and yet realize as I do my many shortcomings I can but feel sorry for Gen P. [who is] served by men worse than I. I am not fishing [for compliments] but telling the exact truth.

Col. R. Inspected camp this P.M. and was much pleased. I was glad as I had not known he was coming so things were just as they usually are.

Patton had a fine athletic field for the soldiers, and they enjoyed it. They had 45 minutes every day for hard-played games, and each man participating worked up a fine sweat. "To day we had a sort of polo on foot using a round foot ball" — he was referring to the game of soccer — "and kicking it was fine exercise. I plaied and found I was shockingly short of wind. I bought some camp clothes and am going to train a little."

He had a good view from his headquarters building "in my town," Bourg — a nice old garden with a statue, an iron fence, and a high terrace looking about 30 miles down a green valley with a lake in the distance and a Roman road down the middle. On a hill about 200 yards away were the ruins of a robber bishop's castle.

Visiting the French tank center at Martigny-les-Bains, he watched an attack maneuver in which four Schneider tanks worked with a battalion of infantry. He was pleased to hear the commanding general of the 18th French Division say that no attack would ever be made again without tanks.

He sent Rockenbach a run-down on some of his thoughts on personnel. He had talked with a cavalry major who was a student at the Army Staff School about joining the tanks, but the major was dubious of his ability and wished to suspend judgment until he saw a tank. Since he was a Regular officer "and almost a temporary Lt. Col. I believe we had better let him make up his mind." A classmate of Patton's who had failed to graduate from West Point was at Langres; he was "quite military and has not got much intelect. He might do well as I believe him brave." Captains Chamberlin and Cramer, old friends of his, were to be relieved as instructors at the Military Academy when they were promoted to major, and Patton suggested that Rockenbach ask for them. Would he please request the transfer to the Tank Corps of Captain Sereno Brett, who was an infantryman, a Regular officer of long service, an expert operator of and instructor in the machine gun and the 37-mm. gun, and who was eager to join the tanks. The only man Patton had who could speak French was Sergeant Major Murphy, and Patton was recommending him for commission as a second lieutenant. Lieutenant Miller had been on duty for three days and seemed well versed in military matters and in paper work. Lieutenant Hebert was neat and soldierly but failed to get on well with some of the company commanders.

Diary

March 17 (Sunday): "Had Elsie Janis [the favorite American singer and entertainer of troops in France] and her mother to lunch. She is not pretty but quite amusing though common in her pronunciation. She wore an artificial Lepord skin coat. Met Secretary [of War Newton] Baker and went around with him for a while. Seemed interested and intelligent."

He wrote Beatrice: "The Sec of War was here yesterday and I saw him. He is a little rat but very smart."

Patton delivered to his officers and men a lecture on discipline, which he defined as "instant, cheerful, unhesitating obedience." Obeying instantly and cheerfully was

very good but it is not good enough, in that you do not obey automatically.

For example: A group of you are sitting talking. An officer approaches, one of you calls "Attention." What happens? You look
about, see the officer, and then come to attention. Your discipline is
good, in that it is almost instantaneous and quite cheerful, but it is
lacking in that it is not automatic. You have failed in the vital thing,
the rest is useless show.

After a long illustration on the response to the quarterback calling the
signals for a football team, he continued:

. . . just as surely as the automatic obedience . . . will give you
the edge on the other team which will win for you, and the lack of
which no amount of star tackling and blocking will replace, so no
amount of bayoneting or shooting will win the battle if you are late,
slow, owing to lack of automatic obedience . . .

Lack of discipline in war means death or defeat, which is worse
than death . . . The prize for this war is the greatest of all prizes —
Freedom.

In battle as in fistfights or football, man cannot reason. What he
does for good or evil he does automatically — subconsciously.

The reason the Bosch [Boche] has survived so long against a world
in arms is because he is disciplined. Since 1805 he has bred this
quality as we breed speed in horses; but he is neither the inventor
nor the patentee of it. Philip of Macedon had as high a discipline
three hundred odd years before Christ. The great Alexander saw its
value and by its aid his phalanxes were victorious against odds of fifty
to one . . .

The legions of Rome were disciplined and conquered because of
it . . .

We cannot wait until A.D. 2018 to breed discipline as they [the
Germans] have done. But we are as intelligent as football players,
far more intelligent than the Greeks or the Romans or the Persians or
the Gauls of two thousand years ago . . . You must get it likewise:
instant, cheerful, and automatic discipline, so that when we the
quarterbacks give the signal of life or death in the near day of battle,
you will not think and then act, but will act and if you will, think
later — after the war. It is by discipline alone that all your efforts,
all your patriotism, shall not have been in vain. Without it Heroism

is futile. You will die for nothing. With DISCIPLINE you are IRRESISTIBLE.

This became a standard lecture Patton gave all new officers and men reporting to the tank center. When speaking to officers alone, he added several paragraphs, stressing that officers could hardly expect discipline in others unless they were capable of imparting it themselves, and pointing out that many officers used unnecessary words when giving commands or directions, for example, "Will you please," or "Kindly."

There is nothing harsh in brief words of command any more than there is impoliteness in the brief wording of a telegram. Commands simply express your desire, your signal, in the briefest and most emphatic language possible. If you are to obtain automatic obedience from your men your language must express your meaning concisely and with emphasis, further each meaning must always be expressed in precisely the same language; so that when you give commands in battle the unreasoning mind of the soldier, unreasoning for the time being on account of the stress of battle, shall automatically carry out the identical directions to which at drill this set of words this signal has accustomed him. On you rests the responsibility, to you goes much of the glory. Hence it is inexcusable for you to express yourselves in an ambiguous or hesitating manner.

These thoughts were impressive, primarily because they were spoken with firm conviction. These were the precepts by which Patton himself lived.

Another lecture he delivered from time to time was on the sense of duty or obligation, which, he said,

are inseparably connected. In fact, duty is but discipline carried to its highest degree. Like discipline also, it must be automatic . . .

The sense of duty is hard to acquire, because it is made up of so many tiny things. But in essence it consists in doing the task set, however small, absolutely, perfectly, and better than it was ever done before . . .

It is not enough to perform a task so that you can get by with it. That is easy and worthless . . .

[For example] to-morrow at reveille, it is raining or cold, and bed is so very pleasant; your undeveloped sense of duty lets you stay in bed two minutes too long. You must make the formation. Have you done your duty? You have not! . . . unless your sense of duty is so undeveloped that you can lie to yourself . . . leniency to self . . . is inimical to duty — hence to victory.

Unless you . . . do your best, the day will come when, tired and hungry, you will halt just short of the point you were ordered to reach, and by so halting make useless the efforts and death of thousands . . .

This imperious sense of obligation is the mark of the thoroughbred in men as in horses. The cold-blooded horse quits in the "Stretch" when the race is all but won. The thoroughbred passes the wire at his best though he dies for it. The thorough-bred man . . . does not argue. He goes until his duty is done or he is dead.

You must develop this thorough-bred sense of duty, otherwise you had better never have been born to wear a uniform you will inevitably disgrace . . .

If this iron conscience, this sense of obligation could not be developed, it would be futile to talk of it, but it can be developed and to beat the Germans, it must be.

Do not talk or think of your rights or your fatigues or of what the other fellow has failed to do. War is the struggle of nations, you are in it but as an individual and hence your feelings as such do not exist . . .

In doing your utmost, even unto death you are conferring no favor, you are privileged to be able to do so much for your Country . . .

To wear the uniform of an officer of the United States Army in any other frame of mind is to live a lie.

Strong words, they were effective in stirring his listeners.

Still another paper Patton wrote in March — whether to deliver orally, to be read by his officers, or simply for his own guidance — consisted of instructions for training the Tank Corps. It was eight pages of single-spaced type containing the principles and maxims on which he himself modeled his actions.

Commanders will train the troops they lead into action. This is a principle which must never be departed from, and nothing in the following instructions, the object of which is to co-ordinate policy and system and so to arrive at uniformity of doctrine, is to be held to relieve Commanders of their initial responsibility . . .

The object of all training is to create a "Corps d'Elite," that is a body of men who are not only capable of helping to win this war, but are determined to do so. It cannot be emphasized too often that all training, at all times and in all places, must aim at the cultivation of the OFFENSIVE SPIRIT in all ranks . . .

The requirements were "a high Efficiency and a high Moral" — plus mental alertness and bodily fitness, discipline, organization, and skill, pride, smartness, and prestige. Lessons must be explained, demonstrated, and carried out as an exercise. Instructions must be interesting. Work requiring brain power should be followed by work entailing physical exertion.

Order is best cultivated by carrying out all work on a fixed plan. Order is the foundation of discipline. Small things like marching men always at attention to and from work, making them stand at attention before dismissing them, assist in cultivating steadiness and discipline . . .

It is an essential part of training for war that the men are taught to care for themselves so as to maintain their physical fitness. To this end the necessity for taking the most scrupulous care of their clothing, equipment and accoutrements will be explained to them.

The importance of obedience to orders will be impressed on all ranks and prevention of waste rigorously enforced . . .

The men must understand that the skill they gained during training would have a result on their lives as well as on the battle. Instruction was not a matter of getting through a definite subject or time period, but of employing time to the fullest advantage.

"Tactics are the foundation of all training, for training has as its object the preparation of the soldier for war." Realism in training must always be sought, for "the value of training is greatly enhanced if the men's interest can be roused."

The principles Patton enunciated in these papers were fundamental to him. On them he staked his career, his hopes, his desires as a soldier.

Writing to Major Daniel D. Pullen — who had defeated Patton in the broadsword tournament finals at West Point, who had been captain of the football team, and who had graduated in the class after Patton's — he asked for suggestions on improving his map course. After explaining his training program in some detail, he concluded, "This keeps everyone pretty well occupied and I have had only one drunk inspite of pay day."

He told Beatrice he hoped to have some tanks soon, though "It will be the greatest surprise in history if I do." He had moved into a new office "in my town," had his adjutant and quartermaster in the same room and his sergeant majors in an adjoining room. "I feel just like Col Pitcher," the post commander at Fort Sheridan.

He closed on what was for him a normal comment: "I have got this place so well organized now that there is nothing for me to do and I am getting nearvous again."

CHAPTER 25

Bourg

"Some times it seems to me that all I have ever done has been in preparation for my present job."

Diary

March 19: "Got telegram from B congratulating me on promotion to Lt. Col. Have not heard of it yet."

Letter, GSP, Jr., to Beatrice, March 19, 1918

I am not so hellish young and it is not spring yet still I love you just as much as if we were twenty two on the baseball grand stand at W.P. [West Point] the night I graduated . . .

I fear he [Willie Horton who had written to ask whether there was a job for him in France] is suffering the fate of rats who cling too long to a sinking ship. He could have come earlier but yearned for the "Flesh pots" of Washington. Still I owe him so much that I will do all I can to help him out . . .

[Tate was living in his house, and Chaffee and Haverkamp were in Langres, together with a lot of other classmates and friends, but] as I am out here [in Bourg] all day I don't see a great deal of them . . .

If I am a lt Col. I have surely gone some and feel like an imposter though dangerous modesty is not one of my many faults.

Well this is the second letter I have written you to day. I only wish it were not necessary and that I could hold you in my arms and squeeze you. I have almost forgotten how soft you are even with corsets on to say nothing of your softness in your wedding nighty. I love you so B.

Letter, Pershing to Mr. Patton, March 19, 1918

George is looking well and seems to be very well satisfied with his new job with the tanks.

Letter, GSP, Jr., to Beatrice, March 20, 1918

Darling Love (Beatrice) I add the parenthesis for fear you might think you were reading a letter to some other lady of my acquaintance. That shows how careful I am even in small details. I have been sitting around all day like an expectant mother waiting the advent of a child in the shape of a train load of tanks but thus far there have been no premonitory symptoms.

Still if the things did get here on time it would probably upset the entire French nation and they would declair a public holiday to celebrate the first occasion on which they were ever on time. Not that we have any thing to boast of in that reguard either.

Some times it seems to me that all I have ever done has been in preparation for my present job. As an instance some of the men could not visualize a contour so I made a mineature hill out of a potato and cut parallel horizontal slices out of it the way Gen. F. C. Marshall [his first company commander at Fort Sheridan] used to do in "K" Troop years ago. And then as now it worked.

I suppose however that in any exact science like war the same would be true and that genius as Napoleon put is is simply memory of detail. I have a hell of a [good] memory for poetry and war.

We are going to have a track meet here on Saturday . . . By having track meets we make the men exercise with out their knowing it.

I have just heard over the phone that the tanks have left Paris so they should be here tomorrow night.

Before the tanks arrived, he received a cablegram from Mrs. Ayer. Beatrice's father had died. Patton wired sympathy to Beatrice and her mother, then wrote Beatrice a fine and sensitive letter.

. . . it is with out question a direct interposition of Almighty God that this war made it necessary and possible for you to be with him for had it not occured you would have been in the Phillippines and absent at the time so priceless to him.

It is a great source of pleasure and pride to me that Mr. Ayer who is the most perfect mortal I know of took an interest and pride in my present work, and his last letter to me will ever be an inspiration to me in this or any other work.

Beatrice Jr and Ruth Ellen should be wonderful children with such a grandfather.

Fearing that Beatrice's sister Katharine would feel guilty over being away from home when her father died, he wrote to his brother-in-law, who was with the State Department in London and toward whom Patton never felt close. "My dear Keith . . . I feel sure she [Katharine] almost sacrificed her love for you in order to stay with her family." But he knew that Mr. Ayer was delighted with Kay's marriage and happy that all his children were happily married.

Especially Kay who had given up so much for him and for Ellie [Mrs. Ayer]. Tell Kay how much I sympathize for her but that I also envie her the satisfaction she must feel in having been such a fine daughter and unfailing source of comfort to her father. I hope she is reconsiled to her absence [from home] and my personal opinion is that her duty is to stay with you but that is none of my d—— business.

Letter, Pershing to GSP, Jr., March 23, 1918
My dear Patton. Please accept my sincerest sympathy for yourself and family especially for Beatrice and her mother in the great loss that has come to them . . . I have cabled to Mrs. Ayer . . .

I am getting sane letters from Anne again and suppose she is over her rage — poor girl, it is hard for her to be anything but open and frank, so I can fully appreciate her abhorrence at anything that looked like subterfuge.

I was sorry you did not have a tank to show the secretary [Mr. Baker] the other day.

Glad to see you looking so well — the trip around with the secretary did me a lot of good, and I have started to ride every day — hope to keep it up.

Sincerely

Letter, GSP, Jr., to Beatrice, March 23, 1918
There is a strange thing that happened on the seventeenth. I was most restless and worried and all the people at the mess noticed it. I thought of you every moment and longed to be with you more than usual which is always a lot.

Of course I don't know when your father passed away. Think it must have been about then. Although at the time of your operation I did not have similar feelings.

Patton suggested to Rockenbach that cutaway models of the parts of the tank engine be furnished to facilitate instruction — specifically, to show the workings of the valves, the camshaft, the oil pump, pistons, spark plugs, carburetor, and so on. One model of each was sufficient because "it is my opinion that after july we will have enough wornout tanks to supply similar models to each battalion if it becomes advisable." He had sent Lieutenant Baldwin to Nevers to get some spare parts, and he requested authority to do so whenever necessary in the future so that at least the driver could draw his two dollars a day — per diem pay — for being away from his home station.

Pershing cabled the War Department on March 22, saying that Patton was the "best qualified officer to command light tank centers, due to previous experience." Pershing renewed his recommendation, initiated earlier by Rockenbach, for Patton's appointment to Lieutenant Colonel, Tank Corps.

On March 23, ten light tanks, so long anticipated, finally arrived at Bourg. They reached the Langres-Marne railroad station about 3 P.M., and Patton arranged to unload them opposite the Bois d'Amour, his training area at Bourg. The train moved to that place at 8:40 and stopped at unloading platforms that Patton had had constructed. All the tanks and spare parts were taken off without accident, and the tanks were run under their own power to the tank park at the center, then camouflaged in the wood. By midnight, the entire operation had been completed. Three tailboards on the flat cars were slightly damaged, but no other injury to the railroad was discovered.

The tanks were in excellent condition, although they lacked jacks, weapons, and turret foreplates for guns. Patton requested Rockenbach to have these deficiencies remedied at once. He called attention to the excellent work performed by all the officers and men who helped detrain the tanks, especially Borland, the Supply Officer of the 1st Light Tank Center.

Diary

March 23: "I backed seven [tanks] off the train and Lt. Baker the other three."

Later versions of the episode had Patton driving all the tanks off the train because he was the only one who had ever seen a tank. After nine of the most experienced drivers were shown the gearshift — it was dark by then — they drove the tanks to the Bois d'Amour, a mile away. "This shows the adaptability of the American Soldier, for totally inexperienced as they were, they drove the tanks by night . . . over two kilometers and landed them without accident at the designated point."

Diary
March 24 (Sunday): Moved tanks into sheds and arranged to have them oiled Monday.

Letter, GSP, Jr., to Beatrice, March 24, 1918
The Tanks are here. Ten of them . . . The french were much impressed [with our unloading] as they said it would take us 15 hours and we did it in just three.

It was a beautiful moonlight night and ideal for the purpose. When the procession of ten started across the fields I was delighted as I have been living on hopes for the last four months.

They certainly are saucy looking little fellows and very active. Just like insects from under a wooden log in the forest.

No one but me had ever driven one so I had to back them all off the train but then I put some men on them and they went along all right. I took one through some heavy woods this morning and it just ate up the brush like nothing.

Tomorrow they will all be oiled up and we will start active business making drivers on Tuesday. It will be fine having something to work with as up to now I have had one old truck [the Atlas] . . . and had to teach all about driving with it . . . I am a little tired to day due to excitement I suppose but am feeling fine.

It was just as well, to help get over his excitement, that he had to take the train to Paris that Sunday afternoon to get his car, which he had left to be repaired. He reached the city in the midst of an air raid. On the following morning, long-range German guns put shells into Paris every fifteen minutes between seven and ten, "but no one paid any attention to it as the chances of it killing any particular person are so small." The shells did little harm because they carried little explosive. The range was said to be 120 kilometers, and the hits were well grouped, most of them near the Gare de l'Est. "It is a hellish affair but a great scientific achievement. Just think of shooting a gun 75 miles and hitting even so large a target as the city of Paris."

Returned to Langres, he assured himself that the tanks were well oiled.
He trained eight men quickly so they could act as instructors in driving.
He arranged a schedule designed to teach, in three weeks, 96 men and 3
officers to drive the tanks and fire the guns.

Letter, GSP, Jr., to Beatrice, March 26, 1918
   My tanks are going full blast this afternoon and I feel very cheerful
over the prospect of getting something done. Of course I have only a
few [tanks] but they are much better than none . . . It is wonderful
how fast the men pick up driving tanks. They will learn it 50%
faster than the French do I feel sure.

He had the tanks working ten hours each day to instruct the men not
only how to operate them but also how to keep them in repair. The latter
would prove somewhat difficult for the tank center was initially short of
monkey wrenches and screwdrivers.

Diary
   March 27 (Wednesday): Started schedule; things did not work
well. Examined the nearby village of Brennes as possible location for
the tank center.

Letter, GSP, Jr., to Beatrice, March 27, 1918
   [Sends letter from Pershing about Mr. Ayer's death, which] was
certainly a nice thing to do . . . the last tribute of the greatest
American soldier to the greatest American civilian. It is a rare priv-
lage for little people like me to have two such associations. I hope I
may be worthy of the good thoughts which I flatter my self these two
men have had of me.
   To day however I hardly feel like I was worth much consideration
as I have been having the duce of a time making things go and one of
the two trucks broke down right in the middle of the morning . . .
   [The YMCA opened a canteen for the men, and he was pleased
because there were no amusements in town.] The only advantage is
that they are working so hard that they go right to bed . . .
   [No disease and hope to keep it out, which is easy if the men take
proper precautions.] Of course I know that your remidy would be
but I don't approve of that as men who are apt to be killed are entitled to what pleasures they can get even if they are not considered
shick [chic] by some.

Letter, GSP, Jr., to Mrs. Ayer, March 28, 1918

We are now wearing a gold V on our left sleeves to show that we have been in the zone of the armies for six months. I wonder how many we will have on before we get through this business? If we get wounded we wear the same on the right arm for each wound. I would like to be hit in some nice fat part so I could get one.

Patton reconnoitered another piece of ground nearby at Brennes, twenty minutes' marching time from a proposed railroad siding in Bois St.-Georges-le-Gros. It would be suitable for establishing billets and training facilities for additional Tank Corps units.

He had six tanks working in training exercises, but firing the tank guns proved a complication, for the French were afraid of stray bullets.

Letter, GSP, Jr., to Beatrice, March 28, 1918

All my present officers are former soldiers [enlisted men] and have no push at all. I have to keep kicking them to get any speed out of them and it is rather a bore and very hard work . . .

Col. Rockenbach is realy fine and does not bother me at all and we get on quite well all things considered especially his reputation [as a difficult man to work with].

He received a letter from Brigadier General F. C. Marshall, his first troop commander at Fort Sheridan, who thanked Patton for the stars — insignia of rank — that Beatrice had sent him upon his promotion to general officer rank.

Patton thanked Beatrice for doing so, saying it was "very thoughtful and like you to do it."

Marshall's letter, sent from the 165th Field Artillery Brigade, Camp Travis, Texas, reproached Patton lightly, but seriously nonetheless, for having gone into the tanks. "I wish you would get out of vadevile [vaudeville] and get into the legitimate — you ought to be preparing for a high command, which you will surely get, if the war lasts long enough, and you have not specialized too much."

Patton was far too busy to answer Marshall immediately. Perhaps he was somewhat displeased that his old company commander should try to throw cold water on what was rapidly becoming a growing enterprise. The Tank Corps overseas was supposed to have more than 15,000 officers and men, including one brigadier general, 4 colonels, 10 lieutenant colonels, 34 majors, 119 captains, 249 first lieutenants, and 505 second lieutenants — not a bad opportunity for an ambitious man.

He had to abandon his training schedule in order, as he noted in his diary, to "groom the tanks," for Rockenbach was bringing Major General W. M. Black, the War Department Chief of Engineers who had come to France with Secretary Baker, to visit the center. To get ready, Patton was in and out of everything. Once when he was under a tank to inspect its bottom, he received about a pint of black oil in his face. After getting cleaned up, he demonstrated how the tank should be operated, and he drove one through some heavy woods to show its power.

Rockenbach had, as requested, obtained Captain Sereno E. Brett for the tanks, and Brett reported in. Patton was pleased to have him at the center helping him run things.

By then he had 98 men in Company A, 99 in Company B, 59 in Company C, and an unspecified number in the battalion headquarters. An additional 23 noncommissioned officers, 6 mechanics, and 30 privates were unassigned. Three more men were under orders to join and had yet to arrive.

Patton suggested to Rockenbach that sufficient privates be obtained to complete Company C and the battalion headquarters. He had enough noncoms and private-specialists. Since 100 light tanks to be constructed in the United States had been promised for delivery to the eastern seaboard by April 15, he suggested that Rockenbach ask for deck space so that the tanks could be shipped to France and put into service at the earliest possible date.

Letter, GSP, Jr., to Pershing, March 31, 1918
I have ten tanks here now and eight of them work every day from eight fifteen A.M. to five P.M. I would consider it an honor if you could inspect them some day. If you would let me know in advance I could arrange a small maneuver for you. I regret that they did not arrive in time for Mr. Baker's inspection. I have had very good accounts of my family especially of Anne. I have as yet no details as to the death of Mr. Ayer. Very respectfully.

A group of celebrities visited his tank center, were curious to see tanks in operation, and seemed much impressed with the show Patton put on.

Donald M. Call, who had volunteered for the tanks, who would later be commissioned, and still later be awarded the Medal of Honor, recalled immediately after the war that when he arrived in Bourg he

found things rather discouraging. The Tank Corps was just beginning to take shape and there were many hardships to go through before things really became organized. There were ten little French tanks and most of the time was spent cleaning and repairing them.

On April 1, Patton visited the dentist in Chaumont and had several teeth filled. He went to Pershing's house for dinner. When General Harbord entered the dining room and saw Patton, he said, "Hell oh Colonel." General Alvord, the adjutant general, came in behind Harbord and confirmed Patton's promotion to Lieutenant Colonel, Tank Corps, National Army, as the result of a message just in from the War Department. The AEF order formally announcing the promotion would be issued two days later.

"I feel more or less a fool being a colonel," he informed Beatrice, "but it will wear off . . . How do you feel being a Mrs. Colonel. We never thought to reach it so soon did we."

His old headquarters troop at GHQ AEF had grown to a battalion of about 2000 men, so he would have been promoted even had he remained with Pershing. But he had no regrets. He was working his men very hard and keeping them very military.

As a matter of fact, he was working his ten tanks so hard that they required more than normal attention. He asked Rockenbach to transfer two first lieutenants who were skilled mechanics to the tank center. Then he changed the training schedule to get even more men at work.

Letter, GSP, Jr., to Beatrice, April 3, 1918
Darling Beat: I got your letter about the horses and at once wrote Pa to sell Cotton but to keep the rest even if it does cost something. I would rather have them and the ponies will be all right for polo even in a couple of years. Though I hope to ride them before that. I would rather kill both Mugador and Spy than to sell them and have them abused. They have both been very honest horses and I owe them something better than the bone yard or the plow . . .

Gen P. had a hell of a time getting me promoted as they said I was too young but he finally put it over.

. . . I wish you would send me a couple of pair of silver leaves [lieutenant colonel's insignia] and send Col S. D. Rockenbach a pair of nice silver stars with his initials on them and the words "Tank Corps."

He will be a B.G. [Brigadier General] in a few days.

I am keeping my gold leaves as I will need them ten years hence when I get to be a major again. At least Williams [my striker] thinks so for he put all my Captain's pins carefully away for future use.

Of course all that depends on the length of the war.

Well there is nothing but the usual thing to say — I love you.

He sent Rockenbach a rough drawing of a device — probably something like a compass — to help a tank crew orient the tank toward its objective when under heavy fire. It was Captain Brett's invention "and is in my opinion mechanically practical and of great value more especially to the Liberty type tank where the visibility [from inside the tank] is bad." He recommended that Rockenbach examine it personally, and that, if he thought it useful, he refer it to the proper source for production. No one at the tank center was capable of making the necessary mechanical drawings, but perhaps someone in the AEF Engineer Section could do so under Brett's direction.

Enough new men arrived to complete Company C. He found the men good, the noncoms poor. They were all somewhat "wild," he wrote Beatrice, but they would soon be put into proper shape.

Am as busy as can be but have to hang around an office too much to suit me . . . It seems funny to think that so short a time ago we thought a Captain was some pumpkins — and will think so again?

Saturday, after the usual personal inspections, he supervised the cleaning of the tanks — they were probably the most immaculate in the world — and worked on plans for a platoon maneuver. He also wrote a formal letter notifying a lieutenant that he was confined to town for two weeks as punishment for an infraction of the rules.

Memo, GSP, Jr., to First Lieutenant Will G. Robinson, April 6, 1918, subject: Absence.

In the military service there can be no hazy uncertainties. Your excuse for your absence comes under that category. Owing to the fact that your service thus far has been excellent, I will not take the action I at first contemplated but will resort to disciplinary measures here. You will not leave the town of Bourg except on a military duty until after retreat at Saturday, April 20, 1918.

Letter, GSP, Jr., to Beatrice, April 8, 1918

[Training] is certainly a cut and dried business and takes a long time to arrange but then this war is not a sparkling affair and so many officers are inexperienced that we have to definately prescribe each seprate movement.

Letter, GSP, Jr., to Beatrice, April 9, 1918

Col. R was down yesterday and was most complimentary and pleased. He threatens to recomend me to be a [full] colonel. I hope he waits a while or people will accuse me of using "influence." But I guess there is little danger of any ones taking him seriously.

I work pretty hard but seem to do so little. Still I have some fine men under me and they are very soldierly.

That afternoon he received a telegram from Beatrice telling him that her mother had died. His letter to her in reply was sensitive and compassionate, all that a letter of heartfelt sympathy could be. In part, no doubt, to divert her thoughts from her mother, in part to express his own deeply felt emotion, he concluded: "I do not think I would care much about keeping on if you were gone. Because if you were not around to admire what I did what the rest thought would make little difference to me."

He phoned Collins and asked him to see whether Pershing would send Beatrice a telegram of sympathy.

On the same day, he received from Beatrice a letter devoted mostly to her father, who had died two weeks earlier. Patton wrote into his diary:

[Mr. Ayer] often read my letter to him saying that his letter to me had decided me to enter the tanks. Last letter he got was one from B announcing my promotion to Lt. Col. He said now that George has his start he will go higher.

Letter, GSP, Jr., to Beatrice, April 11, 1918

It is a source of great pride and joy to me that he [Mr. Ayer] took such an interest in me and I am so glad that the news of my promotion reached him.

Of course he knows what is going on now too but to have had him express his satisfaction in words is fine. I hope his prophicy will come true.

If the war lasts long enough to give me a chance I shall try to justify his opinion . . .

I wish I could be with you [now that her mother was gone] but hope that mama and nita were. They are so solid and natural that I feel sure they would have been a great comfort.

He wrote a long and grateful letter to Colonel Draine, Ordnance Officer of the Tank Corps in Paris, who was helping to expedite shipments of men and matériel to the tank center. He thanked Draine for having sent several replacement depot officers to visit the center, for "Now they know by personal observation just what we are up against. And it is some problem" — meaning it was difficult to find qualified men for the tanks. Captain G. D. Sturdavent, president of the Grant Six Auto Company and a first-class engineer, had come for a few days, and Patton had profited from his advice. Sturdavent was taking to Paris a list of parts and tools needed at the center, and Patton hoped that Sturdavent could return to help him from time to time. Could Draine push the shipment of the first hundred tanks from the United States — or any part of them? He hoped that Draine would at least prod Rockenbach, who

has much more respect for your views than for mine. Please follow example of the British at Cambrai and [in the legendary words of General Elles] do your damnedest.

Of course if the tanks come equiped so much the better but tanks tanks and yet more tanks with or without guns are what we want to train our men on. . . .

It is I hope useless to add that I look forward to a visit from you as soon as possible.

Letter, GSP, Jr., to Beatrice, April 13, 1918

The men of this command are certainly a fine lot and work like the duce. We work saturdays the same as other days and have inspection on Sunday so they don't get much time off . . .

right now I am more like Henry Ford than a soldier only my product is Tankers instead of cars. I think that I might have been a manufacturer if I had put my mind on it but I am glad I did not. Because you might never have married me if it had not been for my brass buttons?

His chest and forehead had been itching for several days, but he entered the hospital only after Captain Joseph Viner reported for duty at the tank center and assumed some of his burdens. He remained in the hospital for three days, staying in bed with a wet dressing applied to his chest, for what the doctors diagnosed as "dermatitis veneneta on anterior chest and left of brow."

Pershing sent a telegram of condolence to Beatrice, adding, "I hope Anne is with you to comfort you."

He also wrote to Patton to express his sympathy for the loss of Beatrice's mother, a hard blow coming so soon after the death of her father.

Patton replied, thanking the general for his kind letter.

There is one good feature connected with the death of Mrs. A[yer] namely that now Beatrice will be able to stay in California [with his parents] which will be a comfort to both she and Anne. Mrs. A's health was so bad that she would have been a constant worry to her self and family so that my statement is not as heartless as it sounds.

Talking his way out of the hospital, he rushed to Bourg to watch a maneuver he had planned. He had secured the cooperation of a battalion of the 16th Infantry, and infantry and tanks were to participate together in a practice attack to seize trenches in the Bois d'Amour and the Bois-sur-Marne, small wooded areas near Bourg.

Diary

April 16: Maj. J. F. Hughes Morris who was to command the infantry got mad at not being met so went home. Maneuver worked out fine.

Letter, GSP, Jr., to Beatrice, April 16, 1918

We had our first tank manuver to day and I came out [of the hospital] to direct it. It went fine better than I had hoped.

I had to have some of my men act as infantry but they did not do well as they had no training [in infantry tactics] . . .

One of my cannon blew up . . . but did not hurt any one much though it scared a lot [of people] pretty well.

This was the beginning of a series of exercises, maneuvers, and practice movements in simulated combat. Patton wrote and supervised the preparation of field orders, instructions, movement directives, and the like, to cover a variety of problems and combat situations. Typical of Patton was a thoughtful detail: "On leaving Bourg, each tank will carry 10 gallons gasoline on its tail in order to start fight with full tanks." It was all very serious.

Patton was finally able in mid-April to reply to his former troop commander, General Marshall, who was at Camp Travis, Texas. He was delighted to get Marshall's interesting letter and to know that he liked his job, and that he had received Patton's letters. "I know how deep your interest must be in the present great battle" — he was referring to the Ludendorff spring offensive, by which the Germans hoped to crush the French and British before the Americans could put a trained army in the field —

and wish that I could tell you about it but I cant for the very good reason that I know nothing and that if I did I could not tell. It is a great effort on the part of the Bosch but in my opinion it is not as so often stated his "Swan song." He is not so badly off in the way of resources as we could hope. Nor have the losses all been on his side . . . There was a brief period of very fine open war and had it not been for the magnificent work of the cavalry of the allies he [the enemy] might have made a hole [through the Allied defenses]. One french division in particular made a most stupendus march and then formed a line dismounted and fooled him [the enemy] into thinking that infantry supports had arrived. This was facilitated by the fact that the Bosch was out of the air [had been denied reconnaissance by planes, either because of bad weather or Allied air supremacy]. So [the Boche] could not tell what was in front of him . . . The bosch cavalry seems to me to have been too cautious. I believe that in their place I would have gone through. The tanks were caught with their pants down owing to their being in the act of changing equipment so did not do so well as could have been hoped. This proves my contention also that the big tank is like a very heavy gun and is also only good for a prepared assault. The light tank on the other hand with its mobility can act like field guns . . .

we have a great general and a great army and when it all gets here he [Pershing] will use it like Gen. Grant would have. I hope to God that I will be in at that time. It will be a great day and some show . . . I was offered the chance [for tanks] when no one else would take it just before [the battle of] Cambrai and it was better than any thing in sight. It gave me a chance to get off the staff. I staid awake all night debating the problem and finally put the pros and cons on a piece of paper and added them up. It seemed to me that the pros had it so here I am. Now I must see it out. I have got a fine outfit and work Hell out of them. In twenty days with only four guns and ten tanks I qualified 88 men who had never seen a tank as drivers gas engine expirts gunners M.G. [machine gun] and 37 mm. [gun] signalers and pistol shots. The British with all the facilities in the world take a hundred days. But then they take tea also. We work from six A.M. to five P.M. and have school at night. We do it saturdays too and have full pack inspection on Sunday. God forgive me [for being so tough on the men].

After the war I am never going to work for a month and then start getting ready for the next [war].

I am inclosing a pistol course which I made up. It is good for quick results and takes no machinery as the men can see the holes [in the targets]. Putting men on fatigue who fail to qualify is also a great insentive. One thing about being over here no one watches you and you can go to hell or heaven in your own way. So long as you do something and get results. I think I have.

I must stop now and get up a lecture for to night. I have 66 officers under me here and nearly two battalions. I will eventually have three, and 116 officers.

With sincere reguards to Mrs. Marshall and Mrs. Page. I am Most sincerely

On April 19, Colonel Maxie brought a battalion of men — students attending various schools in Langres — to Bourg for a rehearsal with Patton's tanks for a tank-infantry maneuver.

Letter, GSP, Jr., to his father, April 19, 1918

This drive [the Ludendorff spring offensive] that is now on is pretty bad but we all hope that it will be stopped eventually and that it will take all the blood out of the Bosch. Still the english have been very roughly handled. Unfortunately we have no tanks so I am out of it though there is consolation in the thought that there are very few Americans enjoying it either. The regiment I would have been in had I gone to the infantry is one of those at it now. That ought to please Mama.

We just got through our first Tank [tank-infantry] maneuver a few moments ago. It worked out fine and we are all very pleased with our selves. It is a very complicated affair to get all the guns and infantry and tanks to the same place at the same time and as I had to write all the orders I was delighted to find how well they worked out. The directing tank got to the first trench with in ten seconds of the time I had planned it would. Of course there was no one shooting at it but on the other hand none of the crews had ever seen a tank on the last day of March and they were the result of my personal effort so I was very proud of them. In fact the Lt. commanding came over [to France] in the Headquarters troop with me. I made him a sergeant then a Lt. and finally a tanker so he is my personal property as much as a man can be.

Sylvia [his horse] thinks the tanks are some new sort of racing animal. She is not afraid of them but snorts in contempt when she passes them as if in derision of their lack of speed. Sim [his horse] wont even get out of the way. They are very sensible horses.

I have had the itch for about a week and had to go to the hospital to get it cured but it is all but well now . . .

With much love to all. Your devoted and disgustingly safe son

Letter, GSP, Jr., to Beatrice, April 19, 1918

Lt. Boland does not belong to the class of society who give dances at the Somerset. He was a sergeant of C.A.C. before the war.

Stanley R.[umbough] is better than he used to be but pretty much of an ass just the same.

We do have games in the athletic period running, jumping, shot putting, hurdle races, rope climbing, socker foot ball, and boxing. We can't play regular foot ball because it is too hard to get clothes and we could not store them if we had them. We also have baseball.

B. Jr had better not be too stuck on being a Miss Colonel as I will probably go back to a Captain after the war.

As I have frequently told you I am not in the battle and very few Americans are . . .

P.S. Here are two poems I wrote in the Hospital. Please don't throw them away. What do you think of them.

Letter, GSP, Jr., to Beatrice, April 19, 1918

I have traveled far and fast since [Mexico] . . . I miss you more all the time and long so to see you but I guess there is little use hoping for any thing but the end of the war. If the Bosch keep on as they are doing the end may come sooner than we want [by] a d—— sight. But I feel sure that they will be stopped and chased the other way shortly. Of course this is the time for them to do their damndest and they are. We can't do a thing for a while yet but will make a fine show when we get started.

Letter, GSP, Jr., to Beatrice, April 20, 1918

We got the parts [probably meaning weapons] for our tanks this morning and now look quite war like on a small scale.

The big hospital at G. H. Q. is giving a dance tonight quite shick [chic] with invitations and I am going. It will get me to thinking about something besides Tanks if it is only corns for all the nurses dance horribly.

Letter, GSP, Jr., to Beatrice, April 21, 1918

The dance last night was lots of fun. We danced till one o'clock and the party was still going on when I left.

I had a letter from Braine [who was in the United States trying to expedite the production and shipment of light tanks] to day saying he had seen [her brother] Frederick and hoped to see you. He also was most discouraging about the tanks but I hope he is pesemistic asto when they will get here. We could use them right now. He needs more money than his travel allowance to see all the people and get things moving so I am going to write him to call on Frederick for a thousand dollars if he needs it. He would be more apt to ask Fred than you and you if he takes it can deduct it as war bonds . . .

We are going to have a big show in the morning. I inclose some of the dope [orders, memoranda, and other papers] in various letters as it comes to hand. You can Peace [piece] the thing together as it is only a problem. It is all right to send it to you and I feel sure it will interest you.

I love you.

The letter from Braine to Patton was a long report. Ordered to Washington on tank matters, Braine had loaded a tank turret, a 37-mm. gun, several tank cannons and mounts, and other pieces of equipment on a train bound for the port of St. Nazaire, then had his things put on a ship. With that as the only cargo and he the only passenger, he sailed to New York.

He obtained a tugboat and unloaded his matériel at Governors Island. He took the train to Washington, where he had difficulty finding the proper ordnance office. He finally saw Colonel Alden, whom he had met in England, and gave him the blueprints of the 37-mm. gun that Patton wanted.

Braine returned to New York, hired a truck, and moved the model gun from Governors Island to Washington. He traveled to Dayton, Ohio, by fast train, taking the turret and turret drawings, plus a list of changes Patton wanted made in the tank. "They were waiting for this information so as to get this turret job into production."

Back in Washington, Braine attended a conference on the truck-and-trailer idea for transporting tanks, then consulted with the Engineer Office on building and producing a machine-shop truck.

After going again to Dayton to answer questions on the turret, Braine proceeded to Detroit to offer guidance on the tank transmission and to try to convince the manufacturer to publish a book of maintenance instructions.

Off to Cleveland, he inspected a sample or mock-up of the tank to be manufactured in the United States.

It would probably be, he estimated, three or four months before tanks were actually in production, longer to get them built and forwarded for shipment overseas. He was attending a production meeting that day of all the manufacturers who were making different parts of the tank. He expected to leave that evening for Chicago and Harvey, Illinois, to see the motor. He would then go on to Peoria and Rock Island.

This is just a hurried line to give you some idea of what I am trying to do, and I believe they will try to keep me over here, but I do not see what good I can do after getting a general line on the whole situation. Please keep me advised as to your wishes. Have been on the move every minute since I arrived, and I doubt very much if I will even get a chance to get home for a few days. Things are now as far along as I had hoped, but will do all that I can to impress upon everyone the necessity of getting some [tanks] over there as quickly as possible. Am taking it upon myself to get around and see as much as I can. This new Department, as you will see by the letter head [— War Department Engineering Bureau, Office of the Chief of Ordnance —], has just been organized; and I may never get any money for my travel and at that will never cover expenses as I am trying to get in with everybody in this whole job.

Diary

April 22, 1918 (Monday): "manuver in heavy rain. Barage of grenades. Fine show. I was much complimented both on the show and on Sylvia's looks [his horse]. About 200 officers were present. One tank fell in a hole but we got it out before five [P.M.]."

Letter, GSP, Jr., to Beatrice, April 22, 1918

Darling Beat: The show came off all right except that it was raining hard and very cold so that one tank got stuck in a shell hole but I had a reserve one ready and every thing went on fine.

We made a fake barage of grenades and burning steam and it worked fine. I was realy more than pleased.

The only accidents occured in the case of general staff officers who fell off their horses. Williams said he saw six fall off. They certainly are rotten riders. I hope you get the copies of the orders for the show as they will interest you a lot. And as I wrote them all and they are correct so you might keep them.

I am all wet and cold so will stop and change my clothes.

I love you.

The copies of the orders Patton referred to were those that defined the exercise, instructed the participants, set the objectives, and gave the starting and finishing times.

He had written to the Director of the Army General Staff College, Lieutenant Colonel A. W. Bjornstad, a few days before the demonstration to advise him that tanks would operate in conjunction with infantry, the whole supported by two battalions of artillery. Bjornstad, as Patton hoped, instructed his student officers to attend and distributed to them orders, maps, and sketches of the exercise, as well as an explanation of tank characteristics, capabilities, and organization — all furnished by Patton. After the demonstration, many student officers examined the tanks and asked questions.

It was a nice package tied to perfection by Patton, not only for training his own men but also for impressing the faculty and students at the staff college. The latter, after graduation, would be staff officers of tactical organizations and would plan attacks that, hopefully, would utilize tanks.

Across Bjornstad's memorandum, Patton later wrote: "1st Problem. Col Maxey [later] killed at Cantigny commanded the infantry in this manuver. The same tactics were used at Cantigny. GSP Jr." Still later he wrote: "I ran this show. It was the first Tank Maneuver ever held in US Army. GSP Jr." He had every right to be proud.

Several years after the war, when he wrote a humorous account of his experiences with "Tanks, Tankers, and Tactics," he referred to this demonstration, saying:

The enemy was unintentionally represented by the members of the General Staff College. These officers, for whose benefit the affair was staged, attended mounted . . . the horses objected to the tanks, and one officer was seen leaving the final objective on foot, after having been thrown five times. He held the record but the competition was close and general.

In a more serious vein, he said he was sure that the maneuver was "largely responsible in convincing a great number of the staff officers who witnessed it, of the efficiency of the light tank."

Somehow in the midst of his activities, Patton found the time to write to Pershing. He invited attention to a lecture presented under YMCA auspices by a Dr. Palmer, who had assured his listeners that the war would end in a year. Patton recommended that lecturers, both civilian and military, be prohibited from prophesying such events.

Four of Patton's officers, Brett and three others, departed to visit a somewhat inactive sector of the front near Montdidier held by French troops. Patton wanted to go too, but Rockenbach forbade it. Brett and the others were gone about a week and returned with valuable information on how the front was organized and how troops behaved in the actual presence of the enemy.

Letter, GSP, Jr., to Beatrice, April 25, 1918
They are certainly piling officers in on me and I am having a hard time putting them away but so far have managed to do it but it is like a sardine factory. This town has only room for eight and there are fifty in it and more on the way.

Still I got a compliment out of it for Col R. told his adjutant that he could send them to me as I had never kicked yet. It is the old thing of the willing horse being ridden to death . . .

[Had an amateur night for his men at the YMCA tent and some boxing matches.] I made a speech. They had a song about me which is most complimentary and says that "We will follow the Colonel through hell and out the other side."

I don't see why they like me as I curse them freely on all occasions. But the drafted man is just like the regular which is a surprise to me.

On April 28, he organized the 1st Light Tank Battalion. His three tank companies were commanded by Captains Viner, Brett, and Herman. Patton himself was the battalion commander. This position was a significant step up the command ladder.

CHAPTER 26

A Glimpse of the Front

"If a person does his best and keeps doing it it usually pays though not always."

Diary

April 29: Lt Sewell suggested that adding to the length of the tail of a tank could make it jump further and therefore cross trenches more easily. None of us had ever thought of it before. He said that it was so obvious he feared to mention it. This is an important discovery and can be done easily. Discussed the essentials of a tank with Major Champlin and wrote them out.

If lengthening a tank gave it the capacity to cross wider trenches, was this really what the designers of tanks ought to strive for? Or were other capabilities more important?

Considering these questions, Patton clarified a significant issue in tank design and grasped an essential tactic of tank warfare.

GSP, Jr., Headquarters, 1st Tank Center, Memo on the bridging of Trenches and the essential qualities of a Tank, April 29, 1918

It appears to me that the single feature of crossing very large trenches easily has so obsessed the minds of the designers of tanks that they have neglected other and more important essentials. In order to discuss this question I set down here in the order of importance the desirable features of a tank as I see them.

1. Mobility of strategic employment.
2. Speed and radius of action on the battle field.
3. Ease and cheepness of construction.
4. Command for the guns and vision.
5. Ability to cross trenches.

With these as the basic principles, Patton went on to say that the strategic mobility of tanks varied inversely with their weight. In other words, the heavier the tank, the less useful it was. "The perfect tank would travel on its own wheels" while moving over roads to the scene of combat "and mount its self on catipillars on entering battle."

This statement was a prophetic vision of the experimental model tank that designer Walter Christie would build in the 1920s and 1930s.

"From this sublime animal" capable of operating both on wheels and tracks — theoretically the most effective machine possible — conventional tanks were useful in a descending scale according to whether they could be transported on trucks or trailers, on standard railroad wagons, or solely on carriages specially built to haul them. Thus, the factor of weight was the most important element in tank construction, for the lighter the tank, the easier and faster it could move — not only in battle, but also in the approach march to the combat zone. For what good was the best tank if it could not quickly get to the battlefield?

Speed of movement, then, both strategic and tactical, was the most valuable tank characteristic, and to that end

we must reduce the vulnaribility of the tank by making it so fast that it like the [naval] cruser is hard to hit. More than this we must give it a radius of action of sixty miles. This means more gass, hence added weight which must be compensated by reductions in useless armour.

Because the tank was a special vehicle-weapon, it was expensive to build. "The perfect tank from the point of view of construction would be a converted truck. The probable tank [in the future] will be a mean between these two."

Tanks had been invented to cross trenches. But huge trenches, like those in the Hindenburg Line, were rare. There was, then, "no reason to make the crossing of such onomolies as [the Hindenburg trenches the] one determinate feature in the design of tanks, any more than it would be sensible to scrap all but huge howitzers in the artillery." In other words, there was no need to make enormous and unwieldy, consequently less mobile, tanks simply to provide a means of crossing large trenches.

Since the Hindenburg Line was a special obstacle, a special solution was better, for example, the use of explosives, which were far less expensive than "huge machines which have many unsermountable defects and the one advantage of great [trench] bridging ability."

The average trench was no wider than nine feet. Therefore, all tanks should be built to cross trenches of that size. To get across wider obstacles, a tank "should be equiped with a bomb throwing catipult and a certain number of large peterds." A petard containing six pounds of high explosive would do enough damage to any trench to allow any tank to cross. The petard, he felt

> should have a perforated outer envelope of some such substance as tin, the space between the two envelopes to be filled with a phosperous compound which would start smoking and squirting fire in three seconds after discharge, while a thirty second fuse would give the tank time to back off out of the way. The explosion would scatter the phosperous and so render the immediate passage of the tank possible.

Five bombs of this sort and the throwing apparatus would weigh about 100 pounds. But each foot added to the length of a tank — the longer the tank, the wider the trench it could cross — would add about a ton to its weight.

From a theoretical engineering point of view, a tank weighing about ten tons and able to cross a nine-foot ditch could be manufactured to go twenty miles an hour on its tracks and thirty on its wheels. Because of

> its speed the chances of its getting hit will be so reduced as to more than compensate for its reduced armour. We have the authority of Col. Fuller [of the British Tank Corps] for the statement that "Any machine which will cross nomans land and make a noise like a machine gun will be fully as useful as the biggest tank ever made."
>
> When I get a machine shop [at the tank center] I request the permission to make such a machine. I will personally bear the necessary expenses and will so conduct the work that it will in no way interfere with the training of any unit under my command.

Patton was exhilarated by his thoughts and discussions of the features of tanks, for tank design and tank tactics were inseparable. The characteristic he sought above all was speed, the cousin of mobility. Movement, maneuver, and firepower became his passions.

Several papers he wrote in May showed his willingness to reduce armor and consequently weight. Compensation for the diminished protection offered tank crews could be gained in part by designing a tank with more favorable angles and a better silhouette, in part by increased mobility.

Letter, GSP, Jr., to Beatrice, May 4, 1918
Don't worry about me. I am disgustingly safe and feel more like a slacker than a soldier.

I have made an invention which I believe is of great value and hope to be able to put it in operation shortly to the great discomfort of the Hun and his friends.

I cannot tell even you what it is but it is a slight alteration where by with an increase in weight of only 250 lbs the value of a machine is more than doubled without the least sacrifice to speed or handeness. It may be a day dream but I think not and I think not on the judgement of men far smarter than my self so far as mechanics goes . . .

I am having a parade followed by inspection this P.M. so must stop and learn my commands.

A letter from Braine prompted him to write: "I think him a very good man and expect a lot out of him when he gets back. I hope he is not so aloof as he was."

Braine was still traveling around the country, to St. Louis, Camp Colt, New York, Washington, and elsewhere, trying to bring some order to the fragmented production of tanks, tank parts, and tank guns. "Not more than twelve people working on all tank work," he later wrote, "including light and heavy, when I arrived in Washington." No tools or spare parts had been ordered. When he insisted that the tank gun be put into immediate production, he was overruled.

He was appalled by the organizational chaos in the Army. Separate groups were working on motor equipment, small arms, ammunition, explosives, cannons, machine guns, automatic weapons, equipment, and supplies, and no one had the authority to coordinate the whole.

After being in the United States three weeks, he discovered, quite by chance, that Colonel Welborn was the director of the Tank Corps in Washington. Braine went to see him and exposed the disunity in the tank program, but Welborn was powerless to weld the various and often divergent, even conflicting, efforts into a single meaningful operation.

Braine finally met Benedict Crowell, Assistant Secretary of War, and, by his description of the haphazard procedures, interested him in the problem of tank production. The arrival of Colonel Draine from Paris helped. Eventually, a civilian was appointed to take charge of the entire work. And, finally, two tanks were constructed and made ready for shipment.

It was Braine who arranged to take these to France. He had some trouble getting authority to leave the United States, for various groups had found him knowledgeable and useful, and they clamored for his assignment to them. But he persisted and succeeded in obtaining clearance.

Traveling to Cleveland, Braine secured the two tanks, personally convoyed them to port, had them loaded on a ship, and himself sailed for France with them. His two American-built tanks would arrive in Bourg and the tank center after the war was over.

Letter, GSP, Jr., to Beatrice, May 5, 1918
Did I ask you to send some sheet music for piano and quartetts of voices for the men. Not very many as there is only one piano.

Letter, GSP, Jr., to Beatrice, May 6, 1918
I am thinking of taking the General Staff course next term if I can manage it. I don't see when I will get the time but hope I can manage it as it is a most valuable course.

But I am getting nearvous. I will have to take a leave I fear or do something different. This thing of doing the same thing every day as hard as I am is getting me a little.

Letter, GSP, Jr., to the Deputy Chief of Staff, GHQ AEF, May 6, 1918, subject: Tank Tactics and Strategy
Presuming upon your interest in the Tank I am sending you herewith . . . a problem which I have gotten up as a basis for further instruction and in the hope of exciting discussion and consequent interest.

In the problem you will notice a halt of eleven minutes on the intermediate objective. Subsequent reflection on my part has convinced me that this halt is an error. The second wave of infantry supported by a line of tanks preceding them should "LeapFrog" on at once. For the reason that if they do not the enemy will have nothing on his mind except the shelling of the tanks and inft. at the intermediate objective, while if the line goes right on he will have something else to think about. Any tanks surviving the attack . . . should help mop up and then go on as fast as possible to thicken the leading line [of] tanks.

The British supports [supporting troops] follow in short columns, the French in skirmish line. I am uncertain which is the best formation and request an opinion from you.

Before the wilderness campaign Gen. Grant told the President that in his opinion the Union Army had never been fought to its limit. Please pardon my presumption in suggesting that the same is true of the Tanks.

About this time he received a letter that pleased him enormously. Captain R. I. Sasse, a cavalry officer with the 1st Division, had made four applications to transfer to the tanks but was being held because he "was needed here." He asked whether Patton could do "anything . . . toward a successful approval of my transfer." Patton would get Sasse into the tanks, and they would become close friends.

Letter, GSP, Jr., to Aunt Nannie, May 9, 1918

I am getting ashamed of my self when I think of all the fine fighting and how little I have had to do with it . . .

[Someone was recently wounded in the fleshy part of the leg.] I rather envie him as now he can wear a wound chevron and pose as a hero . . .

I have a very good place and have been frequently complimented on the good appearance of things and on the discipline of the men.

This is at least satisfying and I hope will lead to something for the good opinion of those above you is a source of great advantage.

I am very well and in no danger of any thing but getting fåt.

Letter, GSP, Jr., to Beatrice, May 9, 1918

We will not get the tanks so soon as we had hoped and that is indeed too bad. Still the "darkest hour is just before the dawn" and we may find that we are getting Tanks sooner than we had hoped.

Yesterday I was all for transferring to the infantry but now think I will not first because probably they would not let me and second because having made my bed I think the sporting thing to do is to lie in it. I have never quit yet that I know of and though it is discouraging to be kept out of the fight so long it may pay in the end. If a person does his best and keeps doing it it usually pays though not always.

Letter, GSP, Jr., to Beatrice, May 12, 1918

I was feeling very low over lack of material but some has just turned up and we ought to do fine. I will have ten times as many machines as I have now. You see luck always changes if you do your best with what you have.

I have been working on a [tactical] problem for 3 days and it is finished so I feel better . . .

Just about a year ago we were rushing around like every thing to get my dress uniforms. I have never had them on since.

Letter, GSP, Jr., to Beatrice, May 13, 1918

I fear that the tanks will not do much for many months except perhaps a few raides for practice.

When "a lot of milk toast YMCA women" came to Bourg to see the tanks, Patton put on a show for them. In the process he experimented with crossing trenches at relatively high speeds. The results were surprisingly good.

Letter, Mr. Patton to Beatrice, May 17, 1918

[Returning some of his son's papers, orders, maps, and poems.] The article on tanks is very interesting and the spelling really spectacular. He certainly misses his "Editor" . . . He was very wise when he left the Staff. What he needs is action — and I have not the slightest doubt he will succeed — He always has.

Diary

May 19 (Sunday): "Col. R came down and talked a lot but said nothing. It was very tiresome. He told me I could go to French front Tuesday."

May 20: Got ready to go. Wrote letter to B which I gave to Viner to forward in case I am killed.

Letter, GSP, Jr., to Beatrice, May 20, 1918

Of course if I am reported killed I may still have been Captured so don't be too worried. I have not the least preminition that I am going to be hurt and feel foolish writing you this letter but perhaps if the thing happened you would like it [the letter] . . .

I think I am too high ranking to be allowed to see much [of the action]. Of course you know I will try to see all I can.

Beatrice there is no advice I can give you and nothing that I could suggest that you would not know better than I. Few men can be so fortunate as to have such a wife.

All my property is yours though it is not much. My sword is yours also my pistol the silver one. I will give Sylvia [his horse] to Gen Pershing and Simalarity [his horse] to Viner.

I think that if you should fall in love you should marry again. I would approve.

I have some money here which Viner will send to you.

The only regret I have in our marriage is that it was not sooner and that I was mean to you at first . . .

If I go I trust that it will be in a manner such as to be worthy of you and of my ideals.

Kiss Beatrice Jr and Ruth-Ellen for me and tell them that I love them very much and that I know they will be good.

Beat I love you infinately.

Diary

May 21: I went home early and sat in sun to cure itch. Gave party in mess. Champagne.

Letter, GSP, Jr., to his father, May 21, 1918

I am leaving in a few moments for the French front to go with a bunch of french tanks. I am hoping that the Bosch will start something but the prospects are not good and besides I have too much rank to see any thing . . . Still there is a great deal of gas in that sector and they may get me. In order to forestall that eventuality I have left some instructions with Capt. Joseph Viner as to my affairs which of course are simple . . .

I left a box containing my dress uniforms and some other things at a fencing room . . . [in] Paris. I have told Viner about it and he will send them to B. if any thing happens. As I said before nothing will.

Patton and five of his lieutenants, Will Robinson, T. C. Brown, W. H. Williams, Nelms, and Morrison, traveled to the Montdidier-Noyons sector.

Diary

May 24, 1918: "Did not speak a word of English all day but talked incessantly."

Letter, GSP, Jr., to Beatrice, May 25, 1918

We are about six miles from the front and you can hear the guns all the time but it is simply a constant roar as there are so many guns you can't distinguish any seperate explosion. At night the sky is quite bright . . . every once in a while you can hear a machine gun above all the other noise . . . All this shooting does little harm but is supposed to worry people. I hope to get up closer for a day or two and can then tell you how it feels when it is hitting nearer.

There are manuvers here every day with Tanks . . .

The French have much less office work than [is] usual with us. This is a command of 3 battalions and it has one typewriter. At my place we have six. All busy.

The French are awfully nice and I get on fine with them. None of the ones here speak a word of English. We get on fine and tell jokes.

Still I some times wish I had gone in the fantry for there is too damned much waiting in the tanks.

Commandant (Major) La Fevre took Patton to St. Martin-aux-Bois. There was a fine eleventh-century church in the village, but "I did not look at it" — meaning he had no time to visit it. On a hill crowned by an old mill, which gave a commanding view of the German lines, La Fevre explained what troops did on entering the front, and "I wrote it all down."

Letter, GSP, Jr., to Beatrice, May 26, 1918

One interesting thing about life is that one can never tell what is going to happen. It is like fishing. You always expect a "strike" yet when it comes you have all the pleasure of surprise . . .

These people know a lot that I should know but it is like pulling teeth to get it out of them . . . They take for granted that one knows it also.

To show Patton what the front was like and, more particularly, where the French usually placed their tanks, La Fevre took Patton in an automobile through St. Martin to Menevillers. Leaving the car — it was unsafe to drive farther toward the front — they walked through a ravine, passing a battery of 155-mm. howitzers well hidden under nets. La Fevre pointed out several good positions for tanks, discussed the reasons why they were good, and talked about the best approach routes to them.

Walking along the railroad in search of additional positions, they saw two batteries of 75-mm. howitzers in action and also several German planes receiving antiaircraft fire.

Letter, GSP, Jr., to Beatrice, May 29, 1918

The French are certainly nice and do everything they can to help us. They are some soldiers too. Personally I like them much better than the British possibly because they do not drink Tea. Which to my mind is a most hellish and wasteful practice . . .

I have hardly spoken a word of english for a week and am quite surprised at my fluency. I can now easily understand conversations between Two French who I happen to overhear. Which is a test of any language.

Diary

May 30: With Commandant La F in auto at 7:30 to Godenvillers; walked along a bayou to a farm near Robescourt; 2 shells fell 100 yards from us; there were many shell holes; we crossed a field on a hill 300 to 400 yards from Bosch but they did not shoot, "which seemed to me foolish as they could have easily gotten us." Neared Ployron while it was being shelled, but when we entered, the soldiers were walking about unconcerned. Visited the Colonel and had some wine; he had a fine abri [shelter].

Letter, GSP, Jr., to Beatrice, May 30, 1918

Darling Beat: I had a most interesting morning. We The Maj. and I left here at 7:30 and went by motor to with in about 1500 yds of the front line. Most of the way the road was screened with camouflage. Sacking about 12 feet high on Frames it keeps the enemy from seeing what is on the road so he can not fire on it. In places there were shell holes in the road quite large perhaps five feet deep and 12 ft accross. We left the machine at last and armed with walking sticks tin hats and gas masks we started accross a wheat field toward the front line. (Our purpose was to locate the departure position for tanks.) The sun was shining and it was as peaceful as could be but no one was in sight. Except for long snake like trenches. Communication trenches — there was no sign of war. Pretty soon we passed some green sacking on the ground. Under it was a whole battery [of artillery] with little caves for the men. They were all asleep. At last we came to the support position about 1000 yards from our front line.

There were lots of shell holes and a whole battalion under some sacking died green to look like trees.

There were several bunches of soldiers walking about armed with walking sticks like picknickers. The guns began to shoot a little just then.

Then we went on up a hill to a farm. It was all shot to pieces. On going round the corner we saw a line of trees about 400 yds away. (The length of the avenue at Pride's.) The Maj said "There are the bosch." It was their line but not a thing was to be seen not even a trench. He said that they could see us which was quite evident so we walked along in the shadow of a hedge.

Two shells came and blew up about 100 yds away at most perhaps less. I went over to the hole and picked up a piece for you. It was still hot. I was not scared but a little thrilled. We went behind the house and you could hardly walk for shell holes but here a rise hid us from the Bosch. We came to a communication trench and I was rather hopeful we would get in it but the Maj said that the walking was better on top so we came to the top of the rise and there was our trench like a ditch for pipe with a little wire in front of it and there was the line of trees — the Bosch, 200 yds away . . .

He then said we had best be going or some "sallebut" [sale bête — dirty dog] will shoot at us. So we went down the rise to my great relief and moved behind it to a little wood where the trench was just in front of it. Here we looked for Bosch 200 yds away but none were to be seen. Behind the wood was a new grave with (Un Soldier Alemande) written on a nice wooden cross. He had been killed by a patroll this morning . . . The Maj. Paused to show me what a magnificent field of fire the Bosch had but I could not help noting that we were the only avalable target and the range was deadly. I hated to have my back to them as it would be awkward to explain a wound in the back. We went diagnally accross this field in plane view. It is the biggest field in the world I think. At least it seemed so. Right in the middle of it the maj. Stopped to fix his legging exposing his bottom in a most tempting way to the Bosch whom he assured me were watching us. To express contempt equal to his I removed my helmet and lit a cigarett. Finally we got over the ridge. Really it is funny to picture a Col and a Maj. strolling along in broad day light the only living things in sight and not a shot. One does not feel scared but has a great curiosity as to why in hell the Bosch don't shoot.

It was about the same thrill as riding a steeplechase.

As we were in the sector of an inft. Col. we knew we went to call on him. As we approached the village two french batteries in the back edge of it opened fire and shot to beat hell for about five minutes.

Then they stopped and the Bosch started shelling the village while we walked towards it. Then they stopped and when we were about 200 yds from the village the French started again. This provoked the major for he said, "Now the Bosch will be shelling back when we get there." In my mind I advocated waiting till the Bosch were through but of course did not mention it. The French stopped and just as we entered the place the bosch started we were in one street and the shells were mostly landing in the next. It was not heavy about 5 a minute. There were lots of soldiers in the place and they didnot pay the least attention but walked about smoking.

The Col. lived in an abri about 30 feet below the ground it was a fine place with bed rooms and telephones. He apologized for having no electric lights but the oil lamps were ample. We had some Ciro and talked about the war in 1914 and how much more chick it was than the present one.

The Maj said "Ah comme j'adore sette guerre de movement, c'etait passionelle. Mais celue ce est tres embetant." [Ah, how I loved that war of movement, it was exciting. But this one is every annoying.] I hope that is the way to spell what he said? All Frenchmen talk of 1914 with longing and never speak of the present "salle affaire."

When we left the col. we watched the batteries for a little while. The performance was must amusing. Every thing is covered with camouflage. The Bosch stop firing. Pretty soon the French rush out of their caves and shoot to beat hell. Then they stop and rush back to the caves . . . They keep this up all the time with out the slightest chance of hurting each other.

The major told me it was perfectly useless but necessary other wise they would forget they were at war. Once in a while they shoot at the infantry trenches but not often. Of course in an attack it is different and they stay by their guns and shoot all the time . . .

This long account gives you an idea of how safe this sort of war is. Also I have been here a year and it is the nearest I have ever been to a bosch so you see I am quite safe. Send this to Papa when you have read it as it may interest him. The whole show appeals to one as funny more than dangerous.

On Friday, May 31, Patton drove through Breteuil to a farm east of Pail-lart, where he visited a French tank unit. These tankers had made an attack two days earlier with part of the American 1st Infantry Division at

Cantigny. The Americans had lost 300 men, including Patton's friend, Colonel Maxie. Patton spoke to the tankers and learned the details of the battle. He discovered that not a single tank had been hit by an enemy shell.

Traveling to the 1st Division headquarters at Le Mesnil, Patton obtained the American side of the tank-infantry operation. He talked with Colonel King, the chief of staff, and Captain Johnson, who had commanded the assault wave of infantry working with the tanks. Johnson was "most enthusiastic" about the machines.

Patton was in Paris on Saturday and went to the theater. After a fairly lazy Sunday and Monday, he returned to Chaumont, where he had a satisfactory talk with Daniel D. Pullen, Rockenbach's new chief of staff. Patton believed that things would move along better now that Pullen was helping Rockenbach.

Then to Langres, where he found everything in fine shape, especially the mess hall, which the officers had decorated while he was gone "as a surprise for me." They had covered the walls and ceiling with camouflage burlap to which they attached branches of trees. But they had refrained from cutting the camouflage material, for they would take it down and use it when they went to war. "One has to be careful not to waste a thing and we don't."

Best of all, he learned that the Commandant of the Army Schools, "Col [Harry A.] Smith [had] said that the Tank Corps was the first [leading] unit in this district and that its smartness and enthusiasm enspired all the other units. I am well pleased as we are having a pretty hard time for not getting Tanks. Still we are doing our damdest."

Smith had complimented Patton's tank center in a memo he had issued "to all concerned":

> Too many officers and men salute as though they had creeping paralysis. All freak salutes will be avoided . . .
> The officers and men at the Tank School rank number one so far as saluting is concerned.

Smith was a man after Patton's heart, and they would become good friends.

"Capt. Viner did well while I was gone so that every thing is in fine shape." After catching up on his correspondence, Patton began translating the French tank regulations for the benefit both of himself and his officers. For several days he ran what he called a "Cook's Tour," showing people around the center and introducing them to tanks. "It is most useful as I use my well known and fatal charm to get them on my side. The last victim was the Chief of Ordnance and he is all for us." Another important visitor thought little of light tanks until he saw them at work, and then, according to Patton, went wild over them and promised to do all he could to help.

On June 6, Patton reorganized the tank center in order to accommodate a second battalion. With this larger command under him, Patton needed a larger staff. He therefore appointed Gibbs his chief of staff, Hebert his adjutant, Knowles reconnaissance officer, and Robinson supply officer. He placed Captain Viner in command of the 1st Battalion — formally named the 326th Tank Battalion (later it would be redesignated the 344th), with Company A under Compton, Company B under Weed, and Company C under English. He put Captain Brett in command of the 2d Battalion — formally the 327th Tank Battalion (later redesignated the 345th), with Company A under Semmes, Company B under Williams, and Company C under Bernard. Lieutenant Baldwin commanded the 301st Repair and Salvage Company, which serviced and repaired the tanks.

With Patton in command of this organization, he became the equivalent of a regimental commander, another significant step up the chain of command.

With two full battalions now formed, with more men and tanks expected soon, he suggested to Beatrice that she stop trying to get to England — "after all the work I have done I should hate to be sent home that way," meaning because her coming might be construed as a breach of regulations.

"Brief Notes on the Tactical Employment of Tanks," dated June 10, indicated the growing maturity of Patton's ideas of warfare, for he was now thinking of how to employ the machines in different types of operations — the assault, the counterattack, the exploitation of a success, advance and rear guards in a war of movement, raids with cavalry or special infantry units, and small, independent operations — and he described how tanks could be so utilized. For example:

We are all aware of the over cautious movements of advance guards. A few shots are fired. The point lays down and signals enemy in sight. The advance party sends out a patrol or deploys and finally perhaps even the support is involved in dislodging a squad with a machine gun in a barn or thicket. Much time is lost and the enemy has made us do just his bidding . . . Time is the great factor in war. The light tank in open war is an uneaqueled time saver.

Unarmored troops working as rear guards performed "a difficult and dangerous proceeding and most exhausting. Also there is the constant menace of being taken in flank by hostile cavalry." But a company of light tanks in this duty was something else.

Cavalry cannot hurt it as a tank has no flanks. The light tank on account of its small size can be hidden in barns thickets or rolls on the ground and from these concealed places will surely take heavy toll of the hostile advance parties . . . It will frequently be put out [of action] but that is the fate of all soldiers and it will cost the enemy untold hours in the priceless element of time.

Speaking of special operations involving a few tanks:

The hostile barrage might put out one tank on the return trip but since it costs only $8000.00 it would be much cheaper than a barrage to cut the wire . . . Besides it would be a complete surprise and hence would reduce the losses of the infantry.

It must never be forgotten that boldness is the key to victory. The tank must be used boldly. It is new and always has the element of surprise. It is also very terrifying to look at as the infantry soldier is helpless before it.

He could have been speaking of blitzkrieg in World War II, 21 years still in the future.

Letter, Will G. Robinson (Secretary, South Dakota Historical Society, Pierre, S.D.) to Lieutenant Colonel Arthur J. Jacobson, July 6, 1961

I went to France in 1917 with the 147th F.A. [Field Artillery] and one day, General Patton, then a captain, came down to Montrichard looking for an adjutant, as St Aignan nearby, was the replacement center . . . He made the Tank Corps look good to me and I got 200 volunteers from the 147th and other troops down there, truck drivers, mechanics and machine gunners and went up to B[o]urg, a little village near Longue [Langres], where the Light Tanks had their headquarters.

Not long after arriving, some Division, or the advance elements came in, I believe it was the 82nd, and they had shoulder patches. The first we had ever seen. Patton, at mess that night, said "I want you officers to devote one evening to something constructive. I want a shoulder insignia. We claim to have the firepower of artillery, the mobility of cavalry and the ability to hold ground of the infantry so whatever you come up with it must have red, yellow and blue [the traditional colors of artillery, cavalry, and infantry] in it." I was billetted with a medico, Lt. Howard and we spent all that evening with some crayons . . . in front of a fire place figuring out use of the colors and a design . . . At breakfast the next morning everybody showed up with their attempt. I guess we were the only ones that had managed to get color on ours. In any event Patton adopted our design [a pyramidal figure] and pulling [out a] $100 dollar bill, the first I had ever seen or at least held in my hand, he told me to take one of the . . . vehicles . . . and go into Longue [Langres] and get as many of our shoulder patches made up as I could get and get them back by Retreat. I managed to get the three colors in felt at the Belle Jardineer a big store on the Place Diderot and took them into a hat and cap shop next door and persuaded the old lady in charge to start her crew making shoulder patches. They did a good job of them and I had one sewed onto my overseas cap, as a possible idea of a new use of them and got two or three hundred of them out to B[o]urg before retreat.

Patton was tickled about it. If there was anything he wanted it was to make the Tank Corps tougher than the Marines and more spectacular than the Matterhorn. That triangle [shoulder patch] was the first step. A few days later he conceived the idea that our overcoats were all too long and he ordered them cut to knee length and the surplus made into belts. We were different all right.

Another indication of his unorthodox methods in some matters:

Letter, GSP, Jr., to Beatrice, June 15, 1918
I am in a little trouble my self over some Pipe I "stole" for the Center here. The Engineers are very mad at me and the inspector General is coming down to investigate the affair. I will probably get repremanded for cutting red tape but it ought not hurt me as I am

only guilty of too much initiative. Which is a quality often missing over here. Don't worry about me. The inspector . . . lived next to us at [Fort] Myer.

Brett moved his battalion to new facilities at Brennes, two kilometers from Bourg. Then Patton arranged for Viner, Brett, Gibbs, and himself to take the General Staff course at Langres.

Letter, GSP, Jr., to Beatrice, June 12, 1918
    Things are very stupid here now and I have little to do but wate and twist my thumbs. I am going to take the next course at the Staff College which starts on the 17th when I will be very busy indeed but that agrees with me more than doing nothing or only a little . . .
    I am certainly living a healthy life. I get up at six go to bed at ten and eat very simple food and drink only water. Not even Port Wine.
    I have to do a great deal of writing on regulations etc as there are none for the tanks, also being a C.O. one can have no friends and though I never much cared for them I find the total loss a little of a bore.

Sometime in June, when it became apparent that there would be no American-built tanks in France in any quantity before 1919, Pershing secured a promise from the French that they would equip two American battalions — Patton's — with Renaults.
    Meanwhile, Patton instituted night combat training and was immensely pleased when a tank company traveled 10 kilometers in just under three hours without straying once from a designated route. That the tankers were able to work through gullies and thick woods under simulated battle conditions indicated a sense of self-assurance on their part that delighted Patton.

Diary
    June 13: Col. Rockenbach came down and said that probably one battalion would get into a fight in August. "I fear we will have no such luck. But hope for the best."

Letter, GSP, Jr., to Beatrice, June 13, 1918
    [Camouflaged tanks were] awful and wonderful to behold close up though at a distance they cannot be seen at all. It is very funny how

the bright crazy colors blend with the most ordinary colors. We had one under a net the other day and some staff officers thought I was lieing when I told them that there was a tank with in 100 yds of them. They could not see it at all.

Letter, GSP, Jr., to Beatrice, June 13, 1918

One year ago to day we reached Paris full of desire to kill Germans. We are still full of desire but so far as I am concerned there are just as many Germans as there were then. Some times I deeply regret that I did not take the infantry last November instead of the Tanks. The regiment I had the chance to join has been at it now for five months. Of course I have done a lot but I keep dreading lest the war should finish before I can realy do any fighting. That would destroy my military career or at least give it a great set back.

The only cheering prospect is that there are very many infantry Battalion commanders and only a few Tank commanders.

If the war lasts long enough it will work out greatly to my advantage but the unknown is always full of terrors and I wake up at night in a sweat fearing that the d—— show is over.

I am having two much routine for my health at least health of mind.

I trust that it is doing my character a lot of good for I keep at it inspite of constant difficulties and descouragements. But unless I get into a fight or two it is all wasted effort.

CHAPTER 27

Bourg and Langres: Staff School

"I will have to develop even a meaner look than I now have but that will only be my official face."

PATTON attended the third course of studies at the Army General Staff College in Langres. It was a good experience, for he came to understand the complex duties of staff work in a modern army, and he came into contact with some of the best soldiers in France.

Brigadier General Harry A. Smith, the commandant, directed a no-nonsense operation that sought to train staff officers, by means of an extremely compressed curriculum, as quickly as possible. A French Mission headed by Colonel J. L. Koechlin-Schwartz and a British Mission headed by Lieutenant Colonel Sir T. A. M. Cunningham contributed the experience of their armies. Major John Millikin, who would command a corps in World War II, assisted. Major Adna R. Chaffee, an old friend of Patton, was an instructor. Visiting lecturers included General Trenchard, the foremost British authority on air power, Brigadier General George Van Horn Mosely, Pershing's G–4 or Supply Officer, Lieutenant Colonel George C. Marshall, who would be the U.S. Army Chief of Staff in World War II, Major Alexander M. Patch, who in World War II would command the Seventh Army during the invasion of southern France and throughout the rest of the European campaigns, and Patton himself, the leading American expert on armor.

Among those who would graduate with Patton's class were Major H. R. Bull, who would be the G–3 or Operations Officer of Eisenhower's Supreme Headquarters, AEF, in 1944–45, Major W. H. Simpson, Patton's classmate at West Point who would command the Ninth Army in Europe during the same period, Captain Joseph Stilwell, future theater commander in China and Burma, and Major John S. Wood, later the commander of the 4th Armored Division and probably the most intelligent disciple of Patton and the most vigorous exponent of his methods of tank warfare.

Although Patton had little interest in becoming a General Staff officer — he wished instead to be a commander — he worked hard at the school. He was motivated by his admiration of and respect for General Smith, who had helped and supported Patton at the tank school. He was motivated too by his professional interest in all aspects of soldiering, and he understood that the immensity of the World War had raised to unprecedented importance the role of the military administrator, organizer, and coordinator — whose functions would, many years later, be combined under the term "manager." Finally, he was motivated by the demon that drove him, his quest for perfection and attainment.

He was extremely busy, so busy that he was unable to write Beatrice as frequently or as lengthily as he wished. He was too busy even to write his normal few lines in his diary; between June 24 and August 20, he made but one entry.

There were several reasons why his time was so fully occupied. Classes at the school started at eight A.M., and the students were usually unable to leave their desks until close to five o'clock. The instructional materials were so concentrated that he marveled how "any one but a regular [officer] of considerable experience" could finish the assignments. Although he would leave the school about ten days or two weeks before the conclusion of the course and the brief graduation ceremony, he would receive credit for the entire work.

Another reason why his days were so full of activity was his continued interest in his tank center and school. He remained in close touch with what was taking place at Bourg and Brennes. In addition, he wrote and delivered lectures to his tankers, drew up drill regulations, and prescribed training exercises and schedules.

"I am now taking a cold bath at six each morning and am feeling fine."

On Monday, June 17, the day Patton started attending the General Staff College, fifteen new French Renault tanks arrived for the center. In less than an hour they were driven off the train and down the ramp and on their way to the tank park. It was a fine performance by well-trained men.

The arrival of the new tanks, giving the center 25 in all, made it possible to have company maneuvers. Patton consequently modified the drill schedule in order to have the companies, in rotation, train as a unit every afternoon, and the platoons, each in turn, work on night maneuvers every day after dark.

From seven until noon, some men from each company took driving instruction while the rest trained on the guns and practiced such activities as message writing, grenade throwing, and gas-mask wearing; from one in the afternoon to six, one company held a maneuver as a unit while the other troops worked with the pistol, learned how to assault trenches, and exercised physically. From seven-thirty to midnight, each platoon had an exercise that featured night driving.

Patton later wrote:

> The spirit of the men during all this time was most wonderful for in spite of working six days a week and having inspection on Sunday and in spite of building roads, buildings, sheds, etc. there was not the least complaint, each man and officer doing his very best each moment of the day.

Some of the lectures he was writing and delivering were on the tactical employment of tanks, the use of ten-ton trailers to move tanks, and the like. One paper, headed "Speaking Notes," consisted of 42 topic sentences, among them:

> 26. I propose instead the following method of employment —
> 27. Diagram V and VI
> 28. But in order to make these actions of the tank useful.
> 29. Here it may be permissable to point [out] a defect I have occasionally noted . . .
> 39. Now I shall take advantage of my position to respectfully propound a question to you. Is the creeping Barrage worth while. [In the later stages of World War II, it was completely eliminated — 26 years after Patton posed the question.]
> 40. Next do you give enough thought to transient targets.
> 41. Do Tanks get as much support as they deserve.

Another paper detailed a training schedule for a nine-week period — with subjects to be studied and hours to be spent listed daily, including recreation — the whole culminating in a week-long battle practice.

So well had he placed his imprint on the men under him that Major C. C. Benson, one of his officers, could himself sound like Patton when lecturing. All company officers must, Benson said firmly, "stay on the job until all machines of the convoy are in . . . Platoon Commander stays on the job until all parts of his groups are parked in camp." Command responsibility in the Patton school of thought could not be delegated.

Letter, GSP, Jr., to Beatrice, June 21, 1918

Things look pretty blue for our getting into the fight soon. We will have to go on training I fear for some time yet.

I must stop now and study.

Letter, GSP, Jr., to Beatrice, June 22, 1918

Still no mail. I know it is not your fault but that of the war. Still I miss hearing from you very much. We had another map problem to day and worked from 8 till 4 with out lunch so feel rather empty. I did not do very well as I am lazy when it comes to stupid details. Still I probably did better than many others.

Enclosed — because it was a "stupid" letter — was the one he had written on May 20 and left with Viner to send in the event Patton was killed during his visit to the French sector of the front.

He was quite tired as the result of doing double work at the college and the center, but he felt that his studies were worth the effort, for he might thereby avoid the necessity of attending the college at Leavenworth after the war. As for tank matters in general, he felt much easier in his mind knowing that Pullen was Rockenbach's chief of staff. To Beatrice he reported talk of giving him six battalions instead of four — "That will be some command. But I can handle it all right if I get the buildings, and the Tanks."

He took a break one Sunday afternoon and rode his horse Sylvia Green to Chaumont. It was a beautiful day and a beautiful ride, 40 kilometers, about 25 miles, along the poplar-lined tow path of the canal. It took him three and a half hours. There were "cows and cow girls in the green fields on both sides. Each girl had at least one soldier in attendance so I fear that more than calves will be approaching in nine months." He had dinner with Pershing, left his horse stabled in Chaumont, and returned to Langres by auto.

Beatrice was thinking again of trying to visit Kay in England, but Patton was against it — unless "you can get things arranged so as not to get me in trouble." He had a bright idea. "I think you had best get a divorce then you can come at pleasure. It realy might be a good idea?"

Letter, GSP, Jr., to Beatrice, June 27, 1918

Four of my officers got put in arrest last night for drinking publicly with women. We are getting full of virtue here. Personally I don't think much of it. The French do as they please so why not we. People who are going to be killed deserve as much pleasure as they can get. This does not mean that I am one of these pleasure seekers but that I approve of the principal.

Letter, GSP, Jr., to Beatrice, June 30, 1918

We have just come back from a most interesting experiment in driving tanks over shell holes at an artillery target range near here. There were a lot of generals and people out to see [us]. The tanks could not have done better. In fact it was as fine a performance as I have seen. Every one was very complimentary. One hole was ten feet deep and over 30 feet across. One tank got stuck in it but another one came and pulled it out in a minute.

They also raised hell with some wire entanglements and had a great time.

I am going over to the artillery school for dinner to day and so must stop and clean up a little.

Letter, GSP, Jr., to Beatrice, July 1, 1918

I am getting to be a regular devil on telephones and use them on all occasions. Remember how I used to hate them. Now I even talk french over them which is a truly great feat for me; both as a linguist or a telephonist.

The Director Army Staff College told me I was doing well. This was a surprise as I have not had time to do any studying . . .

It is remarkable how soon they [his tankers] improve with a little night work.

Letter, GSP, Jr., to Beatrice, July 2, 1918

Next time you go to Washington make it a point to see Brigadier Gen. Hugh S. Johnson who lived with me in Mexico. He is now in very close to the chief of Staff and is also a good friend of mine . . .

You could talk to him quite freely about me and might pump him about John [Pershing] but he is pretty smart so you will have to be careful on the pumping. Still I think that he is susceptable to good looks and you have them. That is one of the many reasons why I love you.

Letter, GSP, Jr., to Beatrice, July 4, 1918

[Holiday] not doing much. I did not get up till eight o'clock which is better than my usual 5:30 habit. Or rather necessity for I never want to get up and never will develop that practice . . .

I have a double sort of existence. With you and away from you. One has a time scale quite different from the other like a creeping and Fixed barrage tables.

I miss you terribly but there is no use dwelling on that as we both know it.

Letter, GSP, Jr., to Beatrice, July 5, 1918

Darling Beat: We have been having much excitement to day. The people to put in my Rail Road arrived also . . . to put in the roades and build houses so I feel like a leading manufacturer putting up a new plant. Which is in fact just what I am at present.

We also did some shell hole stunts for a large crowd of people 250 field officers. The tanks did fine and just played in and out of the holes in a most approved fashion.

It is realy inspiring to see the little beasts climb in and out of the holes in fine style even [though] I always expect them to get stuck but they never do.

See if you can find out why Col. R[ockenbach] is not made a general. He has been recomended time and again and there must be some one gumming up the game. Is it Col. Welborn [chief of the Tank Corps in Washington].

There is another hitch in the mail so I have not heard from you for some days. I love you. George.

Patton traveled to Hammel, where 60 British tanks, 10 Australian infantry battalions, and 2 American infantry companies had carried out a battle operation. He read all the orders and reports, examined the battlefield, inspected several tanks, and talked with participants — the tank brigade commander, the tank battalion commanders, many staff officers, and a few tank commanders. One senior officer explained that too many tanks had been employed on too small a front. As a result, many tanks masked other tanks and prevented them from firing. Two collided. The tanks had nevertheless been of great assistance.

Returning to Langres, Patton wrote a report of four single-spaced typed pages entitled "Tank Action at Hammel." His conclusion: "Infantry well trained with Tanks is the most powerful and least expensive answer to the German machine gun." Then he passed the paper to his battalion commanders, Viner and Brett, and asked them to study the operation and comment on it.

Letter, George to Beatrice, July 7, 1918

A tank which I have had altered will get here in the morning. It has some things on it which render it perfectly silent and it holds more men and gas. If it comes up to my expectations it will be more than twice as good as the present machine and ought to be a truly great invention which will give me prestige as an inventor.

The trouble with me is that I can do too many things fairly well and nothing hellish well and so nothing I have done is of any great use in getting me medals or decorations . . .

It is funny all we do is for the effect it will have on people later. And all I try to do is for the effect it will have on you.

In fact my attitude towards you is more that of a lover uncertain of his chances than of a husband. Still it is a good way to be.

Letter, GSP, Jr., to Beatrice, July 11, 1918

I think you would be a fool to try and do war work in addition to your other duties. There are a lot too many people doing it any way. And the work you could do would have no real value. Most of this alledged war work is realy histeria.

Col P. Echols was here to day to see the tanks. I was very nice to him though he did turn me back a year [at West Point] and keep me from marrying you that much longer.

Col R is now Gen. R having just been promoted to day. I am glad of it as it will give the T.C. [Tanks Corps] more prestige.

Letter, GSP, Jr., to Beatrice, July 12, 1918

We are going to have a map Problem [at the General Staff College] tomorrow which by all indications will be a stinker so I must stop and study it a little. This is the first time in my life I was not after tenths [of points in his school grades] as I don't want to be a staff officer and only am taking the course for general information and to have it on my record. The result is that I am doing very well indeed.

I just got orders to day to arrange buildings for 4 new battalions. That will make 8 here. I don't know whether I shall command all of them or not but I rather think I will. It will be quite a young army about 4000 men. So I will have to develop even a meaner look than I now have but that will only be my official face and not for you.

When about 50 promotions in general officers' ranks were announced, Patton told Beatrice:

the list was fine active men and we ought to do a lot with such leaders. I am afraid people of my time are out of luck. We are too young for this war and future wars will have to use up all these [old] chumps before we get a show. When we do we will be too old to accomplish much.

Letter, GSP, Jr., to Beatrice, July 17, 1918
I shall have to give a lecture to a lot of colonels here tomorrow but as I know my subject I have not the least apprehension but that I shall make a go of it.

Letter, GSP, Jr., to Beatrice, July 18, 1918
I gave a lecture to the Line School to day and five or six officers told me it was the best lecture they had ever heard over here. One said it was the best lecture he had ever heard by soldier or civilian. It was just after lunch and as people are always sleepy I got off a joke every few minutes to keep them awake. The idea worked fine and none of them went to sleep. I had a lot of notes but did not have to use them. I certainly know the subject and could talk right off which is the best way of doing. After wards I had a demonstration for them [at the tank center] and it was a fine performance.

So I feel quite elated over the day . . .

We [in the Tank Corps] will never get any recognition until we have been in a fight and showed that we could do business.

His lecture was on the cooperation between tanks and the other arms, especially infantry. "No claim is made for originality," he began disarmingly.

The ideas are simply a restatement of the ideas advanced by the French and British with some slight changes made necessary by our organization and in conformity to our desire to employ the Tanks more offensively.

There were, he said, "two very patent but none the less frequently neglected truths." These he had presented in his very first lecture — that the advance of infantry was limited by the physical endurance of men, and that the advance of tanks was limited by obstacles incident to the terrain; thus, it was futile to attack where the ground rendered tanks impotent and when infantrymen were expected to follow tanks at a speed or for a distance beyond their endurance.

Tanks in common with all other auxiliary arms are but a means of aiding infantry, on whom the fate of battle ever rests, to drive their bayonets into the bellies of the enemy.

. . . the liaison between the tanks and infantry must be of the closest. It must be worked out in the most minute detail for so complex is its nature that hazy ideas or ill digested plans will become abortive or ruinous in the excitement of the close fighting where the cooperation must be put into practice.

. . . cooperation must be more than a mere matter of routine. Tank and Infantry officers must associate and by conversation at mess and elsewhere interchange ideas and so become thoroughly conversant with all the difficulties which beset their respective arms. . . .

Infantry should enter the [barbed] wire at least fifty yards behind the tank so as not to be tripped by trailings . . . They must not crowd around a tank nor yet follow it like mourners after a hearse. If they do they may change places with the late lamented. They should move up taking advantage of the ground and probably by rushes.

It was a good performance, and it allayed any suspicion that infantry officers might have had that the members of the Tank Corps were about to usurp their missions or claim that tanks could supplant the foot soldier.

Patton was supposed to attend an officers' smoker at the club, but was pleased when he did not have to go. "Pullen was here and we were busy until late on some details caused by things having taken a turn for the better so far as Tanks are concerned."

A lecture to the students at the General Staff College restated some earlier ideas, lifted earlier paragraphs he had written, but his talk was effective.

> In order to properly impress you I shall preface my remarks with the statement that the theory of tanks or of mechanical offensive machines to overcome mechanical defensive measures, was evolved about 300 B.C. That is, during the siege of Tyre by Alexander, moving towers were first used to assault the walls which were so well made as to resist other means of attack.
>
> Now again, that inverted wall — the trench — has become too strong to be overcome by normal means of offence, and we have, once more, evolved a mechanical appliance — the tank — to crush it. . . .
>
> Considering that only 51 [of the 75 tanks in a light tank battalion] . . . go into the fight, we may appear to have an excessive reserve. This, however, is not the case. The tank is a delicate animal, and when you have got your fighting tanks tuned up and ready for action it is best for all concerned to leave them severely alone. Yet since the men must be trained other tanks are necessary, and it is here that the reserve mentioned comes in . . .
>
> The infantry win the fights, the tanks only and always help the infantry to win them. Any other theory of using tanks is utterly wrong . . .
>
> At the Battle of Juvaincourt the tanks were put in arbitrarily by the Infantry Commander, who did not take the trouble to consult the tank officers. The result was a loss of 76% for the tanks and no gain for either the tanks or the infantry. Again at Malmaison, the Infantry Commander, disregarding the recommendations of the tank officers, required the tanks to commence their attack before daylight, with the result that over 50% of the tanks became hopelessly lost in a swamp and did no good to either themselves or the infantry . . .
>
> It must never be forgotten that boldness is the key to victory. The tank must be used boldly. It is new and always has the element of surprise. It is also very terrifying to look at, as the infantry soldier is helpless before it.

Letter, GSP, Jr., to Beatrice, July 22, 1918

I got off my lecture to the Gen. Staff class this morning and it was very well received. In fact I surprised my self at my fluency of utterance but as I have been soaking in Tank dope for a long time I suppose when the plug was removed it naturally flowed out all right.

I was walking around inspecting things just now when all at once a completely new tank tactics popped into my head. It is realy a great idea and I believe it is pregnant with far reaching possibilities. I hope so at any rate. The only thing is that it is so darned simple that I don't see why it has not been thought of long ago. Perhaps there is some equally obvious flaw in it but I don't think so.

All war is simple and we all err by allowing its complexities to divert our minds from the few basic truths . . .

I am going to G.H.Q. Tomorrow and expand this revolutionary theory of mine. For truly it is just that, you may have a genius for a husband yet.

He set down his thoughts at once. "In my opinion the time has now arrived to diverce tank tactics at least to a considerable degree, from the stereotyped formations heretofore thought essential." The proper use of tanks, he believed, should be their employment with a sudden and violent burst of artillery fire mixed with a copious use of smoke to paralyze the German front, which would make possible an assault by light tanks followed by infantry echeloned in density from rear to front. Each jump of the barrage — that is, the progressive advancement of the artillery fire targets — should, he thought, be moved forward, not the standard 100 yards but rather in intervals of 200 to 400 meters, even longer; they should come to rest on defensive lines from 30 minutes to one hour, depending on the length of the jump.

Since he anticipated the utilization of tanks for the most part in enemy territory, he foresaw the need for definite refilling centers for gasoline, oil, and ammunition in hostile country — and this was a new idea also. The large or heavy tanks should take care of establishing these dumps. Each heavy could also tow by chain at least two guns mounted on wheels, plus a supply of ammunition.

"There is nothing original in this mode of progression," Patton modestly wrote, "except the utilization of tanks to produce the effect heretofore produced by machine guns and pack artillery."

But there was, indeed, much more involved, and he directed that experimental training of this sort be conducted at the tank center.

In "Further Notes on the Use of Tanks in Various Operations including Open Warfare" (what would come to be called Mobile Warfare), written perhaps later that evening or later that summer, Patton said, quite contrarily:

The ideas herein advanced are purely original, or if they have been advanced by others it is unknown to me. Hence no virtue is claimed for them but they are simply stated as a basis for criticism in the hope that they may lead to some good results.

Proposing that the light tank could be used in several basic types of operation, he warned:

Tanks must not expect to do these things for nothing; they will be put out [of action] but that is what they are paid for and the loss of a few tanks and men will be a cheap price to pay for . . . [success].

It seems to me that . . . they [tanks] should never be distributed along a front as sort of Pill Boxes in the way the British seem to have done in front of the Fifth Army. Tanks like cavalry must depend on rapidity and shock for success, or as a rear guard in an active retreat but never as adjuncts to a passive defence . . .

Tanks are only partially known and like all new weapons they justify extreme boldness, even rashness, in their employment.

Patton's cavalry upbringing and training were showing, but the qualities of boldness, mobility, and shock action would characterize his deepest military beliefs.

Whatever paper on tactics he sent to Rockenbach's office at GHQ AEF, he received a rapid reply from Pullen, who acknowledged receipt of Patton's outline of proposed new tactics and his belief in their soundness. But he thought that it was no time to propose novel techniques. The first job of the Tank Corps was to get tanks, the second to get tank units into combat. After tank formations had been in several shows, as battles were then familiarly called, the tankers would be in a better position to talk new tank tactics. They would be able to say exactly what they wanted, for

at the present time a great deal of what we say will be looked upon as hot air.

As far as I can find out, the General Staff entirely approves Tanks and is not hostile to the Tank Corps. However, they take the stand that they have approved a Tank program and now it is up to the Tank Corps to produce some Tanks and get them on the fighting line.

What Pullen said made a lot of sense. It was the thinking of the intelligent officer who was well adjusted to and well integrated into the establishment. To him, unorthodoxy, at least at that moment, was out of place. And he was probably right. Patton, the maverick, was out of step, but he had the perception to recognize the truth of what Pullen said.

Letter, GSP, Jr., to Aunt Nannie, July 23, 1918

[His adjutant, Captain Hebert, who was a First Sergeant, Regular Army, for nine years] is realy a most efficient man. I have . . . a lot of officers who were former non coms and with only two exceptions they are fine officers. We never appreciated our sergeants as much as we should. I have one 1st Lieutenant who was a sergeant 27 years and he is a hell of a good officer and one of the best dressed I have ever seen.

In fact all my men are well dressed and I inspect the officers clothes every week.

He delivered a lecture on morality and gambling to his officers, and when he learned that some were losing more than a month's pay in a single night,

I made them stop all together.

They think me very cruel but if they will not play for a one cent limit they must not play at all.

They all think that I am so old that I was probably a class mate of Gen Pershings.

. . . things are looking much better for the tanks now. Some French tanks were in [battle] for thirty hours and only lost eight percent which is nothing . . .

Gen. P. congratulated the 1st and 2d Divisions in a general order. I do hope we can get mentioned when we go in. We will certainly try to deserve it.

But sometimes I fear that we will all die of old age before we get a chance.

He lectured his officers on the points he had earlier raised with Pullen, probably to stimulate his tankers into thinking about the best methods of employing tanks in combat.

When he lost the first of his men, a soldier who died of pneumonia, he published a general order to remark the death and wrote a letter of sympathy to the man's father. In part, it read:

> Though he was not spared to die in battle yet he as truly gave his life for his country as if he had fallen on the field of battle. During the short time he was under my command he impressed me as a very fine type of man and soldier. You should feel proud to have had such a son. I know that in cases such as this sympathy is difficult to express but I beg that you will accept mine and extend it to the other members of your family.

He mentioned this in a letter to Beatrice, then said, "I guess I will have plenty more such letters on this subject to write." His statement was matter of fact rather than callous.

Presenting a lecture to his officers on the "points to be considered in the execution of a tank attack," he concluded:

> Having to the best of my ability told you what to do and so far as is possible how to do it I will now tell you what not to do.
>
> Do not cross trenches diagonally.
>
> Do not cross on traverses. You will fall off.
>
> Do not run away from your infantry.
>
> Do not stall your motor.
>
> Do not bunch. The rally [position] as defined previously is abolished.
>
> If one tank sticks [gets knocked out] thank God it is not your tank and go on.
>
> Do not take prisoners. [There was no way of getting them to the rear.]
>
> Do not go nearer than five yards to a trench when you are mopping up. You may side slip into it.
>
> Do not allow your tank to be taken [by the enemy]. Death is better than a life of shame [being a prisoner of war].
>
> To sum up. You must be elastic like a reubber.

Letter, GSP, Jr., to Beatrice, July 29, 1918

Some of my men deserted the other day in order to [go to the front and] get into the fight. That shows an excellent but lamentable spirit which if persisted in would cause us more casualties than war.

Letter, GSP, Jr., to Beatrice, August 7, 1918

Gen. P. got decorated with the Grand Cross of the Legion of Honor yesterday morning and the president of France kissed him on both cheeks. But the President is so little that Gen. P. had to stoop down. This amused the soldiers a great deal and some who were not in ranks laughed as loud as they could. Gen. P. will have the K.C.B. pinned on him by King George this week also.

He published and had put up on the tank center's bulletin boards a list of 18 *don'ts*. For example: "Don't fool with the magneto or carburetur and don't dissect them . . . Don't tolerate loose wires or poorly made connections. FIX THEM AT ONCE . . . Don't leave your tank standing with motor running." The last one was: "Don't read this only ONCE and think you know all the Don'ts."

Letter, GSP, Jr., to Beatrice, August 10, 1918

Quekemeyer and Bowditch were here yesterday and I think that I impressed them largely [very much] with tanks. I did my best so as to have them in turn make talk at Headquarters as they are both aides to Gen. P.

The way things look now the english and others are doing so well that I fear the war will be over before I get in. That would certainly be a shame. So I shall hope for the best.

There is a fine Rumor that the Staff college will be over in ten days. I hope that this may prove correct as I am getting tired of it and besides would like to devote more time to inspection of Tanks.

The more I see of Gen. R. [Rockenbach] the less I think of him. He is nothing but a good hearted wind bag. I truly believe others would have pushed this show along much better and that we could have been fighting even now.

I hope to hear that Braine and the first lot of Tanks have left [the States] even now and that he and my watch will soon be here.

I must go to school now. I love you.

Letter, GSP, Jr., to Beatrice, August 11, 1918

Darling Beat: A lot of people in the Staff Class were Promoted last week so last night they gave a smoker to which all were invited. It was a very nice affair with only French Beer which as you remember is perfectly harmless. There were also a lot of funny speeches and poems but I am not a gregarious person and such parties bore me to death so I left early at 11 o'clock and went to bed. I slept until ten this morning then got up and had the luxury of dressing for an hour.

Speaking of dressing I often think with regret of how badly I used to dress especially at Ft Myer. In fact Col Vidmer was the first person who impressed on me the virtue of neatness. Now I am a regular Beau Brummel. I wear silk khaki shirts made to order, Khaki socks also made to order. I change my boots at least once during the day and my belts are wonders to see they are so shiney and polished. I have the leather on my knees blancoed every time I ride and my spurs polished with silver polish. In fact I am a wonder to behold.

But the whole army is like that. You can spot a newly arrived officer instantly by the fact that he is not slicked up like us vetrans. I think that among the many good things the war will do an improvement in dress will be most noticable. This is largely due to the fact that having no cits [civilian clothes] at all one takes more interest in ones uniform.

We have a fine big Y.M.C.A. here now and next week the officers are giving a dance to all the nurses and telephone girls at this place about forty five of them in all.

I am going to lunch with some english officers to day so must stop and dress some more.

I love you with all my heart.

Despite his studies at the General Staff School and his duties at the tank center, he composed at least four papers during the first three weeks of August: "Tank Drill Regulations (Provisional)," "Notes for the Guidance of Battalion and Company Reconnaissance Officers," "Instructions on Tank Driving," and "Duties of the Platoon Leader." All were well thought out, detailed, firm, written with spirit, and to the point. He exhorted junior officers to lead at all times by example and instruction, to give careful attention to saluting, dress, and hygiene — "Neat clothes and a clean body help to keep up the spirit of your men" — and to look personally into the health of every man.

Letter, GSP, Jr., to Beatrice, August 13, 1918
. . . we are to put over a big demonstration for a lot of general staff officers on Friday so I have been writing up the problems.

I hope we get time to do the necessary practising to get it down well.

I just got a very nice letter from Gen Harbord. I wrote him congratulating him on his promotion. He has been put in command of the service of supply.

[Henry] Ford is bothering us to death with his machine but I believe it is too small and it would be absurd to run things into the ground with too small a machine [tank].

Pullen has been made a full Colonel and is leaving the Tanks. All my class mates in the Engineers are colonels also. They certainly have been getting rapid promotion.

A full and tiring day was normal. For example, one day Patton was at the Staff College until 5:00 P.M. At 5:15, he rehearsed men and tanks for a maneuver showing tanks and infantry working in cooperation. Because he was unable to secure infantrymen to participate in the exercise, he trained his own men in that role. When the rehearsal was over, he drove to Chaumont to see Rockenbach on business. He returned home at 10:30.

Letter, GSP, Jr., to Beatrice, August 15, 1918
It is remarkable how much easier these [drafted] men are to teach than the old soldiers we used to have. They had no brains at all. These men have plenty . . .

I am certainly some tank profit [prophet] . . . Three months ago I submitted a memo on Tank possibilities to Col. Eltinge. Even he thought I was crazy.

Among other things I advocated night raids by a few tanks. Three weeks later the British pulled one. I said that the second line should be half the strength of the first instead of the other way around after the Fight at . . . The british said it was correct.

I advocated using cavalry & tanks in raids. People said I was clearly crazy. In the present battle the British are doing just that.

Lastly I said that tanks should replace the creeping barrage and that all guns should be used for counter battery. People nearly died of horror at such a thought. Today we had a lecture by a British artillery general advocating my idea in toto.

Hence I have a swelled head for which I ask no pardon. But I still love you more every day.

Letter, GSP, Jr., to Beatrice, August 16, 1918
Here is a poem I wrote a while ago. I went to bed and for a wonder did not go to sleep at once so I composed poetry to put my

self to sleep and rather fancying this [poem] I got up and wrote it, it was a moon light night. I think it is rather disconnected though some of the individual verses sound well.

The officers as I think I told you are giving a dinner dance to night. I did not find out until today that it was for me. All the programs being headed "the Colonels Party." I wish you were here to enjoy it or at least make me [enjoy it]. The guests are rather assorted. One countess two barronnesses. To [two] reporters wives of doubtful cast. The best nurses and telephone girls. I hope that they will have a good time. It may be a sort "of revrilly by night in Belgiums capital" [the night before Waterloo] for some of them as I think one Battalion will be out of here by the 1st of Sept. Of course not many will be killed but if they do their duty some are bound to. Still that rather adds zest to the entertainment as each hopes it will be the other and none are sure.

The demonstration we gave yesterday was a great success. Both the tanks and the infantry did fine and no one was hurt by the grenades. There were over 300 officers looking on and nine generals. Three of whom were Major Generals.

The candy etc you sent by Gen Marshall arrived to day and I have just eaten a lot as I had no time to get lunch.

I have seven or eight sweaters and four or five helmets also some heavy socks so use the wool for something else. In fact stop doing war work and keep young as I am doing.

Patton's scenario of the tank demonstration held for the Army General Staff College on August 16 included such problems as how to replace a dead tank driver and how to knock out an enemy 37-mm. gun. On the program distributed to the observers to enable them to follow the events being staged, Patton had written:

Note to Observers. The infantry taking part are only tank soldiers and may not do as well as trained infantry . . . Other problems have been spoiled by staff officers and other observers getting into the ranks of the infantry and fearlessly braving the supposed barrage. It is requested that this be not done.

At this time he had 900 men and 50 fully trained officers in his center. They were still using only 25 tanks. The French said that tanks had to be completely overhauled and the parts replaced every 50 miles of operational use; Patton's tanks often ran for 500 before being refurbished.

Since July the tankers had been working hard on target practice. At first they fired from a makeshift wooden tank mounted on and rolling along an uneven track, which gave them the motion of a "seagoing platform." Later they worked on a more orthodox range constructed by Major L. K. Davis a few kilometers west of Bourg.

In August, to harden his men physically, Patton instituted a new program. Every morning before breakfast, each company ran one kilometer at double time in a column of squads. It was the forerunner of special physical conditioning that elite units, such as Rangers and paratroopers, later took such pride in.

About this time Rockenbach rated Patton's performance. He wrote:

> The splendid results obtained by this officer in the Tank School show him to be zealous and of good judgement and intelligence. His command is well disciplined and very soldierly in appearance.

Another rating by Rockenbach in the summer of 1918 read that Patton was "energetic, efficient, does much good work with little assistance. Qualified and especially fitted to command a tank brigade."

On Tuesday morning, August 20, while Patton was attending a lecture at the General Staff College, a note was delivered to him. It read: "You will report at once to the Chief of the Tank Corps accompanied by your Reconnaissance officer and equipped for field service."

This had to be a trip to the front at the very least, more probably participation in a "show." It had to be combat; otherwise the note would have told him more. He decided that the summons meant the opportunity at last to lead his tanks in battle and, further, that more tanks were about to arrive in Bourg.

In some excitement, he immediately went to Bourg, where he turned over command of the center to Viner, making him assistant commandant. He also wrote a letter to his father, saying that he had just received a message to go somewhere, a place where there was the

> danger of remaining longer than one wishes on such trips perhaps for ever . . .
> [If I die] please do what is best with any property I may have.

Personally I hope you and mama keep it as beatrice has plenty. I will send her my sword. I will give one horse to Gen. Pershing and one to Maj. Viner. I told you on a former occasion where my dress uniforms are in paris . . .

Of course dont get alarmed over me. I will wire you or Beat. or both of my safe return long before you get this letter.

You and mama and Nita and Aunt Nannie know well my unending love.

VII

Combat

"Things are most interesting and getting more so."

CHAPTER 28

Preparations for St. Mihiel

"This is our big chance; what we have worked for."

AFTER TURNING OVER COMMAND of the tank center to Viner on Tuesday, August 20, Patton, accompanied by Lieutenant Maurice K. Knowles, drove to Chaumont, picked up Rockenbach, and continued to Neufchâteau, where the headquarters of the First U. S. Army was located. On the way, Rockenbach briefed Patton on a proposed operation in which the tanks might take part. The St. Mihiel offensive, as it would be called, was tentatively scheduled for September 5 or 7. It would involve several American corps under the First Army, commanded by Pershing, who would retain also his position as Commander in Chief, AEF.

At Neufchâteau, Patton secured from Colonel Hugh Drum, now First Army chief of staff, maps of the area where the attack was to be launched. While Rockenbach remained to work with the First Army staff, Patton and Knowles drove to Ligny-en-Barrois and reported to General Burtt, V Corps chief of staff. He had dinner with Burtt, an old friend from Mexico, who gave him more information on the action being planned.

Diary
   August 20: "Was rather overwhelmed at size of task [for tanks] but it cleared up after eating."

Wearing field artillery insignia to conceal the plan for using tanks in the impending operation, Patton and Knowles drove to the Third French Army to reconnoiter the battle terrain. With permission to visit the appropriate units in the area, the Americans proceeded to Ancemont and the 10th French Colonial Division. The division commander, General Marchand, impressed Patton enormously, for Marchand had been deco-

rated with five palms, six wound stripes — Patton counted them — and
the Grand Cross of the Legion of Honor. Marchand believed that the
Woevre plain, the ground envisaged for tank action, was too marshy for
the machines.

Unwilling to accept this disappointing news secondhand, wanting to
see the ground himself, Patton received authority to visit the battalion
there. After reporting to the battalion command post, Patton and
Knowles walked to an observation post. Through field glasses they
studied the terrain. Still unable to determine the actual condition of the
ground, Patton asked whether the two Americans could accompany a
patrol that night into no-man's-land.

They joined one of the patrols making a routine sortie beyond the
French trenches after nightfall, and moved about 1500 meters into no-
man's-land. They met no Germans, but several enemy soldiers whistled
at the patrol when some Frenchmen cut a few strands of German barbed
wire. The ground was pretty soft, but Patton decided it might be passable for tanks.

Letter, GSP, Jr., to Beatrice, September 1, 1918
I was out on a patrol in No mans land last week. It was most
interesting and not at all exciting. We went along with the "Burglars crawl" for about a mile and a half till we came to the Bosch
wire. This we examined and the Bosch whistled at us and we whistled back and having seen what we wanted went home. No one shot
at us but we saw some bosch walking along about 100 m. [meters
away]. Both sides were anxious not to disturb the others. Coming
back we came through a village from one house to another by holes
in the walls. The village had been destroyed a long time and looked
like a skeleton in texas.

I picked some dasies for you in the bosch wire and will send them
back . . . it was on the whole a most interesting evening and not up
to expectations.

I rather hoped we would have a patrol encounter but nothing happened. The Bosch seems to be catching it pretty well and is more or
less on the run but is a long way from being dead yet.

A later version by Patton:

The raid itself was a very tame affair, the party penetrated two
belts of wire and was approaching a third when someone in front in

the dark whistled, on this the raid [patrol] stopped and began to retrace its steps. The French noncom in charge explaining that the whistle meant that if the raid had been pushed further the Germans would reluctently be forced to fire . . . Anyhow the raid had been a success, the ground was fine for tanks.

Back in the French lines at 2:30 A.M., Patton thanked the officers at battalion headquarters for their help. Then he and Knowles drove to an American unit, the 59th Railroad Artillery, and found a place to sleep.

They returned to the French battalion on Thursday and walked again to the observation post. Once more, this time for two hours, they studied the ground. Very tired and hot, they proceeded, after lunch, to another OP for still another look at the ground that interested them.

Having examined the terrain to his satisfaction, Patton drove to the rear and, with Knowles, inspected the closest railroad detraining point. It was excellent, not far from the front and hidden by woods. After stopping at Ancemont to pick up more maps and after dinner at Bar-le-Duc, Patton and Knowles reached Ligny. They were tired and went to bed immediately.

Patton spent most of Friday writing a terrain report and a suggested plan for employing tanks. The corps staff members were most helpful; Burtt, Farman, Cotton, and Russell were old friends. That evening Patton returned to Neufchâteau.

Early Saturday morning, he and Rockenbach brought each other up to date. Rockenbach, on temporary duty with the First Army, had studied the operational plans issued by the Army, the corps, and the divisions. A large number of tanks would take part in the attack — three U.S. heavy battalions coming from England with 150 British tanks, three French battalions with 225 light tanks, and two U.S. battalions, both Patton's, with 144 French light tanks. As a matter of fact, the first of Patton's new tanks were beginning to arrive at Bourg that day.

Telling what he had done, Patton said that his reconnaissance "showed the absolute necessity for a tank officer to personally see the ground." All the intelligence reports indicated that the ground to be used by the tanks was an impassable swamp further blocked by dreadful barbed wire; and his observations from OP's confirmed these reports. But his participation in a raid convinced him that the ground and the wire were neither impassable nor dreadful. An attack could be made.

Then he and Rockenbach went over his written report. The proposed battle terrain, according to Patton, was "a very flat and marshy plain drained by numerous small streams" and ditches. Trees and bushes along the waterways offered cover to "prone lines of skirmishers." A protracted hot, dry spell of weather had made the ground hard. Infantry and tanks could easily cross the streams. But two days of rain would "render this sector quite difficult to tanks." Late in September, the wet season would make the area impassable "except along the roads."

He described the roads and the shell craters. Some of the wire entanglements, he said, were strung on iron posts that could "be readily flattened by tanks." The rest of the wire was attached to wooden posts which had been there for several years and were rotten — "It was possible to push these posts over by hand."

After considering the hostile trenches and gun emplacements, which posed no great problem, he mentioned that the villages, all destroyed by shell fire, "were potential centers of resistance" because many walls were still standing.

Patton suggested tank attacks in four sectors and discussed detraining points. He recommended forgoing a long artillery preparation — "it tears up the ground" and made tank movements difficult. He further suggested the use of artillery smoke shells to screen the tanks from anti-tank guns. He hoped that at least "one low flying airplane" would be assigned the duty of maintaining liaison by wireless radio between the tanks and the supporting artillery. He warned that road space should be requested to guarantee the arrival of gasoline trucks for the second day of operations.

After his discussion with Rockenbach, Patton returned to Chaumont, where he talked about the operation with several GHQ AEF staff members during lunch. He then traveled to Bourg.

Letter, GSP, Jr., to Beatrice, August 24, 1918
I have been so rushed for the last four days that I have had no time to write. So you must forgive me. I am perfectly all right and love you very much but some new soldiers are arriving to be trained and I have to work every minute at that. Then there are other things.

I will try and write every two or three days and will wire from time to time.

I love you with all my heart.

With the men at the tank center — officially designated the 302d Tank Center — working feverishly under Viner's direction to tune up the new tanks and get them ready for combat, Patton put Viner in charge of the school and training facility. He placed Brett in command of the 1st (326th) Tank Battalion, and gave Captain Ranulf Compton command of the 2d (327th) Battalion. These two battalions would operate in battle under Patton's headquarters, called the 304th Brigade, Tank Corps (later it would be known simply as the 1st Tank Brigade). Patton was now a brigade commander — like his grandfather in the Civil War.

That evening Patton drove to Ligny, taking Borlan and Heilner with him. They arrived late, but Knowles was waiting for them. The tank operation at St. Mihiel, he said, would be a smaller show than originally planned.

One of the two battalions of American tankers training with heavy tanks at Wareham, England, since April would be, at the end of August, on its way to France with 47 British-built Mark V's. But the unit would arrive too late for St. Mihiel.*

As soon as Rockenbach learned that the heavies would be unavailable for St. Mihiel, he asked the French to furnish four battalions instead of three for the operation — this in addition to the equipment they were sending Patton's battalions. Unable to do so, the French added 12 St. Chamond and 24 Schneider tanks to the Renaults they were contributing to the attack.

Rockenbach was concerned. He feared that the infantry at St. Mihiel might lack sufficient tank support.

Patton moved with the V Corps headquarters to the attack area. His three lieutenants set up a command post, reconnoitered the area, determined the best tank detraining and troop assembly points, located command post sites, traced routes to the front, and laid telephone wires from the corps headquarters to the tank command posts.

Diary

August 25 (Sunday): "wrote plan for attack simply rough draft . . . Billeted in old monestary in a cell with all sorts of praying apparatus. Good bed."

---

* Assigned to the 27th U.S. Division, the battalion would enter battle on September 29 at Le Catelet, working with American and Australian infantry. Later it would operate with the 30th U.S. Division. By October 23, it would have only 12 tanks in operating condition.

Letter, GSP, Jr., to Beatrice, August 26, 1918
I am very well and have nothing to do so will either get fat or nearvous I cant say which . . . I don't think I have changed much unless it is that I look meaner.

Diary
August 27: "Truck arrived with nothing in it. I was very mad."

August 28: "Worked for revised plan on the use of Tanks showing in detail the operation of nearly every Tank . . . Hebert & Gibbs got in at 10:30. But truck and clearks were lost."

Patton issued his field order, indicating in detail the enemy line forming the St. Mihiel salient, the V Corps plan of attack, and his own instructions to the tankers. It was, he later said, quite easy to write, for the Allied front ran along high bluffs overlooking the assault area, which lay spread out like a map.

Memo, GSP, Jr., to V Corps, August 29, 1918, subject: Plan for the Use of Tanks.
The greatest danger to Tanks is from direct fire of A-T [antitank] guns on the flanks or sweeping roades . . . If a creeping Barrage is used it should have a proportion of smoke shells (I believe 20% is about right but that is an artillery question) . . . In each sector where tanks operate there should be a special air plane detailed to fly low and spot anti Tank guns. On locating any it should signal the support battery [of artillery] by wireless or by special light signal. The battery will at once fire on the designated spot with H.E. [high explosive] and smoke.

Rockenbach proposed a tank maneuver at Bourg for the infantry commanders and staff members of the divisions that were to work with the tanks. The infantrymen would thus become somewhat familiar with tank capabilities.

Diary
August 29 (Thursday): "Sent word to have Brett & [his subordinate company commanders] Semmes, Weed, and English to come up. I went to Ligny to see Gen R. [Rockenbach]. He told me to let no

one come up but they had [already] started . . . Gave Brett and his capts a talk on their duties. Truck got in and we got office started."

August 30: "Went to see Gen [Clarence R.] Edwards [26th Division commander] at 1:30. He was most interested and asked me how I wanted him to employ his infantry [with the tanks]. I told him and he was eager to agree. Went to see Gen G. Bell [George Bell, Jr., 33d Division commander] at Tronville. He was also eager to help and I could not have had a better reception. Went to Langres [to prepare tank maneuver for infantrymen] but had motor trouble and did not get in until 1 A.M. Arranged to give shows for officers [of] 26 and 33 Divs."

August 31: "Talked over every thing with Viner & found every thing o.k. Went to see new tanks. All were in but 30. They were in fine shape. Gen R[ockenbach] came to lunch. Had demonstration with one Bn [Battalion]. Every thing went fine. 90 [infantry] officers . . . present.

Letter, GSP, Jr., to Beatrice, August 31, 1918
[The demonstration was] Better than I could have hoped. One tank fell off a cliff and rolled clear over then went on again with out any difficulty . . .

At last we have all the equipment we want even a little more and every thing is coming in fine and fast. The woods are full of tanks over 150 of them all nice and new and in fine shape.

I only got three hours sleep last night so will stop and go to bed.

September 1 (Sunday): "Arranged for Brig[ade] reserve with Viner. Got pigeon baskets . . . Left with Capt. Etheridge at 1:30 P.M. Stopped at Chaumont then came on to Ligny by Joinville & St. Dizier. Passed 200 French trucks full of Americans. Had dinner with Gen R. Saw Col DeWitt G4 1st Army about Detraining [tanks]. Got in at 12:30 A.M.

He was at the V Corps headquarters on September 2 when he learned that the attack zones had been changed somewhat. This required some adjustments in his own arrangements. He moved his office, had Etheridge draw up a memo on detraining and sent him to talk with Rockenbach, and himself reconnoitered the area immediately behind the intended battleground.

Everything was set for the operation—telephone wires were laid, orders distributed, maps disseminated—when without warning, everything was changed. The First Army decided on September 3 that Patton's tanks would work, not with the V Corps, but rather with the IV Corps and in a completely different area. The attack was postponed.

Word reached Patton late that afternoon—as he was picking blackberries. After "some profanity and much regret" because all the preliminary work had been for nothing, he instructed Hebert, his adjutant, to move the tank brigade headquarters to the new area without delay. Patton packed his things and drove at once to Ligny. Pullen met him there, and as they rode together to the IV Corps at Etrouves, near Toul, they discussed the new situation. Pullen had already drawn a tentative plan for the tanks, but Patton objected to the large amount of frontage Pullen had assigned each battalion.

At IV Corps on Wednesday, September 4, Patton talked to the chief of staff and G–3 and had them reduce the length of the tank frontage. Then, still disguised by field artillery insignia, he reconnoitered the terrain near Beaumont, where the new attack would be made.

On Thursday he visited the front, made a daylight inspection in no-man's-land—it was quiet—walked up the fairly large stream called the Rupt de Mad looking for tank-crossing sites, discovered that three smaller streams running through the attack zone were perfectly dry and no obstacle to tanks. The bridge at Marvoisin was intact, but he thought he saw evidence that the Germans were mining it. Since he could not count on the Marvoisin bridge as a sure method of crossing, he found another site 700 yards away where the water was shallow and fordable. After examining the ground from an OP in the Bois du Jury, he decided that the ground would be difficult for his Renault tanks but passable unless it rained. That evening he wrote his plan of attack.

The attack to reduce the St. Mihiel salient—a bulge pushed forward by the Germans into the Allied line—was the first independent offensive to be launched by the First U. S. Army. The salient had been in German possession since September 1914, and though it covered a sensitive position, the Mézières–Sedan–Metz railroad and the Birey iron basin, there had been no large-scale fighting there since 1916.

Pershing hoped to start his attack on September 7, 1918, but bringing the scattered American units together, assembling the necessary artillery support, and constructing a host of new installations — all at night in great secrecy — consumed more time than anticipated. D-day was eventually scheduled for September 12.

On August 29, Pershing moved his First Army advance headquarters from Neufchâteau to Ligny-en-Barrois, 25 miles southwest of St. Mihiel, and on the following day assumed command of the sector. In the attack he would direct three U.S. corps and several French divisions.

The IV U. S. Corps and I U. S. Corps were in position on the southern face of the salient with the I Corps on the right (east). The IV Corps headquarters was at Toul, the I Corps at Saizerais, northeast of Toul. Over on the left and separated from the other American corps by several French units was the V Corps, in position on the western face of the salient. The attack, simply stated, was to have the I and IV Corps drive to the north and meet the V Corps advancing to the east.

Three battalions of the 505th French Tank Regiment, plus one half of the groupement of St. Chamonds and Schneiders the French had added, were to work with the I Corps. Patton's brigade of two U.S. tank battalions, reinforced by the other half of the French groupement — the 14th and 17th Groupes, would work with the IV Corps.

More specifically, Patton's American and French tankers would support the 42d Division, which was in the center of the IV Corps zone, and the 1st Division, which was on the immediate left (west).

Patton disposed his tanks as follows: The 327th Battalion (Compton), less 25 tanks held in Brigade Reserve, but augmented by the French groupes (under Major Chanoine), would operate with the 42d Division. The 326th Battalion (Brett) would be with the 1st Division.

Brett on the left, with the support of the Brigade Reserve, was to cross the Rupt de Mad and lead the infantry to the objectives. In the center, Chanoine's heavier Schneider tanks, which would have more difficulty than the Renaults crossing streams, were to follow the infantry. Compton, operating on the right of the French, was to stay behind the infantry initially, then pick up speed, pass through the infantry, and lead the foot soldiers into Essey and Pannes.

Letter, GSP, Jr., to Beatrice, September 5, 1918
I have been being shelled yesterday and to day but not much. I

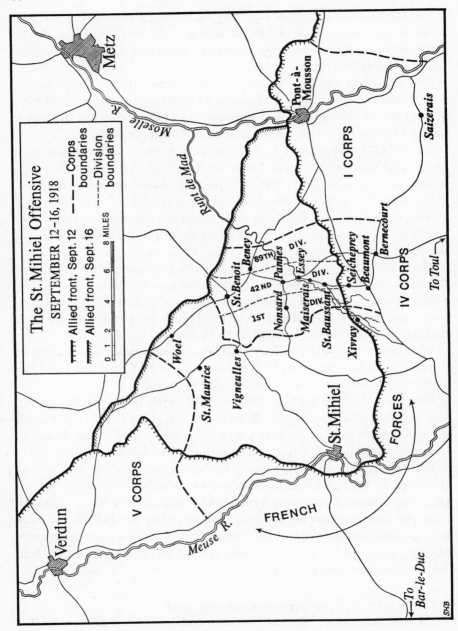

The St. Mihiel Offensive
SEPTEMBER 12–16, 1918

Allied front, Sept. 12
Allied front, Sept. 16

Corps boundaries
Division boundaries

0 1 2 4 6 8 MILES

Metz

Moselle R.

Pont-à-Mousson

I CORPS

Saizerais

Rupt de Mad

Bernecourt

Beney

89TH DIV.

Essey

St. Benoit

Pannes

42ND DIV.

Seicheprey

Beaumont

IV CORPS

To Toul

Nonsard

Maiserais

1ST DIV.

St. Baussant

Xivray

Woel

Vigneulles

St. Maurice

FORCES

St. Mihiel

V CORPS

FRENCH

Verdun

Meuse R.

To Bar-le-Duc

SHB

was out in no mans land to day and it was fine till we started back. I hated the idea of being shot at from behind.

It is funny how little notice one pays to shells after a short experience. I was talking to a major in the middle of a street to day and they were shelling hell out of a church about a block away. The bosch shoot so accurately that when you see what they are aiming at you simply have to avoid that spot and are quite safe for the rest . . .

Things are most interesting and getting more so.

From the configuration of the terrain, it was apparent that the tanks would have to start their attack 300 meters behind the infantry, which Patton disliked. It was also apparent that if the tanks were to move through the marshy ground assigned to them, they would need grousers or mud hooks. Only one had ever been made as an experiment, but it seemed to work. Patton therefore telephoned Viner at Bourg and told him he needed 1000. Viner said, "Very good sir, when do you want them?" Patton had them in three days.

Diary

September 6 (Friday): "Changed [my plan] . . . on advice of Chaffee. Went to see 42 Div C of S [chief of staff] Lt. Col [William N.] Hughes [Jr.]. Thought him an ass. Maj. Chanoine reported. Gen R. [Rockenbach] called."

September 7: Visited 1st Division, saw Gen. Summerall and others, "all most obliging and did all I asked. Went to 42 [Division] Maj Murphy G3. Found that they had adopted my plan in total. Thought Col Hughes less of an ass. Fixed up plan for French . . . Tanks shipped from Langres. Gen. R. called."

Patton was pleased with the cooperation he was getting from the 1st Division, which had worked with tanks at Cantigny. Also, he had complete confidence in Brett, and he was sure that the tanks and infantry would cooperate well together in that sector.

Although the 42d Division was cooperative too, it had had no previous experience with tanks. In addition, he had some concern about Compton. It was these factors, probably, that led him to be somewhat over-solicitous in his arrangements with the 42d Division.

He wrote a memo for the division G–3, specifying certain requirements for moving the tanks from their detraining point to the battlefield. For example, he requested that a bridge be built, pointing out that plenty of trees in the nearby woods were available for the construction. He also worried about the lack of time — everyone was extremely busy getting ready, and this precluded a training maneuver to familiarize infantry commanders with the tanks. He therefore recommended that some of Compton's officers give several brief lectures to the platoon and company commanders of the infantry assault battalions. "No other means of training is available. This will be better than nothing." There was no time even for that.

Half of Chanoine's tanks arrived by train during the night of September 7. Most of them moved to places of concealment in the Bois de la Reine. A small group descended by mistake eight miles away and temporarily fouled up the arrangements for assembling the tanks.

Patton inspected the French units on September 8, arranged to have them move to another wood so that the rest of the French tanks, as well as his own, which had started from Bourg on the previous day, could move swiftly off the trains and into concealed bivouacs.

Still concerned about operations with the 42d Division, he called on the assistant division commander, General Michael J. Lenihan, and spoke with him about getting smoke into the plan. Lenihan referred him to Murphy, the G–3.

Major Grayson M. P. Murphy was a competent officer. A West Point graduate who resigned from the Army after several years of active duty to enter banking, he became head of the American Red Cross in France when the United States entered the war. After organizing that service, he applied for active duty and was assigned to be Operations Officer of the 42d Division. Very busy preparing for the St. Mihiel operation, probably feeling somewhat harassed, particularly by a tank officer who was constantly making suggestions or demands, he refused Patton's request to add a provision for smoke shells in the division plan, which he had to reproduce in many copies and distribute to higher, subordinate, and neighboring units by a certain time.

Diary

September 8: "Maj Murphy told me he could not put smoke in plan as stencil was already cut. The biggest fool remark I ever heard showing just what an S.O.B. the late chief of the Red Cross is. Told Col. Heintzelman [division chief of staff] of remark & said that if tanks fail in 42 Div it will be his Murphy's fault."

He was angry because he was tired and because he was concerned about the attack. The fact that it was raining did nothing to improve his temper and disposition. If the rain continued, the Woevre plain would turn into a quagmire, and the ground would be unable to hold the tanks.

That night the rest of Chanoine's tanks arrived. The rain had become a downpour.

Letter, GSP, Jr., to Beatrice, September 8, 1918

I have been having a hell of a time for the passed two days getting things arranged. I command among other things a French outfit and it is a job requiring great tact but so far I have managed all right.

Yesterday every thing bad which could happen did but I got things clear by supper time to night. Among other things an engine jumped the track and one band of fools detrained eight miles from where they should have.

I met a few militia staff officers who were such polite men that they would say neither yes nor no and refused to do any thing that they could get any one else to do.

West Pointers stand up like light houses in a fog. They do their best and don't shirk responsibility which the rest do all the time . . .

All the Allies seem to be doing very well in deed and the Bosch is catching it on all sides.

Patton issued his field order on September 9, setting forth the missions of his units and how they were to attack.

Diary

September 9 (Monday): Got dump of 10,000 gallons of gasoline; no oil or grease. Very bad weather, wet and raining.

That night two trains bringing half of his battalions reached the area. Since each train could carry one-and-a-half companies, Patton had specified that half of the 326th and half of the 327th come first, the rest later. He had hoped that all the men and equipment would arrive early enough before the attack for the men to get some rest and the tanks some minor adjustments and a tune-up. But frequent delays and sidetracking of trains disrupted schedules. Blocked tracks near the front sometimes required detraining at places other than those selected and consequently meant longer drives to jump-off positions, as well as traffic congestion.

Diary

September 10 (Tuesday): 327th unable to detrain because French had put ammunition on tracks and we could not move up. "Things look bad but we will do our best to get them off." Lt. Colonels Mitchell [commander of the American heavy tanks] and Viner came to observe the operation.

The second section of the brigade was unable to leave the train because French railroad officials would not or could not stop the cars where the tanks could get off. The train engineer was finally threatened with bodily harm and forced to halt. Viner got most of the tanks off.

The last tank company to reach the general area was on the ground at 3 A.M., September 12, a scant two hours before the attack was to begin. The company started at once on an eight-kilometer march to its jump-off point. Patton made a last-minute adjustment in his orders, shifted the company to battalion support, and the tankers got into position at 4:50 A.M. The men had not slept for two nights but were anxious to fight.

Probably the best summary of his activities before the battle of St. Mihiel opened was his own description several days after the attack.

Letter, GSP, Jr., to Beatrice, September 16, 1918

Darling Beat: The news is out so I can give you a brief account of the Battle of St. Mihiel etc. At 10 A.M. August 22 I got a telephone message to report to Gen. R. with my reconnaissance officer ready for protracted field service. I did, at 3 P.M. we were at Army Hq and had been told the plans which as you know contemplated the attack by 3 corps. I was to command the tanks in the 5 Corps. The rest of the tanks were to be supplied by the French. At 6 P.M. I reported to your old friend Gen Burtt (Capt in Mex) who was chief of staff. Next day I went to French Corps Hq. to get permission to visit the Front. On going there I was told it was a marsh where tanks could not move. As I did not believe this I went out with a French Patrol that night to the Bosch wire and found the ground hard and dry though in winter it is probably a marsh. We worked hard and got already to fight also got our tanks. For on August 22 we had only 22. I had to patrol and make plans and then travle back to the center every other night, a four hour ride, to arrange things there. We thought that "D" day would be sept. 7. On Sept 4 I got ordered to leave the 5th Corps and report to the 4 Corps near Toul. Here I got a new job and had to start all over again which was a bore still it had to be done. I walked down the Rupt de Mad by day to the bridge at Xivray which is in no mans land and was not shot at. I had to do it to see whether we could cross the stream.

Then we started to detrain and that was awfull. For 4 nights the French made every mistake they could, sending trains to the wrong place or not sending them at all. The last company of the 327 Battalion detrained at 3:15 A.M. and marched right into action.

Meanwhile, on September 11, the day before the operation was to start, the commander of the French Tank Corps sent Rockenbach a message. Referring to the new tanks recently furnished Patton's brigade, he warned that Renaults required a twelve-day period for breaking in. They should not, he said, be used in action until then. Rockenbach was unperturbed. He replied "that the mud would act as lubricant and that the tanks would operate."

With his tanks moving into position for the attack, Patton issued special instructions. He wanted all cooking completed before dark, no lights or fires to be shown after darkness, no flashlights used. He warned that water in the streams was likely to be contaminated by gas.

Then, having warmed up to exhortation, he concluded:

From a tactical point of view the present operation is easy. A complete success insures the future of the Tank Corps in which all have shown by their long and cheerful work that they are fully interested . . . Remember that you are to make paths in the wire and put out machine gun nests for the infantry; hence do not leave them [the infantry], never get more than a hundred and fifty yards ahead of them and never let them get ahead of you or if they do hurry to regain your place. No tank is to be surrendered or abandoned to the enemy. If you are left alone in the midst of the enemy keep shooting. If your gun is disabled use your pistols and squash the enemy with your tracks. By quick changes of direction cut them with the tail of the tank. If your motor is stalled and your gun broken still the in-

fantry cannot hurt. You hang on, help will come . . . you are the
first American tanks [in battle]. You must establish the fact that
AMERICAN TANKS DO NOT SURRENDER . . . As long as one
tank is able to move it must go forward. Its presence will save the
lives of hundreds of infantry and kill many Germans. Finally This is
our BIG CHANCE; WHAT WE HAVE WORKED FOR . . .
MAKE IT WORTH WHILE.

Diary

September 11 (Wednesday): Viner got tanks off the railroad after
working all day. "I wrote B a letter ate as much as I could hold and
went to see Compton at Bernecourt. Then tried to get to P.C. [com-
mand post] fell in hole and got shelled. It was very lonely in the wet
dark being shelled and all. Found P.C. and went to sleep."

CHAPTER 29

St. Mihiel

*"the feeling, foolish probably, of being admired by the men
. . . is a great stimulus."*

Diary

September 12 (Thursday): "D. Day [Our] Artillery started at 1
A.M. and the Bosch put up pathetic little Flares but made no reply.
At 5 the show started at 5:30 could see tanks beyond Xivray having a
hard time. Moved at 7 to Seicheprey. Saw some prisoners &
wounded . . . got some shelling . . . at 9:30 took Pannes at 10:40
attacked Beney got shot at by m.g. [machine gun] & had to recall
tank as . . . [infantry] would not go in. Saw Brett at Nonsard. He
had 326 T[ank Battalion] up. Reported to corps very tired."

This extremely compressed account of Patton's activities during the
first day of the St. Mihiel offensive was supplemented by several fuller
accounts. Patton sent an interim report to the IV Corps on September 13
and an operation report on the following day, wrote to Beatrice on the
16th and to his father on the 20th. In response to a request from Rockenbach in December, he and other tank officers submitted individual papers
on their personal experiences in the war, including St. Mihiel. Sometime
later he wrote a humorous sketch of the tanks. He also contributed much
to, probably composed by far the greater part of, the less personal "304th
Brigade Operations Report on the St. Mihiel Salient" and the "History of
the 304th Brigade." The substance of all these narratives concerning Patton painted a similar picture. From them emerged the following story.

"We have all been in one fine fight and it was not half so exciting as I
had hoped, not as exciting as affairs in Mexico, because there was so much
company [in France]."

"We attacked at 5 A.M. on Thursday Sept 12" but before that, "at 1 A.M.

900 plus guns opened and shot till 5. It was dark with a heavy rain & wind. I was on a hill in front of the main line where I could watch both Battalions and 30 French [tanks] that I had also under me."

"When the shelling first started I had some doubts about the advisability of sticking my head over the parapet [of the trench], but it is just like taking a cold bath, once you get in it is all right. And I soon got out and sat on the parapet."

Sending periodic messages of the tanks' progress to the IV Corps, he made his first communication by telephone at 6:10, reporting that tanks were passing Xivray, that the French tanks were invisible to him because of the fog, and that the Germans were making very little reply to the American shells.

He telephoned at 6:30 to say that the tanks were advancing.

"I could see them coming along and getting stuck in the trenches. It was a most irritating sight. At 7 o'clock I moved forward 2 miles" — "and passed some dead and wounded. I saw one fellow in a shell hole holding his rifle and sitting down. I thought he was hiding and went to cuss him out, he had a bullet over his right eye and was dead. As my telephone wire ran out at this point I left the adjutant there and went forward with a lieutenant and 4 runners to find the tanks, the whole country was alive with them crawling over trenches and into woods."

At 7:20 he sent a motorcycle messenger with the information that at least sixteen tanks were heavily engaged and that the smoke screen laid down by the division and corps artillery was excellent.

At 8:20, from a hill 800 meters northwest of Seicheprey, he reported that the tanks were preceding the infantry on the fronts of both the 1st and 42d Divisions. Only five tanks were out of action so far as he could tell, but he was unable to determine the cause.

He transmitted news brought by a runner from the 327th Tank Battalion at 9:15 that Compton's tanks — with the 42d Division — were being delayed by bad ground. He himself had a poor view of the action from where he was, and he could see none of the tanks working with the 1st Division.

"I had to see something so I took an officer and three runners and started forward."

"I could not see my right battalions so went to look for it."

"There were very few dead in the trenches as the Bosch had not Fought hard but you never saw such trenches — eight feet deep and 10 to 14 wide."

"We passed through several towns under shell fire but none [of the exploding shells] did more than throw dust on us. I admit that I wanted to duck and probably did at first but soon saw the futility of dodging fate, besides I was the only officer around who had left on his shoulder straps [many officers had removed this identifying mark distinguishing them from enlisted men because they feared that the enemy would concentrate fire against the leaders] and I had to live up to them. It was much easier than you would think and the feeling, foolish probably, of being admired by the men lying down is a great stimulus."

"At the first town we came to St. Baussant the bosch were still shelling and it was not pleasant . . . I found the French stuck in a pass under shell fire. I talked to the Major [Chanoine] and went on. I had not gone 20 feet when a shell 6″ [a large shell] struck the tank he was working on and killed 15 men. I went on towards Essey and got into the front line infantry who were laying down. As there was only shell fire I walked on smoking [his pipe] with vigor. Most of the shells went high."

"I walked right along the firing line of one brigade. They were all in shell holes except the general (Douglas Mcarthur) who was standing on a little hill."

"Here I met Gen McArthur (Douglas) . . . he was walking about too."

"I joined him and the creeping barrage came along toward us, but it was very thin and not dangerous. I think each one wanted to leave but each hated to say so, so we let it come over us."

"We stood and talked but neither was much interested in what the other said as we could not get our minds off the shells. I went up a hill to have a look and could see the Bosch running beyond Essey fast."

He walked to Essey, "then five tanks of my right battalion [Compton's] came up so I told them to go through Essey. Some damed Frenchman at the bridge told them to go back as there were too many shells [falling] in the town. The Lt in command obeyed. This made me mad so I led them through on foot but there was no danger as the Bosch [was] shelling the next town."

It was only later that a story, perhaps mostly legend, arose out of the action at Essey. Someone said that the bridge was mined or prepared for demolition by the Germans. Perhaps some inhabitants thought this was so. Whether Patton was aware of it at the time or only afterward is not clear. His earlier accounts mentioned only the shells falling nearby that discouraged the tankers from crossing the bridge into town.

In any event, he walked across the bridge first, leading the tanks into the village. He said later that he did not believe the bridge was mined.

Still later: "No stage brigand ever moved more light footed or with greater caution than did Col Patton as he walked over it [the bridge] to see if the man [who had reported explosives ready to be detonated] was right — fortunately he was not."

Another version said: "we" — he was referring to himself — "walked over the bridge in a cat-like manner, expecting to be blown to heaven any moment, to our great relief we found that the bridge had not been tampered with."

"Some Germans came out of dug outs and surrendered to Gen McArthur . . .

"I walked behind [the tanks] and some boshe surrendered to me . . .

"I asked him [MacArthur] if I could go on and attack the next town Pannes. He said sure so I started. All the tanks but one ran out of gas."

The other tanks were "out of sight."

"The road from Essey to Pannes was rather a mess; a German battery had apparently been caught by the American barrage and the road was strewn with dead men and horses."

"When we got to Pannes some two miles [away] the infantry would not go in so I told the sgt. commanding the tank to go in. He was nearvous at being alone so I said I will sit on the roof."

"I got on top of the tank to hearten the driver."

"This reasured him and we entered the town."

Another version had it: "Being very tired Colonel Patton, Lt. Knowles and one remaining runner mounted on the tank."

"Lt. Knowles and Sgt. Graham sat on the tail of the tank. I watched one side of the street and they the other."

"That was most exciting as there were plenty of boshe."

"Pretty soon we saw a Bosch who threw up his hands. I told Knowles & Graham to go get him and I went on out side the town towards Beney."

According to another version, as they reached the crossroads in the center of the town, Knowles and Graham dismounted to chase a German running into a house.

Using their pistols, Knowles and Graham took 30 Germans prisoner.

"On leaving the town [Pannes] I was still sitting sidewise on top of the tank with my legs hanging down on the left side when all at once I noticed all the paint start to chip off the other side and at the same time I noticed machine guns."

"I saw the paint fly off the side of the tank and heard machine guns so I jumped off and got in a shell hole. It was small and the bullets nocked all of the front edge in on me. Here I was nearvous."

After "I dismounted in haste and got in a shell hole which was none too large every time I started to get out the boshe shot at me."

"The tank had not seen me get off and was going on. The infantry was about 200 m. [meters] back of me and did not advance. One runner on my right got hit."

"I was on the point of getting scared as I was about a hundred yards ahead of the infantry and all alone in the field. If I went back [that is, returned toward the infantry] the infantry would think I was running and there was no reason [for me] to go forward alone."

"If I did not [rejoin the tank] they [the infantry] would not support the tank and it might get hurt. Besides m.g. [machine gun] bullets are unplesant to hear."

"All the time the infernal tank was going on alone as the men [inside] had not noticed my hurried departure. At last the bright thought occurred to me that I could move across the front in an oblique fashion and not appear [to the infantry] to run [from the enemy] yet at the same time get back [to the infantry]."

"Finally I decided that I could get back obliquely. So I started" — "listening for the machine guns with all my ears."

"As soon as the m.g.'s opened I would lay down and beat the bullets each time" — "laying down in a great hurry when I heard them, in this manner I hoped to beat the bullets to me. Some time I will figure the speed of sounds and bullets and see if I was right. It is the only use I know of that math has ever been to me."

After getting back to the infantry, "I found the Major of the infantry and asked him if he would come on after the tank. He would not [do so] as the next battalion on his left had not come up."

Another version had the infantry commander a captain, who said that the troops on his right had not advanced to his forward position.

"I asked him to send a runner to the tank to recall it. He said it was 'not his tank' " — "he was killed ten minutes later."

"Then I drew a long breath and went after the tank on foot as I could not let it be going against a whole town [Beney] alone. It is strange but quite true that at this time I was not the least scared, as I had the idea of getting the tank fixed in my head. I did not even fear the bullets though I could see the guns spitting at me, I did however run like H ——."

"I went and I burned the breaze too. So did the bullets. I kept the tank between me and the bullets as much as possible."

"On reaching the tank about four hundred yards out in the field I tapped on the back door with my stick, and thank God it was a long one. The sgt looked out and saluted and said what do you want now Colonel, I told him to turn and come back. He was much depressed. I walked just ahead of him on the return trip and was quite safe."

A later and far less disjointed version that was supposed to be humorous:

Colonel Patton, who was still sitting on the top of the tank, here had the most horrible experience; he could hear machine gun fire but could not locate them until glancing down the left side of the tank about six inches below his hand he saw the paint flying from the side of the tank as the result of numerous machine gun bullets striking against the tank. Owing to his heroic desire to make the tank a less enticing target he leaped from the tank and landed in a shell hole a great distance away. This shell hole however was exceedingly small and the Germans took an unpleasant delight in shooting at its upper rim so that the Colonel was greatly perturbed at finding [himself] covered with dirt. His embarrassment was enhanced by the fact that the tank unawares of this continued into the field, while the Infantry which had passed through the village was halted about 200 meters behind the Colonel. He was in a great state of perplexity as if he moved backwards and conducted a strategical withdrawal the Infantry would think a tank officer was running away; should he move forward he would become a distinct target of the four machine guns which he was now able to see about 500 meters to his front. He finally solved the problem by moving sideways until he regained the Infantry. During the course of this movement he was repeatedly forced to seek shelter in small shell holes. On reaching the Infantry he asked them if they would move forward. This they refused to do.

He then asked them if they would send a runner to the tank which was cruising about in the field some 500 meters to the front. To this request the heroic Infantry made this reply "Hell no, It aint my tank." Colonel Patton was then faced with the unfortunate necessity of going to the tank himself. This he did in record time and without accident.

"By this time four more tanks had come up but there was no officer [with them]. I put Lt. Knowles . . . [on them and] asked the infantry if they would follow [the tanks]. They said yes so I started the tanks."

"We now . . . decided to attack the town [Beney]." He arranged the five tanks in line.

"While Col. Patton was arranging the attack on Beney, he handed his haversack to Sgt. Graham, who was guarding the twenty [or thirty] Germans. While the Sgt was capturing another German he saw in a house, the prisoners emptied the haversack and filled it with rocks. The loss was not discovered until hours later." It had contained his flask, razor, and tobacco.

"In the mean time some of our m.gs. had pushed out in front and one tank thought they were Bosch and began to shoot at them. I had no time to get some one so went out again [to stop the tank gunner from shooting]."

"A third time I went out as the tanks were keeping too far to the right but the last time was not bad as the [German] machine gunners were mostly dead or chased away by the tanks."

"The tanks went on to Beney but the infantry swerved off to the right and I sent a Lt. out to change the direction of the tanks. Then I followed the advance on foot but there was not much shooting. The tanks had scared the Bosch away."

"We took the town [and] 4 field guns and 16 machine guns."

Sometime during the foregoing, at 3 P.M., Patton sent his next recorded message to the IV Corps. He reported that he was 3 kilometers northwest of Pannes in what had formerly been no-man's-land. Five tanks had entered Pannes — perhaps he meant Beney — and were proceeding beyond. One tank had captured 30 prisoners in Pannes and had turned them over to the infantry. Some long-range machine gun fire was coming in, but no artillery fire was falling nearby.

"Then I walked along the battle front to see how the left battalion

[Brett's] had gotten on. It was a very long way and I had had no sleep for four nights and no food all the day as I lost my sack chasing a boshe, I got some crackers off a dead one (they had not blood on them . . .) they were very good but I would have given a lot for a drink of the brandy I had had in my sack."

"I was very tired indeed and hungry as I had lost the sack with my rations and my flask of brandy . . . I found 25 Tanks. They had taken the town [Nonsard] and only lost 4 men & two officers but they were out of gas."

"The Major of the left battalion was crying because he had no more gas. He was very tired and had a bullet through his nose [it was a minor wound], I comforted him and started home alone to get some gas."

"All my runners were gone so I started back seven miles to tell them to get some gas [up forward]. That was the only bad part of the fight. I had had no sleep for two nights and nothing to eat since the night before except some crackers I got off a dead Bosch. I would have given a lot for a little brandy but even my water was gone."

"It was most interesting over the battlefield. Like the books but much less dramatic. The dead were about mostly hit in the head. There were a lot of our men stripping off buttons and other things but they always covered the face of the dead in a nice way.

"I saw one very amusing thing which I would have liked to have photographed. Right in the middle of a large field where there had never been a trench was a shell hole from a 9.7 gun. The hole was at least 8 feet deep and 15 across. On the edge of it was a dead rat, not a large healthy rat but a small field rat not over twice the size of a mouse. No wonder the war costs so much."

"When I got to . . . it had been raining two hours and the mud was bad. Here I met an officer sight seeing and he gave me a lift. This was luckey as the car got stuck in a jam and went slower than the men on foot and an air plane dropped a bomb on the road and killed two soldiers who had been walking just back of me.

"I got a motor cycle and got the gas and reported to the Corps."

"This is a very egotistical account of the affair full of 'I' but it will interest you.

"I at least proved to my own satisfaction that I have nerve. I was the only man on the front line except gen McArthur who never ducked a shell. I wanted to but it is foolish as it does no good. If they are going to hit you they will.

"I had in this action 144 tanks and 33 French Tanks quite a command."

Patton's report to the IV Corps of the action on September 12 read in part:

> . . . tanks with the 1st Division delayed in trenches. Attacked M.G. position in Bois Quart de Reserve with Inf. 7 leading tanks attacked and cleared Nonsard before arrival of Inf. Heavy work in trenches, used up gas faster than expected. Tanks were out of gas at 2 P.M. Spent . . . night 800 meters south [of] Nonsard. . . .
>
> American tanks with 42nd Division delayed in trenches. Tanks attacked Pannes with Inf. One tank attacked M.G. nest at Beney but Inf. was not up and tanks had to come back. But Germans stopped firing. 5 tanks attacked Beney at 12:45 P.M. but as Inf. had other objectives tanks withdrew after entering town. 1:30 7 [tanks] attacked Beney with Inf. and cleaned town. All gas exhausted at 3 P.M. Tanks spent night at Pannes. During night 12–13 [September] two tanks dragged up gas by sled from Bernecourt.

The French tanks with the 42d Division, he continued, found the mud so difficult that they followed the infantry to Maizerais. There they were stopped by trouble with their tracks.

Casualties, so far as Patton could determine, were 2 tanks put out of action by direct artillery hits, 3 by engine trouble, 2 French tanks by broken tracks. Forty tanks had become stuck in ditches or trenches but all were being cleared. Thirty were stalled because of lack of gas, but were being filled as gasoline arrived. Eighty U.S. and 25 French tanks were in operating condition for action on September 13.

Four men were reported killed, three officers and four men wounded, one severely.

The tankers had captured more than 150 German prisoners and had turned them over to the infantry for removal to the rear.

Afterward, when more accurate figures were available, the losses of the first day of action totaled 5 men killed, 4 officers and 15 men wounded. Of them, 2 were killed while inside tank, none was wounded there. Of the 174 tanks entering the battle, 3 were destroyed, 22 were ditched so badly that they were out of action all day, 14 had serious mechanical trouble.

The attack on September 12 had gone generally as planned against slight German resistance. The action was no real test of the ability of the tanks as fighting machines, but was interesting and valuable as an exploit in mechanics, driving, and endurance. Designed to cross trenches six feet wide, the tanks actually crossed ditches ten to fourteen feet wide, the first ones being pulled and hauled through by tankers, infantrymen, and engineers, later ones helped by cables that had been brought forward.

Brett had led the 326th Battalion with courage and coolness, walking in front of the tanks to guide them for several kilometers despite enemy machine gun fire, and setting a fine example for his men. His battalion reached its final objective, Nonsard, where Brett himself shot two German machine gunners out of the church steeple.

The French tanks had great difficulty crossing the trenches and never managed to pass through the infantry and lead the foot soldiers. Yet Chanoine's tanks remained close on the heels of the infantry and gave them invaluable support, in terms both of firepower and morale.

Compton's men encountered obstacles in the trenches east of St. Baussant, then entered Essey with the infantry, took Pannes, and, after some gasoline came forward, went on to take St. Benoit at 9 P.M.

All in all, Patton's tankers, known among themselves as the "Treat 'em Rough boys," had done an excellent job. In an initial encounter with the enemy, soldiers usually need at least a day to become familiar with and adjusted to the new and frightening sights and sounds of combat. Patton's tankers were so well prepared and so keyed up that they had performed like veterans.

The only real difficulty, and that was not the tankers' fault, was that the tanks had used up gasoline three times faster than had been expected because of the muddy ground, the large number of trenches and their broadness. Most of the tanks were out of gas by 3 P.M. Some additional fuel arrived by means of sleds dragged first by trucks to the trenches, then by tanks — originally in reserve — across the trenches and into no-man's-land.

All supplies were drawn from the main supply dump at Menil la Tour and brought forward by truck to advance dumps, where the combat units secured rations, ammunition, and other items.

Three trucks loaded with gasoline tried to move to Essey, but military policemen, who were regulating the badly congested traffic, stopped them and refused to let them continue. "This fact materially hampered the operations of the tanks on the morning of the 13th."

Diary

September 13 (Friday): "Saw Compton at 8 A.M. Sent [the rest of] his tanks to St. Benoit. Gen R[ockenbach] came up and we got gas to Brett who started for Vigneulles at 1 A.M."

"On the thirteenth we did nothing."

"The 13th of September was uneventful except that it marked a long struggle to obtain gasoline for the tanks and clearly showed the necessity for having large caterpillar tractors with each battalion to carry gasoline across country since the roads were so congested that it took thirty-two hours to move two trucks of gasoline fourteen (14) kilometers." Some gasoline trucks were on the road since 9 A.M. of the previous day.

Compton managed to get a few tanks from Pannes to St. Benoit during the morning. As a little gas became available, a few others moved to St. Benoit. There they were forced to remain immobile for lack of fuel. About 20 French tanks arrived nearby, and they too could go no farther.

Gasoline arrived for Brett's tanks in the early afternoon. After the tanks were replenished, they rolled through Nonsard to Vigneulles, where 50 were assembled by midnight.

Meanwhile, IV Corps Field Order 26, issued at 4:25 P.M., September 13, announced: "The enemy continues to retreat."

Diary

September 14 (Saturday): "Joined Brett at Vigneulles at 6 A.M. Went on. Passed St. Maurice all bound towards Woel. Here we found we were ahead of our infantry. Sent patrol to Woel. It was attacked. Lt. Grant took up 5 more tanks total 8 . . . I had heard show was over & stopped all tanks moving north. Reported to 1st Div & Corps. Got orders to pull out. Arranged to do so. Had a big row with Gen. R."

". . . on the fourteenth the left battalion personally conducted by me went to hunt for the enemy. We found the only place on the entire front where for the space half a mile there were no troops. We went through and were attacked by the boshe. We drove them six miles, took a town, Jonville, on the Hindenburg Line, [a] battery of field guns [and] 12 machine guns but no prisoners, then finding that we were eight miles ahead of our own line, and that all the canon in that part of Germany were shooting at us we withdrew with only four men hit. I was in at the start of this very fine feat of arms, but not at the finish as I was ordered back just after the tanks started and before we knew the boshe were there. We withdrew that night. Total loses 4 men killed 4 officers and 4 men wounded . . .

"This is a very egotistical letter but interesting as it shows that vanity is stronger than fear and that in war as now waged there is little of the element of fear, it is too well organized and too stupendous."

What had happened was that Brett's tankers on the morning of September 14 were unable to gain touch with the 1st Division headquarters. Impatient to move forward, Patton decided to move Brett's battalion through St. Maurice to Woel in the hope of finding infantrymen along the Woel-St. Benoit road, a logical consolidation line, for Compton's tanks working with the 42d Division were at St. Benoit.

Brett started forward shortly after 6 A.M. At 6:45, Patton sent a message to his adjutant, Captain Hebert, who was holding down the brigade command post, now quite far in the rear. He told Hebert to let the IV Corps headquarters and General Rockenbach know that Brett was pushing ahead with 51 tanks. "I will be back [to the CP] soon as possible wait for me." Then he rushed forward to join Brett's advance.

With Patton accompanying them, the tankers moved through St. Maurice against no opposition. They obtained from a partially burned and abandoned German warehouse some gasoline and a large quantity of cigars, hard bread, and blankets.

They reached the vicinity of Woel — about two kilometers short of the village — by 9 A.M. There, in an auto traveling from Woel Patton recognized Brigadier General Dennis E. Nolan, an original member of Pershing's staff. Nolan knew Patton well and stopped to chat. He asked where the tanks were going. Patton answered they were looking for a fight and for the 1st Division. Nolan informed him that the Germans had evacuated Woel, which was being held by about 20 French infantrymen. He had no idea where the American infantry was.

After telling Brett to conceal the tanks in the bushes and hedges along the road, Patton at 10 A.M. sent a message to the commanding generals of the IV Corps and 1st Division, also to Rockenbach, asking for instructions. He reminded them that the code name of his brigade was "Novelty" and that his headquarters could be reached by telephone through the exchange at "Orphans," no doubt the IV Corps. He hoped that Hebert at his command post would send a runner with any information or instructions that came through.

Patton also dispatched four officers mounted on captured German horses to try to locate some — any — American infantry troops in the neighboring forests.

While everyone was waiting for news from higher headquarters and for the return of the mounted patrol, three trucks filled with gasoline arrived. The trucks had been attacked by a hostile airplane and one soldier had been wounded by a bomb fragment that passed through his arm. The tanks were refueled and the men were given corned beef and coffee.

The officers on horseback returned and reported no infantrymen close by.

Still without word from corps, division, or Rockenbach at noon, Patton sent a patrol of three tanks and five men on foot to Woel. He instructed the men to continue through Woel, then go down the road toward St. Benoit for two kilometers and see if they met any Americans.

The patrol found the town clear of enemy troops and no one on the St. Benoit road. While returning, the tanks encountered a German unit in close-order march, a column with eight machine guns and a battery of 77-mm. cannon. Sending a runner to Patton and Brett, the patrol commander reported that he was going to attack the Germans. Patton dispatched five tanks to assist him.

"These eight tanks unsupported by Infantry attacked the enemy and drove them to Jonville destroying five machine guns and driving the enemy away from the battery of 77's. In attempting to attach these guns to the rear of the tanks two officers and four men were wounded by shrapnel fire and the attempt to carry off the guns was abandoned."

Two tanks, disabled by mechanical trouble, were coupled to a third and towed to the battalion position just below Woel. The enemy began to register shells on the location of the battalion with 150-mm. howitzers, and "as the Commanding Officer had ascertained that he was at least two miles in front of the infantry line, it was decided to withdraw to St. Maurice."

From there Patton returned to his command post. He sent a report of the day's action and commended Brett for his gallantry and tactical sense.

At 9 P.M., he received word that all the tanks were to withdraw from the battlefield and concentrate in the Bois de la Hazelle, near the original jump-off positions. With the exception of three French and two American tanks, which were partially destroyed by direct hits, all the tanks, moving only during the hours of darkness, were in the assembly area by the night of September 18.

According to Patton's humorous account:

The battle field abounded in large and deep shell holes. In those several tanks were lost but all were soon recovered except one. No trace of this could be found until some days later as an Engineer officer, walking over the field was accosted by a lean and hungry soldier who asked the authority of the officer for liberating his two pigeons. He and they were sticking by the lost tank to the last and while he cared little of his own suffering he hated to see the little birdies die. Why he was so secretive or failed to let us know by pigeon of his whereabouts is one of the unsolved mysteries of the war.

In Patton's severely military account of the operation:

Tactical Conclusions. Owing to the fact of the enemy's failure at serious resistance the full value of the tanks was not susceptible of demonstration. In spite of very serious obstacles of terrain the tanks were in a position to aid the Infantry and would have done so had such assistance been necessary. As it was, the tanks entered the towns of Nonsard, Pannes and Benney ahead of the Infantry and captured the town of Jonville unaided by any Infantry whatever.

To Beatrice:

All the losses were small, absurdly so. The great feat the tanks performed was getting through at all. The conditions could not have been worse. Only 40% did it the first day but we had 80% up by morning. The men were fine. Nearly all the officers led the tanks on foot.

This was quite different from the way the British worked it. General Elles, feeling that he had to establish a tank tradition, accompanied the tankers into combat at Cambrai while riding in the lead tank, which was marked with his battle flag and pennant. His chief of staff, Colonel Fuller, had remonstrated against this decision, but later admitted that he had been wrong, Elles right. Tankers belonged in tanks.

But, of course, the British heavies were large enough to accommodate General Elles. In contrast, the French Renaults were built to hold two crewmen. Although Patton — as well as Brett and Compton — might have driven a tank in the attack, he would have lacked the capacity to direct the action, for radio communications from and to tanks had yet to be developed.

> Gen R. gave me hell for going up [with the forward elements] but it had to be done. At least I will not sit in a dug out and have my men out in the fighting.
>
> I am feeling fine and just at present [he was writing on the 16th] I have little to do.
>
> I saved my battle map for you as a souvenir. Here are some cap ornaments I got off a dead German. Personally I never fired a shot except to kill two poor horses with broken legs.

Rockenbach was angry over Patton's conduct during the battle. He believed that a tank brigade commander belonged at his headquarters or in close touch with it at all times. A lieutenant colonel in command of a brigade was not supposed to be running around the battlefield, where it was impossible for higher headquarters, meaning Rockenbach, to reach him — either to gain information or to transmit instructions.

A harsh letter from Rockenbach to Patton made these points: 1) the five light tanks of a platoon had to work together, had to be kept intact under its platoon commander, and not be allowed to split up; 2) when a tank brigade was allotted to a corps, the commander was to remain at the corps headquarters or be in close telephonic communications with it; 3) "I wish you would especially impress on your men that they are fighting [with] tanks, they are not Infantry, and any man who abandons his Tank will in the future be tried [by court-martial]. If a Tank is disabled one member of the crew must stay with the Tank while the other gets out and gets the necessary assistance."

This, of course, was contrary to Patton's instructions to his men who, he had made clear, were supposed to fight, tank or no tank.

Rockenbach was probably right. Tankers fought with tanks, they fought in organized units of tanks, and they fought as directed by a chain of command that needed every link to function properly and effectively. Hebert, left by Patton at his command post to answer the telephone and coordinate routine matters, was incapable of doing more than that. Rockenbach needed a responsive and responsible commander — Patton — at the tank brigade command post or headquarters. For without Patton to receive and transmit the instructions that came to Rockenbach from higher headquarters, without Patton to advise Rockenbach on the feasibility or impracticality of the orders issued by higher headquarters, without Patton at a central location where he could seize the initiative and take immediate advantage of the breaks, Rockenbach — or any other commander in his position — was helpless and lost. In short, by leaving his command post, Patton cut the Rockenbach–Patton chain of command, thereby nullifying Rockenbach's authority over the brigade and his responsibility to the First Army commander.

Patton, on the other hand, felt that too much depended on the performance of his tanks — the whole tank program, his entire training system, the overall meaning of tanks in warfare, the attack itself — for him to remain in the rear largely in the role of observer, reporter, coordinator, and detached director. His concept of leadership was more primitive and personal than Rockenbach's and more suited to an earlier age of warfare, when the melee of combat revolved essentially about the fearless behavior of the commander. Patton's type of commander inspired his men by example, by leading, by being in the thick of the action.

Had he placed Viner as his representative or deputy commander or chief of staff in his command post and had he been able to fashion a better system of communications between his CP and himself, he would have maintained the chain of command even as he personally led his men in battle.

Patton tried to mollify Rockenbach when he saw him on September 15. But by then there was no time to quibble over St. Mihiel. They were already immersed in plans for a new operation.

A day later, when Pershing sent a congratulatory letter to Rockenbach on the successful and important part played by the tanks in the St. Mihiel offensive, Rockenbach got over his pique. He forwarded Pershing's letter to Patton along with an expression of his own appreciation for the magnificent manner in which Patton's tankers had performed.

According to Lieutenant Julian K. Morrison, the tankers had operated with such élan because of the training they had received at Bourg:

> Every day, some Sundays excepted, a fixed schedule was carried out from day light to dark and then for the officers school at night. The writer [Morrison] always got a great deal of encouragement from these lectures, usually given by Col Patton. He [Morrison] was made to understand by the Colonel that a Tank Officer was meant to die. His [Patton's] favorite message to his officers was "Go forward, go forward. If your tank breaks down go forward with the Infantry. There will be no excuse for your failure in this, and if I find any tank officer behind the front line of infantry I will —— [probably 'shoot him']." All Tank Officers know the rest. The result was that each officer left these lectures with the determination never to fall behind the front line of Infantry no matter what happened . . . This message of the Colonel's was passed on down by the officers to their men with the result that in the St. Mihiel drive Tankers could be seen any where from one to seven kilometers in front of the infantry. Everyone fought — cooks, company clerks, mess sergeants, runners and mechanics. So closely was the order carried out that the Tank Corps nearly starved for two or three days afterward. Needless to say before the next fight orders came out to the effect that anyone leaving the post assigned to him would be dealt with by Court Martial. The courage of the Tank Corps having been sufficiently proved.

More than the courage of the Tank Corps had been proved. The St. Mihiel offensive proved the success of Patton's methods of training for and commanding in combat. No troops had better morale, more desire to close with the enemy, a more consistent wish to go forward aggressively than Patton's tankers. They were anxious and eager to fight, and they were disappointed because they saw St. Mihiel as anything but a real battle, a real trial of their strength and mettle. The Germans gave way too easily. It was not much of a fight. The tankers would have preferred a real test because they felt they were ready to take on and to lick the best enemy troops in the world.

This was what distinguished Patton's leadership.

Without the least suspicion that her husband was in the thick of combat, Beatrice sent Pershing a letter on September 13 to wish him happiness on his birthday. "George writes in every letter," she added, "how happy he is in his work. He loves the tanks; and by our [news]papers, they seem to fulfil all his expectations."

Several days later she read an account of St. Mihiel cabled on September 16 by Junius B. Wood exclusively to the Los Angeles Evening *Express* and the Chicago Daily *News*. "Californian Perched on Tank During Battle," ran the headline on a story featuring Patton riding on the tail of a tank. Like a cavalryman.

CHAPTER 30

Meuse-Argonne

"I am reaping what I sewed."

Diary

September 15 (Sunday): "Got ready to move out [of the St. Mihiel sector] and arranged plans etc . . . saw Gen R[ockenbach] at Ligney and went over plans [for new operation] in a hurried way. Went to bed."

September 16: "Studied map [of the Meuse-Argonne sector] and made up plan. Bought a raincoat etc as I had lost mine."

The same tank organization that had operated at St. Mihiel — Brett's and Compton's battalions and Chanoine's 14th and 17th Groupes — would remain under Patton's command for the Meuse-Argonne offensive, but this time would work with the I Corps.

Patton drove to the new battle area and, dressed in a French uniform, inspected the front near Vauquois, making a careful reconnaissance of the ground.

Chanoine's tanks traveled by train to Clermont and detrained in the railway yard. They moved to a nearby place of concealment. The tankers started to work on their machines and prepare them for operational use. In the old area, Brett's and Compton's men, tucked away in a forest, were giving their tanks similar treatment.

Diary

September 18 (Wednesday): Got telephone connected and office and mess running. Expect to be shelled at 9:30 now 10:05 and nothing has happened but they [the Germans] are shelling Paris to the west.

September 19: "Went to Front line and found trenches not very wide. And ground rather better than I had expected."

Letter, GSP, Jr., to Beatrice, September 19, 1918

We are getting ready for another show and I am sitting in the only remaining house of a village. They have not shelled us yet but doubtless will shortly as Americans don't seem to be able to conceal them selves very well. I just got back from a reconnaissance where I was dressed like a Frenchman. I hope I did not get any bugs . . . I fancy our next show will be less easy than the first that is if the bosch fight and I think they will. The ground however is better for us being less of a swamp than the St. Mihiel salient proved to be. Still as it has been raining all the time it may get muddie here also. I just got through writing a report on the last action and recommended certain officers for gallantry. I hope they get something . . .

I must stop now and eat supper before it gets dark as we can have no lights. I will wire you after the next fight as I did this time. I am very well and love you with all my heart.

Diary

September 20 (Friday): "Went up to O.P. [observation post] in A.M. . . . Went to [railroad] station at 12 n. to unload . . . Unloading very badly handled. No plan at all. Much track trouble. Some shelling but all high."

Brett's battalion, now renamed the 344th, and Compton's battalion, now the 345th, detrained in Clermont and moved during the hours of darkness to wooded areas for concealment. While the tankers worked on their tanks in the general wooded area known as the Forêt de Facq, officers reconnoitered routes to their jump-off points.

.   .   .

The Meuse-Argonne attack, the second operation in which an American field army acted as an independent entity, was part of a larger Franco-American offensive. On September 26, along the front stretching from the Meuse River on the east (right) to the Suippes River on the west, the French Fourth Army on the left and the U. S. First Army on the right would attack generally to the north.

The American zone of attack lay between the Meuse and Aisne rivers and included the Argonne Forest, which was in the western part of the sector, near the Aisne.

Pershing assumed command of his front on September 22 and put three

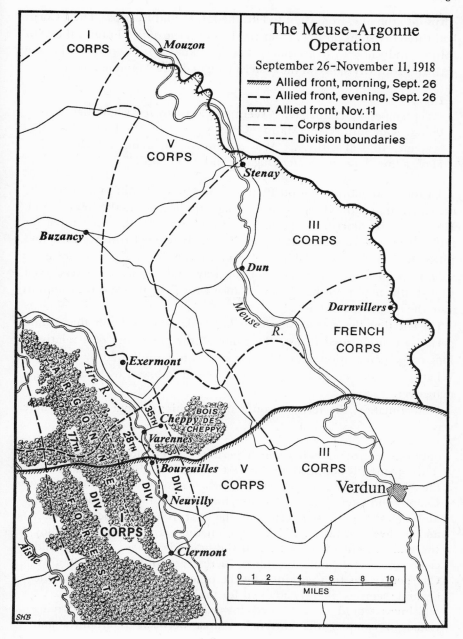

The Meuse-Argonne Operation

September 26–November 11, 1918

- Allied front, morning, Sept. 26
- Allied front, evening, Sept. 26
- Allied front, Nov. 11
- Corps boundaries
- Division boundaries

corps into the line, from right to left, the III, V, and I Corps. The I Corps had three divisions on line, from right to left, the 36th (Traub), the 28th (Muir), and the 77th (Alexander). Patton's tanks would operate with the 35th and 28th Divisions on the eastern fringes of the Argonne Forest.

Diary

September 21 (Saturday): "Went to Corps to see what they were doing. Got lost. Gen [Malin] Craig C[hief] of S[taff of I Corps] very nice to deal with . . . Was told to submit plan. Which I did. Have a fine elephant shelter Dug out and a good bed."

Patton's "Memorandum on Plan for the Use of Tanks" was a lengthy document that showed his usual thorough application to the job at hand. He opened by describing the terrain, which was less than favorable for tanks, for it was "an old battle-ground, heavily seamed with trenches and pitted with numerous shell-holes." Since, however, he had no choice, he would try to dispose the tanks in the way that promised success, even though this might not be "in accordance with most preconceived notions as to the proper use of tanks."

He felt that the correct way of using tanks was in depth that would permit a concentrated thrust. This offered the possibility of a relatively long-range penetration, and this in turn was to be followed by a pursuit. What he wished was to initiate a shock action followed by a cavalry-type maneuver.

Unfortunately, the terrain would inhibit this to some extent. There was

only one narrow opening which permits the employment of tanks. This opening is bounded on the west by the line of bluffs paralleling the Aire River . . . and on the east by . . . the towns of Vaugquois, Cheppy and Exermont . . . The sector to the west . . . is too wooded and mountainous, the sector to the east is cut by deep ravines and by five streams . . . The question then is how best to employ the tanks at our disposal . . . to the best advantage. . . . it would clearly be best to hold the tanks in reserve until the line Baulny-Charpentry has been attained by the other arms. From here on the ground seems excellently adapted for tanks. On the other hand . . . selfishness would be exhibited toward the Infantry, who, having toiled to conquer the entrenched area between Boureuilles and

Varennes, would be deprived of the pleasure of hunting Germans in the open, and this pleasure would be usurped by the tanks . . . There is bound to be fighting on the line Boureuilles-Vauquois. There may not be fighting north of Baulny, because there may be no Germans left to fight. It therefore seems advisable, in spite of the badness of the terrain, to recommend the employment of the tanks against the first hostile trenches . . .

It is respectfully submitted that infantry should progress as if tanks were not present. The tanks, whenever humanly possible, will precede the infantry and do their utmost to reduce the casualties in that arm . . . the latter should follow . . . but not simply as spectators of the fight, as has happened, but rather by the use of their arms, machine guns, 37's and rifles. They should do everything to intensify the fire which the presence of the tanks partially insures.

Patton asked for engineer and artillery support, "a special aeroplane" to communicate with the artillery. He discussed signals — flags, pennants, and pigeons.

The supply of gas for tanks is as important as the supply of ammunition for guns. Both revert to worthless junk without the supplies . . .

Regimental and Battalion Commanders of infantry should be requested to inform tanks acting near them of any orders as to change of plan which may be received by them, as otherwise the tanks will unquestionably become lost and not conform in the best way to changes which may arise.

Briefly, Patton envisaged using his tanks in a relatively narrow corridor, about three kilometers wide, between the Forêt d'Argonne and the Bois de Cheppy, where the ground was least difficult for tank operations. Normally, this opening would accommodate a single battalion. But the Aire River flowed through the length of the corridor and posed a complication. The river separated the zones of action of the 35th and 28th Divisions. Thus, it would make sense to put one tank battalion with one division and the other tank battalion with the other infantry division. But the 35th Division, east of the Aire, had room, that is open ground, suitable for committing two tank companies, while the 28th Division, on the west bank, had space for only one. This led Patton to decide to use a single tank battalion with both divisions even though the tankers on one side of the river would be unable to come to the aid of the others.

Brett was, in Patton's opinion, the more competent battalion commander, and his tanks had seen more action than Compton's at St. Mihiel. Consequently, Brett's tankers were more experienced, while his tanks were more worn and in worse condition.

Patton put Brett's battalion up front, with two of his companies working with the 35th Division and one company with the 28th. Immediately behind Brett would come Compton's men, with the companies deployed the same way across the front. Chanoine's Schneiders, inferior to the Renaults, would bring up the rear.

Although this deployment spread his units in line, that is laterally across the front, rather than in the preferred fashion, in column or depth, Patton sought nevertheless to attain sufficient push and thrust by means of his three waves. He hoped that Brett's battalion could start and sustain an advance to the first objective. There Brett's tanks would probably be mechanically exhausted or knocked out of action; they would be at the end of their usefulness. Patton would then pass Compton's tankers through Brett's for a drive to the next objective. There, where the ground was better for the heavier Schneider tanks, he would leapfrog Chanoine's French groupes through Compton's men for an advance as far as the tanks could go.

Craig, the I Corps chief of staff, approved Patton's plan, had Patton's lengthy memo reproduced, and furnished a copy to each division commander in the corps for information and guidance.

Diary

September 22 (Sunday): "345 Bn tanks not yet arrived. Am very mad. Got 20,000 gal gas sent to Langres for Pigeon baskets. Wrote memo on operation of Tanks. Still madder with Capt. Compton. He is an ass."

Letter, GSP, Jr., to Beatrice, September 22, 1918

Life is just one D—— thing after another. One whole Battalion has failed to show up and I cant find it. The Battalion Commander spent the day looking for a house instead of getting his Tanks. He is a fool but I a greater one to trust him.

Still I am reaping what I sewed. I spoon fed these hounds so much that they are helpless and run to me every time they ought to go to the W.C. to see if it is all right. Some times I think I am not such a great commander after all. Just a fighting animal. Still I will improve in time. At least if one learns by mistakes I ought to be wise. I have made all [the mistakes] there are.

I am getting on fine with the Corps & the Division which is a comfort as things ought to [be] right some where.

One fine example of efficiency nix has just happened. 100,000 gallons of gas arrived in tank cars with no pump. Now we can't get it out except by dippers!!!

It is a good thing I have a cheerful disposition. I have inspite of certain lapses . . .

But I have got a rotten staff and no mistake. Probably my own fault. I have done too much for them. Well I will never do it again if I pull through this. But it is a big if. Hellish big.

Diary

September 23 (Monday): "Got all 345 Tanks unloaded by daylight under shell fire but no casualties. Got lot of mail from home. Five letters from B. Rained all day and a lot of shelling over us at Clermont. Cussed out Brett & Compton for carelessness etc."

September 24 (Tuesday): "Got Corps Plan. Wrote field order & annex. Gen R came up. Things are in pretty good shape but we are very short on men. The Bosch took pictures of us so I guess we shall be shelled or something to night. Wrote B & Mama."

Patton accumulated and stored 20,000 gallons of gasoline in reserve, stocks to be issued after the initial day's action. He ordered each tank moving into battle to carry two 2-liter cans full of gasoline on its tail even though this was dangerous — a bullet penetrating a can might turn the fuel into flame and burn the tank carrying it. But the risk, he decided, was preferable to having the tanks run out of gasoline prematurely as at St. Mihiel.

Patton issued his Field Order on September 24. After giving detailed instructions to each element of his command on routes and methods of advance, Patton gave orders on supply and liaison. The command post then established and the 321st Repair and Salvage Company were to remain at Camp Fourgons, where they were located in a quarry relatively safe from enemy bombardment.

Particularly for Rockenbach's benefit, although he was doing so for his units too, he indicated that he would establish an advance CP at the 35th Division advance headquarters at Les Côtes de Forimont. Then,

After H plus 1 hour the Brigade Commander [Patton] will move forward along the line Route Nationale No. 46, and will be up with the leading tanks at H plus 3½ hours. He will be accompanied by a group of from 6 to 10 runners.

This large group of messengers would enable him to remain in contact with Rockenbach and vice versa.

In an annex to the field order, Patton took up repair-and-salvage efforts, motor transport, supply, administration, and intelligence.

Finally, he made three pungent observations:

All Officers at the Brigade P.C. [command post] are charged with keeping the Corps Commander, the Chief of Tank Corps and the Brigade Commander fully informed as to the state of affairs. By using every means to get information forward some may arrive.

The criminal waste of Government property is a fault of our Army. It will not occur in the 1st Brigade Tank Corps.

The attention of men not in the fight is called to the fact that they have often a more difficult and important part to play than if they were with the tanks. Their good work will not be forgotten.

Rockenbach's strictures over St. Mihiel were neither ignored nor overlooked.

Letter, GSP, Jr., to Beatrice, September 24, 1918

We had a very quiet day except that a shell took of[f] a mans foot for which I am sorry . . .

There is nothing of interest to report so I will go to bed as I shant have another sleep for some time.

Diary

September 25 (Wednesday): Inspected battalions at 9 A.M. 345th very dirty, ordered correction. 344th better but could stand improvement. Gen R called. Went to corps to get H-hour and D-day, also passes for gasoline trucks. Went to meeting at 35th Division. One of our trucks full of runners was hit by a shell 6:15 P.M. Near Neuvilly, no report yet. Had big dinner. Will start soon. Wrote B.

GSP, Jr., "Personal Glimpses of General Pershing," 1924

I personally know of one occasion when the presence of the Commander [Pershing] received a spontaneous tribute. Just at dark on September 25th many of us were lying in the ditches bordering the Flury-Varennes road, waiting for a German concentration [of artillery fire] to cease, when suddenly the big car with its 4 stars came up the road going to the front. Moved by a single impulse we all arose, and regardless of the shells, stood at salute until he had passed us.

On the night of September 25, the tankers moved to their departure positions. During this approach march, it was necessary for four tank companies — about 80 tanks — to cross a bridge at Neuville. As the leading tank arrived at the bridge, a German barrage opened, apparently aimed at the bridge. Some shells landed nearby and killed two military policemen who were directing traffic across the structure. The tanks halted. The moment the artillery ceased, one company rushed across the bridge. The Germans renewed their fire but only at regular intervals. Between these periodic shellings, the tanks raced across the structure without harm.

At their jump-off points, the men tried to catch a few hours' sleep. They knew they would be awakened at 2:30 A.M. by the start of a violent three-hour artillery preparation to be fired by American guns. At 5:30, they would attack.

Letter, GSP, Jr., to Beatrice, September 25, 1918

Just a word to you before I leave to play a little part in what promises to be the biggest battle of the war or world so far.

We kick off in the morning but this will not be mailed until after that . . .

I will have two Battalions and a group of French tanks in the show in all about 140 Tanks . . . I think that after this show we will have a rest. I hope so for the men are tired and all the tanks need over hauling . . .

I am always nearvous about this time just as at Polo or at Foot ball before the game starts but so far I have been all right after that. I hope I keep on that way it is more plesant.

Well if I wrote all night I could not tell you how much I love you and I had better eat a little first as I shant be able to for a few days.

. . .

The artillery opened its preparatory barrage on schedule, and at 5:30, September 26, in a heavy mist, American soldiers moved forward in attack. Some of the leading tanks encountered a mine field just beyond the American trenches, "but thanks to the courtesy of the Germans in leaving up warning signs the tanks avoided this danger."

As long as the mist lasted, the tanks advanced with little difficulty, for the enemy was unable to detect them. But in midmorning, around ten o'clock, the fog suddenly lifted, and the German fires became intense and accurate. American infantrymen, particularly near Varennes and Cheppy, became somewhat confused, panicky, and disorganized.

Patton had said he would remain for at least an hour after the attack started in his advance CP — code-named "Bonehead," it was a dugout on the southern edge of some woods at Les Côtes de Forimont. But he became impatient. He could hear the tanks, the artillery, the machine guns, but the fog was so dense he could see nothing.

Sometime between 6 and 6:30, accompanied by Knowles, now a captain, an attached signal officer named Lieutenant Paul S. Edwards, and about twelve enlisted runners or messengers, some of them carrying telephones and wire, others pigeons in baskets, Patton left his CP and walked northward in the wake of the tanks operating on the eastern side of the Aire River. He and his party followed the tank tracks visible on the edge of the Clermont–Neuvilly–Boureuilles–Varennes road leading toward Cheppy. About halfway between Boureuilles and Varennes, they passed some French tanks, then Compton's support tanks.

Beyond a narrow-gauge railroad cut and near a crossroads just short of Cheppy, the group halted and sat down. Patton sent a message by pigeon, no doubt reporting his location.

Very little was happening in that vicinity. Infantry and tanks were out of sight. Shells were falling, Knowles later said, "to our front some considerable distance [away] probably at least one kilometer." It was desultory firing and difficult to judge how far off and exactly where it was because of the atmospheric conditions.

A handful of tanks came along, stopped for a few minutes to chat, then went on. After they had passed, some shells dropped nearby. Then machine gun bullets came close. Patton ordered everyone to take cover in the railroad cut. Once in the relative safety of that protection, Patton posted Corporal John G. Heming, who would later be commissioned, on the right front, and Private First Class Joseph T. Angelo, his orderly, on the left front. They were to give the alarm if the enemy attempted to advance on or to cut off the small command group.

Several disorganized groups of infantrymen, walking and running to the rear, came through. Patton stopped them and questioned them. The soldiers said they were separated from their units and commanders because of the fog and the machine gun fire. Patton told them to join his group. The shallow and short railroad cut soon became crowded.

As the enemy fire increased in volume and the machine guns began to shoot in short meaningful bursts, Patton led his now considerable number of men, perhaps as many as 100, back about 100 yards to the reverse slope of a small hill. Patton ordered everyone to spread out and lie down. The troops had just done so when machine gun fire began to sweep the area, seemingly from every direction.

About 125 yards to the rear and at the base of the slope, Patton noticed several of Compton's tanks. He sent Knowles down the hill with a message ordering them to come forward at once. Knowles discovered what was holding them up. Two enormous trenches, very deep and very wide, formerly held by the Germans, blocked progress. A French Schneider trying to cross them was bogged down and barring the only suitable crossing place. Some French tankers had started to dig away the banks with shovels, but when shells and bullets landed nearby, they abandoned their work and sat in the trench for protection.

Knowles passed on Patton's message to the American tankers, then continued to the rear to find Compton. He located Captain Williams and delivered Patton's order, then discovered Compton and repeated the instruction.

On the reverse slope of the hill, as time passed, Patton wondered why the tanks were not coming forward. He sent Lieutenant Edwards down the hill to get some action. He also dispatched Sergeant Edgar W. Fansler to find Compton and tell him to get moving.

Like Knowles, Edwards saw what was wrong. While Fansler proceeded to the rear in search of Compton, Edwards talked to the French crew and got no reaction. He walked to the group of five American tanks nearby and talked with Captain Math L. English, who was in command.

Growing increasingly angry because the tanks were still not moving, Patton started down the slope himself. He immediately saw that the infantrymen he had collected were preparing to abandon the hill in panic. If he left, they would flee. So he stopped. He called Angelo and sent him back to get the tanks moved up.

Angelo made little impression on the tankers, and when a volley of shells came in, he prudently jumped into a trench for shelter.

At this point Patton came down the hill himself. He immediately organized a concerted effort to get the tanks across the trenches. He set the French to work. He went over to the American tanks, which were being splattered with machine gun fire, removed the shovels and picks strapped to the tank sides, got the tankers out of their machines, handed them the tools, and put them to work tearing down the sides of the trenches.

All this time, enemy fire was sweeping the area, both artillery shells and machine gun bullets. A hostile plane flew over from time to time to direct the enemy gunners. Some of the men who were digging were hit.

Patton and English, despite repeated requests from Edwards and others to step into the trenches, remained in exposed positions on the parapet directing the work. Several times Patton shouted, "To Hell with them — they can't hit me."

When passages had been dug across the ditches, Patton and English chained several tanks together to get better traction in the mud. Then the two officers, still disdaining the shelter of the trenches, and now joined by Angelo, gave hand signals to help the drivers get across. Miraculously, they were not struck by the enemy fire.

Patton explained the successful crossing as "due to the coolness of the drivers who maneuvered with their doors open" at considerable personal risk.

As soon as English's five tanks were over the obstacles — the Schneider was hopelessly stuck — Patton sent them forward up the hill. Then gathering the men at the trenches together, he led them up the slope.

When the last of English's tanks crossed the crest of the knoll, Patton ordered all the men to spread out and follow him. Waving his large walking stick, which looked like a cane, over his head, he shouted, "Let's go get them, who's with me," and walked forward.

Enthusiastically, about 100 men jumped to their feet and started to follow Patton. Some of Patton's command group wanted to join their colonel, but they were unarmed. Sergeant William V. Curran was carrying a telephone and some wire, Sergeants L. T. Garlow and Lorenzo F.

Ward were loaded down with pigeon baskets. Sergeant Harry M. Stokes was in a shell hole bandaging a wounded infantryman's leg.

Patton's force swept over the crest of the hill. They went no more than 50 or 75 yards when the incoming machine gun fire became terrific. Everyone, including Patton, flung himself on the ground and let the wave of bullets wash over the hillside.

It was probably at this moment that Patton had his vision.

GSP, Jr., "My Father," 1927
Once in the Argonne just before I was wounded I felt a great desire to run, I was trembling with fear when suddenly I thought of my progenitors and seemed to see them in a cloud over the German lines looking at me. I became calm at once and saying aloud "It is time for another Patton to die" called for volunteers and went forward to what I honestly believed to be certain death. Six men went with me; five were killed and I was wounded so I was not much in error.

When the noise of the firing abated, Patton picked himself up. Waving his stick and shouting "Let's go, let's go," he marched forward.

This time only six men accompanied him. Among them was Angelo. As they walked ahead in a miniature charge of the light brigade, Angelo noticed that the others were dropping to the ground as they were struck by enemy fire. Finally just he and Patton were left. "I told him they were all hit but us."

"We are alone," Angelo said.

"Come on anyway," Patton said.

Why? What did he hope to accomplish?

He and Angelo could certainly not hope to eradicate the hostile machine gun nests and stop the enemy fire. He himself was armed with his walking stick, although he wore a pistol in his holster. Angelo carried a rifle. Together in that hail of bullets they resembled Don Quixote and his faithful servant Sancho Panza.

Or did Patton believe that he and Angelo led charmed lives? They had, after all, both stood on the parapet at the trench below the other side of the hill and had urged the tanks across the ditches. Nothing had harmed them. Could they then pass safely through this rain of steel too and make their way up forward to the leading tanks where, surely, more work remained to be done?

Was Patton unwilling to admit defeat, to lose face with the others on the hillside, who were even now crawling frantically back across the crest to the relative safety of the reverse slope? Was he merely stubborn? Did he expect the men to see how easy it was to walk through the bullets? Did he think they would eventually join him?

Or was he seeking to be hit? Was he inviting the glory of death or injury on the field of battle? Was he fulfilling his destiny?

Or was it the thoughtlessness and mindlessness of battlefield madness, the pull and power of taut anger, barely controlled rage, overwhelming hatred — so strong that it makes a man tremble — that drove him toward the enemy?

"Come on anyway," he said.

No more than a few seconds passed when he felt the jolt of a bullet strike his leg. He took a few steps, struggled to maintain his equilibrium, kept going on nerve alone for several yards, and fell.

It was probably around 11:30 A.M. The place was a few hundred yards short of the village of Cheppy.

Angelo helped him into a small shell hole in the middle of an open field, cut his trousers, and bandaged his wound, which was bleeding freely. It was difficult and dangerous work, for there was little protection in that slight depression a shell had scooped out of the earth. Every time Patton or Angelo moved and exposed himself, German soldiers in a railroad cut about 40 yards away fired at them.

After a while that seemed like eternity, some tanks came by. They had crossed the trenches at the bottom of the slope, climbed the hill, and were following Captain English. The appearance of the tanks prompted a decline in the level of intensity of the enemy fire — no machine gunner in his right mind was going to expose his position to the tank guns. In that lull, Patton sent Angelo out to tell the tankers where the enemy gunners were located. Informed by Angelo of lucrative targets, the tankers departed.

More time went by. Sergeant Schemnitz, obviously looking for the colonel, came along. Angelo hailed him, and Schemnitz hurried over. Patton told him to carry the word back that he was wounded, that Major Brett was to take command of the brigade, and that no one was to come to carry Patton back because he would attract enemy fire.

Schemnitz ran back with these instructions. As he crossed the crest of the hill to the reverse slope, where Knowles, Edwards, and the runners were waiting, he shouted the news in great excitement — the colonel was wounded, Major Brett was in command, and nobody was to go near the colonel until the fire died down. He rushed off to find a stretcher.

Garlow released a pigeon with a message that Patton was wounded.

At the shell hole, a few more tanks passed nearby. Patton again sent Angelo to attract the tankers' attention and tell them where to go. Compton was in one of those tanks, and, following Angelo's directions, placed a few well-aimed shells and silenced a machine gun that had been harassing the two men in the hole. The tanks then continued on their way.

A medical aid soldier named John L. Close, who was working with the infantry, wandered through the field. He stopped, looked at Patton's wound, and changed the bandage. Patton thanked him courteously, and Close went on.

After about an hour or so — it was difficult to estimate the passage of time — the work of all the tanks in the area eliminated the machine gun fire. About 25 German machine gun nests were believed destroyed. The hostile artillery shelling became erratic as the gunners seemed to be ranging on the tanks up ahead.

Only then did Schemnitz, accompanied by Sergeant First Class Ely and Corporal Heming, return to the shell hole with a stretcher. These three men and Angelo placed Patton on the litter and carried him back to the reverse slope of the hill.

Edwards went off toward the front in search of Brett, whom he found at 2 P.M.

Fansler relieved Angelo on one corner of the stretcher, and these five men took Patton three kilometers to the rear and delivered him to an ambulance company.

While the others returned to their duties, Angelo stayed with Patton. Before Patton would go to a hospital, he insisted on being taken to the 35th Division headquarters so he could report conditions on the front.

An ambulance drove him and Angelo there, and an officer came out and talked with Patton. Then he allowed himself to be moved to Evacuation Hospital Number 11. Angelo took his pistol and his money for safekeeping.

Diary

September 26 (Thursday): "Started forward at 6 A.M. H plus ½ hour. Heavy fog. Found men coming back and took them along with me. Heavy fire all around from m.g. Found mine field with

Bosch notice on it. Got to R.R. cut near Cheppy sent pigeon message. Was fired on heavily and 35 Div came back on the run. Moved back about 200 m. [meters] Heavy m.g. [machine gun] & Art. [Artillery] fire. Lots of Dough Boys hit. [Captain] English & I got tanks forward. 20 men hit. Tried to make inft charge and got shot. Lay in shell hole an hour. Could hear bosch talk. Went to hospital and was operated on by Dr. Elliot of N.Y."

September 27 (Friday): "Woke up to find Capt Semmes on my right. Capt. Gilfillen on my left. Both wounded. Slept a lot. Wrote Beat. Tried to wire but could not."

Letter, GSP, Jr., to Beatrice, September 28, 1918

We went into our second fight on the morning of Sept. 26 at 5:30 A.M. It was terribly foggy and in addition they were shooting lots of smoke shells so we could not see ten feet. I started forward at 6:30 to see what was doing but could see little. Machine guns were going in every direction in front behind and on both sides. But no one could tell who they belonged to. I had six men — runners — with me and a compas so I collected all the soldiers I found who were lost and brought them along. At times I had several hundred.

About 9:30 we came to a town called Cheppy. I went passed the infantry as we were supposed to have taken the place. But all at once we got shot at from all sides.

With m.g. and shell also but still we could see nothing. Pretty soon some of our infantry came running back. So as none of my men had any rifles I went back with the inft. but stopped before they did. Also I stopped in a better place just back of a crest.

When we got here it [the weather] began to clear up and we were shot at to beat hell with shells and machine guns. Twice the inft started to run but we hollored at them and called them all sorts of names so they staied. But they were scared some and acted badly, some put on gas masks, some covered their face with their hands but none did a damed thing to kill Bosch. There were no officers there but me. So I decided to do business. Some of my reserve tanks were stuck by some trenches. So I went back and made some Americans hiding in the trenches dig a passage. I think I killed one man here. He would not work so I hit him over the head with a shovel. It was exciting for they shot at us all the time but I got mad and walked on the parapet. At last we got Five tanks accross and I started them forward and yelled and cussed and waved my stick and said come on. About 150 dough boys started but when we got to the crest of the hill the fire got fierce right along the ground. We all lay down I saw that we must go forward or back and I could not go back so I yelled who comes with me. A lot of dough boys yelled but only six of us started. My striker, me and 4 doughs. I hoped the rest would follow but they would not. Soon there were only three but we could see the machine guns right ahead so we yelled to keep up our courage and went on. Then the third man went down and I felt a blow in the leg but at first I could walk so went about 40 ft when my leg gave way. My striker the only man left yelled "oh god the colonels hit and there aint no one left." He helped me to a shell hoel and we lay down and the Bosch shot over the top as fast as he could. He was very close. The tanks began getting him and in about an hour it was fairly clear [of bullets].

Some of my men carried me out under fire which was not at all plesant.

Finally I got to a hospital at 3:30. I was hit at 11:15.

The bullet went into the front of my left leg and came out just at the crack of my bottom about two inches to the left of my rectum. It was fired at about 50 m[eters] so made a hole about the size of a [silver] dollar where it came out.

It has hurt very little and I have slepped fine. I will be out [of the hospital] in ten days.

Have tried to telegraph you but so far with out success.

CHAPTER 31

The End of the War

"I have always feared I was a coward at heart but I am begin-
ning to doubt it."

Thomas M. Johnson, staff correspondent of the Evening Sun, *with*
the American First Army at Verdun: "Col. Patton, Hero of the
Tanks, Hit by Bullet — He Crawled into Shell Hole and Directed
Monsters in Argonne Battle," October 8, 1918.

Lieutenant Colonel George F. Patten, Jr. [sic] of Pride's Crossing,
Mass., one of the first officers of the American tank corps to be
wounded, gave a splendid example of courage and self-sacrifice to the
officers of this newest branch of the service which he did so much to
build up.

At 11 o'clock in the morning of Sept. 26, Col. Patten was with a
number of tanks south of Varennes in the Aire Valley. It was the first
day of the Verdun attack and vitally important that the tanks get
forward.

The mist, however, was so dense and the fog so thick that Col.
Patten walked ahead of them choosing their route and also assembling some and leading forward infantrymen who had got lost.

The tanks were being heavily shelled and had also come within
reach of the Hun machine guns. As Patten walked forward a bullet
struck him in the right leg. He walked about forty yards further, and
then crawled into a shell hole. His orderly, Joseph Anzelo [sic] of
New York, bandaged the wound, whereupon Col. Patten lighted a
cigarette and remained in the shell hole for some time, issuing orders
to the tanks to spread out so as not to make so large a target.

He coolly looked about for the German machine guns, directing
the tanks how to wipe them out. Finally the pain became intense
and Patten at last consented to go to the rear.

Col Patten was one of the organizers of the tank corps, and had studied tanks on both the British and French fronts. He developed four new devices improving tanks which were adopted by the French and British. For some time he conducted the American tank service school where the corps now fighting so gloriously was developed.

Even though he was wounded and removed from the battlefield, he was surely present in the minds of his tankers, who carried out the precepts he had so firmly implanted in them. He would later write, "we broke the Prussian guard with the tanks," and his assessment was essentially correct. The tanks had helped the First Army gain a significant victory.

Although Patton had planned to commit his battalions in successive lines of attack in order to reach a series of objectives, serious German resistance, particularly near Cheppy and Varennes, made it necessary to bring all the tanks into action on the first day of the battle. The tanks on the western (left) side of the Aire River working with the 28th Division had run into strong concrete enemy pillboxes. It was the first time American tanks met this type of defenses, and the tankers mastered the obstacles and silenced the German gunners by employing a new technique — firing 37-mm. high explosive shells through the portholes of the bunkers. Tankers with the 35th Division helped materially in the capture of the strong position at Vauquois and the reduction of stubborn opposition at Cheppy. In the process, the brigade lost 43 tanks, some to enemy action, others to mechanical failure.

Brett, who would command the brigade for the remainder of the war, wrote:

> The entire 1st Brigade suffered that first day, for at the end we learned that the Brigade Commander, Colonel G. S. Patton, Jr. had been seriously wounded while heroically attempting to rally disorganized Infantry to attack a machine gun nest.

On the second day of battle, eleven tanks west of the Aire advanced along the edge of the Argonne Forest, knocking out machine guns and capturing their crews, which they turned over to the infantry. On the east bank, the tanks received repeated calls for help from the infantry, but no concerted effort was possible.

With only 83 tanks in operating condition on the third day, the brigade "took the town of Apresmont five times before the infantry would enter, consolidate and exploit the success." At the end of that day, Rockenbach withdrew the 14th and 17th Groupes because of the complete mechanical exhaustion of those tanks.

After a massive repair-and-salvage operation lasting all night, the two American battalions fielded 55 tanks for the fourth day of fighting. They helped the infantry establish a consolidated line, then withdrew from the battlefield and entered reserve positions, where they remained inactive for several days.

The men worked hard to get their machines in fighting condition, and on October 1, 89 tanks returned to combat. Fifty-nine were lost that day, and the tankers retired once more. On October 5, the brigade committed the remaining 30 tanks and lost almost half. With but 17 tanks left, Rockenbach called the brigade back.

A final action took place on October 16, when a provisional company, consisting of about 20 tanks, 10 officers, and 140 men, under Captain Courtenay Barnard, supported the 42d Division. Ten tanks reached their objectives, but — a familiar refrain in the Tank Corps — "The infantry did not follow and the tanks returned. Large bodies of the enemy were dispersed during this advance."

The excellent performance of the tankers, who had gone on until they had exhausted their machines, could be traced to the spirit and skill of Patton who had instructed them and inspired them, and their success was a reflection of his accomplishment.

. . .

Brigadier General C. D. Rhodes, who had been commandant of the Mounted Service School when the Pattons were at Fort Riley and who now commanded a field artillery brigade, tried for several days to ascertain how seriously Patton had been wounded. He finally learned from General Craig that Patton was all right. Rhodes immediately wrote to Beatrice — "Dear Mrs. Georgie" — and assured her that her husband's condition was good. Rhodes had seen Patton the day before the battle:

He looked well — hard and muscular — but his hair at the temples has grown quite gray — and he said it was due to being so scared in the St. Mihiel drive — when the Huns, he alleged, knocked him off the top of the tanks . . . Now he's better off with a good honorable wound . . . and [he will] be the envy of everybody . . . I really envy Georgie that fine wound!

After spending three days at the evacuation hospital, Patton was transferred to Base Hospital Number 49 in Allerey.

Diary

September 30: "Was put on cattle train in rain and had a rather bad night as the iron bars of the stretcher hurt my back and I could not move."

On that day, Rockenbach recommended that Patton, Captain English, and Lieutenant Edwards be awarded the Distinguished Service Cross for gallantry and exceptional heroism in the Meuse-Argonne offensive.

Diary

October 1: "Breakfast on train consisted of bread and molasses. Got to Allerey at 11 A.M. was put in nice bed and felt better. Dr. Greenbourg dressed my leg. A nice little Jew who was careful not to hurt. Had two drains put in my leg. The powder [in the bullet] burned my skin badly."

Letter, GSP, Jr., to Beatrice, October 2, 1918

Here I am . . . missing half my bottom but other wise all right.

We staied at the evacuation hospital just back of the line from the night of the 26 till the night of the 29. Then we left by ambulance to the train. The train was box cars and we were put in racks three high. I got a top. We were in stretchers and they are not comfortable. We left in the freight [cars] at 7 P.M. and got here at 11 A.M. on the 30th. It was a pretty tiresome trip but as it was raining there was no dust. They fed us once during the trip on coffee and molasses and bread. It was good enough but not up to the pictures of red cross trains. This hospital is pretty nice but there are only two nurses for 50 officers. I got washed to day for the first time and I am the senior [officer in the hospital].

Still it might be worse though just how I cant see. The hole in my hip is about as big as a tea cup and they have to leave it open.

I just wrote to Boyd [one of Pershing's aides] to come and have a look at this place and get some books to the men and let them smoke . . .

One fellow died in the next bed to mine. His back was broken. It is strange that the "gentlemen" make less noise over their wounds than the others. But there is little howling even on the train I heard hardly any noise.

There is a fellow next to me with a smashed hip. He suffers a lot but jokes. I suffer none at all except when they dress the wounds.

I look as if I had just had a baby or was unwell . . .

This is a stupid letter but it is hard to write.

Letter, GSP, Jr., to Beatrice, October 4, 1918

I am getting on fine and will be sewed up in about a day or two. Now they spend their time taking "cultures" of my bottom to see if there are any bugs.

This is a rotten place with a cemetary just out side where they bury people all day long.

Also the food is very poor but I get on fine as I always do. And I am doing a lot of sleeping.

I think I am not very sensative by nature as I seem to suffer less than most people . . .

My scar wont ever show unless the styles change. I surely am a lucky fellow . . .

Will we have any money after the war so we can go on a Honey-moon. Lets us do it any how. We will have to get used to each other.

I love you.

I wired you on the 29th Sept. "Slightly wounded no danger love"

I love you George.

Letter, GSP, Jr., to Beatrice, October 10, 1918

I am sitting out in a wheeled chair in the sun smoking and it is quite nice and comfortable. We moved to a new ward yesterday and it is much better. There are more nurses and orderlies so all goes well. Also we are out of quarenteen for meningitis which makes it much nicer.

I had seven Captains two majors and my self in the fight. Of these all are hit but one capt and two majors . . . Capt. English was killed and Capt. Higgins got both eyes shot out. Two Lts. were killed and 15 wounded. But the tank corps established its reputation for not giving ground. They only went forward. And they are the only troops in the attack of whom that can be said.

I feel terribly to have missed all the fighting. It seems too bad but I had to go in when I did or the whole line might have been broken.

Perhaps I was mistaken but any way I believe I have been sited [cited] for decoration either the Medal of Honor or the military [Distinguished Service] cross. I hope I get one of them.

Letter, Pershing to Beatrice, October 10, 1918

George . . . was exceptionally gallant and was leading a body of men to attack a machine gun nest when he was shot in the leg; I think not very seriously. It was a gallant thing to do, and he has received all sorts of praise from those who know of the incident. You are to be congratulated and should be prouder of him than ever.

Letter, GSP, Jr., to Beatrice, October 12, 1918

Peace looks possible but I rather hope not for I would like to have a few more fights. They are awfully thrilling like steeple chasing only more so . . .

One of my men came to see me to day. He was a gunner in a tank and got his right thumb shot off. He did not know it until he went to pick up a shell and found he had no thumb.

I am getting on fine.

On October 13, Rockenbach recommended that Lieutenant Colonels Henry E. Mitchell, George S. Patton, Jr., and D. D. Pullen be promoted to Colonel.

Letter, GSP, Jr., to Beatrice, October 15, 1918

Your letter sent by [Lieutenant Elgin] Braine came to day and I was glad to get it. I have not seen Braine yet but will do so shortly I trust.

I think I told you that Rockie has recomended me for a Colonelcy. I would like it in a way but the more rank one gets the harder it is to get into a fight and fights certainly are fun. That is not a pose either. It is actually so and one of the few things I could enjoy. As you know I like most things solely for the results.

They took another culture of me to day. I hope they report no bugs . . .

I am feeling fine and do not suffer at all.

Letter, GSP, Jr., to Beatrice, October 16, 1918

My d—— wound is still full of bugs so they can't sew me up. It is most Provoking.

I have just been in to cuss out the surgeon but it does no good. As it is impossible to give special attention to any one here.

I am feeling fine and want to get out.

Letter, GSP, Jr., to Pershing, October 16, 1918

[Thanks for kind letter which came at right time and which Patton will treasure.] It is hard to have so much nice fighting going on and be in bed with a darned old hole that will not close as fast as I want it to. You see I was about thirty or forty yards from the gun that hit me and it naturally took out a lot of beef. I feel fine and eat too much. I respectfully request that you leave some Bosch to be beaten after I get out. With sincere thanks for your kindness and congratulations for your great victories.

On October 17, Patton was promoted to Colonel.

Letter, GSP, Jr., to Beatrice, October 17, 1918
What do you think of me. I just got my colonelcy over the wire and am not yet 33. That is not so bad is it. Of course I have class mates in the engineers who are colonels but none others. So I feel quite elated though as a matter of fact I don't believe I deserve it very much. I could have commanded just as well as a Lt. Col. Well after the war the slump will be all the greater. [I will go] back to a captain.
Tell B & R.E. so they can be haughty while they have the chance. As "Je reviendra capataine apres la gare." [I will go back to captain after the war.]
I do hope I get the decoration. I would prefer it to the promotion.

Letter, Mr. Patton to Pershing, October 18, 1918
I want to thank you very much for all the family for your cable as to George's wound. Our first information was indirect through a New York newspaper followed by a notice from Washington reporting him wounded "degree undetermined." So your cable came as a great relief to our anxiety.

Patton asked General Smith, commandant of the Army Schools, to try to get him transferred to Base Hospital Number 24 at Langres. Smith did so, and Patton was moved.

Diary
October 19 (Saturday): Spent the day at Bourg and played my new phonograph. Very nice. Felt tired.

Letter, GSP, Jr., to Aunt Nannie, October 19, 1918
I don't know whether I told you all in my last letter that I am a

full colonel. Which is not bad for 32. Though I had always intended to be a general at 26. Of course I will probably drop back to captain after the war but that can't be helped.

Capt. Braine has just telephoned that he was coming to see me as he has just landed. I will get some late news. He saw B just before he sailed.

I have only 80 men out of 834 fit for duty in my T. Brig. Of course many are only wounded or sick but some are dead.

I am still unsewed up but hope to be soon.

Letter, GSP, Jr., to Beatrice, October 19, 1918

. . . to day I was worrying over what I would do after I get out [of the hospital]. And making all sorts of difficulties [for myself] when I remembered. What Gen R. [Rockenbach] once said namely that "most worries never happen." I guess I must have aged in apperance. All these doctors thought I was 45 but that is probably on account of not being able to shave every day and because I am thin.

I am a lot older in some things, for example when we were in Washington before we came over. Barnett told me about commanding a battalion of militia and I wondered at the time if I could have done it. Now I know that I could command a Division. Things realy are much easier than they appear. Hence why worry. C. D. Rhodes is a Maj. Gen. speaking of worrying.

I just got a telephone from Braine saying he was coming to see me, so I will get some first hand information.

Letter, GSP, Jr., to Beatrice, October 20, 1918

Braine got here at 10 P.M. last night and brought a lot of letters from you.

I asked him how you looked and if you had any gray hair. He said no. At least that you had fixed them . . . I always think of you as Undine so I don't want you to look 33, even if I do.

He said you wore a black dress like a neck tie. I could not tell whether he ment in texture or in size.

. . . I also am much relieved to know that you have that much money after all the taxes etc.

I must be getting about $400 a month now as a colonel . . .

We have a phonograph here to night and it plaied some of the songs you used to sing . . .

Your childish procilivites of which you boast do not interest me at all. I love you too much and I am jealous or something of children . . . Your only chance [to have another child] is accident or emaculate conception. You ought to be complimented but being pig headed I suppose you are not.

I love you too much.

. . .

Finally returned to France after his odyssey in the United States, Braine had fulfilled his role in the Tank Corps. Rockenbach sent him to Varennes on the Meuse-Argonne battlefield to inspect the disabled tanks still there. Braine analyzed the causes that had put them out of action, the mechanical reasons as well as the structural weaknesses in the armor protection. He then went to the 302d Tank Center for duty. The two American-built tanks he had brought reached Bourg on November 20.

Braine reorganized the mechanical and tank-driving courses at the school. He improved the efficiency of the tank-repair shed and machine shop. He created a central stockroom, established a salvage department, opened a central gas and oil station, and took charge of motor transportation.

He always felt that the Tank Corps had been cheated. It had "never had a seat at the [production] table and therefore did not get a fair showing" in the war.

Although he would reappear once or twice again, he gradually moved from the prominent place he had formerly occupied on the tank scene, and eventually he faded from sight. He was separated from the Army on June 30, 1919, and placed on the Emergency Officers' Retired List on July 31, 1928. A quiet man who had truly been one of the founders of the American Tank Corps, almost as important as Patton, Brett, Rockenbach, and Viner, Braine died in Columbus, Ohio, in May 1932 at the age of forty-four.

Letter, GSP, Jr., to Beatrice, October 23, 1918

I am back at a hospital in my "own home town" and my wound is nearly healed up.

I feel a lot better as I can see my officers and do a little work. I ought to be out in a few days.

I worked on one of my friends to get me transfered here, it is a better hospital and not so crowded . . .

My brigade . . . got a lot of nice letters from the division we fought with so we are feeling fine and are anxious to get at it again but I fear it will be a while yet.

Here is a nice letter I got from Maj. Brett who commanded after I was hit.

It is a very generous letter. He is mistaken as I still command the 1st Brig[ade] . . .

P.S. My dear classmates are reported as being very jealous of me. I don't blame them.

Letter, Sereno Brett to GSP, Jr., no date

Col Patton: Please allow me to congratulate you on your promotion, I'm damned sorry to see you leave the 1st Brigade, but happy to the same degree that you received a well-earned promotion.

Don't worry about the old Brigade. It fought them until we had no personnel left and then we organized the remnants into a Provisional Company and gave them another whirl for their money. Just now the company is laying back at Exermont waiting to tear into them again.

Was mighty sorry when your runner arrived announcing that you were wounded, but was not surprised at all. Its a miracle you weren't killed. Peculiar, but I was only about 100 meters to your right when the accident happened trying to corral a few tanks and send them forward. Of course, I didn't know you were there. But it was the hottest little hell I have ever burned in, and believe me I wouldn't have given three cents for my future pay vouchers for a while.

The Brigade has been mighty highly complimented by all around here, and I'm happy I can convey this appreciation to you as I know it will bring pleasure to learn that your work with the Brigade has been productive of such excellent results. I am sending you a copy of a letter the Brigade received from General Summerall, who [commanded the 1st Division and] is now commanding the 5th Corps.

Best of luck to you, Colonel, and I sincerely hope you will be out among 'em again by the time this reaches you.

Brett.

Letter, GSP, Jr., to Beatrice, October 24, 1918

I would never have gone forward when I got hit had I not thought of you and my ancestors. I felt that I could not be false to my "cast[e]" and your opinion. At the same time I did not realy think I would be hit. One has a sort of involuntary fear of the bullets but not a concrete fear of being hit. While I was waiting on the hill before I went back to get the tanks I remembered some story by Kipling where the officers smoked to reasure the men. So I smoked like a factory. We were then being shelled heavily from in front and were under rifle fire from both flanks and in front. But I kept saying to myself I am not to be hit I know it so I felt better but it was quite bad. Men were falling or rather being blown to bits all around.

Military education shows at such times. The hill in this section [of the front] was like this [drawing a hill in profile]. I put my men just back of the crest . . . there were no trenches there but I remembered Balastics [ballistics] and that a shell just clearing the top could not fall . . . [there] while they were falling at [the bottom] every second. Yet the foolish dough boys staied . . . [at the bottom of the hill]. None of my men were hit and at [the bottom] it was a regular shambles so I went down there and made the doughs move up. Then they got killed less.

One of my officers was in yesterday and told me during the fog we sat on the roof of a dug out that had a battalion of germans in it. We had only nine men. Some luck.

My wound is getting on fine and is nearly healed. The Dr. says that he can't see how the bullet went where it did with out crippling me for life. He says he could not have run a probe without getting either the hip joint, the siatic nerve or the big artery yet none of these were touched. "Fate" again. I have never had any pain and can walk perfectly . . .

P.S. I was not altered by the gas as I was not gased. Some were, but none of my men as I made them all use the masks.

Letter, GSP, Jr., to Beatrice, October 26, 1918

Just one month to day I was hit and I was out walking just now and feel fine. They have decided not to sew me up but to let it fill up its self so I ought to be out in a few days . . .

I met a lot of my friends to day and they were all sore at me for getting promoted. It makes me mad.

If they had wanted to risk their skins in fighting instead of looking for staff jobs they might have been promoted too.

Letter, GSP, Jr., to Beatrice, October 26, 1918

Dear Beat: I just got your letter with a coppy of R[ockenbach]'s letter to you. It was a nice letter was it not. He is quite a poetical old cock . . .

I had four men recomended for the medal of honor and about 20 for the D.S.C. Two of them are dead.

I had a nice compliment from a Col. Keochlin-Swarts of the french army to day. He called on me and said "My dear Patton I am so glad you were wounded. For when you left I said to my wife that is the end of Patton he is one of those gallant fellows who always get killed."

Rather nice what. They all seem to think me quite a fellow for walking in front of the tanks. As a matter of fact it was the only thing to do. You say the Bosch will quit. Listen to this. One of my tanks was attacking a machine gun when the gun in the tank jammed so the men decided to run down the machine gun. The two Bosch fired to the last and the tank went over them. Next day they were found still holding their gun though dead.

There could be nothing finer in war. My men buried them and put up crosses. "Salute the brave" even bosch.

There are few d—— f—— [few] husbands who write twice a day to their wives even when their wives wear such low dresses as B [Jr.] says you do.

Please keep it till I get home or get a lower one. George.

Letter, GSP, Jr., to Nita, October 26, 1918

I have about forty letters from you to —— which I have not transmitted as I only got them. They had been following me from hospital to hospital . . .

I was out walking twice to day and feel fine. My wound is still open but only a little . . . It did not cripple me at all, the dr. said that it seemed impossible [not to]. . . . I was borne to be hung.

Had a [I] had a hemorage I would have bled to death as I was only 30 yds from the Bosch and every time I turned over to try to put on a dressing they shot at me. So I staied there for an hour with one of my tanks sitting by guarding me like a watch dog. That first Brigade [of tanks] was some bunch. Six captains out of seven were hit the first 3 days and 30 Lieutenants out of 35 also got hit, we ended up after 14 days with 80 men and 6 officers out of 800.

Of course not many were killed. Only 3 officers and 18 men so far.

I got a nice compliment from a french colonel. He . . . said "I am so glad you were only wounded. You are one of those gallant men who always get killed. But you will get it yet." I will not however . . .

One of my tanks broke their gun while they were attacking a Bosch Machine Gun. The Bosch held on to the last and we squashed them but even in death they were holding to their gun. My men burried them and put up a cross "To two brave men though S.O.B's." Quelle sentimente!

I will call and tell your friend about you.

Letter, GSP, Jr., to his father, October 28, 1918

Dear Papa: Your letter of Sept 28 has just reached me and as usual was most interesting. But instead of being in the fight as you thought I was in a hospital with a whole bath towel stuffed in my bottom and bleeding like a stuck pig. Still as usual at such times I slept which was the best thing to do.

I left the hospital to day and resumed command of my brigade or what is left of it. I am here in my own room and feeling fine though I can't walk much yet and lost about 30 pounds of weight which I will soon get back.

My letter written after St. Mihiel will have reached you by now. For once I out did the papers. I rode on top of the tank not on the tail and so riding I mopped up a town Pannes which the infantry would not enter later . . . I got shot off the top of it by the bosch but was not hurt, only scared.

Every one has been telling me what a heller I am for the Verdun-Argonne show that I am beginning to believe it. But if I had not thought of you and mama & B and my ancestors I would never have charged. That is I would not have started for it is hell to go into rifle fire so heavy that one fancies the air is thick like molases with it. After I got going it was easy but the start is like a cold bath.

Maj Brett who has been in all the while says that was the heaviest fight of the whole battle. There were 12 m.g. [machine guns] right in front of me at about 150 yds. backed by a battalion of guard infantry. While from fifty to 150 machine guns were firing at us from the flanks.

My "Guardian spirits" must have had a job to keep me from getting killed so one can't blame them for letting one slip by and hit me in the leg.

Gen Ellis of the British tanks said of it that it was "Splendid but not war." The same thing that was said of the Light Brigade. However he was wrong. An officer is paid to attack not to direct after the battle starts.

You know I have always feared I was a coward at heart but I am beginning to doubt it.

Our education is at fault in picturing death as such a terrible thing. It is nothing and very easy to get.

That does not mean that I hunt for it but the fear of it does not — at least has not detured me from doing what appeared my duty.

My brigade will not be able to fight for a while yet so dont worry about me for a month after my birthday [November 11] . . .

My class mates are all soar as hell at me for getting promoted and probably lay it to Nita['s influence with Pershing] or some other hellish plot.

With much love to all your devoted son

George S Patton Jr. D. S. C.? Perhaps.

Col Tank Corps.

Commanding First Brig[ade]

. . .

Patton did not wait long after getting out of the hospital to make his presence known to his men. On the very next day he issued a formal order to the tankers in the units as well as the tankers in the training center. His subject: "Concerning dress, comportment and discipline of this command, most of which is extracted from Memoranda issued previously on the same subject." He wanted everyone to keep his shoes, leggings, and belts polished, his uniforms clean, his face shaved daily, and his hair cut short. Sweaters were not to be worn on top of but underneath the khaki shirt. Straw in the bedding in quarters was to be changed frequently. Military courtesy was to be observed at all times. And finally:

There is a widespread and regrettable habit in our service of ducking the head to meet the hand in rendering a salute. This will not be tolerated. In rendering salutes the head will be held erect. The hand will be moved smartly to and from the head-dress or the forehead, if uncovered.

He also wrote a letter to Mrs. Math L. English, Fort Casey, Washington, whose husband was killed in battle After confirming Captain English's death, Patton continued:

It may, however, help ameliorate your grief to realize in what very high esteem Captain English was held by all the officers and men with whom he came into contact. I believe that the Brigade is unanimous in attributing to him all the highest virtues of a man and officer . . . You and his children should always guard [the memory of his gallant action] as a perfect example of heroism and soldierly devotion to duty under the most trying circumstances . . . Please allow me, my dear Madam, to close in again assuring you of my heartfelt sympathy for you and my unbounded admiration for your gallant husband.

Patton sent a copy of this letter to Beatrice and added a handwritten note at the bottom: "This is a copy of letter I wrote Mrs English. He was a very fine man. He used to be a 1st Sgt. But was insured for $10 000. Still it would be nice if you wrote his wife. He had a litle boy I think GSP."

Letter, GSP, Jr., to Beatrice, October 29, 1918
Your two letters of Oct 10 & 11 came to day and I am dreadfully sorry to have shocked you so . . .
The account in the paper is correct except that I was carried off when they could get to me. The fire was so heavy for an hour that no one could come to me except the tanks. It did not take much nerve to direct them against the machine guns as that was what I was there for and there was nothing else to do. I could not walk as my leg would not work. I don't even limp now.
My orderly had two pigeons and it was funny when you think of it to be sending up "Doves of Peace" from a hole right under the nose of the Bosch.
My wound never hurt a bit but I have three boils that do . . .
Also I smoked a pipe not a cigaret.

On November 3, Patton sent a formal letter to Rockenbach recommending awards to members of the 1st Brigade, Tank Corps, for gallantry in action. Recommended for the Medal of Honor were Captain Harry H. Semmes, whom Patton cited for two actions, Second Lieutenant David M. Bowes, and Private First Class Joseph T. Angelo, whose citation read: "For dragging his wounded commanding officer into a shell hole at a range of about 40 metres from the German machine guns and for thereafter remaining with him under continued shell fire for over one hour, except when he twice left the shelter of the shell hole to carry orders to the tanks which were passing at a distance of about 50 metres."

Recommended for the Distinguished Service Cross were Commandant Chanoine, French Army (cited for two actions); Major Sereno E. Brett; Captain Newell P. Weed (with two citations), Captain Math L. English (Killed in Action and cited twice), Captains Harry H. Semmes and Dean M. Gilfillan; First Lieutenant Robert C. Llewellyn (Killed in Action), First Lieutenants Paul S. Edwards and Tom W. Saul; Second Lieutenants Julian K. Morrison, Darwin T. Phillips, and Edwin A. McClure; Sergeant Raymond C. Chisholm (Killed in Action) and Sergeant Charles C. Young; Corporal Harold W. Roberts (Killed in Action) and Corporal William E. Brophy.

. . .

About this time Patton wrote a paper entitled "German and Allied Theory of War." In it he sought to explain the course of World War I. Whether a lecture or a piece simply for his own meditation, it demonstrated his understanding of the tactical developments of the war.

When the French and Russians became allied, he wrote, Germany had to gain a prompt decision over one or the other in order to deal with the remaining one at some leisure. To that end, Germany concentrated military thought and training to produce an army "national in numbers and yet professional in ability." The end was to crush the French by a decisive battle or series of battles "likened to the knock-out blow of a pugilist and it obviously required great smash and driving force." This required "unlimited reserves at the point of impact," or forces massed in depth, and this policy contrasted with French and British theories of maneuver.

The tactics of the two combatants were equally at variance. The Allies looking on fire as a means of movement. That is, they fired only enough to permit them to close and finish with the bayonet. The Germans on the other hand looked to movement as a means of fire. That is, they moved their skirmish lines so that its withering flame might consume nearly all resistance and they looked to the bayonet simply as a means of giving the coup de grace . . .

Happily for the world their plans were brought to naught by 1st: The delay in Belgium. 2nd: The heroic value of the French and

British Armies. 3rd: The fact that short maneuvers had taught the
Germans to over-estimate the endurance of their men which consequently resulted in the over-marching of their command. 4th: Their
error in converging their vast numbers in an attempt to reach Paris,
consequently causing complication in supply.

Those causes coupled with the necessity of sending men to Russia
made the German assault a failure and they were forced to assume
the defensive on the Western Front which attitude they maintained
with the exception of the 1916 Verdun Offensive until the beginning
of the present year.

The ensuing developments made the struggle "the most futile form of
war which history records." Allied efficiency diminished because of the
large number of untrained men who had to be quickly trained as specialists. "These coarse creatures increased and multiplied . . . There were
bombers who could not shoot and shooters who could not bomb and Staff
Officers who could do neither. All of these claimed that they were the sole
means to ending the war and that all others were useless and in the way."
The result was the set-piece attack, the rigid rolling barrage, and the
limited objective. Artillery pieces increased in numbers, the trench system kept pace, preparatory barrages were lengthened, shell expenditures
grew, and combat became expensive.

Tanks were invented to relieve the intolerable situation "and to supply
mobile firing power . . ." But the mechanical deficiencies of tanks and
their scarcity in numbers made it necessary to continue the barrages before attacks, and warfare remained expensive and static.

The Germans, having disposed of Russia and Rumania and having
checked Italy by the winter of 1917–18, had to end the war before the
United States became the dominant factor. They therefore developed the
tactic of surprise. They concentrated their attacking forces in a rear area
so they could move toward any one of several attack points. When the
decision was made on the point of attack, the troops moved there by night
marches, padding the wheels of wagons and gun carriages with straw and
taking extraordinary care to conceal their movements. With this, they
launched their several successful surprise attacks, the first and greatest of
which occurred on March 21, 1918.

"The old wrestling maxim that there is a block to every hold remains
true however," and the Germans were blocked because "First that they

did not realize the elasticity of the Allied defense and having made a hole of considerable depth they presumed the line to be broken and instead of pushing on until it was really broken they turned to the flanks to widen the wedge which they had punched. This gave the Allies time to close the nose of the salient . . . The second thing was . . . that" Allied artillery was able to concentrate shells in the path of the German attack and block them.

We will now consider how the tactics just described which were our own tactics when we assumed the offensive, may be used in future "Efforts to maintain Peace." A look at the map of the world makes it fair to assume that nowhere but in Europe will armies without flanks be encountered. Where this situation arises it will be possible by the uses of cavalry, armoured motor cars and light tanks to get behind the enemy and prevent the concentration of guns which have heretofore checked the successful advance of infantry. Also in wars in less civilized countries than Europe it will never be possible to have or move such quantities of artillery as now exists or to maintain the huge supply of ammunition which they daily consume. The same is true with machine guns and automatic rifle ammunition. Hence we will again revert to the Infantry skirmish line strengthened and made more deadly by automatic rifles and machine guns. Strategical maneuvers will return with the diminution of front[al] attacks but it will always be fire backed by the threat of bayonet which now as in the time of Gustavus Adolphus decided the fate of war.

Three pages of single-spaced typescript emerged from his machine on November 7. Entitled "Notes, Entraining and Detraining at Night," they were explicit and detailed instructions on how to get tanks on and off trains.

On the following day, he submitted a letter to the Assistant Chief of Staff G–5, the Training and Plans Officer at GHQ AEF, on the subject of "A suggested method of attack."

In suggesting the following form of attack it is not my purpose or desire to infringe upon the prerogatives of infantry or artillery officers. The plan as set forth is regarded from the point of view of a tank officer, and the changes recommended are those which my meagre experience in battle with tanks causes me to believe are perhaps useful to all arms concerned

He went on to discuss the use of infantry working behind tanks, the method of advancing by rushes, and the proper application of overwhelming strength.

Two days later, in a paper entitled "Practical Training, Tank Platoon," he defined the duties of a tank platoon in combat when operating over broken ground.

> Tanks must watch their infantry. If the latter is held up there is a reason; the tanks must go back and find out. They must also always watch for helmet and rifle signals from the infantry. It is perfectly useless for tanks to attack more than 200 M[eters] ahead of the Infantry. Tanks can take almost anything but they can hold practically nothing. Hence they *MUST STAY WITH THE INFANTRY*.

Ordering practice attacks to be held at the tank center, he wrote:

> In all of this practice battle conditions will be supposed to exist. Officers must use signs and cover and not run about with an heroic disregard of imaginary bullets. While it is not the intention to make officers timid they must nevertheless conserve their lives until the supreme moment. When as heretofore they will not hesitate to expose themselves [to enemy fire].

· · ·

It was all well meant but too late. The war came to an end. It terminated on his thirty-third birthday. And that seemed like a fitting date. Somehow it linked the war to his fate and destiny and made the biggest conflict in the history of man a personal event for him.

For Patton, the war had been a glorious experience. He had established the Tank Corps in the U. S. Army and proved its combat value. He learned and saw much, grew a great deal, achieved much, and earned both high honor and rapid advancement. He organized men and shaped them and led them and did all this expertly. He succeeded in his profession and passed the test of battle.

Yet the war had been frustrating too. Despite all the dedicated effort and the expended energy, all the thought and devotion he had given to his job, all the problems he had overcome, he had been in action less than five days. That was rather disappointing.

But surely there would be another war. There had to be if only for his sake so that he could profit from the maturity and wisdom he had accumulated and thereby fulfill his destiny or fate.

Diary

November 11 (Monday): "Peace was signed and Langres was very ex[c]ited. Many flags. Got rid of my bandage. Wrote a poem on peace. Also one on Capt. English."

VIII

Postwar France

"I fear that laziness which ever pursued me is closing in on me at last."

CHAPTER 32

The Prize

"I realize that one is apt to attatch too great importance to ones own exploits. If I am guilty, as is probable, of thinking too much of my self please forgive me."

Letter, GSP, Jr., to Beatrice, November 16, 1918

We are going on almost the same as usual [now with peace] but it is not so easy to get up in the morning as it used to be especially on saturday. I fear that laziness which ever pursued me is closing in on me at last. It will be funny [back in the United States] to command 74 men in a troop of cavalry after having commanded a thousand and more in battle and to be through by noon each day.

To avoid so far as possible the devil of idleness I am going to write a book. For in prose it is the pen which makes the sword great in peace. So if I write a good book I might get to be a general before the next war now. If I start the next [war] as a Brigadier General and hit the same pace I gained in this I will make three grades or end up as a full general. This is necessary to keep pace with Nita. Or at least her present hopes.

I inclose the chapters of the book with the subjects to be treated in each chapter. It ought to reach several volumes. Which no one will buy in all probability.

The idea of writing a book originated, no doubt, in a project he was working on with Brett. They were preparing a history of the 304th Tank Brigade operations in the Meuse-Argonne campaign. Patton knew the beginnings, Brett the later stages, and as Patton learned in detail what had occurred after he was wounded, he was impressed by what his men, the men whom he had formed and inspired, had accomplished during his absence.

The after-action report, issued on November 18, bore the unmistakable imprint of Patton's intelligence and style. Of 141 American tanks actually engaged with the enemy, 140 were accounted for — the one that was missing was swallowed up in an enormous shell hole or trench or lost in the underbrush of a forest, perhaps captured by the enemy. "The supplies of gasoline and equipment to the tanks and of rations to the troops" — the *sine qua non* of sustained operations — "was excellent, the chief difficulty arising out of the congestion of the traffic and the bad condition of the roads."

There were nine "Tactical Conclusions":

1. Infantry officers lacked understanding and appreciation of tank capabilities, for tanks needed infantry operating with them at all times to be successful — which subtly, probably unconsciously, foreshadowed a shift in doctrine from the use of tanks to support infantry to the contrary conclusion that infantry should be used to support tanks; but this idea would remain obscure until clarified with terrifying suddenness by the German blitzkrieg tactics in World War II.

2. A lack of liaison between tanks and infantry hampered efficient operations.

3. "Infantry should act as though tanks were not present and not expect tanks to overcome resistance and wait expecting tanks to attempt to consolidate a success."

4. Tanks were too valuable because of their strengths in firepower and mobility and too weak in mechanical reliability to be dissipated in reconnaissance missions.

5. The distance between readiness positions and the line of departure should be reduced, for "tanks cannot sustain a prolonged march without being overhauled and put in order."

6. A thorough preliminary reconnaissance on foot of the terrain to be used by tanks was absolutely indispensable.

7. "The enemy artillery is the dangerous adversary of the tanks." Therefore, strong supporting artillery ready to deliver counter-battery fires, as well as screening smoke, was terribly important to insure tank success.

8. The value of tanks as attacking units and as a fighting arm had been demonstrated.

9. Some slight changes in tactical employment were necessary, those looking toward a better utilization of tanks in mass and in depth.

Letter, GSP, Jr., to Beatrice, November 17, 1918

Lininger was wearing his D.S.M. [Distinguished Service Medal] for [his service in] Mexico. He had just gotten it and it is a very pretty ribbon. I wish I had one for killing Cardanes. Perhaps I will get one. It is one degree lower than the D.S.C. [Distinguished Service Cross] but apparently I may not get that either though I think I will.

There are all sorts of Rumors about our going home very soon. I hope there is truth in them.

As to my needing money. I don't I have plenty as nothing has cost me much lately and I am getting on all right. And have a couple of thousand left. I may buy you a present?

The history of the tank brigade and Lininger's medal prompted Patton to make two requests.

Letter, GSP, Jr., to Pershing, November 17, 1918

In considering the two favors I am going to ask please treat me as a simple officer of the army. That is I do not want to presume on the fact that I have been on your staff. Nor do I wish to presume on your constant kindness to me.

First, if Pershing was satisfied with the performance and achievements of the tankers at St. Mihiel and the Meuse-Argonne, would he please write a letter of commendation that Patton could distribute to every man.

I realize however that most of your army are equally deserving and that perhaps I am selfish in asking so much of you.

The second favor is entirely personal and hence less deserving of your consideration. Lt. Col. Lininger . . . has been awarded the D.S.M. for his services in Mexico. I believe that my accidental encounter and killing of Col. Cardanes at San Miguel on May 16, 1916 might equally be considered as a service to the Government in that by good luck I was able to do in one morning with nine men what a whole regiment of cavalry . . . had failed to do in one week. I would not dare bother you with this were it not that it is only you and Gen. Cabel who know anything about it.

I realize that one is apt to attatch too great importance to ones own exploits. If I am guilty, as is probable, of thinking too much of my self please forgive me.

Letter, GSP, Jr., to Beatrice, November 18, 1918

The most terrible thing has happened to me. I heard last night that I will not get the D.S.C.

Why I don't know as one is not even supposed to know that one has been recommended. I think that R. [Rockenbach] was in too big a hurry and put in [for the medal] with out sufficient data. Or else some one got me from behind. The worst part of it is that once rejected you cannot again be recomended. I woke up last night feeling that I was dying and then it would occur to me what had happened. I cannot realize it yet. It was the whole war to me. All I can ever get out of two years away from you.

But I will be G.D. if I am beat yet. I don't know what I will do but I will do something. If not I will resign and join the French army as a Captain or something. Gen. R. thinks my colonelcy is a compensation but it is nothing. I would rather be a second Lt. with the D.S.C. than a general with out it. It means more than an "A" [his West Point letter] and it would be of vast value in future.

I am sorry to bother you but I had to get it off my chest, onto yours even at long range by letter. I love you.

Letter, GSP, Jr., to Beatrice, November 18, 1918 — "Night"

Darling Beat I wrote you such a desolate letter that I must hurry to tell you of what has just happened. It is not all I want but it is something. Gen Smith who has been commanding the schools is leaving so I called on him to say goodbye as he has been very nice to me. I also told him of my trouble and asked him what to do. It may work [yet]. Then just as I was leaving he said "It is against orders but I will tell you that I have to day recomended you for the D.S.M. for having had the finest spirit and discipline in your command that I have ever seen." Of course I may not get it either but then I may. And now I feel less alone in the world than I did. I just said my prayers for them both [both decorations]. I have a crude religion.

But an everlasting love for you. George.

Although the distinction was sometimes blurred between the Distinguished Service Cross and the Distinguished Service Medal, the former was generally awarded for gallantry in combat, that is, for action in direct contact with the enemy, the latter for distinction in a post of high responsibility.

Patton wanted both, but he wanted the Distinguished Service Cross more. He had distinguished himself on the battlefield against the enemy, and he therefore deserved the D.S.C. and the recognition and honor it bestowed. According to his values, those who aspired and who succeeded merited the tangible reward.

He had his wound and he proudly wore the wound stripe on his sleeve as his badge of sacrifice. He had his promotion and he proudly wore his eagles on his shoulders as his badge of excellence. Now he wanted the Distinguished Service Cross as his badge of courage.

It was characteristic of him that he wished not the highest decoration for heroism in combat, the Medal of Honor, which he never actively sought. He desired rather the second best, which was still a considerable honor. It resembled his quest at West Point for the position not of First Captain but rather of Adjutant, which still carried recognition. It was as though some innate sense of inferiority prevented him from seeking the highest place.

Perhaps he feared too much to be disappointed. Perhaps he had a clear and honest notion of his capacities. Perhaps he was too sensitive to risk unbearable hurt.

Diary

November 20: "Got letter from Nita in which she said Gen. P wrote her. 'I know of no one who has as much courage as George.' "

. . .

GSP, Jr., Lecture, "Tank Tactics," November 20, 1918

Historically the tank is in conception a very old idea. At the siege of Tire by Alexander the Great in 318? B.C. walls had already become so formidable an obstacle to the siege artillery of the time that it was necessary to devise some more efficient mechanical means for their reduction and the moving tower was invented.

The first year of this war again so enhanced the power of passive resistance capable of being offered by that inverted wall the trench that artillery again proved helpless to cope with it and the mind of man following the inevitable cycle of cause and effect reinvented the moving tower in the shape of the tank to cope with it.

Such at least in its inception was the purpose of the tank, but we shall show that like many other inventions it proved of vast utility in spheres of activity which its inventors never claimed for it . . .

The French . . . thought of it as a means of carrying infantry accross a relatively narrow Nomans-Land and then of dumping these soldiers like the Greeks from the Horse on the heads of the disgusted and demoralized Germans . . . To accomplish this end the tank evolved had no need to cross trenches and at the time of the origin of the idea Spring 1915 artillery was much less heavy than laterly so the shell craters to be encountered were negligable. Unfortunately the french plan was made abortive by two causes. First the British sprung their first attack with six tanks before the French were ready and second the artillery became so heavy that the French carriers could no longer negotiat the shell holes. They then were confronted with the necessity of converting their tanks into make shift fighting machines and of following as well as might be with these monstroci-ties the tactics of the British.

From the beginning the british had thought of the Tank as a fight-ing machine and the more enthusiastic and less well educated from a military point of view went so far as to dream of mechanical armies. The first essay of the machine in battle proved the absurdity of such notions and the tactics of Tanks to meet the then existing conditions were at once evolved. With out going into minutee as to the drill formations of tanks I shall now explain to you the determinant fac-tors in the evolution of tactics and call your attention to the steady changes in these factors with the corresponding change in tactics noting that nearly always the tactics lagged one stage behind the con-ditions they were destined to encounter.

When tanks first appeared upon the scene the defensive had out-stripped the offensive. In spite of barrages so long drawn out and so terrific that the whole face of nature was changed there always re-mained some men some Machine guns and some wire which had es-caped destruction and whose presence not only made attacks over the front trenches terribly costly in man and material but also so har-rassed and shattered the morale and formation of the attacking troops that they were unable to reach the hostile gun positions where victory lies but were also easly victims to hostile counter attack. These counter attacks in turn were made possible by the notice of the impending attack given long in advance of D day by the mighty alarm bell rung in no uncertain terms by the Artillery preparation.

To recapitulate: At the moment of attack the infantry was always held up by some or all of the following obstacles and resistances. Wire, rifle fire, Machine Gun fire, counter attack and artillery. To facilitate the attack of the infantry then the Tanks had to do the following things. 1. They had to cut wire. 2. They had to help keep down the hostile fire from rifles and machine guns. 3. They had to help mop-up as doing this without them wasted too much time. 4. They had to repel counter attack. 5. They had to get into the hostile artillery positions and so disorganise them that they would be impotent to destroy the infantry while they were consolidating. But all these things they had to do as an AID to the inft. For now as in the time of Hanibal or as in the times to come it is the infantry and only the infantry — the man on foot with the hand arm — who wins the battle. This is true even and perhaps more so since I who say it am first a cavalryman and next a Tanker.

These duties of the tank were well understood from the beginning but due to the fact that all new weapons are reguarded with suspicion not much credence was placed in the power of the tank to accomplish its task.

This lack of faith was not very troublesome to the tank except in that part of it which insisted on tremendious artillery preparations. These bombardments were very bad. They cut up the ground to an almost unbelivable extent there by ditching many tanks and so exhausting the infantry by causing them to walk for miles from crater to crater that they were physically unable to progress the requisite 10,000 M. [meters] to the hostile guns. Also they gave the alarm and nice well arranged counter attacks were always waiting to rebuf the few tanks and infantry which succeeded in surviving the efforts of their own artillery as demonstrated in the conversion of level fields into bogs and mine craters.

On Nov. 20 1917 the light dawned and Cambrae [Cambrai] was fought with out artillery preparation and from a Tank standpoint was a great success.

One would think for a moment that the problem was solved but it was not. Two things intervened. The brain of the Bosch and the Trench mortar.

This latter animal began to appear in force and under various names about the time of cambrae or earlier. With his nondelay fuse he was the answer to wire and hence to rigid front line defense. His character needs no higher approval than the German offensive in the spring of 1918. He was the father begetting of Necessity the defense in depth . . .

Herretical as my statement may appear there is nothing new at all in the machine gun. It is only the latest solution to the age long riddle. Supremacy of fire. The men who invented the sling beat those who threw stones by hand. Those of the bow and arrow destroyed the javlen men. The transendent genius who thought of the ballista which shot ten arrows at a time was in his day the master of the world. So it goes down the ages this incessant striving to have one man as effective as many men. And why? simply to reduce losses. Simply arithmetic. If one man can shoot as much as ten men and at the same time offeres one tenth the target down goes your losses. Here is the raison D'etre of the defense in depth. The front line can no longer be held on account of the belchings of that metal toad the T. M. [trench mortar]. If the defense were moved back just beyond T.M. range nothing would be gained as the toads though very awkward can hop a little and would soon be [moved forward] near enough to hit the line. Moreover a line in order to stop good troops must be dense even with machine guns and this causes losses also it eliminates surprise. Hence defense in depth. An area miles deep dotted with machine guns each mutually protecting every other. The front line while still held is only a rotting husk. The real line well to the rear is the place from which to launch counter attacks on troops disorganised and decimated by passing through the machine gun zone.

How did the tanks answer this question for answer it they did as the Peace [the Armistice] proves. Unfortunately they answered it not by subtly playing the game but rather by bulling through relying on their great margin of superiority over the machine guns but costing them selves and their infantry too dearly.

That lack of confidence or [that] conservatism which I have before alluded to made tanks think that because they had attacked held positions and cut wire at Cambrae and Himmel they should always do so, even when these trenches were no longer occupied and the wire had been blown to bits by trench mortars. They did this to the glory of God and the extreme satisfaction of the Hun. The result was that a large number [of tanks] were left stranded in the trenches which they could have easily crossed in column and the rest too weak in numbers arrived late to help the infantry and often with most of their gas exhausted. But this was not the end of the mistakes of the tanks. Having finally reached the infantry they were filled with a noble fire and hurried on to conquer the world. Forgetting the unvarying truth that tanks exist to help infantry. They cannot help a mile in front any more than a mile behind.

Now when the tanks went on with out the infantry the Germans often did not shoot at them [for the Germans were] waiting for the infantry. Tanks are at least 50% blind so many machine guns were not seen. Those that were were attacked and the [gun] crews killed or driven off. But the tanks often could not drive directly over the gun. When they had passed by the germans remanned the guns undestroyed; the guns unseen were still there and both sets opened up on the infantry. After some time possibly hours the tanks returned to help the infantry and this time having the infantry there to help point out the guns the attack was more successful but time had been lost. And something worse than time had been gained. The tanks in their first trip had attracted the notice of the Hun guns. These opened a barrage on the place where they had seen the tanks and when the tanks appeared proudly leading the infantry the latter caught hell from the barrage so kindly arranged for them by their tanks.

Now was it inevitable that these things should have happened? Yes it was since we are all poor weak mortals after all. Was it necessary? No.

Here is the French solution which not being my own I am at liberty to crytacise . . .

[He explained how time was lost and how bypassed enemy machine guns took attacking infantry in the flank. The French idea was to have tanks work with the reserve infantry battalions, those coming behind the assault elements to mop up.] Hence I say that this method of using the tanks while it has some virtue is not the correct method and hence I condemn it.

Here is the correct method. The answer to the [defensively] organised area and the way we would have attacked had the bosch given us the chance. I still hope he does . . .

[Patton's solution was to have infantry and tanks operate together, with infantry scouts ahead pointing out machine gun nests to be destroyed by tank fire or by tanks rolling over them. The best method was to get tanks across the few front lines of trenches so they could move into areas where few trenches existed. There the tanks could roam at will and demoralize the enemy.]

I will now point out to you a few of the more thrilling phases of tank tactics such as we will use in Mexico perhaps.

•   •   •

His lecture notes ended there, and from there, no doubt, he extempo-rized.

There was much of interest in what he said. He believed that the prin-ciples of war remained immutable and valid. Fundamentally, then, there was nothing new in the art of war. A military leader proved his genius or his lack of it by the way he adapted constantly emerging new weapons to the determining principles. How the combat leader organized his troops into formation and how he committed them to battle decided the out-come of warfare.

He still held the idea that the tank was a weapon designed to support the infantry. As one of his young captains would explain early in 1919, "Tanks are to assist the Infantry. If the Infantry needs no assistance don't employ tanks."

Although Patton was to cling rigidly to that principle, which would inhibit his military thought — preventing him in the end from breaking through to a new concept — there were already intimations in his think-ing that tanks need not be tied always to the slow pace of riflemen on foot. This idea would remain undeveloped until the opening weeks of World War II, when the Germans — Guderian and others — displayed and demonstrated how tanks in conjunction with closely sup-porting airplanes, self-propelled artillery pieces, and motorized infantry-men could break defensive lines and roam at will through enemy rear areas, completely demoralizing outflanked and confused combat troops and command nerve centers.

Patton was also convinced that the likelihood of another war in western Europe, where good roads existed, was slight. He saw rather the prospect of war in underdeveloped regions of the world, for example, in Mexico, and there the close cooperation of tanks, cavalry, artillery, and infantry, he believed, would produce a type of warfare much like the somewhat primitive mechanized warfare in World War I.

These themes would characterize Patton's thinking throughout the two decades between the two world wars.

. . .

Letter, GSP, Jr., to Beatrice, November 20, 1918

I am leaving in a few moments to see Gen Leroy Eltinge about a subject you can well imagine. I hope I get something out of it besides gigles. But I am . . . loosing faith in men . . . every one is your friend until you want something and then you have only your self for friend.

Some of the T.C. [Tank Corps] is going home shortly but I doubt if it is my outfit. We will be held [for the occupation] I fear . . .

Yesterday the big [heavy] tanks said they could beat the Renaults so they laid out a course. We followed and beat hell out of them.

The subject he discussed with Eltinge was the Distinguished Service Cross. What had happened, he explained, was this. Three days after Patton was wounded, Rockenbach hurriedly collected several certified statements and affidavits from those who had witnessed Patton's heroism. Knowles, Edwards, Angelo, and a few others contributed firsthand accounts that were quite generalized rather than specific and detailed. Attaching these as documentary proof of Patton's gallantry, Rockenbach wrote a proposed citation and recommended the award — all normal procedure. Rockenbach sent the papers on September 30 to the commanding general of the First Army, who was Pershing.

On the same day, Rockenbach placed in Patton's official file his assessment of his wounded subordinate. "This officer," Rockenbach wrote, "is recommended for the Distinguished Service Cross for conspicuous courage, coolness, energy and intelligence in handling troops in battle."

Four days later, Drum, the First Army chief of staff and a longtime friend of Patton, added his favorable recommendation to Rockenbach's and forwarded the papers to Pershing. As a routine matter, they went to the adjutant general who disapproved the recommendation, probably on the ground of inadequate documentary proof.

On October 24, Rockenbach resubmitted the papers to the First Army commander, who was now Hunter Liggett. Five days later, Liggett's adjutant general returned Rockenbach's recommendation with the statement "In view of the fact that this recommendation has been disapproved by the Commander in Chief, no further action will be taken in the premises." Presumably, "premises" meant the First Army headquarters.

That seemed like the end of the road.

Heartened by his conversation with his good friend Eltinge on November 20, Patton went immediately to see Rockenbach. He convinced Rockenbach that the recommendation might be approved if it traveled directly to the AEF adjutant general with fuller and better documentation of

Patton's battlefield exploit. To expedite his request, Patton presented Rockenbach with a draft letter he had prepared for Rockenbach's use.

This letter read, in part, as follows:

> During the course of this opperation the progress of the Tanks was stopped by three lines of trenches. Colonel Patton reconnoitered a passage accross these trenches. He then supervised the work of digging a passage through them and during the course of this work encouraged the men first by starting to dig him self when the men showed fear at exposing them selves and later by mounting on the top of the parapet the better to give directions . . . It was necessary to get more shovles and as the men hesitated to leave the trenches in order to get the tools from the tanks against which the bullets could be plainly heard striking Col. Patton made three trips to the tanks each time bringing back shovles. During the whole course of this work he was exposed to rifle and machine gun fire which was effective as some twenty men who were engaged in the work were hit. His actions and encouragement to his men added materially to the success of the enterprise.
>
> These facts were ascertained by Brigadier General S. D. Rockenbach, Chief of the Tank Corps U.S. Army from the statements of Capt. M. H. Knowles TC, 1Lt P.S. Edwards, Signal Corps, Sgt. E. W. Fansler, Headquarters Section, 304th Tank Brigade, Pvt. J. T. Angelo, Headquarters Section. All eye witnesses of the affair . . .
>
> I am of the opinion that Colonel George S. Patton, Jr. Tank Corps USA, has so distinguished him self by his extraordinary heroism in connection with the above military opperations that to an extent justify the award recommended.
>
> signed, S. D. Rockenbach, etc.

Attached to this was his own memo to Rockenbach:

> During the course of this opperation five tanks having crossed the trenches moved forward to the attack of Cheppy. About 300 men of the 35th division who were on the reverse slope of a hill at this point failed to accompany the tanks. Col. Patton urged them forward to the crest of the hill but here as the fire increased the men halted again. Col. Patton asked "Who will come with me" or words to that effect and started forward. Six men accompanied him. After advancing about fifty yards all the men were hit except Col. Patton and his

orderly. At this time Col. Patton was shot through the upper part of
the left thigh but continued to advance until his leg failed him and
he fell about forty yards from the German position. And was
dragged to a shell hole by his orderly.

Using this account by Patton as the basis for rewriting his recommendation, getting Knowles, Edwards, Angelo, and the others to redo their certificates and affidavits in fuller and more detailed form, and securing
additional accounts from other members of Patton's command group,
Rockenbach sent his request forward again. Attached were no less than
eleven eyewitness reports of the battlefield incident.

Letter, GSP, Jr., to Beatrice, November 21, 1918
I inclose what purports to be copies of my citations [for the D.S.C.]
at least they will be something like that. Of course do *not* let them
get in any paper but you can show them to your friends if you want
to. I do wish they would hurry up and give me something. If they
dont I will see that John [Pershing] gets hold of it and does something as from a letter of his of which I have seen a copy he is most
nice about the affair.

We are working as hard as ever in order to keep the men interested
but it is a hard job as war was the great stimulant and replaced to a
degree the lack of inherent discipline from which we have always
suffered.

As a matter of fact had it not been for the regular army officers we
would have been in a very bad fix indeed . . .

I have bought my three stripe chevron for 18 months in France
which I can put on the ninth of Dec. pretty soon now.

I hope you see me before I get a fourth stripe.

Letter, GSP, Jr., to Beatrice, November 22, 1918
To morrow I give a lecture to some generals followed by a demonstration of an attack with a battalion of tanks. One of Braines new
American tanks will be there also to show that we did build
them . . .

I wish you would get over this fool idea of war work. And attend
only to your self. Your hair, your chin and your tummie. I have
done plenty of war work for the family.

I don't know whether there will be a regular tank corps or not and
if there is I don't know if I will stay in it. I would rather be a captain

of cavalry than a major of Tanks but a Lt. Colonel of tanks might be different. Although tanks in peace time would be very much like coast artillery with a lot of machinery which never works. Still "Il faut voir" [we will see].

Patton's lecture at the Staff College to a group of general officers who had no specific assignments started as follows:

> The amount of nerve required by a Captain [his Regular Army rank], even though camouflaged as a Col[onel] in attempting to lecture to so august an assembly is such that I respectfully suggest that someone of you recommend me for a medal for gallantry in lecture. However in the words of General Ellis at Cambrai, "I shall do my damndest."

Tanks, he continued, were the last word in shock troops, the modern equivalent of the Greek hoplite or Carthagenian elephant. He described the battle of Cambrai and British tank tactics. He indicated that the Americans had adopted, then adapted, the British tactical methods. And he insisted that tanks must be used boldly.

Letter, GSP, Jr., to Beatrice, November 24, 1918
Yesterday I gave a lecture on Tanks to a bunch of Generals followed by a demonstration. It was a rotten affair as they all went to sleep. They were the culls and they looked it.

Tonight the 344 Battalion is giving a dinner & dance to which I am envited. The ladies will not be much class being telephone operators and nurses but still that is better than nothing . . .

We are getting up a football team here also. I am Captain [of the team] . . .

I got a letter from Col. J. E. Carberry Air Service. He was a year after me at West Point and is the only person around my time who has written to me. So if you see him be nice to him.

The weather remains fine and we could do lots with tanks if there was only a war on as the ground is hard and they can cross nearly any thing.

We tried out some American Renaults yesterday and they were O.K. faster than the French machines and better built.

If we could only have had a few hundred of them during the war it would have been something.

The following day he received a letter from Lieutenant Skinner, one of the British officers who had entertained him in the Tower of London, another from General Harbord, formerly Pershing's chief of staff, then commander of the Services of Supply. Patton felt better, less alone, to have these indications that friends thought of him and wanted to remain in touch with him.

Letter, GSP, Jr., to Aunt Nannie, November 24, 1918

My leg is much better. So well that I played foot ball yesterday and ran a nail in my foot but not far. As it was in my left foot I still limp on the same side.

We had a dinner last night and there were some Y.M.C.A. women and nurses at it. One of the former told me that the soldiers thought a lot of me because I walked accross a bridge at Essey to see if it was mined. I had forgotten the incident and was pretty sure it was not mined. Soldiers are funny.

. . . I just got a wire from Beat saying she had moved to Washington.

Letter, GSP, Jr., to Beatrice, November 25, 1918

We had a very nice time and danced until mid night with telephone girls, YMCA females and nurses. One of the Y.M.C.A. ladies sat next to me and told me that all the soldiers attatch great glory to me for something I forgot to mention. When we got to Essey we thought that the bridge was mined and the tanks stopped so I walked accross the bridge to see if it would blow up. It did not. So many more interesting things have happened since that I forgot to speak of it. I was pretty sure it was not mined. If it had been it would not have hurt me at all as there would have been nothing left to hurt. It is funny that this small thing should stick in the minds of the soldiers.

Letter, GSP, Jr., to Major S. E. Brett, commanding 344th Tank Battalion, November 25, 1918

My dear Major Brett: . . . I want to take this opportunity of putting in writing what I have long felt in my heart. I consider the enviable record of the 1st Brigade, Tank Corps, both in peace and war, has been due more to your earnest and constant efforts in training and valorous conduct in battle than to that of any other man or officer. Not only did you work here when we had nothing, not even hope, without a murmur, but, in battle you fought the Brigade until there was nothing left and even after that, you fought on. As far as I know no officer of the A.E.F. has given more faithful, loyal, and gallant service. Please accept my heartfelt congratulations and thanks.

Letter, GSP, Jr., to Beatrice, November 26, 1918

I took a long ride this morning and it did not hurt my tail much so I feel incouraged. Miss Green [his horse] wanted to jump all the mud holes she saw which was not very easy on my but[t]. She meant well . . .

I have been writing orders for a tank battalion attack all afternoon to use in a lecture I am going to give. I wish I had known as much when I was fighting as I do now but there was no one who knew and we had to learn by experience. I have been reading some German documents about tanks and they furnish the greatest compliments we could have received. They under estimated the tank and it cost them the war perhaps. At least it hurried the end.

I inclose copies of all the letters [of commendation] we [in the brigade] got as they are quite nice. Lots of them don't belong to me by right as I was out of it but I trained them and taught them all they know. Which is a satisfaction in a way. It was most interesting and very original. Realy it is almost as much fun working out manuvers as it [is] working out fights only the denouement is not so nice as in the case of a fight.

Well this is a hellish stupid world now and life has lost its zest . . . I think I will get fat lazy but I hope not. Don't you dare do so. I love you.

Diary

November 27: "Rode horseback and hurt my leg. So I do not feel very flip."

November 28: "Went on bore [boar] hunt . . . and killed a rabbit. Ate a huge dinner and felt very stuffed."

November 29: "Col Taylor came down to see about changing D.S.C.s to M Hs [Medals of Honor for] English, Morrison, Weed, Semmes, Corp Call and Lt. Boss. He also took some evidence about me. I hope I get it."

November 30: "Col Taylor left. Got Black male [blackmail] letter from a Mr. Whiting. Who in hell is he? Bill Reed says not to worry about it."

Letter, GSP, Jr., to Beatrice, November 30, 1918

I just had a great surprise. Some irate frenchman wrote me a letter accusing me of all sorts of things with respect to his wife. It was most interesting as I had never heard of the lady but he seems to have a lot of dope on me. . . . I was worried about it but Bill Reed said to pay no attention. To be insulted greatly one should at least be guilty . . .

I begin to think that I have a chance of getting the M.H. [Medal of Honor] after all. Some Col. Taylor who knows [knew] you and Nita at El Paso is president of the board now and seems very fair. All I want is fairness not partiality. I would surely like to have the blue ribbon with the white stars.

The appearance in draft form of a manual on tank tactics prompted him to indicate certain errors in the text:

While the equation for tanks shows they can climb at 60% slope, no earth I have ever encountered will sustain the tracks at such an angle. Figure should read 40 to 50% . . .

I believe that no wire entanglement can stop a Light Tank . . .

The American Renault can also create a smoke barrage for defensive purposes by injection at will of a smoke producing substance into the hot muffler . . .

Tank obstacles also consist of concrete walls burried, 1 to 2 meters high, 2 meters thick, with railroad iron embedded in the walls and sticking out in the direction from which the tanks will approach . . .

While it is right and proper to place Tanks under Infantry Units the relation of the Tanks and Infantry must be clearly defined. Infantry Commanders may simply tell the tanks what to do and not how to do it. Also they should be prohibited in requesting Tanks to do Patrol and Guard Duty which is not one of their functions.

Diary

December 1: "Left with Maj. Brett at 6:45 A.M. for Varennes . . . Went over field South of Cheppy in P.M. Took pictures of my shell hole and trench where English was killed. Varennes is where Louis XVI was made prisoner when he tried to leave france. Little of it left now. Very bad mud."

December 2: "Went to Vauquois . . . most interesting and stupendus. More than 48000 French & Germans killed in fighting there.

Went . . . to Landres-St. George & St. Georges which were the scenes of the last Tank attacks. The U.S. Barrage was most terrible. We went . . . to look at the Bosch positions and they had lost much material."

December 3: Went to Verdun and San Mihiel. Trench system is most interesting. French did more digging but Bosch better and they had better shelter for the men also better wire.

Patton and Brett returned to Bourg on December 4 just in time for Patton to learn he had won the prize. Someone, probably Rockenbach, no doubt telephoned from Chaumont to give him the good news.

Diary
December 4: "Got D.S.C. Wired Beat to that effect."

On the following day, confirmation came in writing:

Diary
December 5: Got letter saying I had D.S.C.

Letter, GSP, Jr., to Rockenbach, December 5, 1918
My dear General: Please accept my sincere thanks for the trouble you took in my behalf with reference to the D.S.C. I shall always prize it more than any thing I could have gotten in the war. My gratitude to you is based on the fact that with out your earnest effort I should not have gotten it. Thank you again . . .
With renewed thanks I am most sincerely, G. S. Patton, Jr.

Diary
December 6: "Left for Paris on 2:18 train [for one week of leave, rest and vacation]. Gen. R. let me wear my D.S.C. Ribbon."

CHAPTER 33

The Wait

"Generals are made — by themselves . . . by a life of ceaseless effort at the military profession."

SOON AFTER PATTON, wearing his D.S.C. ribbon, left for Paris, Rockenbach rated him. "This officer is very efficient, but youthful. He will, I believe, sober into one of highest value."

The process of sobering an exuberant young man into an officer of highest caliber was already at work. It could be seen in Patton's serious application to his professional duties.

He lectured regularly at the General Staff College. He gave formal talks to his own officers and men. He assiduously collected British and French training notes, and he would continue to add to his collection of materials, operations reports, and after-action histories, to expand his knowledge of tank warfare. He gathered — and apparently studied in fascination — citations awarding soldiers decorations for bravery in combat. He continued to be interested in technological improvements. He frequently directed exercises at the tank center.

Diary

December 5 (the day before he left for Paris): Gave lecture to General Staff College. They asked to have it printed. Had manuver in P.M. quite successful. Wireless tanks worked for first time; sent and received messages while in motion. Staff very inattentive due to end of war probably.

For his presentation at the Staff College, Patton wrote two lectures on the subject of "Light Tanks in Exploitation." One was a draft lecture, the other he actually delivered. Each was interesting in its own right.

The draft lecture notes — later marked by Patton, "This was not given as here shown. GSP" — advanced his thoughts on tank doctrine almost to the blitzkrieg concept. His proposal or thesis: once the tanks and infantry, working together, crossed the line of trenches composing the forward enemy defenses, thereby breaking the hostile defensive positions, the tanks ought to take advantage of their mobility and exploit the victory.

Exploitation signifies that the situation is such as to at least justify the hope that there is something to exploit. In other words that the crust has been broken and we are about to eat the pie. This occurs when the Infantry and Tanks have passed the first organized positions and are rushing headlong on the harrassed and fleeing enemy . . .

Before proceeding further to tell of these thrilling exploits, it may be well to try to picture as vividly as possible the actual position of the defeated enemy as seen close up.

Above our heads the constant roar of our barrage fills the air and we hope kills the enemy. Unfortunately I have yet to see our own shells bursting. As after the first hour of progression, our barrage has invariably been from two to four miles ahead of us.

As to the enemy, he is only represented by a few shells falling in unpopulated fields. For the rest, the country is empty and uninteresting dotted with clumps of trees, ruined houses and perhaps a camouflage bordered road. The tanks and Infantry advance. The latter in platoon columns; the former in skirmish lines. Finally the Tanks gain sufficient distance (150 meters) ahead of the Infantry, deploy and then proceed to form there a grotesque line. All is progressing as on the drill field when suddenly the hostile shells become more numerous and inquisitive and then from several places at once the put put put of the Boche machine guns.

The defeated and demoralized enemy has been run to earth; we are upon him; it only remains to finish him; but where in hell is he. He is apparently all around and for once appearances are not deceptive. He is not in those dense waves of surging green humanity so vividly depicted by newspaper reporters and other fiction writers, but scattered in groups of a few men armed with one, two or 4 machine guns or automatic rifles admirably placed and almost totally concealed.

This is the form of battle called Exploitation or at least the first phase of Exploitation. The name is apt . . .

Having thus sketched in my most charming style the toute ensemble of the scene, I will attempt by the use of the blackboard to show how all around fire above referred to is arranged. If I have appeared frivolous, it is because being a graduate of this institution I know that the [student] . . . prefers amusement to instructions and a lecturer who would not have his voice drowned in a barrage of snores must try to amuse for at least the first five minutes.

. . . Four to eight Kilometers back of this [front] line is the real defended position, usually a naturally strong line enhanced by skilfully prepared trenches linking together well organized villages and backed by a numerous artillery and well placed machine guns, but in the area between the first line and this second one is the organized zone where we must make our first essay in exploitation . . .

These men [on the defensive] are often described as being in "Checkerboard" formation. To me this term is misleading as it presupposes regularity of distribution. There is no regularity. The guns are arranged solely to attain two things. First: concealment so as to avoid discovery and destruction. Second: mutual support . . . nearly always the forward ones are on reverse slopes with a short field of fire to the front and relatively longer ones to one or both flanks. Each gun position has been selected with the greatest care . . . The guns are placed in a position to kill or be killed. When first the Tanks advance through this area preceding the infantry these guns do not fire but . . . fire only on Infantry targets after the passage of the Tanks. For this reason it has often happened that tanks have gone forward meeting no resistance from machine gun fire while the Infantry following them have been decimated by a tempest of machine gun bullets.

. . . this solitary advance of the tanks while apparently a very useful operation is in reality a perfectly futile one. Tanks can take nearly anything. They can hold absolutely nothing. Furthermore the visibility from within a Tank is not over 40%. Hence at least 50% of the machine guns remain unseen by the Tank . . . if the Infantry and Tanks enter the fight firmly impressed with the fact that they are mutually necessary one to the other and take proper steps to maintain contact, the problem of the organized area is solved.

The Tank is the answer to the machine gun but like any other solution it must be rightly applied . . . the tanks must see more than they now do. This can be accomplished by placing a line of

Infantry scouts from 100 to 150 meters ahead of the tanks . . . the infantry taking a hostile machine gun should act as a catcher behind the bat. He makes all preparations to catch the ball and does catch it unless the bat, in this case the tank, interposes . . . if the tank is successful the infantry which has been lying supine has lost distance and distance in war means time and time means victory.

The above are the tactics of the first phase of exploitation of the Light Tank. Proceeding in this manner the tanks and infantry arrive at the main line of resistance . . .

If the tanks have been successful in quickly reducing machine gun resistance, this main line of defence will have lost much of its virtue because it is constituted not to resist vigorous attack of unbroken troops but rather to check the straggling assault of troops wearied and weakened by the machine gun infested area in front of it. Hence it too will fall to the vigorous attack of the Tanks aided by the infantry using all its arms, which means an overwhelming fire of rifles, machine guns, automatic rifles and 37's concentrated with the aid of the tanks upon certain strategic points of the second line of resistance.

Assuming then that we have successfully negotiated the organized area and the line of resistance, we arrive at a second organized area, but a much less highly developed one . . . and there should be no difficulty in continuing the same methods to maintain the continuity of our progression.

Finally we have reached we will say the corps objective, but night is falling. It appears injudicious to attack at night so we must use the night as a means of preparation for renewing activities at dawn. From the tank standpoint these preparations consist of refilling the tanks with gasolene, oil and ammunition. This is the most difficult task as anyone who has ever seen an axial road must admit but upon the solution of this question the next day's operations of the tanks wholly depends. It never yet has been fully solved because the mechanical means to the solution have been absent. If we had had ten ton munition tractors capable of carrying sufficient gasolene, etc. and negotiating the fields on either side of the road, the solution would have been easy. These tractors should move forward as soon as the hostile fire permits and should arrive at the tanks before midnight. With them should come sufficient extra men and company mechanics to thoroughly groom and refill the tanks while tank crews snatch a few hours sleep.

When morning comes the exploitations of our dreams has perhaps arrived. The enemy's artillery positions have been passed. Any fire he may direct upon us is not based upon carefully prepared firing data but is either direct over the sights which is futile or is indirect based on very insufficient information. We may then push rapidly forward along the roads. It is impossible for his infantry or artillery to stop tanks under such circumstances but it is futile for the tanks to advance faster than their infantry can follow them. If then during the night new infantry has arrived to proceed forward say at two miles an hour behind the tanks we may progress indefinitely . . .

The hostile infantry deprived of the support of the artillery is powerless against the tanks even if they fortify themselves in the upper stories of the houses of villages. They will be cut off by the infantry, who is pressing forward on either side, need only leave a party of moppers-up and may continue their march with practically no delay.

The only thing that will stop this progression will be a river without bridges or a Hindenburg Line or an artillery resistance where the guns have been placed long before and have accurate firing data for all approaches by which the Tanks could menace them.

The vision emerging inevitably out of this prospect was to use tanks in long-range thrusts of exploitation through the enemy rear areas. It was a thrilling view, for the tanks could advance indefinitely until they reached an impassable barrier. If the obstacle was a river, bridge-laying engineers accompanying the tanks could get the machines across in quick time; if a concrete wall, engineers could demolish it.

One unsolved problem burst the bubble of using tanks as long-range instruments of mobility and shock. That was how to refuel the tanks so they could continue to advance with only short and few halts. The difficulty would be overcome only in World War II.

In 1918, the notion of a deep penetration by tanks was too radical for general acceptance, and Patton decided to give as his lecture a more conventional presentation. He used an earlier talk, which stressed the employment of tanks as supporting weapons for the infantry. The more original thought, that infantry could support tanks in long-range thrusts, was merely intimated.

Letter, GSP, Jr. (Hotel Lotti, 7 & 9 rue de Castiglione), to Beatrice, December 8, 1918

. . . this is the only place I could get a room. Paris is terribly crowded with every sort of people. You should see how the civilian clothes have blossomed since the Peace . . .

The most melancholy thing I have ever tried is amusing my self alone. I doubt if I stay the entire seven days [of leave] I have coming . . .

I called on the Boyds [Colonel Carl Boyd was an aide to Pershing] this morning and Anne is quite cute . . . She is a very nice little girl and quite a relief being American.

I am going to Zig-Zag at the Follies to night. It is all in english and they say it is good. I had to pay 18F for a little folding seat.

Diary

December 11: Semmes, Weed, and Castle came to tell me good by. They are all on the way to the States.

Letter, GSP, Jr., to Beatrice, December 11, 1918

[Bought a police dog named Char for $200; he has a long pedigree.] Since marrying you I have never been satisfied with any thing but the best . . . I also bought you a little present a folding cigarette holder in gold. It is very chick and pretty . . .

Paris is terribly expensive. A lunch for one with beer costs 50F. at any good resteraunt . . .

I lunched with John [Pershing] . . . and had a very nice talk with him. He says we shall all be home in less than a year.

Diary

December 14: Went to Place de la Concorde to see the President. There was a large crowd but little noise. Gen. P. was in fifth or sixth carriage. "Pres [Wilson] looked fine and very much a man."

Woodrow Wilson had sailed from the United States to take part in the peace talks. He would remain in France until mid-February, 1919, then return home. After less than two weeks in the United States, he would come again to France early in March, this time staying until the end of June.

Letter, GSP, Jr. (Hotel Plaza Athénée, 25 avenue Montaigne), to Beatrice, December 14, 1918

Darling Beat: I have just seen the deflade [défilade] of Le President Wilson. It was quite interesting but very little yelling. I was on the street in the crowd and the smell of bad tobacco was fierce . . .

The crowd is funny as it is made up of people one never sees usually. It reminds me of Kiplings story of the earth god's at sea where all the funny creatures were thrown up.

. . .

War Department General Orders No. 133, December 16, 1918

By direction of the President, under the provisions of the act of Congress . . . the distinguished-service cross was awarded by the commanding general, American Expeditionary Forces, for extraordinary heroism in action in France to the following-named officers and enlisted men:

George S. Patton, jr., colonel, Tank Corps. For extraordinary heroism in action near Cheppy, France, September 26, 1918. He displayed conspicuous courage, coolness, energy, and intelligence in directing the advance of his brigade down the valley of the Aire. Later he rallied a force of disorganized infantry and led it forward behind tanks under heavy machine-gun and artillery fire until he was wounded. Unable to advance farther, he continued to direct the operations of his unit until all arrangements for turning over the command were completed.

GHQ — Tank Corps, AEF, General Orders 24, December 17, 1918

[The Commander in Chief, AEF] in the name of the President has awarded the Distinguished Service Cross to the following Officers and Enlisted Men of the Tank Corps, U.S. Army, for the acts of extraordinary heroism described after their names:

Colonel George S. Patton, Jr., Tank Corps, No. 1391. For extraordinary heroism in action near Cheppy, France, September 26, 1918.

Colonel Patton displayed conspicuous courage, coolness, energy and intelligence in directing . . .

By command of Brigadier General Rockenbach.

At the tank grounds at Bourg, now known as Camp Chamberlain, all the troops of the 304th (1st) Brigade, Tank Corps, and of the 302d Tank Center were present at a review held on December 17. They honored seventeen officers and seven enlisted men who were decorated with the medal.

Diary

December 19: Battalion manuver; "it went very well and showed possibilities of Light Tanks in bad country in open war."

Letter, GSP, Jr., to his father, December 20, 1918

I mailed you under seperate cover a copy of one of the lectures on Tanks which is quite good I do not read my lectures but deliver them and amplify the text. They are all thought to be very good and I am perfectly at ease lecturing to any old thing that comes up to major generals. I must inherit your "gift of gab." It is quite a gift.

I am sending one company of tanks for a review which is to be held for the president of the Republic on the 25th. I hope it does well. I inclose a copy of my citation order also a D.S.C. ribbon as a Christmas present for you all. I could get hold of nothing else worth sending.

Diary

December 20: "Gave lecture to a bunch of artillery officers. They were all most interested and it was a pleasure to talk to them. Had demonstration in P.M. which was not well staged as the tanks bunched too much."

December 22: "Went to Chaumont to have uniforms tried on. Had to wait two hours there was such a crowd."

December 24: Braine and I talked over our last Christmas eve. I read a Book B gave me "The Kingdom of the Blind."

December 25: "Ate [Christmas] dinner here [at Bourg] at one. Went to Gen P's for dinner at eight . . . Got some nice presents . . . Left at 12:30 A.M. in snow storm. Char [dog] had eaten my shoes."

Letter, GSP, Jr., to Aunt Nannie, December 29, 1918

My Xmas box came on the 27th and all the presents were very nice and in good shape. I also got a lot of Presents at the Generals house. Last Christmas I was the only one who gave presents so this year I decided not to and every one else did.

I got a cigarette case, a pocket book and cigars and handkerchiefs in profusion also a nice scarf from J.J.P. We had a lot of fun at the dinner. The generals nephew and I were the only out siders and we had a lot of fun. We shook dice and danced after dinner . . . I ate so much plumb pudding that the general ordered the waiter to give me no more there by saving my life.

The General had on most of his ribbons and they made three and a half rows on him and looked fine. I was the only D.S.C. there so was well pleased with my self.

Quekemeyer gave me two guard Corps Bosch helmets brand new. They are very fine. There are all sorts of rumors about our going home soon. I hope they are correct as I would like to rest up a while before the next war when ever it may be.

I hope I do as well next time as I did this. I ought to get the D.S.M. and [the] two stars [of a major general]. I surely am some soldier if I say so my self, and my shape is a great help.

Diary

December 31: "End of a fine year full of interest. I hope it will be the only one in which I am away from B. for such a long time. Sat up until 12 reading French history from 1814 to 1914. Got letter from Frenchman again accusing me of all sorts of vice and saying he would write Gen. P. I hope he does."

Rockenbach assessed Patton as an officer "believed to possess ability to render good service in any position." General H. A. Smith, former school commandant in Langres, called Patton "A strong forceful active young officer. One of our very best."

Diary

January 3: Order to be ready to leave (for the United States) on short notice.

January 6: Started infantry training in "gang" attack tactics.

Letter, Maj. Gen. André W. Brewster, Inspector General, AEF, to GSP, Jr., January 6, 1919

Thank you for your letter of the thirtieth with the inclosures, which I have taken the liberty of having copied; if you have any objection to this I shall destroy them. I needed no certificates of witnesses to establish in my mind the fact of your gallant conduct both before St. Mihiel and in the Argonne. It was the talk of the men of the different divisions with which your brigade was serving and it caused me no surprise. I was very happy to see you get your decoration, both from the point of view of an Inspector who likes to see justice done, and, personally to see a friend get a decoration which he had so gallantly won.

I wish in turn a very Happy New Year for you and yours, and I hope that you will receive earned promotion.

Sincerely your friend.

Letter, GSP, Jr., to his father, January 8, 1919

So far the question of my returning to the united states is very uncertain. The Tank Troops are to return and in fact are now under orders but there is a general order to the effect that regular officers will turn over their commands at the port of embarcation and be given other duty in France. Gen. Rockenbach is trying to have an exception made in our case so the chances are about fifty fifty that we come home. I hope we do.

I am sending you in two seperate packages A bosch 105 shell case arranged as a tobacco jar. I hope you will like it. I also sent you a knife with a silver blade in it to eat oranges with. The handle is ivory and the steel very famous.

I hear that the tanks which were shot up in the fighting are to be shipped to America and that various cities are to get them as trophies. The cities will have to pay the cost of shipment. I suggest that the Los Angeles Chamber of Commerce at once ask for one. As I may be clamed as a citizen and I commanded the American Tanks in the first two actions in which they fought and in the only actions in which light tanks participated. A bronze plate with some such screed on it should be attached to the Tank by my grateful fellow citizens. If they want one they had best apply to the chief of Ordnance at once and specify RENAULT TANK.

All the troops in France were paraded at 3:00 P.M. to day and held in parade rest for Twenty one minutes while the 21 minute guns were fired in honor of the death of President [Theodore] Roosevelt.

. . . I am very busy writing a book on war and also a Tank Manual both at the same time . . .

I think that in six months we will have to go to Russia for a war. So I hope I can be back [home] for a little while any way. Then I must come back [to Russia] so as to get the Medal of Honor which I missed getting this time on account of all the witnesses getting killed or being Bosch.

Patton was enormously pleased when Beatrice sent her reaction to his D.S.C. citation and to his crossing of the supposedly mined bridge at Essey:

As I read the letters & citation & your own about the "little affair of the Essey bridge" which you say you "forgot to mention," I am [struck] dumb — if you were only near enough for me to whisper it to you.

Georgie, you are the fulfillment of all the ideals of manliness and high courage & bravery I have always held for you, ever since I have known you. And I have expected more of you than any one else in the world ever has or will.

He copied the last paragraph into his diary, adding, "I am glad she likes me."

Diary

January 15: Started writing lecture on German Tactics. Gen. Eltinge told me I was to be inspector of Military police 3 army (Third Army in the Occupation). Col. Grubbs said I was going home.

Trying to keep busy, Patton read British, French, and German tactical papers and reports of all kinds, avidly studying the art of war. He received from Mitchell, now Rockenbach's chief of staff, a training note written by Fuller for the British tanks; Mitchell had scrawled across the bottom: "Patton Here is some thing that may amuse you for a while. Mitchell. Keep it if you want to." Patton read it and put it into his files, recognizing the soundness of Fuller's views. Fuller was the tactical brains of the British tank service; he would continue his tank work and teaching after the war and would eventually be regarded as the father of tank doctrine.

Diary

January 16: Went to manuver with Tanks and 82 Div. (Infantry). Men took no interest and showed no idea of what they were doing.

Patton and Mitchell left on January 17 for the Second U. S. Army headquarters at Toul and a visit with units to give lectures and demonstrations on the functions of tanks. In their travels they were with the 35th Division at Commercy, the IX Corps headquarters at St. Mihiel, the 88th Division at Gondrecourt, the 79th Division at Souilly, and Patton became familiar with the terrain of that part of France, ground over which he, as an Army commander, would lead his troops 25 years later.

Letter, Colonels H. E. Mitchell and G. S. Patton, Jr., to Second Army
G–3, January 24, 1919, subject: Notes on Tanks

. . . The tank, in other words, is the answer to the machine gun. Tanks are then a separate weapon as truly new and original as the aeroplane. They are not mechanical cavalry, neither are they artillery or armed infantry . . .

[Tanks, like Stokes mortars, and] other abnormal weapons, have a debilitating effect on the infantry soldier, who, seeing himself supported and propped up by numerous auxiliary arms, loses pride in himself . . .

Success in the attack of tanks on infantry depends chiefly on three factors: 1st — determination and dash on the part of both tanks and infantry, 2nd — tanks keeping in touch with their infantry. To do this the tanks must get on the Infantry skirmish line, and not vice versa. 3rd — Infantry must maneuver promptly and boldly, so as to take immediate advantage of the opportunities created by the tanks . . . Like all other phases of war, success in the operation of tanks with infantry depends on teamwork.

At the bottom of this paper, Patton wrote some years later: "Col. Mitchell signed but did not write this report. GSP."

Continuing his trip, Patton, presumably still accompanied by Mitchell, drove through Pont-à-Mousson, Metz, Thionville ("the cleanest town I have seen"), Esch, Diekirch ("a very nice town as are all in Luxembourg much like America"), and Luxembourg City, all of which would figure prominently in his 1944–45 campaign.

Diary

January 28: Went to Trier. Went to the theater. A very nice town like an American [town]. Some fine Roman ruins.

Letter, GSP, Jr., to his father, January 28, 1919

Right now I am in the north end of Luxembourg. It is a very rich country and has also many mines. The people speak German and look it. You know my feelings toward the Germans before the war. Well they are more so now . . .

This whole country looks cleaner, more modern, and more like America than any other place I have been since I left home.

I am billeted with an old lady whose son in law commands the Luxembourg army. He is a major. He said it was very hard on him as last week all his soldiers went on strike and were discharged so now he has nothing to command except the policemen.

This is the first country in the world to have no army. It is a horrible example of what not to do.

Returned to Bourg, Patton received word that he was about to be relieved from duty with the Tank Corps and sent to Germany for the Occupation.

Rockenbach asked the AEF chief of staff to hold up Patton's reassignment for at least a month and explained the reason for his request. There were 1355 men in the tank brigade and only four Regular officers.

This is not a sufficient number of officers to enable me to enforce discipline to keep the men exercised, entertained, and in a sanitary condition. As you know Colonel Patton exercises a great deal of influence not only in his own Brigade, but also in the Tank Center, which I estimate, will have for approximately one month a total of nearly 5000 men.

The chief of staff agreed with the cogency of Rockenbach's statement. If Patton had not already complied with orders to proceed to Treves for duty, he could remain with the tank brigade until the tankers departed for the United States. At that time, Patton would go to Germany.

This information reached Patton as he was leaving on another round of conferences. He wrote in his diary: "Just before starting found that I would have to go to Treves after Brigade goes home. God-Dam."

He was in a foul mood during his trip. "Officers in billet were drunk and kept me awake." The officers in the billet were drunk again the following night. Officers were uninterested in their work. This officer was "a dead one," another was "dead and a fool." The weather was cold, and his wound "hurt like the duce."

Letter, GSP, Jr., to Beatrice, February 7, 1919
I have not had a chance to write for the last couple of days as I have been on the go all the time and have slepped in places with no lights.

Letter, GSP, Jr., to Beatrice, February 7, 1919
I wrote you a brief note this morning from Toul . . .

You poor thing you surely have a hell of a time. [Beatrice had been ill.] Please die your hair. I am going to [do the same] . . .

I just heard the French translation of Y.M.C.A. "Ilya moyen coucher avec." [They can be slept with.] That shows the way they are thought of here . . .

As to J. and Nita. It is possible that the game is up. You see he could get anyone in the world and they are after him. Ambition is a great thing and without soul. I have no reason for knowing this but ??? "C'est possible."

It is a good thing you and I are safely married?? — Other wise I would have to have proposed to you all over again for having seen the world I have yet to see your equal. I love you.

The book Patton worked on between November 1918 and March 1919 grew to 26 single-spaced, typewritten sheets on the subject of "War As She Is," which was very close to the title of the book his wife would publish shortly after his death, *War as I Knew It.*

The incomplete manuscript contained Patton's deeply held beliefs on patriotism and warfare. Much of it was trite, much synthetic. What was based on his experiences revealed originality of thought and expression.

GSP, Jr., "War As She Is," Bourg, France, spring 1919

Foreword

War, to quote Clausewitz, "is but the continuation of policy by other means." Hence logic demands of us that in approaching our subject we consider these other means; namely the soldiers and officers which are the molicules forming the Body Military.

Having dealt with these we must consider War in general and finally the duties of the various arms which combine to produce the only admissible result — VICTORY.

It thus appears that we have set ourselves a task of no mean proportion and one which would tax the ability of a far more learned author. Therefore, we hasten to disavow any attempt at a full exposition and purpose simply to set down some thoughts on this vast subject which our limited experience and reading has taught us to regard as specially important.

It is hoped that our modest effort will perhaps find approval in the eyes of that large class of readers, who while not soldiers, yet take a patriotic interest in our means of national perpetuity — the ARMY.

Chapter I. The Soldier.

The success of armies and consequently the existence of states depend upon the caliber of the individual soldier. Therefore it seems self evident that soldiers should come from the people, the whole people and nothing but the people.

To entrust our most sacred possession — National Existence — to any one class is as foolish as to entrust our legislature to a class of men who legislate for personal profit not for national benefit . . .

Thus far our professional hired army has held untarnished the highest traditions of American manhood and patriotism. But the cycles of history are inexorable; the day will come when due to unjust prejudice and small pay the class of our enlisted will fall . . . When that day arrives a second [battle of] Zama will write a crimson "FINIS" to all our proud hopes and noble ideals . . .

With wars on the present scale there is no nation rich enough to pay the vast masses of men necessary to maintain an active army and competent reserve adequate to its defense . . . for national health the army must be composed of all the able bodied citizens whose age and physique permits to them the privilege of bearing arms . . . What manner of man is it who when insulted, hires another to shoulder his responsibility? Even the despised jackall protects its young personally and not through the interposition of some more courageous animal hired by the offer of some choice bit of carrion.

. . . there must be a uniform and fundamental belief that the highest privilege of man is to perpetuate his native land even at the forfeit of his own life. The soldier in the service must be actuated by this belief else he prostitutes his high office and goes to battle an unwilling slave . . .

. . . the man who has served his country for a year [in training] with sweat and some discomfort feels truly that he has a part in his country . . . and he is a Patriot . . .

The boy who has served his time as a soldier has stood on his own feet . . . He has seen rich and poor doing just what he is doing. He is considerate for the democracy of the squad room . . . and the man who carelessly disturbs his sleeping comrades by a late and noisy entrance will gain a most valuable lesson as to the rights of others in the form of a well aimed marching shoe. These things bring a realization of the fact that liberty means equality for all, not license for one . . .

. . . the man who serves his country serves also himself. But to get the maximum results presupposes two things. First the willingness to serve, bred of early training in patriotism and second disciplined instruction . . .

Discipline may be defined as "Prompt, cheerful and AUTOMATIC obedience." . . . if each man of a company of 250 delayed thirty seconds in finding his place it would take two hours to form the company . . .

. . . the training of the soldier must be absolutely uniform . . . Interchangeability of working parts of industrial machines has long been recognized as an economic necessity. Men are the working parts of an army.

. . . one of the salient reasons for a national army is the prohibitive expense of a hired one. Neither we nor any other nation can afford to pay men enough to make them willing to die . . . Men so venial as to deliberately barter their lives would be equally open to similar offers from the enemy. This statement would seem to cast disparagement on our present regular army but such is not the case. The men of our regular army serve from a spirit of adventure and a genuine liking for the service. The pay to them is incidental. It seems highly improbable that a decided increase in pay would in any way effect the number of enlistments . . .

Since we cannot pay enough to secure soldiers we must resort to compulsion and rely on a general improvement in patriotic education to make that service less grudgingly rendered and trust to the final educational influences of the army itself to insure the cheerful giving of life itself if the need arises . . .

. . . The soldier, being a citizen, owes the country service and whatever he gets in return is a gift, pure and simple . . .

All pensions and bonuses voted soldiers . . . are most detrimental to public morality and national thrift . . . [They are] bribary . . .

This does not apply to pensions or support tendered soldiers actually incapacitated while in line of duty . . .

The above sentiments will doubtless be unintelligible to those who regard the nation as a convenience to the individuals . . . The nation is the one common possession of all the citizens and as such they are all bound to insure its maintenance — not it, theirs.

. . . The nation owes all an equal chance but is not responsible for the faults and follies of those who fail to avail themselves of these opportunities.

Chapter II. The Line Officer.
. . . The officer's sense of patriotism, discipline and self-sacrifice

must be no cosmus incoherent shape, but clear and vital so that its lambent flame may distill that most vital of all his attributes — a sense of OBLIGATION . . . [which] is inseparably connected with discipline . . . [which] is made up of so many tiny and apparently trivial things. In essence however, it consists in doing the task set, however small, absolutely, perfectly, and better than it was ever done before. Here is the heart of the whole matter — a perfect performance . . . perfect also in the light of your own conscience . . .

. . . leniency to self . . . is inimical to duty, hence to victory.

. . . In war there are no individuals and consequently their feelings as such do not exist. The least and the most that is required of an officer is a perfect performance of his duty. Not excuses, or failures, but results must be forthcoming. In doing his utmost, even to death, the officer is not conferring a favor, he is privileged to be able to give that much for his country . . .

. . . man is a poor thing at best and loves his little span [of life] better than he will usually admit. The word fearless is a misnomer; all men fear, some show it less than others, hence when we say that officers must be brave we mean they must show fear less — be more stoical. And this too may be developed . . . we must make officers so proud of their calling that the fear of disgracing their cloth shall be more potent than that of the animal shrinking from imminent dissolution . . .

Each year a sufficient number of soldiers who have completed their service and who desire to further serve their country as officers should be sent to military academies similar to West Point. The idea in this requirement is to insure complete democracy among officers and to produce a thorough understanding [among officers] of the viewpoint of soldiers . . .

Upon graduation these cadets will . . . for at least two years serve as officers . . .

. . . [Then] those desiring to, should return to civil life and be given preference for employment in all branches of state and Federal government. (Average age 24). Those who remain in the service should be promoted or retired according to their deserts. But all who leave the service should . . . be available to return to the colors . . . in cases of emergency.

. . . [Some people] insist that a few weeks training makes them competent to command in war . . .

Suppose some eminent broker has surgery for a hobby and reads it two evenings a week and attends several clinics during the year.

Which one of you with an inflamed appendix will select such a man as your surgeon? If there is any such, our definition of Courage will have to be revised along with our estimate of his sanity . . .

This is no reflection on the thousands of gallant officers who led our armies in the World War. On a desert island . . . one layman may, and must, operate upon another . . .

It seems incredible that in America the land of specialists, trained men are demanded for every occupation but that of officers. Yet only in the army is lack of trained specialists paid for with the blood of our first born and the tears of our people . . .

The road to high command leads through a long path called the "History of War." Like all long roads the scenery is not always interesting; there are desert stretches of prosaic facts, but now and again the traveler reaches eminences where he sees the most sublime panoramas ever vouch safed to mortal — the deathless deeds of the great who have passed to that Valhalla which is death but not oblivion.

To be useful in battle, military knowledge, like discipline, must be subconscious. The memorizing of concrete examples is futile for in battle the mind does not work well enough to make memory trustworthy. The officer must be so soaked in military lore that he does the military thing automatically. The study of history will go far towards producing this result; the study of mathematics will not.

But the above study must continue after entry into the service and last until the day of retirement . . .

Here it is well to call attention to the possibility of falling into an age old error. Namely that of presuming that all future wars will be an exact replica of the most recent past war . . . when the foam of freak expedients has been blown away by the sterile breath of retrospection, war settles back to the same old bitter draft, the ingredients of which, have been, are, and ever shall be — DISCIPLINE, SIMPLICITY and BOLDNESS.

Strategy and tactics do not change, the means only of applying them differ. A sound and profound historical education should have as its end an absolute grounding in the immutable principles of war comprehended so that they are sufficiently flexible to permit of having implaced on them the transitory expedients which evolution from time to time produces. The uncontrolled specialist is one of the greatest menaces to an army . . .

While it is a patriotic duty and privilege to be an officer we are all human and if the path to glory is beset with its normal hardships coupled to poverty, the temptation to let some other patriot wear the shoulder straps [of an officer] will remove many a good officer from the service.

Chapter III. Staff Officers.

The Staff Officer, as a class, is probably the object of more criticism than any other officer in the service. This criticism is partially justified and partially the result of misunderstanding . . .

Like Line Officers, staff officers should first be soldiers, next officers, and finally, as the result of special training and aptitude, staff officers . . .

To be efficient and avoid criticism the general qualifications of the Tactical Staff are as follows, arranged in order of importance:

a) A personal knowledge of troops, learned by actual command . . .

b) . . . loyalty to the chief they serve. Nothing is so subversive of discipline as criticism of superiors by juniors . . .

c) . . . TACT . . . to give direction or instructions to officers of superior rank . . . The sight of a bumptious Staff Major airing his views to a General of Division is one of the most nauseating of spectacles . . .

d) . . . they must stick absolutely to facts, unadorned by anamus, sympathy, or enthusiasm.

e) The following pun always elicited great applause in the World War: "If bread is the Staff of Life, what is the Life of the Staff? — One long loaf." . . . Staff Officers should constantly visit the troops to keep in first hand touch with the situation . . . The presence of Staff Officers in the field has both a real and a physological [psychological] influence. The information so gained is reliable, the difficulties of the soldier are realized and the actual sight of the Staff Officer makes the soldier more trustful of him. The Staff Officer is the Servant of the Line . . . he must see all and then while others rest he must translate the information gained by his eyes into orders by his brain. This task ought to be the more willingly performed since though the hours of work for the staff are longer the surroundings of that work are more pleasant.

THE CHIEF OF STAFF . . . The Commanding General should be relieved by his general staff of all vexatious details in the working out of any project . . . In the exercise of his function as coordinator, the Chief of Staff must often act with repression upon many brilliant schemes, excellent in themselves, but not well balanced as viewed from his general point of vantage . . . the Chief of Staff must guard against the habit of becoming too repressive. The habit of constant negation is an insidious disease and if allowed to florish unhindered may do more harm than good.

. . . the Commanding General should be required to spend a minimum of time in his office and hence have much leisure to personally inspect and supervise the training and marching of his soldiers. It is only by such personal contact that he may instill confidence and devotion in them — hence fulfill his duties as a General. . . .

ASSISTANT CHIEF OF STAFF G–1 . . . The services are created to serve the troops. Battles are won by troops, not by services. It is the duty of G–1 to see that the troops are served . . .

ASSISTANT CHIEF OF STAFF G–2 . . . it would be useless to plan the most splendid cavalry raid in country which G–2 knows to be waterless . . .

ADVISORY STAFF OFFICERS . . . Chaplain, charged with fighting the Devil. (Usually unsuccessful.)

Chapter IV. Generals.

. . . an attempt to define what have appeared to us the leading characteristics in varying degrees and combinations of American Generals with whom we have had the honor to be associated.

. . . first impressions are of vast importance . . . a general [must] have a soldierly bearing and typify in his person as well [as] possess in his mind the highest qualities of a soldier . . .

To this soldierly bearing should be added that indescribable something which we call Personal Magnetism. Men admired Wellington but they worshipped Lee.

Tact . . . [but not] that cheap and disgusting fawning on the men practised by some, to their own ruin, for the men are the first to perceive and ridicule such procedure . . .

Finally . . . Impartial Justice . . .

. . . actuated by the highest ideals as to life, patriotism and duty . . . final decision as his final responsibility is for him alone and not to be taken by a vote of advisers like a club election. Clive said he had only called one council of war and fortunately had not abided by its decision.

. . . utmost fixity of purpose . . .

Health . . .

A desire to fight . . .

A trained military mind soaked with the theory and practise of war by daily study and environment so that no matter what the circumstance, the mind will think in a military way, automatically.

. . . Generals are made — by themselves.

. . . they acquired them [the above virtues], not at birth, but by a life of ceaseless effort at the military profession.

Chapter V. War.

. . . we are not concerned with the causes of war for these are provided by statesmen . . . and are always just . . . From the time Paris stole Helen to the time William [of Germany] tried to steal the world, the peoples at issue have believed implicitly in the justice of their cause. Nothing but this inhereent idea of the justice of their cause can explain the sacrifices made throughout the ages by all peoples. The fact that half these assumptions must have been wrong in order to have the other half right in no way detracts from the fact.

. . . On the decision and courage of a Boy Lieutenant hangs the success or failure of the General's plan. But . . . during battle the General is powerless to direct this Boy. He is, however, none the less responsible, for he should have trained his Lieutenants to do the right thing . . . as a result of habit.

First in importance of these vital habits comes the automatic instinct of forward movement . . . Men who think only of going on, will be victorious or killed. They will be victorious more often than killed.

. . . It is the failure to do something offensive instantly, whether right or wrong, that has lost more battles than any other one fault and this failure is due to just two things: lack of courage and lack of habit . . .

Victory alone will come through the will to conquer relentlessly and automatically applied in battle.

Note on Chapter VI. Combat General.

In spite of the kaleidoscopic changes in the outward semblance of war, it in fact remains the same in principle and these principles are — have been — and ever shall be the following:

First — getting the largest force of the right sort to the right place at the right time. We must however, be careful in our definition of force. It is not of necessity numbers . . .

. . . force in the form of fire, must so discomfort opposed forces in the same form that it [the latter] gives back and that this recession must be followed by numerical force, killing and bluffing other opposed numerical force . . . inaccurate fire of whatever nature is not force but noise — useless — impotent.

. . . Our moving force in fire and flesh [in the offensive] advances over the enemy's front positions but in his back positions we are met by concealed fire beyond the range of our own concealed fire [artillery] and we must overcome this force also before we can get to the place where we may overrun the enemy by a display and use of stone-age brawn.

In trench war the solution of this difficulty was usually sought by the use of limited objects. Such attacks failed because the undisturbed concealed fire in the back area was superior to ours and we were slaughtered while consolidating. This form of attack failed also because limited objectives disregard psychology in omitting the ultimate threat of beef [more numbers of men].

. . . In wars without such flankless lines penetrations or encircling movements by cavalry and tanks will, I believe, be sufficient to break up to a large degree the great gun concentrations and thus permit moving fire and force to gain decisive results.

In other words, cavalry and tanks would restore mobility to the battlefield. The next conflict would be unlike the trench warfare in France. If Patton saw clearly into the future, and certainly if he had his way, the next war would be a war of movement.

CHAPTER 34

Going Home

"I will get a M.H. [Medal of Honor] in the next war. I hope."

WRITING A DETAILED INSTRUCTION — eight typed pages, single spaced —
for his troops on how to prepare for their return to the United States
made Patton feel blue and depressed. He wanted to go home too. Yet he
was scheduled to be part of the forces occupying Germany.

He traveled to Chaumont to deliver to Pershing some shells his men
had turned into tobacco and cigar boxes for presentation to President
Wilson. Arrived at the AEF headquarters, he was invited to attend a
luncheon Pershing was giving to the men who had been awarded the
Medal of Honor. He accepted, of course. He had a chance to chat for a
few minutes in private with Pershing who "talked to me of Nita and I
wrote a letter advising her to enter YMCA." He also decided to write a
letter to his friend General McAndrew, Pershing's chief of staff, "about
my going home."

Letter, GSP, Jr., to Commander in Chief, AEF (through channels),
February 10, 1919, subject: Return to United States of America

Request that instead of being detailed on Provost Marshal duty at
Treves, as at present ordered, I be allowed to return to the United
States with the Tank Corps troops, and that Col H. E. Mitchell, TC,
be given my detail as he desires to remain in Europe.

REASONS: I have been in France since June 18th, 1917. During this
time my wife has lost both her father and mother and is at present in
very poor health. Prior to coming to Europe I had been in the Mexican Punitive Expedition from beginning to end so that with the exception of about three weeks I have not seen my family for more than
2½ years. I have been in the Tank Corps since its inception and

would feel great pride in being allowed to accompany it to the United States.

For the above reasons request my application be given consideration.

Letter, GSP, Jr., to Beatrice, February 10, 1919

I had a most interesting day. I went up to the generals house to take him some shell cases . . . When I got there I found that all the medal of honor men had been invited to a boufet lunch. Besides [the Medal of Honor recipients] there were present Gen P., Gen Bullard, Gen Ligget, Gen Summeral . . . Corps commanders and a lot of staff generals. The generals helped serve the M.H. men all of whom were soldiers or lieutenants. I helped also. All of them were young except one captain and one corporal. The rest were just boys but all had fine clear eyes. It struck me as a splendid contrast the Brains of the army and the brawn . . . One of mine [that is, a tanker] was there Lt. Call. The other [who was awarded the Medal of Honor] is dead. Gen Summerall asked me to present Call to him and I did. The general was very nice to Call who is a fine looking youngster. I wish I had gotten an M.H. but one can't have you and every other good thing too. At least not all at once. I will get a M.H. in the next war. I hope.

I have just wired you "Have Nita stay with you till letter arrives, Love All. Patton."

I talked to the General and he said wives could not come over. He also said that he would be here until late next fall.

Then he said "Why can't Anne come over in the Y.M.C.A.? I want her and I could arrange her coming so that no one would know I had." I said "General she can't come unless it is known [because] she belongs to a distinguished family in her state and it would cause remark. That is why she has not come. Out of consideration for you." He said "I think she could come from Washington all right and all those rumors are dead any how." I said "you are wrong but I don't think any thing can hurt you. Shall I write?" he said "Yes do." I am.

This seems to me to settle the facts of the case so far as his continued affection is concerned. Now this is what I think. You may not like it but here it is.

Nita loves him and he her (or she). It might be unpleasant for her to come but it would be more unpleasant for her to loose him. He is great and much sought after. One more year of seperation might ruin two lives and loves. It is better for her pride to suffer a little than for her to loose such a Great man. Therefore I say tell her to come. One word from her and he can fix it. This is my best judgment in the matter. If she comes they will be married here. I am sure or nearly so. If she does not [come] who can say what may not happen.

I inclose a letter I just wrote [to General McAndrew] trying to get home. It is the only chance. No leaves will be granted and there is no other way. Consider what I have said [about Nita] from your *head* not from *sentiment*.

I love you.

Letter, GSP, Jr., to Beatrice, February 11, 1919

In addition to writing you last night I also wrote Mama. I am still of the same opinion as when I wrote.

I wrote a personal letter to Gen. McAndrew the Chief of Staff asking him to consider my official letter favorably and I hope and trust that he will.

Bowditch [one of Pershing's aides] just called up saying that the Prince of Wales would be dining with Gen. Pershing on Thursday and asking if I could come and bring some of my minstrels to entertain H.R.H. . . .

One of my men is an artist and he is going to make a picture of me . . . I must stop now and pose.

Letter, GSP, Jr., to Beatrice, February 12, 1919

. . . if I get to go I ought to be home in a month. It seems too good to be possible but I hope it is just the same. If I learn anything definate I shall wire you at once which ever way it is.

We had a dinner last night to the original officers of the 304 (1) Brigade and to the other officers who were here prior to August 21, 1918.

There were numerous speeches etc. I made every one pay 3 francs and I paid the difference to the amount of 900 francs.

We also got up a souvenir book which we will print. My picture is the frontice piece.

As there is nothing much to do now I am getting worthless the same as I got in Mexico. I hate to feel this way.

Patton was one of six American officers invited to a reception for the young Prince of Wales, future King Edward VIII, who would abdicate his throne to marry the woman he loved. The Prince's evening with Pershing and his staff was postponed several days because of a sad occurrence.

Diary

February 13: Bowditch telephoned that Carl Boyd [one of Pershing's aides] died last night and for me to come up and go to Paris with them for the funeral. Sent B. my picture drawn by Corp. Land. Had dinner with Gen. and got on the Special train at 10:30. About 25 officers were on it all going to funeral.

February 14: Arrived Paris 9 A.M. Went to Generals House 73 Rue de Varenne. Went to Hammonds & got my Blouse also a regulation Over coat. Lunched at house. Went to church at 1:30. Went to cemetery. Cars stuck on the hill. We pushed them up. Mrs. Boyd did well at funeral. I spent the evening with them, Ann sat in my lap and cried about 2 hours. Asked Gen McAndrew if I could go home. he agreed.

February 15: Took Ann for walk in morning. Called on Gen. Rhodes. He is a fright to look at. Gen. [F.C.] Marshall came also. Saw Floyd Gibbons. Queck and I went to the Boyds and I told stories for 3 hours and got them to laugh. Got on train at 11:30. The H.R.H. [Prince of Wales] had not yet arrived. He was at a dance.

February 16: Met Prince of Wailes and his aid Capt. Sir Claud Hamilton Cloudstream Guards as they left the train. Saw Gen. R[ockenbach] at his office. Lt. Col. Bowdich and I took the Prince to lunch with Gen. H. T. Allen 8 Corps. Saw some good [prize?] fights. I rode back with Prince. A very nice fellow. Reception at Gen P's house. Dinner at 8 P.M. I had the itch.

February 17: Gen. P. the Prince, Capt. Hamilton, Queck, Bowditch and I went to Commercy to review the 35th Division. Had lunch with Gen. Dargan Division Commander. Rode around Division. Then inspected on foot. All [men] were in fine shape and perfectly equiped. On way back rode with Gen P. for 2½ hours. He talked all the time and told me a lot of recent history. I asked him if I could go home. He said Haugh [a grunt or something equally noncommital]. Returned to Bourg.

Letter, GSP, Jr., to Pershing, February 18, 1919

Please allow me to thank you for letting me have the sorrowful pleasure of attending the funeral of poor Boyd and the honor of having met the Prince of Wailes. I talked so much about my self yesterday that I think I had better reinforce my statements. Besides I like to appear well in your eyes. For both these reasons I am inclosing the statements of two men [Angelo and Edwards] who were with me on the 26th of September. Some day if you have time I should appreciate it if you would read them.

Letter, GSP, Jr., to Nita, February 18, 1919

I have been having a very historic time. Col. Boyd died of pneumonia on Wednesday and Gen. P. asked me to go up with him on his special train thursday night . . . The funeral was on Friday and I spent the rest of the day consoling Mrs. Boyd and Ann. Next day I called on Gen. Rhodes who fell out of an Airplane and lost most of his nose. He is a sight . . . Then I took Ann for a walk and later told stories to her and her mother until eleven P.M. when I had to walk most of the way to get the special train. The Prince of Wales and his aid Sir Claude Hamilton were on the train.

Sunday when we got to Chaumont Col. Bowditch and I took the H.R.H. over to the 8th Corps . . . for lunch . . . On the way back I rode with the Prince and he told me a lot of stories supposed to be bad. Some were. He said "Bein a dashed prince rather cramps one style What?" There was a reception and later a dinner. After the dinner the prince and several of us danced to a phonograph and then he wanted to play poker but none of us knew how so we shot craps sitting on the floor. The H.R.H. got a hundred and fifty of my francs and then went to bed. He did not have much money and had to borrow to start the game. I stayed at the house all night and the next day we left for Commercy to inspect the 35th Div. There were twenty thousand men in ranks and we walked about seven miles to inspect every man. Every one with a wound stripe was talked to by the Gen. and the Prince . . . On the way back I rode in the Machine with J. and we talked for about three hours. He told me all sorts of secret history . . .

When I left after dinner the Prince said "I should like awfully to nock about with you in america on the border." He possibly says that to every one. J. made a fine speech to the Division and the P. said a few words.

I am inclosing for you all a couple of copies of the statements of two men who were with me when I was hit. Dont loose them.

I realy think it would be a fine idea if you would come over here in the Red Cross or the Y.M.C.A. . . .

I dont know yet whether I am going home or not. If I do I shall leave here a week from to day. But that would not interfere with your coming and might make it easier for you to leave Pa and Ma. In fact that is a good idea. You might write some one and then he would send me home. I still have the itch but otherwise am well.

Much love to all your devoted brother

Diary

February 19: 305th Tank Brigade, commanded by Col. H. E. Mitchell, left this morning for home.

Letter, Mr. Patton to GSP, Jr., February 20, 1919

My dear Son — When your cable came — asking Nita to wait a letter — we all decided to stay [in the East] — & hope your letter will arrive now any day —

Nannie is sick in N.Y. & Mama & Nita are with her and I am here with B & the babies. I hope . . . you are coming home — or that B can join you soon — leaving the children with us.

. . . Among other things I have been worrying for fear that the "gift of gab" you have developed may get you in trouble — unless restrained such a gift is always dangerous The temptation to say smart or striking things is hard to resist — and it is only next day — that cold reason condemns. You are now 34 — and a Col and the dignity going with your rank invests what you say with more importance so I hope in your speeches you will be very careful & self restrained — for your own good & for your future — Another gift you have developed I really regret — and that is the ability to write verse upon vulgar & smutty subjects. That is very dangerous. The very men to whom you read & recite such stuff as your last one will laugh — and apparently enjoy it — but you have really lowered yourself in their eyes — above all it lacks *dignity* — and you need to cultivate that especially in view of your rank.

All my life I have known such instances — and never has it failed in my experience — that the Club wit — who indulges in smutty stuff hurts himself. You may some day want to enter public life — but you must couple with your talent . . . great self restraint &

sense of dignity — Most men have no real sense of humor — & fail to distinguish little matters of this sort — from realities & judge one accordingly. All the really big men I have known — abstained from repeating vulgar stories — and all who were facile in speech — cultivated great reserve — or if they sometimes forgot themselves — always suffered for the lapse. I dont want to preach and will say no more but I am sure your own judgment — upon reflection will agree with mine —

B is much improved & if you could come to her or she go to you, I think she will be as good as ever . . .

February 21: Request to go home with brigade disapproved by Lt. Col. Obrien.

February 22: Went to Chaumont about going Home. No one there. Heard that Gen. McAndrew would return at 8 P.M. Telephoned him. He said I could go but that Mitchell would Stay. I told him Mitchell had already gone and he said it was o.k. anyhow. Wired B.

February 23: Inspection of all Property to be taken home. The rest to be turned in. Heard definately that I was to return to the U.S. Heard dogs not allowed on boat.

Letter, GSP, Jr., to Pershing, February 23, 1919

Thanks to your permission I am leaving France with My Brigade . . . [and thanks also for] all your kindness and consideration . . .

I have attempted in a small way to model my self on you and what ever success I have had has been due to you as an inspiration . . .

[Is not quitting Pershing's service, but] I beg that you will permit me to count my self as one of yours . . .

[Regrets Pershing's absence from Chaumont making it impossible for Patton to say goodbye in person; hoping to serve again under Pershing] in America or else where.

Diary

February 24: Wrote letters to Gens. Summerall, Burtt, Brewster, Conner, Harbord. Lt. Colonels Collins Reed Shallenberger. Gen. Nolan. Gen. Rockey [Rockenbach].

February 25: Finished packing and got out Train order. Hope this is my last night at Bourg. Gave Maj. L. K. Davis blank check on Morgan-Harjes bank to close my account. Had my hair cut so I will look neat when I land. Will have to be up at 4:45 A.M.

Patton specified the regulations to govern the conduct of the brigade and of the attached units and casuals en route to the port of embarkation. All men, formed in units, were to be at the train siding at Bourg at certain designated hours. Uniform for officers was to consist of overseas cap, overcoat or trench coat, side arms (pistol) on Sam Browne belt, gas mask, trench helmet, and hand baggage. Uniform for enlisted men was to be overseas cap, overcoat, field equipment, trench helmet on pack, gas mask. Guards were to be posted to keep the men on the train. There would be four kitchen cars and three days' travel rations. Men were not to ride on the roofs of the railroad cars or sit in the doors with their feet hanging out. All personnel were to maintain a soldierly appearance

and will not appear at the doors or windows of cars or on the station platform unless their uniforms are buttoned throughout. The efficiency of the Command is judged by its soldierly appearance. All men and Officers will make special efforts to remain clean and neat. Military courtesies will be strictly observed. No liquor of any kind, including beers and light wines will be allowed on the train . . . All men must be instructed to guard against Venereal Desease by abstinence and when they have failed to do so by prompt use of the Government Propholaxis.

Diary

February 26: Got word at 4 A.M. that train would not be in until 8 A.M. Notified battalions. Train got in at 11 A.M. Morale very bad. Got loaded and left at 1:45 P.M. Two cars jumped track and it took 3 hours to put them on. Fed men. Got to Langres at 6 P.M. put on second coach. 30 officers 1470 men. 37 baggage cars, 36 American 1 French. Two 2d class coaches for officers.

February 27: On train all day. Two men missed train. Passed Lyons. Everything nice. Men very well behaved. Good food. Made men keep buttoned up and neat. Ate sandwitches and had a nice time. Weather fine and rather clear.

February 28: Arrived Marseille at 12:30 P.M. Met at once by R.T.O. [Railroad Transportation Officer] who told us just what to do. Found that we were to sail on S.S. Patria next day. Held vermin and I.G. [Inspector General] inspection of men at once finishing at 8 P.M. Adjutants worked on rolls all night. I went to bed at 4:30 A.M. and got up at 6:00 A.M.

Telegram, Harbord to GSP, Jr. (at Marseilles), February 27, 1919
Letter received good bye good luck go to see Mrs. Harbord at sixteen sixteen twenty first street Washington.

The authorities at Base Number 6 were efficient and polite. They directed officers and men to proceed to the Marseilles Breakwater in a column of twos on March 1 for embarkation aboard the SS *Patria* — 65 officers and 1475 men of the 304th Tank Brigade, plus five casual companies, totaling altogether 71 officers and 2010 men. Barracks and tents vacated were to be thoroughly policed and cleaned one hour before departure.

A board of officers convened by the base commander inspected the *Patria,* due to sail March 1 from Marseilles via Gibraltar with a crew of 200. It had a capacity for 150 officers in first class, 204 enlisted men in second class, and 1749 in third class — 2103 in all. Patton was designated the commanding officer of all the troops sailing and would be responsible for discipline aboard ship and for compliance with regulations.

Diary
March 1 (Saturday): Went to Boat with Lt. Bowes & Simmons at 7:45. Went over entire boat and found it very clean and well appointed. Quarters for men excellent. Mix up on state room. I lost mine to Mr. Moore a Mason 33°. Supposed to sail at 6 P.M. failed to do so account of strike of crew. Tried to get mess Sgt. Allenby on board but could not do it account passport.

The men were aboard ship by 10 A.M., a record, for they had been at the base camp only fourteen hours. The base commander told Patton that his contingent was the best disciplined unit he had seen pass through.

Although Patton would not know it until much later, he was awarded the Distinguished Service Medal that General Smith had recommended — for

exceptionally meritorious and distinguished services . . . energy and sound judgment . . . very valuable service in his organization and direction of the Tank Center at the Army Schools at Langres. In the employment of Tank Corps troops in combat, he displayed high military attainments, zeal and marked adaptibility in a form of warfare comparatively new to the American Army.

Diary

March 2: Captain told me we would know at noon when we could sail. Put one man on shore with fever 103°. Arranged bed space for men and had a lot of bother account of worthless officers. Food for men good.

March 3: Had a good deal of difficulty getting men straightened out in quarters. Boat very steady and comfortable. Sea perfectly quiet and weather warm.

March 4: Reached Gibraltar at 8:30. Let most of officers and 150 men go on shore. Lot of Bum boats came and sold brandy. Men got drunk and we had pretty bad time. Found over 40 quarts on board. Some officers arranged to go to Tangier on mail boat.

While the ship took on coal, Spanish entrepreneurs sold the soldiers bottles of brandy hidden in baskets of oranges. Eight men became very drunk.

Letter, Beatrice to Mr. Patton, March 4, 1919

Here are the two letters from Georgie for which we have been waiting [with respect to Nita and General Pershing]. Don't worry, we are not going to do anything about it at all until this Roman business is settled [there was a possibility of Mr. Patton's becoming ambassador to Italy], as it doubtless will be soon, one way or the other. *Don't* write Nita to break it off.

I have just seen Mr. Hammond & this is the situation. [Thomas Nelson] Page is anxious to get out as soon as he can & the question of the appointment will presumably be settled as soon as Wilson lands on the other side. Vance McCormick, now in Italy is believed not to want it. Your only chance *not* to get it is that [Colonel Edward M.] House may have committed himself to another man. If not, you are sure to get it. Walsh is doing all he can & Mr. H[ammond] all *he* can & he says your being here [in Washington] would make no difference at all. If you are offered the job you will have to decide at once & you may get the offer *quite* soon. Mr. H. has been through the figuring end of it exhaustively with one of the secretaries of the last three ambassadors (Page inc[luded]) & he says that, to live as you would want to you would spend about $30,000 yearly outside your salary. Now this would be for 2 years only. Mr. H. says that, at this period of the world's history he would think it worth while to make great sacrifices to take the position.

Now, if you go to Rome: it will be: 1) The best thing the country could do for itself. 2) Great for Italy. 3) Just what you deserve. 4) Would make Aunt Ruth [Mrs. Patton] proud & glad. 5) Might make a difference in G's whole future. 6) G. & I would see one another a lot & I would love it. 7) Just what I've always wanted for the babies. 8) Last & most important right now — the most dignified way for Nita to go abroad & the only thing extraordinary enough to put her back on her feet if the worst should happen. *And* would make *some* impression on John [Pershing].

You will have to decide quickly when you get the offer & I hope for all our sakes that you will take it.

I should not mention the financial side if I did not feel that that would do much to decide you. But it would be only fair for us to halve the bills & it would *not* be fair for you to turn it down for that reason. Its all in the family & I would like to have some fun of that sort & may never have another chance. And it would make a difference in G's whole future.

As for Nita — you can see by these letters what it would mean to her: a dignified, suitable way of seeing John again, or a great diversion if she doesn't marry. Uncle George, you *couldn't* turn it down? & it would make us all so happy . . .

[P.S.] I asked Mr. H. what "sacrifices" he would be willing to make in your shoes. He said *"any* sacrifice of personal wishes or comfort for the time being. I would borrow money on my securities."

Diary

March 5: I went on shore [at Gibraltar] and called on Naval C.O. Went up rock. Place could be taken by Synide [cyanide] shells shot on face of cliff so that drainage could poison water. Command of sea would be necessary. Nothing in town to see or buy. Maj. Benson shot at Bum boats to keep them off. I will throw coal at them in the morning.

He explained later: "we fired at the water near them [the Spanish sellers of brandy] and they left. It was safe to fire as they had no recourse at law being without license [to sell fruits]."

March 6: Let 172 men go on shore and got very nearvous for fear
that they would not come back. All returned. 3 men got mumps.
We left Gibraltar at 7 P.M. I hope nothing stops us until we get in.
Hardly any young officers can be trusted to obey orders.

March 7: Weather very rough and nearly all the men sick. I had to
leave the table at noon and was sick but got up at 3:30 and inspected
the ship. About half the men were able to eat supper. I was very
nearvous and tired when we left Gib and drank a quart of claret for
supper. This I think upset my stomach. Also I got up too late for
breakfast and ate candy instead.

February 8: Weather fine and bright. Had fire drill that is boat
drill at 2:30. The crowding is such that in case of a real alarm there
would be trouble. Saw soldier eating a huge sandwitch at 9 A.M.
Asked him if he had had breakfast. He said yes but not yesterday.
Got Wireless that one man had been left at Gib. Felt strange not to
have to write B a letter daily.

February 10: men sick on food in 3d class but believe it due to fact
that they are not hungry as they do no work.

February 12: Found worms in the beans of the men.

March 13: Felt very worthless all day until 4:30 when I did some
exercises and climbed a stay on the smoke stack. This made me feel
better.

March 15: Mens meat full of worms so we had to stop it. Some of
men were mad. Menu has been Meat-maceroni, bread, coffee & jam
or marmelaid. I would like to know what is in the future and where
I will be ordered. This will be the 10th time I have had to start
fresh.

Typed Statement, aboard S.S. Patria, *March 16, 1919*
A testimonial of personal affection for Colonel Patton for his
energy, his leadership, his courage, his constant attention to the welfare of his officers and men, his understanding and foresight, his sterling sense of justice and fair-play.
[signed by Major Sereno E. Brett, Major C. C. Benson, and 48
other officers.]

Diary

March 16 (Sunday): All work on reports completed at noon. Passed fire Island light ship at 3:30 P.M. Ambrose Channel at 6 P.M. Capt Murray came on board with instructions. The end of a perfect war. Fini.

The ship docked on March 17, a misty day, at the foot of 31st Street, Brooklyn. Welcoming boats had dignitaries and bands of music.

Form letter, 2d Captain S.S. Patria *to Commanding Officer of Troops (Patton), March 17, 1919*

This is to certify that this ship has been left in proper state of police [cleanliness].

The return home of the tankers created a minor sensation, and there were many news stories about the men and their machines.

There was also a somewhat unpleasant incident, an expression of dissidence among some members of Patton's contingent. According to the New York *Tribune*'s headline: "Troops Spurn Hylan-Hearst Welcome Body — Protest Signed by 500 on the Patria Tossed to Committee on Police Boat — 'Take That to Mayor' [Hylan] — Returning Tank Fighters Silent as City Officials Greet them with Gifts."

The story read:

Soon after the midday meal was finished on Saturday, when the troopship Patria, from Marseilles, was some five hundred miles east of Sandy Hook, 40 officers and 450 men of the homecoming 304th Brigade of Heavy Tanks got together and prepared resolutions on William Randolph Hearst.

This tank organization, which had "treated 'em rough" throughout their assault on the Hindenburg Line, had had many informal discussions during the voyage concerning the position Mr. Hearst occupies on the reception committee. They decided that they would express their indignation to Mayor Hylan as soon as the brigade came ashore . . .

[The resolution drafted and signed aboard the *Patria* read] We the undersigned officers, noncommissioned officers and enlisted men registered our unqualified disapproval of the designation of William Randolph Hearst as a member of a committee formed for the purpose of welcoming members of the American expeditionary force returning to the United States. The protest is registered because of the conviction that he has proved himself to be un-American, pro-German and inhumanitarian, and therefore totally unfit for membership on a committee of the above character.

. . . Colonel George Smith Patton, jr., an officer of the regular army, whose home is in San Gabriel, California, did not sign the document. It was said that as an army officer in command of troops he did not feel that it was proper for him to align himself with any factional protest.

This was not what he wrote Pershing about a week later. Unknown to Patton, he told Pershing, some men had composed a round-robin letter which they threw into one of the boats. The message said that they wanted no welcome from Mr. Hearst. "I knew nothing of it until I saw it in the papers next day. I was very worried but so far I have not been tried [by court-martial] or any thing."

He was still upset when he wrote to his father on April 1.

I was very much worried about that foolish round robin about Mr. Hearst which some of my men sent.

I knew nothing about it until I read it in the papers. Of course had I had any idea what they were [up] to I would have prevented it. It was most uncalled for and ungrateful. My idea is that it was gotten up by a small minority of the men who had it in for me on account of my severe discipline and who took that means of getting even.

None of the regular officers on the ship had heard a word of it.

I heard some reserve officers talking about Hearst and I told them that what ever their opinion they ought to be gentlemen enough to appreciate what Hearst was now doing for the returning soldiers and not critacize him. They said they would do nothing and I thought no more about it, but as I said some fools must have heard them and done it to get me in trouble.

As to the poem I don't know where it came from.

I hope I don't get hit for something of which I was perfectly inoscent.

The poem to which he referred was doggerel, several verses, each ending with the line "For the hand that shook Bernstorff's [the former German ambassador to the United States] will never shake mine."

By then the affair was all but forgotten. What everyone remembered was the delight to be home. What everyone recalled was the joy on the faces of those who welcomed them.

Patton was surrounded by newspaper reporters, and he loved the attention. The New York Evening *Mail* quoted him as having said: "The tank is only used in extreme cases of stubborn resistance. They are the natural answer to the machine gun, and as far as warfare is concerned, have come to stay just as much as the airplanes have."

The New York *World* quoted Patton as saying: "I was wounded on Sept. 26 in the Argonne, while on foot with the tanks. Lying there, helpless, I was picked up bodily by Private Joseph Angelo of Camden, New Jersey, who dropped me into a shell hole. He stuck by me for two hours while I continued to direct operations from that shell hole."

The New York Morning *Sun*, after telling how Patton chained three tanks together and brought them out of a shell hole where they had been embedded, quoted him as saying that tanks "have come to stay on land just as the airplane has come to stay in the clouds and below them."

The New York *Herald* ran a story headlined "Colonel Patton Tells How Big Machines by Hundreds Attacked the Germans" devoted more than half of the coverage to him, featured his photograph, described his battlefield exploit, mentioned the Distinguished Service Cross, and noted that he had "also been cited by the French for the Croix de Guerre."

The Washington *Post* gave Patton prominence. The Los Angeles *Times* reported: "Southland Man is Back a Hero. Col. Patton Wounded in Tank Action in Argonne. San Gabriel Officer's Gallantry Wins Recognition." The Los Angeles *Herald:* "Victory of Tanks is Described by Patton — L.A. Colonel Tells How Argonne and St. Mihiel Battles were Won." Patton had supposedly said: "The American soldiers were the best equipped and best rationed in Europe, and, while other nations may produce as good fighters, they are not superior." The Richmond *Times-Dispatch* told all of its story in the headline: "Returned Officer Tells of Exploits of Tanks — Col George Smith Patton on Foot Led Huge Juggernauts Through Argonne Forest. Has D.S.C. and Wound Stripe — Believes Steel Machines will Prove as Useful as Airplanes in Future Wars."

The marvelous publicity culminated in a letter Patton received several days later:

Dear Sir — I shall greatly appreciate it if you will permit me to have your photograph together with the details of the exploits which won you citations, for the Sunset Magazine [which had a large circulation among Californians]. They take excellent care of photographs and it will be returned to you in good condition.

Thanking you for the courtesy of an early reply, I am, Very truly yours.

Telegram, Aunt Nannie (New York) to Mr. Patton (Pasadena), March 17, 1919

George landed today at noon Gone to Camp Mills for few days Beatrice met him and says he looks well and happy.

IX

The Immediate
Postwar Years

"People seem to be trying to put the army on the bum as hard as they can."

CHAPTER 35

Camp Meade

"War is the only place where a man realy lives."

THE SPRING AND SUMMER of 1919 were a time of transition and adjustment for Patton. The war and the glory were behind him, although there would be moments when he relived the past. The peacetime army posed problems for his own future career — what would the role of tanks be in the postwar military establishment and should he remain with the Tank Corps or return to the cavalry?

After a week at Camp Mills, Long Island, Patton traveled with the tank brigade to Camp George G. Meade, Maryland. Located between Baltimore and Washington and close to both cities, the camp was particularly convenient for the Pattons, for Beatrice had established a home in Washington.

At the Benjamin Franklin Cantonment, which was the tank part of the post, troops were demobilized. The AEF Tank Corps, drastically reduced in size, was then merged with its U.S. counterpart, including elements moved from Camp Colt, Pennsylvania, to Camp Meade.

With Rockenbach remaining in France, the tankers came under Colonel Welborn, who had offices in Washington, and Colonel W. H. Clopton, Jr., the post commander who acted as Welborn's deputy. Next in rank to them was Mitchell, who commanded the heavy tanks. Then in order of seniority came Patton, who commanded the light tanks.

Writing to Pershing and warning him "there is nothing important in the letter so don't bother to read it unless you have time," Patton passed along some observations of how Americans regarded Pershing. "Your picture and statues of you — all very bad — are in the store windowes." At the Hippodrome Theater in New York, moving pictures showed Theodore Roosevelt, President Wilson, and Pershing. "T.R. got most applause," Patton candidly reported, "you next, and Mr. W [was] a poor third." St. Mihiel had "made you solid with the people." His mother and sister were coming tl..t afternoon to see Patton for the first time. "Please excuse the frankness of this letter. It is designed to show you how things are here . . . so far no other man in the sense you were a man had yet been born."

A few days later, after repeating his injunction — "There is nothing important in this letter, so dont read it if you are busy" — Patton talked about a combined recruiting and Liberty Loan drive that he found "a most week kneed performance." "A lot of flannel mouthed officers" had sought to sell re-enlistment on the advantages of travel, vocational training, and fun in the peacetime Army. "The whole thing was peculiarly norsiating to me as I believe in compulsory service as a national duty." He assured Pershing that "every one I have seen has it in for Gen. M. [Peyton March]," who was Pershing's arch rival. Patton was concerned about the development of a split between Regular officers who had served abroad during the war and those who were kept at home. He liked the new mathematical rating scale for officers.

And finally, he had been to West Point and talked with the Superintendent, who mentioned public pressure to shorten the course at the Military Academy. Patton hoped that could be resisted.

> What West Point makes is a soul. We the graduates are efficient because we can't help it. We dont run away because we are a lot more afraid of our own conscience than we are of the enemy. The Soul cannot be built in on[e] or two years. It would be much better to have several West Points [if the Army needed more Regular officers].

He added that his mother and sister were staying with him and were quite well, then concluded:

> I went to a war Play last night and the noise of the shells and the machine guns made me feel very homesick. War is the only place where a man realy lives.

Probably stimulated by his remark that he believed in "compulsory service as a national duty," Patton wrote a paper headed "Notes on the

Desirability of Universal Service." Perhaps he delivered it as a talk to officers on post or to townspeople near Camp Meade. It stated in part:

It is the common experience of mankind that in moments of great excitement the conscious mental processes of the brain no longer operate. All actions are subconscious — the result of habits. Troops whose training and discipline depend on conscious thought become helpless crowds in battle. To send forth such men is murder. Hence, in creating an Army, we must strive at the production of soldiers so trained that in the midst of battle they will still function . . .

[A soldier] is in the midst of thousands of shells and hundreds of corpses . . . He is tired, in a strange environment, hungry and for days has been working himself up more or less to a nervous state in the expectation of battle and possible death. The training which will produce habit and that will operate under such circumstances must assuredly be longer and more intense than the practice necessary to you as a motorist . . .

He may learn his multifarious duties in three or four months . . . but it takes innumerable repetitions, or soaking in the idea for a long time, at least a year, before he can perform them without thought. Since he can not think in the midst of battle he is worthless as a soldier until he has reached this state . . .

The salute . . . is the mark of brotherhood, the cryptic hand shake exchanged between members of the most patriotic of societies — the Army . . .

The soldier at attention, saluting, is putting himself in the same frame of mind as the [football] player — alert, on his toes, receptive.

In battle the officers are the quarterbacks, the men the disciplined team on their toes, with that lightning response to orders which means victory, and the lack of which means death and defeat, which is worse.

Now we come to the greatest of all reasons for universal service, namely, the fact that it makes patriots . . . The man who has served a year with sweat and some discomfort feels that truly he has a part in his country, that of a truth it is his — and he is a patriot. . . .

At the end of his year of service the boy emerges a man, courteous, considerate, healthy, and moral. To get these results in a democratic way service must be absolutely universal. There is some phase in the vast mechanism of the Army where all may serve; the lame, the halt, the weak, and even the blind . . . the year he serves his country and renders it great and sound . . . can only be looked upon as a year well spent.

Letter, GSP, Jr., to his father, April 1, 1919

I am very much ashamed not to have written before, but being in America has upset my habits to such an extent that I have neglected to do so. I have thought of you all the time and am most anxious to see you . . .

Mama and Nita seem fine. Beatrice is much better. I hope to get a leave soon but things are so upset that I can't fix a date.

With much love your devoted son.

Letter, GSP, Jr., to his father, April 1, 1919

I am in favor of Nita's going to england as that will finally settle the matter one way or another.

For the present I shall stay in the Tank Corps as I will thus probably keep my rank and besides I owe it to the Corps. Also if I went to the cavalry now I should find my self on the border at once. As I have no friends over here.

There is a good chance of my getting detailed in Washington to write a Tank Drill regulations. This would be fine for Beat and for me. Also I have been away from the "flesh pots" so long that I rather yearn for a bath tub and warm water to shave.

I bought a Pierce Arrow automobile as I can afford it and believe in enjoying my self between wars.

Camp Mead[e] is only an hour and a quarter from Washington by trolley or auto so even if I stay here it is not bad.

If I get the Detail on the Drill regulations I shall not be able to take a leave until that is over. If I don't I might get a leave pretty soon but things are too unsettled to say yet.

Patton was flattered to receive a letter from a board of officers in France who canvassed his opinions on cavalry tactics, armament, and organization, and its future role in warfare. He replied at once, explaining: "This paper did not reach me until I had returned to the U.S. As I am deeply interested, I am taking the liberty of answering."

His response was oriented toward the use of cavalry in a future war in Mexico and concerned with gaining "great fire power and mobility." He recommended that the newly developed air-cooled machine gun replace the water-cooled barrel, that the number of automatic rifles in a cavalry division be increased drastically, that the Stokes mortar be added to cavalry squadrons, and that the saber be retained to stimulate "morale and dash. It is worth its weight." He hoped that cavalry would concentrate its operations in terrain impassable to armored cars and tanks and that the troop (or company) would be expanded

> to 5 officers and 150 men so as to ensure getting 100 men into battle . . . Our pre-war theories were correct but more emphasis must be placed on daring and reckless bravery . . . Cavalry must attack always and not dig in and howl for help. Cavalry is an arm of bluff and must make that bluff good . . . The [mounted] attack must be delivered with more emphasis on speed and violence than on cohesion. . . .
>
> The killing or wounding of a few men and officers at drill [or training] should not be regarded as a national calamity . . .
>
> In my opinion the prompt decision is the essence of training, for more losses will occur while seeking a perfect solution than will occur by using an inferior solution promptly.

Somewhat significantly, for it betrayed his indecision over his own future place in the Army, he signed his paper "Col. Tank Corps (Maj. Cav.)."

While still in France, Patton had filled out a card to indicate: 1) the branch of service in which he preferred to serve, and 2) the special duty he desired within that branch. Somewhat boyishly, he had put down: 1) "Tank Corps," 2) "Fighting."

Now he filled out a more detailed "Personal Report" to set forth his professional qualifications and his wishes for future duties. He indicated that he spoke French fluently and Spanish slightly, read French rapidly and Spanish slowly. He had special knowledge of the sword, horsemanship, gas engines, and tractors (tanks). He was a graduate of the Army General Staff College at Langres, France. He was 6 feet 1 inch in height and 170 pounds in weight. He had achieved expert rating in the rifle and pistol in 1913 — "No oppertunity to fire [for scores] since."

Perhaps to avoid the necessity of choosing between the tanks and the cavalry, he said he preferred duty as a military attaché in London or, even more, as a student at the Army School of the Line at Leavenworth, Kansas.

. . .

Sometime in April Patton drove, probably in his new Pierce-Arrow, to Camden, New Jersey, where Joe Angelo lived, and listened without interrupting, no doubt amused but not daring to show it, as Angelo told newsmen in his hometown how Angelo had won the Distinguished Service Cross. The newspaper featured the story under the headlines "Camden Soldier Called Bravest Man in the Army — Tank Commander Lauds Boy who Saved His Life when Wounded."

Angelo's recollections were somewhat hazy. He said he had gone over the top at 6:30 with Patton and 15 men and 2 first lieutenants, along with 150 tanks moving through a dense fog. Angelo walked beside Patton until they reached a crossroads, where Patton told him to watch for Germans.

Two American infantrymen came along, and Angelo asked what they were doing.

"Just mopping up," they answered.

"Well," Angelo said, "if you don't get out of here, you will get mopped up. The Germans are pouring plenty of lead over our way."

The infantrymen took shelter in a shack nearby. Moments later, a shell struck the building and blew it to "atoms."

Angelo saw two German machine gunners behind a bush. They fired at him. He returned the fire and killed one. "The other one," he said, "beat it."

Patton had gone ahead, and he reappeared on top of a knoll and shouted, "Joe, is that you shooting down there?"

Almost immediately, Angelo "thought sure hell had broken loose." Bullets were flying all around.

"Come on," Patton yelled, "we'll clean out those nests."

Angelo followed him up the hill. Patton was sore because the infantry had not taken care of the enemy machine guns. It was their job.

Then Patton saw that several tanks were not moving. He sent Angelo to see Captain English and find out why. Angelo discovered that the tanks were stuck in the mud.

Patton went to the tanks, almost hub deep in the mud, grabbed a shovel, and began digging the tanks free. Other men and Angelo began to dig. German fire started to fall in, but they got the tanks moving and over the hill.

When Patton found some infantrymen wandering around without officers, he rounded them up. He told Angelo to take about 15 riflemen and clear out the machine guns.

Angelo did so but soon returned. "They have all been killed," he told Patton.

"My God!" Patton said. "They are not all gone?"

Yes, Angelo said, they were all killed by machine gun fire.

We'll clean out the machine gun nests ourselves, Patton said.

"I thought the Colonel had gone mad and grabbed him. He grabbed me by the hair and shook me to my senses. Then I followed him. We went about 20 yards and the colonel fell with a bullet in his thigh."

Angelo assisted Patton into a shell hole and bandaged his wound.

Patton passed out. He revived two hours later. He told Angelo to find Major Sereno Brett and tell him to assume command of the Tank Corps. Angelo did so, then returned to Patton.

Two American tanks and a French tank came up and camped about 20 yards from their hole.

"Jump out there," Patton ordered Angelo, "and scatter those tanks or they will be blown up."

Angelo rushed out and told them to do so. The American tanks got away, but the French tank was shot to pieces.

Patton told Angelo to take a tank and wipe out the machine gun nests. Angelo did so.

Then he ordered four infantrymen passing by to carry Patton to the rear.

Angelo, the newspaper stated, had been employed at the Du Pont powder works before the war.

In mid-April, together with Lieutenant Colonel James E. Ware and Majors Viner and Sasse, Patton reported to Welborn in Washington to formulate tank regulations and prepare a drill manual and a course of instruction for the tankers. Taking Patton's place as commander of the Tank Corps at Camp Meade until Clopton returned from leave was Lieutenant Colonel Dwight D. Eisenhower.

The Tank Board worked for a month in Washington on the basic doctrine that would shape the training and employment of tank units. Then, augmented by Mitchell, the board members proceeded to the Rock Island Arsenal, Illinois, and to the Springfield Armory, Massachusetts, to inspect Tank Corps matériel in development and production.

Letter, GSP, Jr. (Hotel Blackhawk, Davenport, Iowa), to his father, June 2, 1919

I am out here with the rest of the Board looking at the Mark VIII Tank. It works much better than we thought. I went to Peoria, Ill. Saturday to see the Holt factory and had a nice time though I felt sick all the time. When I got here I went to a Dr. and he told me I had Chicken Pox. I was delighted to find that I was still young enough to have it. He says that I am practically over it but had best stay here a day or two to get looking decent again. I am all swelled up now . . .

Nita must be over [in England] by this time and things always come out for the best. Even the Pox is giving me a good rest.

GSP, Jr., Poem, "Written while I had the chicken pox, Daven port, Iowa, 1919"

A Soldiers Burial

Not midst the chanting of the Requiem Hymn
Nor with the solemn ritual of prayer
'Neath misty shadows from the oriel glass
And dreamy perfume of the incensed air
Was he interred.

But in the subtle stillness after fight,
In the half light between the night and day,
We dragged his body, all besmeared with mud,
And dropped it, clod-like, back into the clay.

Yet who shall say that he was not content,
Or missed the priest, or drone of chanting choir,
He, who had heard all day the Battle Hymn
Sung on all sides by thousand throats of fire?

What painted glass can lovelier shadows cast
Than those the Western skys shall ever shed,
While mingled with its light, Red Battle's Sun
Completes in magic colors o'er our dead
The flag for which they died.

Later that month Patton wrote Pershing to suggest that he consider running for President. Patton had recently been in Chicago, where Leonard Wood was being boomed for the presidency on the basis of his great organizational ability. What about you? Patton asked. How about Pershing's great organizational ability as demonstrated in the Philippines, in Mexico, and in France? "The last time I was with you I told you that you did not advertise [yourself] enough. I respectfully repeat that statement. There are too many others who are using it to hurt you."

Pershing was, obviously, pleased by Patton's remarks. When he replied, he said he thought that all presidential booms were premature. It was better, he believed, to wait and see what the people wanted, better too because the Army required a complete reorganization in terms of the lessons of the Great War, and this Pershing intended to carry out.

He informed Patton that he had seen his sister Ann in England recently at the Keith Merrills', Beatrice's sister and her husband. They had all had a pleasant visit. Nita was very keen on her work, though perhaps somewhat lonesome. Her plans, Pershing said, were indefinite, and so were his.

The Holt Manufacturing Company of Peoria, Illinois, proudly advised Patton that a five-ton caterpillar tractor had gained the summit of Pike's Peak despite fifteen-foot snow drifts during the last two hours of its climb.

Perhaps stirred by this feat, which foreshadowed remarkable improvements in automotive and tank designs, Patton wrote a formal letter asking to be sent as a student to the School of the Line at Fort Leavenworth that September.

Welborn endorsed his request favorably, saying that he considered Patton especially fitted for the course of study. He was one of the best informed officers on the operations of tanks, and he would prove particularly valuable in helping to formulate the general course of instruction.

No action was taken.

Early in July, Patton showed his concern over former noncommissioned officers who had been commissioned during the war, who were known as Class III officers, and who were about to be discharged from the Army. Patton was indignant because separation from the Army would "work an injustice on many efficient men and at the same time result in a great loss to the service." The former enlisted Regulars had proved their merit as instructors in peace and as commanders in battle, had learned no other profession, had families for whom they had provided by "blood and sweat." Now that the war was won, they were given solely the opportunity to re-enlist as privates or noncoms if they wished to practice their profession. Many would probably depart the military service altogether, and that would be a real loss to the Army, for they were all well disciplined and highly trained, and all of them had performed

> always in a most efficient and loyal manner . . . This letter is submitted in the hope that it will aid in calling attention to the condition of so many fine officers and that something may be done to hold them as temporary officers, perhaps with the loss of one grade each, until such time as a definite policy may properly place them.

He wrote much the same thing informally to Harbord, who was again Pershing's chief of staff. Patton hoped that Pershing could do something to safeguard the commissioned grades of former noncommissioned officers until legislation could provide some way for them to remain on duty.

Patton told Harbord that he had gone to the War Department and visited seven offices. Each passed the buck until someone in the seventh office referred him to the office where he had started —

> and I blew up. On this they said that they would consider it [Patton's suggestion] . . . I talk like I was a class three officer My self but it is only due to the old dictom that the good soldier should look out for his horses and men.

Harbord passed Patton's letter to Pershing, but nothing could be done. The country was interested in retrenchment and economy after the exertion and expense of the war.

Soon after Patton's departure from France, Rockenbach had rated him according to the new mathematical scale and in July Patton's new superiors did so. His capacities and performances were scored as follows:

	Physical Condition	Intelligence	Leadership	Character	General Value to Service	Total
Rockenbach	12	12	15	14	32	85
Welborn	14	12	15	14	32	87
Clopton	13	14	14	15	35	91

The perfect officer, theoretically nonexistent, would accumulate 15 points in the four personal categories and 40 for general value, giving a total of 100.

Requesting leave for 45 days, Patton listed these reasons to justify the fifteen days beyond the normal leave period: first, while he had been in France, Catalina Island, of which he was part owner, was sold; his share of the sale, "which is a fair sum," had never been invested, and he wished to do so; second, in 1915, he had started a farm in California to raise thoroughbred horses; he now had nineteen, many of which he had never seen. One month's leave, of which ten days would be consumed by travel, would give him insufficient time for these concerns.

Welborn approved Patton's request, and so did the Adjutant General.

Letter, GSP, Jr., to Aunt Nannie, July 11, 1919

Everyone will be back to their old rank on or before Sept. 30, 1919. So if I want to show off as a colonel I had best get home before that time . . .

It is very stupid sitting around. Doing nothing. I hope Ma does not break her neck in her Electric [auto] as that would be a sad fate. Monday Beatrice ran into a truck with the Franklin and busted Off the lights and the bumper but did no other harm. It made her very mad especially as it was her own fault but it might have been much worse.

Writing Rockenbach about the men who had been recommended for awards but who had failed to receive them because their exploits were deemed insufficiently meritorious for the decoration, Patton said:

I do not believe however that any officer of the Brigade would recommend men unless they had shown merit above the ordinary. It has therefore occurred to Major Brett and myself that it might be possible for you to get out a general order from Headquarters Tank Corps, mentioning these men by name and saying something about their meritorious service, the idea being that the possession of such an order would enable each man specifically named therein to wear one silver star on his victory medal. I believe that you will agree with me that this is the least that can be done for these men. Major Brett just at present is taking the trip across the continent with some motor trucks trying to recruit men for the TC.

Letter, GSP, Jr., to his father, July 12, 1919

I just received a letter from Gen. H. A. Smith saying that he had just heard that I had been given the D.S.M. for which he had recommended me last August. If he is correctly informed as must be the case I am delighted as the number of people with both [D.S.C. and D.S.M.] medals is very limited.

I am inclosing a draft for $1500.00 which is the rest of the amount I owe you on that Benson loan. I got it from the sale of the Packard to the Government in France.

I got the tickets today to leave here on the night of Friday the 18th. we should arrive [in Los Angeles] 22 or 23 I don't know which. We leave Chicago on the limited Santa Fe Saturday night.

I was only able to get a months leave but Col. Welborne is letting me fudge about six days three each way. Besides I shall telegraph for an extension. Still a month is better than nothing . . .

Beatrice is having her Picture Painted so is having a fine time.

Letter, GSP, Jr., to his father, July 17, 1919

Inclosed is a copy of my citation for the D.S.M. So far as I know the only other man with the two decorations is Gen. McArthur, of course there are probably others but in a very limited quantity.

I inclose also two poems which I wrote at speed but which have the unusual merit so far as my poems are concerned of being short.

We leave tomorrow evening [for California].

The citation, issued by GHQ AEF on June 16, 1919, read as follows:

Under the provisions of Cablegram No. 2830, received from the War Department, March 1st, 1919, the Commander-in-Chief, in the name of the President, has awarded the *Distinguished Service Medal* to you for exceptionally meritorious and distinguished service . . .

He later wrote:

Col Patton was awarded the D.S.M., and it is common knowledge that it was never earned by him but was the result of the generous and splendid manner in which the Tank Corps carried out the orders as to dress and deportment. They won the medal, fortune pinned it on him.

GSP, Jr., "My Father," 1927

Beatrice, the girls and I came home on leave in June [July] 1919. Papa and I had long talks about the war. He had followed it carefully and was a delight to talk with. He insisted that I have my picture taken . . . He was so proud of me that he embarrassed me. When he presented me to his friends he always said: "Mr. so and so you remember my son Colonel Patton."

Neither he nor mama ever made an actual fuss. The nearest I can recall is when one day Mama called me "Her hero son."

The Pasadena *Star-News* welcomed Patton home with a spread featuring the headline "U. S. Tank Leader is Home with High Army Honors," and showing a photograph of him standing beside a tank; the caption read: "Col. G. S. Patton Jr. Who Led First American Tanks into Battle Is Visiting Parents at their Home in San Marino." He had arrived in Pasadena accompanied by Mrs. Patton, and with his German war dog, Char.

The Los Angeles *Times* ran a big story headlined: "Col. Patton Designing American Super-Tank — Pasadena Hero who had Iron Cavalry in France Says Warfare with Mobile Forts is Yet in Infancy," and showed Patton standing in front of a tank. He was quoted as saying that tanks were as far behind the times as planes had been ten years earlier. He said too that he had acted as aide to the Prince of Wales who was "a very democratic young man . . . I also met King George and found him to be democratic."

He spent quite a bit of time during his vacation fishing off Santa Catalina Island.

Returning east on the train, the Santa Fe Limited, Patton wrote a poem while riding through Kansas:

Marching in Mexico

The column winds on snake like,
Through blistering, treeless spaces;
The hovering gray-black dustclouds
Tint in ghoulish shades our faces.

The sweat in muddied bubbles,
Trickles down the horses rumps;
The saddles creak, the gunboots chafe,
The swinging holster bumps.

At last the "Halt" is sounded.
The outpost trots away;
The lines of tattered pup-tents rise, —
We've marched another day.

The rolling horses raise more dust,
While from the copper skies
Like vultures, stopping on the slain,
Come multitudes of flies.

The irate cooks their rites perform
Like pixies round the blaze,
The smoking greasewood stings our eyes,
Sunscorched for countless days.

The sun dips past the western ridge,
The thin dry air grows cold.
We shiver through the freezing night,
In one thin blanket rolled.

The night wind stirs the cactus,
And sifts the sand o'er all,
The horses squeal, the sentries curse,
The lean coyotes call.

Back at Camp Meade, Patton discovered that Rockenbach was in the United States and was the new Chief of the Tank Corps, U. S. Army, replacing Welborn, who became his deputy.

A concerted effort was made throughout the Army to get official files in good order, and several of Patton's superiors submitted reports on his past performance.

Clopton, who had earlier that year cited Patton as having worked "excellently," called him "an excellent energetic ambitious officer. His only fault is his impatience when unable to pursue his work along his desired lines, thus failing to appreciate the details of team work." Clopton nevertheless judged Patton "average" in judgment and common sense, and "above average" in physical energy and endurance, attention to duty, initiative, organizational ability, and capacity for command.

Welborn, who had said that Patton's work as a board member in Washington "was well performed," wrote: "This officer is enthusiastic about any work he has to do and will accomplish results." He marked Patton "superior" in energy and endurance, as well as initiative, "above average" in his attention to duty and capacity for command, "average" in judgment, common sense, and organizational ability.

Rockenbach characterized him as "intelligent, active, and gallant. Possessing great dash and courage." He scored Patton "superior" in all categories except judgment and common sense, which were "above average." Patton had performed his duties "most excellent and gallantly," and was fitted for either staff or command assignments.

Major General J. W. McAndrew, who as commandant of schools in Langres had been Patton's superior, wrote: "Colonel Patton is an exceptionally fine soldier and has demonstrated his ability in the field. He is an unusually efficient leader of men in action, and his great usefulness lies in that direction rather than in General Staff work." McAndrew thought him "above average" in physical energy and endurance, judgment and common sense, "superior" in all other qualities. He added that Patton was best fitted for service with troops or tanks, duties he had performed "exceptionally well. The Army Tank School of the A.E.F. owes the greater part of its success to Colonel Patton Jr."

Brigadier General Harry A. Smith, who had succeeded McAndrew at Langres, wrote: "One of the strongest most active and forceful officers in the service . . . Organized and directed the Tank School in a superior manner." He gave Patton "superior" in all categories. He added, "One of the strong officers in the Army."

Pershing marked him as "an able officer especially adapted for active field work." Patton was "superior" in physical energy and endurance, attention to duty, initiative, organizational ability, and capacity for command; "above average" in judgment and common sense.

These testimonials were flattering and merited, but they seemed to belong to a bygone age, for, in September 1919, Patton was appointed a member of a board of officers, headed by Mitchell, to investigate into and report upon ordnance equipment for tanks. It was hardly thrilling work, but Patton, as usual, threw himself wholeheartedly into it. The language of the board's proceedings, findings, and conclusions indicated that Patton took a lively part in and probably dominated the discussions.

At one meeting, for example, the board suggested putting a lock on tanks, changing the type of grease cup on the pump, shortening the handle of the gearshift by six inches; also "Modify gear shift mechanism so that gears can be shifted into proper place without driver looking at them."

If this was tedious, it was necessary, for Patton was convinced that the tanks had to be brought out of their mechanical infancy and fashioned into reliable and hard-hitting instruments of warfare.

Occasionally, there were interesting exercises. For example:

Letter, GSP, Jr., Commanding Officer, 304th Tank Brigade, to the Chief of the Tank Corps, September 20, 1919

The recent operation, conducted by this Brigade, of moving 27 tanks by trailer from Campe Meade to Washington and return has I believe finally demonstrated the unsuitability of this form of transportation.

The move was 31 miles each way, 23 miles of this distance was over concrete boulevard and city streets. The shortest time for either leg of the trip was six hours. The longest was fourteen hours going and twenty-three hours returning.

There were seven accidents of a serious nature. Two cupling poles were broken. Three trucks were ditched or wrecked by the trailers running into their rear ends. Two trailers were badly ditched from side slipping. These accidents accounted for the long duration of the trip in the case of the slowest trucks and also sent two men to the hospital with serious injuries in the form of broken legs . . .

[During this march, as well as in recruiting marches, especially good roads were selected and used only by day.] In war necessity not desirability dictates the roades to be used. In my experience the roades are always bad and crowded and the marches must be made at night. Both these facts will militate still further against the efficiency of trailer transportation . . .

I desire to go on record as believing that neither truck nor trailer transportation for tanks will prove efficient except over metaled roades. For long halls or where dirt roades are to be expected railroad transportation is the only solution.

Letter, GSP, Jr., to Aunt Nannie, September 20, 1919

I was in the parade in charge of the tanks and we made a pretty good show except that one tank just missed taking down the triumphul arch . . .

We saw in the paper that Pa. had been recomended for secretary of commerce along with two other men. I do hope he gets it and accepts the job. It would be fine for him and not for long enough [meaning only until the end of the Wilson administration] to make him sick.

Beatrice and I are having a party at the Chevy Chase club to night for her cousin Beatrice Banning who is a very nice girl and quite pretty. Gen. R. [Rockenbach] is going to party and will stay all night with us.

Col. Collins is back at the war colledge as captain and I am delighted.

I am inclosing a copy of a new poem which I have written.

Letter, GSP, Jr., to the Secretary, Naval War College (through channels), September 24, 1919, subject: Naval Tactics

[It is possible that in the future tanks will combat each other.] In my opinion such an engagement will partake somewhat of the nature of a sea fight with much diminished ranges . . .

If possible I request information as to suitable maneuvers and formations for attacking a line of hostile tanks in similar original formation. Assuming that at the beginning of the fight it was known that hostile tanks were to be encountered request information as to the best original formation for the approach and for subsequent maneuvers.

How to improve the tank and how to employ it successfully in battle would occupy much of Patton's time between the two world wars. He would read a great deal, write much, and think even more. But his activities would, for the most part, be somewhat hidden. They were off-duty interests for much of the period.

While his quest for professional knowledge, his search for military perception, his desire to learn better his trade as a soldier would continue unabated, he would suffer the disappointment of frustration and even the bitterness of what must have seemed like betrayal. The Army in the 1920s and 1930s would be moribund. This would appear to him as a kind of rejection of himself and of his contributions to the art of tank warfare in the World War. Yet he never explicitly complained.

In compensation for the inertia in the Army, he would find other outlets for his energy, ambition, and drive. His fate or his destiny, he must often have thought, had deserted him. Yet he had to move on in pursuit of glory, for if that eluded him, what else would remain?

CHAPTER 36

Camp Meade: Goodbye to Tanks

"Our calling is most ancient and like all other old things it has amassed through the ages certain customs and traditions which decorate and enoble it, which render beautiful the otherwise prosaic occupation of being professional men-at-arms: killers."

VERY ACTIVE in his thinking, writing, and lecturing on tanks in the fall of 1919 and the first half of 1920, Patton was trying to establish a doctrine or methodology for their employment. He never quite managed to systematize a coherent theory, in part because he was unable to resolve satisfactorily some of the basic questions, in part because the Army failed to solve some of the fundamental problems.

If tanks were auxiliaries designed primarily to help the infantry, their functions could be classed with those of the artillery. If tanks were a separate and distinct arm capable of independent missions, they required a life of their own. If they were the mechanical equivalent of cavalry, they would best be joined to that branch of the service.

These issues, which provoked discussion among a very small coterie of American officers during the next twenty years, were never properly worked out for the U. S. Army before World War II. As a consequence, Americans made few advances in tank warfare. Even their machines — in a country where the automobile became king — remained rudimentary and primitive, primarily because the appropriations furnished by Congress for research and development were small.

In grappling with the problems of using tanks, Patton came close to creating a new and convincing technique. Despite his ardor and perception, in the end he failed — in large part because he grew persuaded that lack of funds and interest would block an imaginative approach to tank warfare and rob the Army of its capacity to advance.

Unlike Billy Mitchell in the Air Force, he was unwilling to risk his career for an idea. Unlike J. F. C. Fuller in England, whose dogged work and stringent logic, despite the discouraging obstacles thrown up by the conventional military leaders, produced tank principles that were publicized by Liddell Hart and eventually brought to life by Guderian in Germany, Patton lacked patience and forbearance. His self-discipline generated quick action and decisive movement rather than intellectual rumination and wide-ranging thought. What sharpened his insights was actually working with formations of men on the drill field and maneuver ground, as at the tank center in Bourg.

The Army between the wars would fail to provide machines and soldiers in sufficient quantity and quality to permit experimentation. Held back by the inertia around him, finding little stimulus and, finally, little reason for creative solutions, he would turn increasingly aside from the problems and look elsewhere, concealing his disappointment and frustration in a life of physical exertion.

His papers and lectures showed how near he came to enunciating an original view of tank tactics.

In September 1919, speaking on "The History, Employment and Tactics of Light Tanks," probably at Camp Meade, Patton described

briefly the latest views on the imployment of tanks in the various phases of war. These ideas are not final as they are ever subject to changes imposed by improvements in the tanks themselves and in the means of combatting them.

Tanks could be used in purely offensive operations or in defensive warfare for counterattacks. They were simply an auxiliary arm to assist the advance of infantry. Suffering more from wear and tear than from hostile fire, they could and should be employed sparingly and only when necessary, only in decisive moments.

Tanks like all other arms must be deployed in depth . . . [to] insure the constant and uniform feeling of the front line and at the same time to have forces available to exploit to the front and flank and to repel counterattacks.

Against hostile tanks, he postulated, tanks provided the best defense. He visualized combat between machines as resembling a naval battle.

Tanks are not motorised cavalry, or armoured infantry or accompanying guns; they are tanks — a new auxiliary arm whose purpose is ever and always to facilitate the advance of that master arm the Infantry on the field of battle.

Thus, he saw tanks primarily as supporting weapons designed to assist the infantry — the mission they had performed in the World War.

A lecture entitled "The Effect of Tanks in Future Wars" took a somewhat different course.

In view of the prevalent opinion in America, that soldiers are, of all persons, the least capable of discussing military matters and that their years of special training are as naught compared to the innate military knowledge of lawyers, doctors and preachers; I am probably guilty of a great heresy in daring to discuss tanks from the viewpoint of a tank officer. I am emboldened to make the attempt, however, not from a bigoted belief in the infallibility of my own opinions, but rather in the hope that others will assail my views and that the discussion engendered will in a measure remove the tanks from the position of innocuous desuetude to which they appear to have been relegated by the general public.

The specific reasons for the present paper are that during the time which has elapsed since November 1918, I have heard not a few experienced officers poo poo the idea that tanks will ever again be used, or that if used they will have any material effect. Admitting that my intimate relation with tanks may perhaps cause me to be over sanguine as to their future, it still appears to me that to utterly disregard them is a very serious error . . .

The infantry are peculiarly susceptible to the attack of tanks, and are perfectly impotent to withstand them, except insofar as they are assisted by the accompanying gun. The discovery of other means for combatting tanks appears, then, to be vital to the infantry; and in view of the improved tank which we shall discuss, to the cavalry also. Artillery, while less likely to suffer from tanks, is equally interested in their development, because artillery is the weapon most dangerous to tanks, hence best adapted to combatting them.

I have neither the ability nor the desire to point out to the arms above mentioned, tactical improvements designed to assist or combat tanks. My purpose is simply to call their attention to what appears to be a lack of effort in that direction; to show some of the causes which have led to this lassitude, and to suggest, in a very sketchy manner, certain tactical uses to which tanks will be set in future wars.

. . . the lack of interest in the future employment of tanks is due primarily to the following: Comparitively few American units operated with tanks. The tank of 1918 — a war production — had many grave mechanical defects. Tank warfare, the necessities of which caused the invention and construction of the tank is, never the less, peculiarly ill adapted to tank combat . . . the great mass of people are totally unaware of the great improvements made, and [in the] making, in the tank. Only those of us who doctored and nursed the grotesque warbabies of 1918 through the innumerable inherent ills of premature birth know how bad they really were, and by virtue of that same intimate association, are capable of judging how much better they are now, and how surely they will continue to improve.

. . . tanks now exist in several countries, capable of a speed across country of from twelve to fifteen miles per hour, and, on the road, up to twenty miles. They are impervious to small arms bullets, and shell fragments. They can cross trenches up to twelve feet. They have fine interior visibility, and all around fire from both cannon and machine guns, and finally they have a radius of action of more than two hundred miles, without resupply of any sort. Such machines exist, and others will surpass them. It is futile to ignore the dreadful killing capacity of such arms . . .

[Tanks] are laboring . . . from unimaginative conceptions as to future wars. Too many people vainly fancy that future unpleasantness will follow as sealed patterns of the World War. With trenches, barriers and plasticine maps. With air photographers so accurate that the latest activities of some careless rabbit are easily discernable. Wars of preparations, concentrations . . . of air raids, welfare workers and Big Berthas. . . . wars with endless intrenchments and flankless armies.

They forget that not in Asia, Africa, or America, can such a war be staged. Because all the above luxuries depend upon two things. First, ROADS — hundreds of good metalled roads to carry the limitless supplies. Second, FRONTS short enough to be continuously occupied . . .

In the continents just mentioned the scanty network of inferior roads precludes the first; and their vast size prevents the second . . . In such regions the fragile line of rails, . . . the Placenta of the army, harrassed by aerial bombardment, cavalry raids, and the vassitudes [vicissitudes] of weather will prove inadequate to the double task of feeding the maw of the guns and the bellies of the troops.

. . . there is strong presumption that the possible loci of some, possibly most, future operations, will be continents which only admit of the use of the various arms in something very closely approximating their pre World War proportions . . . battles will be gained by rifle, automatic rifle, and machine gun fire, unaided by artillery to any marked degree . . . surprise and uncertainty will prevail to a degree unknown in the World War. To guard infantry and supply columns from the unsupported raids of fast tanks accompanying guns will have to be distributed at short distances along the columns, reconnaissance will have to be wide and completely new tactics will have to be evolved and tanks will be necessary . . .

There is no belief on the part of any tank officer that the tank has replaced in the least degree any one of the existing arms. It is distinctly a new instrument added to the full chorus of the Military Band. But having appeared the new pieces composed by future generals will demand the peculiar tone of the tank instrument for the proper rendition of their compositions.

The tank is new and for the fulfillment of its destiny, it must remain independent. Not desiring or attempting to supplant infantry, cavalry, or artillery, it has no appetite to be absorbed by any of them . . . Absorbed . . . we become the stepchild of that arm and the incompetent assistant of either of the others . . .

The great expense of tanks precludes the possibility of their being equably distributed to all units of the other arms. Hence their hyphenation with any such arm will lead to an unequal distribution.

The [Tank] corps should be kept, as was the case among all armies in the World War, a separate entity and be assigned [in battle] by higher authority to that unit where their presence will add the most to the general good. Like the air service they are destined for a separate existance. The Tank corps grafted on Infantry, cavalry, artillery, or engineers will be like the third leg to a duck, worthless for control, for combat impotent.

As he urged the continued independence of the Tank Corps despite his view that tanks supported infantry and perhaps even cavalry, he realized that the primary problem underlying all questions of tank warfare was how to get machines that were mechanically reliable and operable for longer periods of time. Despite their size, frightening appearance, and steel construction, they were fragile creatures, breaking down at the slightest hint of trouble; and their guns were merely adaptations of infantry weapons.

Patton therefore threw himself with zeal into the deliberations and study of the Tank Corps Technical Board of Officers selected in September to consider how to improve tanks. Late that month, the board — Patton, Mitchell, Grubbs, and Sasse — traveled to Aberdeen, Maryland, and inspected ordnance equipment of various sorts, including guns specifically suitable for tanks. A few days afterward, the board recommended that the Browning tank machine gun be equipped with special ammunition designed to increase the tank's firepower.

The board met frequently in Washington through the final months of 1919 and the early months of 1920, looking into such items as periscopes, fan belts, a handrail for the engine compartment, a bracket wheel for the sun pinion, how to prevent a clutch from sticking, the radiator, exhaust manifold, brake drum, speedometer cable, and other essential items. The members visited repair shops, studied preventive maintenance, recommended changes in the ammunition storage system, the driver's location, the engine, the eye-slits, the foot accelerator, the ground clearance of the axles, the movable roof, the pistol ports, the antiaircraft protection, the seat suspension, the small-arms ammunition racks, and the placement of tools.

Letter, GSP, Jr., to his father, September 29, 1919

What do you think of my new [writing] paper? [The sheets were headed "Colonel George S. Patton, Jr., Commanding 304th Brigade, Tank Corps."] I got it too late as the latest news is that we will all be busted on the 31 of October and repromoted according to length of commissioned service. That will make me a junior or more probably a senior captain. I believe that I shall still command the brigade but according to the latest dope that will be a skeleton. In fact people seem to be trying to put the army on the bum as hard as they can. A congressman shook his fist in the face of an officer the other day and in every way they are trying to lower our authority and reduce the discipline of the men. I told John Rogers that if he did not look out the army would strike and if they do that is the end. He had never thought of that, none of them have. But it is true just the same.

Senator Phelan Gave B and I a dinner with the Secretary Of War and two assistant secretaries of state present also two senators. It was very nice of him but we did not know till next day that we were the guests of honor.

. . . you cant make a gentleman in one generation . . .

I am inclosing for your benefit a copy of a lecture I wrote. It is the best I have written so far. Also a copy of a poem. B has sent most of my poems to a publisher to see if he thinks them worth publishing.

They will not appear under my name . . .

B and I will meet Nita [returning from Europe] so you need not worry about that.

He collected about 30 poems for publication and prefaced his work with the following disclaimer:

Preface. These rhymes were written (over a period of years) for his own amusement by a man who having seen something of war is more impressed with the manly virtues it engenders than with the necessary and much exaggerated horrors attendant upon it. They are offered to the public in the hope that they may counteract to a degree the melancholy viewpoint so freely expatiated upon by most writers. If such slush is left unanswered it is feared that it will have a detrimental influence on the spirit of our youth, who in the cause of freedom, may again be called on to battle for the right.

When he mentioned "the right," he was hardly thinking in the political terms that owed their origin to the way the parties were seated on the right and left of the French Chamber of Deputies. He meant the moral right — God, liberty, and the United States. Yet the leaders of what came to be the parties of the right would unconsciously echo his words. Mussolini in Italy and Hitler in Germany would shout that war was the noblest activity of man. Although Patton had interest in neither their politics nor their social and economic panaceas, he agreed with this aspect of their thought and propaganda.

A typical poem in Patton's collection was entitled "Fear."

> I am that dreadful, blighting thing
> Like rat-holes to the flood
> Like rust that gnaws the faultless blade
> Like microbes to the blood.

There were several verses, all in the same vein.

Having sent off his poems — no publisher would accept them — Patton composed a series of eleven lectures for delivery to the officers of his tank brigade. "The Obligation of Being an Officer," dated October 1, revealed his thoughts on the profession of soldiering and, rather gently for Patton, laid down some ground rules prescribing conduct and etiquette, for example, what was expected of a young officer in the matters of social calls and invitations at an Army post.

. . . we, as officers of the army, are not only members of the oldest of honorable professions, but are also the modern representatives of the demi-gods and heroes of antiquity.

Back of us stretches a line of men whose acts of valor, of self-sacrifice and of service have been the theme of song and story since long before recorded history began . . .

In the days of chivalry — the golden age of our profession — knights-officers were noted as well for courtesy and gentleness of behavior, as for death-defying courage . . . From their acts of courtesy and benevolence was derived the word, now pronounced as one, Gentle Man . . . Let us be GENTLE. That is, courteous and considerate of the rights of others. Let us be MEN. That is, fearless and untiring in doing our duty as we see it.

. . . our calling is most ancient and like all other old things it has amassed through the ages certain customs and traditions which decorate and enoble it, which render beautiful the otherwise prosaic occupation of being professional men-at-arms: Killers.

. . . Some of the more common and most frequently neglected [customs] are the following.

MESSES. Officers should behave in as polite a manner at mess as they would if dining at home with the ladies of their family. They should not tell smutty stories, or swear, or pick their teeth. Above all it is the height of bad manners to refer to any lady by name at mess . . .

QUARTERS. Officers should live in a neat way, their rooms should . . . not look like the cells in an insane asylum . . .

GOSSIP. Gentlemen do not gossip. It never does any good and is unfair; many men who would never think of hitting a man from behind will nevertheless stike a deadly blow at his character from behind his back . . . It is the lowest form of sin no matter what cause prompts it.

GROWLING AND CRITICISM. The man who always whines about what he has to do usually is incapable of doing anything. The man who criticises his superior in the presence of soldiers or junior officers is disloyal to his oath as an officer and is doing more than a bolshevic to destroy discipline.

DRINKING . . . never taking a drink when on duty, or about to enter on any duty. Officers of different grades should not drink in company. . . .

MONEY MATTERS. Too much emphasis cannot be laid on the sacred nature of Government money . . . If you must borrow money go to a bank . . .

MILITARY COURTESY. . . . Toothpicks like tooth brushes are for private use. To sport one in the mouth in public smacks very much of the idea that the officer so doing is proud of being able to have bought a meal. . . . Such acts [as saluting, standing at attention, and the like] show that you are a soldier, not simply a uniformed person.

PROMPTNESS. This is always referred to as a military virtue. But like the buffalo it appears to be becoming extinct . . .

EXAMPLE . . . You have no idea how men watch you. If you grow a beard half the company will have beards . . . if you curse so will they . . .

DRESS . . . No one respects a tramp and soldiers will not respect a dirty officer. The rougher the work especially in the field the more inspiring to the men is the sight of a clean, well-shaved officer.

EDUCATION . . . Do you imagine that the successful broker spends his evenings studying the progress of the National League? Hardly. He studies the market . . . Few are born Napoleons, but any of us can be good company commanders if we study. When we are that [company commanders], try for the Battalion and so on, for Four Stars. Hence read military history and books on tactics. I am making out a list of such which I will give you and some of which we will study together. But I earnestly advise you all to read military subjects 3½ hours a week . . .

DON'TS. Don't try to gain success by "Pull" or accuse others of doing so. The man with the alledged pull usually has the goods too.

So far as I know the above remarks do not apply to any one here, but we are none of us perfect . . .

Telegram, GSP, Jr., to his father, October 13, 1919

Ship two horses by express to Camp Meade Maryland valuation two hundred a piece. See that horses have necessary medical certificates also that they will be fed enroute. Wire date of shipment and whether collect or prepaid. All well.

Letter, GSP, Jr., to his father, October 15, 1919

Inclosed is check [for $672] for shipment of horses if you have prepaid them . . . I was sorry to miss Nita and Mama but could not get to Washington [he meant New York] before 6:05 P.M. and they left at 6:00 P.M. I will write as soon as I get time. Love

Letter, GSP, Jr., to Nita, October 18, 1919

Dear Anne: I am very sorry that I did not get the chance to see you in New York and also that I have been so long in writing to bid you welcome home. The earliest train that I could catch landed me in New York at 6:05 P.M. just too late to see you. I of course had no Idea you would get accomidations so soon. I hope that you take a good rest after you get home for the sort of work you have been doing is more trying on a person than they always realize at the time. Then if you feel full of energy I would get into business. Real business. I would suggest the Blankinhorne-Hunter Company. You have shown that you possess ability and the best way to stay contented is to use that ability.

The United States in general and the army in particular is in a hell of a mess and there seems to be no end to it. We are like people in a boat floating down the beautiful river of fictitious prosperity and thinking that the moaning of the none too distant waterfall — which is going to ingulf us — is but the song of the wind in the trees.

We disreguard the lessons of History — The red fate of Carthage; the Rome of shame under the Pretorian guard — and we go on reguardless of the VITAL necessity of trained patriotism — HIRING an army. Some day it too will strike and then the end. FINIS written in letters of Blood on the map of North America. Even the most enlightened of our politicians are blind and mad with self delusion. They believe what they wish may occur not what history teaches will happen. We dined with John Rogers last night. He said that my views were interesting but impossible. What gets me is the fact that I being a loyal fool will be among the first to decorate with my highly intelligent head the arch of Triumph of some future COMMUNE. What a pitty that such a splendid receptical of Military knowledge should be doomed to putrify in such a place.

We are loosing all hardihood! To day at the races I saw a jockey killed. A large healthy man near me shuddered and said that steeplechasing was so dangerous that it should be abolished. Such squemishness is fatal to any race.

I have been very busy lately trying to teach military art to my officers. The only one that is profiting is my self. Still it makes time pass rapidly.

I hope Aunt Nannie is still improving and that the rest of you are well. Some one stole Char so I am desolate.

When Rockenbach asked Patton his opinion on certain procedures at Camp Meade — duty hours, the number of officers required on post, administrative practices — Patton replied in his usual manner, with zeal and thoroughness. Many officers would have regarded the subject as rather trivial, especially after combat service in France, and if asked would have answered quickly and effortlessly. Was Patton then unable to differentiate between important and relatively unimportant matters? It would appear that whatever distinctions he might have made, he regarded all his obligations as requiring his best, his utmost. This, of course, contributed on occasion to a useless expenditure of energy, but he had more than enough vigor for all his activities.

He sent out a barrage of technical papers, sometimes in reply to a request, other times without prior request, bombarding the Chief of the Tank Corps with suggestions on how to improve not only the mechanical aspects of the fighting machine but also the effectiveness of tank formations. For example, he recommended changes in the eye-slits in tanks for increased visibility and a better method of assigning renovated tanks to the tank battalions.

Patton also pondered the question of how best to keep tanks supplied in battle.

The most striking example of the necessity for direct action by the tank corps in obtaining supplies not delivered by normal channels is the case of ammunition for this brigade at the beginning of the St. Mihiel operation. Ammunition estimated as necessary . . . was requisitioned some weeks in advance. On Sept. 9, 1918 this ammunition was not on hand and could not be traced. In order that we might enter the battle [on the 12th] it was necessary for the chief of Tank Corps to send his adjutant to Paris to obtain the ammunition from the French and deliver it by truck to the Brigade. It arrived if my memory is correct on the morning of the eleventh. Had normal channels been resorted to in this case we should have entered the battle with less than half the necessary ammunition and no case shot at all. Similar situations are bound to recur in war . . .

Just before the St. Mihiel operation the Brigade commander . . . made a personal reconnaissance of the sector . . . He found that to move in the very greasy ground each tank would have to be equipped with 16 steel "Grousers." Had it not been for the fact that the Chief of Ordnance A.E.F. turned over the entire machine shops at Is-sur-Tille to the tank corps for the making of these "Grousers" the 2304 "Grousers" necessary for the success of the operation would not have been made. This prompt action was only possible by use of the telephone and prompt support from the Chief of Ordnance. Normal channels would not have worked. A workshop under the Chief of Tank Corps would have removed the danger of a hitch.

Tanks are so new in war that special arrangements will constantly be necessary; the work thus required can only be obtained from shops under the Chief of Tank Corps.

Absolute liaison with the G–2 and G–4 of the units with which the tanks are operating is vital to remove misunderstandings as to use of roads, priority of supplies etc. In the St. Mihiel lack of such liaison delayed our resupply of gas for more than thirty two hours.

Liaison with the signal corps is necessary to prevent the tanks [from] destroying the ground wires.

Genuinely interested in perfecting the tank, Patton struggled with the fact that the Ordnance Department, rather than the Tank Corps, produced tanks, delivering these and other equipment to the Tank Corps. Ordnance demands for safety, versatility, and structural solidity in tanks were often in conflict with the requirements or wishes of the tankers, who wanted instant modification of features that took months of lead time to produce, even when sufficient funds were on hand for research, development, production, and purchase. The Congress would be penurious toward the Army in general and the Tank Corps in particular.

Sometimes the tankers themselves were unable to agree on certain aspects of matériel. For example, the Technical Board approved new tables of allowances at one meeting, decided that the subject of gasoline capacity needed further research, and clashed over the best kind of gun to mount on a tank.

This meeting apparently prompted Patton to write a paper on the "Desirable features in Proposed Tank." He listed certain basic desiderata under five categories: armament, hull, suspension, motor, and speed.

The armament, he believed, should be a single cannon, preferably a model similar to that used by either the infantry or artillery in order to "simplify the ammunition supply." A tank should also have two heavy Browning machine guns much like those currently in use.

The hull, he wrote,

requires the most careful study. Heretofore it has been made to conform to the motive power. This is an error. The Hull should be designed: first from a tactical view point, i.e. it should afford the greatest facility for the use of the arms and for control and visibility; second: from a balestic [ballistic] and weight standpoint, i.e. it should afford as fiew straight surfaces susceptable of normal impact to hostil projectiles as possible . . . in the next war antitank weapons of heavier calaber than the rifle will surely be encountered. The only answer to such weapons is the construction of a body which precludes normal impact. If it were attempted to thicken the armour as a counter to such weapons the weight of the Tank will become prohibative . . .

My own experience and observation leads me to the firm conviction that the turret mount is the only one admissable for tank guns . . .

It is my firm conviction that the cannon and one of the machine guns on the Proposed tank should be mounted on the same trunions and operated by the same gunner using one sight — preferably telescopic — with ranges for the cannon on one side of the vertical hair and ranges for the machine gun on the other . . . tanks rarely have more than one target at the same moment . . . [if] both [guns] are always on the target the gunner has but to choose which class of fire will be the most effective. Further this method of mounting will eliminate one machine gunner . . . The second machine gun should be in a seperate turret and have . . . the duty of firing at targets not covered by the other guns and further be so located as to be able to sweep with its fire the top of the tank to repel assault. It should be at the rear of the tank and the gunner should be also charged with keeping liaison with the infantry. Both turrets should be provided with perescopic sights for both observation and firing under intense hostile fire.

The problem of suspension required further study and experiment.

The motor, Patton felt, should be of a heavy type with reliability for a minimum of 500 hours of "unskilled driving with out the need of readjustment. The Best tank is but a pile of junk when the motor stops . . ." A tank motor needed a self-starter. The tank also needed an internal lighting system. Shaft drives, he believed, were superior to chain.

As for speed, a tank should be able to run on wheels as well as on tracks. Road travel on wheels or special tracks should offer the possibility of running at 20 miles per hour. Cross-country driving should have the same maximum speed, "if attainable."

The Army would adopt the idea of a single gunner controlling both the tank cannon and one machine gun, and the American tank in World War II would embody this feature.

Probably the most significant development in tank design between the wars occurred on October 30, 1919, when Patton, Benson, Brett, Captain Barnard, and Lieutenant Hahn made a thorough investigation of a new type of tank known as the Christie gun mount. In a report dated the same day, their recommendations and remarks were enthusiastically favorable.

The Christie gun mount is, so far as we know, the first attempt in the field of self-propelled mounts or tanks where the entire machine and each component part there of has been designed and constructed solely from the military standpoint. In other words it is a production job, not an assembly job. This fact is noteworthy . . .

The power plant is unique in three particulars: First: it is set in across the length of the machine, thus saving much space and also the necessities of diverting the power through a right angle by the use of beveled gears. Second: the power plant is completely equipped with large ballbearings at all points of friction. Third: the motor and transmission are mounted on a sub-frame or chasse [chassis] and are not bolted to the armor . . . The transmission is separate for each track: running through two separate sets of gears situated one at each length of the crack [crank] shaft . . .

The christie arrangement gives added simplicity by doing away with one clutch and two trains of reduction gears, and adding one transmission. The saving in space is obvious.

Further, this machine gives four speeds forward and four reverse, by the simple addition of one idle gear . . .

The control is effected very simply by two combined clutch and
steering levers, one gear shifting lever and one reverse lever . . .
The entire motor and transmission which are combined in one crank
case may be taken out as a whole by the simple removal of one of the
side plates. This is very important from a tank point of view.

Suspension. Six of the eight wheels or track rollers . . . have independent spring action on the spiral springs . . . the Christie machine obviates both these difficulties [the problem of friction and the
condition of having axles too close to the ground — by having better
track rollers and also rubber tires on the wheels]. The ability which
the Christie machine possesses of running on tracks or wheels is interesting, but from the tank point of view, hardly essential . . . [This
may have been a sop to the Ordnance Department.]

Recommendation. The board is of the opinion that much good
will be accomplished if Mr. Christie is empowered to design and construct a tank combining the mechanical features and masterly construction of his present mount with the tactical ideas of the Chief of
the Tank Corps.

Impressed with the Tank Corps enthusiasm, the Ordnance Department
prepared to award a contract to Walter Christie of the Front Drive Motor
Company of Hoboken, New Jersey, who was to construct a tank with a
combination wheel and track mechanism, that is, a vehicle that could run
either on wheels or on tracks, which were interchangeable and could
quickly be alternated even in the field. Before final approval was given
and the contract was signed, the Ordnance Department had some second
thoughts. In a memo from the Tank, Track, and Trailer Division to the
Chief of the Tank Corps Tactical Staff, the Ordnance Department
pointed out that several features and specifications of the Christie tank
failed to meet Ordnance standards. Would the Tank Corps take these
under consideration?

The memo came to Patton who replied at once. He stressed the excellence of Christie's basic design. Even though the Christie tank failed to
meet, exactly and rigidly, the specifications of the Tank Corps, as well as
of the Ordnance Department, it was nevertheless worth pursuing. Once
the machine was built, it could be improved and perfected. It could also
be altered to conform with the specific Ordnance requirements.

Reinforcing Patton's statement was a memo, prepared by Sasse and
signed by Rockenbach, that the Tank Corps was favorably impressed by

the Christie tank primarily because it represented a novel and promising departure from the tanks then in existence. Even though "it is believed that the Tank Corps has been required to answer questions involving technical details, which have always been a function of the Ordnance Department," the Tank Corps saw the Christie tank as the best approach to tank development quite apart from compliance with "technical details." The Tank Corps hoped that the Ordnance Department would go ahead.

Learning that the Ordnance Department was still worried about the specifications on the Christie tank — Ordnance had too little money for adequate research and experimentation and had to be careful with its funds — Patton sent a strong letter of encouragement about a month later.

On June 15, 1920, the contract between Walter Christie and the U. S. Army, represented by the Ordnance Department, was finally executed. The contracting officer certified that he was satisfied with the value of the rights and services the contractor proposed to furnish and also with the terms of payment, which he deemed fair and just. Letters of patent had been granted to Christie on April 6 for a tractor and gearing transmission. Now Christie was to build what might become a prototype for an altogether new American tank.

Patton was elated by the letting of the contract. But by then, he was no longer directly involved with tank development.

Letter, GSP, Jr., to his father, October 29, 1919

The horses and boxes arrived here in fine shape last night. Apparently they had a perfect trip. I rode Bouvard from the station to the stable a distance of about two miles and he went perfectly fine. I went to Boston Saturday night and returned Sunday night. B and I spent the day in going over the 395 Commonwealth house and selecting things. I am going up again Friday night to be at some races that Freddie [Beatrice's brother] is riding in on Saturday.

There is considerable unrest here over the Labor situation and we are doing a little extra work [in anti-riot training] on some [tank] crews in case of necessity. That is Private . . . It is funny that it is impossible to arouse any of the Congressmen to the Gravity of the situation. Also the business men think nothing will happen simply because it would be so bad for them if it did.

Patton presented the American Legion Post #19 (Tank Corps) in Washington, D.C., with its colors. On that occasion, where Semmes and other friends who had been in the brigade were gathered, Patton's remarks to the veterans included the following statements:

Discipline which is but mutual trust and confidence is the key to all success in Peace or War . . .

The Flag is to the Patriot what the Cross is to the Christian.

Letter, GSP, Jr., to his mother, November 6, 1919

Dear Mama: I have been pretty bad about writing lately but realy I have been flying around so much that I have some excuse. I have been to boston the last two Saturdays and was at Long Island the week before that. Last week at Freddies we had a fine time. First there was a race meeting in which Fred won the heavy weight steeplechase then there was a hunt in which I rode and then a Hunt Breakfast at which I made a speech and finally a dance. At the Breakfast and dance I was pursued by a man in a Pink coat who wept bitterly and protested that I was the Goddamdest Officer he had ever met and the only one whom God had endowed with Braines equal to his own. He would then wipe his eye with the tail of his coat and take another drein from a cutglass bottle about two feet long which he carried in the tail of his coat. He said he had heard me lecture in Langres at the [staff] college and had then and there decided to moddle himself on me which he was doing at the time . . .

We have had great luck in tanks lately. A man who is an inventer came here and after he got our ideas as to what was necessary from a fighting viewpoint he designed what I think will be the greatest machine in the world. It is far ahead of the old tanks as day is from night. And for a wonder there is lots of room in it . . .

Newtie the Cootie [Secretary of War Newton D. Baker] pins the D.S.M. on me officially tomorrow at 3:30 P.M.

Letter, Major General C. P. Summerall (Commanding the 1st Division, Camp Zachary Taylor, Kentucky) to GSP, Jr., November 8, 1919

My dear Patton: I am very glad to receive your letter of November fifth, in which you have recommended for citation Major Brett and Captain Barnard. It gives me great pleasure to enclose the citations requested, and I beg that you will deliver them with the assurance of my deep appreciation of the services which they rendered the First

Division and the 5th Corps. I am also enclosing a citation which I consider that you richly deserve in the operations which resulted in the reduction of the St. Mihiel Salient.

Very sincerely yours.

The citation naming Patton for gallantry in action and devotion to duty read as follows:

An officer of superior courage, dominant leadership and technical skill. During the operations of the First Division in the attack on the St. Mihiel Salient September 12th 1918, he commanded the Tank Unit assigned to the Division. By his gallantry, his superior organizing ability and his determination he overcame great difficulties and contributed effectively to the success of the Division in crossing the enemy's trenches and wire and in giving protection to the advancing Infantry while bridging and crossing a difficult stream.

Colonel Walter H. Gordon of the Inspector General's Department rated the efficiency of officers on duty at Camp Meade above the grade of major and gave Patton "Very Good."

The Pattons had a nice Thanksgiving. Beatrice and Beatrice Junior came to dinner at the mess and later all three went riding. He obtained a three-day pass to go to the Army-Navy football game. When he returned, he and Beatrice had General and Mrs. Harbord, General and Mrs. Fox Conner, and Mr. John Hays Hammond to dinner.

Early in December, when a brief flurry of trouble arose on the border, Patton suggested a method of recruiting tank soldiers. "In view of the, not unlikely, commencement of Hostilities with Mexico," he wrote, letters should be sent to the old members of the brigade offering re-enlistment in their former units. He was sure that 60 percent of the enlisted men and 80 percent of the officers with the brigade in France would return. Those who volunteered could come directly to Camp Meade for refresher training. "This would enable us to put at least nine companies in the field with in two weeks of the declaration of war."

There was, of course, no war.

Mitchell rated Patton as having performed his duties "Excellently." He was a "very well informed; capable, energetic; very high type of officer and gentleman. Known [him] intimately for 10 years." Patton was "superior" in military neatness and bearing and in general value to the service; "above average" in physical energy and endurance, judgment and common sense, attention to duty, intelligence, professional knowledge, leadership, force, initiative, handling men, performing field duties, instructing, training troops, handling troops tactically, equitation, topography, map reading, machine guns, army regulations, and military intelligence; "average" in tact, administration, and executive duties.

Christmas was a painful time for Patton. Three days before, according to the doctor's report, "While riding horse on target-range, Tank Corps, Camp Meade, Md. . . . the animal 'bucked,' and the officer [Patton] was thrown forward on the pommel of the saddle and sustained injuries to his testicles." The condition resulting was called "Orchitis, bi-lateral" and it was "moderately severe." Even though "The disability: Incapacitates officer for all duty," the doctor was certain that "With proper treatment and absolute rest in bed . . . the condition is entirely curable." Patton received a month's leave of absence.

In the spring of 1920, Patton's parents visited in the East. He and Beatrice and his mother and father and sister drove "to Winchester and saw the Grave [of his grandfather]. I was still a Colonel and had my Picture taken by the side of the two other Patton Colonels [his grandfather and his Uncle Tazewell, Colonel, 7th Virginia, killed at Gettysburg]." They went to Gettysburg, to Fredericksburg, and to Richmond "and looked at the many graves of our ancestors there and at the statue of General Mercer . . . I have always regreted that we did not go to Lexington."

Letter, Leonard Wood (written on train en route to Cleveland) to GSP, Jr., April 1, 1920

Dear Colonel Patton: Thank you for your letter of the twenty-second. I can hardly imagine their taking the saber away from the Cavalry. From present indications, there is little or no attention paid to outside recommendations. Things are run not in accord with the views of the majority of those in the service, but quite otherwise. I will do what I can for the saber. Sincerely yours,

This was Patton's last direct contact with Wood, who sought the presidential nomination of the Republican Party that year and came close to getting it. Appointed Governor General of the Philippines by President Harding, Wood remained in the islands until his death in 1927.

Tanks in the Great War, a book by Colonel J. F. C. Fuller, impressed Patton to such an extent that his notes, made from his close and careful reading, covered seven pages typed single-space. The salient points that appealed to him were diverse.

He found it funny but true that some soldiers welcomed the end of the war because they could now get back to *real* soldiering in peacetime, with its spit and polish. To those officers lacking imagination or the warrior frame of mind, war was an aberration. To the dedicated professionals, on the other hand, the main problem of war was how to strike blows against the enemy without receiving them. Patton remarked:

> Gun powder rendered armour carried by men useless but it took from the end of the 12th to the beginning of the 14th century for this fact to perculate. Will it take a similar period to show the futility of unarmoured men against armoured machines? Probably.

Leonardo da Vinci in 1482 had described imaginary covered and invulnerable armed chariots, which forced large armies to retreat, thus allowing infantry to advance in safety and without opposition. "The motive power is not staited [by Leonardo] but it is a clear description of a tank written 350 years before the first apperance of the successful TANK."

When Napoleon was elected to the French Institute, he selected as his subject for the initial paper he delivered "The automobil in war." In October 1914, Swinton proposed "catapilar drawn machines. The Tanks developed from this idea were first used Sept. 15, '16. The british tanks from this date to end of war fought 85 actions."

Tank tactics, Patton wrote,

> may be summarized as "Penetration with security." Due to present machanical defects tanks should be used in Groups not smaller than two. After penetration tanks must widen hole by opening out to one or both flanks. If the defense is in depth reserves of tanks must be used for this opening out further in [the enemy positions].

This was, in essence, the "expanding torrent" concept made popular by B. H. Liddell Hart, and it became the basic tactical principle of German blitzkrieg in World War II.

Still drawing from his reading of Fuller, Patton said that the considerations affecting a battle between tanks were suitable ground, enemy guns, smoke, minor objectives, appropriate departure positions, and surprise. "No well planned tank attack has ever failed. Each has brought in more prisoners of war than the casualties to the attacker."

Staff preparations required for a tank offensive included reconnaissance, movement, secrecy, supply, communications, assembly of forces, tactics and training with infantry, reorganization. The tank staff had to be on the field before and during the action to ascertain and report actual conditions and results. Airplanes and tanks had always to work together for information, protection, and, possibly, supply.

This too became a fundamental part of blitzkrieg warfare.

In World War I,

> The German [antitank] methods tipify lack of forethought. They never imagined the consequences of possible improvements in the type of tank . . . This same lack of imagination is the besetting sin of our army with respect to tanks and means of aiding or combatting them at the present time . . . Slowness of american construction of tanks is shown by the fact the time which it took to get twenty american renaults to France was longer than the time it took from the first drawing of the British Mark I in February 1915 to its apperance in France in August 1916.

As for armored cars — "They can do nothing that a tank cannot do and they cannot do many things a Tank CAN DO."

Yet an armored car was less expensive than a tank, and in the 1920s and 1930s, the U. S. Army would have to make do with armored cars, and Patton would become a vigorous exponent of using armored cars as an adjunct of cavalry action.

In summary, Patton wrote:

> He [Fuller] goes on to elaborate on the use of tanks in what is doubtless a possible but at present impractical extent, because Nations of sufficient wealth and resources to provide such mechanic armies are by the very nature of their wealth those nations [which] are incapable of looking on war in a serious manner and are willing to devote to it only their minimum effort. His ideas as to the use of tanks in small wars are less chimerical but his entire views are extreme and though sound will not be realised in our generation. The lesson to be drawn from his book is the necessity of using our imagi-

nation in an effort to combine mechanical with muscular means of combat. Tanks Gas and Automatic weapons are all in their infancy. In planning their future use we must be guided less by what they have done than by what they reasonably will do. And above all we must remember that the will to win is the basic element of victory and that this will must be DISCIPLINED to be useful. A mechanic[al] army manned by mechanics who were not at the same time soldiers would be a MESS.

Patton was delighted when Summerall wanted a tank company as a demonstration unit to show infantrymen of his 1st Division how tanks worked. Always interested in promoting tank-infantry coordination, Patton personally selected Captain Barnard as the most suitable young officer for the detached service.

Letter, Major General C. P. Summerall to GSP, Jr., April 14, 1920
My dear Patton: I am greatly pleased by the receipt of your letter of April 10th, and I beg to assure you of my deep appreciation of your congratulations upon my permanent appointment [as a major general]. My chief reward lies in the approval and the good will of my old friends, and I especially prize the sentiments that have ever existed between us.
We are extremely glad to have Captain Barnard and his Company, and I hope that they will be happy with us.
Mrs. Summerall joins me in regards to you and Mrs. Patton and the children.
Faithfully yours,

A welcome break in Patton's routine occurred in April when, as a member of an Army team, he went to New York City and took part in a Duelling Sword Competition.

The May issues of the *Infantry Journal* and of the *Cavalry Journal* — the magazines exchanged articles because of a paucity of material being written and offered — carried Patton's article on "Tanks in Future Wars." The ideas were drawn from papers and lectures he had previously prepared, but he was pleased to see them in print, together with his name, pleased to have his thoughts recorded and disseminated throughout the Army for the benefit of the relatively few officers who read professional journals and discussed developments in warfare.

The situation in the country became even more discouraging for serious career officers. Money appropriated by Congress for the military services was scarce and so was public interest. A training exercise held at Camp Meade on May 14 illustrated the Army's difficulties. The mock order of attack, which gave unit objectives and boundaries and provided the other information needed for the maneuver, observed: "NOTE: Due to lack of troops, only [the] first assault line will be indicated by infantry."

As though that was hardly bad enough, a heavy rain almost washed out the practice. Four radios, the Technical Board later reported, "were entirely put out of action, due to the rain storm which came up shortly after the maneuver began, and it was several hours before the apparatus could be dried sufficiently for further operation." Instead of recommending the development of a waterproof radio, one that would work effectively in damp weather, which would be an expensive endeavor, the board contented itself with an expedient and cheaper solution, suggesting that a cover be provided for the tank radio to prevent water that leaked into the tank from short-circuiting the radio.

It was perhaps a sense of discouragement that led Patton to consider seriously whether he ought to leave the Tank Corps. A "Personal Report and Statement of Preferences" he filled out late in April indicated his continuing wish to be the military attaché in England or a student at the School of the Line at Leavenworth, Kansas. Perhaps it was hardly surprising that he wrote: "When returned to Cavalry," he hoped to be assigned, in the following order of preference, to Fort Myer, Monterey, California, or Fort Riley.

Lieutenant Colonel E. G. Beurat of the Inspector General's Department investigated the efficiency of officers at Camp Meade. Patton, he reported, was regarded by his commanding officer as "An efficient officer." Beurat's evaluation: "Efficient; keenly interested in the development of tanks. I consider him average."

Toward the end of May, Patton took seven days of leave and went fishing at Fort Myers, Florida. He needed some time to think, some leisure to ponder the future of the Army and the future of his own career. For things were about to happen that would abruptly change the course of both.

On June 2, Congress passed the National Defense Act of 1920, one of the most important laws in American military history. Among other provisions, the legislation established the Air Service, the Chemical Warfare Service, and the Finance Department as new branches; it abolished the Tank Corps. Tank units and personnel were assigned to the infantry. From now on, tankers would be designated as belonging to the "Infantry (Tanks)." Rockenbach's position as Chief of the Tank Corps was eliminated, and he moved to Camp Meade to become the post commander and de facto chief of a branch of the service that was no longer independent.

The law created several new positions, among them a Chief of Cavalry, who would serve at the War Department as principal adviser on cavalry matters to the General Staff; and a Chief of Infantry.

The act instituted the postwar military reorganization.

Teams of doctors examined all officers on active duty to determine their fitness for retention and promotion. Patton was certified as being physically qualified to hold any grade.

At the end of June, he was discharged as a Colonel in the Tank Corps, National Army; he reverted to his basic Regular Army grade of Captain of Cavalry. Late in August, he would be promoted to major, with rank from July 1, together with 44 other officers, among them his classmates Devers, Baehr, and Philoon.

After the reductions in rank, Rockenbach showed great consideration for Patton. He retained Patton, now a mere captain, in command of the 304th Brigade, while Mitchell, reduced to major, remained in command of the 305th Brigade. What Rockenbach did was to assign the majors to his own headquarters or to Mitchell. Otherwise, that is, if a major had been placed in Patton's brigade, he would have outranked Patton and would have had to receive command of the unit. Therefore, Rockenbach assigned Majors R. L. Collins, D. C. T. Grubbs, and C. P. Chancler to his own General Tank Corps Headquarters; and Major Daniel W. Colhoun to Mitchell's brigade. The result was that Rockenbach, a colonel, had 3 majors, 3 captains, and 2 first lieutenants in his headquarters; the 305th Brigade had 2 majors, 7 captains (among them Eisenhower), and 12 lieutenants; the 304th, headed by Patton, had 9 captains (including Benson and Floyd L. Parks) and 16 lieutenants. The arrangement was a thoughtful kindness on the part of Rockenbach.

Detailed to a board meeting at Camp Meade to determine the temporary officers to be retained on active duty and those to be released, Patton informed Pershing, who was now in Washington, that it was "Hard and nasty work especially as I am recorder and the president of the board is an old man who has been dead for years." His main reason for writing was to congratulate Pershing on the "fact that so many of your old men [like Summerall, Harbord, and Conner] have been definately recognised [by promotions]. It certainly is fine." Patton was living at Camp Meade, which he liked better than staying in Washington. Beatrice and the children were in California for the summer. Would Pershing care to come out some day and ride over the lovely Maryland countryside with Patton?

Letter, Pershing to GSP, Jr., August 3, 1920

My dear Patton: I have your very kind letter of July 16th and am glad that the list of promotions meets with the approval of the Army in general, which I think is really the fact — although many of the older set naturally feel disgruntled. However, there is little doubt that in time all those who deserve promotion will be recognized.

Nothing would give me more pleasure than to go to Camp Meade and have a days trip somewhere out in the country with a Troop of Cavalry, or a ride over the hills in that vicinity . . . but I am very busy myself with various Boards and have been held down to the vicinity of Washington almost all summer.

With very many thanks for your letter, and with affectionate regards to Beatrice and the children, I remain, as always, Sincerely yours,

Early in August Patton suggested to Rockenbach that he try to secure a unit citation for the 304th Tank Brigade for its wartime service. This award would honor all who had served in combat.

Having thereby symbolically discharged his debt to his brigade and his men, Patton wrote a formal letter through channels to the Adjutant General on August 15. He asked to be relieved as soon as possible from his present assignment with tanks and returned to duty with the cavalry. He gave the following reasons 1) The Tank Corps was now part of the infantry, and Patton had no wish to transfer to that branch. 2) Having wanted to return to the cavalry as early as September 1919, he had refrained from applying for a transfer because the 304th Tank Brigade had been in the process of reorganization, and he had believed it his duty to assist; since then, the brigade had been built up by recruitment from one company to its full strength of thirteen companies, and therefore his obligation was complete. 3) He had been with the Tank Corps nearly three years; to remain longer, he believed, would benefit the tankers little and himself less, for he would lose all touch with the cavalry. If he could be useful to the tankers because of his experience in the war, he would be happy to act as an instructor delivering courses of lectures and directing or judging tank demonstrations — as a matter of fact, he would like very much to do so.

. . .

What really motivated his desire to return to the cavalry? The niggardly funds appropriated by Congress for the Army in general and for tank development in particular disturbed him. The War Department decision to put the Tank Corps under the infantry upset him.

Was his resentment on both counts evidence that he was divesting himself of the idea that tanks had to be tied to infantrymen? Or was he concerned because he knew relatively few infantrymen, particularly those who were important and could help him advance in his career? Perhaps he felt that cavalrymen would have better chances for promotion and advancement as soon as Pershing became Army Chief of Staff, a post he would assume in 1921.

There was something else. The Tank Corps loss of its independent status negated Patton's standing as one of the few high-ranking and experienced tank officers who could reasonably hope for promotion into the general officer ranks. Disappointed, he preferred to go "home" to the cavalry, where he could play polo, participate in horse shows, and hunt. Being a cavalry officer would facilitate these pursuits in a way that service with the infantry would not, for cavalrymen were expected to be prominent horsemen.

Furthermore, he and Beatrice liked Washington, nearby Fort Myer was a cavalry post, and they knew enough leading people in the capital to have a fine and exciting social life.

To a large extent Patton was intuitively inclined toward the cavalry. The tanks were far from being reliable machines. Until they were perfected, they would remain relatively fragile mechanisms, unable to take to the field to fight anywhere, any time, and under any conditions.

In contrast, horses could go everywhere. Unrestricted by terrain and weather, they were dependable The cavalry was mobile. And he expected the next war to take place in primitive areas of the world, where the absence of roads, while hampering tanks, would restore the cavalry to importance. In particular he kept anticipating an outbreak of hostilities with Mexico, perhaps because he had first enjoyed combat and glory there.

In the tanks, a man was tied to engines and gasoline and oil, to masses of troops and machines, to careful coordination, planning, and protective maintenance — as in France. In the cavalry, a man on horseback was an individual, relatively free, able to charge recklessly and mordantly while waving a saber — as in Mexico.

If Patton had hoped that the tanks might be transferred to the cavalry instead of to the infantry, he had only himself to blame. To a large extent, his papers and lectures had helped persuade the Army that the proper role of tanks was as auxiliaries to assist the infantry. Although the field artillery played that role, it managed to retain its independent status as a separate branch of the service. In contrast, the tanks were new; they lacked the traditions that might have argued successfully for independent status.

Absorbed into the infantry, the tanks were there regarded as "armored infantry" and as "accompanying guns." And thus they tended to lose their mobility. Had they instead gone to the cavalry, they might have developed the mobility that had characterized Patton's thinking in the World War and that would characterize the German blitzkrieg.

Had the tanks been shifted to the cavalry, Patton might well have remained a tanker. Instead, like most cavalrymen, he became tied to the horse and associated with those who were obsessed by the horse cavalry.

To Patton's request for transfer to the cavalry, Rockenbach added his approval on the first indorsement. He recommended that the change take place on October 1. The letter traveled to the Adjutant General, and from that office went to the Chief of Cavalry, who also approved the transfer. His executive officer consulted with the Chief of Infantry, who had no objection to Patton's transfer from the infantry (Tanks). The Adjutant General then issued orders on September 4, 1920, assigning Patton to the 3d Cavalry at Fort Myer.

Letter, GSP, Jr., to Quartermaster General, September 15, 1920
When I left the Mounted Service School, Ft. Riley Kan. in 1915, I

expected to go to the Philippines and shipped some of my furnature at my own expense to Topeka Kan. for storage. It is still there.

After returning from Mexico I was on duty at Camp Stewart Tex. While on Leave from that station I received telegraphic orders about May 18, 1917 to Report to Gen. Pershing for duty — Copy of telegram is lost. I accompanied him to europe and my wife shipped my furnature from El Paso to my fathers home at San Gabriel California on private B.L.

Since returning to the U.S. in March 1919 I have been on duty in the field and have had no property shipped.

I am now ordered for duty to Fort Myer Va. . . .

Request authority to have furniture etc weighing about 4500 lbs shipped on Government B.L. From Pasadena California to Ft. Myer Va. And for a shipment of similar property to the weight of about 2500 lbs shipped on Government B.L. from Topeka Kansas to Fort Myer Va.

Should the weights of these shipments exceed my allowance of 7200 Lbs I will pay the difference.

Letter, GSP, Jr., to Aunt Nannie, September 19, 1920

We started to get ready to move yesterday and expect to be moved by the second or third [of October] depending on when I get back from the Bryn Mawr Horseshow which starts on the 29 and lasts till the second.

We will probably have the same house we had as lieutenants. It is not as large as we could wish but will have to do.

Becoming interested in whether tanks could be used to advantage in street fighting, particularly in Latin American cities, Patton wrote:

Owing to the peculiar conditions and general lack of preparedness which exist in Latin-American countries, it will be possible in the use of light tanks to have them depart from the general principle of avoiding main streets because anti-tank cannon and tank traps will probably not be found. Hence, unless Intelligence reports clearly point to the presence of the above named tank defences, the tanks should co-operate with the Infantry Street and Roof Detachments.

His methodology for operating on broad and narrow streets, as well as "In the attack of churches and public buildings surrounded by plazas," was concerned only with fulfilling the mission; it paid no attention to the possible destruction of lives and property. He advised:

You will find that in Guerrilla warfare or riots that the average street-fighting does not force you to contend with much real military preparation or Artillery . . . [Tanks were to] form a bulwark for the Infantry advance and shield the Infantry from hostile fire from the front.

Letter, GSP, Jr., to Pershing, September 24, 1920

I trust that you will excuse the personal vanity which emboldens me to intrude this upon your valuable time. But as I am one of the few officers who has ever registered hits on a human target I am very anxious to have that fact on my record.

In short, he would consider it a great honor to have a statement from Pershing placed in his official file on the Rubio affair in Mexico. Would Pershing please write to the Adjutant General? To stimulate Pershing's memory, Patton sent an account of the Rubio ranch action. He said that it came from his diary, but it was a recapitulation of his letters to his father and to Beatrice at the time.

There are quite a few references to me in the above but then it was my diary. I trust that after the Great War you will not consider me too childish in mentioning this matter to you.

I trust that when I get to Fort Myer I shall be able to see you and perhaps take you for a ride [on horseback].

Pershing was nice enough to have an aide look up his own report of the fight. He then sent a quoted paragraph for inclusion in Patton's file. This formed the basis for the award, which Patton later received, of the Silver Star decoration.

Letter, GSP, Jr., to Rockenbach, September 28, 1920

My dear General: It is rather hard to tell you goodbye and express to you my sincere appreciation of your long suffering and great kindness to me during the past three years. While serving under you I have had the most vivid and interesting experiences of my life and shall always remember your considerate treatment of me and my various vageries.

I believe I have learned much of value and what ever I have learned has been due to the latitude and councils and example you have given me.

I hope to continue along the lines I have learned from you. Please believe that I shall ever remain most grateful to you for the oppertunities you have [give]n me and for the support you have ever been ready to tender.

With best wishes to you and the Tank Corps, I am

Affectionately,

GSP, Jr., Parting Speech to 304th Brigade, September 28, 1920

I could not deny myself this oppertunity of seeing you all once more, for though you probably think me the meanest man in the world I assure you that you exagurate. I have a great pride and sincere affection for the brigade and the men and officers composing it. Neither now nor at any other time have I thought it necessary to apologize for my acts since what ever I have done has been the result of an honest effort to perform my duty as I saw it. When I have cussed out or corrected any of you, men or officers it has been because according to my lights you were wrong, but I have never remembered it against you. I have never asked any of you to Brace more, work more, or fight more, than I have been willing to do my self; with the result that in keeping up to you in France I had to get shot. You have always responded and consequently where ever the brigade or any part of it has served it has been an example of discipline, courage and efficiency. In consequence of the splendid work of the Brigade in France I was given the Distinguished Service Medal, but be sure that I realise it was the Brigade not I who won it. For the future you have only to mould your conduct on the past. If you do so, and I am sure you will, the members of the Brigade, dead or departed will have nothing more to ask and our pride at having been of you will ever increase. God bless the 304th Brigade.

Letter, Beatrice to Aunt Nannie, September 29, 1920

Your idea about moving to Washington is o.k. We expect to be there two years & I wish any or all of you w'd come . . .

They have some fine pictures of G's last review here. I am having prints made for you all. It was very impressive; &, on the night of the 27th there was a big hop for Col. Mitchell & us. The 305 Brigade officers gave Col. M. a silver vase . . . & the adjutant of our Brigade made a speech saying that G. & I were to have a present, delivered at Myer on Nov. 11th! & then gave me a huge bunch of roses!! We nearly died. Also, I had to lead the grand march with Gen. Rockenbach!!

Next day, G. assembled all his men — 700 — and made a very touching farewell speech. (He will send you a copy.) Then the headquarters Sgt. Maj. & 2 others advanced and presented me with a beautiful cup. About a foot high, solid & very heavy. On one side was etched a light tank. On the other was "To Colonel & Mrs. George S. Patton, Jr. from the enlisted personnel of the 304th Brigade." I made a little speech, & we all cried some, especially G & me & the Sgt. Major. . . . It was very touching.

This A.M. I went to the hospital & thanked all the sick men for their share in the cup . . . They certainly do appreciate G. . . .

G. went to Philadelphia last night & I certainly am glad. I hope he'll have lots of fun & we'll be all settled when he lands [in Washington] Sunday. If he had to move us all up, after the emotional strain he's been under this last week I w'd be sorry. The horse-show [in Philadelphia] seems heaven-sent. And I don't even have to clean the house, so many are helping us. Everyone wants to help. And bags of apples sweet potatoes & pears & eggs & chickens are pouring in . . . to go on the truck tomorrow.

It was quite a wrench for Patton to authorize the publication of General Order 9, Headquarters 304th Brigade, Tank Corps, Franklin Cantonment, Camp Meade, September 30, 1920, in which he relinquished command of the brigade. To the formal order he added a sentence that was somewhat unconventional. "In leaving the Brigade with which he has been associated since it's existence, his regret at parting is only exceeded by his pride at having commanded such a unit."

CHAPTER 37

Fort Myer Again

"Insist on . . . BOLDNESS . . . THE ENEMY IS AS IG-NORANT AS YOU . . . BE BOLD . . . YOU ARE NOT BEATEN UNTIL YOU ADMIT IT, Hence DON'T . . . The 'Fog of war' works both ways. The enemy is as much in the dark as you are. BE BOLD!!!!! . . . War means fighting — fighting means killing, not digging trenches . . . YOU MUST HAVE A DEFINATE PURPOSE . . . Try to make fenatics of your men. It is the only way to get great sacrefices."

IT TOOK PATTON less than a month to make the transition between tank training and cavalry drill. After returning from the Bryn Mawr horseshow on October 3, 1920, Patton relieved Lieutenant Colonel Harry N. Cootes in command of the 3d Squadron (or Battalion) of the 3d Cavalry, and he and his family moved into quarters #5 at Fort Myer. Three weeks later he was instructing his officers and men on the art of warfare and the practice of soldiering with the same enthusiasm and flair he had demonstrated to his tankers.

His goals were to inculcate respect for standardization and uniformity and to stimulate desire for imagination and initiative among his troops. His program would show careful attention to the progressive feature of Pershing's training in Mexico, an orderly sequence from the smaller to the larger units. His method of imparting knowledge was by example and practice, and he would insist that his officers be clear in their explanations to the men and thorough in their supervision of the exercises.

Patton started with the essentials of platoon combat, the mutual support required between a base of fire and a maneuvering element.

Offensive combat consists of FIRE and MOVEMENT. The purpose of FIRE is to permit MOVEMENT. When a group of a rifle platoon is rushing [forward in the attack] the fire produced by rifles is diminished despite the fact that the portion of the line not rushing should increase its rate of fire. To maintain or augment the intensity of fire at such times the Automatic Rifles should be used in full force. Hence they must not rush at the same time the riflemen rush. They must be in position and firing during rushes . . . [to keep] the enemy's heads down [and] thus facilitate the advance of their comrades . . .

The foregoing applies to an attack against an enemy in line in open country; where the hostile resistence consists of isolated groups or in closed country an automatic rifle may steal forward . . . and by taking the enemy in enfelade [enfilade] may facilitate the advance of the whole line . . . more brilliant and complicated methods cannot be specified but are up to the initiative of the officer on the spot. Mention is made of them here to awaken inventive interest.

He told his officers to "Explain Par[agraph]s. 2 and 4 to the men. I will question some of them to assure myself that this has been done."

Dissatisfied with the appearance of his squadron, Patton specified in detail how personal gear and equipment were to be packed and precisely what items a cavalryman carried.

Having determined the strengths and weaknesses of his unit, he opened a school for his officers and scheduled 22 lectures and lessons for a single month. He delivered 16 himself — on hippology, marches, stable management, parts of the horse, shoeing, orders for the attack, military hygiene, orders for the advance, the rules of land warfare, outposts, riot duty, division attack, and advance and rear guards.

Next followed troop (or company) instruction, including the proper methods of fighting on horseback and dismounted. His exposition on how to make the approach march, how to conduct a reconnaissance, how to select objectives, how to attack, how to deploy and commit the reserve was thorough.

These words to his officers were typical:

Take all the time you want but attend to these details. Read C.D.R. [Cavalry Drill Regulations] Pars. 650 to 670 inc, and Pars. 716 to 735 incl. Also I.D.R. [Infantry Drill Regulations] Provisional 1919. Pars 358 to 360 and 361 to 371 inc. Explain to the men what you are trying to do.

Throughout his training program, Patton avoided blind conformance with the regulations. He insisted always on the thoughtful consideration of problems, each of which was unique and had its own solution. For example:

Now while column of fours may occasionally be used as an approach formation its use will be exceptional because if Cavalry has gained, as it should have, a suitable position before dismounting it will be too near the enemy to justify column of fours . . .

Since the duty of the cavalry is to retain mobility by means of a quick decision and since conversely its mobility should enable it to select a point of attack where a quick decision is possible, the approach march for cavalry will ordinarily be shortest [shorter] than that for infantry . . .

Of course this is a violation of the principle to avoid normal formations, on the other hand men must have something to go on or they can never improvise an attack.

After discussing "fan wise" formations, "maximum useful density" on the firing line, and other technical matters, he directed his subordinates to "Read the Paragraphs in the manuals referred to above and get the idea in your head. Now apply it" — in exercises and maneuvers.

After the charge assemble the men and explain to them what has been done and why. If you have time repeat problem on way home. If you carry out this exercise slowly and with attention to detail men will learn it in one trial.

During the first three months of 1921, Patton put his squadron through a series of problems and exercises. He invented mock situations, supervised the maneuvers, and criticized the solutions his subordinate officers offered. These theoretical situations — worked out near Merriefield, Dunn Loring, Gallows Road, Annandale Road, Bailey's Crossroads, and Holmes Run — forced his officers, as well as himself, to think about the art of command, to learn the art of war, and to reflect on the art of leadership.

In a game played on January 16:

if things go badly Gen. D. must ride up and rally his men personally. In the event of a panic he should show the greatest resolution and if necessary get killed. If his men should break in the withdrawal which is more than possible Gen. D. SHOULD NOT SURVIVE IT. THERE IS NOTHING MORE PATHETIC AND FUTILE THAN A GENERAL WHO LIVES LONG TO EXPLAIN A DEFEAT.

A problem game a month later, this one on how to prevent or delay the capture of Alexandria, Virginia, involved making certain estimates — of the situation, friendly forces, morale on both sides, the terrain, and alternative courses of action — all of which were preparatory to reaching a decision. According to Patton:

The plan adopted is that of a desperate man and is only justified by desperate conditions and a will to fight. The placing of the guns is particuarly faulty but if they hold out till run over they will enfelade [enfilade] at rifle range any attack on his right which is his weak flank and will give his line the appearance of great length.

Instructions for another:

We must approach the consideration of this problem by the admittance of one unalterable fact and the acceptance of one arbitrary assumption. Troops moving at night are confined to roads.

At the conclusion of his three-month course in tactics, Patton examined his officers. After questioning them on the problems and the exercises, he then presented several supplementary lectures and lessons to correct the deficiencies uncovered by the tests.

Somewhat later, he issued a squadron-training schedule for four consecutive weeks. Its purpose was dual — to comply with training requirements imposed by higher headquarters and to train his junior officers to develop individual initiative. His troop commanders were to turn in weekly reports showing their compliance with the drills specified by Patton and indicating those exercises they had personally devised for the remaining and unallotted time.

Patton's final maneuver, called a tactical ride, set up a theoretical situation in which the Potomac River separated two hostile states at war. Assigning Troop A the task of covering the Ballston–Halls Hill–Chain

Bridge Road against an attack launched by the rest of the squadron proceeding via Upton Hill to the Leesburg Pike, Patton wrote a scenario that
posed problems not covered in the drill regulations. For example, you
meet a civilian in an automobile; what do you do? Stop him? Interrogate
him? Pay no attention to him? The object was to test officers in situations
likely to be met that could be handled only on the basis of alertness,
imagination, and common sense.

∙ ∙ ∙

Colonel W. C. Rivers, the regimental commander of the 3d Cavalry and
Patton's immediate superior, rated Patton at the end of 1920 "below average" in tact, "average" and "above average" in most characteristics, and
"superior" in general value to the Army. Feeling that his evaluation
somehow did less than full justice to Patton's capacities, Rivers added
another category of his own invention, "mental energy," and in that he
graded Patton "superior."

Patton was, according to Rivers,

An officer of more than usual power mental and physical. I estimate him to be of good habits — pleasing personality — has many
attributes of a natural soldier and is much interested in his profession. Good type of officer to have in a command — gets good results
and aids in keeping things on a good general plane of efficiency.
Keen on both athletics and on military work — a desirable and not
too frequent combination — has power and push.

On March 4, 1921, the troops at Fort Myer took part in the Inaugural
Parade. A newspaper photograph showed Patton riding a horse beside
the automobile carrying Presidents Wilson and Harding to the White
House.

Later that month, Rockenbach returned to Patton a manuscript that
Patton and Brett had written on the history of the 304th Tank Brigade.
Rockenbach wanted two additional points incorporated into a revised
narrative. First, it was Rockenbach who had taken Patton around to become acquainted with the British tank school system, not the reverse.
Second, after Patton was wounded, it was Rockenbach who personally
directed Brett's operations.

Your paper illustrates one of the most important considerations to be used in handling soldiers, that is, to keep them thinking they are the whole show, but I think it is an error if the impression is made that the Tank movements were not all carefully planned and given the necessary direction. I think it is quite important to emphasize the fact that, due to throwing everything in that we had and using it to exhaustion, we had to get additional mechanical assistance and from necessity, I was able to get mechanical reinforcement of one motor mechanic company.

In other words, Rockenbach wanted to make sure that his role in the combat employment of tanks was neither slighted nor overlooked in favor of those who commanded the troops on the battlefield.

Mitchell, who had also returned to the cavalry and was assigned to Fort Myer, rated Patton "superior" in equitation, "above average" in all the other categories except tact, which was "average." Patton was "a very well informed, gallant, loyal officer."

Major H. H. Pritchett of the Inspector General's Department made a three-day examination of Fort Myer, and his report carried this observation:

Particularly deserving of commendation was the orderly and clean condition of quarters, store rooms, kitchens, stables and equipment of the troops composing the 3d Cavalry [Squadron], commanded by Major G. S. Patton, Jr.

A notebook Patton maintained in 1921–22 recorded some of his thoughts on warfare. "Success in war," he wrote, "depends upon the Golden Rule of War. Speed-Simplicity-Boldness."

He listed the personal equipment he carried as a cavalryman. On his belt, a pistol, four clips of ammunition, a knife, wire cutter, and first aid pouch. Around his neck his identification tags, a compass, and field glasses. In his right pommel pocket a mirror, "raisor, sharpner, shaving brush, tooth brush, tooth powder, nail brush, match box, hair brush, listerine." In his left pommel pocket long silk drawers, socks, clothes brush, handkerchiefs, flashlight, candle, coffee, salt, "sacerine," saddle soap, sponge. In his dispatch case maps, pencils, map measurer, message book, notebook, Field Service Regulations, Cavalry Drill Regulations, and small camera. In his bedding roll 1 shirt, 1 blouse, 1 sweater, 1 pair of breeches, 1 pair of long silk drawers, 1 wool undershirt, 1 bath towel, 1 sleeping bag, 1 extra blanket, 1 small pillow, 1 canvas bucket, 1 rubber basin, 2 shoe laces, 1 pair of shoes, 1 pair of leggings, 1 "housewife" (probably a sewing kit), handkerchiefs, hay fever "medicin, asparin, laxatives, toilet paper, stamped envelopes, writing paper, large flash light, extra battery, army regulations, manual [of] courts martial, 1 flask brandy." In his pockets a knife with can opener and hoof pick, a mechanical pencil and fountain pen, toilet paper, "$100 preferably gold." On his right wrist a whistle. On his left wrist a watch.

He wrote instructions to himself:

> Insist on: Maximum distances; BOLDNESS; Prompt and accurate reports. Speed is more important than the lives of the [men at the] point. THE ENEMY IS AS IGNORANT AS YOU. Do not halt on the near side of a river below a hight . . . You must not be delayed by blufs. Bluf your self . . . BE BOLD. Camps unless screened by trees are sure to be noted by enemy airplanes. They will then be bommed. BILLITS for this reason are preferable. . . . YOU ARE NOT BEATEN UNTIL YOU ADMIT IT, Hence DON'T . . . The "Fog of war" works both ways. The enemy is as much in the dark as you are. BE BOLD!!!!! . . . War means fighting — fighting means killing, not digging trenches . . . YOU MUST HAVE A DEFINATE PURPOSE . . . "THE ROAD TO THE BAYONET IS PAVED BY FIRE SUPERIORITY" Patton. . . . Remember that the information you get is for instant use not for history. . . . Try to make fenatics of your men. It is the only way to get great sacrefices. . . . OFFICERS MUST BE MADE TO CARE for their men. That is the sole Duty of All Officers.

Rivers judged Patton in June 1921 as "superior" and "above average." Patton was "physically and mentally a powerful officer: good habits and pleasing personality: a superior type of officer. Excellent both on mental and physical side of an officer's development; keenly interested in riding and polo, but also progressive in tactics and in studies."

Patton played on an Army team that participated in the polo tournament at Meadowbrook, Long Island, that summer. He was one of nine officers authorized to participate in the American Junior Polo Championship Tournament at Philadelphia. The performance of the Army team was disappointing.

In order to improve the caliber of the Army's polo, the players were solicited for suggestions that might make the Army a contender for the championships next year.

Letter, GSP, Jr. to Colonel J. R. Lindsey, October 10, 1921, subject: Polo

I have played polo in a humble sort of way since the Spring of 1905 when I began it at the Military Academy. Due to good luck I have usually been on the first team and have always had to work hard to stay on it. Still as a result of the above I had come to entertain the belief that I knew something of Polo.

But subsequent to my brief acquaintance with REAL Polo my golden illusions have been shattered and I KNOW — not think — that I know nothing of Polo.

Admitting than that I am probably the only polo "ATTEMPTER" in the Army who has grasped none of the following self evident truths I yet take the liberty of recounting them to you with the belief or perhaps hope that you may see fit to call them to the attention of others who while they probably think they already know them have none the less never in my observation practised any of them.

Before starting however, I desire to place my self on record as one who recounts the exploits of others and in no way poses as a performer of similar merit.

RIDING OFF. There is a wide spread falicy among us that . . . we [Army officers who play polo] are rough. Compared to good players we are as lambs to raging lions . . .

Instead of so maneuvering as to come into a man at an angle sufficient to give him a bump which will loosen his fillings we come up parallel and try to "Two Track" him off the ball . . .

We do not start at top speed, whip and spur, to catch the loose man, unless he is easily caught. We simply follow him trusting that an ever merciful God will cause him to miss; unfortunately God is seldom on the job . . .

SPEED. In polo we never realize what a football coach once told us: "You don't have to hurry, you have to run like hell" . . .

STARTING . . . We must learn to start at full speed. It will be objected that **our horses** are not up to this. True they usually are not because we **do not** require it of them . . .

DISCIPLINE. Strange as it seems the average Army team has less discipline than the average good civilian team . . .

MYSELF. I have never done correctly one of the things for which I criticise others. I just have hopes.

The remedy for the above is fast polo on good fields by as large a number of Army players as possible, drawn from as many sources and localities as possible . . . We have the ponies now . . . We have the physique. We have in undeveloped form the mental quickness. To date we have not the practice.

Next summer two or three teams with substitutes, men and horses, should be sent to Meadowbrook, put in camp and placed under training conditions as to early hours and prompt attendance. In addition to polo ability the men selected should be responsible and earnest. For the simple purpose of winning the Junior next year one team would probably be all who should compete. But from the broader and more important standpoint of developing polo and more teams that enter, the better for the Army.

Horse shows occupied much of Patton's time. In September he rode at Syracuse, in November in Madison Square Garden, New York. He won cups and ribbons. He also fell with his mount, injured his hip, and was forced to withdraw from the competition.

The rotogravure section of a New York newspaper showed "A Who's Who in the Kingdom of the Horse Scene at the Annual National Horse Show Breakfast" held at the Hotel Biltmore. Gathered about a horseshoe-shaped table and a miniature tanbark ring was "Practically Everybody Who is Anybody in the Exhibition of Horse Flesh in the United States." Patton was there.

A letter from Beatrice informed Pershing that the Pattons were busy with horse shows and "collecting cups."

The Pattons attended — he was on duty — and were moved by the ceremonies on November 11 for the Unknown Soldier, whose tomb was established at the amphitheater in the Arlington National Cemetery.

Letter, Chief of Cavalry to Commanding Officer, 3d Squadron, 3d Cavalry, November 18, 1921, subject: Appearance of Command at Ceremonies

. . . noted with appreciation the excellent reports concerning the

appearance and conduct of your command during the ceremonies incident to the Burial of the Unknown Soldier at Arlington and the
meeting of the Limitation of Armaments Conference.

*Letter, Brigadier General H. H. Bandholtz, Commanding General,
Headquarters District of Washington, to Commanding Officer, 3d
Squadron, 3d Cavalry, November 14, 1921*

. . . appearance and marching of the third Squadron, 3d Cavalry,
under your command on November 9th and 11th, 1921, were in every
respect most satisfactory . . . I am highly pleased with their snap
and military bearing, and that I have received many favorable comments from officers on the appearance of the men, horses, and equipment.

Rivers indorsed both letters and transmitted them to Patton with his
own commendation.

GSP, Jr., Lecture, "The Cavalryman," 1921

[The superior cavalry officer had to] possess a combination of
qualities not often found in one individual.

He must have a passion — not simply a likeing — for horses, for
nothing short of an absorbing passion can make him take the necessary interest in his mount . . .

He must be a veterinarian in theory and practice; a farrier and a
horseshoer better than any man in his troop, a stable sergeant and
horse trainer, a saddler. Above all he must possess a sense of obligation to his mount, which, with the whip of a remorseless conscience
makes him — him personally — seek the welfare of his horses above
his own.

No one acquires these qualities at teas or card parties, or by slapping his leg with his whip.

Such knowledge can only be acquired by reading books on horse
diseases, on horse management, on conditioning and training. By
association with horsemen of all sorts and conditions wherever
met . . .

But . . . he is neither a stable sergeant, nor a horseshoer, nor a
veterinarian; such arts are but means. The end is to become a cavalry officer who will be a success in war.

. . . why?

Because success in war depends on getting to the right place at the right time . . . Nearly all the remediable failures of the world result from being LATE.

. . . affection for the horse; tenacity of purpose; a studious mind; a feeling of obligation and a sense of time . . .

A thorough knowledge of war by reading histories, lives of cavalry men, by the study of the tactics of his arm and by the constant working of problems . . .

He must train himself into the possession of a GAMBLER'S Courage.

. . . the successful cavalryman must educate himself to say "CHARGE." I say educate himself, for the man is not born who can say it out of hand . . .

Civilization has affected us; we abhor personal encounter. Many a man will risk his life, with an easy mind, in a burning house who recoils from having his face punched. We have been taught to restrain our emotions, to look upon anger as low, until many of us have never experienced the God sent ecstasy of unbridled wrath. We have never felt our eyes screw up, our temples throb and had the red mist gather in our sight.

And we expect that a man . . . shall, in an instant, the twinkling of an eye, direct [divest] himself of all restraint of all caution and hurl himself on the enemy, a frenzied beast, lusting to probe his foeman's guts with three feet of steel or shatter his brains with a bullet. Gentlemen, it cannot be done — not without mental practice . . .

Therefore, you must school yourself to savagry. You must imagine how it will feel when your sword hilt crashes into the breast bone of your enemy. You must picture the wild exaltation of the mounted charge when the lips draw back in a snarl and the voice cracks with passion . . .

When you have acquired the ability to develop on necessity, momentary and calculated savagry, you can keep your twentieth century clarity of vision with which to calculate the chances of whether to charge or fight on foot, and having decided on the former, the magic word will transform you temporarily into a frenzied brute . . .

To sum up then, you must be: a horse master; a scholar; a high minded gentleman; a cold blooded hero; a hot blooded savage. At one and the same time you must be a wise man and a fool. You must not get fat or mentally old, and you must be a personal LEADER.

A paper entitled "Tactical Tendencies," dated November 26, 1921, stated a significant point in Patton's thought, his belief in the inherent superiority of tactics over strategy.

. . . while Strategy needs occupy the minds only of the more exalted of the stellar officers; tactics is the daily lot of all. Splendid strategy may be made abortive by poor tactics, while good tactics may retrieve the most blundering strategy.

Tactical officers had little choice in selecting their forces, but they would, in time of war, be responsible for using them. Predominant force of the right sort applied in the correct way at the proper place at the right time was the basis of all military success. "A mistake of yards or minutes . . . may blight our career and butcher our men."

While I do not hold with those who consider the World War as the sealed pattern of all future efforts to maintain peace, it is nevertheless, our most recent source of information, and the tactical tendencies shown by its last phases will most certainly color to a considerable degree our initial efforts in the next war.

As soon as the first battle of the Marne was won, the World War became a special case, due principally, in my opinion, to two reasons.

Fixed flanks which prevented maneuver; and the splendid rail and road [system] on both sides which permitted a very heavy concentration of men and a relatively easy ammunition supply. Without these good roads and short hauls it would have been impossible to have fed and supplied the vast armies and the war would have taken a different course . . .

The restricted area, long deadlock, and vast resources, permitted the employment of masses of guns and ammunition which probably during our life time cannot be duplicated, certainly not in any other theater of operations. The great results apparent and real accomplished by these guns has so impressed the majority of people that they talk of future wars as Gun wars. To me, all that is necessary to dispel such dreams, or at least limit their sites to western Europe, is a ten mile drive along country roads in any state of the Union except perhaps a favored half dozen along the coasts.

Tactics then based on a crushing artillery are impossible except in one place [Western Europe]. But even where roads permit its use in mass, the effect of artillery alone is negative, so far as offensive victory is concerned . . . all the artillery ever built cannot defeat an enemy unaided . . . Little as it may please our self love to admit it [in the Cavalry], the "Dough Boy" wins the battle. Hence, if we aspire to high command we must know his tactics.

The Guns are the greatest auxiliary — but only that . . .

Another feature resulting from the war and which also has left its mark is the evolution of the SPECIALIST.

His birth is the result of an unholy union between trench warfare and quick training . . .

Our own men, thanks to the genius of General Pershing, were less troubled by the specialist disease . . . but due to lack of time many of ours were not and could not have been well rounded open war soldiers . . .

The outstanding Tactical features of all these great battles [in 1918] were First, Open War methods, and second, Surprise made possible by secrecy and deception. Notice that all three of these features are as old as war . . .

Yet even with the locking of armies in the west and the total absence of flanks, there were chances for cavalry . . .

In Russia and under Allenby, Cavalry was as important as ever in its history . . .

A general survey of the Tactical tendencies at the close of the World War seems to me to point to greater and not lessened usefulness and importance for Cavalry.

The necessity, due to air observation, for more marches of concentration being made at night adds vastly to the destructive power of the mounted man, for charges with the saber or pistol or surprise fire by machine rifles will be terribly effective and most difficult to prevent.

The importance of airplanes in war was bound to increase, and consequently, wooded country was bound to become the best terrain for cavalry action, as well as for the action of infantry. Thus, cavalry tactics would probably be one of the following: delaying or harassing action against infantry; attacks against flanks or thinly held sectors; actions against enemy cavalry, "ALWAYS OFFENSIVE" — "the cavalry man who dismounts in the face of a mounted opponent gives his birthright for a mess of potage"; action against enemy lines of communication; against strong positions where cover or obstacles prevented maneuver.

The charge itself is simply the blind stampede of furious and exhausted men initiated on the spot by a few brave spirits who start going and are followed pell mell by the rest. And unless the enemy is so situated that he cannot get away he departs before the Bayonets ever reach him. At least that is how I have pictured it, how I have heard it described, how I once saw it enacted by about twenty Americans against a group of machine guns and how it felt when I was in one — which failed to arrive as all were hit . . .

The Bayonet Charge and the Saber Charge are the highest physical demonstrations of moral victory. The fierce frenzy of hate and determination flashing from bloodshot eyes squinting behind the glittering steel is what wins. Get as close as you can to the objective, unseen or helped by covering fire and then CHARGE in line in column or in mass it makes no difference.

At the end of 1921, Rivers judged Patton "superior" as a squadron commander, "above average" in field duties, and "average" in tact. In addition to being a "loyal type," Patton was

An officer of superior mental and physical qualities, [a] high class man devoted to his profession. Very capable all round man; while he is known as an exceptional horseman and swordsman he is also keen on military studies and keeps well abreast of the times by intelligent industry. Studious man fond of study and reading; yet Major Patton can take a horse, or a saber, or a rifle, or a pistol and equal or surpass any man — officer or N.C.O. or [enlisted] man — in his squadron with either or all.

General Bandholtz, the District of Columbia military commander, added his indorsement: "I concur in above report. An unusually accomplished and capable officer."

Letter, GSP, Jr., to the Chief of Cavalry, subject: Machine Rifle Pack, January 22, 1922

I have the honor to inclose a description and pictures of an improvised Pack for the Machine Rifle. So far as I know no such pack exists. The one submitted is cheap and easily made and might be of use to the service.

While at the New York Horse Show I talked with Major A. R.

Chaffee and he asked me to send him some description of this pack which I had described to him. I am inclosing three copies and request that if the idea of the Pack meets with your approval your office send Major Chaffee one set of Pictures with description as it seems to me such information should first pass through your hands.

Col. W. C. Rivers has often examined the pack and has authorized its use in this Squadron of his regiment as an experiment.

I have two additional sets of Pictures should you desire them for the Cavalry Journal or the Cavalry School.

Automatic Rifle Carrier, Improvised.

Since each Troop of Cavalry is now supplied with four Automatic Rifles, and has a separate Platoon designated to use them, some method of carrying these weapons is necessary.

Up to the Present Time no Ordnance Pack for this purpose has been issued, hence the following improvised Pack has been designed.

About a year ago one such pack, and one similar, except with more complicated ammunition Packs was constructed at Fort Myer, Va. These two Packs were given a test of daily use at drill on the same horses for a period of three months, no sore backs resulted. As a result of this test the troops of the 2nd Sqdn., 3rd Cavalry, at Fort Myer, Va., are now equipped with four such packs each.

The cost of construction of the packs is *nothing* as they are made of expendable issue articles throughout, except the iron straps forming the forks, the iron for this purpose was "SECURED" free of cost. The saddles used are not hurt in any way.

. . . any average troop saddler and horseshoer can make the packs, at least they were so made at this post.

It is not claimed that the pack is perfect . . . Above all they COST NOTHING . . .

This carrier was designed by Major Patton, Sqdn. Sgt. Maj. Negus and 1st Sgt. McCormick, all Third Cavalry.

On January 26 and 27, Patton suffered a temporary shock and cardiac weakness from an allergic reaction — probably from eating shellfish. The doctors called it a "protein sensitization manifested by swelling of loose areolar tissue of face and of mucous membranes of mouth and respiratory passages." He was puffed up and had difficulty breathing, but the condition soon passed.

Although he was still shaky, he worked throughout the following night of January 28, when the Knickerbocker Theater disaster occurred.

More than two feet of snow had fallen on Washington, and at 9 P.M. that Saturday, the overburdened roof of the Knickerbocker movie house gave way and fell on the audience, killing nearly one hundred persons and injuring many more. Pershing came to the scene of the catastrophe about an hour later and, seeing the urgent need of help, telephoned General Bandholtz and directed him to order out all available troops. Soldiers, sailors, airmen, and marines came promptly from Fort Myer, the Washington Barracks, Bolling Field, the Navy Yard, and elsewhere to assist the police and firemen in clearing the debris and removing the dead and the injured.

Letter, Brigadier General H. H. Bandholtz to GSP, Jr., January 31, 1922

It affords me great pleasure to send this letter of appreciation of your highly efficient services during the rescue work following the Knickerbocker Theater disaster. All reports indicate that the work of yourself and of the officers and men under your command, was of the highest order, and that without it many of the injured would have died. It is the cause of much gratification to me, as it must be to you, to feel that the Army, in such a disaster, carried out the best traditions of the service.

1st Indorsement, February 2, 1922

Transmitted with the commendation of the post commander, Rivers.

Patton sent Pershing a book entitled *The Desert Mounted Corps* because it reminded him "of you and your methods in Mexico and France. It is the greatest military book I have ever read and believe should be a text book at Riley." He had marked parts of the book for Pershing, especially "all the thirty three Mounted Charges with the SABER." Mailing, he said, a great cavalry book to a great cavalryman,

I am also impelled by the desire to emphasize the importance of CAVALRY; for western Europe is very small and in all the rest of the world there will be fine chance, to stick the enemy from the horse.

Letter, Pershing to GSP, Jr., February 14, 1922

My dear Major Patton: . . . I heartily agree with you that it is a very interesting book. It especially appeals to those of us who have learned by experience that the saber is a valuable part of cavalry equipment.

Letter, GSP, Jr., to Beatrice, April 16, 1922

Darling Beat: I went to the Cat & the Canary [a play] with May and Dick, it was fine and I enjoyed it very much. The people were very much keyed up and a little girl in front of me screamed several times.

I . . . went to the tank corps where I had a very dull time. All they want to do is to talk of their passed life which is far from exciting.

I hid the [Easter] eggs down in the gulley. B found hers and put them in a pile while she went for a basket. Tank [the dog] found the pile and took a good "hark" on it. So she fed him the eggs.

I saw Mrs. Harbord and she said she was very sorry you had to go [Beatrice went abroad because her sister Kay was ill] . . .

You behaved fine [when she left] and I never saw you look prettier.

Patton played his first polo game of the season at Fort Myer. He informed Mrs. Charles Dawes, wife of the future vice president, who had asked Beatrice to lunch, of Beatrice's absence. The children went to the egg roll at the White House but there was such a crowd they all came away at once. "I escort Jofre [Marshal Joffre] on Wednesday so will have to put up a good show."

Letter, General H. A. Smith (Commandant, Army War College, Washington) to GSP, Jr., May 11, 1922

I hope with you that in the next war we may again serve together. If I could have had a few more officers like you in France, the schools at Langres would have been much more of a success.

Letter, GSP, Jr., to Beatrice, May 15, 1922

Darling Beat: I had a better day to day getting three ribbons and a cup.

Ball Room got second in Local Saddle horses being beaten by that same black mare that beat him last winter.

In the military jumping eight 4 foot jump both Allahmande and Dragon went perfectly clean.

Allahmande made a really wonderful performance. He changed

his gate [gait] the whole way and took every jump in his stride. Several people left the stand to congratulate he and I.

Dragon went almost as well. He got too close to the wall but got over it. I lost in the polo class . . . Still I feel less depressed. I think I put up a very fine ride.

I am well, hope Kay is better

I love you.

Commendation [by Inspector General's Office, July 19, 1922]
Major George S. Patton, Jr., 3rd Cavalry, is to be commended for the excellent condition of equipment, fine appearance of men and animals, and cleanliness and orderliness of Barracks and stables.

That summer Patton was one of eight officers, together with enlisted personnel, mounts, and equipment, ordered to Mitchel Field, New York, to train with an Army team for the Junior Championship Polo Tournament to be held at Narragansett Pier in August. In charge of the group was Major C. L. Scott, who would command the 2d Armored Division in the opening years of World War II.

Letter, GSP, Jr. to Beatrice, July 4, 1922
I have been dining and lunching with Belmonts, Harrimans, Penn Smiths, Stoddards, Brice Wings, etc to a great extent. These are the nicest very rich people I have ever seen. Their houses are very simple and they drive Fords and Dodges with out chauffeurs. All the women do something to their hair to keep it from getting gray. Other wise they don't make up except their lips . . .

I have gotten nice and thin and only weigh 165 in my polo clothes. But I am perfectly well.

Letter, GSP, Jr., to Beatrice, July 5, 1922
Booker [Pershing's orderly in Mexico and France, now working for the Pattons] told me with great pride that he had sent you an account of Newman's death. I had not intended you to see it. The fact that a man is now and then killed at polo makes it no more dangerous. Further the accidents always happen in the slow games with the bad ponies. I am playing in fast games on splendid ponies so don't worry.

Letter, GSP, Jr., to Beatrice, July 7, 1922
I hope I put up a fair game and am not self conscious. I will hope for the best any way.

I think it is perfectly certain that I will not go to Riley until December.

Letter, GSP, Jr., to Beatrice, July 24, 1922

It was fine practice to play with or against the greatest Players in the world. I got cussed less often than I had feared.

Letter, GSP, Jr., to Beatrice, July 28, 1922

I mailed your letter to Mrs. Newman. I am glad you have so much sense about Polo. I am being very careful.

Letter, GSP, Jr. (from Washington), to Beatrice, July 30, 1922

Every thing was so nice and the post so pretty and green that I realy felt most depressed at the thought of having to leave in January. I think we are established better here than any where we have ever been and I have enjoyed it very much.

G. S. Patton, Paper, "Polo in the Army," autumn 1922

In retrospect it seems a far cry from polo as we first knew it on the ten dollar ponies and skinned fields of the western garrisons to the polo of the Army Team at Point Judith which won the Junior Championship in 1922.

. . . There is little or no similarity in American Polo opportunities and that obtained in the British Army with whom we are so often disparagingly compared.

The vast distances which separate our posts make inter-regimental matches difficult or impossible. The constant changes of personnel in these same regiments prevents the development of teams of men used to one another's play . . . Further the majority of our mounted troops are of necessity stationed far from the centers where good civilian polo is played and hence we lack high class competition.

The above drawbacks are indigenous and cannot be overcome . . . But there are also other facts which have retarded our development . . .

Most of our officers do not take the game seriously . . .

Now from the standpoint of the Army officer, polo is not simply a game; it is a vital professional asset . . . it is the nearest approach to mounted combat which can be secured in peace . . .

Further there are constant and real physical hazards in polo and talk as we will of the necessity for cold judgment in combat it is none

the less a fact that no man can stay cool in battle unless he is habituated to the exhilerating sense of physical peril. No sport save possibly hunting and football is so good a school in this respect as polo.

War also demands quick decision while engaged in rapid movement under the disconcerting influence of profuse perspiration resulting from vigorous exercise. Such practice is not acquired behind
the steering wheel, at golf or while riding at a walk.

. . . The officer who . . . trains and conditions his horses acquires
more knowledge of present and future value to his Government
through the actual practice of polo than from the study of a hundred
easily forgotten treateses on horse management.

An officer's efficiency is measured by his activity and as he is an
investment by his useful life . . .

The War Department, then, in encouraging polo is doing a very
economical thing. The civilian polo player by helping and supporting the Army in the same line is not only doing a very sporty thing
but is also of vast assistance in rendering more efficient a body of
men, on whom should war recur, the honor of his country will depend.

GSP, Jr., Paper, "Army Polo. (No. 2)," autumn 1922
. . . The great improvement in the play [of the Army team] was
due chiefly to three things. The assistance of the War Department in
permitting the assembling of selected players. The efforts of the
American Remount Association in producing and making available
more suitable horses for polo and for war. The generous support of
civilian players in helping and playing with the Army Team . . .

This element of personal risk is not a drawback but a decided advantage. No matter how brave a man may be he is none the less a
creature of habit. If his most lethal experience prior to battle has
consisted in dodging automobiles on city streets the insinuating whisper of bullets about his sacred person will have more disquieting influence on him than would be the case had his same person received a
few cuts and broken bones on the polo fields.

This last statement seems a trifle harsh but such is the nature of
truth.

After visiting her sister in England and touring the battlefields in
France, Beatrice returned home at the end of August. Patton took a three-
day leave of absence and met her in New York.

Letter, Major General C. J. Baily, Third Corps Area commander (Baltimore) to GSP, Jr., December 3, 1922

[Deep appreciation of] the splendid appearance which they [Patton's men] made in the parade in this city on Army Day, December second, and in the formation in the Stadium. I realize that this command had to be put to considerable trouble and personal effort in marching over to Baltimore in order to appear mounted in the parade. I need hardly say that the appearance of the squadron was a distinct feature of interest to all concerned, and especially so on account of its well-known record for fighting in all the wars of our country since it was first organized prior to the Mexican War.

In December, Rivers judged Patton "superior" as a squadron commander, and an

officer of good habits and agreeable personality, and of superior mental and physical powers, superior type of officer. Keenly interested in and superior in riding, polo, etc; and also a hard student of his profession — devotes himself assiduously to military studies in winter season. Have had to get after him about supervising troop paper work and troop fund books better occasionally. Minor deficiencies called to his attention [from] time to time: immediate improvement resulted.

Bandholz concurred in his endorsement.

In mid-December, the Pattons, together with their children, left Washington to spend Christmas in California. Early in January 1923, the family traveled to Fort Riley, Kansas, where Patton enrolled in the Advanced or Field Officers' Course at the Cavalry School.

Attendance at the Cavalry School indicated that he was once again integrated into his basic branch. His work at Fort Myer had been recognized and approved, and his selection for schooling meant that he was marked for advancement.

Letter, Beatrice (303 N. Jefferson Street, Junction City, Kansas) to Pershing, January 22, 1923

Georgie is getting well started at the school. He has been at work a week today, and is sitting opposite me as I write [studying a map and], coloring rivers in purple.

X

The Middle
Years

*"I am an enthusiastic if not a good
Cavalryman . . . success . . . hinges
on the taking of calculated risks."*

CHAPTER 38

Riley, Leavenworth, Boston, Hawaii

*"Sad to say, it [my photograph] is not so fierce as I had hoped
though it has a more or less Prussian expression."*

IF THE FIRST THREE DECADES of Patton's professional life consisted of an
apprenticeship for high command, if his career before World War II was
preparation for his unique leadership, the 1920s expanded his horizons
despite the confining nature of his work. His schooling and staff assignments restrained and tempered his natural inclinations, at the same time
disciplined his character and intellect without destroying his ebullience.
Perhaps it was his physical exertions, his hard play on the polo field, that
permitted him to maintain the patience required for the sedentary tasks
imposed on him.

He attended the Cavalry School at Fort Riley, Kansas, during the first
five months of 1923, and completed the Advanced Course. The single
paper remaining from that experience was the draft of a lecture he delivered to his fellow students.

I am going to talk about Napoleon's marshals. In this school we
deal with great plans and projects, theories and organizations, and I
have taken this subject lest we forget that in war the personal element is most important.

After recommending *The Three Musketeers,* that highly romanticized
account of combat, as proper reading background to understand the marshals, he showed pictures of Napoleon in 1796, 1809, and 1815. To explain why Napoleon was less than at his best during the last three years of
his active career, Patton suggested:

that large protuberance about the waist line . . . may be becoming and not at all harmful to a lawyer, a doctor, a banker or a chief

justice, but to a military man it is ruinous. When you see one gradually coming upon you two measures are necessary; eat less, exercise
more.

Taking the marshals in turn, Patton characterized their special gifts.
Berthier had "the ability to present in a simple manner the most complicated situations." Murat had no intellectual capacity, understood nothing of strategy, but could maneuver 20,000 cavalrymen in the field to
perfection. Having discussed them all, Patton concluded that their
fathers' occupations had had no influence on their attainments — "a
great leader may be inherited from a notary or a noble, a mason or
a manufacturer, a lawyer or a landowner and . . . no walk of life has a
monopoly on military talents." Nor was formal education necessary for
military leadership, except in staff duty.

The great danger in military schools is that they will become narrow, too much concerned with teaching . . .
The personal element is given too little consideration in peace
time training and in schools, yet it is the most important element in
war and no where in history is this better exemplified than in Napoleon and his marshals.

Nowhere would this be better exemplified than in the case of Patton
himself.
Upon Patton's graduation, Brigadier General Malin Craig, the commandant, rated Patton:

Very energetic, enthusiastic and versatile officer. Does everything
exceptionally well. This report is the combined opinion of 28 Instructors, 4 Directors [of courses] and the Commandant.

Colonel Guy V. Henry, the assistant commandant, certified to Patton's
"marked proficiency" in tactics, marksmanship, map reading, sketching,
and field fortifications.
His high standing in his class led to his selection to attend what had
been called the School of the Line, was then named the General Service
Schools, and would become known as the Command and General Staff
College, at Fort Leavenworth, Kansas.
Before reporting to Leavenworth early in September, Patton spent

three months of leave in Massachusetts, where he and Beatrice performed a heroic act. They were sailing off Little Mission rocks near Salem in a twelve-foot catboat when a sudden squall almost swamped them. As they turned and headed for shore, they heard cries and saw three boys — two were sixteen years old, the other was ten — whose boat had capsized, struggling in the water. The youngsters had managed to turn their dory over and, about three-quarters of a mile from land, were standing in the boat in water to their waists, waving their oars and shouting.

The Pattons went to their aid. The wind was so uneven and uncertain that they had to go past the boys, then tack back. They took the young-sters aboard with great difficulty and at some personal danger, then brought them and their boat to land. "Their deed, especially Mr. Pat-ton's," one of the boys later stated, "was one of fine skill in handling the boat in such weather and also one of courage and of almost self-sacrifice."

Beatrice had affidavits drawn up and signed by the rescued boys, each of whom gave his version of the incident. Then she transmitted the docu-ments to the Secretary of the Treasury, who awarded Life Saving Medals. Her own narrative stressed the bravery of her husband, who, she knew, was fond of decorations, recognition, and fame.

No more was heard of the occurrence for some time.

Beatrice, who was expecting their third child, remained in Massachu-setts when Patton traveled to Leavenworth.

Letter, GSP, Jr., to Beatrice, October 7, 1923

If you come here you will be very lonely for a while as I go to school at 8:30 usually get out at 12:00. Go back at 1:00 P.M. and get back at 5:00 and then have to ride or play tennis to get exercise. Except of course on Saturday and Sunday when there is nothing to do.

I am not telling you this to discourage you but simply as a warn-ing.

He had their house at Leavenworth painted so it would "be less of a shock to you than would other wise be the case. I even got them to make the bath room all white."

Letter, GSP, Jr., to Pershing, October 23, 1923

As I have frequently told you I am an enthusiastic if not a good CAVALRYMAN and this fact together with the knowledge that I am not grinding any personal axe emboldens me to write you about the next chief of CAVALRY. I have talked the matter over with Quek [Quekemeyer, a former aide to Pershing in France] and we both think that *if* Gen CRAIG is not available that Col Henry would be *next* best. The only thing I can see against Col Henry is that he is too cold. It seems to me that we want a good soldier and also a good mixer for the next chief. To my mind General Craig is both. Of course I know that it is none of my business and that my opinion will not divert you from what you think best but I think that all cavalry men owe it to them selves to get the best chief possible.

I am getting on fairly well here and DONT like it a bit but suppose it is a necessary disease like measles.

Letter, Pershing to GSP, Jr., November 27, 1923

. . . you are not only a very enthusiastic but a very good cavalryman, remembering one particular instance . . . when you brought in 2 important Mexican dead strapped on to the front of your automobile . . .

Craig seems to be the general choice, and if things work out as I think possible, he will probably be selected. Of course, all this is confidential — only for you and Quekemeyer — but you know I have the interests of Cavalry at heart and shall always do everything possible for my old branch of the service.

Patton bought his daughter Ruth Ellen a police dog five weeks old. "When I let him out to look at him he left the others and bit a cow in the leg. The cow kicked him over and instead of howling he growled and bit her again: this decided me that he must be a good dog."

Beatrice arranged by mail with Patton's manservant Booker to give Patton a surprise party on his birthday.

Letter, GSP, Jr., to Beatrice, November 11, 1923

I got enough candy from Cal[ifornia] to keep me sick until Christmas . . . It is after 12 [midnight] as I was reading so I must stop. I think you were fine to arrange for the party. Inspite of my advanced age I still love you.

Letter, GSP, Jr., to Beatrice [November 1923]

Darling Beat: I have just mailed you by seperate package one of my recent Photos. Sad to say it is not as fierce as I had hoped though it has a more or less Prussian expression.

He wrote to General Hines, the Deputy Chief of Staff of the Army who would soon succeed Pershing as Army Chief of Staff, asking to be detailed, upon the completion of the course at Leavenworth, as military attaché in England. In a quite long and friendly letter, Hines replied that someone else had already been promised the job.

He had Thanksgiving dinner with John Lucas and his family. Lucas would command the VI Corps in Italy during World War II and be relieved at Anzio.

Letter, GSP, Jr., to Beatrice, November 26, 1923
I have the usual unthankful feeling of having vastly over eaten and not had much exercise . . . I hate to write such a stupid letter but don't seem to have many ideas. I do however think I have a lot to be thankful for and hope that I am properly grateful . . . The most thankful thing I have is that you love me.

In December, Patton sent Beatrice a letter of congratulation he had received from Pershing on the impending birth of the new Patton baby. "You ought to keep it for 'it,' " he wrote, "(notice avoidance of gender)."

Gen. [Malin] Craig wrote me that he was after the job as chief of cavalry. So if you see Gen Brewster talk him up. Of course it is secret. I hope he gets the job. So far I have done pretty well [at Leavenworth] but the marks are so close that one may slip at any moment.

He spent Christmas vacation with Beatrice, who gave birth on December 24 to a boy, George S. Patton IV.
Mr. and Mrs. Patton, Nita, and Aunt Nannie were there, and Mr. Patton "insisted on having George IV baptized at once. This was done in the house. Papa wrote some nice things in the baptismal book but it was burned."

Letter, GSP, Jr. (Leavenworth), to Beatrice, January 1, 1924
I enjoyed my Christmas very much and am especially glad that you had so little trouble [with the delivery of young George].

Patton worked hard on his studies, and he mentioned his efforts in almost every letter to Beatrice.

So far I have done better than I have expected on almost all the problems though I doubt if I stand as high relatively as I did at Riley. Still I hope to improve and I think some of the others will crack — I hope so . . . Gen Smith [the commandant] gave us another lecture to day about not worrying. I have not done so yet and I hope I shant.

Again:

I certainly busted all my rules about studying to day.

I studied from 2:30 P.M. to 6:00 P.M. and from 7:15 to 11:45 and have [seven] or eight hours in all but I know the subject so it is all right and don't happen often.

Once more:

I have been getting "A" again so feel much more mental than I did though I can still stand to improve. However I am not taking it at all seriously . . .

Had a nice letter from [Ralph] Sasse today full of advice. He is some soldier and ended up with real emotion saying that I was the only man who could speak his language.

Later: "I have been studying to beat hell."

Finally:

I never seem to get through any more. It is now 11:30 and I have just finished. Either I study harder or the lessons are harder. We had our physical exam to day. I was perfect as usual.

Letter, Joseph J. Angelo (2415 Sherman Ave., Camden, New Jersey) to GSP, Jr., February 3, 1924

Dear Col. P. We received your letter and sure thank you for your check as it helped us a lot. As it put us on our feet. Hoping I can some day return you a favor. Am sending the other letter [attesting to Angelo's character and recommending him for a job] to the fire dep't. Am very glad to hear that you have a son and hope he will some day be an officer like his father . . . I will let you know if I get in the Fire Dept and I am looking for a job every day willing to take everything. I know you are working hard in that school as I remem-

ber how hard we worked in the tank school . . . Bettey is doing
nicely outside of a cold. With Best wishes for all I remain Your
Friend always Joe.

General Frank Parker, commandant of the Army War College, wrote
and thanked Patton for his kind and complimentary letter of congratulations on Parker's promotion. "I especially appreciate your letter," Parker
said, "as it comes from a man for whom I have a very high regard personally and professionally."

Letter, Rockenbach to GSP, Jr., February 5, 1924

My dear Patton: I am very much pleased to see that school has not
dulled your capacity to estimate the situation correctly, for I was
wondering why I had not heard from you and I assure you that your
congratulations, though much belated, are highly valued. [Rocken-
bach had been promoted to Brigadier General.]

I have gotten my promotion, as some of my stupid friends inform
me, in spite of the Tanks, but I believe in Tanks, I believe that the
machines that we have in manufacture at the present time are going
to win many of our opponents and are going to force you, cavalrymen, to adopt them. Consequently, I believe that my promotion is
connected with the Tanks and will make others think more of them.
I have delayed going to Washington, with a view to letting the Army
get accustomed to the fact that a Brigadier-General is a suitable officer for the command of the Tank School.

I am wearing the first stars which you gave me and also the Tank
insignia.

Don't let it get into your crazy head that I don't need the approval
and sympathy of my juniors. I often felt in my long period of waiting [for promotion and for recognition of the tanks], that had they
[his juniors] known the amount of scrapping I did to get them what
I consider their well-merited reward, at a time when there was a mad
rush to grasp the decorations, they would have realized that all the
time I was behind them, looking after them, and ready to get into a
fisty cuff with any one who was derogatory in his remarks.

I shall leave here probably next Monday but there are two things
that I want your active assistance in: the first is, to keep alive the
interest in Tanks and the other is to get up a suitable memorial in
Arlington [Cemetery] for our men who died in France . . .

Let me know what your plans are on leaving the School there.
There are a good many things in the District of Washington that

will have to get more snap and pep into them and assuming that the various schools you have gone to have had a beneficial exterior effect on you, without curbing your Napoleonic spirit when the fight is on, I may have to call on you.

With regards to Mrs. Patton and yourself. Sincerely yours,

In September, Rockenbach would be appointed commanding general of the District of Washington. He would retire from the Army in 1933. Until his death in May 1952, he was convinced that Patton was his protégé and had gained fame because of what Rockenbach had taught him.

Patton was an honor graduate of the 1923–24 class at the Command and General Staff College, standing 25 of 248 students, with an average overall grade of 88.948. This high mark placed him in the General Staff Corps, a status much sought after. Colonel Charles M. Bundel, the Director of Instruction, judged him to be "a superior officer of marked ability." In his endorsement, the commandant, Brigadier General Harry A. Smith, concurred, adding, "In my opinion he is one of the ablest and best officers of his grade in the service."

Malin Craig, the new Chief of Cavalry, congratulated Patton, saying:

. . . you have added additional prestige to our branch of the service.

I consider it the duty of every Cavalry officer to take advantage of the courses of instruction made available to them — a matter of duty to the Cavalry service. Furthermore, I firmly believe that lasting individual honor and preferment are gained only through individual effort to improve the efficiency of the service at large.

Shortly before Patton's graduation, Smith had written in behalf of "one of our best students," Patton, to Major General Robert L. Howze who commanded the 1st Cavalry Division at Fort Bliss, Texas. Smith wanted to keep Patton at Leavenworth as an instructor, but the War Department had decided instead to assign him to duty as a General Staff officer. Smith recommended that Howze request Patton as his G–3 or operations officer because he believed that Patton would be valuable and

because I am very fond of him personally; second, he was one of the best subordinate officers I had in France and one of the most outstanding; third, he is a high class student here and has demonstrated that he understands the theory, as well as the practice, of war. He is a fine man to have around, aside from his military ability, and I regret exceedingly that I cannot keep him here.

The War Department would transfer Patton to the I Corps Area head-quarters in Boston. As soon as he heard of his assignment, he wrote to the corps commander, his friend Major General André W. Brewster, who had been a member of Pershing's staff.

Letter, Brewster to GSP, Jr., May 27, 1924
Dear George Patton. Thanks for your letter. I am expecting to see your order [assigning Patton to the I Corps Area] very shortly and shall be glad to have you by my side. We have taken the old Proctor house at Prides and Fred Ayer told me last Sunday that he had got the Brown "Mansion" nearby for you. It has a fine swimming pool. I am glad that you are all pleased with the detail [to the I Corps Area]. Give our love to Mrs. Patton and the children.

In Boston, Patton became the G–1 officer concerned with personnel and manpower management, including plans to control the mobilization of all the reserve units and installations in the New England area.

When Pershing retired from the Army on his sixty-fourth birthday in September 1924, an editorial in the Boston *Transcript* marked with lavish praise his distinguished career.

Letter, GSP, Jr., to Pershing, September 22, 1924
At the request of the paper I wrote the editorial . . . I tried to express in a very restrained manner my enthusiastic admiration for you as the Greatest American Soldier. The restrictions of publication however prevented me saying all I feel. In my opinion the greatest honor a soldier can have is to have been privaleged to serve under you as I was allowed to do. While you were on the active list I did not tell you my feelings as I did not want to be thought guilty of bootlicking for my own benefit . . . With renewed expressions of my sincere admiration, I am Very respectfully.

Letter, Pershing to GSP, Jr., September 30, 1924
. . . it is particularly pleasant and somewhat rare to hear such

good things of oneself while still alive. In this connection, I cannot let this opportunity pass to repeat my warm congratulations on your own splendid services to the Army and the country, and I want you to know that I am particularly grateful for the very loyal and efficient support you have always given me.

Having established firmly his sense of belonging to the cavalry, Patton began to look again toward the tanks. Perhaps he was stirred by Rockenbach's promotion and letter. Perhaps he always felt that machines of one sort or another could hardly be excluded from warfare in the future.

A paper he wrote sometime that year and published in the *Cavalry Journal* on "Armoured Cars with Cavalry" opened with a futuristic fantasy. He described Major General Alonza G. Gasoline sitting in his command car, gas-proofed against chemical agents, watching the screen of a radio motion picture projector. The film was being photographed by a camera on an observation helicopter hovering over a battlefield. Close support planes were flying low and squirting liquid fire — an aerial flamethrower of the equivalent of the more modern napalm. Many tanks were meeting in head-on combat.

These visionary events led him to his main question: How could the Army adapt and use the numerous mechanical inventions due to appear, he was certain, in the near future?

Waging war depended on the existence of roads, and roads were restrictive. If Grant had had all the trucks in the AEF, he could not have supplied an army in the Wilderness campaign much larger than the one he actually had and kept supplied with wagons. Wheeled transportation was no better than the available roads.

What released a field army from its bondage to roads were caterpillar tracks, and

the time may conceivably come when in the immutable cycle of military endeavor we shall see small professional armies of highly trained mechanical soldiers operating simple yet powerful machines again dominate the battle field as did their prototypes the heavy cavalry of the armies of Belesarius and Narses. Or again we may see the roadless machine with all its apparent potentialities sink to a position analogous to that occupied by the submarine which but a few years since was so touted as the future mistress of the sea.

Lieutenant Patton in Mexico, 1916

Lieutenant Colonel Patton in France, July 1918

Tank Corps training, summer 1918. Colonel Patton is in center

Reception for the Prince of Wales,
second from left, France, February 1919.
Colonel Patton is third from left

The Tank Corps at Camp Meade, Maryland, 1919.
Colonel Patton is fifth from the right, Lieutenant Colonel
Eisenhower is fourth from the right, both second row

Major Patton, Fort Riley, May 1923

The Patton family, 1929. Major and Mrs. Patton, daughters
Beatrice and Ruth Ellen, and son George IV

Presentation of the Argentine Polo Cup to the War Department "Whites," winners of the 1931 tournament. Left to right: Major John Eager, Lieutenant Gordon B. Rogers, Major George S. Patton, Jr., and Major Jacob L. Devers

Master of Foxhounds,
Cobbler Hunt, Virginia,
1932

Sailor and navigator,
aboard the *Arcturus*

Father of the bride, daughter Beatrice's wedding, 1934

Commanding Officer, 5th Cavalry, Fort Clark, Texas, 1938

Fort Myer Horse Show, benefit for infantile paralysis fund, January 1939. Left to right: Colonel Patton, commanding officer, Fort Myer, President Franklin D. Roosevelt, and Colonel Edwin M. Watson, White House Military Aide

Colonel Patton and members of his staff, Fort Myer, June 1940

Fort Myer review, June 1940

He was, he said, confining his comments to armored cars working with the cavalry, for "Regretfully . . . at the present time there is no tank AVAILABLE FOR ISSUE in this country which can keep up with any unit of cavalry." Neither could the armored car, but it could be easily and cheaply constructed from existing motor vehicles with limited armor plate and with existing machine guns — an "assembly [line] proposition, not one of [individual] manufacture."

What he hoped for was an armored car built on a stock chassis, that is, a commercial two-ton truck, which would insure an abundant supply of spare parts. He would accept pneumatic tires and the absence of a roof and a protective floor. He would dispense with anything that impeded mobility. And this the developers of new weapons failed to understand. "Unfortunately," he remarked sarcastically, "inventors don't have to fight [with] the things they make." What they failed to realize was that every ounce of extra weight on an armored car or tank reduced its fighting strength.

The important quality was mobility. "A quail is not doomed to death because he has no armour, neither is a Destroyer. An armoured car with cavalry is a land Destroyer." Men who fought in tanks would willingly dispense with 50 percent of protection in order to gain 5 percent of mobility. "To be useful in any of the above capacities the car must be mobile practical and simple of repair; not a costly hypothetical monstrosity."

This was one side of his ambivalent feelings. Showing his versatility, he displayed the other when he lectured in Boston on "Cavalry Patrols." According to General Grant, he said, war was very simple; it consisted of locating the enemy, then hitting him as hard as possible, and continuing to push him. In this context, cavalry and the air service — "in bad weather [only] the cavalry" — were responsible for finding the enemy, and this the cavalry did by patrols.

Cautioning his listeners against being unduly influenced by the Great War, he said they were unlikely to find

a situation in which when conflict is imminent a courteous G–2 will hand us a large scale map artistically marked out in red and blue and accompanied by fifty pages of mimeograph information as to the exact location of the enemy's latest efforts in the line of new latrines or machine gun emplacements. When such *modern conveniences* exist cavalry reconnoissance will be as useless as it will be impossible.

Only in western Europe were "such refinements" possible, for elsewhere in the world the opposing forces would be separated by mountains or forests, by deserts or prairies, by farm lands or swamps. And in this rough terrain lacking good roads and railways, the cavalry would have the task of learning where the enemy was and in what strength.

Patton touched humorously upon some common errors made by patrols. "Because these defects are mentioned in lighter vein," he warned, "is no reason for their being so regarded."

When you set out to find the enemy . . . remember that he is as much lost in the Fog of War as you are. He has no ghostly scouts to penetrate unseen the trackless woods and lurking in every cover to instantly report your slightest move. His men get just as tired and hot and dusty or cold and wet and stiff as do yours. His patrols as yours will follow the easiest way — the ROADS and it is there that you will find him.

Further remember that maneuvers [in peacetime] to the contrary notwithstanding — a man does not die every time a gun goes off — not by several thousand rounds . . .

Remember success with cavalry hinges on the taking of calculated risks. History proves that such risks may be great — "FORTUNE FAVORS THE BOLD" . . .

Patroling is both physically and nervously exhausting, neither men nor horses can remain on it indefinitely so we must provide reliefs for mind you, a reconnoitering detachment will be out days, not hours . . .

It is a cardinal principle that tactical unity must be preserved . . .

Attention is here called to the fact that eye sight is a God given sense intended to be used and that the Signal Corps has aided the Almighty by the issue of field glasses. Take every good occasion to follow the advice so freely displayed at railroad crossings: "Stop-look-listen"; and when you so stop remember to cover the patrol with a modified form of march outpost . . .

If the enemy is so strong that you cannot charge him it is folly to fight him on foot . . . If you are not destroyed you will surely be made useless for information is not gained by shooting competitions. WHEN A CAVALRY PATROL IN SEARCH OF INFORMATION CANNOT CHARGE IT MUST RUN . . .

A patrol is not working for an historical society. Most of the information it gets while priceless today will be worthless tomorrow . . .

During the battle of Custozza in June 1866, 104 Austrian Cavalry met a column of 10 000 Italian infantry on a wood road. The meeting was a surprise and the Austrians charged instantly in column of fours. In thirty minutes they had ridden through the column and back and still had sixteen men in the saddle . . .

And finally, what was to become one of the Patton bywords in World War II: "get around if you can't get through . . . IT IS THE DUTY OF CAVALRY AND SHOULD BE ITS PRIDE TO BE BOLD AND DASHING."

His tour of duty at Boston lasted only eight months. He expected to be sent to the War Department General Staff in Washington, but late in January 1925, he was abruptly ordered to sail in March to the Hawaiian Islands. Beatrice was not feeling well, and he would travel alone.

His annual physical examination disclosed a long and impressive history of injury: 1905 — fractures of the radius and ulna at heads, just below the right elbow joint; fractured nose; 1906 — dislocation of the left ankle; 1907 — fracture of the left radius; fractured nose; fractured sixth left rib; 1910 — fracture of the third right metacarpal; 1911 — prepatellar bursitis; 1912 — lacerated wound, five inches long, sagittal suture region, 16 sutures; 1914 — concussion with partial paralysis of the right arm; 1915 — lacerated wound, head, 5 sutures; 1916 — lacerated wound, left eyebrow, 3 sutures; second-degree burn of head and neck, third-degree burn of ears; 1917 — lacerated wound right side of neck and over right eye; 1918 — penetrating gunshot wound, left thigh; 1920 — left hydrocele cord tapped; 1921 — fracture of arch of pubis, left; 1922 — lacerated wound, head, 2 sutures; lacerated wound, penetrating, upper lip; 1924 — fractures of eighth and ninth left ribs; lacerated wound, head, 3 sutures; severe sprain, left knee.

The physicians discovered that he had a long tumor formation over the ascending arch of the left pubic bone, probably caused by injuries received from a horse, which had fallen on him at drill, resulting in a probable fracture and massive callus formation.

He had mild myopic astigmatism, which was corrected by glasses, stood 72½ inches tall, weighed 179 pounds.

Letter, GSP, Jr., to Beatrice, February 17, 1925

I suppose you are about ready to leave the Hospital and hope that you wont be too strenious . . .

It hardly seems six years since I got back from France and we stayed in Moose's house at Mitchell Field but such is the case. We are well Preserved considering the time.

Colonel C. D. Roberts, chief of staff of the I Corps Area, rated Patton as a "superior" officer, "an experienced, well educated, accomplished officer. Excellently fitted for General Staff work or high command."

This first mention of his qualification for high command reflected the rigorous schooling he had successfully completed at Fort Leavenworth. A graduate of that esteemed institution was, per se, capable of assuming high command.

Patton boarded the ship *Château-Thierry* in New York on March 4.

Letter, GSP, Jr. (from Panama), to Beatrice, March 11, 1925

Mrs. Simonds and Tracy Pope came to meet me (they thought you were along too). We had dinner and drove around. It is perfectly beautiful and most attractive. I almost want to be stationed here. If Hawaii is better it must be fine . . .

It is lovely beyond words and very different to what I had pictured. I saw an aligator. Have your opera glasses repaired as they will be useful. Cameras are useless as things are on too large a scale.

Letter, GSP, Jr., to Beatrice, March 15, 1925

Every one on board is Bridge crazy and Play all day. Several of the ladies have fights and the children holler all the time . . . It is foolish to write when the letter wont be mailed for a week however as I think of you all the time it is well to write once in a while.

Patton debarked at San Francisco and made a quick trip to see his parents, sister, and aunt — "Papa and I drove a lot together" — then returned to board the army transport *Grant*.

Letter, GSP, Jr., to Beatrice, March 27, 1925

When I woke up yesterday I found the ship stopped and on going on deck found much smoke pouring from the after hatch and learned that she was on fire. There were four hose lines into the hold. On inspecting after breakfast we found about eight feet of water in the hold with two automobiles and your Pianow floating happily around. All the rest of our things are drenched with water but were not floating. It is hard to say how much they are hurt but unquestionably they are all damaged to a degree. There is no need to worry about it as nothing can be done. They are drying out the place as much as possible. I am not sure that the books were in that hatch as I could not find them nor could I locate the chests of Blankets. If on opening the stuff I find that some things are permanently ruined I will write you. We were luckey on the Packard. It was so big that it could not be put in the hatch so was on deck and not hurt any by the fire. I radioed Fred [Ayer, Beatrice's brother] for information asto the name of the company in which we are insured and for information of what to do and to send me papers. I am sorry to write you such bad news but thought you would want to hear and would be excited over the Radio to Fred . . . The ship is nice and I have a room and bath so am very comfortable.

Letter, GSP, Jr., to Beatrice, March 29, 1925
    The men who dared this ocean must have been great fellows and fine seamen. At least one of the book boxes was burned all to pieces but I think that the water did less harm than I at first thought.

The passengers sighted land on the afternoon of March 31. Patton smelled Hawaii's fragrance six miles offshore. To him, it looked like Catalina Island, but with heavier surf. It was dusk by the time the ship docked, and the lights of the city were on. He was met by a friend who had a wreath — a lei — for him and an automobile and who said that Patton was detailed to Schofield Barracks, where the headquarters of the Hawaiian Division was located. The headquarters of the overall command, the Hawaiian Department, was at Fort Shafter.

Schofield Barracks was on a big flat with high mountains on each side. The post was constructed along loops, but a single loop was as big as all of Fort Sheridan. The verdure resembled that of southern California, that is, southern California with rain. Honolulu was not quite so good as El Paso; it was 21 miles from camp on a concrete road. Waikiki beach was much smaller than he had imagined.

Letter, GSP, Jr., to Beatrice, April 2, 1925
    The climate while seeming cool is very sweaty. If you walk seven or eight blocks you are very wet like a melon in an ice box . . .

Asto coming here: I think it was not the intention of the W.D. [War Department] but was some inside politics of the island. The man I am replacing who goes to the [War] Department as G–4 (the place I was to have had) is supposed to be the meanest man in the Army. I think it was a scheme to get rid of him. The official family here seems to me to be much too large and in a sort of cat fight. We get a new Chief of Staff soon which may help though all of them except me are ex Coast Artillery men. While I was not supposed to come here I think it was the luckiest thing in the world that we did as it is cooler and in all ways nicer [than Washington] except asto houses . . .

I have made this rather long as I doubt if you get any more mailed to Boston. However I shall write one or two more there and then write to California. I am well and hope you will like this place.

After he rode around half the island, he thought the scenery looked like Mexico and Florida. The beaches were excellent for swimming. There were all sorts of places to "picknick and even I might be tempted to do it. There is a valley full of burial caves where chiefs in their armor were buried. No one seems to go there." Hawaii was "a swell place and I am sure we shall have a good time." The polo was not much. "I am well and not over worked."

Letter, GSP, Jr., to Beatrice, April 7, 1925
. . . as distance removes sorrow to a degree I had just as well tell you [after uncrating the furniture] that practically every thing is ruined. Water was still seaping out of the linen and blanket chests. There is mildew on about a third of the things rust on some and die off hangings and pictures frames on some. About half the linen is so stained I sent it to the French laundry just now . . . I had to stretch string in five rooms and hang up every single thing to day in the house as it is raining steadily out side. The big mahoginy table is busted all to little pieces. My shaving [stand] and bureau are busted we may be able to save one by using part of the other. The graflex [camera] and typewriter are junk. The gold frame mirrors are no more. The two big screnes are not worth repairing. The backs are off 75% of the books and they swelled so much that most of the book boxes are burst open. Your bureau and the one with brass handles are not hurt. Your sewing cabinet is all right. The two sets of nested

tables are all right. So is the oval table with the glass tray top. All the chairs including my leather one seem all right. The Davenport is not hurt much. The Hoover and all the electric irons are ruined but perhaps can be rewired. The highboy is not hurt much. Neither are the mattresses or pillows. All the clothes I sent and all the hangings you sent have been soaking in salt water for two weeks but may recover. I can't tell till they dry. However we have still more than enough furnature to get on with or we can buy it here. The insurance appraiser seemed to me very broad minded and I think we will get 2500.00 or 3000 damages which will realy replace every thing. I am doing the best I can to fix up what is left so you may find things better than this letter indicates. I told you all the horrors as distance will soften them and you may find that time and a good carpenter has repaired some damages.

He added that Schofield Barracks was quite a military place, with no less than eight marching bands in existence, and with 13,000 men in ranks for a division review. He had no servants in his house, but was taking his meals at the officers' mess, which was close by and quite good. "I don't think much of the C.O. nor of the chief of staff but they might be worse. I should like very much to be detailed as G–3 [operations officer] and may manage to work it as the present one leaves soon." He added a postscript: "The Bed is not *hurt at all*."

Patton was fortunate to be transferred to Hawaii. In the continental United States, the Army was dispersed in small detachments across the country. Training major units such as regiments, brigades, and divisions was consequently impossible. In contrast, the Army posts in Panama, the Philippines, and Hawaii were relatively large and accommodated sizable numbers of troops. Exercises of the important formations were periodically undertaken. Even though the weapons used were left over from the World War and were becoming increasingly obsolete, even though there was little opportunity to test new equipment and doctrine, training was feasible.

Patton arrived in time to observe the large-scale maneuver held annually by the Hawaiian Division.

Lieutenant Colonel J. B. Murphy rated him as a "superior" officer, then continued:

Major Patton served as my assistant during the Grand Joint Army and Navy Exercises April 1925. I had an excellent opportunity to observe the manner in which he performed his duties as a general staff officer. His tactical judgment is superior, he is well balanced, and he is a quick and enthusiastic worker. Major Patton is well educated along tactical lines and he would be a superior Chief of Staff, G–2 or G–3 of a Corps during combat. While I have had no opportunity to observe him in command of troops, it is my opinion, based on general observation, that he would be an excellent commander of combat troops during war.

Patton sent General H. A. Smith, under whom he had served in Langres and Leavenworth, an informal report of the exercises, together with photographs and documents, plus some desultory thoughts about the next war.

Smith replied and said that he was about to depart Leavenworth regretfully for Washington. "I dislike the War Department very much and if my choice friend, General Hines [the Chief of Staff], were not there, it would be still more distasteful." But he hoped to land at the Army War College and, further, to welcome Patton to the course. He warned Patton somewhat jokingly but with an undertone of seriousness not to become so accomplished a staff officer that he would get only that kind of duty in the future. "I note with a great deal of pleasure what you say about the next war and I hope that you are a good prophet. If I get either one of those jobs [you predicted] you will command the First Division."

Meanwhile, Patton was appointed Acting G–1 (personnel officer) and G–2 (intelligence officer) of the Hawaiian Division, positions that kept him working with papers of one sort or another but left him enough time for riding, polo, and other strenuous exercise.

Colonel Howard L. Laubach, acting chief of staff, cautiously rated Patton's work as "above average." Several months later, when Laubach knew him better, he considered Patton an "average" G–1 and G–2, but thought him to be

an upstanding gentleman of courteous, well-bred demeanor. Very loyal and dependable. A student of his profession. This officer is a man of energy and action and in my opinion is better qualified for active duty than the routine of office work.

In November, Patton was placed on detached service with the Hawaiian Department, where he remained as acting or temporary G–1 for almost a year.

In a lecture at Schofield Barracks, "On Leadership," Patton categorically fixed the foremost trait of a military leader as

> the possession of a superiority complex. . . .
>   . . . what other traits are necessary [?] . . .
> Perhaps the attributes he should possess are best illustrated by a comparison to the ignition system of a gasoline motor. No matter how carefully designed and accurately machined and assembled it may be, the motor is but iron sloshed with oil until fired to powerful and harmonious activity by the electric spark — the soul of the leader.
> For this reason the vigorous possession of a self confident combative instinct is more important to the commander of any army than to the commander of a squad for in the former case the voltage must be higher in order to overcome the resistance of inertia in the mighty mass whose functioning is dependent on his vitalising power.
> The wires which, so to speak, conduct this energy are five fold: Habit, Personality, Example, Fear, and Reward . . . In practice they are inexorably commingled and mutually dependent.

Habit, he said, induced a sense of responsibility in the leader and made it "impossible to fail in the discharge of his trust." He cited as an example the high proportion of officer casualties when compared to that of soldiers.

Personality, an intangible quality, consisted of

> charm, reserve, tact, consideration and aggressiveness in combat. It enables its possessor to be in but not of a group; it produces an aura of authority . . .
> The lifelong habit of command and responsibility, produces in the better sort, a command personality. Since we cannot breed our leaders, our efforts must be bent towards the fullest possible development of this trait . . .
> The leader must demonstrate his superiority in the technique of combat. He must be a better rider, shot, scout, cook, etc. than any of his men . . .

. . . the ability to make quick and correct tactical decisions, producing thereby a self confidence which battle may reduce but cannot destroy [is fostered by solving problems in service schools and makes for] a sense of demonstrated ability . . .

The battlefield alone offers him [a leader] the opportunity to make a reputation for dauntless courage without which it is impossible to obtain the uttermost from his men. For despite the calming influence of excessive civilization, the human animal still retains his age old admiration for heroism, seeing that in the dark beginnings of our race it was the one prerequisite to success in the stark battle for existence.

Few men are by nature devoid of physical fear. The blistering heat of battle withers many a budding reputation when the poor shrinking flesh fails to sustain the soul midst the myriad forms of dissolution in which the reaper seems to stalk the field. To combat this it behooves us to develop an antitoxin to fear and with it to inoculate our men. The best virus is a mixture of race consciousness, a mind saturated with former deeds of heroism, an abundant sense of obligation and an insatiable desire for present distinction and posthumous celebrity, so that in the fateful hour he may subdue his weaker self with that mighty potion — fear of fear.

Like a cold bath the first plunge is the hardest. Later, if he live, custom, fatigue, fatalism and pride will make him master of his emotions, for devoid of fear no normal man can ever become. Once on the morning of battle an officer asked Turenne if his knees shook from the cold and the veteran replied: "No my friend they shake from fear but if they knew where I shall this day take them they would tremble more."

Opportunities for reputation are not prevalent in the dug-out, nor do they flock to the leader with the reserve. Glory and death are brothers and their abiding place is the front line. The man who would qualify as a leader must lead — lead not by the cold incandescence of his super-refined intellect but by the fiery passion of his blazing manhood — a very king of beasts . . .

We do not stress enough the necessity for personal exposure and rash boldness on the part of our officers. Man loves life and too often yields to the sophistry of the subtle demon Fear, when he whispers, oh! so temptingly: "Your men need you, you must save your self for them" forgetting that the inspiration of an heroic act will carry men to victory . . . forgetful too that the blood of heroes like the dragons teeth will sprout new leaders to replace his loss.

War is elemental in its physical aspect and responds alone to psychology based on physical means . . .

There is no inspiration in the squeaking voice made dim and quavering by a mile of [telephone] wire nor can the most impressive personality accompany the wiggling atoms of a six hundred meter radio wave through the dreary wastes of interstellar space . . .

Courage as in the day of our neolithic ancestors is the greatest and most prized of virtues; lacking it, a shoulder full of stars is impotent to make a leader.

The recruit, in a new and strange environment, sought an ideal to copy and he looked to his officers. Courtesy, smartness, and promptness — "in a word discipline" — were best indoctrinated by example, but courage above all evoked imitation. Therefore, the leader must

never deviate from the role of a perfect soldier. He is always on parade. His orderly will report the number of his baths and the cleanliness of his undershirt. The mess waiter will recount the shinyness of his leather at meals and so on; while ten thousand men will hear and see and copy.

There was only one way to handle fear, and that was by prompt and public punishment, linked with ignominy and ridicule. "Punishment is not for the benefit of the sinner but for the salvation of his comrades." And this Patton would act on in the summer of 1943 in Sicily, where he slapped two soldiers in public for what he believed was cowardice on their part.

And finally, speaking of reward, Patton said:

The vital influence on morale and hence on leadership inherent in decorations cannot be overstated. Nor does the person exist to whom these baubles are repugnant. Our service has never realized nor capitalized [on] this fact . . . if a dime's worth of ribbon will make a hero of a craven it is the best investment in the world.

This does not mean that we would cheapen the decorations but it does mean that we should be more prompt and generous in their distribution; have more of them if need be . . . Deterred by the fear that one coward will benefit, we let a hundred heroes starve of their due, the inspiration of their lives, their half inch of ribbon.

Patton spent the Christmas holidays with Beatrice and the children at his parents' home. "Papa and [young] George had great fun together."

Soon after Patton returned to Hawaii in January 1926, he replied to a memo circulated by the G–2, who proposed that a school be organized in order to qualify selected junior officers in foreign languages. Patton had two main objections. First, "Personal experience in the study of two foreign languages convinces me that no useful working knowledge can be received save by residence in the Country concerned and the absolute separation from all English speaking companions." Second, junior officers were already overburdened with administrative and school duties requiring excessive indoor or clerical work. Enlarging on the latter point:

> wars are won by the physical courage, energy and initiative of junior officers and . . . such qualities are only engendered in the young male animal . . . by much recreation and violent physical exercise. The previous enviable record of our Army is in my opinion largely due to the fact that prior to the World War, young officers were less confined and by leisure stored up a reserve supply of energy and enthusiasm which enabled them to conquer in battle.

Beatrice and the children were now in Hawaii with Patton and life was more than pleasant for all of them. "We are going to a big dance at the opening of the new Royal Hawaiian Hotel tomorrow night," he wrote his father, "and will stay at Walter Dillinghams for the night." But if Patton was playing polo and frequently sailing with Beatrice, he was also reading and studying and occasionally giving lectures. He talked to a group of artillery officers on the "History and Employment of Light Tanks," a lecture he had originally written in 1919. It had then consisted for the most part of history, plus a few general principles of employment. He now had something more to say.

> . . . the notion [is] too prevalent, among military men, that the last war no matter where fought is the final word, the sealed pattern of all future conflicts . . . and [it] has infected to an alarming degree both our tactics and our organization . . . [We are] seeking so hard for an approved solution that will avoid the odious task of thinking . . . The characteristics of the next war are as insoluable as are those of an unborn babe. From his parents we can deduce his probable color. For the next war we can alone be certain that it will consist of wounds, death and destruction. How the baby will think, or how the war will be fought are veiled. But as surely as we know

the child will have hands so are we certain that the war will have tanks . . . Whether the tank shall precede or follow the infantry or even be associated with it is irrelivant. When the next war comes some of us, God willing, will have the Tank ready to our hands as one of the instruments with which to inflict wounds, death and destruction. As Forrest well put it: "War means fighting and fighting means killing." Let your best thought and keenest ingenuity based on principles and untrammeled by all labored memory of past *tactical details* be bent to the employment of the instruments of combat; infantry, cavalry, artillery, air service and TANKS in the best way most suitable to kill the enemy.

This was the idea of the combined arms, the combined use of all the weapons in the Army to make war on the battlefield, and it would characterize the operations in World War II.

The Treasury Department transmitted to Patton in February a silver Life Saving Medal of Honor — "in recognition of the gallant conduct displayed by you in bravely rescuing three boys from drowning in Salem Harbor, Massachusetts, August 21, 1923." Major General Edward M. Lewis, who commanded the Hawaiian Division, ceremoniously pinned the decoration on Patton, in the presence of a host of friends and a regimental infantry band.

Walter F. Dillingham, a resident of Hawaii, a polo player who had become one of the Pattons' best friends, wrote to congratulate Patton and to tell of his delight in what he called the merited recognition to Patton and his heroic wife. "I am prepared to decorate the whole family for bravery on general principles, but I had always thought of your special forte as being one of killing rather than saving lives. It must be a fine sensation to know that one is a well rounded hero."

CHAPTER 39

Hawaii: Schofield Barracks

"There are probably as many ways of winning a war as there are of skinning a cat."

GSP, Jr., Lecture, "The Secret of Victory," March 26, 1926

Despite the years of thought and oceans of ink which have been devoted to the elucidation of war its secrets still remain shrouded in mystery.

Indeed it is due largely to the very volume of available information that the veil is so thick.

War is an art and as such is not susceptible of explanation by fixed formulae. Yet from the earliest time there has been an unending effort to subject its complex and emotional structure to dissection, to enunciate rules for its waging, to make tangible its intangibility. As well strive to isolate the soul by the dissection of the cadaver as to seek the essence of war by the analysis of its records.

Yet despite the impossibility of physically detecting the soul its existence is proven by its tangible reflection in acts and thoughts.

So with war, beyond its physical aspect of armed hosts there hovers an impalpable something which on occasion so dominates the material as to induce victory under circumstances quite inexplicable.

To understand this something we . . . shall perchance find it in the reflexes produced by the acts of the Great Captains . . .

Not in the musty tomes of voluminous reports or censored recollections wherein they strove to immortalize and conceal their achievements. Nor yet in the countless histories where lesser wormish men have sought to snare their parted ghosts.

The great warriors were too busy and often too inapt to write contemporaneously of their exploits save in the form of propaganda reports . . . biographies were retrospects colored by their vain striving for enhanced fame, or by political conditions then confronting them.

War [is] . . . violent simplicity in execution [and] . . . pale and uninspired on paper. . . .

The white-hot energy of youth which saw in obstacles but inspirations and in the enemy but the gage to battle, becomes to complacent and retrospective age the result of mathematical calculation and metophysical erudition; of knowledge he never had and plans he never made . . .

Colored by self deception, shaded by scholarly book worms our soldiers stand before us as devoid of life as the toothless portraits of Washington which adorn the walls of half our school rooms . . .

Disregarding wholly the personality of Frederick [the Great] we attribute his victories to a tactical expedient, the oblique order of battle . . . accounts of valor mellow with age . . .

Yet . . . the history of war is the history of warriors; few in number, mighty in influence.

Alexander, not Macedonia conquered the world. Scipio, not Rome destroyed Carthage. Marlborough not the allies defeated France. Cromwell, not the roundheads dethroned Charles . . .

. . . the tendency . . . to consider the most recent past war as the last word, the sealed pattern of all future contests to insure peace . . . all unconscious of personal bias we of necessity base our conceptions of the future on our experience of the past.

. . . personal knowledge is a fine thing but unfortunately it is too intimate . . . So with war experiences . . . [we forget that] it was the roads and consequent abundant mechanical transportation PECULIAR to western Europe which permitted the accumulation of enough gas shells to do the strangling . . .

Due either to superabundant egotism and uncontrolled enthusiasm or else to limited powers of observation . . . [the specialists] advocate in the most fluent and uncompromising manner the vast FUTURE potentialities of their own weapon. In the next war, so they say, all the enemy will be crushed, gassed, bombed or otherwise speedily exterminated, depending for the method of his death upon whether the person declaiming belongs to the tank, gas, air or other special service.

. . . many of them possess considerable histrionic ability and much verbosity [and] they attract public attention. The appeal of their statements is further strengthened because . . . they deal invariably in mechanical devices which intrigue the simple imagina-

tion . . . [and their schemes have] a strong news interest which insures their notice by the press . . .

. . . [newspapers have a] tendency to exploit the bizarre . . .

To . . . [pacifists] the history of the race from the fierce struggles
in primordial slime to the present day is a blank . . . the lion loses
his appetite and the lamb his fear, avarice and ambition, honor and
patriotism are no more, all merge in a supine state of impossible tol-
eration. The millions who have nobly perished for an ideal are fools,
and a sexless creature too debased to care and too indolent to strive is
held up for emulation . . .

There is an incessant change of means [in warfare] . . . [but] the
unchanging ends have been, are and probably ever shall be, the securing of predominating force, of the right sort, at the right place, at
the right time.

. . . High academic performance [in the study of war] demands
infinite knowledge of details and the qualities requisite to such attainments often inhabit bodies lacking in personality. Also the striving for such knowledge often engenders the falacious notion that capacity depends on the power to acquire such details not the ability to
apply them . . .

. . . no soldiers ever sought more diligently [than the Germans]
for prewar perfection. They builded and tested and adjusted their
mighty machine and became so engrossed in its visible perfection, in
the accuracy of its bearing and the compression of its cylinders that
they neglected the battery till when the moment came their master-
piece proved inefficient through lack of the divine afflatus, the soul of
a leader . . .

We require and must demand all possible thoughtful preparation
and studious effort possible . . . Our purpose is not to discourage
such preparation but simply to call attention to certain defects in its
pursuit . . .

In acquiring erudition we must live on not in our studies. We must
guard against becoming so engrossed in the specific nature of the
roots and bark of the trees of knowledge as to miss the meaning and
grandeur of the forests they compose . . .

All down the immortal line of mighty warriors . . . [they] were
deeply imbued with the whole knowledge of war as practised at their
several epochs. But also, and mark this, so were many of their defeated opponents; for . . . the secret of victory lies not wholly in
knowledge. It lurks invisible in that vitalising spark, intangible, yet
as evident as the lightning — the warrior soul . . .

Dry knowledge like dry rot destroys the soundest fiber. A constant search for soulless fundamentals, the effort to regularise the irregular, to make complex the simple, to assume perfect men, perfect material and perfect terrain as the prerequisites to war has the same effect on the soldier student . . .

War is conflict, fighting an elemental exposition of the age-old effort to survive. It is the cold glitter of the attacker's eye not the point of the questing bayonet that breaks the line. It is the fierce determination of the driver to close with the enemy, not the mechanical perfection of a Mark VIII tank that conquers the trench. It is the cataclysmic ecstasy of conflict in the flier not the perfection of his machine gun which drops the enemy in flaming ruin . . .

. . . Hooker's plan at Chancerlorsville was masterly, its execution cost him the battle. The converse was true [with Napoleon] at Marengo . . .

Staff systems and mechanical communications are valuable but above and beyond them must be the commander; not as a disembodied brain linked to his men by lines of wire and waves of ether; but as a living presence, an all pervading visible personality . . .

. . . Napoleon Bonaparte and Stonewall Jackson stand preeminent in their use of . . . time . . .

In war tomorrow we shall be dealing with men subject to the same emotions as were the soldiers of Alexander; with men but little changed . . . from the starving shoeless Frenchmen of 1796. With men similar save in their arms to those who the inspiring powers of a Greek or a Corsican changed at a breath to bands of heroes all enduring and all capable . . .

There are certainly born leaders but the soldier may also overcome his natal defects by unremitting effort and practice . . .

Loyalty is frequently only considered as faithfulness from the bottom up. It has another and equally important application, that is from the top down. One of the most frequently noted characteristics of the great who remained great is . . . loyalty to their subordinates. It is this characteristic which binds with hoops of iron their juniors to them.

A man who is truly and unselfishly loyal to his superiors is of necessity so to his juniors and they to him . . .

A man of diffident manner will never inspire confidence. A cold reserve cannot beget enthusiasm . . . there must be an outward and visible sign of the inward and spiritual grace.

It then appears that the leader must be an actor and he certainly

must be. But with him as with his bewigged counterpart he is unconvincing unless he lives his part . . .

The fixed determination to acquire the warrior soul and having
acquired it to conquer or perish with honor is the secret of victory.

These sentiments, expressed publicly, burned within him. The deeds
of derring-do he dreamed of contrasted with the routine duties he performed as a staff officer, a G–1, who was concerned with matters of personnel and administration. Sitting at a desk was anathema to him and to
his vision of the warrior. Yet accompanying his drive for battlefield greatness was his loyalty to the Army and to his superiors that gave him the
patience to endure. As he wrote to Aunt Nannie, "The present indications are that I shall be kept on this down town job for another three
months which is a great nusance but there is no help for it." With as
much good grace as he could muster, he performed the functions required
of him.

He did, of course, a great deal more. He led an extensive social life.
"Gen and Mrs. Howze are over here visiting their daughter and we are
giving them a party on Saturday with all the rank in the army coming."
He was president of a riding club. He devoted a great deal of time to
polo, not merely to playing the game but also to the details connected
with arranging the matches.

He continued his professional reading. Annotating Swinton's *Study of
War*, Patton commented: to live meant to fight tenaciously, disarmament
was disastrous to nations, and countries had constantly to prepare for
war.

Patton reviewed for the *Cavalry Journal* Captain B. H. Liddell Hart's
The Remaking of Modern Armies, saying in part:

> . . . many of its ideas are radical. In other words, their thoughts
> must be chewed to be digested, for if swallowed whole, like patented
> foods, their nutritive qualities will either fail to develop or else they
> will overstimulate and produce mental colic . . .
>
> We are informed that "Sudden and overwhelming blows from the
> air — could destroy Essen or Berlin in a matter of hours." Having
> learned by experience and by reading, the difficulty of destroying
> anything and the obstacles incident to the production of overwhelm-
> ing instruments, one is tempted to suggest [that] . . . a steam roller
> . . . would be as useful and as attainable . . .

The question he asks as to the future of the French Army might, with some limitations, be asked of our own. The answer is fraught with great moment.

In the same issue of the *Cavalry Journal,* Patton reviewed with great charm and literary facility a biography of Major General Sir Frederick Maurice, soldier, artist, and sportsman.

Of Major B. C. Deming's *The Future of the British Army,* he wrote:

There are probably as many ways of winning a war as there are of skinning a cat. Some of us pin our faith on an accurate use of commas, others on grease or gas, on footease or saddle soap, and in the ardor of our enthusiasm for our especial panacea forget that the way to skin a cat is to remove his hide, and the way to win a war is to beat the enemy. Whether or not we belong to those who pin their faith on grease, and mechanization as the surest means to future victory is, however, immaterial to the fact that any soldier will be benefited and interested by reading [the book under review].
. . . our future triumphs or disasters depend on whether or not we are able to compromise, to select the virtues of the new and add them to the merits of the old — to mix grease with footease.

The last was a subtle reference to the place of the gasoline engine in warfare. Still interested in machines, Patton could not afford to be altogether outspoken in his advocacy of mechanization if he wished advancement in the cavalry.

The Hawaiian Division commander signed a letter prepared by his G–1, Patton, recommending a revision in an Army Regulation to prevent "an unduly rapid flow of promotions among reserve officers, thereby doing an injustice to them by making them eligible for commands in war for which their training does not qualify them. And at the same time militating against public interest by the placing of the lives of our soldiers in untrained hands." At the bottom of the paper in Patton's handwriting was the notation: "Form proposed and written by GSP Jr. Approved with minor modifications." He may have disliked staff work, but he took pride in his minor triumphs.

Colonel A. G. Lott, chief of staff of the Hawaiian Division, rated Patton as "above average" — "an officer with 'a punch' who is better suited for duty with Cavalry than for peacetime administrative details.'

Early in 1926, Patton learned that the Commandant of Cadets at the Military Academy was soon to be transferred. He immediately sought the post. He telegraphed three influential friends, Generals Harbord, H. A. Smith, and Malin Craig, asking them for help.

Harbord regretfully said that he had already committed himself to support another officer, for it had not occurred to him that Patton wanted the assignment. Otherwise, Harbord would have been for him. Quekemeyer, he informed Patton, had been selected but had died very suddenly of pneumonia.

Smith wrote to the Superintendent of the Military Academy and recommended Patton without reservation. Patton, he said, was "one of the best informed officers in his profession that I know." He was a hard worker and extremely loyal, had a fine personality and a delightful family.

Smith also talked with Fox Conner, the new Deputy Chief of Staff — "He is for you, as you know I am, and we will do whatever we can for you."

Telegram, Malin Craig (Fort Riley) to Major General Robert C. Davis (War Department), March 4, 1926

Following cable received from Honolulu Quote Please recommend me for commandant of cadets signed Patton Unquote You know Patton so foregoing is for your consideration.

Letter, Malin Craig (Washington) to GSP, Jr., March 16, 1926

My dear George: Your cable reached me at Fort Riley where I was making an inspection. All I could do was to transmit it by wire to Davis with the necessary recommendation. I regret I was not here, as I would have gone to General Pershing, though of course Davis [a member of Pershing's staff in France] knows you. As you know, the detail has gone to a man named [Major Campbell B.] Hodges of the Infantry, who, I understand, was the personal selection of General Stewart [the Superintendent]. I regret very much that circumstances existed as they did as you are one fellow for whom I am always ready to go to the bat. When the next thing comes off I would naturally like a little more time as it is astonishing how details are prepared for and sewed up in advance.

Letter, Major General Fox Conner to GSP, Jr., June 15, 1926

My Dear Georgie . . . I am afraid the poor old Regular is in for hard sledding . . . As a matter of fact our whole trouble is one of money. I think we have ourselves largely to blame for we have, in the past at least, wasted a H— of a lot of money . . . I notice that the French Air Service have not yet knocked the Riffs out [in Morocco, where natives were in revolt]. Something must be wrong. Perhaps they [the Riffs] refused to be anchored! [He was referring to their mobility.] As far as I can make out China is the place to be now. Drop me a line on how you size up the maneuvers [in Hawaii]. Much love to the family.

Letter, GSP, Jr., to Eisenhower, July 9, 1926

Dear Ike: Your letter [following Eisenhower's graduation from the C&GS College] delighted me more that [than] I can say. As soon as I saw the list I wrote you congratulating you on being honor[ed] but I had no idea that in addition you were no [number] ONE. That certainly is fine.

It shows that leavenworth is a good school if a HE man can come out one [in his class].

You are very kind to think that my notes helped you though I feel sure that you would have done as well with out them. If a man thinks war long enough it is bound to effect him in a good way.

I am convinced that as good as leavenworth is it is still only a means not an end and that we must keep on. I have worked all the problems of the two years since I graduated and shall continue to do so. However I dont try for approved solutions any more but rather to do what I will do in war. This applies both to formations and to verbage of the order. Orders in battle must be written wholly by the general him self not by a committee of his staff. Hence they must be short. Further in battle par 3 not par 2 is the important point.

As for par 4 let them live off the country and in par 5 state that the CP is the head of the maine blow. [He was speaking of the paragraphs of the standard field order.]

You know that we talk a hell of a lot about tactics and such and we never get to brass tacks. Namely what it is that makes the Poor S.O.B. who constitutes the casualtie lists fight and in what formation is he going to fight. The answer to the first is Leadership that to the second — I don't know. But this I do know that the present Infantry T.R. based on super trained heroes is bull. The solitary son of a bitch alone with God is going to skulk as he always has and our advancing waves will not advance unless we have such superior artillery that all they have to do is to walk.

First Read Battle Studies by Du Pique (you can get it at Leaven-worth) then put your mind to a solution. The victor in the next war will depend on EXECUTION not PLANS and the execution will depend on some means of making the infantry move under fire. I have a solution for the Artillery and cavalry but only a tentative one for the infantry. After you tell me what you can make of it I will send you mine.

You did not say in your letter where you were going? I think prob-ably an instructor ship is the best. The G.S. [General Staff] is punk. You and I will never have a G.S. [assignment] at least not as now invisioned.

With renewed congratulations and best wishes, I am

Most Sincerely, G S Patton Jr.

P.S. I gave you the last copy of my notes. Since they have been so useful I should like to get hold of a copy. Do you think you can locate one for me. If so I would like it. GSP

Letter, GSP, Jr., to Major Jack W. Heard (Cavalry Board, Fort Riley), August 12, 1926

I have made rather profound studies on the subject of Saber and Bayonet charges and it is my opinion based on history that the cases where two lines will meet will be VERY exceptional. One side will loose its nerve and run. In the rare instance when the lines meet, it will be at a very reduced pace or at a halt as the big majority of horses will refuse the shock. In either case, then a light handy saber will be more useful than a long awkward one. The above remarks in no way imply that I have lost faith in the saber. I have however decided that it is the enemies soul rather than his body which is de-feated. For the same reason the formation which a charge is executed is immaterial; determination and speed are the only requisite. *The leader must be in front.* It is interesting to remember that the mounted bowmen never closed nor did the pistol fighters of Maurice of Nassau — Reason — the weapons they used could be discharged at a distance. In both cases they were put out of business by the charge with the steel NOT because the steel was more *deadly* but because the determination to use it, being of a higher order, broke the spirit of the enemy. Pistol fire, if effective, would kill more enemy than the saber. Rifle fire from the hip would kill more enemy than the bayo-net but man, being what he is, will never close to effective range unless he knows that his weapon is useless at any other. It is the apparent menace of death rather than actual death which wins battles. The vicious saber charge wins long before the lines touch; and having won, anything is sufficient to stick the enemy in the back. Sincerely yours,

The last point came directly from the writings of Ardant du Picq, military thinker and writer who fathered the idea of élan, the spirit of the charge, who died during the Franco-Prussian War, and whose concept was adopted and fostered by Grandcamp and Foch — so that at the beginning of World War I, the professional French officers, convinced of the superiority of men over machines and of the necessity of the offensive, threw away thousands of soldiers against the machine guns that mowed them down.

And yet, who could deny that one of two opposing lines usually broke and ran. The steady — meaning Regular — troops of the French and British employed in far-off lands and romanticized in the 1920s and 1930s by such novels as *Beau Geste,* always withstood the howling mobs attacking them and sent them streaming back in confusion and defeat before physical contact was made.

Patton's letter to Heard was probably his clearest exposition of this point of view.

Colonel Lott rated Patton as "above average" — "an enthusiastic soldier with a 'punch,' and a serious student of his profession, exceptionally well fitted for duty with troops of his arm (cavalry)."

The polo was splendid during the summer of 1926, and Patton's Army team defeated the two civilian teams in competition and captured the Island championship. To the senior officers in Hawaii, the games were not merely amusement but rather a "creditable exhibition of fine sportsmanship, leadership, and team play, qualities essential to success in the military profession."

Letter, H. A. Smith to GSP, Jr., October 26, 1926
I enjoyed your letter very much, and when I read Mrs. Smith the sentence, "May we soon have a war so that you can exercise command" she said, "You needn't read any more. I know George Patton wrote that." However, maybe we can kick up a good war. I am thinking some of starting a filibustering expedition to one of the Central American States. How would you like to go along on that?

Smith was only joking.

Letter, GSP, Jr., to Beatrice (visiting in Massachusetts), November 2, 1926

I have always hoped that as the result of a great war I would secure supreme command and such fame that after the war I would be able to become President or dictator by the ballot or by force. In that case we would not have needed a house for we would have persuaded a grateful people to build us a marble Palace at the flag pole at Fort Myer. However as I approach [the age of] 41 and there is no war I almost doubt the Palace and fear that I shall live to retire a useless soldier. In which case as we could still hunt it would be nice to have a place in the hunting country. As inspite of polo ponies, boats and Squash Courts you don't spend ¼ of your income I think the house might be fine and certainly no extravagance.

Letter, C. P. Summerall to GSP, Jr., November 4, 1926

My dear Patton: I deeply appreciate your very good letter congratulating me upon my appointment as Chief of Staff. It has been one of my peculiar privileges to serve with you under varying circumstances and difficulties, and I have always felt the most sincere appreciation of your loyalty and admiration for your efficiency. Indeed, it is to you and to the officers and soldiers with whom I have served that I owe whatever success may have come to my efforts. I can only place my reliance upon you for the support and cooperation that I shall need in my future tasks.

Letter, GSP, Jr., to Beatrice, November 16, 1926

Darling Beat: I got three letters from you to day one with the clippings about the Riley Races. What is the matter with your eyes [in one of the photographs], are they crossed?

Beatrice and young Bea traveled from Massachusetts, Patton, Ruth Ellen, and young George came from Hawaii, and all met in southern California for Christmas.

GSP, Jr., "My Father," 1927

In the spring of 1926 Papa Mama and Nita visited us at Schofield. Papa was very feeble and his tongue used to get black and we would joke him about it. He suffered a lot with constipation. One day he went swimming with us and once he and I took a ride of about an hour. It was his last ride. We drove all over Oahu. Papa had a little Oakland Coupe which we rented for him.

After they left for home in July, Papa wrote me much less often and his writing was much less firm and clear. Mama wrote that she was much worried about him. He went to the hospital and was cured of his constipation but his bladder became inflamed and he underwent a thorough physical examination. In November he wrote me that he hoped we would all come home "so that we could have one more Christmas together."

While we were home last Christmas [in 1926] he seemed to improve. Still he was very weak and worried about trivial details. He and [young] george used to walk in the Cannon gorge with a pop gun and they would pretend to kill lions as I had once done. Papa took me with him when ever he could always asking me to drive to the Post Office with him for the mail. One day I was lazy and did not go. The sorrow in his voice when he said "All right son never mind I will be right back" Haunts me.

In 1922 Papa [had] bought himself a Hup Roadster. He used to write me about it and took a lot of interest in it. So far as I know this was about the only present he had ever bought just for him self. He and Mama drove all over the country in it especially on Sunday Morning when they would most frequently drive towards Duarte. In 1926 it was old and stiff so Beatrice and I made him turn it in and we got him a new Hup Eight. Papa protested violently that his old car was good enough for him but I shall never forget the pleasure of his smile when the new one came and he walked around it poking the tires with his stick and saying "it is a gentleman's car." He liked it a lot and used to tell mama that it was the best sort of car. He and I took several drives in it, once to Duarte, but at the time of his death he had driven it less than a thousand miles. The memory of his pleasure at it is a great happiness to me . . .

The morning after we arrived Christmas morning 1926, papa took me to his office and told me that the examination he had taken disclosed the fact that he had T.B. in his left kidney. He asked me not to tell any of the family as it would worry them. I went to see the doctors and after consulting with them and with Nita and Beatrice we decided that it was better not to operate as we feared he would fret so in the hospital that it would kill him; besides some of them said that sun baths might arrest or cure the disease.

At this time he was more interested in affairs than he had been for some time. He wanted to make a trade with Mr. Huntington so as to get the bottom of the Cannon [canyon] back of the house especially as it would improve Nita's place. And he was again interested in the

Pyramids and their significance and had several new books on them which he read in connection with Biblical prophecies.

He had always expressed to me his belief that the very fortunate career I had had in the army was Fate and that I was being specially prepared for some special work. He and Mr Gaffey felt that the end of our Civilization was at hand and that war was sure. When I used to bemoan the fact that wars were getting scarce and that all the time I had spent getting ready would be wasted for lack of opportunity he used to assure me with the greatest confidence that I would yet be in the biggest war in history. He was most convincing and I believed him, particularly as I have always felt the same thing concerning my self . . .

This same Christmas period he took me to his office and showed me the relics he had about his father and family.

One evening when the rest had gone to bed he said to me wistfully "Son you had more experiences and saw more of life in two years in France than I have in all my seventy years." He was not bitter or complaining, only wistful. He had a romantic and venturesome spirit which had been curbed by circumstances and a sense of duty to those he loved. I am sure he felt that death was the only adventure left for him and yearned for it with out fear and with great curiosity and anticipation being only deterred from so expressing such feelings by his love for his family and his fear of wounding them.

One evening I made him dictate to me all his memories of the civil war as he saw it as a boy. I have this at schofield [Barracks] and will type it and file it with this.

After we left Papa became much worse and suffered intensely . . .

Letter, GSP, Jr., to his father, February 6, 1927.

As I wrote you the other day I can arrange to get off any time and come home either to go east with you or to be present if you have an operation. I have already gotten the permission from General Smith . . . I cannot urge too strongly my earnest hope that you realy exercise your will power to take care of your self. You are such a good arguer that it is too easy for you to reason your self out of doing things that are a nusance. And you are then perfectly convinced that you are doing the right thing when in fact it is not so. When you were a cadet [at VMI] you did what you were ordered with out question. Cant you ORDER YOUR SELF to take a regular course of treatment what ever it may be and then TAKE IT. The surest way in my opinion is to set aside a certain hour and then arrange things so that in spite of hell or high water you can do it. There are too many people who love you for you to disregard their wishes and kill your self by carlessness. I hope you will forgive my preaching and do your duty to your self.

Long-distance admonition from son to father had little effect, and sometime in February, Mr. Patton wrote and asked George to come home if he could. Unknown to Mr. Patton, Nita wired the same to her brother. A few days later, feeling he was inconveniencing his son far too much, Mr. Patton wired him not to come. George disregarded his father's telegram.

When Patton reached the family home at Lake Vineyard, he found things better than he had expected. All the doctors consulted or in attendance favored an operation.

Thin, weak, and suffering from pain, Mr. Patton, according to his son writing to Beatrice,

has gotten over his idea that the family is financially ruined . . He thinks he is not eating but so far to day has eaten more than I have . . .

After he sent me the wire not to come he was terribly worried for fear I would pay attention to it so, as usual, you were right in telling me to come. He does not know that Nita wired me to come and thinks that I did it in response to a letter [from him]. I am certainly glad I came as it seems to have done them all good. I think that Pa has a very good chance for recovery. If not it would be better for him to die than to suffer, or think he suffers, the way he does.

GSP, Jr., "My Father," 1927

I was in the room with him when the attendants came to wheel him to the operating room. I kissed him and as he went out the door he waved his thin brown hand at me and smiling said "Aurez War [Au revoir] Son." The courage of that act would have won the Medal of Honor on any field of battle. He was seventy, had never been operated on, so dreaded it, and he was very weak; yet going to what he thought was death he tried to cheer me with out thought of self.

Mr. Patton came through the operation nicely and slept quietly immediately afterward. Mrs. Patton was in good spirits "and did not show any

excitement." Patton had a room next door to his father's in the hospital.
After a bad night, Mr. Patton improved.

GSP, Jr., "My Father," 1927
   I stayed with him every day till the thirteenth when I left for San
Francisco. He suffered a lot the first five days but then seemed much
better. The last afternoon I was with him I was smoking and he
asked me to fill his favorite pipe for him and we smoked together.
That night I kissed him for the last time and said good by. He
smiled and said he would take care of him self. Next day I called
him on the long distance from San Francisco. The last words I ever
heard him say were: "Good by Old Man take care of yourself."

Letter, GSP Jr. (on the Dollar Steamship Line steamer S.S. President
Polk) *to his father, March 17, 1927*
   I have read two books and written some notes on the defense of
columns against Air Planes. I hated to leave before you were completely well . . . I never saw one go out to die with as much calm-
ness and assurance as you did. When they wheeled you out of the
room you waved your hand to me and said "Aurey vois" with a smile
and in a perfectly natural voice. Now please as a favor to all of us use
that same high courage to get well and strong so that you can enjoy
life and we can enjoy having you.

Letter, GSP, Jr. (in Honolulu) to his father, March 21, 1927
   You ought to be like me and not worry. In getting off the steamer
a friend offered me a bottle of whiskey so I put it in my overcoat
pocket and was arrested on the dock. I was very polite and all that
happened was that it cost me five dollars no publicity or any thing.
Beatrice did not even know that it had happened nor does she yet
for that matter for she is like you and would have at once started to
picture the penetentiary court martial etc. Worrying does not help
any thing and hurts every thing. STOP IT . . . Everyone seemed
glad to see me back and my new assistant is a very good officer and
seems willing to do all the work while I get what glory there is.

Letter, GSP, Jr., to his father, April 22, 1927
   I hear that you have got your self on your mind and dont eat etc.
Of course if you want to die that is the best way to secure the end
desired. You will now say that I dont understand you and that you

cant help it. You can if you will. With all the people who love you and want you to live it is selfish and poor sportsmanship to act as you are doing.

He invited his father to come for a visit and promised he would not ask him to ride or to swim or to do anything but sit in the sun. He had just returned from the island of Hawaii, where he had spent eight days buying horses for the post. He had purchased 66 animals and had had a nice time staying with Mr. Alfred Carter who ran the Parker ranch of 500,000 acres, quite a "fudal" place.

He wrote again on April 27, telling his father that he and Beatrice had sailed in two races on Saturday and Sunday and had finished third and fourth in a field of eleven boats. The 66 horses he had purchased had arrived, "and every one thinks that I am a famous horse buyer . . . The longer we stay here the more we like it and hate the thought of leaving. We have not yet decided whether or not to ask for a fourth year."

Letter, GSP, Jr., to his father, May 24, 1927

I am sorry that you had such an awful trip [here last year] for when you are well [and can come for another visit] you will like it here. Right now it is lovley.

Mr. Patton died early in June, and his son went home, too late for the funeral.

GSP, Jr., "My Father," 1927

The morning I arrived I wore my uniform and went alone to his grave. The whole lot was covered with flowers all of which had wilted save the pall of red roses over the spot where he lay. These to me seemed fresh, vivified by the great soul of him who lay beneath them.

For an hour I stood there and the knowledge came to me that the grave no more held Papa than does one of his discarded suits hanging in a closet. Suddenly I seemed to see him in the road werring his checked overcoat and with his stick which he waved at me as he had been used to do when he was impatient and wanted to go some where.

I knelt and kissed the ground then put on my cap and saluted not Papa, but the last resting place of that beautiful body I had loved.

His soul was with me and but for the density of my fleshly eyes I could have seen and talked with him.

As I write this in his office where we talked and smoked so often he is here. I like to remember not the symbol of his gallant spirit which I saluted in the church yard but Rather Papa as he was wheeled out to die perhaps, and to think of his words so true of our present temporary seperation when he smiled at me and said "Aurevoir Son."

Oh! darling Papa. I never called you that in life as both of us were too self contained but you were and are my darling. I have often thought that life for me was too easy but the loss of you has gone far [to] even my count with those whom before I have pitied.

God grant that you see and appreciate my very piteous attempt to show here your lovely life. I never did much for you and you did all for me. Accept this as a slight offering of what I would have done.

Your devoted son

G S Patton Jr

July 9 1927

Letter, Pershing to GSP, Jr., July 12, 1927

No one could meet your father without feeling his personality, and no one could know him, even casually, without recognizing his high character and great ability. I know the high esteem in which you yourself held him and knew him well enough to understand fully the reasons for your great admiration and affection. Please accept for yourself and extend to your mother and sister my deepest and sincerest condolences in the great loss that has come to you, to his friends, to the State of California, and to the nation in his passing.

Letter, GSP, Jr., to Pershing, July 25, 1927

While all sympathy is most grateful when it comes from the first soldier of the age it is truly delightful . . .

I can imagine no more pleasant and instructive place [than Hawaii] to serve. While I am on the Staff — a place for which God never intended me — I can with the Hawaiian Division still see quite a lot of the troops.

CHAPTER 40

Hawaii to Washington

"In war death is incidental: loss of time is criminal."

Letter, GSP, Jr., to Beatrice, November 1, 1926
The order is out to day making me G–3 — at last.

He was excited by his assignment to the G–3 post, which he had long hankered after. That staff section was concerned with operations, plans, and training. Although staff work frustrated Patton, the functions of the G–3 were closest to his peacetime interests — preparing troops for combat in a future war. Although he would suffer from the lack of direct contact with units and soldiers enjoyed by commanders, he would at least be directly involved in what he considered to be the most important activity — training. As G–3, he was the division commander's adviser on tactical matters — a subject which encompassed a great many affairs — and as such he could speak in the name of the commander to all subordinate formations and commanders in the division. Relishing his new status, Patton immediately made his presence remarked.

The 22d Brigade of the Hawaiian Division held an exercise in mid-November on how to conduct the advance guard. The demonstration displeased him immensely. As the staff representative of the division commander, he was free to make comments, and according to his observations, certain obvious deficiencies required correction. He minced no words in his written remarks to the brigade commander, who was a brigadier general, and this was a procedural error on Patton's part. He should have had the division commander sign the paper. For a major to "correct" a brigadier general was inadmissible. His action was tactless and created much ill-will toward him.

What he wrote was this:

The normal purpose of an attack is the infliction of death wounds and destruction on the enemy troops with a view to establish both physical and moral ascendency over them. The gaining of ground in such a combat is simply an incident; not an object.

The following remarks are not confined to advance guards nor are they wholly orthodox. They are submitted for what they may be worth . . .

[The attempt by soldiers to use cover was not warranted in most cases, for the] primary efforts are directed to fancied self preservation rather than towards killing his enemy . . . In battle a man going forward enters a lottery, with death the stake, and the odds the laws of probability. The only saving clause in his venture are the time and the effect on the enemy's nerves of his rapid approach; why waste these benefits in futile sacrifices to lost Gods of Indian wars . . .

In battle the dead do not run but the living do and for them to so perform it is necessary that they be scared. These considerations seem to indicate that the present method of using machine guns is not the last word, the best arrangement. Serious thought should be given to supplying each platoon with self contained man transported machine guns . . .

[Howitzer platoons] seem to absorb more men from our depleted regiments than their killing value justifies. . . .

There is much talk to the effect that the fire of guns, machine guns, stokes mortars, etc make certain places impassable. History proves that fighting men can go anywhere. The technique of deploying, fire, cover, etc [in our training exercises] seems to overshadow the paramount idea of KILLING. Advances are too unenthusiastic. This tendency is enhanced by the fact that most exercises stop at the deployment. Actually it is in stages subsequent to the deployment where the fighting and the trouble starts. It is thought that all exercises should be conducted with this idea in view.

Again in his capacity as G–3, Patton instructed all brigade, regimental, and separate unit commanders to correct certain derelictions in military bearing among officers and men: poor adjustment of Sam Browne belts worn at drill; poor saluting by officers who frequently failed to come to attention during the salute; poor manners on the part of officers who smoked while instructing or while supervising instruction — "They shall only smoke during rest periods where the same privilege is allowed the men."

Lieutenant Colonel S. T. Mackall, the acting chief of staff, rated Patton "above average" as G–1, G–2, and G–3 — "an ambitious officer, aggressive disposition, well read, perfectly loyal [to his superiors]."

As G–3, Patton tried to solve a problem that plagued all headquarters — how to deal satisfactorily with the mutually conflicting tasks of housekeeping and training, that is, how to have the minimum number of troops on supply and administrative details required to keep a post operating, while at the same time retaining the maximum number at military instruction. At Schofield Barracks, only about half the men were attending drill and other military exercises at any given time; the rest were on kitchen police and similar duties. Patton suggested two alternatives: set aside certain days when all purely administrative and routine activities would cease, thereby having all the men available for training; or form provisional units to train the relatively few men available from each company for military instruction.

These suggestions were probably too radical to be accepted.

A report issued by a board of officers studying how a division could gain protection against low-flying airplanes impressed him unfavorably. The board, headed by Major Henry H. Arnold, who would command the U. S. Army Air Corps in World War II and be a member of the Joint Chiefs of Staff, recommended that ground troops disperse at once when spotted by planes.

Patton wrote in the margin of the report: "This is a poor paper and views the whole thing in a negative way. 'War means fighting and fighting means killing' GSP." What he was saying was that passive defense — dispersing and taking cover — was no solution.

The board also recommended that two .50-caliber machine guns be mounted on light motor vehicles, that these accompany troop units, and that the gunners be ready at all times to engage low-flying planes. Patton's comment on the margin: "only good idea so far."

In May 1927, Patton devoted thought to the problem. In a long memo to the chief of staff, he said that the history of war was replete with lags, that is, periods when a new means of attack or defense gained a temporary ascendancy simply because it was novel rather than irresistible. The latest instance was air attack of ground troops, effective because the sudden appearance of planes gave them the advantage of surprise and because the ground troops offered no opposition. Air attacks were not terribly impressive in lethality; they were more expensive and less productive than ground attacks. Therefore, there was no need to be alarmed that airplanes might replace ground troops. Nevertheless, the vulnerability of ground units to aircraft made it desirable to see what might be done to counter the air weapons.

Most of the important troop movements in the World War, Patton continued, were made at night. This gave soldiers immunity from air observation and attack. But perhaps aircraft had since improved and were now capable of night operations against moving columns, the most lucrative target for planes.

What could be done? It was impossible to think of concealment, for that played into the enemy's hands. Nor was it feasible simply to disregard air attacks, for no discipline was sufficiently strong to keep men from scattering under strafing. The only solution that made sense was to devise some method of attacking the planes from the ground. How?

The speed of planes, which were capable of flying at 200 miles per hour, required ground soldiers to have instant warning of their approach. This meant that at least some troops had to be trained to identify enemy planes and to be on constant lookout for them. Once they gave the alarm, troops had to deploy from their march formation to a fighting formation; they had to do so in less than half a minute. Thus, the transition from march to combat formation had to be a simple procedure that could, with practice, be executed automatically. Whatever combat formation was selected, it had to enable all the men — not just part of them — to participate in the attack against the aircraft. What seemed instantly apparent to Patton was that almost everyone had to turn his weapon against the planes; a few soldiers would have to blindfold the horses and mules to keep them from panicking.

To this end, Patton composed a set of simple principles to regulate the switch from marching to fighting.

He warned, "The purpose of this memorandum is to stimulate thought; not to stifle it with dogma so that the sketchy regulations set out below are to be considered as provocatory rather than manditory in nature."

He added a note:

> In writing this a studious attempt has been made to avoid the use of defensive expressions . . . [which] should never be used as they

ingender a defensive frame of mind. The same is true of talk of
concealment or the avoidance of splinters from bombs. Under normal shell or machine gun fire men do not or should not hide. The
same is true in the case of air attacks. It is not recommended that
practice against baloons or towed target be indulged in. In peace the
hits will be so low asto reduce confidence. In war the volume of wild
fire and the less adroitness of war time aviators [likely to be reserv-
ists] will secure us more hits. Care should be exercised that enemy
aviators shot down should not be taken alive.

Patton proposed an exercise to determine whether his idea was practi-
cal, and the Hawaiian Division commander, Major General William R.
Smith, after issuing a letter prepared by Patton on the "Ground Attack of
Airplanes," ordered a demonstration.

On May 26, as the 3d Battalion, 35th Infantry, and several planes of the
18th Pursuit Group tested the effectiveness of Patton's notion, he observed the maneuver. On the following morning, he wrote a scathing
criticism of the results obtained. Having learned his lesson, Patton submitted his comments to General Smith, who had his adjutant general sign
the paper and send it to the proper brigade commander.

According to this letter, the officers in the battalion that had taken part
in the exercise had failed on a number of points. They had failed to use
every available weapon — only one machine gun of the machine gun
company had been mounted for firing against air targets; they had failed
to arrange to place all the machine guns instantly into action on a stable
platform, from which they could fire more effectively against planes; they
had failed to guard against a stampede on the part of the animals — the
mules had not been blindfolded; they had failed to insure maximum
speed and order in assuming the combat formation; they had failed to
give fire commands and halts in an authoritative manner.

As a result of these defects, the impression was inescapable that the
officers and men had not grasped the spirit of the proposed regulations.

. . . order, volume of fire, and rapidity of transition from march to
combat and back to march conditions are the essential elements in
the successful combat with air planes. Order depends on instant exact and subconscious obedience to specific commands. Volume of fire
depends on the utilization of all available means. Rapidity depends
on automatic obedience. Conversation with the officers and men

forces the opinion that the men of this battalion were not trained or prepared to combat airplanes and did not visualize the situation. Further that what notions they did have were negative and showed too much thought of danger. The reason stated for the column leaving the road was that in this way they would avoid ricochets. More complete immunity could be secured by not having enlisted. In war death is incidental: loss of time is criminal.

This was strong language, particularly from a relatively young staff officer. It was common knowledge that the exercise was the G–3's baby rather than the division commander's; and so were the comments.

As muttering among some senior officers against Patton grew, General Smith removed Patton from the G–3 position and appointed him G–2, giving as his reason that Patton was too positive in his thinking and too outspoken in his remarks.

The chief of staff, Colonel Francis W. Cooke, rated Patton "average" in all categories as a G–3 and added, "He has had unusual opportunities to acquire both a theoretical and practical knowledge of General Staff work. He is affable and makes friends readily."

But Patton was badly hurt by his removal from the G–3 post. He showed his resentment in a letter to Beatrice: "Gen S. [Smith] must think he was wrong as he had had both Floyd [Parks?] and Capt Coffey tell me that it was only dire necessity which made him relieve me as G–3. Of course he is either a fool or a liar probably both."

Friends of Patton, far more sympathetic to his personality and professional outlook, would soon take control of the Hawaiian Division. Major General Fox Conner would become the commander and Brigadier General George Van Horn Moseley would be chief of staff.

Letter, GSP, Jr., to Brigadier General Harold B. Fiske, September 30, 1927

My dear general Fiske: While I fully realise that generals do not require the approval of majors I am presuming on the fact of my acquaintance with you in France to tell you how very timely your article in the last issue of the Infantry Journal appears. Both my experience in the World War as a training officer and my present occupation as a General Staff Officer . . . have forcibly impressed me with the slowing and emasculating effect on operations and personal leadership inherent in large staffs. As you point out, one of the chief defects in staff work arises from the fact most recent graduates from the different schools seem over impressed with formularism. Their chief concern is to write an order in the nature of an approved solution without regard to the men who must execute it and without considering that successful combat depends on energetic and timely execution rather than on wordy paragraphs. My observation of the schools since the war impresses me with the opinion that this is due, in the vast majority of cases, to the fact that the students have no background of military knowledge as obtained by reading . . . instead of applying teachings to pictured situations and pondering their application they simply memorise the methods . . . better results might accrue were student officers required to read more either at the schools or else before going to them. Also while at the schools that they were impressed with the idea that over half of a staff officers responsibility consists in inspections with a view to assuring his chief that the orders issued are understood and promptly executed . . . I hope you will forgive my temerity in inflicting this long letter on you and attribute it simply to professional interest. Very respectfully.

GSP, Jr. Lecture, "Why Men Fight," October 27, 1927
With the causes and effects of war we are not concerned. Its continued existence is inevitable and its results for good or evil are beyond all human power to avert or change . . .

Help for the helpless springs from love of ourselves . . .

Battle is an orgy of disorder. No level lawns or marker flags exist to aid us strut ourselves in vain display, but rather groups of weary wandering men seek gropingly for means to kill their foe. The sudden change from accustomed order to utter disorder — to chaos, but emphasize the folly of schooling to precision and obedience where only fierceness and habituated disorder are useful.

Superiority in all endeavors, particularly in war, was hereditary. A man's class would show in gentlemanly behavior and sacrifice and leadership. The lower classes had to be schooled to instant and unquestioning obedience to authority. Men fought for food and sex, out of patriotism, habit, or simply obedience, and decorations for valor were important.

. . . a coward dressed as a brave man will change from his cowardice and, in nine cases out of ten, will on the next occasion demonstrate the qualities fortuitously emblazoned on his chest . . .

We must have more decorations and we must give them with no niggard hand . . .

War may be hell; but for John Doughboy there is a heaven of suggestion in anticipating what Annie Rooney will say when she sees him in his pink feather and his new medal.

The truly great military men were

biological incidents whose existence is due to the fortuitous blending of complementary blood lines at epochs where chance or destiny intervenes to give scope to their peculiar abilities.

Americans were handicapped in their search for leaders because of the absence of class distinctions in American society. Increasing the number of graduates from the Military Academy and from ROTC training at colleges and granting more noncommissioned officers Reserve commissions were methods of conferring class distinctions, and leaders so designated acted in consonance with the highest ideals of gentlemen.

It may well be that the greatest soldiers have possessed superior intellects, may have been thinkers; but this was not their dominant characteristic . . . [they] owed their success to indomitable wills and tremendous energy in execution and achieved their initial hold upon the hearts of their troops by acts of demonstrated valor . . . the great leaders are not our responsibility, but God's . . .
    . . . the soul of man is changeless. Our difficulties differ in manifestation but not in nature from those Alexander experienced and Caesar knew. Our success or failure in the next war will depend on our ability to face the naked facts as they exist, and to utilize our means not as we would, but as we may.

This lecture appeared in print, and Patton's friend Sasse commented on the article, saying that men fought because they saw their buddies wounded or killed and they wanted to destroy those who had been responsible. A far less romantic view of men's motivations in combat than Patton's, Sasse's explanation would correspond to the findings of sociologists a generation or so later.

Patton requested a year's extension of his assignment in Hawaii, hoping thus to stay for four years. Was he motivated simply by the extremely pleasant life? Did he cherish the opportunities to observe and participate in relatively large-scale training exercises, which enabled him to have some contact with troops and troop formations? Or did he believe that his staff duties were good discipline, steadying him and restraining his impulses?

Whatever his motives, the War Department turned him down and notified him that he would be transferred to the Office of the Chief of Cavalry in Washington, D.C. at the completion of his Hawaiian tour of duty.

His final few months in Hawaii were notable for his work in amphibious operations, his studies on supporting weapons for assault troops, his thoughts on a reorganization of the division, and a renewed interest in tanks — all of which anticipated developments in World War II.

A series of training exercises on landing an invading force on Hawaii had Patton on the side of the invaders. He issued a series of field orders, signing them "Major General." The situation, sham, of course, resembled in remarkable fashion Patton's invasion of French Northwest Africa on November 8, 1942.

In the same maneuvers, he signed subsequent field orders "Viscount and Lieutenant General" and admonished his subordinate commanders to remember that "violent offensive and rapid movement spell victory."

One set of plans in the war games gave the objective as Pearl Harbor and concluded, in Patton's words: "The Emperor expects the most dauntless courage and vigorous leadership from all his officers. We shall not disappoint him. G. S. Patton, Jr., Viscount and Lieut. General, Commanding [the] Corps." It was a strange intimation of the reality at Pearl Harbor fourteen years in the future.

This was the beginning of Patton's study of amphibious assault techniques, and it would culminate in an expertise that would enable him to plan and lead invasions of North Africa and Sicily in World War II with such conspicuous success.

Devoting thought to the support of infantry assault units in the attack, Patton saw the tank as a vital instrument of firepower support, but was impressed too with its deficiencies.

Any one who fires tank machine guns in war at 500 yards should be tried [by court-martial]. The best range is from 25 yds down . . .

The idea of two shots is based on the assumption that accuracy is desirable, IT IS NOT. Therefore bursts of five shots are better because they tend to be inaccurate. I cannot refrain from adding the following remarks though I feel that since they are based on war experience they are not apt to be well received by the shooting specialists. The tank is primarily and only a shock weapon. Its efficiency resting on its ability to produce mental shock by the never realised threat of physical shock. For this reason all firing should be from a moving tank at ranges from 150 yards down. A tank which stops to fire gets hit.

This led him to experiment with a device he called a Sled Machine Gun Mount, designed to give the infantry assault echelons adequate self-contained firepower. Infantrymen provided with mobile machine guns capable of accompanying them in the attack and furnishing close and direct fire support — as distinguished from indirect machine gun fire from a distance — would have better fire control, more volume of fire, and, consequently, improved morale. In order to avoid fabricating an entirely new weapon for use up forward where the combat action was — a new weapon would consume time and money — Patton invented his sled mount for the existing machine gun. He had an enlisted blacksmith construct one from scrap material, and it worked quite well. Light, simple, and cheap, it could be pushed along the ground by a single man, packed on a horse, and carried by two men. It was also suitable for antiaircraft fire.

Fox Conner witnessed the sled mount used in a practice maneuver, and recommended to the War Department that it be given a trial and accepted or rejected as it was.

Attempts to improve it by the addition of various alleged improvements are foredoomed to failure. Major Patton is now under orders to take station in Washington. He will take this mount with him. It is recommended that extensive tests with the mount be held at some suitable place in the vicinity of Washington.

Letter, GSP, Jr., to Major General Robert H. Allen, Chief of Infantry, January 30, 1928

My dear General Allen: The night after the standings of my class at Leavenworth were published in June 1924 I was talking to you at the dance and you congratulated me in the following words: "Patton, it is a real pleasure to me to see a 'He' soldier graduate in the honors." I have always treasured this remark and have tried to live up to the standard you allotted me. I trust that in sending you direct the enclosed account [description] of a Sled Machine Gun Mount which I have devised I shall not forfeit your esteem. As I see it, the mount is adapted to the use of "He Soldiers" and will, I hope, help them to additional successes in the next war. The original letter was sent to the War Department through channels, but as I felt that you and the Chief of Cavalry would perhaps be interested, I secured permission from Gen Fox Conner to send you and General Crosby a copy direct. Asking pardon for my temerity, I am Very respectfully,

Allen cordially replied and said he was having the Infantry Board look at the sled mount. "I congratulate you on this additional demonstration of your practical ability as a 'He soldier' and wish you continued success along that line."

Letter, GSP, Jr., to Major General Herbert B. Crosby, Chief of Cavalry, January 30, 1928
My dear General Crosby: I have been experimenting on the construction of a machine gun mount sufficiently mobile to accompany the firing line. General Fox Conner was quite pleased with it and I obtained from him permission to send you the enclosed copy of the letter I wrote forwarding it to the Adjutant General. I also sent a copy to General Allen. Due to the lack of pack saddles here I have not been able to experiment with packing this mount on a horse, but I think that it can be readily placed astride the top of a pack. To do this it may be necessary to spread the runners a little. If it proves to be easily packed I suggest that it may prove a much better weapon for the Machine Rifle platoons than the arm they now carry. Its quick adaptability to antiaircraft fire certainly makes it very useful to cavalry. I trust that you will pardon me for bothering you personally with this subject. I was emboldened to do so by the fact that you would perhaps be interested. I am looking forward with great enthusiasm to serving in your office. My tour here ends April 1st and I should be in Washington around the end of the month, depending on the boats. Very respectfully.

Crosby wrote Patton that the sled mount appeared interesting. But far more important to Crosby was his implication of why Patton had been selected to serve in his office — "Mechanization looms very large in the

War Department today, and your past experiences will serve you in this."
And Crosby, although he left this unsaid, was happy to have Patton because no one could better refute the apostles of mechanization — who
were claiming that the horse had become obsolete in modern warfare —
than the premier American tank expert in the World War, Patton,
widely known to be a proponent not only of the tank but also of the
horse.

Probably asked why machine guns on the front line were necessary, why
sled mounts were needed, Patton broadened his thinking and considered
the larger problem of how best to wage warfare, which to him meant executing the attack. A long paper, entitled somewhat inaccurately "Drills
for Fighting," presented the outlook of a mature and thoughtful professional officer. Starting with how to revise training to gain greater realism,
that is, how to make exercises approximate actual conditions in combat,
he proceeded to look at warfare in the large, what it was and how wars
were best fought. This in turn took him into matters of organization, the
ideal numbers of men for units, the functions of units, and the nature of
leadership.

The study was divided into seven sections and had five tables appended. It was written humorously, sometimes with savage sarcasm, and
it represented Patton's distilled thoughts at age forty-two, his prime. Virtually all of the ideas had been expressed previously in piecemeal fashion,
but he now brought them together in a unified view of combat that
stressed the contrast between the ordered uniformity of the drill field and
the chaotic reality of the battlefield.

1. Battle as per Training Regulations:

The scouts appear advancing with unerring intelligence despite their
unfamiliarity with the terrain, and employing . . . methods of progression often depicted on the burlesque stage as those employed by burglars.

Eventually, this line of tiptoe dancers exasperates the enemy to the
point of firing . . .

Crawling and wiggling, on the [scouts] press, the superlative excellence
of three months training manifesting itself in the precision with which
they invariably avail themselves of the redundant protection of sundry
blades of grass and dandelion stems.

Eventually they reach a well sighted [sited] line from which with marvellous accuracy they bring a devastating fire . . . upon the enemy, whose exact location and range they have determined by sundry occult methods well known to map problems.

. . . the leaders in rear . . . assemble their several staffs and, heedless of whispering bullets and bursting shells, engage in erudite cogitation, whose result is . . . academic orders chiefly remarkable for the surprising information they contain relative to the position and intentions of the yet unlocated enemy.

These orders, transmited by all possible means from pantomine to radio, are clearly received and promptly comprehended; with the result that the leading sections of the assault echelon dribble accurately to a line on or near that established by the scouts, and having ascertained the range and targets from these prescient individuals, coolly set their sights and bring to bear on their doomed opponents an accurate and well distributed fire of awe-inspiring intensity.

After . . . this meticulous killing, sundry infallible signs of enemy weakening in the form of diminishing and less accurate fire and movements to the rear become manifest to the Napoleonic corporals and lieutenants. Immediately they engage anew in pantomine while their dauntless soldiers, apprehending the wishes of their leaders by their third eye conveniently placed in the back of their heads, either advance anew or else redistribute their fire to cover those so doing.

. . . A support element materialises itself and, maneuvering with utter disregard to hostile fire, assaults that Achilles Heel, the flank, with a hurricaine of bullets and grenades until the recalcitrant foe becomes quiescent and the line moves on.

. . . that modern Ariadne, the Artillery Observation Officer, moving ever forward at the end of his strand of copper and in collusion with the infantry commander, keeping his guns informed of the changing requirements of the fight. At times the wire is inadequate to voice his emotions and he has recourse to a varied assortment of fireworks which he and his satellites carry with them for such emergencies.

. . . . machine guns which, advancing by bounds on mules bred from salamanders, if one judges from their immunity to fire, support the attack with staccato deluges of distant animosity; while from time to time their cackling is punctuated with the crack of a one pounder or the cough of a stokes [mortar].

2. Obviously in the foregoing we have been guilty of a degree of exaggeration, but our offense was premeditated, for by this means we hope to throw in to sharper relief some features of our present regulations which appear inapplicable to the strident realism of war.

. . . . the manifest inadequacy of the self-contained means at the disposal of the assault echelons for the carrying out of their stupendous task.

. . . while for the purposes of dissection and examination the several acts are treated separately, it is important to remember that they are all mutually interwoven and interdependent.

a. Dispersion:

The deployment into a [firing] line . . . places the large majority of the men . . . beyond the direct physical and moral influence of the platoon commander. The subsequent operations . . . must therefore depend on his delegated influence as diluted and transmitted through section and squad leaders. In theory . . . [they] are capable . . . In practice . . . this will hardly ever be the case . . . the sergeants and corporals will . . . be largely chosen from men of superior educational rather than moral qualifications; because in the brief time available for training, mental quickness is more readily discerned than moral hardihood . . .

In actuality, the principal influences [on a firing line] . . . will depend on instinct and a sense of duty.

Without in any way disparaging the valor of our soldiers we affirm that the inexorable record of war proves that neither instinct nor a sense of duty flourish[es] very luxuriantly under the chilling influence of a corpernical blizzard.

Perhaps the lieutenant and 20% of the men will be sufficiently immune to this numbing influence to advance. In addition a certain proportion of the others . . . will follow the example of the natural fighters. The rest will stay put or else advance later when the action of their more dauntless comrades has lessened the danger. With each successive advance a number of the leading spirits become casualties, so the influence of their example steadily diminishes . . .

b. Cover:

. . . Due to subconscious memories of his prehistoric arboreal existence, man possesses an inherent instinct for secretive movements.

Owing to this fact instructors are prone to display exaggerated interest and ingenuity in hide-and-seek tactics. Who has not seen a scout or a patrol spend hours in stealthy and circumlocutory meanderings at places where hostile observation was highly improbable and completely unimportant; forgetting while so engaged that time and energy the inexorable functions of military operations were being ruthlessly squandered.

Over-stressing the value of concealment . . . has a further disadvantage due to the psychological effect produced. Just as children often evolve terrors from the fertility of their own imaginings . . . so do soldiers produce in themselves visions of an omnipresent and deadly foe . . . The desire for self-preservation is a fundamental instinct which the first whistle of a bullet impels men to exercise. If, to this natural reaction is added a long course in the avoidance of danger by concealment . . . we shall possibly produce complete invisibility at the cost of absolute cessation of movement . . .

The utilization of cover from fire when that cover is bullet proof is commendable and necessary so long as undue hankering for it does not produce inaction . . .

In battle the soldier enters a lottery, with death the stake . . . the only saving clauses in this gamble lie in time, and the demoralizing effect produced on the shooting and staying qualities of the enemy by the rapid and uninterrupted advance of the attacker.

c. Fire Power:

So far as we are aware, no research of any American attack in the world war substantiates the vaunted assertions as to the death dealing efficacy of small arms fire on the part of the assailent . . . [because] there was nothing much at the actual front with which to fire.

. . . the conditions under which he [the defender] delivers his fire are superior to those of the attacker . . . his firing line is so sighted that all its occupants can fire all the time. . . . his men are not breathless with exertion, he knows the exact range and his machine guns are close enough so that both he and the attacker are audibly and visibly aware of their presence. Under such circumstances . . . the attacker can only advance according to one of the following assumptions.

First, in the case where the defender is morally weak and an outrageously bad shot.

Second, by the result of attrition secured by a constant feeding of the [attacker's] firing line. . . . [this] is bound to be unduly expensive . . .

Third, by the aid of maneuver . . .

Fourth, by means of supporting weapons, mainly artillery . . .

. . . our present firing line does not contain in itself sufficient lethal energy to produce an advance with a normal expectancy of success, due to the fact that it does not contain the killing facilities in adequate density . . .

d. Machine Guns:

The ensanguined ingenuity of our ordnance experts and the fulminations of the pacifists to the contrary notwithstanding, the anomalous fact remains that corpses do not produce panic save in a very indirect manner. It is the fear of becoming corpses that turns men's hearts to water.

. . . this condition is rather generally appreciated [but], we still seem to find our machine guns employed on a generally contrary hypothesis. Furthermore their employment for the ends they seek largely defeats its own purpose . . . as a result of the combined heritage of 1870 when the French used the Mitrailleuse as a cannon because it looked like one, and of the largely defensive traditions of machine guns in the World War our machine guns in the offensive are in but not of the Infantry. This rearward emplacement of our most powerful offensive small arm is further accentuated by . . . the bias of a mechanical age [which] makes men cling with great tenacity to such gadgets as aiming circles, range finders etc. and in the use of these devices to find valid reasons for not exposing his person to the deadly blast of short range hostile retaliation.

The result . . . is that in the inception of an assault, the attacking machine guns are brought well up and the rifleman steps off . . . but from this stage onward they become less and less an integral part of the infantry . . . due to the real and fancied difficulties attached to its [the machine gun's] progression, it usually follows [the riflemen] at too respectful a distance.

. . . As the chorus of his own machine guns dies away the refrain is taken up by those of the enemy, rising ever in volume as he advances . . .

To send men with hand weapons whose accuracy is adversely affected by each throb of physical or mental excitement up against impersonal mechanical means of destruction, while at the same time depriving them of much of the real and all the moral support and threat of their own machine guns, is to ask too much. If, finally, the line does charge home the impetus impelling it is more apt to arise from what Du Picq calls "a retreat forward" than from the creation of fire supremacy.

e. Maneuver . . .

In the many books devoted to the larger military operations . . . what the older writers called "Grand Tactics" we find much reference to maneuver, particularly . . . envelopments and flank attacks.

Unquestionably, much of success in war is due to a just use of such movements, or rather to the fact that, due to these movements, the elan and fighting power of the troops was most happily exploited. But just as the grandeur of a natural landscape becomes tawdry and uninspiring when depicted through the medium of a small water color, so does the maneuver of an army fail to inspire when scaled down to that of a squad.

If, for example . . . the 1st Blue division . . . destroy the first Red brigade by an enveloping attack, we shall always find that, in addition to the invariable stupidity of the Reds certain other conditions were requisite for the success of the masterful maneuver . . . [as] listed by Maurice about 600 A.D. . . .

[These are] . . . the enveloping element . . . moved to its assault position . . . under the cover of darkness, superior artillery fire, or terrain features. . . . [or] the outer flank of the enveloping force was not menaced; or else was covered by a superior force of cavalry. . . . [or] the moral stimulus of a superiority of two to one, measured in regiments, existed. So much for the landscape, now let us consider the water color . . .

It is therefore well worthy of considering whether the losses sustained by the leading element while awaiting the questionable relief due to a menuver [that is, an envelopment], will not exceed those which would have resulted from an immediate [frontal] assault . . . If the firing line is to advance as a result of its own efforts, it must do so by maintaining superior means of killing in its own hands . . . The chief deterrent to the advance is in automatic fire of machine guns. This must be countered by machine guns in the firing line.

f. Supporting Arms:

The firing line in its present may still attain success if its self-contained lack of fire power is made good by that of supporting arms, particularly by artillery.

However . . . it takes from the infantry both prestige and initiative. . . . terrain conditions may well arise which will prevent the massing of sufficient artillery to insure the requisite support.

In the World War the adequate system of metaled roads failed to emphasize different conditions, highly probable of existence in theaters of war where no such roads prevail. Again, in France operations were in general so methodical that ample time could be found for the collection of large stores of ammunition. In a theater where lack of roads prevents the maintenance of continuous fronts, the time element will be much more vital; while the same lack of roads will necessitate much greater periods for the collection of munitions and the movement of guns. In this sort of war, units will frequently engage with only their organic artillery and that limited in ammunition to the amounts present with the artillery batteries . . .

The same considerations which have induced the infantry to hinge their tactics on a practically unlimited artillery support have also predisposed the artillery to utilize methods that will be of doubtful practicability under many conditions of war. What we refer to is the apparent tendency towards the utilization of excessive ranges where the efficacy of fire is contingent on lengthy and unsimple methods of communication . . .

The tendencies towards distant positions received further stimulus from the "gadget" complex . . .

. . . both in consideration of the time lost and of the small effect secured, better results would accrue were the infantry so armed and instructed that, once the artillery has made its lift [lifted its preparatory barrage], they were able and accustomed to go on without second thoughts as to the possibility of a renewed bombardment.

g. Leadership:

At first blush one would scarcely expect to find in the behavior of a piece of cooked spaghetti an illustration of successful leadership in combat . . . it scarcely takes demonstration to prove how vastly more easy it is to PULL a piece of cooked spaghetti in a given direction along its major axis than it is to PUSH it in the same direction. Further, the difficulty increases with the size of either the spaghetti or the command . . .

The splendid motto of the Infantry School: "Follow Me" certainly refutes . . . training and maneuvers . . . [where] there are a good many backward glances for inspiration.

To us it seems that a fungoid over-growth of that devilish device the command post is largely responsible for this condition.

. . . when we find commanders as low as company and battalion more interested in securing command post accommodations than in injuring the enemy, something is wrong . . .

. . . Officers were and are taught that thinking is superior to doing; that brains outrank guts. The natural corollary to these notions is that constant reports must flow from front to rear . . . the message center has replaced the leader . . .

The birthright of leadership is sold for the pottage of formalism.

While to-day battle fields are vast and more or less vacant, a great deal can be seen by earnest lookers. But . . . All of us are accustomed to acquire knowledge by reading and listening, not by seeing; and to impart this knowledge by writing, not by acting.

. . . [Instead of] "By their deeds ye shall know them" . . . "By their reports shall they be selected." We are apt to reach a state of mind in which we will prefer a mimeograph [machine] to a [Stonewall] Jackson.

3. Possible basis of Present System:

. . . our thesis in making the above criticism of present regulation[s] is the belief that the firing line as now armed and used is inadequately equipped for its functions under conditions where artillery support is lacking or insufficient . . .

Prior to the world war, our combat methods were the outgrowth of the legendary ability of all Americans to hit a squirrel in the eye at 100 yards. . . . [Thus we adopted] a doctrine predicated on the belief that the aimed fire of infantry rifles supported in a desultory manner by the fire of a negligible number of cannon and machine guns would be able to secure and retain sufficient fire superiority to permit the advance of the firing line.

On entering the world war, we found these views modified by several circumstances . . .

First; time, facilities, and instructors were lacking with which to train efficient shots.

Second; the foreign instructors who infested our camps had neither experience of, nor confidence in, the efficacy of aimed rifle fire.

Third; the special circumstances existing in France in the way of numerous railroads and metaled highways, permitted the attacker to collect at the desired place such a numerous artillery that its preparatory and supporting fire was sufficient to derange the defense to an extent permitting the advance of the infantry with little actual assistance from the killing weapons in the hands of the foot soldiers.

Since the infantry, following in the wake of the shells, suffered its chief losses from artillery and automatic weapon fires; neither of which it was their primary function to subdue, it became expedient to so spread them over the landscape, that their losses from these agencies would be reduced to a minimum; regardless of the fact that such formations were inimical to the effective use of their own hand firearms.

At the present time, the minds of all military thinkers are still strongly imbued with both our pre-war theories and our war practice; so it seems reasonable to believe that our present attack formations are the fruit of an unholy union between a firing fighting line and a shell-proof formation.

4. Fundamental principles of fighting:

Due to the facility with which men, material, and even situations may be created on paper, many writers produce these on war as admirable as they are impractical. Due also to our school experiences where such intangible factors as morale, training, discipline, fatigue, equipment, and supply cannot be considered, we adopt the simple course of first omitting reference to these factors, and later of assuming them all satisfactory . . .

Duped by the historians who explain defeat and enhance victory by assuring us that both result from the use of PERFECT armies, the fruit of super-thinking, we never stop to consider the inaptness of the word perfect as a definition for armies.

So far as we can recall, only Alexander, Frederick and Napoleon inherited complete armies. Of these the ever victorious Macedonians came nearest laying claim to contemporary perfection.

While the Prussians, though they performed well, were far from being universally successful, and the final outcome of the Seven Years' War was more the result of Allied bickerings than of German superiority.

Napoleon's army was an unwashed mob, whose superiority lay in their elan born of revolutionary exhilaration, which found in the histrionic Corsican a peg on which to drape itself. In each of these armies there was an example of perfection, but it was that of an individual, not of a system. Also, the opponents of each were below the average of their respective epochs . . .

All through history there have been recurring cycles of two schools of war; the one tending towards the adoption of small professional forces relatively well trained. The other toward the utilization of masses and mob psychology. Both schools have usually foundered on the rock of compromise, when the first sought to increase its numbers and the second its discipline . . .

. . . we are personally disposed to favor the use of small trained . . . armies. Certainly, wars conducted with such forces would be more mentally stimulating, much cheaper, and vastly less bloody . . .

Another solution . . . consists in the use of a highly tempered spearhead of long service troops, backed by a horde of amateurs to do the holding and the drudgery . . .

The illusory security of our isolation and the short term of office of our law-makers make them unwilling to burden their constituents and prejudice their own chances of re-election by imposing present financial burdens to fend off future national catastrophies. Under their benevolent despotism our voteless army is bound to pine in a coma of incipient dissolution.

Since, then, our next war will be fought on the quantity rather than the quality basis, it behooves us to determine the best methods of warring with the amateur masses our destiny has foredoomed us to control . . .

. . . victory results from the infliction of a series of moral shocks to which the infliction of death wounds and destruction are but contributory influences . . . we must therefore first demonstrate our ability to kill, and then threaten its inevitable accomplishment.

. . . If the theory of evolution is correct, it is highly probable that our arboreal progenitors did grapple in a mele[e]; but since the dropping of tails, man has always earnestly striven to do his killing at a distance and has devoted incessant ingenuity to the devising of means which will permit [him] to accomplish this desire. None the less, the theory of the necessity of hand to hand fighting is so completely accepted, that resistance can only be overcome by the threat of its imminent accomplishment.

To take a position, we must convince its defenders with our ability to effect an apparently inexorable progression towards physical shock . . . to date the fact remains that victory without movement is as impossible as movement without fire.

In utilizing our horde, then, we must seek SIMPLE means to produce the will to move, and the fire to make it possible.

5. A solution:

Our present mobilization plans contemplate the enrollment of masses so vast that the feeding, to say nothing of the maneuvering, of the host envisioned will be impossible save in the most highly civilized locations. Further, while awaiting the advent of our embattled farmers over a period ranging from seven to twelve months, we contemplate holding the foe at bay with our attenuated regulars and ill-trained national guardsmen. . . .

However pacific a citizen may be, he usually becomes quite belicose when first donning a uniform. In order to capitalise on this fleeting emotion we should start warlike training on the first day. That is, instead of saying: "This is a rifle, its nomenclature is thus and so; it takes three counts to put it on your shoulder and four to take it off" and so on, we will have to talk in this wise: "Take this rifle and get into a line even with Corporal Jones. He is your boss. That bush is an enemy machine gun. It is up to you to kill its crew." At this point Private 1/c Brown (regular) will inform his neighbors as follows: "Hey you bozos! Put that wooden part agin' your shoulder. . . ."

To paraphrase the famous remark at Balaclava: "It is horrible but it is war." At first the bush will be fairly safe, but by night the ex-civilians will have an idea of what they are trying to do and till Taps and later they will be arguing, asking questions and, best of all, making fun of each other. Day by day, in every way, they will be better and better. And the men who train them and learn to know them will be the men, who, in the near day of battle, will lead them . . .

Irrespective of plans and organization, all battles quickly resolve themselves into a series of more or less isolated head-on conflicts between small groups of combatants . . .

6. Proposed training and organization:

Without in any way aspiring to enter those pellucid regions inhabited by Genius . . . we strive to devise a scheme of: "Utilizing the means at hand for the accomplishment of the ends sought."

. . . in our previous paper on "Why Men Fight," we have striven to divest war of its non-essentials and to strip it to a tangible, if uninspiring contest between artificially enraged males . . .

The necessity for this course is particularly important to us as a nation, since we are congenitally opposed to any form of useful preparation . . .

[Then followed a detailed discussion of the elements composing a division, with certain recommended changes, including the elimination of the regiment.]

So far we have assigned to the division three infantry brigades [each consisting of three infantry battalions] and occasionally perhaps some units of medium artillery. [Actually, the reorganization of the infantry division in the early 1940s, when the so-called triangular or McNair division replaced the square division of World War I, eliminated the brigade and retained the regiment (which, unlike the brigade headquarters that was capable only of tactical functions, was able to handle tactical, administrative, and supply duties), each regiment consisting of three battalions of infantry, plus a cannon company — much as Patton was here suggesting.]

Considering the reduced personnel, considerable curtailments in the medical regiment will be possible . . .

. . . we propose replacing the engineer regiment with an engineer company plus a detachment of engineer officers to act as advisers on simple engineering projects, for which the line troops will furnish the labor . . .

The tank company should be eliminated because, as now armed, it is inadequate in strength to the tasks proposed and of either march or combat mobility it is wholly innocent. Moreover, encumbering of a division with the permanent tanks, irrespective of the intrinsic worth of the type imagined, is as irrational as would be the permanent issue to all soldiers of arctic overcoats. The tanks and the overcoats are only an occasional necessity. Tanks are in reality a modern version of heavy cavalry, as that arm was understood by the first Napoleon. When satisfactory machines are available, they should be formed into a separate corps and used, when terrain permits, for the delivery of the final shock in some great battle; when so used they must be employed ruthlessly and in masses. [This was in striking similarity to Patton's initial conception of how to use tanks in World War II.]

The retention of an air corps unit with the division is vital. We believe that, in addition to the observation squadron which is also capable of a limited amount of attack and light bombing, a pursuit unit should be added as the surest means of safeguarding our marching columns from the growing menace of enemy air attack. [This too foreshadowed Patton's use of supporting air forces in World War II.]

The functions proposed for the augmented air unit are exactly analogous to that of a cavalry unit so frequently required by a division, in that they both furnish reconnaissance and protection in their separate spheres of action, and that by making them integral with the division, the integrity of the main striking force of the arm is left intact, since it will not be constantly depleted by demands for local protection . . .

7. *Battle as per proposed regulations:*
. . . After a moment's pause to permit this orchestra of death to reach its crescendo the line of bayonets rises and led by the major [in command of the battalion] rushes to its final task gruesome only in anticipation [for the enemy will have fled].

With the semi-stillness of the charge our ear suddenly perceives the insinuating whine made over head by . . . fifty calibre bullets from the brigade machine guns whose devilish whispering is punctured now and again by the hoarser murmur of a lobbing shell from the accompanying howitzers.

Appended to this study were proposed tables of organization and equipment for the infantry rifle company, the infantry battalion, the infantry brigade, and the infantry division. Then followed a comparison of the current and his proposed divisions, showing that the latter, that is, Patton's recommended division, would have a total strength of 9715 men as contrasted with 19,417 in the current organization; at the same time, the firepower of the recommended organization would be far stronger.

This was precisely what the triangular division of World War II sought to attain — more bang with fewer men.

. . .

Several weeks before his departure from Hawaii, Patton delivered a lecture at Schofield Barracks on "Tanks Past and Future." It foreshadowed his forthcoming involvement in Washington with mechanization and motorization, with tanks and armored cars.

Forerunners of the modern tank, he said, were the Trojan horse conceived by "Liarte's" (Laertes') godlike son Ulysses, which was itself the forerunner of the movable towers used by Alexander against Tyre, and certain engines called the Sow, the "Bore" [Boar?], and the Cat, which were intended for siege warfare in antiquity and medieval times.

The British Museum had a picture dated 1456 of a "Cart of War," a vehicle propelled by horses with a platform above their heads to support a weapon and a crew, the platform being protected by sideboards. "So far as I know this machine is the earliest form in which the light or open warfare tank appears. I have been unable to find any evidence that it was ever used in battle."

A similar engine driven by windmills operating wooden gears was described in Italy in 1492. One hundred years later, Simon Stevens depicted a land ship with masts, sails, and guns mounted on wheels. Unfinished notes of Leonardo da Vinci spoke of a land ship or battle car propelled by an engine of some unspecified sort.

As an aside, Patton mentioned that in France in 1918, he had been directed to report on the military value of a machine called the Moving Fort and Trench Destroyer. He examined an elaborate set of blueprints showing a caterpillar-propelled box covered with two-inch armor, bearing six 75-mm. howitzers, twenty machine guns, and a flamethrower. In the midst of the drawing of this contraption was a rectangular box labeled, "Engine not yet devised."

After the laughter of his audience subsided, Patton said,

I do not know whether atom bursting was known at that date. If it was I feel sure that an engine actuated by that sort of energy must have been intended as no other form of power occupying so small a space could have propelled the 200 ton estimated weight of the fort. In my indorsement I stated that the lack of an engine was considered a defect and further pointed out that while it would unquestionably crush trenches it would just as surely squash a considerable part of France in its journey to the front.

The drill, he continued, for tanks in the British Army — "Colonel J. F. C. Fuller, Chief of Staff of the Tank Corps, is my authority for the following description" — resembled training described by Xenophon and attributed by him to King Cyrus in 500 B.C. But the British tactics at Cambrai were not applicable to American doctrine. The British had the infantry formations conform to the tank capabilities, whereas Patton in France had reversed the conception, primarily because the American tanks were small and unlike the heavier British tanks. He had also rejected the French method of moving tanks behind the infantry until they were needed forward, because this meant that one or two hours elapsed between the need for them and their time of arrival.

Patton had therefore devised an American system of tank employment, which, though far from perfect, had worked satisfactorily. Certain mistakes were nevertheless committed. It was an error to have tanks precede the infantry against weak trenches, for the infantrymen could cross them after an artillery barrage. Tanks were needed primarily for the enemy machine guns sited behind the front.

"In future," he interjected, "it will be better to have the tanks follow the infantry over the front . . . and then deploy ahead for the passage through the delaying area."

This would be the normal procedure in World War II, notably in the COBRA attack, launched on July 25, 1944, in Normandy.

"It is the unconquerable soul of man and not the nature of the machine he uses which insures victory," Patton said. Yet tanks were useful in combat, and he hoped that tanks in the future would be mechanically rugged, have great cruising radius, be light in weight and mobile for roads and cross-country operations, have speed, armor, and gun power.

Finally, ending on a pessimistic note, he was dubious whether the United States would ever have first-rate tanks in sufficient numbers. "The chief drawback under which the whole military profession is now laboring arises from a too unimaginative conception of the probable nature of the next war." The next war was likely to be "trench warfare, which God forbid."

Grading Patton as G–2, Colonel Cooke had thought him "above average." Perhaps because Patton was held in such high esteem by Fox Conner, or perhaps because Cooke now knew Patton better, he marked him "superior" in most categories and "very active both mentally and physically; widely read in military history; an expert horseman. His outstanding qualities are those of a commander."

The endorsement read: "I concur in the above report. I have known him [Patton] for fifteen years, in both peace and war. I know of no one whom I would prefer to have as a subordinate commander. Fox Conner, Major General commanding."

These words from Conner, naming Patton as the subordinate commander he judged best of all the officers he knew in the Army, were exceedingly important for Patton's career. A gray eminence in the Army, whose power was indirect and often concealed, Conner wielded immense authority during the years between the World Wars.

The last efficiency report rendered on Patton for his Hawaiian tour of duty rated him "above average" and "superior." According to Lieutenant Colonel S. T. Mackall, the acting chief of staff, Patton was "an outstanding officer; a student of military affairs, well above the average; intensely interested in his profession; he has taken full advantage of serving in Hawaii to become familiar with the military problem in the Islands."

Letter, GSP, Jr., to Aunt Nannie, March 5, 1928

So far we have not secured a house [in Washington] but hope to do so on the Virginia side [of the Potomac] as it is cooler there and there will be less calling.

Beatrice is still very busy writing her Hawaiian ledgends in french. I hope she succeeds in getting them published. It will be a great dissappointment to her if she does not.

With no horses to ride [apparently the horses were already en route from Hawaii to Washington] I find more time than I have been accustomed to here but as soon we will have to start packing it will be an advantage.

While he was packing the family's possessions, he listed the military, horse, and boat books he owned. There were 321, and from the marginal notations, most of them had been carefully read.

Patton's three years in Hawaii were a pleasant social interlude and a sobering professional experience. The ferocity of his play on the polo field, which became legendary, was in large part the sublimation of his frustrations as a staff and desk-bound — chairborne, the Army calls it — officer, denied the joys of commanding troops. Everyone who mattered in the Army recognized his natural qualities as an active and forceful leader of troops. Everyone also realized that his professional attainments, his loyalty to his superiors, his zeal toward his duty, whatever that happened to be, were outstanding — Patton always gave his best. He had matured but without losing his essential dash.

CHAPTER 41

Washington: The Lure of the Machine

"Oil and Iron do not win battles — Victory is to men not machines."

IN WASHINGTON, after moving into a house at 3117 Woodland Drive Northwest, Patton reported for duty to the Chief of Cavalry and was assigned head of the Plans and Training Division of that office. He left almost immediately for Mitchell Field, Long Island, where he played on the Army polo team all summer.

Lieutenant Colonel H. C. Pratt, probably the nonplaying manager, rated Patton "satisfactory," judged him capable of being a colonel in peacetime and a brigadier general in war — but no higher, and thought him "an unusually energetic and active officer; well-versed in his profession, and always endeavoring to improve himself."

Patton returned to Washington in September and became acquainted with the details and routine of his job.

Letter, GSP, Jr., to Beatrice (in Massachusetts), September 3, 1928
    I am delighted that you will not hunt. I realy hate to have you hurt more than to be hurt myself. As a matter of fact it does not hurt me to be hurt . . .
    Ike Eisenhower and I are going down the river [sailing] on Sunday.

A month later, on October 6, Mrs. Ruth Wilson Patton died. Patton left no record at that time of his sorrow at the loss of his mother. He would do so three years later.

Sometime during the autumn of 1928 or the following spring, George and Beatrice Patton purchased in South Hamilton, Massachusetts, a house and sufficient acreage for riding and hunting. They named their place Green Meadows, and it became their home, their permanent residence.

By virtue of Patton's assignment to the Office of the Chief of Cavalry, he became intimately involved in probably the most significant controversy that occupied the Army until the eve of World War II. The question constantly debated was the importance of mechanization in future warfare. Should machines replace horses, and if so, to what extent?

The discussions took place in the Army, in the congressional committees concerned with military expenditures, and in the press. On one side were ranged the automobile manufacturers and their lobbyists, the advocates of the car, the truck, the tank, and the airplane, who insisted that machines made horses obsolete. On the other were the polo players, hunters, riders, breeders, farmers, and their associations that publicized the virtues of horseflesh, argued that horses were more reliable and cheaper than machines, and supported congressional parsimony with respect to research and development.

In the center of the debate, Patton would be emotionally torn for more than three years by the conflicting attractions of the intriguing yet contrasting notions over the place of machines and horses in the Army. His superior was the Chief of Cavalry, his own branch was cavalry, he loved horses passionately; he relished the slash of the saber and the reckless abandon of the mounted charge. But he was beguiled by the engines of war too. How could he deny or renounce the achievements of the tanks in France?

As he wrestled with the currents of change, he sought to fulfill his sense of loyalty to the cavalry without betraying his obligation to the Army and its capacity to wage war. On occasion, he mirrored excruciating pain. He preferred not to choose. Throughout his tour of duty, he would seek the path of compromise, trying to offend neither the conservative horsemen nor the radical mechanists.

It was a tricky business, and Patton's gifts were hardly suitable for so devious a course. He was neither subtle nor discreet enough to avoid a wavering commitment, first to one, then to the other. If a single beacon guided him, it was his loyalty to his boss, the Chief of Cavalry. And in the end, despite himself, he became identified with the horse. This bond to the horse cavalry almost cost him his chance for fame in World War II.

For Patton, the whole disagreeable yet fascinating activity started in November 1928. He worked on the War Department Mobilization Plan and suggested that the cavalry secure young and vigorous accomplished horsemen to form "an aristocracy of valor, vital to the success of Cavalry." He was also appointed to a board of officers — with Lieutenant Colonel James J. O'Hara, Majors C. C. Benson and Harry A. Flint — to inspect the Christie caterpillar mount for its suitability as a heavy armored car; as before, he found Christie's machine a promising development.

There was little difference between the Christie tank and the Christie car except semantics. The proponents of change in the cavalry were restricted to armored cars because the tanks had been transferred to the infantry. Forbidden to have tanks, the cavalrymen simply called them armored cars. Yet they were smaller and lighter than tanks, consequently more mobile and more appropriate for a branch of service that prided itself on its ability to move and maneuver.

Thus began a persistent fiction, also a continuing struggle between the infantry and cavalry for control of the means of armored warfare, no matter how the vehicles were designated. The contest would eventually be decided by the branch of the officers who would be selected for and assigned to the armored forces. That fight would take place largely within the Office of the G–3, the War Department Plans, Training, and Operations Section. There, Major Adna R. Chaffee, son of a former Army Chief of Staff, old friend of Patton, and well-known cavalryman, horseman, and polo player, would play a principal role in the activity.

The question of mechanization had become important because the Secretary of War, Dwight F. Davis, had observed during the summer of 1927 the maneuvers in England of the British Experimental Armored Force, a rudimentary organization of mechanized units. Davis was impressed by what he saw. Influenced also by the advances in the motor vehicle industry, the advent of better roads in the United States, the abundant American oil resources, and the increasing displacement of horses and mules by farm machinery, Davis directed the Army to create an armored force in 1928.

The Army assembled at Camp Meade a composite force made up of small units — tanks, cavalry, field artillery, air corps, engineers, ordnance, chemical warfare, and medical corps. Because of insufficient funds and obsolete equipment, little was done in the way of welding these elements into a single unit of combined arms. Yet merely gathering the force together was a symbolic act that would prove beneficial to the Army.

Absorbed by both horses and machines, Patton was sufficiently enthusiastic over the horse cavalry to propose:

The use of Army Cavalry in driblets or for indefinite missions is to be deprecated. When opportunity for decisive results offers, or occasion demands, cavalry must be ruthlessly expended.

At the same time, he cherished and saved the paper that announced the Secretary's approval of a plan — after tests at Fort Leonard Wood, Missouri, and Fort Myer — for the Chief of Cavalry and the Chief of Ordnance, in cooperation, to procure the Christie chassis and equip it as an armored car.

Patton copied this letter and kept it in his personal papers. He wrote on it: "Probably a very momentous paper. GSP Jr. Feb 21 1929."

He was destined to be disappointed, for the Army would fail to buy the chassis in sufficient numbers to keep Christie solvent, and he would eventually be forced to sell his invention elsewhere, to the Russians, English, and Japanese.

Armored cars seemed an obvious solution to the major problem of funds; cheaper to build than tanks, they offered mobility and firepower, plus a degree of protection to their crews. Stimulated by the Secretary's decision, Patton listed their advantages and disadvantages, probably to clear the air of misconceptions.

A normal armored car rolling on wheels was an effective offensive weapon capable of rapid movement on roads; gave partial protection to its machine gun or small cannon; had a relatively long cruising range; provided secure and rapid messenger service; could delay enemy units operating without tanks, penetrate enemy rear-guard forces, ambush enemy troops and transport, and make distant raids; was an excellent rear-guard weapon; added firepower to mounted units; and was cheap to manufacture, thereby easy to build in large numbers.

The special tracked and wheeled vehicle, Christie type, was expensive to manufacture, therefore wasteful to employ for messenger service. Its ability to move off the roads improved its capacity for reconnaissance, helped it to avoid ambush and gain surprise. It could menace deployed lines of troops, launch independent raids, accompany cavalry, thereby adding fire and shock, cover a withdrawal, and act as a powerful mobile reserve.

A normal or wheeled armored car was liable to stall on unimproved, frozen, or wet roads; could be stopped by simple obstructions; had limited mobility at night; was susceptible to ambush, useless in swampy, rocky, or forested country, and certain to provoke enemy attack. Its killing power was limited.

Having set forth the characteristics of armored cars, Patton pushed forward in a paper entitled "Tactical Employment of Armored Cars, Experimental." He prefaced his remarks with a typical opening:

Oil and Iron do not win battles — Victory is to men not machines. No perfection of mechanism nor metriculosity of training can replace courage. The heart which animates a chauffe[u]r is only a bilge pump. If the A.C. [armored car] degenerates into a perambulating source of fire power it has belied its cavalry birthright. Movement, not fire, is its primary weapon.

The armored cars had to have complete liberty of action and "act with the uttermost boldness." They moved by bounds, by accordion or by inchworm methods. The armored car commander had to consider his machine and its weapons as a trooper regarded his horse and arms. "The analogy is complete: grooming, cleaning, feeding, oiling and fueling; training; adjustment."

Armored cars personified "the age old dread of monsters." They should follow the precept "Audacity and the threat of contact are far more potent means of combat than are fire or armour." Fire fights should take place only at close range.

After accompanying several armored cars making an experimental march from Washington, D.C. to Camp Meade, Maryland, Patton set down additional remarks. He warned against making the vehicle too heavy — "any military machine has a tendency to overload itself with spare parts, whether they are men or material." He recommended against having crew members equipped with the Thompson submachine gun, for that would encourage them to fight as infantrymen rather than as armored car operators. Fuel was as important as ammunition, if not more so, because "an armored car which stops to fight is lost."

He was caught up rather short in his enthusiastic promotion of the armored car by a question asked by General Crosby, the Chief of Cavalry. Would Patton consider the "Limitations of Mechanization"?

Responding, Patton offered a key thought:

Without in any way detracting from the capabilities of mechanical
and mechanized units when employed under conditions of terrain
and weather which render their use possible, it is none the less pertinent to point out certain characteristics of the machines which detract from their universality and limit their spheres of action.

He said what he had said often before. Machines could not operate in
certain kinds of weather and terrain, and thus horses were still necessary
for military forces that wished to preserve their capacity to fight anywhere
and any time.

This became the standard cavalry formula — no objection to developing gas-engine weapons like tanks and armored cars so long as the proponents of mechanization and motorization recognized the basic contribution of the horse.

This led to the idea of using machines with horses, and in 1929, the
cavalry tentatively adopted the Christie car, which could go 40 miles per
hour cross country on tracks and 70 miles per hour on highways on wheels.

Asked to write an article on the new vehicle for the Hearst papers,
Patton turned out an unpublishable effort. In it he justified the development of war machines by his own peculiar logic:

. . . it must never be forgotten that all weapons and devices are
only of secondary importance. Now as ever the fate of the nation
depends on the heroic souls of its sons not on the weapons they wield.
None the less in order to justify ourselves in demanding of them the
supreme sacrifice we must in honor see to it that we give them every
assistance which our wealth and ingenuity can provide.

He meant not only the armored car but all the weapons and equipment
that enabled the American fighting man to face with confidence any
enemy equipped with first-rate matériel and weapons.

So drawn was Patton to the need for machines in the Army that he
worked on a table of organization for a mechanized cavalry regiment designed to operate with horse cavalry units.

Early in 1929, Patton said that Americans in peacetime could afford
only the essential parts of the military machine. In wartime, with large
funds and great numbers of men available, "we may indulge ourselves in
experimental accessories, but, in peace, any part which cannot meet this

question of absolute indispensability must be ruthlessly scrapped." If all that was claimed for all sorts of new machines and weapons were true, there would be no reason to retain the horse cavalry. Yet this could hardly be the case.

"It is pretty well agreed that the next war will be a war of movement." Since air forces and mechanized forces were bound to play important roles in the future, it was necessary to understand both the powers and the limitations of those new means of waging war.

> I wish it distinctly understood that nothing I shall say is spoken in disparagement of these branches. We recognize the extreme importance of the air corps and mechanized forces . . . we go further — we are endeavoring with all our might to include in our [cavalry] scheme of things all air and mechanization developments.

In all wars, no matter what sort and where fought, certain functions had to be performed, and only cavalry was capable of doing them in all kinds of weather and terrain. Therefore, cavalry remained an indispensable part of the military establishment.

Patton developed this theme in a paper he called "Cavalry in the Next War." In his opening he established his belief that

> the ROAD in all its forms from marble to chicken-wire has played a predominant role in the bellicose meanderings of mankind. The invention of the motor car and its variants has not only failed to alter this condition but has in fact emphasized it.

Contrasting as he had before the experiences in Mexico, where roads were primitive, and in France, where the roads were so good that they "give us an exaggerated idea" of how easy it was to use trucks, he said that in both areas the roads did not come under attack — "so that in this respect our experience lacks finality." Yet it was certain that the general condition of roads "in any theater save Western Europe" would approximate more nearly those in Mexico. It would, therefore, be foolish to expect mechanized vehicles to move with facility.

> It is realized that these statements will be challenged by the vast fraternity of motorists who spend their Sundays in pleasant perambulations along our arterial highways. But let these skeptics try our

vastly more numerous byways and the valor of their ignorance will be abated. Moreover, let them remember that the difficulties they encounter are as nothing to the conditions that would confront the hundredth truck of a convoy [that has churned up and destroyed a road].

Roads were the alpha and omega of military operations,

and their number and condition will absolutely determine the character of the next war . . .

Vast concentrations [of men], such as we saw in Europe cannot exist if they cannot be fed. Hence in most parts of the earth contending forces will be smaller or else tied like unborn babes to the placenta of a railway or river line. This reduction of forces will result in making . . . flankless lines [as on the Western Front] impossible.

As a consequence, maneuver will reappear. Time will again become the vital factor [in war].

Emphasizing that he had no intention of belittling the importance of motor transport in war, recognizing the need for "the employment of the utmost usable number of motor vehicles," Patton foresaw difficulties "undreamed of on a holiday tour."

. . . it seems relevant to advert on[c]e more to history in order to definitely confound lithesome theories of the self-styled mechanists or academic warriors who are so exhilarated by the gaseous exhalations of their pet machines as to be oblivious to the necessity for more prosaic arms.

It is confidently asserted that if any one of these gentlemen will take the trouble to personally examine the districts made famous by the Peninsular and Bull Run campaigns . . . of the Wilderness campaign . . . he will have to admit that no machine yet made or dreamed of could have replaced to any appreciable degree the man on foot or the man on horseback. . . .

Having had the honor of commanding tanks in action we are the last to belittle their importance, but knowing their limitations as we do we are unalterably opposed to the assigning to them of powers which they do not possess. Such action not only foredooms them to failure but also condemns the army which relies solely on them to disaster and defeat . . .

Of yore the chariot, the elephant and, later, gunpowder were severally acclaimed as the mistress of the battlefield. Within our memory the dynamite gun and the submarine were similarly lauded. Now gas, the tank and the airplane share . . . this dubious honor. The glory of the skyrocket elicits our applause; the splash of its charred stick is unnoticed . . .

The wrestling adage that: "There is a block for every hold" is equally applicable to war. Each new weapon demands a new block and is mighty potent until that block is devised. The development these new weapons and their counters . . . are desirable in that they add to the repertoire of our attack and defense. They are dangerous when they cause us to pin our whole faith on their efficacy . . .

The proportion of automatic weapons in our cavalry is now much larger than in any other cavalry of the world. This will have most striking results. Formerly we were weak in fire power and that which we attained was paid for at the price of immobilizing a large number of our men. Now the use of automatic weapons permits us to develop a formidable fire effect while at the same time leaving the great majority of our men mobile, thus giving us a double threat in the offensive and making us more tenacious on the defense.

We have already incorporated the wheel-type armored car into our cavalry divisions and at this writing are carrying the process one step further by adopting a combined wheel and track machine for use with cavalry corps and, perhaps, divisions. This latter weapon is ideally suited to play the part of an offensive reserve and may on occasion be used for reconnaissance.

Finally, the partial motorization of cavalry supply trains will have a far reaching beneficial effect on our mobility.

From here, Patton went into a consideration of "the several functions of cavalry in the sequence in which they will occur during our next attempt to insure the peace of the world by combat."

Cavalry, he wrote, was useful for distant reconnaissance despite the airplane, which was useless in storms, fogs, darkness, and forests. Planes were properly regarded as the ally of cavalry for strategic reconnaissance, and they would help cavalry troops to gain and maintain contact with the enemy, to locate and report the enemy's movements and condition. When the road network permitted their use, wheeled-type armored cars would "add strategic feelers to the cavalry." They enjoyed an intermediate place between the plane and the horse, but they were unable to live off the country and a mechanical breakdown was likely to be disastrous. In contrast, "A lame horse loses one trooper." Still, they were excellent for supply and messenger services, and they could fight "as naval cruisers, possibly in pairs," fighting enemy cars by "Nelsonian tactics and close shooting rapidly."

The essential idea governing the use of these reconnoitering detachments is to furnish a control force and mobile base for patrols. Perhaps if we picture an ambulatory beehive moving down the road with small groups of bees going in and out searching for the honey of information, we will form an accurate notion of such a detachment. Like the hive, too, it can be stirred into vindictive activity against any interference with the endeavors of its members . . .

. . . in story books, map problems, and other works of fiction, patrols are supposed to move over hill and dale like a skiming swallow or agile fox examining . . . every hedge, barn and manure pile, and maintaining at the same time the fabled rate of five or six miles an hour.

In practice this is impossible because horses lack spare parts. Roads are where the enemy will be; why seek him in bogs?

As for the masked batteries and lurking machine guns which are popularly supposed to make movement by roads impossible, they do not exist. No enemy, however malign, has enough of such trinks [tricks or trinkets?] as to be able to secrete them about the countryside in the fond hope of bagging poor Corporal Smith and his trusty squad.

Patton then described the correct method of patrolling. "Notice," he said,

that there is no Boy Scouting, no crawling or entwining the hat with a wreath of poison ivy in a futile endeavor to impersonate some Pan or Satyr. In war men will have neither the training nor the time for such frivolities.

If the patrol met a small enemy force or an enemy patrol of like size, he continued,

Instantly the corporal should gallop at this with all his men, emitting while so doing ferocious noises . . .

If our corporal gallops the enemy and does it first, and hell for leather, the chances are 99 to 1 that the foe will run and later justify his tumultuous departure by reporting to those who sent him that he was attacked by a platoon or possibly a troop — such is the nature of man.

If the patrol encountered a machine gun in position, "it must take its losses, which will be surprisingly small, and beat it out of range." But then the patrol must discover the size and nature of the force grouped around the gun.

In an aside, Patton gave his opinion that "Night patroling should be more emphasized in peace training." Then he made a statement, later to be quoted widely and frequently misunderstood because of being taken out of context. "Our personal feeling," he said, "is that even if the enemy were not trying to stop us, we would attack him. War is a question of killing, and the sooner it starts the better." What he meant was that victory usually belonged to the side on the offensive, and the side that got the jump on the enemy in launching an offensive was more likely to win.

He also summarized his tactical thinking in a single aphorism, and it too would be quoted later in World War II — usually in vulgar form — as personifying Patton's unorthodox and fiercely aggressive views:

> In reading of the tactics appropriate to . . . a fight we are apt to find ourselves enmeshed in a mob of strange words, such as the "Pivot of Maneuver," "The Mass of Maneuver," etc. If instead of this we describe the tactics appropriate by saying: "Grab the enemy by the nose and kick him in the pants," we sacrifice purity to precision but we express the idea.

Once a position had been gained in the enemy's rear, "there is but one solution: the mounted charge."

For this attack the saber is more appropriate than the pistol because the psychology of the bayonet and saber are identical — you have to get close to use them. The actual killing potentiality (not effect) of a line of infantry firing from the hip while charging is far greater than a similar line trusting to the bayonet, but human nature being what it is a charge so conducted would never get home. For when the bolt refuses to close, signaling an empty magazine, the hero will stop to reload and in nine cases out of ten he will never restart . . .

. . . [the charge] should be executed at the utmost speed of every horse. To follow the theory that the pace should be that of the slowest horse in order to attain so-called cohesion, is foolish. By such methods all the fierce elemental emotions of the stampede are lost. To charge effectively a man must be in a frenzy; you cannot have controlled frenzy . . .

In our opinion the headlong charge applies also to operations against mounted opponents. The efficacy of the charge rests in very great measure on the psychological effect produced. There is an exhilaration in speed and it utilizes the enthusiasm of the natural fighters both to afright the enemy and to hearten their more cautious comrades . . .

If the unlikely happens and a melee follows the charge, it is individual killing ability and savagery — not formations which will determine the issue.

Patton noted that "the increased use of machines [in future wars] will put a high premium on gasoline. Its destruction will be worth a great effort."

The German Ardennes counteroffensive in December 1944 would threaten important stocks of Allied gasoline.

Mechanized forces, Patton predicted, would have difficulty forcing the passage of obstacles, for example, creeks and gulches, and would have to do so by establishing bridgeheads. These would require the presence of "portee infantry" or "Tank Marines" or, more simply, motorized infantrymen. These in turn would demand "numerous non-fighting vehicles, with a corresponding elongation of the [marching] column." And this would seriously delay the speed of march and the rate of deployment.

Furthermore, "Without gasoline machines are junk." They could not fight at night. And "the battle command of Mechanized Forces offers tremendous and as yet unsolved difficulties."

Cavalry, Patton indicated, could fight mechanized forces if the cavalrymen followed certain principles — attacking only at night, harassing tankers, giving them no rest, destroying bridges behind them, intercepting their supply columns, and the like.

Of course the cavalry will not get off scatheless. Sad to say no effective means of fighting without killing and getting killed has yet been invented.

. . . it is our firm belief that the independent employment of Mechanized Forces is so largely illusory that it will never be seriously employed. Certainly not after a few trials.

The true metier of these forces is in the form of effective reserves to be used in the final stages of a general battle to strike the decisive blow.

The effect of airplanes on cavalry, Patton prophesied, would be to force cavalry units to move while dispersed into small march units and concentrate at a desired point, no great difficulty. Bivouacs would have to be spread to offer poor air targets. "The days of nicely ordered cavalry camps on the open sunny slopes of a hill are as defunct as the buffalo among whom they used to flourish."

The best method of countering enemy aviation was to have "our own" aviation — but whether he meant planes controlled by cavalry or simply Army air forces, he did not specify.

As for command, communication, and supply, he stressed that objectives "must be few and simple; the means of attaining them must be vigorous and direct." Simple orders and personal example were the keys to success.

We can give men ideas if not brains. In this case we must imbue our officers with restless energy. An old football coach once said to a lineman: "If you don't know what else to do, throw a fit — do something."

Approvingly, he cited Marshal Foch as having said that most military information was received from historians — after the war. But "Lack of orders is no excuse for inaction. Anything done vigorously is better than nothing done tardily."

Thus, more than a decade before World War II, Patton's thought and expression had attained mature originality. In the "next war" he so confidently expected, he would apply with conspicuous success these beliefs he phrased as aphorisms.

Replying to a published article advocating mechanization, Patton wrote:

It would be foolish for us to be uncompromising toward mechanization with non-existant vehicles when we can still utilize existant

horses. There is a probably psychologic influence at work in favor of
mechanical war which takes its sources in the natural reluctance of
mankind to be killed. Consequently man attributes great efficiency
to machines which he thinks will reduce the number of combatants
and, therefore, materially lessen his chances of being called to fight.
Also there is no question but that all of us today feel the lure of the
machine.

Chairing a conference in the Chief of Cavalry's Office on the impact of
mechanization on cavalry, Patton repeated most of what he had already
said in writing. He had some additional materials.

The statement that most regular officers know everything about
the last war and nothing about the next was never truer than to-day.
The sooner we disabuse our minds of trenches and barrages; of endless lines of boundless supplies; of cigarettes and chocolates — and
get back to mud, marches and bacon — the better are we apt to be off
the next time Mars sounds revellie on a disillusioned world.

He gave special attention to the armored-car squadron. "Much of the
experimental work on its component parts," he said, "was done right
here," and the squadron was now an integral part of every cavalry division. There were 36 fighting cars in each armored-car squadron, divided
into three 12-car troops (or companies). There were two types of cars,
light and medium.

After discussing the various functions carried out by units, Patton
closed "with a brief excursion into the unexplored realms of tomorrow."
He touched upon the effect of airplanes on marching columns, admitting
that his ideas were "largely conjectural." Any theorist would be biased,
depending on whether he was a pilot or a horseback rider, but since
Patton was both an amateur pilot and a rider, he was likely to be less
biased. Thus, he believed that planes would force the cavalry to march in
shorter columns, to make more marches at night, and to disperse its units.
Yet

the multiplicity of missions which fall to the air corps in war will not
leave it with unlimited time or planes in which to chase columns.
Furthermore, if all columns fight back instead of running, the joy of

column strafing will diminish — there is no pursuit so keen as that of the unresisting. Finally, our own air forces will certainly afford the best and surest protection against their kindred of the clouds.

He believed "beyond the shadow of a doubt" that mechanized forces would be used in the next war, but how they would affect cavalry or how cavalry would influence mechanized forces was

problematical. Having both the cavalry and the tank viewpoint I shall not try to argue either way but shall simply point out certain phases of the question which appear to warrant more notice than our army has so far given them.

He remarked the congestion of mechanized forces on roads, the difficulties of supply and command, and the virtual impossibility of fast cross-country movement. But, he warned, if "a mechanized force gets deployed in fair country, cavalry will have to clear out."

The armored cars, light and medium, Patton concluded, were weapons of the future, and he looked for

a combined wheel and track vehicle capable of real work across country as well as high speed on the road, where it will normally be used. Obviously such a vehicle is in no sense a tank, since the mobility we demand of it will inhibit the use of really bullet-proof armor. We also realize that since such a type will be a non-commercial product we shall never have very many of them, certainly not at the beginning of a war.

Such a weapon will restore the cuirassiers to the cavalry and I confidently believe that at no distant day we shall see troops or squadrons of them charging in line as of old and bursting a hole through which our equine squadrons will thunder to victory.

It was a thrilling vision; part of it would come true.

Undoubtedly he managed to establish an equilibrium within himself on the conflict between horses and machines. It permitted him to ride horses and be their advocate while at the same time it enabled him to keep a notebook filled with materials on the Christie tank and the tactical employment of mechanized forces.

The armored car was imperfect, but "Mechanical progress can only result from physical experiment." During the spring of 1929, the 1st Armored Car Troop of the 1st Cavalry Division — the only armored car unit in the Army — was patrolling the border between El Paso, Texas, and Hachita, New Mexico, with five small, open cars, five small pickup trucks, and one larger truck, all quite innocuous.

The Christie car was better, even though some highly theoretical factors still remained to be solved.

> The reason for this state of uncertainty is due to the fact that in the Christie car we are buying a principle not a vehicle. The vital thing is the track and wheel suspension. This we have secured and will build around it an appropriate body with armament, armor, crew, engine, gasoline supply, etc. in proper proportion.

"The use of armored forces," he wrote, "is likely to restore mobility to its preeminent place in warfare." The greatest chance for victory would lie with the side that had developed mobility to the maximum extent. For mobility enhanced surprise. Sweat saved blood, and so would gasoline.

He disagreed with his old friend Brett, who wrote on "Anti Tank Defense" and suggested using tanks to counter enemy tanks. To Patton, tanks were not defensive weapons, they were offensive tools. Bodies of water, marshes, forests, and mountains would serve as strategic tank defenses, and in actual tank combat, delayed fuze shells and white phosphorous rounds (which burned at extremely high temperatures) would be the best defenses, especially if command tanks were singled out and knocked out and if tank assembly points were bombed by planes.

Reacting to an article by Colonel C. M. Bundel on strategy, Patton found himself in disagreement on four points. Bundel said that surprise was unnecessary if a military force had sufficient superiority; beside that statement, Patton wrote: "But it adds to superiority." Bundel said that every commander in contact with the enemy had to hold forces in reserve to counter unexpected developments; Patton wrote: "I do not at all agree with this." Bundel said that it was essential for a soldier in a republic to keep the head of government accurately informed on all military matters; Patton added: "Or to depose him." Bundel said it was necessary to use every man in combat; Patton wrote: "Twice."

An article by Marshal Foch on the conduct of war prompted Patton to observe that the fundamental truths underlying the art of war remained unchanged, that victory came from the ability to prepare for offensive battle, then to launch the decisive attack during that battle, and that generals who fought willingly were not easy to find.

Material describing the British Experimental Mechanized Force led him to postulate that the human factor in war could not be disregarded, that long-service professional soldiers were necessary for mechanized units, that mechanized forces were sensitive to ground conditions, that all the functions of the horse were still unable to be borne by machines, that a stationary gun always had the advantage over a moving gun, and that tanks had to become cheaper to manufacture and less cumbersome to operate if they were to become the decisive factor in combat.

Another treatise caused him to agree that war games were valuable for training, that it was difficult to design problems for practicing command in a war game, and that commanders were likely to control ground troops from the air in the future. But he was unimpressed by the tendency "to use the word 'VAST' in speaking of the numbers of tanks. (One could win a war with a 'VAST' number of trained worms.)"

Patton acquiesced warmly with a statement that a mechanized force was useful only in the attack and that cavalry units bolstered by mechanized elements were doubled in value. He noted that during the siege of Rhodes in 304 B.C., Demetrius had constructed an enormous rock-throwing machine moved by 3400 men; the enemy destroyed the engine by making it fall into a hole.

He cited Seeckt, father of the postwar German Army, as authority for the statement that mechanization was a catchword against which thinking soldiers had to fight. The Army of the future was sure to be small, professional, well trained, and highly mobile, with cavalry a vital element.

After looking at the courses offered by the Air Corps Tactical School, Patton commented on the need for armor-piercing ammunition for all antiaircraft guns. He noted that radios and planes still failed to work well together. He felt that an observer in an aircraft being used for reconnaissance had to be an expert in radio, photography, flying, the tactics of all the other arms, and a good machine gunner — "for which profundity of knowledge he only gets 50% increase in pay and that only for a little while." Observation missions in the air would, he thought, be hampered by fear of interference from hostile pursuit planes.

Patton believed that an effective military leader was an artist rather than a scientist. Unfortunately, the intricacies of mechanization were apt to involve soldiers in techniques that were more scientific than artistic. While the fighting value of units depended on many elements, the prime determinant was the sort of leadership they had.

It is very easy for ignorant people to think that success in war may be gained by the use of some wonderful invention rather than by hard fighting and superior leadership.

Fifteen years later, when signs multiplied that Germany was losing World War II, Hitler would constantly promise and the German people would believe that new miracle weapons were about to appear and change the course of the war.

Emphasizing leadership, Patton wrote:

. . . the attempt to make mahoginy boxes out of pine is analogus to the attempt to make leaders out of a large percentage of students [in the military schools] . . . Leadership demands a balanced consideration of all means — a complete mastery of technique. The military specialist who is blind to the defects or virtues of all arms but his own is a menace, a dangerous menace . . . Wars are not won by maneuvers but by fighting. Education cannot make though it can help a genius . . . It is cheaper to beat an enemy by war of maneuver than by trench warfare but in our enthusiasm for maneuver we must not forget that trenches will be used to defend vital localities and most of all as points around which to maneuver.

The papers, articles, and reports he studied reinforced his long-held beliefs in the importance of mobility, speed, and surprise, the importance of the soldier rather than the machine, the importance of command, communications, and supply, the importance of air warfare and ground mechanization, and the continuing importance of the offensive, the attack.

Had the environment — the United States, the Army, the cavalry, his own friends and associates — been more stimulating, less negative, more open, less constricting, more alive, less bound by tradition and inertia, more encouraging in funds and in spirit, what contributions might Patton have made to the military thought and the art of war of his times?

CHAPTER 42

Washington: Cavalry and Tanks

*"It is just Tank propaganda and was hard to write as I did not
want to do any thing that could be used against the horse."*

*Letter, GSP, Jr., to Henry L. Stimson, Secretary of State, March 29,
1929*

My dear Mr. Secretary: Knowing, by previous experience, your
fondness for exercise and riding, I am taking the liberty of offering
you the use of my horses and squash court, at any time and as often as
you may find convenient. The court and horses are situated at 3000
Cathedral Avenue (the old Newlands Place), not far from the War[d]-
man Park Hotel. Of course the court cannot move but the horses can
meet you either at my house or at any other place you may elect . . .
Please believe me when I say that in accepting either of these invitations you will be conferring a favor upon me. Both the court and the
horses need exercise. Mrs. Patton joins me in sincere regards to Mrs.
Stimson and yourself. Very respectfully,

Letter, Stimson to GSP, Jr., April 6, 1929

My dear Major Patton: Many thanks for the kind offer of horses
and squash court. Some time in the near future I hope to be able to
avail myself of the use of the horses . . .

It has been a pleasure to get back to Washington and to have the
privilege of enjoying the hospitality of my old Army friends . . .

[Handwritten] P.S. Apr 8. I had a delightful ride on Gaylord
yesterday.

Patton attended the twentieth reunion of his class at West Point, then
traveled to Fort Riley to inspect training activities for the Chief of Cavalry. He talked with many officers, "all old friends," on how well the
Cavalry School was fulfilling its missions, and he observed the classroom
and outdoor activities.

When he returned to Washington, he recommended certain changes. Assigning students to the Advanced Equitation Class, he thought, should be deferred until later in the school year because some students developed slowly. Horses should not be classified as jump or school horses but be used for whatever purpose was required. More time ought to be set aside for riding during the year-long course — "After all, the chief characteristic of the cavalryman is his horse-induced mobility."

Due to the constant change in station, to the small pay and the great amount of duty at stations where horses may not be maintained, the present cavalry officer gets far less riding and knowledge of the horse than did his predecessor of ten or twenty years ago.

More riding halls, whether temporary or permanent in construction would help. Polo received insufficient official encouragement; the Cavalry School should have the best polo team in the Army.

I realize that in making this statement I can be accused of bias. However, I honestly believe that my opinion in this particular case is impartial. Polo is . . . the great equestrian game, and it seems therefore very appropriate . . . at our great equestrian school.

Better quarters on post were required for the noncommissioned officers.

Even the very senior non-commissioned officers are forced to inhabit buildings of a very temporary and dilapidated nature. The class of non-commissioned officers at the Cavalry School and with the school detachment is particularly high and every effort should be made to facilitate their comfort and self-respect.

More cavalry maneuvers were needed. The students who came from the 1st Cavalry Division were better prepared for their studies because of the frequent exercises along the border.

Discussing the school programs for the coming academic year, Patton said that "long and intimate association with scholastic subjects leads to an obliteration of perspective. The purpose of instruction (killing) becomes lost in the means of imparting it (talking)." Therefore, he recommended that the courses be reduced from 180 to 140 hours in length, with the exception of military history, which should be increased "as a means of inculcating esprit de corps and of developing a resourceful mind." He thought it made sense to increase the hours devoted to mounted and combined arms warfare, to decrease the hours concerned with staff and logistics. As for fortifications, "The less cavalry knows about digging the better." Cavalrymen had no need of technical knowledge of machines, but they needed to know how to employ armored cars tactically. He recommended that riding and scouting classes be held at night and in bad weather at least ten times during the school year.

Crosby rated Patton a "superior" officer who was competent to hold the rank of major general in the cavalry and brigadier general in any other arm and who was capable of holding any General Staff position. He was:

> A most energetic and forceful officer with a thorough knowledge of his profession. He possesses a combination of physique, determination and daring, coupled with a knowledge of his own and other arms that make him one of the few officers I know who would make an ideal commander of a Cavalry Division in war.

The campaign in the Army, the Congress, and the press to modernize the military establishment by machines seemed to pick up in intensity, and a rebuttal appeared in the Washington *Post* of Sunday, July 7, 1929. A story called "The Juggernaut of No-Man's-Land" purported to show what had been learned about tanks since the World War, what the latest developments were, and how they would be used in the "Next Great World Conflagration." There was a large photograph of Patton standing in front of a tank in France. The reporter had obviously talked with Patton, and certainly it was from Patton that the following sentence came: "In a country like the United States, which owns 21,000,000 horses and 4,000,000 mules, the tank and the motor vehicle will not soon supplant all animals for military purposes."

In a formal rebuttal of the case for mechanization in August, Patton referred at length to the inability of machines to traverse all kinds of terrain in all conditions of weather. He offered the observation that horses required no experimental or developmental costs. The horses necessary for a patrol of four men cost $600; an armored car capable of carrying four men cost at least $1500; a tank cost anywhere from $12,000 to $15,000. Furthermore, "It would be folly and a great hardship to the farmers if we fail to utilize the natural and existing productions in the shape of horseflesh." He concluded with words that had become second nature to him:

> . . . each new invention from the chariot to the airplane — from gunpowder to the gas engine — has been heralded as the final solution, and yet in no instance has the adoption of a new weapon materially affected war. The wrestling maxim that "there is a block for every hold" still holds true. We may say without exaggeration that the first appearance of any new weapon in combat marked the zenith of its effect, though usually the nadir of its efficiency. This is due to the fact that now, as always, surprise is the primary means of attaining military success.

He worked much the same thought into a somewhat different format in a paper entitled "The Value of Cavalry." He started by quoting "expert opinion" — statements by high-ranking officers who testified to the continuing importance of cavalry. The list of cavalry supporters was impressive — Pershing, Harbord, Summerall, Liggett, Parker, Haig, Allenby, French, Foch, Pétain, Hindenburg, Weygand, Ludendorff, Kluck, Seeckt, and others. For example, Summerall had said, either in a letter to Patton or in an address: "There has been a great deal of misinformation broadcasted relative to the cavalry. It is a fact that cavalry is of far more importance than it has ever been."

Continuing, Patton must have been hurt by his need to turn so savagely on Fuller and Liddell Hart who were espousing theories of tank warfare in England.

> There is not a single known statement of any soldier of combat reputation which is derogatory to Cavalry. Surely the remarks of Colonel J. F. C. Fuller (British Army) who during the course of four years' war replete with opportunities attained only the rank of Lieutenant-Colonel, or the opinions of such a hack-writer as Captain Lyle Hart seem puerile when compared with the forceful statements of the elite of the military world. Despite this fact the effects of often repeated misstatements and halftruths are so far reaching and so readily swallowed by a gullible and motor minded public that a critical examination of the value of cavalry as compared with or modified by the so-called scientific arms is necessary in order to reach a definite conclusion.

He then went into his song and dance. Cavalry could operate anywhere whereas "Mechanical forces do not possess this universal availability." Unimproved roads were hard on motor transport, for they reduced the rate of speed, deteriorated rapidly under military wear, destroyed vehicles "through unwonted stresses," and exhausted drivers. Bridges were rarely strong enough to sustain the weight of motor vehicles. Vehicles could neither ford nor swim streams. "In the next war the destruction of roads and road bridges will be as common as was the destruction of railways and railway bridges in the last."

The last statement was an accurate prediction.

Cavalry, Patton went on, had augmented its firepower by increasing the number of automatic weapons it handled, now used armored cars, and was hoping to obtain tracked armored cars to form strong mobile points of maneuver.

> The limitation inherent in . . . vehicles, such as their inability to operate at night, to live off the country, or to penetrate wood and mountains indubitably stamp them as auxiliaries and not as supplanters of Cavalry.
>
> The individual mobility of cavalry and its universal adaptability are unaltered . . .*

Patton's paper was vehement because the cavalry was fighting for its existence. Lack of funds since the National Defense Act of 1920, and reductions in authorized personnel had cut the mounted arm back, and the advocates of mechanization, particularly the airmen, were clamoring to decrease the horse cavalry even more. As authorized numbers of wagons and pack animals were severely limited by public and congressional pressures, the cavalry compensated for its losses by adding small trucks and automobiles.

Coming events cast long shadows. Even though the combined arms assembled at Camp Meade to test concepts of mechanization were unable to

---

* Appended to this paper was an Addendum in Patton's handwriting: "Note: a great friend of mine was in G–3 when this paper came in. He simply had it coppied and submitted it as the belief of his section. Gen. Edward King then G–3 took the paper to Gen. Crosby Chief of Cav and showing it to him said this is a great paper why can't one of your office write it. Gen. Crosby showed Gen. King the original with my name to it. Neither King nor my friend A.R.C. [Adna R. Chaffee] ever apologized to me. GSP Jr."

accomplish much, a War Department Mechanization Board, appointed to study the results of the experiment, recommended that a permanent mechanized force be established despite the general lack of funds.

It was even impossible to keep the tanks (infantry) as a large and concentrated striking force. When the War Department decided to send eleven tank companies to various posts in order to facilitate training with infantry divisions, there were insufficient machines and men to carry out the plan. Tank companies were dispatched from Camp Meade to four Army installations. But the tank "companies" transferred to five others, as well as that left at Camp Meade, consisted only of tank platoons — five tanks instead of twenty.

For a few weeks during the summer of 1929, Patton was in charge of the Army polo team at Mitchell Field. Putting aside his visions of tanks and armored cars, forgetting for a short time the collection of photographs, drawings, and blueprints of experimental machines in his files in Washington, he concentrated on horses, the joy of riding, the thrill of competition. He played hard.

At the end of the polo season, he went to Green Meadows for a month of leave. While there, he answered a letter from the Chief of Cavalry.

My dear General Crosby: Pardon my delay in sending you the following answers to the questions . . . It is only too true that when one has lots of time one has no time.

He sent Crosby a ten-page staff paper on organization, division trains, motor equipment, vehicles, roads, marksmanship, gunnery, courses of instruction, motorized infantry, and national defense. "Aviation cannot take prisoners or hold ground," he wrote. "Again therefore it can aid but not replace cavalry." He was perfectly frank when he could not answer a question — "I have no data here on which to base recommendations for motorizing Cavalry Division trains." He admitted that "the consolidation of the Field and Coast artilleries is not susceptible of discussion by me." He thought that certain economies could be gained by reducing unit movements and personnel transfers, by cutting the number of officers attending service schools, and by abolishing military bands.

Early in October 1929, he traveled to Fort Bliss, where he attended meetings of the Polo-Horse Show Association and observed maneuvers held by the 1st Cavalry Division.

Letter, GSP, Jr., to Beatrice, October 9, 1929

Darling Beatrice: We had a very interesting manuver yesterday. The 8th Cav in trucks went up to Finlay to stop the 1st Cav mounted. There were 4 armored cars with the eighth [Cav]. Due to the utter lack of imagination of the Colonel of the 1st . . . the cars so delayed them that there was no battle. However it proved that my ideas both asto fighting with and against armored cars was correct . . .

Our old house at Sierra Blanca is still standing but you would hardly know the town. It has grown to be quite a place and has a golf club. Dick Love now lives in Mexico and Dave Allison has at last been killed.

I am getting on fine. I love you   George.

Letter, GSP, Jr., to Beatrice, October 12, 1929

The value of the commander is most evident. When he is active the manuvers are fine. When he is slow . . . they are a wash out.

Letter, GSP, Jr., to Crosby, October 18, 1929

My dear General: Feeling that you will not now be able to attend the maneuvers and knowing your great interest in them I am sending you this [which] is a brief and probably ill-digested account of the features which have attracted my notice thus far.

Armored Cars: These vehicles have an almost unprecedented capacity in this terrain. They function not only as cars but are also capable of assuming frequently the role of tanks. They are much more effective on the defense than in the attack. In combating them it is axiomatic that troops (Cavalry) must refrain from playing their game. That is the cavalry must keep off the roads — well off. Captain Holt has established excellent relations with the Ordnance. If he can secure two hundred dollars from the Ord. he can make some most desirable changes in the cars here. I believe Gen. Williams [Chief of Ordnance] will let you have this money . . .

Pursuant to your ideas I persuaded Col. Brown . . . to put his saddle packs in the train in one maneuver. The effect was marked in the excellent condition of the horses . . .

Envelopment: It is my opinion that in some cases cavalry is too timid about extended deployments. Too much memory of distances used in the schools . . . A notable exception was an attack made by the 10th Cav. under Lt. Col. L. Brown. In that case he got completely behind the enemy before he was ever seen . . .

So far as I can see control and mobility are inimical. We should admit this and . . . let the two principal elements work independently . . .

Comments from some of the Corps and War Department heads harped on the subject of more caution. This is an error. All men are cowards; the first whisper of a bullet will awaken all the caution we need, probably much more than we want. At maneuvers we should be over bold so that in war the tendency to over caution may to a measure be counteracted . . .

If a division can't operate 18 miles from a good road it is in a hell of a fix . . .

The training of the [cavalry] division is excellent, the discipline fine, the conditions of the mounts exceptional . . . The arrangements were worked out in the most minute details and worked without a hitch. The umpires and observers were cared for to a superlative degree. If we had had this division in Mexico in 1916 there would be no border question to-day. All officers were most regretful that you could not be present. In closing I repeat that this is a very hasty summary liable to error. The general impression [I have of the Cavalry Division] is of an efficient contented and powerful machine. Very respectfully,

After refereeing a polo game, then giving a dinner party for eighteen people to pay off social debts — it was expensive, cost $83, "but they all had a good time," Patton departed by air for Los Angeles and a brief visit with his sister and aunt. While flying over Arizona, he wrote Beatrice: "You can see the tops of all the hills we have so often wished to climb and look into the secrets of all the little can[y]ons. One gets so much better an idea of the lay of the land."

Letter, GSP Jr. (Woodley, Washington), to Beatrice (Green Meadows), no date.

Enclosed is a copy of an article I wrote for the Hearst papers by request. It is just Tank propaganda and was hard to write as I did not want to do any thing that could be used against the horse.

As I wrote it in two sittings and failed to have your help either in criticism or punctuation it is not much good but if it is accepted I get $250.00.

The untitled article started with a sketch of tanks moving to position for jump-off in battle:

. . . a machine gurgles and dies while its frantic crew, sobbing curses like apoplectic mule skinners, wiggle and sweat to replace some refractory magneto or erring fanbelt. Presently an officer arrives to lend his muffled profanity to the task of rekindling the defunct spirit of the motor . . .

She tops the parapet and exposing six feet of slimy belly teters for a moment until with the grace of a baby hippo she plunges forward and courtesying clangorously to the void wabbles on again for all the world like some huge Galapagos turtle, swaying the gun proboscis of its turret head from side to side in search of prey . . .

The "Baby Tank" as the French affectionately called the little Renault [during the war] was an infant in more respects than size . . . all the faults of adolescence; feeble clumsy and near sighted, it only survived due to the indomitable will of the men who fought and tended it . . .

[Those at Camp Meade recently saw the latest example of] the metal saurian make its debut . . .

Long, low, its eight wheels articulating with the rhythmic abandon of the legs of a water beetle it flew past us not at four, but forty miles an hour.

Report, GSP, Jr., to Crosby, Tactical lessons derived from the Cavalry Division maneuvers, October 1929, November 27, 1929

Armored Cars. In dry weather the country along the western section of the Mexican border — that is from Marfa to the Pacific Ocean — is particularly well adapted to the employment of armored cars. Their ability to move over this region is extraordinary and permits them to partake of the nature of fast, light tanks. The operations are further facilitated by the fact that few of the roads are ditched so that they may be entered and left at will . . .

The best place to locate barricades for the purpose either of checking or upsetting armored cars is on the far side of blind curves, or just beyond the brow of a steep rise . . . A tree or telegraph pole felled across the road will serve as a basis for such a barricade.

In engaging armored cars by fire the targets should be the tires, wheel-hubs, eye slits, and differential or radiator, even when protected . . .

Envelopments. Excessive pursuit of "A's" [good grades] at sundry schools have had the pernicious effect of making our officers timid . . . The function of cavalry is to get behind the enemy . . . wide and risky movements are necessary . . .

Advances by bounds. This method of progression exists only on paper . . .

Control. There was much comment by all the observers upon the lack of control in action . . . we have for so long been accustomed to . . . the dream soldiers of map problems that we forget the many defects in poor human flesh. As a matter of fact, in war we shall have much less control than at the maneuvers. The sooner we accommodate ourselves to this fact and arrange our methods of war so that they will function despite lack of information, the better we'll be off.

Camps. No effort was made to cover or protect camps from air attacks . . .

Supply . . . Unfortunately, when rain occurred, making the roads difficult, the maneuvers were called off; so no test of supply during inclement weather was obtained . . . some engineering trucks . . . were stuck for some two days not over seven miles from a hard road.

Due to the ill-advised attempt to make World War conditions of static combat applicable to cavalry, staff command was overstressed . . . Much time was wasted. The essence of cavalry combat as has been demonstrated by all successful cavalrymen, of whom there are a very limited number, depends upon spontaneous cavalry leadership. Attempts to smother and delegate authority and staff command is fatal.

GSP, Jr., Lecture to the Pennsylvania National Guard Convention at Reading, December 6, 1929, "Cavalry in the Next War"

. . . should any of you chance to believe one-tenth of the current bunk about cavalry and war, you might well paraphrase the title of my remarks into: "The Extinct in the Impossible." . . . piffle to the contrary notwithstanding, cavalry will bear its part in that war as it has done in all that have preceded it. For, as Field Marshal Earl Haig once said to me: "My boy (I was one twelve years ago) Infantry and Artillery can win battles, but only cavalry can make them worth winning." Less cryptically he meant that the man who runs in fear of death can always outstrip the man who pursues, unless the pursuer can provide more rapid means of locomotion . . .

Battles without successful pursuit are futile . . .

I have had as much experience with mechanized forces, both in war and peace, as has any man in our army; therefore when I tell you that machines have defects as great as their advantages, I deserve your attention . . .

An unfed motor stops; a starved horse takes days to die.

Remount magazine carried a piece by Patton on hunting, "The Sport of Kings." It was marked by humor — "the first horse a man owns is apt to share the fate of the first child and be killed by misplaced attentions and undigested education"; by common sense — his fears over his adequacy to complete a course of schooling were countered by the remark "Just look at the dumb-bells who have graduated"; by exaggeration — a small error leads to "folly"; by individual turn of phrase — timidity was "intuitive reluctance to adventure in the unknown"; and by the need to be perfect in every action undertaken — one became perfect by constant study and practice.

By the end of the war, Patton had completed what he called the "First Phase of Study" of a long treatise entitled "A Study of the Combat of Cavalry up to and Including the World War." An ambitious project, the initial part alone consisted of 249 typed pages, single space. It was typically Patton in phraseology and content. For example: The mission of armies was to win battles, for all military operations culminated in battle. Cannae was won "by a supreme confidence [of the soldiers] in their leader, Hannibal." At Pharsala, Pompey and Caesar exemplified that "Strategy merely leads up to battle. The end of all effort and maneuver in war is successful combat or to cause the enemy to give up because of his fear of that combat."

A lecture he wrote early in 1930 re-used parts of earlier papers. There was nothing new except his form of expression. For example, novelty was a form of surprise, "and it is surprise, not power which appalls us." Airplane observers saw a great deal but very badly. Armored cars went fast and far but only if and when the roads permitted. Seeing a charging line, troops would

usually act like Macbeth's dinner party and depart without waiting on the order of their going . . . Think . . . of how few places there are in the world, except target ranges, where one can see every foot of ground from zero to a thousand yards . . . Extensive obstacles such as creeks, gullies, and wooded draws should be held in force. At such places mechanized forces can be stopped. If they know their business, however, they will not attack but go around . . . [Command] must be extremely personal and extremely decentralized . . . Anything done vigorously is better than nothing done tardily.

These statements had become his clichés, and he reiterated them constantly. Whether he actually believed that the horse had a place in modern warfare, or, as everyone was saying, in the next war, or whether he was forced into defending the horse against his convictions with respect to tanks and armored cars was probably something he himself could not have said with assurance.

There is no doubt that he believed in mechanization to some extent, perhaps to a large extent, and to this end he worked actively with Christie, perhaps even to the degree of partially subsidizing his work.

So he straddled the issues. And was apparently comfortable enough in his dual role as traditionalist and innovator to handle both sides with ease. In February, while he was working on the proper sequence of training regulations for mounted troops, he marked one of six glossy prints of Christie tank bodies in his handwriting as "My model of Christy Type for Cavalry." Whether he was expressing a preference or whether he had actually contributed to the Christie design by advice or funds remains a matter of conjecture.

In March, Patton was appointed a member of a board to review and revise the development, organization, and equipment of the permanent mechanized force that the War Department had approved. Perhaps it was this that led him to come close to conceding defeat for the horse cavalry. In a memo on antitank and anti-armored car operations, he wrote: "Mechanization is now so universally adopted that we will probably encounter a certain number of fighting vehicles in the ranks of any possible enemy."

How successfully he had managed to defend the horse and to advocate the machine was obvious in Crosby's rating of his performance. Crosby repeated what he had earlier written — that Patton would make "an ideal commander of a Cavalry Division in war." This time Crosby added: "While he is an outstanding horseman he is also outstanding as an authority in mechanization due to his varied experience in France with the Tank Corps and to his continued interest in and study of the subject of mechanization."

CHAPTER 43

Washington: Horses and Machines

"It would be cheaper to dress our men in overalls, but it would be a saving too truely bought, for without pride soldiers are useless."

WHATEVER PATTON'S DIFFICULTIES may have been with respect to machines and horses, a way out suddenly appeared in a letter from an old friend.

Letter, Ralph I. Sasse (West Point) to GSP, Jr., March 18, 1930
Dear Patton: For the last two months my tongue has been tied on a definite promise to one of rank here at West Point — yesterday I heard additional news which may be stale to you, however here goes. Richardson is due to leave here as Commandant of Cadets. The following have been mentioned to replace him — Charlie Thompson — Tom Catron — Jake Devers, Buckner and yourself. General Rivers [Patton's former commanding officer] has probably gotten wind of what is taking place, as he told me last Saturday evening that he had recommended you to the Superintendent, though no reaction was obtained. Col Whipple, The Adjutant here is one of my best friends and the Supt. acts upon his advice in many matters. Accordingly I have swung Whipple in line for you. I would like to see you come here. The place needs some red blood and hard common sense. With you as Commandant I believe we could produce a few soldiers. Besides I need a squash partner. Best to Beatrice and the gang. Cordially,

Patton tucked away Sasse's phrase "red blood and hard common sense" in his mind, then went to see General Crosby. He asked Crosby to recommend him for the job.

It was not a moment too soon. Crosby was retiring from the Army in two days. He wrote immediately to the Superintendent, Major General

William R. Smith, who had commanded the Hawaiian Division and who had removed Patton from the post of G–3. Being Commandant of Cadets, Crosby wrote, was the most sought after assignment among young field officers, and many had asked him to recommend them for the position. He felt he could at last recommend two officers,

> either Chaffee or Patton — two of our outstanding cavalrymen — for the place. Both of them, as you know, had brilliant records in France and Patton especially, one that should make him a hero to the Cadet. As a result of his service under you in Honolulu his friends tell me he is less positive in his ideas and in his expression of them. He is certainly loyal to you and has been most loyal to me during his two years in my office. With apologies for butting in to what I know you will decide and decide properly for yourself, I am, Cordially,

For the second time, Patton would fail to get the assignment.

Major General Guy V. Henry, an old friend of Patton's became Chief of Cavalry, and the pleasant relations Patton had enjoyed with Crosby would continue.

Patton's professional study during his years in the Office of the Chief of Cavalry was enormous. He now wore glasses when reading. In the spring of 1930 when he suffered from a slight conjunctivitis, an inflammation of the eyes, the doctor recorded that the probable cause was Patton's staying up with his books until one o'clock every morning

He avidly went through G–2 reports compiled from military attachés in England, France, Germany, and Japan, and appended to many of these papers, which Patton kept in his personal files, were his own typed notes, usually a page or half-page, sometimes more, generally a digest of the substance. For example, one sheet was headed "Thoughts aroused by the foregoing" and contained the statement that advocates of mechanization believed they would have a monopoly on heroes in the future. "Mobile A.A. [antiaircraft] units are excellent Anti Tank Units," which was a concept for a dual-purpose gun able to engage both air and ground targets.

With cavalry under heavy attack and Patton busy fending off efforts to declare the cavalry obsolete, he wrote draft lectures for Henry to deliver. He had Henry saying that machines, guns, tanks, armored cars, and planes only made cavalry stronger.

We are now the most powerful cavalry and, in my opinion, the most powerful arm in the world. The path to fame and glory lies before us, if we have but the intelligence to follow it.

As a committee member studying the development both of weapons and of communications and their influence on strategy and tactics, Patton stated:

A Study of the evolution of tactics . . . naturally [but it would be natural only to someone like Patton who was steeped in military history] leads me to use the Seven Years War as a mile stone since at this point we just find the powder propelled missile assuming a predominant place in warfare.

A summary of conclusions appended to a report on firepower read:

In art it often happens that a sketch by the very baldness of its portrayal gives a better likeness than does a finished painting. Just so when we view war objectively . . . we denude it of its non essentials and bring into vivid relief the thoughts of Frederick and Napoleon which we still paraphrase to read: "Fire is every thing as a means to securing victory through movement."

He thought it a mistake to expose immobile masses of humanity to machines and believed that as science placed additional inventions at the disposal of the Army, greater demands would be made on the soldiers who used them.

His miscellaneous notes written on various occasions, most of them un-dated, contained aphorisms, including:

. . . articles and pictures . . . far out horror the reality of war.
. . . rifle fire in war . . . is not to be taken too seriously, because in addition to the almost complete absence of targets all the partici-pants have their nerves and muscles strained to the breaking point by fatigue, sleeplessness and lack of food to say nothing of the insinuat-ingly suggestive hissing and screeching of shell fragments and bullets.
. . . in a war of position cavalry is about as useful as railway artil-lery would be in a war of movement.
Battles are won by fear.

[Victory in the Boer War was actually a] triumph of discipline cohesion and the offensive spirit.

In April 1930, he delivered a speech to the American Remount Association, and it was music to the ears of his listeners. He cited progress in breeding, the numerous horse shows, the flourishing state of polo competition, the popularity of horse racing, the appeal of hunting, the growth in bridle paths in cities, and called this equine revival pleasing to horsemen everywhere because it benefited the population in health and pleasure, brought wealth to breeders and to the farmers who grew the forage, and helped train young men for the next war.

He then swung into his sermon, a hard-hitting talk consisting of arguments "to refute the blithe assertions of the motor enthusiast that the horse has no place in war and hence is not a necessity," to rebut the "unlimited belief in and enthusiasm for machines as a cure-all for future unpleasantness."

The World War was not the first conflict that prompted the inventive genius of mankind, and he recalled the chariot, longbow, ballista, armor of various sorts, Greek fire, and gunpowder — all of which in their day had much the same impact on warfare as gasoline motors, tanks, gas warfare, airplanes, and machine guns.

To me it seems that a person who says that since machines are faster than horses, horses should be scrapped and machines only secured is on a mental parity with the poor man who on seeing an overcoat of undoubted warmth in a second hand store sells his pants to purchase the coat only to find that in summer it is burdensome and not wholly satisfying even in December . . .

The horse is not useless neither is the machine. What is wanted is better types of both run by men who know their powers and limitations and who instead of decrying each others capacities aid one another.

In May, Patton wrote a lengthy rebuttal to a study submitted by Colonel James Kelly Parsons, who proposed the creation of six tank divisions, one for each of the six field armies envisaged in the General Mobilization Plan. Patton's major objection was that there were "only three [possible] theaters of war in which we could utilize such a mass of men" — Western

Europe, Asia, and the United States, and he showed in great detail why he thought six tank divisions would be "redundant." Furthermore, tanks like battleships became obsolete. At the close of the World War, the Army had had 900 Renaults and 100 Mark VIII tanks; their current value was *"zero."* The tank, he said, was a better machine in 1930 than in 1918, but it was less effective, because there would be many heavy machine guns in the next war — they were "cheaper and quicker to make than tanks," and they could knock out tanks.

> The expenditure of twenty seven million [dollars] on lightweight .50 caliber machine-guns would probably do much more toward the winning of the next war than will the expenditure of two hundred and seventy million on tanks.

Soldiers were trained in the Great War to fire at the hulls and eye-slits of tanks. "This was playing the tank-man's game." In the next war, soldiers would aim at "the running gear and will secure results for less ammunition. A stalled tank is junk!"

Exactly how conservative Patton was — whether by necessity or by inclination — became apparent when he rejected the idea of having "infantry integral with the tank division." Unlike the Germans who were organizing units of closely coordinated tanks and infantry, Patton felt this was "a grave mistake." He would change his mind in World War II.

Attached without comment to a letter from Patton to Beatrice in June was a newspaper article. The clipping was headed "Joe Angelo Pleads for Veterans."

Angelo appeared before a congressional committee investigating unemployment and the bonus claims of veterans. According to the reporter, "The veteran [Angelo], who weighs 107 pounds, said he had walked 180 miles to Washington to state that the ex-soldiers 'do not want to rob the treasury. We just want to work.'"

He had been out of work for a year and a half. He was married and had a child. He had built a home when he returned from France, but he was likely to lose it because he was unable to pay the taxes he owed on the property.

Medals covered Angelo's breast. When asked how he had won the Distinguished Service Cross, he replied that he had saved the life of Colonel

Patton, who was now stationed at Fort Myer. Angelo showed a watch he had received from the colonel's wife and a stickpin with a bullet mounted in gold from the colonel's mother.

Angelo said he could make money bootlegging. Or he could go to Fort Myer and get all the money he wanted or needed from Patton. But that wasn't right. He wanted to work. Or if work was unavailable, he wanted the money due him according to his service certificate. He wished to have at least part of the $1424 coming to him for his war service.

Congress refused to authorize an immediate cash bonus for veterans. For the moment there was little more than vague unrest about the hard times in the country. But demands for the federal government to ameliorate the economic conditions would soon reach a strident insistence, and Joe Angelo would figure in it. He would have a symbolic confrontation with his old Tank Corps colonel.

In the War Department, Patton was considering "the tactical role of armored cars and the characteristics deducible therefrom."

It is patent that any assumptions made must be tentative, until the test of battle shall have given its verdict. None the less it is believed that we now have enough information to justify us in certain assumptions. Such a course will at least service the purpose of giving us a datum plane from which to measure progress . . .

The history of war is a history of an age-old duel between defensive and offensive devices. Each new arm traces its birth to the necessity of countering some temporarily decisive invention. The tank was conceived and born to counter the .30 caliber machine-gun. Conversely, the .50 caliber machine-gun was devised to counter the tank. To continue the construction of vehicles only capable of resisting .30 caliber fire is absurd. On the other hand, an attempt to wholly protect them against short range .50 caliber projectiles is impossible. A compromise must be effected on grounds analogous to those used in the Navy. That is, we must make an harmonical arrangement of our four defensive means: armor, speed, gun fire, and low silhouette.

. . . The nose of our machine must then be heavily armored. To do likewise to the tail would not only overload our machine, but also would have a bad moral influence. Remember Cortez and his burned ships [which forced his men to advance into the interior of Mexico].

Together with C. C. Benson, Patton wrote a paper entitled "Mechanization and Cavalry." It was published in the *Infantry Journal* in June 1930. The final paragraph read:

The fighting machine is here to stay, and if our cavalry has not lost its traditional alertness and adaptability, we will frankly accept it at its true worth. If the 14th Century Knight could adapt himself to gunpowder, we should have no fear of oil, grease, and motors. Confident of our own power, we should give the fighting machine the serious thought that it deserves.

Letter, GSP, Jr., to Beatrice, June 30, 1930

Darling Beat: Our [boat] trip was most successful We left . . . at ten minutes to 5 Sunday morning and got to our destination Smith's Creek, beyond St. Mary's at 10:30. We looked over Col Latrobes prospective place for a couple of hours got gas and returned . . . at 7:15 having gone 160 miles in 10½ hours. The moku [boat] went fine.

The place on Smiths creek is very beautiful though terribly run down and owned by the largest man I ever saw. Remind me to tell you about him. The house is on a peninsula with a private bay nine feet deep right at the house.

There are private oysters in the bay.

Col Latrobe and Palmer Swift make a fine crew. Palmer loves to steer and Col Latrobe to cook so I had nothing to do. This did not keep me from missing you and thinking how much nicer a trip it would have been had you been there . . .

It is realy very hot here but not too much so.

I love you   George.

Henry rated Patton a "superior" officer — "outstandingly energetic and forceful. A thorough student of his profession — dependable and loyal. Suitable for most any duty."

Over the long Fourth of July weekend, Patton met and talked with John Pell, associate editor of the *North American Review*. Pell was impressed by the thesis that Patton articulated — that every weapon was most useful though least effective when it was introduced into combat. Would Patton write an article for the journal emphasizing the application of that theory to the airplane? Patton agreed.

He sent the article, saying:

In accord with your suggestion . . . I have attempted to express my views . . . I fear without too happy results. My chief critic and leading punctuator, Mrs. Patton, is away so that probably much is left to be desired in this connection.

Entitled "The Effect of Weapons on War," the article opened beautifully:

When Sampson took the fresh jawbone of an ass and slew a thousand men therewith he probably started such a vogue for the weapon, particularly among the Philistines, that for years no prudent donkey dared to bray.

Although the rest of the piece was vigorous in language, it was so obviously addressed to military men that the *Review* could not publish it.

Letter, GSP, Jr. (Washington), to Beatrice (Massachusetts), July 21, 1930

Darling Beat: It is 108 in this office so they have closed the offices and I am only waiting to write you before I take to the cellar at home. The heat is something fierce . . .

I hope I did not leave you with the impression that I thought you were either a poor sailor or mother. I think you are perfect in these rolls as in all others. I will even "bend" so much as to sail with you in the Dont Esk if you want me.

I love you. George.

Letter, GSP, Jr., to Beatrice, August 5, 1930

Gen Douglas MacArthur is announced as the next Chief of Staff. I don't know just what effect that will have on the cavalry. He is not favorable to polo but I heard that he said that if he became chief of staf: he would try and convince the army that the war was over. Meaning that now too much work is required.

In a memo to Henry he argued that automatic weapons, contrary to general belief, enhanced rather than reduced the need for and value of cavalry. Speaking of economy, he said: "Unquestionably it would be cheaper to dress our men in overalls, but it would be a saving too truely bought, for without pride soldiers are useless."

Patton could well have said he had gained an international reputation as a military expert, for the British *Cavalry Journal* in its October issue gave a précis of an article of his in the American journal and called it a well-reasoned paper with a sane outlook.

When Captain B. H. Liddell Hart stated that cavalry had become too susceptible to air attack for continued usefulness in war, Patton took issue.

In my opinion Captain Lydell Hart assumes his conclusions and then writes articles to prove them. This is a very common practice among all writers. I think that he probably overstates his ideas with a view of creating argument.

Asked to comment on a new experimental cavalry saber, he said it seemed superior because it was lighter and stiffer, but actually it was inferior because the hilt was attached to the sword by an outmoded method instead of by the kitchen-knife method used in the 1913 — his — model.

I am very much opposed to the fancy grip suggested. For several thousand years men have been killing each other with out finding thumb grooves or finger bumpers necessary. A simple hard rubber grip is cheaper better and lighter . . .

Note: In 1912 when I was working on the saber I designed one almost identical with the Experimental model. I also had a metal scabbard. Gen. H. T. Allen and E. St. J. Greble were on the G.S. [General Staff] and insisted that I make a double edged sword so it would pull out easier (This was theory as they had never tried in bodies of pigs as I had — the single edge pulls out equally well). These same two also forced the wooden scabbard. The temper refered to by the board is not very essential. Softness is better than brittleness. It is a simple matter to straighten a saber blade with a foot. We also do it with dueling swords.

He wrote, probably on instruction from Henry, to several influential commanders asking them to exert pressure on the War Department to help keep the cavalry branch from losing men to the air corps. To Fox Conner, commander of the First Corps Area, he added:

You told me years ago that the next war would be fought with
smaller armies of professionals. Now is a chance to save a few of the
"Brutal and licentious soldiery" for that happy occasion.

Under his signature, he wrote, jokingly of course, "Maj[or] of
Pac[i]fists."

*GSP, Jr., Lecture, "New Developments in Cavalry," delivered at the
Quartermaster School, Philadelphia, December 17, 1930*
Were I to begin by saying that there are no new developments I
should probably both surprise and please you, while at the same time
I would be telling the truth — but not the whole truth . . .
Our so-called new developments . . . are not new, only recur-
rent . . .
The trench is but a rampart upside down while belts of wire are
moats . . .
. . . the railway train is the epitome of reliable speed. Yet if the
coal fails, the tracks are pulled up, or the engine injured, our mighty
contrivance becomes junk. Moreover, it has no liberty of direction:
it follows a predestined course.
The same thing applies in varying degrees to all machines. Further, being devoid of intelligence and sensory nerves machines can
not move freely at night without lights — what lovely targets headlights make! Finally, they have no ears and their own noise deadens
those of their operatives.
. . . A Swallow can out-maneuver an eagle but he is not feared.
Speed and mobility not linked with fighting capacity are valueless.
Wars are won by killing. . . .
Some bewail the advent of machines while others proclaim them as
the final solution to the age-old problem for safe success. As usual
both are wrong. The new abets but does not supplant the old.
. . . In the cavalry we are doing everything financial restrictions
will permit to develop to the full our part of mechanization . . .
. . . success depends very little on complicated tricks of procedure
and very much on stark fighting ability. Victory comes to rough and
simple methods executed by disciplined and heroic soldiers. The
Bosch call it: "The will to victory." The vulgar call it "guts."
. . . many writers on mechanization picture the enemy as static
and unarmed, while gasoline grows on trees and bridges are constructed by a wave of the hand.

A battle in which the enemy is not destroyed is a more or less futile affair . . .

I invariably find myself feeling sorry for the enemy: he seems in such an awful fix. But really my tears are wasted. His cavalry with its cars is on hand to oppose ours, so it is a fight once more and the best man wins . . .

In closing I can but repeat that the ends we seek and the methods we employ are as old as winter and as young as spring. Only the technique and the weapons change a little, but neither are vital. Battles are won now as always by the indomitable heart of man, the oldest weapon.

Memo, GSP, Jr., to Chief of Cavalry, December 31, 1930

The other day while hunting in the snow I saw some people putting cup grease in the bottom of their horses feet. On asking the reason I was told that it prevented the snow from "Balling." I tried it and found that it worked. [It cut down slipping. Some winter campaign in the future might depend on some such expedient for success. Recommends test at Cavalry School.] No expense is involved as grease is expendable or at the worst waste cylinder oil can be used.

GSP, Jr., Lecture, "Modern Cavalry," delivered at the Marine Corps School, Quantico, Va., January 9, 1931

. . . the saber and the bayonet are . . . the symbols of implacable determination . . . but it is more the fear of their questing points than the wounds they produce which induces the enemy to leave . . .

The mobilization, feeding, and movement of [huge armies] . . . is a stupendous task, while the cost and delays entailed are out of all proportion to the results attained.

For example, the ratio of men behind to men in front increases out of all reason. At time[s] during the war it reached the ridiculous figure of five behind the three fighting. [In World War II, the proportion required would be, roughly, ten to one.]

The inertia inherent in such armies leads inevitably to stabilization with its attendant high costs and lack of conclusiveness.

The inert human masses become fodder for their equally inert masses of machines. The only road to victory lies in attrition — the sausage machine method.

Again, while the development in weapons is continuous, the cost of perpetually rearming hoards [hordes] with new arms is beyond the powers of the richest; so mass armies must, perforce, fight with obsolescent tools.

Finally, the complexity of the new weapons and of the methods best adapted for their employment is beyond the capabilities of short term troops.

The outstanding lesson of the World War was its indecisiveness and, since this is largely traceable to the use of "Nations in Arms," soldiers seeking a solution tend more and more towards a return to smaller mobile armies capable of maneuver . . .

In closing let me say that the greatest ill-luck I can wish those who think cavalry is dead, is to be against us in the next war. They will be the corpses, not we.

Letter, Fox Conner to GSP, Jr., January 1931

I hope that the powers that be will never lose sight of the fact that we need, above all, things that will work under all conditions.

This was exactly what Patton had been preaching.

In mid-January, Patton almost had the dubious distinction of being challenged to a duel. A member of the Spanish embassy, Ramon Padillo, had unexpectedly stopped at a jump during a hunt and had almost caused Ruth Ellen Patton to collide with him. She barely avoided the possibility of serious injury. Her father who was nearby rode up and gave Padillo a severe and profane tongue-lashing.

Apprised immediately afterward that the Spaniard would be quick to take umbrage, Patton wrote him a note, asking him please to accept his apologies for any remarks he may have made. In sport in America, Patton explained, it was the custom to speak out and those who did so were not considered impolite. Had he known that Padillo was a foreigner, he would not have so spoken. He gave renewed expressions of his regret.

He was, more than likely, himself disturbed by the savagery of his outburst.

Padillo answered on the same day, addressing his note to "Major G. S. Patterson, Jr." He thanked Patton for his letter. "I did not consider myself the least offended by your remark at the hunt." He explained his own behavior by saying that he had not known whether it was the custom in Washington to halt at each jump.

A potentially nasty situation was avoided.

Commenting on March 4 on a draft manual, Patton wrote, with some unnecessarily harsh words:

> A manual should state WHAT to do and HOW to do it. It should not state WHY nor should it give alternative methods. Men who will use this manual in war will belong to the honest 80%. The smart 10% need no manual; the stupid 10% cannot use one.

Letter, Vice President Charles G. Dawes to GSP, Jr., March 22, 1931

My dear Patton: I hope you will excuse my delay in answering your letter but my sister, Mrs. Gann, informed me she had accepted your invitation for dinner and told you we would attend the Polo Ball. She looks after all my social engagements. It will be a pleasure to attend the Ball and indeed a great pleasure to have dinner with you and Mrs. Patton. With kindest regards, I am Very truly yours,

In April 1931, the argument over machines and horses seemed to come to some kind of tentative resolution. Following the recommendation of the War Department Mechanization Board and shortly before his retirement, General Summerall, who was then Chief of Staff, directed in October 1930, that a mechanized force be stationed permanently at Fort Eustis, Virginia. A strong proponent of the infantry-artillery-machine gun team, which had been effective in the World War, Summerall was convinced that tanks must be included in that team of combined arms. Since the infantry presumably was less interested in mobility than the cavalry and since mobility was the rage in conversation about how to avoid in the next war the static conditions of the last, a cavalry officer, Colonel Daniel Van Voorhis, was appointed the first commander of the mechanized force. Yet to insure infantry participation in the venture, the executive officer or second in command was Patton's old friend Sereno E. Brett, an infantryman who had taken command of the tank brigade in France after Patton was wounded.

Perhaps to press the issue of mobility, to confirm the control of cavalry over mobile mechanized forces, and to guarantee the notion that horses and machines would work together, Patton composed a memo entitled

"Notes Regarding Cavalry." It was for Henry, the Chief of Cavalry, to submit to the Chief of Staff, now General MacArthur. In great detail, Patton analyzed the occasions when machines were superior to horses and when the reverse was true. He concluded:

> As a result of derogatory articles, preposterous claims by inventors and loose talk by officers, many junior cavalrymen are greatly exercised over the future of their arm. My purpose in submitting these notes to the Chief of Staff is the hope that he will either approve my ideas or else give me definite instructions as to those changes he may elect. Armed with such a statement I can calm my juniors and shape my course to conform to the wishes of the Chief of Staff.

Henry was apparently dissatisfied with this paper and asked Patton to turn out another. Patton wrote a memo called "Information on Mechanized Forces," which in slightly altered form took a somewhat different approach.

These two papers were put together and revised, then sent to MacArthur. The Chief of Staff returned it at once. What he wanted to know was how much progress had been made on re-armament and re-equipment in the cavalry. He meant mechanization and motorization.

Henry, probably with Patton's help, complied.

By then, the future of cavalry seemed altogether precarious. The War Department proposed to consolidate the cavalry, field artillery, and coast artillery branches. In a staff paper, Patton argued heatedly against the idea. His reasons were less than cogent and somewhat superficial, but actually amalgamation made very little sense and had been prompted by a desperate search for economy.

With the swing accelerating toward mechanization, and perhaps because his tour of duty in the Office of the Chief of Cavalry was coming to an end, Patton decided that machines could no longer be wished away, that the cavalry had best make peace with that fact, and that more armored cars had to become part of the old horse cavalry. Categorically, he wrote: "At the beginning of a war with any first-class power armored fighting vehicles will be met."

For Henry's information, Patton noted the composition of Van Voorhis' Mechanized Force at Fort Eustis. There were a headquarters company, a troop of cavalry armored cars, a company of tanks (infantry), an infantry machine gun company, a self-propelled artillery battery, an engineer company, an ordnance company, and signal, chemical warfare, and quartermaster detachments.

The whole contained 36 officers, 648 men, and 167 vehicles — 20 passenger cars, 11 armored cars, 15 motorcycles, 23 tanks, 7 caterpillar tractors, 33 carrier cart trucks, 2 generator trucks, 4 kitchen trucks, 4 radio trucks, 5 trailers, 3 antiaircraft machine gun trucks, 15 tank carriers, 1 machine shop truck, 1 wrecking truck, 1 caterpillar wire-layer, 11 six-wheel machine gun trucks, 11 Class B trucks, and 31 additional vehicles due to arrive, mostly light quartermaster trucks with four-wheel drive.

It was by any standard a pitifully small force.

Writing to the captain who commanded the armored car troop, Patton wanted to know whether a car could cross a river even if the exhaust was six inches below the water's surface. Could a hose be attached to the exhaust and raised above the water level? If the batteries, generator, and self-starter were first removed, was it possible to tow an armored car — by man, horse, or motor power — across a river when the water covered the engine?

No doubt the captain experimented.

Patton closely followed the activities of the Mechanized Force. He kept a file of newspaper clippings on its work and the comments it prompted. He exchanged notes with others interested in the experimental composite Force. He was quite well aware of the politicking that surrounded its efforts.

Despite the appointment of Van Voorhis as commander, which made the cavalry the dominant arm, the infantry was still trying to gain control of the Force. Despite the dubious effectiveness of the Force, which had yet to be proved, congressmen were increasingly talking about abolishing the cavalry horse regiments.

These were perhaps peripheral matters to the real work required, but Van Voorhis had to deal with them in order to carry out his experiments. Furthermore, he had to be careful not to destroy the horse in the process.

Beyond that, Van Voorhis had to grapple with the problem of developing a doctrine, a methodology of how to plan, as Patton phrased it, "the use of machines for which there is no historical precedent." Doctrine could emerge only after units of precise size and composition were firmly established.

What hampered Van Voorhis, Patton believed, was that his tactical "ideas are extremely nebulous." Van Voorhis, for example, thought of mobility as meaning speed, whereas the correct definition, according to Patton, was fluidity, a more inclusive term derived from the French language.

> Finally I believe that Colonel Van Voorhis attaches too much importance to the technical skill of officers and men serving in mechanized regiments. If war were as difficult as specialists seem to think we would need no League of Nations to prevent fighting.

Patton cautiously conceded in May:

> the advent of the airplane and radio have so facilitated the transmission of information that raids other than local night affairs cannot in the future be effectively executed by horse elements of cavalry.

In the same month, Chaffee, Patton's old friend, left Washington for Fort Eustis to replace Brett and help Van Voorhis cope with the problems of the Mechanized Force. For Chaffee it would be the beginning of a new career. During the next ten years, he would work extremely hard to develop and promote concepts of mechanized warfare. He would sponsor and champion mechanization, motorization, armor, and the use of the combined arms in a hard-hitting striking force. In the process he would become known as the Army's foremost tank expert. He would thus hold the position at the beginning of World War II that was comparable to Patton's place in World War I.

Late in 1931, General MacArthur dissolved the Mechanized Force because of a lack of funds. Harking back, probably unknowingly, perhaps not, to a suggestion made in passing by Patton, MacArthur directed all the arms and services — that is, all the branches within the Army, whether combatant or noncombatant — to adopt mechanization and motorization as far as they could with the limited appropriations, men, and equipment at their disposal.

In compliance, the cavalry in 1932 would adopt the mechanized regiment as its basic experimental unit. Similar in organization to the horse regiment, the new unit would have 35 combat or armored cars. Later, an armored car troop would be added to the cavalry division, along with a tank company, and still later an air observation squadron would be programmed. Retained with these mechanized forces were two horse bri-gades.

Thus, the idea of using horses and machines together, a cherished no-tion of Patton's, came into being.

In 1933, the cavalry would develop and test combat vehicles at Fort Knox, Kentucky, and early that year, the 1st Cavalry Regiment would arrive from Texas and begin to replace its horses with machines. The movement toward the Armored Force had begun. In the course of that development, Chaffee, as the cavalry's expert in mechanization, would figure prominently, Patton would arrive late.

Letter, GSP, Jr., to Colonel Pierre Lorillard, Jr. (Tuxedo Park, New York), May 14, 1931

Dear Pete: All this stuff [in the press] against the horse hurts the General [Guy Henry] beyond words, both because of the discourag-ing effect it has on his officers and also because, while many of the quotations used in the papers are authentic, they are frequently re-moved from their proper contexts with a deceiving effect. As you know, the General has more physical and moral courage than any Chief we ever had. Also, he is the pre-eminent horse-soldier of the Army. On the other hand, he is intensely loyal and, since the state-ments quoted, however perverted, are alledgedly those of his military superiors, his hands are absolutely tied insofar as making rebuttal statements in the press. The same things apply to any of us here in the office. Anything we write or say is of necessity attributed to him. Personally, I think that we will have to grin and bear it until the accumulated effect causes horsemen outside of the Regular Army to write the "powers that be" — namely, the Secretary of War, the Chief of Staff, and General Moseley — explaining to them the vital need for further explanatory statements to the press by way of correcting the idea that the horse is to be immediately supplanted. The in-closed copy of a radiogram sent to all cavalry regiments is clear and self-explanatory. Since it is confidential it should not be quoted but it can guide you in forming any letters you may write or cause to have written. You probably feel that I am passing the buck. Hon-estly, Pete, I am not; and, most emphatically, General Henry is not. We are "muzzled." The only comfort we can get is our belief that you and your friends will again come to the front and help us with the same enthusiasm which you have always shown. This is not "Bull."

Throughout the spring of 1931, Patton enjoyed considerable success and publicity as a horseman. He won first prize in a show in nearby Virginia. Near Baltimore, he scored what the New York *Times* called "a notable triumph" in hunter trials.

That summer, his tour at the Office of the Chief of Cavalry came to an end. Henry judged him "superior" — "A man of outstanding energy. A hard-worker and a great reader of military literature. Very progressive and has an extensive knowledge of various subjects. He will accomplish what he sets out to do."

After a month of vacation in Massachusetts, he would enter the Army War College as a student in the 1931–32 academic course. This was the top Army school. Attendance would terminate his formal military education. Selection to attend the school meant that he was deemed suitable and completion of the course would make him eligible for command at the highest levels.

CHAPTER 44

Army War College and the Bonus March

"If you must fire do a good job — a few casualties become martyrs, a large number an object lesson."

Letter, GSP, Jr. (Washington) to Beatrice, August 31, 1931

Darling Beat: I got here last night at 9:30. I had to leave the boat at Cape May the entrance to the Delaware.

The winds were light and heading all the way so we had to use the motor all the time except one day.

I had a devil of a time persuading Capt S. [Stimpson, paid skipper] to leave N.Y. [to sail] down the Jersey coast. We waited 24 hours while he tried to hire an extra man. At last I said I was going alone if necessary so we started going down the bay. He swore the compas was 20° out and wanted to turn around but I said we would allow for that and we kept on.

I think that he is a fair weather sailor who hates to loose sight of land. When we got to Deleware and he heard it was all in side he was full of fire again.

At Gravesend Bay I met a Bolshiviki sailor working on a fishing scooner. My costume led him to believe I was a sailor too so he told me how wicked it was to own a yacht and be a capatalist when he was only getting seven dollars a day rigging a boat. I told him it was wrong all right but that the wrong part lay in his getting 7.50 for a job worth 1.50 and that I was a capatalist and that if his theory was correct we ought to fight it [out] at once and see who was best and that I was redy to start. He then got very friendly and offered to work for me at 8.00 dollars a day.

I liked the boat very much. She keeps you busy and is very good in a sea and a blow. Though we had only moderate ones. Capt S. with a toothless wonder I hired to help him up the [Potomac] river will arrive on Wednesday.

I have hay fever.

I love you. George.

Soon after Patton entered the Army War College, he began to maneuver to get the post of Commandant of Cadets at West Point upon the completion of his course of study. General Harbord wrote to Major General William D. Connor, Army War College commandant, who was rumored to be the next Superintendent of the Military Academy:

> I consider him [Patton] the outstanding man among his contemporaries that I include in my acquaintance. He has always been an outstanding soldier and has had such a broad experience for a man of his age that I am sure his fitness for the duty has probably already occurred to you. He has a very charming wife, and it is no drawback to the family that they have means enough to keep up their end, as the saying goes.

General Drum, who now commanded the Fifth Corps Area, spoke with Connor about Patton's desire and extracted the promise that if Connor could make the selection, he would put Patton's name second on his list. If Connor's first choice was unable to accept, Patton would have the appointment. "Will you please keep this confidential?" Drum asked Patton.

This effort too was in vain. Patton would fail to get the assignment.

General Henry confided to Patton that he feared he had reached the end of the line as Chief of Cavalry and would receive no further promotion. Patton sent a confidential letter in behalf of Henry to Malin Craig, who had been Chief of Cavalry and who now commanded the Ninth Corps Area. Could Craig, Patton asked, offer any advice that Patton could pass on to Henry?

Craig acknowledged "your very thoughtful, generous note concerning General Henry." He understood Henry's concern, and he suggested that Henry go directly to MacArthur and tell him frankly that he hoped his current tour would not interfere with his selection for promotion, which had always been his ambition.

> I did the same thing with the Chief of Staff the very day I reported in Washington to take over the duties of Chief of Cavalry, and while the Chief of Staff seemed a bit startled he, nevertheless, recommended my promotion at the time he thought I was entitled to it . . .

I wish to repeat that MacArthur is absolutely straight-forward and fair and, to the best of my knowledge, he will never play a favorite at the expense of his fairness while he is Chief of Staff.

Henry, it turned out, would receive no further promotion.

Aunt Nannie Wilson, who was a dear old lady and rather pathetic in her later years, addicted somewhat to sherry, died on November 26, 1931. Patton traveled to California for the funeral, staying while he was there with his sister Nita.

When he telephoned his daughter Ruth Ellen to inform her of Aunt Nannie's death, he said, "I never knew, until I saw her in the majesty of death, what a noble face she had."

During his visit to the family home, Lake Vineyard in San Marino, Patton wrote a letter to his mother, deceased for three years, and put it in her trinket box.

Letter, GSP, Jr., to his mother, November 30, 1931

Darling Mama. Here with your things before me you are very near. I never showed you in life the love I really felt nor my admiration for your courage and sporting acceptance of illness and losses. Children are cruel things. Forgive me. I had always prayed to show my love by doing something famous for you, to justify what you called me when I got back from France, "My hero son." Perhaps I still may, but time grows short. I am 46. In a few moments we will bury the ashes of Aunt Nannie. All the three who I loved and who loved me so much are now gone.

But you know that I still love you and in the presence of your soul I feel very new and very young and helpless even as I must have been 46 years ago.

Nothing you ever did to me was anything but loving. I have no other memories of you but love and devotion. It is so sad that we must grow old and seperate.

When we meet again I hope you will be lenient for my frailties. In most things I have been worthy.

Perhaps this is foolish but I think you understand.

I loved and love you very much.

Your devoted son G. S. Patton Jr.

Patton worked hard at the Army War College. At the end of February 1932, he passed in a 56-page study entitled "The Probable Characteristics of the Next War and the Organization, Tactics, and Equipment Necessary to Meet Them." It was an ambitious work that drew together his cherished beliefs.

As was his practice, Patton started by drawing on history. Armies, he said, had oscillated between those based on quantity and those based on quality. Mass armies were composed of hastily raised and incompletely trained individuals who looked upon war as a secondary occupation. Since the World War, it appeared that smaller, more mobile, better trained armies would fight short, decisive wars. The current interest in mechanization reflected this feeling.

Size and strength, he said, were not synonymous. Small professional armies were thoroughly trained, gave their members long association together that enhanced solidarity and mutual confidence in the ranks, were suited for mobility and maneuver, were ready immediately in time of emergency, and had a better chance of achieving quick and decisive victory. They would be used in the next war, he predicted, because equipment was becoming more complex and costly. Equipping masses of men with the latest weapons was financially impossible, but smaller armies could be kept up to date.

According to some military thinkers, it was useless to study warfare before 1870, for the lessons before that date were no longer relevant and practical. To Patton, history moved in cycles; therefore, styles in warfare recurred. Without perspective a painting was valueless; and so it was with things military. Ancient tactics were hardly to be copied, but professionals had to be familiar with them and with the reasons for their adoption. For the basic nature of man had changed but little during the course of recorded history.

Starting with 2500 B.C., Patton classified wars after the types of armies involved, that is, mass or professional. He ran through the Egyptians, Syrians, Greeks, Macedonians, Romans, Africans, Goths, Byzantines, Franks, Vikings, Mongols, Swiss, Turks, British, French, Spanish, Dutch, Germans, and Americans — ending with the Boer War. From these historical examples, he extracted certain lessons. For example, professionals fought better in protracted operations, in campaigns where supply was difficult, and in wars where discipline was more important than emotional inspiration.

He had asked many officers, including students and instructors at the War College, why mass armies were desirable. No one could say.

So far as he could tell, the advantages of large conscript armies were: 1) the sense of power and security raised in the popular mind by an armed force numbering in the millions; 2) the opportunity to arouse popular enthusiasm and support by placing the burden of war on all alike; 3) the benefit of producing a homogeneity of national character among recruits; 4) the safeguard afforded political leaders, who could say, if things went wrong, that everything possible had been done to insure success; 5) the widespread conviction that a national army was the cheapest form of national security; 6) the fact that a large army could fight on several fronts simultaneously; and 7) the belief that big battalions were the same as strong battalions.

On the other hand, small, highly trained, lightly equipped, professional armies were more easily supplied, less tied to the roadnet, and better disciplined. They had the ability to disperse on the battlefield, a requirement now forced on ground troops by the airplane; the capacity to maneuver in order to gain surprise and, as a consequence, decisive victory; the capability to function in dire cases of stress, when habitual or automatic responses to emergencies were necessary. They could, in short, better cope with all the conditions of war, for "Battle is an orgy of organized disorder."

Small, mobile, largely self-contained units were therefore indicated for the next war. They were better too because they offered military leaders the opportunity to exercise great initiative. Commanders could operate on the assumption that "a simple mediocre solution instantly applied is better than a perfect one which is late or complicated."

Frequent conferences between an overall commander and his subordinate commanders were necessary in order to indoctrinate all concerned in the methods selected to meet a few general situations. Battles were fought mainly by junior officers who carried on without specific orders. The overall leader, Patton believed, could personally influence only one or two units. He therefore had to depend on subordinates who exercised command by their personal efforts — through the influence of example. Inspiration for them and for the troops came not from coded messages but from the visible personality of the overall commander.

For the history of war was a history of warriors, few in number, mighty in personality. In small professional armies, leaders would often be killed, but the death of high-ranking officers whose primary aim was to win, not simply to survive, had great inspirational effect on men.

In sum, small professional armies would restore mobility to the battle-field in the next war, which, as a consequence, would be shorter and more decisive than the World War.

The sincerity of purpose and the hard work that went into this paper were obvious, and in April the commandant of the War College informed Patton:

> An examination of your individual staff memo recently submitted indicates that it is of sufficient merit to warrant consideration by the War Department. Accordingly the memo, by direction of the Chief of Staff, has been forwarded to the War Department for such use as the Department may see fit to make of it. You are hereby commended for work of exceptional merit.

This was high honor indeed.

Patton was also chairman of a student committee, which, as part of the regular course work, presented a report on mechanized units. The Patton touch was everywhere in evidence. For example: "The Austro-Prussia War of 1866 furnishes the only instance, in wars between two civilized opponents where weapons played the decisive role."

The task of the committee was to study and assess the current interest in mechanization and to make several direct and practical recommendations to the General Staff on the subject.

Since "mechanical warfare," "mechanization," and "motorization" were terms often used interchangeably, the committee first defined them. A mechanized force "not only . . . [is] transported in motor vehicles, but also fights from some or all of its vehicles . . . having armament [weapons] and protective armor." A motorized force, in contrast, was transported, in whole or in part, in vehicles to the scene of action; the troops dismounted from their vehicles to fight.

In the following year, the War Department would accept these definitions and make them official.

The tank in the World War and mechanized forces in the postwar period, the committee said, were attempts to restore maneuver to combat in order to shorten wars and lessen attrition.

Armored fighting vehicles were special, costly machines with no commercial use. Of them, the tank was "peerless" for shock action. In order to stimulate as much experimentation as possible, the committee believed that each arm should develop its own mechanized units according to its own missions and expected capabilities.

This was what Patton had earlier recommended and what MacArthur had directed the Army to do.

The committee's conclusions, which were very much like Patton's convictions, were: a large and independent mechanized force had no role in current warfare; mechanized units assisting infantry and cavalry had vital roles; mechanized units could not replace existing arms; mechanized units should be developed by the existing arms.

The committee's single recommendation was that the mechanized units developed by each arm should be used in combined maneuvers to determine their tactical and strategic capabilities and characteristics.

Rating Patton's performance as a student, the War College commandant judged him "superior." He was, Connor wrote,

> An aggressive and capable officer of strong convictions. An untiring student. Proficiency in theoretical training for High Command: Superior, for War Department General Staff: Superior. Special aptitude for any particular class of duty: Command. Qualified for duty with any civilian component. Academic rating: Superior.

He was, in short, a first-rate, all-around officer capable of exercising high command and competent to discharge the responsibilities of an important staff position.

In his official personal file was noted "Work of Exceptional Merit."

Now Patton had completed his formal military education. If there was to be a next war, he would be assured of a high and important place in it. Unless, of course, he failed somehow to measure up to the high standards he had set for himself or failed somehow to meet the high expectations of his superiors.

On July 8, 1932, Patton reported for duty to Fort Myer, Virginia, as executive officer, second in command, of the 3d Cavalry Regiment. Less than three weeks later, he was a central figure in the Bonus March incident.

With the country in the depths of the Great Depression and economic distress rampant, several thousand members — somewhere around 20,000

— of the Bonus Expeditionary Force, an informal organization, arrived in Washington. Unemployed and poverty-stricken veterans, they came to the capital to influence Congress into voting each former serviceman a cash payment, a bonus, computed according to length of war service. The money had been voted, but only for disbursement in 1945. The Bonus Marchers wanted it at once.

The influx of veterans, who camped in a "Hooverville" of shacks and tents on the Anacostia Flats, who occupied abandoned and partially dismantled buildings in the heart of downtown Washington, and who lived in other parts of the town and on the outskirts, seemed to threaten the peace. It was not so much that they were disorderly or unruly; it was rather that they were present, a large and restless group of surly men who might turn into rioting mobs. President Hoover, Secretary of War Patrick J. Hurley, and Chief of Staff Douglas MacArthur regarded them as subversives and potential revolutionaries.

When Congress adjourned without voting the bonus, many marchers departed Washington, probably more than half, and the attitude of the government, War Department, and city officials hardened toward the veterans who remained. On July 28, there was a scuffle between police and some marchers who were camping in and refused to leave government buildings being demolished for a park downtown. A panicky policeman fired his revolver and killed a man. This triggered a call for troops to help the police restore order.

According to an account written by Patton, he said, to "commemorate" the successful "quelling of the domestic disturbance," the operation, from a military point of view, was a complete victory.

> Owing to a total misconception of mob psychology General Glassford, then Chief of the Metropolitan Police Department, temporized with the Marchers. As time went on they violated more and more laws and regulations, and finally marched on the Capitol and the White House . . . In my opinion, the majority were poor, ignorant men, without hope and without really evil intent, but there were several thousand bad men among them and many weak sisters joined them.

Like Hoover, Hurley, and MacArthur, Patton believed that Communist agents had infiltrated the ranks of the Bonus Marchers and were inciting them to revolution.

For some weeks . . . the troops here [at Fort Myer] were held in the Post in readiness to move. The horses had been practised in moving against mobs, and the men were equipped with gas masks and a few gas grenades.

Therefore, the men were ready for action on July 28 when the 3d Cavalry commanding officer, Colonel Cootes, received a telephone call at 1:45 P.M. from the 16th Infantry Brigade commander, General Perry L. Miles. Miles asked that all available cavalry troops on the post be sent to the Ellipse, just west of the White House. Accompanied by Patton, the troops crossed the Memorial Bridge into Washington and reached the Ellipse 55 minutes later.

. . . we moved in column of fours without security detachments; the tanks in trucks followed by themselves at [a distance of] about one mile. No outpost was established. We dismounted at the Ellipse.

While the cavalry — a total of 14 officers, 217 enlisted men, and 213 horses — waited for infantrymen to arrive from Fort Washington, about twelve miles below the city on the Maryland side of the Potomac, Patton rode off alone. Stiffly and unsmiling, he trotted down Pennsylvania Avenue to 3rd Street, where several thousand veterans were congregated. They greeted him with mixed cheers and jeers.

Having made a reconnaissance of the terrain and an estimate of the situation, Patton returned to the Ellipse.

. . . the battalion of 12th Infantry from Fort Washington arrived in trucks, having passed right through the Bonus Camps. After a pause of another hour the troops were ordered to march up Pennsylvania Avenue and clear it as far as 3d Street. So far as I know this was the only order issued for the first operation.

The clearing action started at 4:05 P.M. Cavalrymen wore steel helmets, carried gas masks and carbines at the sling, and held drawn sabers. Infantrymen wore gas masks and carried rifles with bayonets.

The cavalry moved first in column of troops with the tanks in trucks between the last two troops [companies]. The infantry followed in colum of fours. The avenue was a sea of people. It took us half an hour to clear them out, and we . . . had to use force. As we passed the occupied buildings [where the scuffle had taken place] the Marchers cheered us and called, "Here come our buddies." The civilians in the crowd hissed us in a mild way.

After a halt of half an hour at 3d Street the infantry put on their gas masks and, advancing in assault formation in two waves, using gas grenades, began clearing the buildings . . . Soon the gas got to work, and they all ran and formed along the second street south of the Avenue. Major Surles [who commanded the 2d Squadron] then moved his cavalry to push them on. We were doing very well when the infantry halted to reform, and the mob, angry by now . . . were very nasty and brandished clubs, iron bars and bricks, and cursed us in a most wholehearted manner. The soldiers were magnificent. They set grimly on their horses and made no reply except to poke an occasional Marcher who tried to grab a horse by the head. Things kept looking worse as the infantry was still not up and our flank was turned. Suddenly, without a word of command, the whole line surged forward. Bricks flew, sabers rose and fell with a comforting smack, and the mob ran. We moved on after them, occasionally meeting serious resistance. Once six men in a truck threw a regular barrage of bricks, and several men and horses were hit. Two of us charged at a gallop, and had some nice work at close range with the occupants of the truck, most of whom could not sit down for some days [afterwards].

The cavalry, moving via the streets, and the infantry, through the shacks, pushed the crowd to the railroad where all resistance ended.

It was then decided to capture the camp [across the Anacostia River] at night. The men were fed, and General MacArthur came up and gave explicit orders for the operation.

When we crossed the bridge at the Navy Yard the infantry was in front and had to use grenades to force the spectator crowd out of the way.

The cavalry formed at the north end of the [Bonus Marchers'] camp with its right flank on the river, while the infantry moving south along the edge of the water turned by the left flank and started to clear the camp. At this moment we were ordered to halt as the Marchers said that if they were given an hour they would withdraw. During this hour many left but some set fire to their tents.

When the time was up the infantry moved forward in a long line of skirmishers, using grenades from time to time. If, during this operation, a single shot had been fired many would have died, for in the dark on a flat plane [plain] fire discipline could not have been maintained, and there was no cover.

It speaks volumes for the high character of the men that not a shot was fired. In justice to the Marchers it should be pointed out that had they really wanted to start something they had a great chance here but refrained.

On the following morning, groups of veterans began to leave the city. Troopers from Fort Myer routed out a large encampment at Oakcrest, Virginia, and these Bonus Marchers crossed Key Bridge into the city and walked up Wisconsin Avenue and out of Washington.

It so happened that Joe Angelo was in Washington, and the newspapers played up the Angelo-Patton relationship. One headline read: "Major Ousts Vet Who Saved Life; Bonus Seeker Flees before Officer He Rescued on Battlefield."

From this moment on — if not already as early as the occasion when Angelo had appeared before a congressional committee two years before — Patton became hostile to his wartime orderly.

If any letters came to Patton expressing objection to his role in the action against the Bonus Marchers, he saved none. But he kept a letter from Al C. Stiller.

Writing on stationery headed Stiller & Strickland Tire Company, El Paso, Texas, Stiller said that he had been the initial First Sergeant in charge of the Casual Company (soldiers awaiting assignment) at the tank center in France and later First Sergeant of two other companies. He had been wounded at Varennes, where his tank was destroyed. He had thought often of Patton since the war, would be mighty glad to see him again, and hoped that Patton had fully recovered from his wounds. He added that he would have liked to have been with Patton to throw the veterans out of Washington because they were "rif raf" and not the kind of men who had done the job over there in France.

Ten years later, Al Stiller would be Patton's aide-de-camp. He would serve with Patton throughout World War II.

Sometime after the election of November 1932, probably immediately thereafter, Patton wrote a paper on "Federal Troops in Domestic Disturbances." It was designed as two lectures to officers, one on the history

and training of this type of duty, the other on the tactical aspects of operations of this sort. It was, in many respects, a savage document.

From the Whisky Rebellion, he wrote, until the Bonus March, federal
troops had been called out more than one hundred times

> to participate in that most distasteful form of service . . . We of the
> Army should take pride in the fact that not once in all these cases
> have our predecessors either failed or been guilty of unnecessary vio-
> lence. It must be our aim to maintain this proud tradition whenever
> it shall be our unfortunate duty to be called on for such onerous
> service.

When the Army was effective, Patton continued, liberty flourished.
When soldiers failed in their duty, insurrection and national chaos ensued.

> When, under Marius, Rome's first Regulars blotted out in blood the
> mobs roused by those generous and misguided brothers, the Grac-
> chae, she prospered, and, from a debating society, became the mis-
> tress of the world, and so remained until at last the venal and dis-
> loyal Praetorian Guard sold the purple to the highest bidder and
> thereby destroyed the power no foe could conquer. When the foolish
> and genial Louis XVI lost his head and the Seine ran crimson to the
> sea, the fault lay not with the people but with the soldiers . . . the
> success of the Bolsheviki in 1917 was due wholly to the hesitating and
> weak character of the Russian officers. While in Germany, on the
> other hand, a loyal and well led Army destroyed the course of Com-
> munism ere it could raise its ugly head above the ruins of a war
> weary nation . . . [Soldiers] have never yet bitten the hand which
> starved them, or failed in any way to support constituted authority.
> Even in the Civil War when more than twenty percent of the officers
> went south not a single enlisted man deserted the flag . . .
>
> The military is used [in domestic disturbances], not to *displace*
> existing laws, but to *sustain* them when by reason of obstructions
> their effectual administration by normal legal methods becomes im-
> possible . . .
>
> TRAINING REGULATIONS: Strange as it seems this loquacious
> document is very reticent on Domestic Disturbances. All it has to say
> is found in TR 10-5, paragraph 9 — "Troops of the combat
> branches, in addition to their training for war, will be trained in the

tactics for the suppression of domestic disturbances, the guiding method to be employed being a demonstration of force, followed, if necessary, by its application in a speedy and decisive manner."

HABEAS CORPUS: This is the next item that arises to plague us . . . If you have captured a dangerous agitator and some misguided judge issues a write of Habeas Corpus for him . . . there is always danger that the man might attempt to escape. If he does see that he at least falls out of ranks before you shoot [him]. To be soft hearted might mean death to your men. War is war after all . . .

Throughout history, good soldiers have quelled riots and often, as a result, have achieved promotion and fame. Bad soldiers have failed, and as a result their countries have perished . . . As juniors we simply obey the orders of our superiors. As independent commanders, there is a very remote possibility that we may have to back our judgement with our commissions. Officers in command of troops on riot duty should remember the following points:

Civil officials and National Guard and Reserve officers could give Regular troops proper and legitimate orders only if they had been mustered into the federal service. Regular officers were to cooperate with police and state troops, but the Regulars, not the police or state troops, were to judge the amount and character of the cooperation to be rendered. They were to insist on having all orders in writing.

Before firing at a mob warn them of your intention, and tell innocent people to "beat it" . . . Designate in advance certain sharpshooters to kill individual rioters who fire on or throw missiles at your men. Have even this firing done only on your order, or that of a commissioned officer . . . Should some orator start haranguing the crowd and inciting them to violence grab him even if it brings on a local fight. Small fights are better than big ones. Words cunningly chosen change crowds into mobs . . .

Do not enrage reporters . . . They dislike tear gas and are not provided with masks. Finally, do your full duty as you see it, and damn the consequences.

Crowds could usually be dispersed by strong patrols and kept from reforming. But if a crowd suddenly became violent and destroyed a patrol, it had to be punished instantly. Otherwise, it would develop a false sense of power and become dangerous.

. . . try to arrange your axis of approach so as to drive the mob
into the poor quarter [of the city] and away from vital areas . . .
Gas is paramount . . . While tear gas is effective, it should be
backed up with vomiting gas.

If gas failed to move a mob,

open fire with one man per squad from a frontal attack while, at the
same time, have men previously stationed in nearby buildings shoot
into the rear ranks selecting apparent leaders. Always fire for effect
[that is, to kill] . . . If you must fire do a good job — a few casualties become martyrs, a large number an object lesson . . .

When a mob starts to move keep it on the run, but always leave it
a line of retreat — a cornered rat will fight desperately, while on the
other hand movement to the rear engenders panic . . . use the
bayonet to encourage its retreat. If they are running a few good
wounds in the buttocks will encourage them. If they resist they must
be killed.

When guarding buildings, troops should mark a line and announce
clearly that those who crossed would be killed. "Be sure to kill the first
one who tries, and leave him there to discourage the others."

If intelligence indicated that mob leaders were gathering for a meeting,
"A night raid . . . will be most useful — no prisoners should be taken."

FINALLY: Never take a drink at any time, or allow your men to
do so. Close all drinking establishments. This is illegal but necessary
. . . An armed mob resisting federal troops is an armed enemy. To
aid it is treason. This may not be law, but it is fact. When blood
starts running law stops, because, by the fact of bloodshed, it has
demonstrated its futility.

His ultimate judgment on the action against the Bonus Marchers:

In spite of faulty methods the high training and discipline of the
soldiers and officers secured a complete and bloodless (mostly) triumph, which, by its success, prevented a war and insured the election
of a Democrat [Franklin D. Roosevelt].

CHAPTER 45

Fort Myer, Hawaii, Massachusetts

"I think that a little blood and gutts would be good for cadets."

PATTON spent nearly three years at Fort Myer, and they were filled with social and sporting events and activities. He played polo, sailed in the Chesapeake Bay, participated in horse shows in Washington, West Point, Tuxedo Park, and elsewhere, hunted in the lovely countryside of nearby Maryland and Virginia — Mrs. Curtis Dall, President Roosevelt's daughter, presenting him on one occasion with the first place ribbon for winning the Hunter Trials at Bradley Farms, Maryland. Beatrice was prominent as a sailor, and, with her daughters acting as crew, raced in the Women's National Sailing Championship competition at Cohasset, Massachusetts.

For the Pattons, the highlight of those years was the Cobbler Hunt, an organization he and Beatrice formed of civilians and military people who rode to the hounds, usually twice a week. The course was on the adjoining estates of friends who lived near Delaplane, Virginia.

Patton kept a diary for the 1932–33 season and recorded the first hunt, taking place on September 26, when the Pattons and two others gathered at 7 A.M. "This was the first time I acted as M.F.H. since 1912 at Fort Riley."

October 1: "The jumps were very hairy and pace fast."

October 19: "The best run so far and one of the best I have ever had."

The cub hunting having ended, the regular season opened with 41 riders present, and many more spectators in motor cars, coming for breakfast. According to a newspaper account, the Pattons were "clad in scarlet coats and derbys"; a photograph in the New York *Times* showed them dressed alike in formal hunting attire.

Patton attended a dinner in New York for Masters of the Fox Hunt. At the end of March, the season closed with the Cobbler Hunter Trials, various races and competitions arranged and directed by Patton.

The Cobbler Hunt had another successful season in 1933–34. A message posted at Fort Myer by Patton invited all officers and their ladies to hunt with the Pattons. "Any horse able to jump three and one-half feet is capable of hunting in Virginia."

Letter, Colonel C. L. Scott to GSP, Jr., no date ("after Cherry Blossom Festival Show, 1934")

Dear Georgie. Want to thank you and your whole family for your entries and support in the Hunter Trials last Saturday . . . the winning of the class or the loosing of the class was a small matter compared to the sportsmanlike way in which the Patton family accepted the judges decision — after all the kicking and crabbing one generally sees and hears in events of this nature it is a pleasure and an encouragement to occasionally see some real sportsmanship show up.

Young Beatrice was married to Lieutenant John Knight Waters on June 27, 1934, at St. John's Church in Beverly Farms, Massachusetts, and a reception took place immediately afterward at Green Meadows, South Hamilton.

Letter, GSP, Jr., to Beatrice, July 7, 1934

From my view point as "wedding guest" I want to say again what a realy great organizer I think you are. No show could have gone better and it was a very large show too. Also no mother of a bride ever looked better or cried less.

The Cobbler Hunt had a third season. According to Patton's diary, there were seven runs during the cubbing and 39 during the regular season, ranging in duration from 15 minutes to an hour and a half. The twelve horses belonging to the Pattons were all scrupulously noted on a work sheet so that each was exercised regularly.

The opening of the season had 50 guests gathered on a spacious lawn against a background of the Cobbler Mountains. After the hunt, about 2500 persons assembled for a giant barbecue. Later, a tournament featured charging knights, about 30 horsemen driving forward to place a lance through a ring. Among those present were General Leon B. Kromer, the Chief of Cavalry, Colonel Kenyon Joyce, commanding Fort

Myer, General Hugh Drum, Deputy Chief of Staff, and General Billy Mitchell.

On November 27, Patton recorded that the weather was rainy with a heavy fog on that scheduled hunt day. He waited until 10 A.M. for the field to show, but no one came, so he went out with two attendants. "Coming back I tried to shut a gate on Hukupu [his horse] and he got mad and rearing fell on a woven wire fence with me under him. He got all four feet caught but kicked him self clear and ran away till he hit a second fence when I caught him. Neither of us was hurt."

The Pattons resigned as masters at the end of the season. "Beatrice and I both feel that the cost of hunting for the last three years as Masters has been more than offset by the pleasure abtained which no inflation or confiscation can ever take away from us."

Letter, Walter Huston (a leading actor on Broadway, writing from the Waldorf-Astoria Hotel, New York) to Beatrice, February 1, 1935

Dear Mrs Patton. We will be very happy to join you after the show Thursday Feb. 7th. We Both send our Regards to you and your family and will be glad to see you again. Sincerely,

. . .

GSP, Jr., Speech to the American Legion, Alexandria, Virginia, November 11, 1932

To most of us November 11 is a day full of mixed emotions.

Joy when we think of it as commemorating the victorious termination of the World War.

Sorry when we remember all the young lives extinguished to achieve the victory . . .

Certainly no one who was privileged to see, as I did, the solumn grandure of todays ceremonies at Arlington could help being deeply moved. Though possibly in my case the remembrance of the fact that I very nearly caused my dear mother to wear a gold star may have enhanced my appreciation . . .

Until we have more, much more tangible proof of a change of mental attitude disarmament is folly. Perpetual peace a futile dream.

Yet . . . groups of internationally minded pacifists are constantly working to change Armistice day into Disarmament day.

A limited number of these deluded [persons] . . . unsatisfied with making us physically helpless . . . are seeking to render us morally unworthy . . . They hold to scorn the deeds of our fighting ancestors, of our dead comrades. They make a mock of courage, a joke of patriotism. This too we must combat or else contend with China for the prize as leading jellyfish of the world.

Do not misunderstand me for in spite of the fact that I am what is sometimes referred to as a brutal and licentious mercinary I am not hunting trouble or advising others to do so. I do however regard with horror a state of affairs which would make our country both unready and unwilling to defend its honor . . .

Most of us think of [the next war] in terms of France, of conflicts between huge immobile masses of men engaged in a butting match and abundantly supplied with every sort of contrivance from Gas, Tanks and Airplanes to cigarettes, chocolates and Red Cross girls . . .

There will be much more walking than fighting [in the next war] and armies will be numbered by thousands rather than by millions. Similarly . . . we will have less shells, less gas, less chocolates and less Girls. It will be a most unpleasant war. An investigation of the Bolsheviki-Polish war of 1920 or of the operations in China last year proves this contention. Man as an individual not munitions decided those conflicts.

Also it is well to disabuse our minds of the fanciful picture of wholesale destruction conjured up by certain writers and attributed to such inventions as Gas, Tanks, and Airplanes . . . It is man not his machines that conquers.

Most men and all armies are goosey, they fear an attack from the rear. Since the continuous fronts in France prevented rear attacks stalemate resulted.

Many eminent soldiers realizing this fact are now seeking not bigger but more mobile armies. The very evident dread with which France with her large conscript army views Germany with her small professional one is cumulative evidence on this point.

Hence since we are not particularly likely to again fight in Europe and since if we do we are apt to meet small highly trained forces it seems reasonable to turn our minds to the need of such a force ourselves . . .

Personally I believe that our form of preparation lags in the maintenance of the adequate and immediately available regular army and navy with which to get to the fire [war] quickly and hold it in check until our national man power in smaller numbers and with better training becomes available.

. . . there are countless other solutions equally good. The point is to adopt one of them and then see that it is carried out . . .

When our time comes to sleep in Arlington we can lie down with quiet minds content in the knowledge that as soldiers and citizens we have done our full duty.

A long letter, with illegible signature, reached Patton in January 1933, and bemoaned current military trends, asking how in the world the dedicated horsemen in the Army could stop mechanization. The field artillery was ready to become motorized. The National Guard was motorizing its field artillery units. "We [in the cavalry] may soon be the only mounted arm." Congressmen were talking of having lots of machines — planes, tanks, armored cars — in storage and a small army of highly trained, technical personnel ready to wheel them out when needed. What they failed to realize, these advocates of mechanization, was that machines, not horses, became obsolete. But the lobbyists, especially General Motors, were exerting pressures, and "these are critical hours for our cavalry."

GSP, Jr., Lecture, "Mechanized Forces," delivered at Fort Myer, Fort Humphreys, and Washington, D.C., January, March, and August 1933

Many soldiers are led to faulty ideas of war by knowing too much about too little.

A picture without a background is both uninteresting and misleading. Hence in order to paint for you an intelligent picture of Mechanization as it exists today we must provide an historical background . . .

. . . the want of perspective . . . still induces most of us to visualize future battles as simple repi[ti]tions of the butting matches of the World War while soldiers who talk of forces smaller than groups of armies are considered pikers . . .

New weapons are useful in that they add to the repertoir of killing but be that tank or tomahawk weapons are only weapons after all. Wars may be fought with weapons but they are won by men. It is the spirit of the men who follow and of the man who leads that gains the victory.

Cootes rated Patton "excellent" and capable of being a colonel in peacetime and a brigadier general in war. "Possesses force, fine military bearing, excellent horseman, superior as instructor in tactical work. Fine leadership. Excellent in every way, very loyal and outstanding officer."

Letter, William Floyd, Arlington, Virginia, to GSP, Jr., December 13, 1933

[Sincere thanks] for every consideration shown my son in his severe moment of distress. When you came into the room where Captain Hickey, myself, and the boy were the night of the tragedy I thought you might be a stern, severe officer extending little sympathy, but when you called me out and had a little talk with me I appreciated what a real flow of sympathy there was in your heart and, Major, you will possibly never know what your words meant to me at that time.

On March 1, 1934, having been a major almost fourteen years, Patton was promoted to lieutenant colonel.

GSP, Jr., Lecture, "Mechanization," April 11, 1934

Let us not become so bemused with technical and administrative details that we forget this fact. In the last analysis the successful soldier is the courageous fighting man — the killer.

GSP, Jr., Lecture, "The Probable Characteristics of the Next War," 1934

The object of maneuver is to get . . . behind [the enemy] . . .

Men not machines win battles. Let us strive to be men and worthy leaders of the other men who follow us.

Patton spent almost the entire month of May 1934 at the Cavalry School, Fort Riley, Kansas, observing a series of maneuvers by mechanized cavalry units belonging to the 1st Cavalry Regiment (Mechanized). "Just to be around with a bunch or rather selected lot of officers who talk and think nothing but of war," he wrote to Beatrice, was exciting. He was going out on the first exercise that evening, an all-night affair, "and [it] promises to be very wet as it is raining hard now and is quite cold."

He spent a weekend at Fort Leavenworth, where he visited a horse show, watched a horse race, and saw a lot of old friends. He learned that he might be sent there the following year as a chief of section. Gen [Guy] Henry thinks I should go if asked for. I hate the idea but it might be worse I suppose . . . Most every one on the post was "oiled." I was not. We leave at 8:00 o'clock A.M. for a three days manuver. As it is raining hard I think we will have quite a time . . . I smashed my little finger in the lock of the car but it is not serious.

Colonel Kenyon A. Joyce, who had replaced Cootes as commander of the 3d Cavalry and of Fort Myer, rated Patton "superior." Patton was "an officer of outstanding physical and mental energy who is intensely interested in his profession. I believe this officer should be counted upon for great feats of leadership in war."

As Patton's tour of duty drew to a close, Joyce rated him once more. Again he scored Patton "superior." He changed his description but slightly, saying, "an officer of broad attainments who has extraordinary mental and physical energy. In my opinion he is absolutely fearless and could be counted upon for great feats of leadership in war."

Patton was then fifty years old. His weight varied between 170 and 180 pounds. He wore a partial denture. His hairline was receding. His vision was myopic.

When Patton learned he was to be assigned to Hawaii again, he purchased a 52-foot schooner, the *Arcturus,* and had it moved from New England to the west coast by steamer. With Beatrice, Mr. and Mrs. Gordon Prince of Boston, and Joe Ekeland as crew members and himself as navigator, he sailed from California in May 1935 and reached Honolulu a month later.

The Pattons discovered that Hawaii was as pleasant as they remembered it. They found many old civilian and military friends. It did not take them long to settle down.

Patton was detailed to the General Staff Corps and assigned G–2 or intelligence officer of the Hawaiian Department at Fort Shafter.

He arrived in Hawaii in time to observe the June maneuvers. Since the commanding general asked all staff officers to report their personal reactions, Patton was quick to oblige. His observations, all critical, ran to five single-spaced typed pages.

He criticized the lack of mental flexibility among commanders. They showed "rigid adherence to methods of procedure current in the World

War and applicable, if at all, only to situations involving very large bodies of troops in semi-stabilized operations." For example, while the division was launching a counterattack of five battalions of infantry, the staff remained in the headquarters 4½ miles from the scene of the combat, made no effort to conduct ground reconnaissance, and established no forward command post.

He pointed out the absence of imagination in the exercise. The troops demonstrated "utter disregard for the probable effect of enemy fire." For example, "From 4:00 P.M. on, Kolekole pass and the road leading to it was jammed with transportation. It is certain that any enemy capable of forcing a landing would have the means and intelligence to interdict the pass . . . artillery units adjacent to the road were making meticulous efforts to camouflage their battery positions, which . . . they had moved into in broad daylight with columns well closed up." Infantry and artillery counterattacking forces camped in close formation and made no attempt to conceal their bivouacs. "Camps were brightly illuminated and their fires unscreened." The units posted no gas sentries and employed no security detachments.

He cited the misuse of motor transportation. All units used vehicles greatly in excess of the number required, and many carried equipment inappropriate to war, for example, iceboxes, field safes, and the like.

He deplored the pervading philosophy of "comfort first." "Sumptuous eating, sleeping and clerical conveniences everywhere" included folding cots, bedding rolls "of monumental proportions," blackboards, mess tables, chairs, and typewriters, all of which "took transportation — needless transportation."

He was pained by the appearance of "Undigested Education." "Many officers have acquired information that they are either unwilling or mentally incapable of using. The result is that they try to remember rather than to think." The brigade field order was far too long, drawn without the benefit of reconnaissance, and issued too late. "The operation was conducted as a map problem because our officers are familiar with them, not as a war problem because our officers are not familiar with maneuvers."

He remarked the excessive use of signal wire. "The craze for wire is largely due to the inordinate demands made by higher units for reports from the front . . . If higher commanders would go up and look they would do some good, at least they would inspire the men . . . the place of the brigade commander is with his men, not with his telephones."

He made some pungent comments on the effect of motorization on war. "To utilize the full power of strategic mobility inherent in trucks, columns must move under fire or else we must readjust our estimates as to their speed of employment." As for tactical mobility, "the normal human tendency to avoid perspiration is very apt to induce the utilization of machines in tactical stituations where their use would be suicidal."

He concluded: "The army exists to kill men — not to groom vehicles."

GSP, Jr., Speech to the American Legion Convention, August 7, 1935
The chief trouble with the thousands of honest peace advocates is that, due to lamentable ignorance of history, they confuse the apparent with the actual causes of wars . . . the causes leading to wars are as obscure and far more malign than are the germs which result in cancer or tuberculosis. The pimple or the cough to which the uniformed attribute their ailment is but the last and superficial evidence of the long continued presence of the disease within their system . . . [War is] the culmination of convergent commercial and political interests. Wars are fought by soldiers but they are produced by business men and politicians.

GSP, Jr., Paper, "The Causes of War," November 27, 1935
. . . it seems hardly fair to assume that through all those bloody years thousands of Trojans should have laid down their lives in order that a somewhat discredited prince might enjoy the bedfellowship of a lady; or that countless Greeks were equally willing to die in order that Menelaus might regain his lost, aging and besmirched light o' love. In actuality the causes which produced the war may be ascribed to the fact that the Trojans were becoming too successful in competing with the Greeks for the carrying trade of the Aegean Sea.

Patton went on and talked of the destruction of Carthage, the First Crusade, the long years of undeclared war between Spain and England, the rivalry between English and Dutch fleets, the American Revolution, the Napoleonic conflicts, the war with Mexico (due chiefly to land hunger, he said), the Civil War (King Cotton not Uncle Tom), and the Franco-Prussian War.

[It is impossible to predict] just where or when on sea or land some trivial incident will once more induce Mars to sound his tuneless horn . . . Our lack of prescience is immaterial and we can but regret and, if we are wise, zealously prepare for the cataclism which will inevitably occur when any pair of the several nations now moving on lines of convergent political and commercial interests collide.

A classmate of Patton, Lieutenant Colonel Robert L. Eichelberger, who was serving as Secretary of the War Department General Staff and who would command the Eighth Army in the Pacific during World War II, sent Patton a radiogram in February 1936 to tell him that the post of Commandant of Cadets at West Point would soon become vacant.

Without waiting to hear further details, Patton dispatched an immediate telegram to the War Department:

> Just learned that I am on list for Commandant. If I am otherwise acceptable hope you can prevent the use of any Adjutant General policy from preventing my detail on the ground that I am on foreign service or the General Staff. I have had more foreign service than most officers of my grade and this is my second tour on the General Staff. Am willing to return [to the United States] at own expense. Please do what you can.

Eichelberger had already mailed a letter explaining the situation more fully to Patton. It was that Simon Bolivar Buckner — who would command the Tenth Army in the Pacific during World War II and be killed on Okinawa — was the current Commandant of Cadets and would soon leave West Point. The job had been offered to Eichelberger, who found it tempting but was unable to accept. Patton was being considered but, unfortunately, he was out of the country on what was considered a foreign assignment. Someone had been chosen to succeed Buckner for only a year. Eichelberger would be going to West Point for a visit in the spring, and he would let Patton know what he could find out about the next appointment. "I feel that you would grace the job with your usual 'becoming dignity and efficiency.'"

Upon receipt of Patton's telegram, Eichelberger cabled him:

> Prior to receipt of your radiogram General Connor [West Point Superintendent] had asked for detail of Colonel McCunniff as Commandant of Cadets and his detail has been approved for one year.

There was nothing to do but wait. By November, feeling that McCun-niff's tour of duty was drawing sufficiently toward its close, Patton solic-ited Pershing for help in obtaining the appointment.

Letter, GSP, Jr., to Pershing, November 12, 1936

I hate to be always asking favors but as I still am anxious to amount to something before I retire I am going to do it . . .

You were good enough to write Gen. Conner in my behalf last year so I hope you will feel able to do it again this year and if you will, also write to Gen. Craig. The best argument I have for my selection is based on the fact that I think the fact of having had close in battle service under you in both Mexico and France would be a drawing card with the cadets. Since the World War none of the officers de-tailed as commandant have had such service. True it was not their fault but their misfortune but none the less I think that a little blood and guts would be good for cadets.

Trusting that you will forgive my bothering you and with all good wishes, I am, Very respectfully,

Five days later, Patton wrote Pershing again. He had heard that Gen-eral Connor had recommended Captain Butler of the engineers to be Commandant of Cadets. Butler was "a very nice man," but his service had consisted for the most part as aide to Connor, and this, to Patton, appeared inadequate preparation for the position. Butler was a member of the class of 1920, which had graduated in November 1918, after two years at the Military Academy, and this was hardly enough time, in Pat-ton's opinion, to absorb the West Point tradition and outlook. Butler had not graduated from the Command and General Staff College and therefore probably lacked maturity. Butler had no war experience com-parable to Patton's, and officers with active combat such as Patton were much more looked up to by the cadets.

If Pershing wrote to Connor in Patton's behalf, would he please refrain from mentioning Butler's name because that would implicate Patton's friend at West Point who had tipped him off. Meanwhile, Patton had written to Craig telling him the whole story. If Pershing could talk to Craig, it would certainly help Patton's case.

"I have only wanted three things in my life very much," Patton con-cluded. "The first was to go to Mexico with you, the second was to ac-company you to France."

Pershing's aide answered Patton on December 1, saying that Pershing had left Washington for Lincoln, Nebraska, and from there was going to Arizona to spend the winter. The aide in Washington had forwarded Patton's letter to Arizona.

The letter reached Pershing, and he answered. A handwritten note on Patton's letter contained these words of Pershing: "Wrote him [Patton] in general terms nothing definite as there is nothing definite I could write. J.J.P."

On February 25, 1937, Patton acknowledged with thanks — he could not thank Pershing enough — Pershing's letter, which the general had written in his own handwriting. Patton was having it mounted between two pieces of glass, not to exhibit it but "to pass on to my descendants as a priceless souvenir of our greatest soldier."

He was pleased to learn that Pershing and Harbord had both recommended him to be Commandant of Cadets. But he was pessimistic over his chances.

> I have gained the impression that possibly the fact that I am very outspoken is held against me in some quarters, but as I never noticed you doing very much pussyfooting, I do not take this criticism to heart as much as I should. Possibly the candor of a fighting soldier is not too well received in peace.

At the end of March, he wrote Pershing to tell him he had just learned that Charles W. Ryder — who would command the 34th Division in World War II — was to be Commandant of Cadets. When some people failed to get something they wanted, Patton continued, they lost interest in those who had tried to help. "I want to assure you that I appreciate your efforts very much and only regret that I put you to unnecessary trouble." He hoped to be in Washington soon and "shall give myself the pleasure of calling on you to thank you personally."

A job he wanted with all his might, it escaped him for the fourth and final time simply because of chance. What was important about this last effort on his part to obtain the post was the emergence of the term he coined — "blood and gutts."

Although Patton wrote several papers on mechanization — in one he predicted accurately the development of self-propelled howitzers — his notable professional preoccupation at Hawaii was his study of amphibious

operations, a subject into which he had delved during his earlier tour of
duty in the Islands. It was a natural interest, for the defense of Hawaii
was very much on the minds of those responsible for this American outpost. Yet, characteristically, Patton was concerned less with how to repel
an invasion than with how to get ashore.

His first step in 1935 was to look into history. He selected several landing operations, summarized the salient facts, and extracted, then evaluated the lessons. Sir Francis Drake, he found, succeeded at Cartagena,
Colombia, in 1588, because he utilized surprise, command of the sea, and
ferocious attack. The French took Cartagena in 1697 even though they
failed to gain surprise — because they had command of the sea and met
no resistance on the beaches. The British admiral Vernon was defeated at
Cartagena in 1741 for a variety of reasons. The British attack at Antwerp
in 1809 was significant for command of the sea and beach resistance.
Winfield Scott's invasion of Vera Cruz in 1847 showed careful planning
and cooperation between Army and Navy, was mounted on a broad front,
and profited from command of the sea.

Patton considered the French and British operations 40 miles south of
Sebastopol in 1854, during the Crimean War; the Japanese landings in
1904, against Russia, and particularly the Japanese capture of Tsingtao;
the British crossing of the Tigris River in February 1917; the German
operations in the Baltic in September and October, 1917; and the Japanese amphibious behavior in the Shanghai incident of 1932.

What interested him most of all was the Dardanelles operation, usually called the Gallipoli campaign:

> Foisted on a reluctant government by an enthusiastic but visionary
> politician [Winston Churchill] who did not scruple to use disingen-
> uous methods to attain his desires. Conducted by a gallant but in-
> capable general [Ian Hamilton] initiated without plan or adequate
> means. The operation was still born and preordained to failure . . .
> more repleted with a strange mixture of valor and stupidity, of sac-
> rifice and unselfishness, than any other campaign of which history has
> a record.

Patton then summarized the lessons he had derived. Command of the
sea, surprise, night landings, energetic leadership, Army-Navy cooperation, naval fire support, broad front landings, artillery and machines with
the leading waves, special boats and other equipment, and transports

close to the landing beaches were all necessary for successful invasion. In the future, the side that had command of the air would have an overwhelming advantage.

Daylight landings, an absence of surprise, landing on a narrow front, the failure of naval fire support, inflexible plans, inept leadership, and poor Army-Navy cooperation led to defeat.

Applying his observations to Hawaii, he concluded that if the Japanese attacked the Islands, they would utilize air attack and try to block the sea channels in the Pearl and Honolulu harbors.

Actually, his forecast of amphibious doctrine in World War II was accurate. Allied operations, uniformly successful during that war, capitalized on all the factors he listed — command of the sea and of the air, surprise (gained by elaborate deception plans), close inter-service cooperation (gained by the principle of single or unified command), heavy naval fire support of ground forces, broad front landings, a large proportion of artillery and tanks and other heavy weapons going ashore with the leading elements, a variety of special equipment, and the anchorage of ship transports relatively close to shore. Night landings were at first deemed essential, but as the Allied domination of the sea and air became overwhelming, later amphibious operations were conducted during daylight.

To what extent Patton's study influenced the amphibious doctrine during World War II, or whether it had any impact whatsoever, is impossible to say. At the very least, his informal discussions and conversations with his fellow officers stimulated thought of a technique that was to have an important bearing on the outcome of World War II. Certainly his knowledge of amphibious operations was a factor that led to his selection as commander of the Western Task Force, which invaded the coast of North Africa near Casablanca in November 1942. By 1943, after the invasion of Sicily, where he led the American troops ashore, Patton was regarded as one of the leading amphibious experts on the Allied side.

Fascinated by the Gallipoli operation, Patton studied it more deeply. In August 1936, he completed a paper of narrative and analysis that ran 128 pages. So thorough and thought-provoking was this work that it was mimeographed, bound into a booklet, and disseminated to officers in Hawaii for their instruction.

Patton's conclusion on Gallipoli:

At Suvla Bay it was not the Turkish army which defeated the British, but it was Von Sanders, Kemal Pasha and Major Willmer who defeated Hamilton, Stopford, Hammersley and Sitwell. Had the two sets of commanders changed sides it is believed that the landing would have been as great a success as it was a dismal failure.

Leadership, above all, he was saying, was the decisive factor in warfare.
After the annual major exercise in April 1937, Patton specifically investigated Hawaii's vulnerability to attack. Crediting Drum, who was the Hawaiian Department commander, with the vision to draw attention to the strategic importance of the Islands, with the knowledge of amphibious operations to understand Hawaii's danger, and with the foresight to warn of Hawaii's value as a hostile advance base, first for enemy aviation, later for amphibious forces attacking the United States mainland, Patton wrote of

the inescapable assumption that complete surprise offers the greatest opportunity for the successful capture of these islands. It is reliably reported that during the last four years three or more Japanese divisions were embarked, moved to the coast of Asia and disembarked without any military attache, consular agent, foreign press correspondent or any other foreigner living in Japan being aware of the fact until the troops were in action in Asia. Some of the Mandated Islands, about which absolutely nothing is known, are only 2500 miles distant, seven days' steaming over the loneliest sea lanes in the world. Who can say that an expeditionary force is not in these islands now?

He invited attention to "the necessity of establishing certain precautionary measures against surprise attack," including providing infantry, artillery, and air troops with at least half a day's fire in ammunition — actually in the hands of the troop units; storing lamps and candles in barracks and supply rooms, flares or floodlights for depots and hangars; and creating an alarm system designed to get troops to their wartime posts in a hurry.

For the Japanese, he demonstrated in some detail, could invade and occupy Hawaii.

It is realized that the events above enumerated [how the Japanese could take Hawaii] are not likely of occurrence. On the other hand the vital necessity to Japan of a short war and of the possession at its termination of land areas for bargaining purposes may impel her to take drastic measures. It is the duty of the military to foresee and prepare against the worst possible eventuality.

The attack on Pearl Harbor was four and a half years in the future, and Patton's estimate was a shrewd and thoughtful perception.

The world seemed to be marching toward war. Japan had conquered Manchuria and invaded China. Italy took Ethiopia by force. Civil war had broken out in Spain. And Hitler in Germany was preparing for violent expansion.

The U. S. Army, long dormant, was beginning, but slowly, hardly visibly, to reawaken and rearm.

Patton's ratings at Hawaii were uniformly high. Brigadier General Daniel Van Voorhis, chief of staff of the Hawaiian Department judged him an "excellent" G–2 — "ambitious, progressive, original, professionally studious; conscientious in the performance of his duties — fine appearing — the most physically active officer I have ever known . . . An officer of very high general value to the service."

Colonel James A. Ulio, who succeeded Van Voorhis as chief of staff, graded Patton twice "superior" and called him "an outstanding officer of high professional attainments. An indefatigable worker and reader as to his profession. A most active officer physically. Loyal, zealous and efficient."

Drum wrote: "Heretofore I have noted on this officer's Efficiency Reports a weakness in 'Tact.' In the last year he has overcome this weakness in a satisfactory manner. Colonel Patton has those qualities so essential to a superior combat leader."

Patton was reassigned to the Cavalry Board at Fort Riley, and in June 1937, he, Beatrice, young George, Francis "Doc" Graves, cook Suzuki, and deckhand Joe Ekeland sailed from Hawaii in the Patton *Arcturus* and headed for the mainland.

Beatrice Patton, Voyage of Arcturus, *Honolulu to San Pedro (California), 1937 (in the form of a letter to the children)*
June 13: We left on the dot yesterday at nine A.M. . . . over two hundred people on the dock to wave us goodbye. We had 180 leis

and presents galore, books, soap, (salt and fresh water), iced cakes, candy, liquor, lifesavers, grapefruit peel, cap nets, jam, macademia nuts and everything you ever dreamed of. Joe said we had more flowers than a gangster's funeral! We were making one giant lei of all the little ones to throw overboard off Diamond Head, when all of a sudden . . . seven airplanes swooped out of nowhere and sailed right over us, all changing their positions directly overhead — an Aloha!

[Escorted now by porpoises and birds. Ran engine 10 hours to get clear of land. Have to go north 600 miles before turning east with the westerly winds.]

June 15: so far this cruise is just the way I have pictured a cruise ought to be — lovely weather — everyone happy and comfortably sunburned — and the whole situation most pleasant and congenial.

June 22: Doc is a great joker, he swore he could see Latitude 34 when he looked over the side . . . (Back in 1898 on the River Nile, Uncle Freddie and I took turns all one day hanging over the rail of the Dahrobiyeh, watching in the muddy water for the Tropic of Cancer. Our tutor, Mr. Bentinck Smith told us to look for a dotted line.)

June 27: [third wedding anniversary of B and Johnnie Waters, who were at West Point.] we shall probably have to drink to your health in lavender water, as the regular stuff is running low.

July 9: [getting radio stations; learned that aviatrix Amelia Earhart had crashed.]

July 12: [arrived Los Angeles and were met by Ruth Ellen and Nita and others.]

Patton had arranged in Honolulu to sell the *Arcturus* on the mainland, and this was done. After a brief stay at San Gabriel, the family traveled to Massachusetts. Patton had a leave of absence for one month and fifteen days, to end early in August.

On July 26, he telephoned the headquarters of the First Corps Area in Boston to report that he was in the hospital at Beverly with a broken leg.

His stay in hospital, he said, would be without expense to the government, he wished his status changed as of July 25, the date of his accident, from leave to sick in hospital, and since he was under orders to proceed to Fort Riley for duty, would the War Department notify the commanding general of his injury.

The corps area commander assumed that Patton had broken his leg playing polo, and he so advised the War Department. About a month later, on August 19, he instructed the commanding officer of the Harbor Defenses of Boston at Fort Banks to appoint a board of officers to determine whether Patton's injury was in line of duty. A normal procedure, the investigation would establish whether there was a good reason and just cause for the accident or whether Patton was hurt as the result of some foolishness.

Two coast artillery officers and a Medical Corps officer, comprising the board, proceeded to the Beverly Hospital. Patton appeared before them and was sworn to testify.

On Sunday, he said, July 25, he, Mrs. Patton, and Lieutenant John K. Waters were riding on his estate near South Hamilton when Mrs. Patton's horse, which was just ahead of him, bolted suddenly, kicked, struck Patton's right leg, and inflicted a compound fracture of front and back bones. An ambulance was summoned, and it carried him to the hospital.

The doctor who had been on duty when Patton was admitted to the hospital was then called and sworn in. He said that Patton was absolutely sober and not under the influence of narcotics when he arrived. The doctor had administered anesthesia for an operation to reduce the fracture of the right tibia and fibula before applying a plaster cast. He believed there might be some permanent partial disability as the result either of the fractures or of a subsequent swelling in the pelvic veins.

The medical diagnosis was fracture, compound, right tibia, middle third; fracture simple, multiple of right fibula, upper and lower thirds; thrombo phlebitis, acute, of the pelvic veins, with resultant edematous swelling of the right leg.

The board of officers returned to Boston, met again, and reported their findings. Their unanimous verdict was that the injury had been incurred in line of duty. There was no misconduct on Patton's part. He had not been under the influence of drugs, narcotics, or alcohol at the time of the accident.

Letter, Lieutenant Colonel W. J. Froitzheim, commanding General Dispensary, U.S. Army, Boston, Mass., to Commanding General, Fort Riley, Kansas, November 15, 1937, subject: Sick Report

Report that Lieutenant Colonel George S. Patton, Cav . . . was admitted to the Beverly Hospital, Beverly, Mass., from July 25th to November 4th, 1937, inclusive. Upon his discharge from this particular hospital he was marked "sick in quarters" and at the present time is remaining in quarters . . . LD [Line of Duty] — yes.

Date of final disposition will be furnished by this office at the proper time.

Pershing wrote to Patton in December, saying he had just heard of Patton's accident and hoped he was on the road to recovery. General Kromer, the Chief of Cavalry, had given a small dinner at the Army and Navy Club the night before to which were invited several men "with whom I have been rather intimately associated . . . You would, of course, have been one of the party if you had been available."

Letter, GSP, Jr., to Pershing, December 30, 1937

My leg is realy much better and though I still have to wear an iron brace I can put a little weight on it and expect to go to Riley on dismounted duty about the tenth or fifteenth of January.

Now I have to bother you with a personal problem. Gen. Drum has always been more than kind to me and took me to Hawaii on his staff. As you know he is most anxious to follow Gen. Craig as Chief of Staff. So far as I can see the choice lays between him and Gen. De Witt. Yesterday Gen. Drum wrote me and asked if I could find out from you how you felt toward him in respect to his ambition. My loyalty to Gen. Drum makes it incumbent on me to ask you this question but since you are the center of all my loyalty I do not wish to place you in a position which might prove inconvenient to you. If you care to write me some statement which I could quote to Gen. Drum it would be helpful to me in my relations with him. If however you do not feel disposed to say any thing I shall understand your position and will simply have to say to Gen. Drum that I did not feel able to ask you such a question. I trust that you will forgive me being thus frank and assure you that what ever action you will take will be perfectly satisfactory to me.

Pershing chose to make no response. Eventually, in 1939, George C. Marshall would succeed Malin Craig as Army Chief of Staff.

On January 31, 1938, having been ordered to report to the Fort Banks Hospital for a medical survey to determine his fitness for active duty, Patton entered the hospital. He walked with a decided limp, although his general condition appeared good. He complained of a slight weakness in his right leg while walking and of a slight pain and swelling after walking.

According to the notes of his medical history, he had been under treatment in the Beverly Hospital for 103 days, and after discharge had been at home, walking on a caliper splint and cane. During his hospitalization, he had had a severe phlebitis due to an embolus in his right leg and a pulmonary embolus had lodged in his left lower lung. Recovery from both was complete. He appeared capable of limited duty, that is, of work requiring neither constant standing nor riding.

His eyesight was 20/30, uncorrected for distant vision, but corrected by glasses for near vision. His figure was medium, his frame heavy. He was 73 inches tall, weighed 196 pounds, and his normal chest measurement was 40 inches, 42½ inches when expanded, 38 at exhalation.

As for his recent injury, his recovery was very satisfactory. The function in his right leg was good. There was a limitation of motion in the right ankle because of the prolonged fixation of the leg. At the moment he was not qualified for duty. He was to have moderate exercise and refrain from riding. He was to elevate his foot and leg when his edema (swelling) was troublesome. He should be under medical supervision until he recovered completely.

On February 2, the War Department relieved Patton from assignment to the Cavalry Board and detailed him to the staff and faculty of the Cavalry School and to additional duty with the 9th Cavalry, which was stationed at Fort Riley as school troops.

There is no personal record of this six months of enforced inactivity resulting from Patton's broken leg and, what was frightening, his embolism. He must have read a good deal. He must also have pondered his future with a depression close to despair. He must certainly have wondered whether he would recover sufficiently to exercise his profession, to sustain the active pursuits that were the heart of his active duty. He must have painfully relived all his disappointments, his failures, his errors, and the occasions where he had displayed a lack of tact.

The world seemed to be drifting toward "the next war" he had anticipated with relish. And there he was, isolated and incapacitated, fifty-three years old, and perhaps over the hill. Could he recover his élan, his spirit, his robust health, his stamina, his zest for physical exertion? And could he do so in time to answer with confidence and vigor the peal of opportunity, the call of his destiny, his fate?

XI
The Approach
of War

"The thing we want is to retain our mobility."

CHAPTER 46

Fort Riley, Fort Clark, Fort Myer

*"He certainly seems to have taken a shine to me and I have
developed into the greatest YES MAN."*

PATTON'S RECOVERY was quicker than might have been expected. He arrived at Fort Riley on February 8, 1938, and became executive officer of the Academic Division and of the 9th Cavalry, and a member of the faculty and staff of the Cavalry School. Although he remained at his desk much of the time, he soon took brief rides, which he lengthened progressively. By March he had regained much of his old form and was displaying his customary energy and enthusiasm. After being examined by a board of officers, he was certified qualified for promotion.

In July, Colonel Clarence Lininger, assistant commandant of the Cavalry School, rated Patton "superior" in all categories except physical endurance. "Broken leg last summer from kick of horse," Lininger explained. "Rapidly approaching recovery. He rides hard now and it interferes little or not at all."

*Letter, GSP, Jr., to Major General John A. Herr, Chief of Cavalry,
spring 1938*

My dear General: The three swords of which I wrote you are forwarded today under separate package for your inspection. They are not made of sword steel but are simply mild steel which I procured from the Union Pacific shops, roughed out with a cutter and then ground to shape. At first I made wooden models but decided that I could not judge the balance so had to revert to the steel . . .

. . . There are several advantages to this bayonet idea. In the first place it might be easier to issue a bayonet to the cavalry than it would be to restore a saber. In the second place it would give the cavalry a very nasty arm for close combat dismounted should they become involved in such an operation, which heaven forbid. Third, it has the greatest chopping leverage of any blade I have ever seen . . .

Trusting that the models may be of some satisfaction to you, and assuring you that it was a great pleasure for me to make them, I am Very respectfully,

That spring, for his own edification or for the consideration of the staff, he set down his thoughts on what was wrong with the methods of instruction at the Cavalry School. The teaching was generally colorless, without emphasis on leadership and individuality. Not enough time was devoted to the personality of leaders. The problems to be solved by the students were too long and far from clear cut; too much information was given — "It is not necessary to have a history of the war to fight it." He had the impression that staff officers were becoming operators and were tending to usurp the functions of commanders. "Only God can make generals," he wrote, reversing his thought of two decades earlier, "the duty of this school is to make captains and majors."

Letter, GSP, Jr., to Beatrice (with her daughter Beatrice at the birth of the second Waters child), April 27, 1938

Here is George's report card which as he feared is not too good but on the other hand it might have been worse . . .

I had all the Heads of departments, the Gen., Col Rodney, Col. Holderness and Col Stayer and their copious wives in yesterday afternoon to drink the health of the offspring . . . Honeycutt and Nelly Richardson got promoted. So did Gens Van Voorhis, Ben Lear and Walter Grant all Cavalrymen. Col. Lininger was pretty well cut up as the selection of Richardson definately passes him up as it does Col Rodney too. Someday I may be in their shoes so feel sorry for them.

Significant changes were occurring throughout the military establishment as Japanese and German aggression pushed the world toward war, and the promotion of Van Voorhis to major general — he would receive his second star in July — was linked to a decision respecting mechanization. Early in 1938, the War Department directed the cavalry and infantry — no other branches — to develop mechanized forces. In compliance, the cavalry formed two mechanized regiments at Fort Knox and organized the 7th Cavalry Mechanized Brigade. Because of Van Voorhis' earlier experience with the Mechanized Force at Camp Meade and Fort Eustis, he was given the command of the unit.

Van Voorhis would remain a short time. In September, he would move on to Columbus, Ohio, to command the Fifth Corps Area.

Chaffee would take his place. Chaffee had served at Forts Eustis and Knox for three years, then on the War Department General Staff for four. When he replaced Van Voorhis, he would be promoted to brigadier general. Soon Chaffee would be put in charge of mechanized units of both the cavalry and infantry, and he would, in effect, recreate a new Tank Corps augmented by motorized infantry.

Despite Patton's interest in mechanization, he appeared to remain wholly a cavalryman. This too had its rewards. On May 12, in a memo addressed to the Adjutant General, subject: George Patton, General John K. Herr, the Chief of Cavalry, wrote that he wanted Patton promoted so that he could command the 5th Cavalry. He considered Patton "the only suitable officer for this assignment." Since no one in the military was supposed to be indispensable, Herr crossed out the "only" and substituted "most available." Therefore, Herr was recommending that the restriction currently in force against giving an officer a permanent change of station until he had served at least two years at his current duty post be waived in Patton's case.

On July 1, 1938, Patton was promoted to colonel. Ten days later he was assigned to the 1st Cavalry Division. He arrived at Fort Clark, Texas, on July 24, and assumed command of the 5th Cavalry.

Letter, GSP, Jr., to Beatrice, July 24, 1938
San Antonio is very quaint and I think you will like it . . . [Fort] Clark is 138 miles due west . . . I think we will like it. Gen J. [Joyce] runs the post and I run the regiment which makes it very nice. The Joyces were delighted to see me and are more human than [they were] at [Fort] Myer . . . All one can do here is to Ride-Read Write & Swim.

Letter, GSP, Jr., to Beatrice, August 4, 1938
One of us [Joyce or Patton] has to be here as . . . the next ranking officer is not considered suitable to command the post. However he is doing all right for me . . .

[The house is beginning to look] swell. I had a new room built for a butler's pantry and bought a sink for it. I also am having the garden fenced with a 6 foot latice fence which should be finished by the end of September. All work here has to be done by soldiers. So as not to make them hate me I have them do the work on their own time and pay them for it. I got an extra month's furlough for George Meeks [his orderly] so he will be here until I return. Last night the Joyce's and I went to Eagle Pass and had dinner at El Moderno with Gen. Canones the Mexican commander. You will like him and his wife and also the town. It is just as foreign as Saumur or more so. I am striking up numerous friendships with the ranchers who while crude are real people and have plenty of shooting and fishing to trade for a little politeness. The Joyce's cant see this which is their misfortune. The sherrif and the County judge and the policeman are already my friends.

Letter, GSP, Jr., to Beatrice, August 8, 1938

[Brigadier General Kenyon A. Joyce] certainly seems to have taken a shine to me and I have developed into the greatest YES MAN unhung but it is the best way to get along with him and as a matter of fact he is very nice but I am makeing mental notes what I will do to two members of his staff if he ever leaves them in my clutches. He seems to think he will get Gen Lears job commanding the Division in November or december and if he does I may be in command here for a long time alone which will be somewhat less complicated than at present.

Patton had been sent to Fort Clark in order to take part in a series of maneuvers staged by the Third Army in Texas. The overall aim of the sham battles was to test concepts of troop mobility, concentration, and deployment under conditions of simulated warfare.

Letter, GSP, Jr., to Beatrice, August 15, 1938

This is the second day of the [mock] war. Yesterday we marched 35 miles in the worst heat I have ever seen and secured our objective with out a fight. Said objective is a stunted oak forest on a ridge but owing to ground rules we have to sit in a windless vally. I have been here ever since 5 A.M. I think that the infantry wont get up for another 18 hours and as the enemy who is 4 miles north of us wont fight I guess we will just sit. Tomorrow night we may march around his flank but it will be a very long trip over slippery roads. Still at night it is cool.

Letter, GSP, Jr., to Beatrice, August 23, 1938

We are now at Savenal which is sixty two or three miles from [Fort] Clark. So as I am making two thirty mile marches we will be in on the 25th. Actually I am at Clark now having driven in the regimental Car to get a bath which God knows I needed . . .

The last day of the Maneuvers I had a swell time. The 12th was in front on a flank march which I had advised the first day and was only put over on the fourth. It got held up for three hours and then they put B [Troop] and the Machine Gun troops of the fifth [cavalry] in the advance guard. I went along as sort of huntsman. We moved about ten miles mostly at a gallop and one horse died but we got right into the enemy rear areas and captured two battery kitchens one battery one battalion all of National Guard artillery and then scooped up the colonel and the command post of the 69 Regular artillery AA [antiaircraft]. In galloping over a wire fence the man next me got a bad fall but I was having such a swell time I never saw the fence which was low and my horse jumped it all right. The colonel of the 69th was very mad and refused to surrender to Capt Doyle till I came up and stuck my white pistol in his face then he was very quiet especially as I paroled him as I had no men to guard prisoners.

Gen Joyce expects to get back the 13th [of September] and I can start [on leave] immediately . . . Let me know what riding and evening clothes I have at G.M. [Green Meadows] as I expect to fly and want as little baggage as possible.

At the close of the maneuver, Major General George Van Horn Moseley, the Third Army commander, conducted the critique and concluded that the horse cavalry had demonstrated its continued usefulness for close-in reconnaissance. Patton's strenuous endeavors had, no doubt, contributed to that judgment.

Letter, GSP, Jr., to Beatrice, August 27, 1938

Last night I had my first experience in twenty years of being the old man [senior officer] at a party. I drank beer till my teeth floated but nothing else and along about midnight I found it expedient to go home . . .

The awnings have made the house cooler but still you sit and drop from two to four daily which is the hottest part of the day.

Letter, GSP, Jr., to Major General Daniel Van Voorhis, Fort Knox, Kentucky, August 29, 1938

We had a great war in the Third Army Maneuvers and on the last day got right back of the enemy and into his gun positions. It was great sport and the funny thing was to see the utter surprise of the enemy. They had so absorbed the bull butting tactics of the World War that they forgot they had to keep their pants buttoned or else get buggared. The more people decry Cavalry, horse or mechanized, the more we will bust them up next time. The thing we want is to retain our mobility for the last ten miles.

You can count on me to keep the torch burning [for mechanization?] . . .

The only out about Fort Clark is the heat but I suppose it is no worse than Brownsville and you survived that. Anyhow, it is swell for the figure; mine has dwindled perceptiably . . .

Some times I almost think that there will be something doing here [along the border] in a little while. Of course I have hoped so more or less ever since 1911 and it has only happened once, but now again I think there may be a flare up. If you command the army of occupation don't forget to take the Fifth Horse and loan us a few combat cars; anything you can spare.

With sincere regards to yourself and love to the family, I am Very respectfully,

Letter, Major General Ben Lear, commanding 1st Cavalry Division, to GSP, Jr., October 30, 1938

My dear Patton: Before leaving the Cavalry Division I desire to personally express to you my appreciation for the most generous loyalty, the many kindnesses, and the real assistance which you have given to me and to the Cavalry Division throughout the period we have served together . . .

I have the warmest feeling of friendship towards you and your personnel, and wish for you and the members of your command much real happiness and success in the days to come.

Please permit me the privilege of sharing with you an admiration of your splendid command, and a gratification over it's many outstanding accomplishments.

Sincerely yours,

Patton enjoyed Fort Clark and its outdoor life, which restored him to health. He thrived in a position of command, and commanding the 5th Cavalry Regiment gave him great satisfaction, particularly because it was a combat organization, a tactical unit that was expected to be ready at all times for operations. Although Patton experimented with new organizational and operational concepts, he had plenty of time to hunt and fish and ride. He enjoyed his associates and friends.

His hopes for remaining in Texas, close to Mexico, where he continued to expect hostilities to break out, came to an abrupt close. On November 1, the War Department suddenly relieved him from assignment with the 5th Cavalry. He was instructed to report to Fort Myer, Virginia, in December, and take command of the post and of the 3d Cavalry stationed there.

Shortly before he left Texas, a board of officers examined him and found him qualified and eligible for promotion to brigadier general.

Letter, GSP, Jr., to General of Brigade Jesus Jaime Quinones, Piedras Negras, Coahuila, Mexico, December 2, 1938
I regret from the bottom of my heart that circumstances are such that I cannot call on you in person but can only express my gratitude by the written word. I must also take this occasion to bid you farewell. It is a source of profound sorrow to me to leave here and so deprive myself of seeing more of you. With renewed expressions of thanks and esteem, I am, my dear general, your devoted admirer.

Joyce, who succeeded Lear in command of the 1st Cavalry Division, hated to see Patton leave. "Professionally it was grand to have you with me and personally it was a real joy."

He rated Patton "superior" and "an outstanding leader who has great mental and physical energy. Because of his innate dash and great physical courage and endurance he is a cavalry officer from whom extraordinary feats might be expected in war. A deep military student who is intensely interested in his profession. He is thoroughly qualified for the grade of brigadier general. Of outstanding value to the service in every way."

Patton reached Fort Myer on December 10, just as General Jonathan Wainwright, the previous commander, was leaving. The 3d Cavalry was drawn up in trim lines from Wainwright's house to the post gate, and his automobile was preceded and escorted by four scout cars.

The formation, while indicating the respect his officers and men had for Wainwright, reflected in large part the ceremonial nature of the duties performed at Fort Myer. During Patton's tour, he and his men would serve as escorts to the President of Nicaragua and to the King and Queen of England during their visits to Washington in 1939, they would provide the solemn trappings for military funerals, and they would lend military glamour and security to official receptions at the highest levels of the government.

While absorbed with these details and with the normal preoccupations of a post and unit commander, Patton was able to meet with important persons in the capital. The Army Chief of Staff had his quarters at Fort Myer. The War Department was nearby. And the city and its dignitaries were close at hand.

Drum, who was at Governors Island in New York and who was hoping to succeed Craig as Army Chief of Staff, wrote Patton and expressed pleasure that he was back in Washington, where he knew many influential people in high social and government circles.

He was glad, Patton said in reply, that Drum thought his stay at Fort Myer would work out well. He added that he would

do my best to make your wish come true. Also, I am most hopeful that the opportunities to see one another, of which you speak, will not be those resulting from my occasional visits to New York, but rather will be the consequences of having you living at Fort Myer [as Army Chief of Staff].

To Chaffee, who commanded the 7th Cavalry Mechanized Brigade at Fort Knox, Patton wrote: "My dear General Adna," he was grateful to have Chaffee's letter welcoming him back to the Washington area. He would have preferred to serve under Chaffee, for together they could have made the brigade "a very warlike rather than a show-off outfit. However, don't tell General Van Voorhis what I have said." As for his assignment to Fort Myer, "I was as much surprised as anyone when I was ordered from Clark here, and have yet to find out why it happened."

It was all too obvious why Patton had been brought back to Fort Myer. The post was a show place. It featured a ten-week season of drill rides, mounted spectacles featuring impeccable troopers and spirited horses, that attracted congressmen and other governmental officials. The social obligations of commanding the installation were such that no colonel living solely on his Army pay could handle the position. Patton had an outside income. Wainwright, it was rumored, had departed from Fort Myer in debt.

The exhibition drill season opened in January, and Patton invited Major General James Kelly Parsons, the area corps commander, to come down from Baltimore as the guest of honor. He and Mrs. Patton, he wrote, would be happy to have Parsons and his wife, his chief of staff, and anyone else Parsons wished to bring, to lunch at their home.

Early in February, Patton informed General Malin Craig that the members of the Senate Military Affairs Committee and their wives were to attend the drill after lunching with the Pattons at their quarters.

Since I thought it might prove a good chance for favorable propaganda, I have asked the Deputy Chief of Staff, the Assistant Chief of Staff G–3, the Chief of Cavalry, the Chief of Field Artillery (who cannot accept), and Gen Murray [who commanded the troops stationed in the Washington area] to have luncheon with us at one o'clock and attend the Drill afterwards. Mrs. Patton also asked Mrs. Craig who is coming. I wonder if it would be too much of a favor to request that you, too, come. I would have asked you sooner but I hated to keep bothering you.

General Orders 5, Fort Myer, Virginia, March 18, 1939
The Commanding Officer congratulates all the members of the command on the superlative quality of the individual and combined efforts demonstrated by them during the exhibition drill season just concluded. The outstanding success of these drills was wholly due to the fine spirit of discipline, initiative and cooperation for which this garrison is famous. Troops animated by such spirit are invariably successful in peace or war.
Signed: G. S. Patton, Jr., Colonel, 3d Cavalry, Commanding

[Handwritten on one copy sent to Joyce] Dear Gen Joyce: How is that for a little back slapping that I learned from a former Colonel of the Third [Cavalry — meaning Joyce] . . . GSP Jr.

[Handwritten from Joyce] Dear Georgie: Done like the master that you are! . . . KAJ

Whatever Patton's efforts in behalf of Drum, Brigadier General George C. Marshall, the Deputy Chief of Staff, was selected to succeed Malin Craig as Chief of Staff on September 1. Early in May, Patton wrote to Marshall. Extra funds, Patton said, had been allocated for the Chief of Staff's house at Fort Myer, and Patton suggested that the money be used to replace the coal furnace by an oil furnace, to repair two bathrooms, and to paint the rooms. He thought this could be done without disturbing General Craig. He also told Marshall who the servants were — the drivers, the cook, the butler, and so on. "I trust you will forgive me for bothering you with these details, but I believe that your knowing of it now will permit you to make more intelligent plans."

The announcement of Marshall as the new Chief of Staff led to some inevitable jockeying among Army officers. Patton, who was on the scene, who was in contact with Marshall, not on policy matters but rather on housekeeping affairs, and who was, by virtue of his position, rank, experience, and standing very much in the social swim, thus became important to his friends. A chance remark or a private conversation might provide that slight push that could bring about a choice assignment or an advancement in rank.

Joyce, for example, wondered in a letter to Patton where he would be transferred if he were promoted to major general. He preferred, he said, the Ninth Corps Area. "How is Marshall in the matter of the horse and horse cavalry? While I know him very pleasantly I know him but slightly in an official way."

"It would certainly be splendid if you could get the Ninth Corps Area," Patton replied. "What I say will possibly carry little weight but I shall find occasion to bring the subject up in conversation with General Marshall, whom I know very well."

Joyce, it turned out, would be transferred to that post the following year.

There was more involved than a gesture for a friend. International tensions provoked by the aggressions of Germany and Japan were having their effects on the U. S. Army. During his tenure as Chief of Staff, Malin Craig had succeeded in securing increasing budgets for military expenditures. Although the Army was still small and ill-equipped, it was growing.

The National Defense Act of 1920 had authorized 280,000 enlisted men on active duty, but the actual strength of the Army had remained far below that figure. General MacArthur had recommended in 1933 that the Army be built up to at least 165,000 men, and that level was finally attained five years later. Not until June 1939 would the Regular Army total 200,000 officers and men.

Even though the troops were scattered in relatively small parcels among 130 camps, posts, and stations, the Army was stirring after years of doldrums. There was serious talk of preparedness for the next war. New units were being formed, large-scale maneuvers — such as the ones in Mississippi and Texas in 1938 — were being planned, and for the Regular officers, an invisible excitement that contrasted with the sober demeanor of the newly selected Chief of Staff ran like a tremor through the military establishment.

Happy to be near the center of power although constrained to operate on its fringes, Patton looked longingly toward the horses — the 1st Cavalry Division, which Joyce commanded; and toward the machines — the 7th Mechanized Brigade, which Chaffee commanded. Both were operational units devoted to training, and it probably would have made no difference to Patton if he could have worked with either — or, for that matter, with any of the units that were scheduled to participate in a variety of exercises to test combat doctrine, weapons, and equipment. He waited impatiently, hoping desperately to be chosen for a field command, where he could dispense with the glitter and pomp of a show place like Fort Myer and get into the excitement and reality of combat preparation.

While waiting, while performing diligently and loyally the functions of his assignment, he wrote numerous letters of congratulatory flattery to old friends and new, trying somehow to attract notice so that he too could be part of the almost imperceptible expansion of the Army that was starting.

He wrote to Van Voorhis to express regret that he had been away when the general had visited the post. Patton hoped that what the general had seen of Fort Myer "accorded with your own standards insofar as copying perfection is possible."

He wrote to Brigadier General Robert C. Richardson, Jr., to say that he had heard that Richardson was doing "wonderful things for the [Cavalry] School as we all knew you would."

He congratulated Frank Andrews on his promotion to brigadier general. He congratulated John Millikin, who was elevated to colonel and who would command a corps in World War II. He congratulated General George Grunert, Fourth Army commander, who wrote back, "we oftimes wish you were here to pep up action and add color to the otherwise drab exercises." He congratulated Thomas M. Robins, George R. Allin, and others. His good wishes were genuine, yet there was an unmistakable undertone of query: when would he have something important to do? When would he enter into the ranks of the general officers?

His most faithful correspondent, and probably his best friend at this time, was Joyce. Soon after leaving Fort Clark, Patton had conveyed his thanks:

> I always find myself quite incoherent in expressing my appreciation and gratitude, and when I say that never have I had more delightful and instructive service than during my two tours under you I am understating it. I sincerely hope that I may again have the honor and pleasure of serving under you and in a war.

Joyce cautioned him about his health. "Don't be a nitwit and play any hard polo with that leg! In other words, be sane and don't jeopardize your chances for the sake of a little fun. My advice would be to do some equitation and jumping but otherwise confine yourself to indoor sports."

"I intend following your advice about polo," Patton replied, "and shall only play enough to keep my stomach under control."

When Patton learned, unofficially, of course, that Joyce's chances for promotion were good, he wrote, "I am saving up for your extra stars."

In the midst of his correspondence, Patton found time to look after his subordinate officers. For example, he wrote to Richardson about a captain who was a member of Patton's command and who had recently been detailed to Fort Riley. The captain, Patton said, was

> an outstanding competition rider. He has the rare ability of doing better under pressure, and I believe that the Cavalry School is fortunate in getting his services. As a Troop Commander I rated him very satisfactory [not a high rating] due to the fact that his interest in individual horsemanship somewhat clouded his attention to troop duties. I am writing this letter because I feel that should you see his efficiency report without having the information contained in this letter you might possibly get an adverse reaction to him. I think this

would be a mistake for on the job on which [he is] detailed I consider him very superior. Trusting that you will pardon my writing to
you, I am, Very respectfully,

He wrote to one of his lieutenants who was temporarily at Fort Riley,
telling him not to worry for even a moment about asking for an extension
of leave because of his wife's condition; he was not to hesitate to ask for
another extension if necessary.

He wrote to Colonel W. C. Crane, who was vacationing at Woods Hole,
Massachusetts. The recent movement of Crane's battalion from Fort Belvoir to Fort Myer had resulted in the loss of fourteen horses in one battery
because of heat exhaustion. A board had been convened to determine the
responsibility for this excessive loss. What were the exact orders, Patton
asked, that Crane had issued for the march? Was the entire battalion to
move as a unit? Or were the batteries to proceed separately? "I do not
believe the situation demands your return [from vacation], but write me
all the information that occurs to you."

Patton managed to give some attention to professional matters outside
the scope of Fort Myer. He sent the Chief of Cavalry a copy of the new
"Infantry Drill Regulations" and suggested that the cavalry ought to
have a similar book "instead of having to look through a public library to
find out how things should be done." Seen handling the new cavalry
saber-bayonet in the Office of the Chief of Cavalry, he was asked to submit
a short article for the *Cavalry Journal*.

He found time to look into the case of three soldiers who annoyed two
visitors to Washington. "I personally feel," Congressman Anton J. Johnson of Illinois wrote Patton, "that it was through your untiring efforts
that these soldiers were apprehended and punished, and the way the
whole thing was expedited speaks again of the high efficiency of the
United States Army."

"Probably no one," Patton replied, "regrets the incident more than I
do. I am proud of being a soldier and therefore I particularly dislike
incidents tending to bring disgrace on that splendid profession."

*Letter, GSP, Jr., to his son (at the Hill School, Pottstown, Pennsyl-
vania), May 19, 1939*
Your frank and manly letter was very pleasing to me, and I was
glad to get it. If you can't like the Smith boy, leave him alone, because no matter how good a fighter he is, the people at the school

consider him an under dog. It never pays to fight an under dog. You can fight for them, but never against them. It is very foolish, but quite understandable that one should run around raising h——l, but it gets one nowhere and betrays a lack of self-confidence. A man who is self-confident does not run around with a gang. It is much better to be a lone wolf than a coyote. Thanks for the money you sent me. I have already spent it. Hoping that you will not get into any more trouble, I am, Very affectionately,

He and his daughter Ruth Ellen rode at horse shows, and during a single week, between them, collected fourteen ribbons and a reserve championship, plus what he called several pieces of tin.

He rejoined the Capital Yacht Club. After spending a month of leave in Massachusetts, he and Beatrice sailed their boat, a two-masted schooner named *When and If,* from Cape Ann above Boston through the Cape Cod Canal, past Cape Charles, into the Chesapeake Bay, and up the Potomac to Washington.

Brigadier General Maxwell Murray, who commanded the Washington Provisional Brigade, judged Patton "superior" in all categories and qualities. Patton was "a vigorous, forceful and conscientious officer, whom I consider an outstanding leader. He is loyal, courageous, and gives his best effort to his profession."

General Parsons endorsed Murray's rating.

In the midst of Patton's activities came a poignant reminder of the past. A former captain living in Merchantville, New Jersey, wrote Patton that he had met Joseph T. Angelo, who had a job with the Works Progress Administration "pushing mud on the riverbank." He had tried to help Angelo because of Angelo's war record and sunny disposition, which the captain found attractive despite the man's lack of education. Angelo had asked nothing, "as he seems to still have some pride." But any financial help that Patton could send would be a good deed. Angelo lived at 834 Homan Avenue, Camden.

Instead of writing directly to Angelo, Patton wrote to the former captain. He referred in some disdain to Angelo

who I believe saved or materially aided in saving my life there [in France]. I am sorry to hear that he is on relief. As he told you, my mother and I helped him considerably, but due to changed conditions I am not able to do as much for him now as then. I am enclosing a check to his order for $25.00 which I should appreciate your handing to him.

Angelo was capable of the grand gesture too. He spent more than he should have to send Patton a telegram: "Thanks for money much needed now hope you are well. Joe Angelo."

Letter, GSP, Jr., to General G. C. Marshall (Acting Chief of Staff, U.S. Army), July 20, 1939
Major Gay, the Quartermaster here [at Fort Myer], informs me that your property will be moved to the house from town on the 28th. That being the case, it occurs to me that you will have no place to stay. All my family are away, but my house is open and running, and I am there. I can give you a room and bath and meals, and should be truly delighted to do so. I shall not treat you as a guest and shall not cramp your style in any way. Hoping that you will give me the pleasure of your company, I am Very sincerely yours,

Letter, Marshall to Patton, July 24, 1939
I have just found your letter of July 20th, with its hospitable invitation for me to "batch" with you while I am getting my house established at Myer. I will be glad to accept and will talk to you later over the 'phone. You are very kind to invite me. Faithfully yours,

Letter, GSP, Jr., to Beatrice, July 27, 1939
I have just consumated a pretty snappy move. Gen George C Marshall is going to live at our house!!! He and I are batching it. I think that once I can get my natural charm working I wont need any letters from John J. P. [Pershing] or any one else.
Of course it may cramp my style a little about going out but there are compensations . . .
You had better send me a check for $5000.00 as I am getting pretty low.

Letter, GSP, Jr., to Beatrice, July 29, 1939
Gen M.[arshall] is just like an old shoe last night he was dining out and instead of having a chauffeur he drove him self
He is going out in the boat with me to day [Saturday]. He does not seem to have many friends.

CHAPTER 47

Fort Myer to Fort Benning

"If we can get the platoons so they can fight anywhere and the men convinced that they are the best on earth and are willing to get killed to accomplish their missions, we will be a great success."

AS PEOPLE EVERYWHERE during the summer of 1939 watched with growing indignation and anguish the threatening posture of Adolf Hitler, Patton pursued his normal occupations, waiting all the while for some mark of attention, some sign of notice, some gesture of assurance that he was deemed worthy of something more than the direction of ceremonial duties at Fort Myer. He seemed to have reached a dead end in his career. Out of the mainstream of military developments, he performed his official functions, mingled with the upper elements of society, and pined for excitement.

His most interesting activity that summer took place near Fort Belvoir and Manassas, Virginia, where he participated in maneuvers conducted by the III Corps. These games were a smaller offshoot of a major exercise engaging the First and Second Corps near Plattsburg, New York. The entire training program was under the direction of the First Army, commanded by Drum, and its chief aim was to give the staffs of higher headquarters — divisions, corps, and field armies — practice in moving and deploying units in simulated combat.

As early as May, when Drum was planning the exercises, Patton wrote him to make a suggestion. He had been studying maps of the probable areas of the summer maneuvers, and he thought that if Drum imposed imaginary boundaries on the flanks of the troops involved, he would be committing a mistake. Arbitrary lines confining the maneuver area would inhibit and limit the possibility of flanking marches, and thereby seriously handicap the cavalry units, whether horse or mechanized. Similar restrictions placed on the maneuver forces the previous year in Texas, he said, had prevented the proper use of mobile troops.

Knowing your interest in realism [in training] I am taking the liberty of making the above suggestion so that we can attack from the rear, which, in my opinion, is the proper direction of attack for horse and mechanized Cavalry. Trusting that you will forgive my temerity in writing you direct, I am, as ever, Devotedly and very respectfully yours,

Drum replied that he was glad to have Patton's remarks, which, he said, he would bear in mind.

But Drum was less interested in mobility than Patton was. At the conclusion of the maneuvers, Drum would report to the War Department that it would be desirable to develop the highly mobile, hard-hitting striking forces that intrigued Patton. But Drum's overall conclusion was that the bulk of the Army ought to be organized for sustained and prolonged combat much in the manner of World War I.

During the exercises in Virginia, called the First Army Maneuvers, Third Corps Phase, Patton commanded a mobile unit — probably at least part of his 3d Cavalry — supported by attached artillery. He carried out his assignments with vigor and verve, playing hard, conducting in his aggressive way wide, sweeping movements designed to outflank his opponents.

In the course of the war games, he was unintentionally brusque, perhaps even rude, to Albert H. Stackpole, a well-known National Guard officer and military writer. Concerned over the possible damage to his public image, for he was highly conscious of Stackpole's power with the pen, Patton later apologized. Stackpole gracefully acknowledged Patton's note, saying, "Apologies are not at all necessary. I fully appreciate that while a war is being fought the commanding officer can't be bothered with casual observers."

At the conclusion of the maneuvers, Patton wrote to Major General Edward Martin, who commanded the 28th Division, Pennsylvania National Guard, which had been on the opposite side of the sham battles. Patton congratulated Martin on the spirit and efficiency of his men. Martin replied, "I can reciprocate the remark relative to the enthusiasm, energy, and sportsmanship shown by our command. The same applies to your officers and men."

Brigadier General Maxwell Murray sent a "Commendation" to the War Department to cite the "superior" performance of Patton during the exercises. "His tireless energy, prompt decision, and clear grasp of the situations presented were noteworthy," Murray wrote, "and I consider that his work as commander . . . in most difficult terrain, was outstanding. I recommend this officer for early consideration for appointment to the grade of brigadier general."

Letter, J. W. Stilwell (Carmel, California) to GSP, Jr., August 23, 1939

My dear Patton, That was really an unfair advantage I took of you and Carberry [when they were cadets at West Point and returning at night from an unauthorized expedition]; I was running on a nice smooth path, and you were leaping over rocks all the way. And how you two did put out! My belated thanks for an exceptional feat of agility and an interesting recollection. [Stilwell had then been an instructor and was nice enough to have pretended he could neither recognize nor catch Patton and Carberry; otherwise, he would have had to report them for punishment.] Many thanks for your kind words about my promotion, which is of far less importance to me than the approval of old friends. I appreciate your having taken the trouble to write. Best wishes, and hoping to see you again some where soon.

Joyce wrote on August 25 to thank Patton for the delightful party he had given for him several weeks earlier when Joyce had been in Washington. "Our mutual friend is most interesting, and I am sure will make a great Chief of Staff . . . Do not fail to get Pa Watson [Brigadier General Edward Watson, soon to be promoted. He had graduated in Patton's original class of 1908, had been Roosevelt's military aide and was now his Secretary] on your side. This is confidential, but most important. As things are now you are nicely fixed [with influential friends] I know."

Letter, GSP, Jr., to Colonel James A. Ulio, Office of the Adjutant General, Washington, D.C., August 31, 1939

My dear Jimmy: Paragraph 4 of the enclosed letter of commendation is, I believe, of vital importance to me, because, while General Murr[a]y gave me a wonderful efficiency report on June 30th, he failed to mention the general officer part. Since it is highly probable that I shall be up for consideration [for promotion to brigadier general] prior to next June 30th I wish you would discover some way of getting a copy of this letter before the Chief of Staff, or at least have it recorded with my current efficiency report. This letter is certainly doing me no good sitting in Baltimore [at Headquarters, Third Corps Area]. On the other hand, I cannot ask the new Chief of Staff, Col Allin, to do anything as he might consider that I am stealing his thunder [affecting Allin's eligibility for promotion]. Since you are sure of being made [a general officer], I believe that I can call on you without misgiving. Do your damnedest. Most sincerely,

The German invasion of Poland on September 1 opened the hostilities of World War II. And still Patton remained unaffected by the hectic changes occurring everywhere.

Early in September, as German mobile mechanized forces were overrunning Poland, President Roosevelt raised the U. S. Army's authorized strength to 227,000 men. At the same time, General Lesley McNair started planning a program to reorganize the combat divisions from square to triangular type. Instead of four regiments, a division would now have three, and each regiment would have three battalions instead of four. The result was a saving in manpower and a gain in flexibility. Improved weapons would increase the division's firepower, and more vehicles would give it greater mobility.

McNair's program would be carried out late that year, and the new look would make possible genuine corps and army maneuvers in 1940, something more than the earlier extemporized exercises.

Meanwhile, Patton was writing to the Chief of Cavalry to suggest that four officers at Fort Myer ought to attend the Army War College. However, one of the four, he said,

will probably be taken care of by the President, or could be if you had no hole [space] for him. In any case he is of more value to the Cavalry in his present position as a riding companion for Mrs. Roosevelt than he would be at the War College, at least for the next few years.

Patton wrote to Chaffee on a flimsy excuse. Chaffee was coming to Washington to give a talk at the War College, and the Pattons hoped he would stay with them.

Chaffee was unable to avail himself of Patton's hospitality. "I am counting on seeing you, though," Chaffee wrote, "and talking over a lot of things with you." He was, no doubt, referring to armored things, for Chaffee was working hard on mechanization at Fort Knox.

When Marshall officially assumed his post as Chief of Staff and became a four-star general, Patton had a set of sterling silver stars — eight in all — sent to him from New York. Patton also presented a set of stars to Joyce upon his promotion to Major General.

Letter, General G. C. Marshall to GSP, Jr., September 23, 1939
Dear Patton: As I told you yesterday, I tried to get you over the 'phone to thank you for that whole firmament of stars you presented to me. I appreciate very much your thoughtfulness and generous gesture, and I trust that I will wear these stars with satisfaction and honor to the Army.

Letter, Joyce to GSP, Jr., September 27, 1939
[Thanks a thousand times for the stars.] I trust I shall be able to return the compliment with a pair for your own wear in the very near future. I have just returned from [Fort] Clark where I had two glorious dove shoots on Otto Postell's ranch. They tell the story at Clark that when Mrs. Postell recently used some strong language she promptly explained that she had learned the words from you.

Letter, GSP, Jr., to Marshall, October 12, 1939
My dear General Marshall: With the rapid approach of the social season in Washington it occurs to me that you might require the temporary service of an aide to attend to your engagements and to keep the appointment book for both yourself and Mrs. Marshall.

First Lieutenant Loren F. Cole has had considerable experience, knows everyone in Washington, and is a very charming gentleman. Should you see fit I would be very glad to detail Lieutenant Cole as an acting aide until such time as your permanent aide reports for duty.

Trusting that you will not consider me too intrusive, I am Very respectfully,

Letter, Marshall to GSP, Jr., October 16, 1939
My dear Patton: I received your note of the 12th regarding Cole. I

appreciate your thoughtfulness and I will talk to you about it at some later time. Faithfully yours,

Letter, Sterling Larrabee, Master of the Fox Hounds, The Old Dominion Hounds, Crest Hill, Virginia, to GSP, Jr., October 15, 1939

Dear George: Your question as to the best ration for foxhounds is indeed a nice one, and probably has as many answers as there are Masters of Hounds. After experimenting with various rations during the past fifteen years, I have arrived at the ration as shown below, which has proven satisfactory in this particular country and this climate — I fancy the climate and other conditions at Fort Knox are somewhat similar . . .

[Then followed a detailed, three-page, single-spaced, typed letter on the feeding of hounds.]

I sincerely trust that you may get some dope out of the above which you can cull over and pass on to Adna Chaffee, who (Hitler permitting) may get some good sport out of organizing a pack at Fort Knox. Those mechanized gents ought to get some real exercise, anyway.

Life went on as usual for Patton. In November, he went to New York and attended the National Horse Show in Madison Square Garden, participating in several events and judging the Open Jumpers Classes.

In December, a board of officers certified that Patton was eligible and qualified for promotion to brigadier general. This was the second year he had been so designated. What he needed was a job, an assignment, that called for that rank.

He was well regarded. His official file was full of "superior" ratings and comments. "Everywhere I hear mention of the fine record you have built up and are continuing to maintain," Colonel J. A. Green, editor of the *Infantry Journal*, wrote him.

Yet nothing happened. His status remained unchanged. Marshall seemed to ignore him even though he searched for young and vigorous officers to fill vacancies in an expanding Army. Perhaps it was because he thought Patton too old, or too wedded to the horse cavalry; perhaps because he was aware of Patton's efforts to impress him; it may have been that Marshall was testing Patton's patience, or, indeed, that nothing suitable for him was open. Then too there was vague talk — from Pa Watson? — that the White House considered Patton too outspoken, too flamboyant, possibly even erratic; and his social and political connections through his wife to prominent Republicans in Massachusetts would hardly have worked in his favor. Whatever the reason, Patton stayed at Fort Myer.

The new year arrived, and he conducted the drill exhibitions. In his spare time, for his own amusement, he drew up his "idea of what the proper course of instruction" in the pistol should be.

Letter, Lieut. Col. John J. Bohn, Cavalry School, to GSP, Jr., March 22, 1940

Dear George: Your recent study on instruction of the pistol has just passed over my desk en route to the Cavalry Board. I cannot refrain from expressing to you in a personal note my appreciation of your succinct murder of the present valueless course in cavalry pistol instruction. In addition, I strongly feel that the simple, sensible and practical course of instruction proposed by you for cavalry pistol instruction should be adopted at once. The plan needs no selling. The improvement is apparent to anyone who has ever fired a pistol, and I look forward to its speedy adoption.

Several events in the spring of 1940 would finally change the direction of Patton's career. First, the Third Army Maneuvers in Georgia and Louisiana in April and May precipitated a break in the close relationship between Patton and Joyce.

The split had become visible, although it was far from a rupture, as early as the previous autumn, when the tactical thinking of Joyce and Patton began to diverge. Joyce's 1st Cavalry Division had engaged in war exercises in Texas, and shortly thereafter, Joyce summarized for Patton's information some of the relevant experience.

He himself had commanded the cavalry division, which had opposed a force of motorized and mechanized infantry and artillery. In the course of a "battle," a relatively small task force of "enemy" infantry and artillery had made a wide turning movement of 100 miles to get on the flank of Joyce's horse cavalry. If successfully prosecuted, the sweeping advance would have struck the cavalry flank and thereby have, theoretically, destroyed Joyce's unit. Yet when the "hostile" task force arrived in position to menace Joyce, his troops stopped the flanking movement cold and separated the enemy task force from the main enemy body, thereby, again theoretically, making the small outflanking force vulnerable to destruction. In short, the mobile unit had failed to carry out its aim, and Joyce's cavalry had "won" the battle.

Knowing Patton's penchant for wide envelopments or turning movements, Joyce admitted in his letter that there were, of course, many good arguments in favor of this sort of venture. But personally he believed that it was too risky.

Joyce then tried to smooth over the difference. Both sides, he wrote, had made mistakes, "as there always will be in maneuvers or in wars, and all learned by the experience. The good soldier does not make the same mistake the second time."

If Patton felt offended by Joyce's having questioned one of his deepest convictions — the value of mobility to permit hard-hitting forces to strike at the enemy's flank and rear — he made no immediate retort.

In February 1940, as evidence of his friendly feeling toward Joyce, Patton passed along some news, some inside information that, strictly speaking, it was not altogether fair to disclose. John S. Wood, chief of staff of the Third Army and a friend of Patton, had been in Washington and had talked about the maneuvers to be held that spring. According to Wood, Joyce's 1st Cavalry Division would participate and have the assignment of covering or protecting the assembly and concentration of an infantry corps. Joyce's division of horse cavalry would oppose Chaffee's mechanized brigade. Wood has said that the initial concentration points of the opposing forces were 100 miles apart. But he had hinted that the covering action by Joyce would start before the main troops on both sides reached those positions.

This was valuable advance knowledge that Joyce was not supposed to have, for it gave his forces an unfair advantage over Chaffee's. Patton promised to let Joyce know anything further that he might learn.

Patton continued:

It occurs to me that, since mechanized cavalry depends for its success on a very large use of radio, much advantage could be obtained over them should you be able to set up radio interference. I am informed that the sets in the scout cars are strong enough to be used for this purpose if they are tuned in on the same bands. I think it would be a great joke if our friendly enemy on wheels and tracks could be totally deafened [by radio jamming]. Colonel Wood also

informs me that there is a river running through a considerable portion of the maneuver area, and that this river will probably be
unfordable except by swimming. Perhaps you could find some place
near [Fort] Bliss where you could practice this and so steal another
march on Chaffee, Millikin and Company . . .

Trusting that you will not consider me presumptuous for the foregoing and with all good wishes for the success of the horse cavalry, I
am, as ever, Very respectfully yours,

Thus, Patton was motivated in his desire to have Joyce win both by his
friendship for Joyce and by his attachment to the horse cavalry.

*Letter, GSP, Jr., to Lieutenant Colonel John S. Wood, Third Army,
Atlanta, Georgia, March 19, 1940*

Dear P: While I have not received my order I definitely know that
I shall be an Umpire [in the forthcoming maneuvers], so don't forget
to give me a good job.

Write me prior to March 25th as to what uniforms I should take,
do I need woolen o.d. blouses as well as breeches, do I need a cap as
well as campaign hat; do I need a bedding roll, and any other pertinent information that you may think will be of value to me. Please
answer at once.

As ever, in a hurry, yours,

On the following day, he received the order detailing him to the Third
Army on temporary duty as a control officer or umpire.

Upon receipt of Patton's letter, Wood wrote that mimeographed instructions had probably reached Patton. There was little he could add,
except that it was chilly in Georgia in April and hot in Louisiana in May.
"Please give my love to Bea. I hope that you are both well. It was a great
pleasure to see you two again and to have had such a delightful evening
with you."

The Third Army Maneuvers were staged in two phases, the first near
Fort Benning, Georgia, between April 12 and 25, the second near Camp
Beauregard, Louisiana, between May 5 and 25. These games had as their
prime purposes the testing of organization, doctrine, equipment, and the
performance of units, commanders, and staffs. They were designed to
train the new type of corps, composed of triangular divisions, to deploy
large bodies of troops over long distances against a mobile enemy, and

were particularly oriented on the operations of the few mechanized units in existence. The maneuvers would help in determining how mechanized forces and combat aviation could best work together. They would also evaluate the usefulness of horse cavalry against motorized and mechanized troops.

These aims stemmed from the shocking success of the German blitzkrieg in Poland the previous year, which was a sobering sight for the U. S. Army. An isolationist Congress, niggardly with funds, had deprived the Army of the means with which to develop and produce in large numbers tanks, self-propelled artillery, trucks, close-support planes, and other new weapons and pieces of equipment, together with the units to use them. There were but few mechanized forces with rudimentary equipment, and they had had little experience working with close-support airplanes.

Chaffee's 7th Mechanized Cavalry Brigade from Fort Knox and a Provisional Motorized Tank Brigade created by the infantry at Fort Benning dominated the Third Army maneuvers. These two units were formed into an improvised armored division, and the success of this force coincided with the crashing explosion that marked the end of the Phony War in Europe. In May, as Chaffee's machines were defeating Joyce's horses, the German forces attacked France. In six weeks, with an astonishing rapidity, the Germans defeated the British, Belgian, and French armies and forced the evacuation from Dunkerque. Professional soldiers in general and tank enthusiasts in particular advocated with increasing clamor the need to form true armored divisions.

This was what the Third Army commander, Lieutenant General Stanley D. Embick, recommended — that the mechanized brigades, one cavalry-sponsored, the other infantry-sponsored, be expanded into armored divisions. Embick also suggested that the horse cavalry be retained to perform the subordinate and limited function of reconnaissance, and that the horse units be further motorized and mechanized.

Patton's presence as an umpire in the maneuvers was extremely beneficial to him. He saw precisely how the new mechanized units were organized, how they operated, and what could be expected from them. Joyce's horse cavalry had been unable to stand up against them, in part because Joyce lacked the punch and the slashing, driving aggressiveness that characterized Patton's thought and behavior. Yet, no matter what the deficiencies of Joyce as a commander, no matter whether Patton might have done better if he had been in command, it was obvious to everyone, and to Patton as well, that the machine had replaced the horse in warfare.

Disenchanted with Joyce's leadership and with the horse cavalry operations during the maneuvers — the two were tied together — Patton nevertheless made an effort to keep his friendship with Joyce intact and close. In the following month, Patton sent Joyce a training memo he had drawn up for his own regiment of horse, the 3d Cavalry at Fort Myer.

Joyce's reaction to Patton's training program was negative. The memo, Joyce wrote, contained much advice for the young, but some statements were so general as to be misleading.

> What you say in paragraph "M" relative to saddle bags and cantle rolls is just 100% wrong. The individual mounted soldier should not be dependent on a truck in any way for periods up to 48 hours . . . This belief that the cavalry soldier must have a truck with him all the time is as bad as the infantry soldier having to ride up to the firing line in a truck. We must get away from such stuff. Save the horse — YES, but in any active service have the individual fighting man self-supporting in every way and ready to go.

A decided gap had opened between the doctrinal thinking of the two men. Joyce remained conservative in his views. Patton modified his traditional outlook by broadening his focus and by adjusting to the reality that Chaffee's machines had made Joyce's horses look bad.

This perception prompted Patton to switch his allegiance. He began to look with increasing longing toward Chaffee's tanks. This was the second event that affected Patton's career.

Meanwhile, Patton was collecting "superior" efficiency ratings and commendations for his manner of performing his duties. As an umpire in the maneuvers, he was graded "superior" for his contributions to the successful exercises. Shortly thereafter he received an official compliment on the appearance of his troops during a parade.

Letter, Brigadier General Maxwell Murray, Washington Provisional Brigade, to GSP, Jr., June 5, 1940, subject: Commendation

The review held at your station [Fort Myer] on the morning of June 4, 1940, in which the 3d Cavalry . . . 1st Battalion, 16th Field Artillery, 3d Battalion, 12th Infantry, and Troop F, 10th Cavalry participated, was a superior demonstration of precision and nicety of detail, always desired in Army ceremonies, yet too seldom achieved. The appearance of the troops, their precision of march and exactness of formations were so exemplary in every detail as to unequivocally establish claim to a high state of training, morale and discipline. Mindful that such standards of proficiency are only attained through long and tedious hours of instruction and training, with a high spirit of cooperation throughout, I wish to commend you and through you the commanding officers and enlisted men of the units concerned.

Two weeks later, Murray composed for Patton's official file another "Commendation" in appreciation of Patton's faithful discharge of duty. Patton, Murray wrote,

has filled this difficult assignment [at Fort Myer] in a manner which reflects great credit upon himself and the military service . . . I feel that I have been very fortunate in having had Colonel Patton serve under me in the important post he has occupied.

Still later that month, Murray formally rated Patton "superior" in all categories, and called him

a most enthusiastic, energetic and able officer. He has decided opinions, and expresses them frankly but carries out loyally any decision of his superiors. He maintains himself in remarkable physical condition, and through personal leadership builds a high esprit in his command. He is well fitted for higher command in peace or war.

But a "higher command," for the moment at least, eluded him.

The training memo he had sent to Joyce appeared in the *Cavalry Journal* under the title "Training Memoranda to His Regiment." It was an attempt — his last — to restore the faltering prestige of the horse cavalry. "My observations at the Maneuvers in Georgia and Louisiana," Patton wrote, "induce me to re-stress the following points which are so obvious they are never remembered."

Scout cars, he said, were not combat cars. They were supposed to find and report information about the enemy. They were to fight the enemy only when combat was unavoidable. "It is not necessary," he said in illustration, "to push your nose against the glass to see through a window. Observation from a distance is just as efficient and much safer."

Reconnoitering elements, he counseled, should stop on the friendly side of a crossroads so that the enemy could not use the lateral road to cut them off. Units had to guard their security by putting out flankers during a halt. "If attacked by enemy planes, fire at them with everything you have. If you are under cover [and undetected] keep quiet." Crew members of scout cars ought to fill their gasoline tanks at every opportunity. If withdrawing, they should destroy all the gasoline they could not use.

"The secret of success in mounted operations," he reiterated, having made the same statement several years earlier, "is to GRAB THE ENEMY BY THE NOSE AND KICK HIM IN THE PANTS." As soon as horse cavalry struck opposition, it had to pin down the enemy in the front with a minimum of force and get around the enemy flanks. Against motorized columns, the objective was always the trucks, which were usually just around the first bend or just behind the first hill. If the wind was favorable, troopers could set fire to anything that would burn toward the enemy.

Imbedded in his text were aphorisms:

> Always fell trees and burn bridges on roads leading to your position or bivouac . . .
> Anti-tank guns are deadly at 1000 yards. The guns in tanks are not . . .
> Next to a windshield a khaki tent is the most visible object from the air . . .
> It is not soldierly to send a two-ton truck for a can of beer, but it is done all the time. This must stop . . .
> It must be borne in mind that the surest way to avoid losses is to inflict losses on the enemy by your own fire.

These were hardly profound observations. They were practical, down-to-earth statements that were immensely applicable to field soldiering. They repeated his continuing belief in the efficacy of mobility, the value of wide sweeping maneuvers, and the benefit of overwhelming firepower to defeat the enemy.

Despite his continuing interest in horses, his responsibilities as post commander, his satisfying contacts with prominent people in Washington, Patton was restless. He had been at Fort Myer a year and a half. He had everything under control. His life was pleasant enough, but offered little

challenge. His duties were routine. Furthermore, the dedicated horsemen with whom he had been closely associated throughout his career
seemed to have lost touch with and to be out of step with the times.

Motivated by his boredom and by his newly awakened appreciation of
the capabilities of mechanized forces, Patton wrote on June 26 to his
friend Chaffee. Perhaps Patton had learned informally that Chaffee
would on July 10 become Chief of a newly organized Armored Force,
which was built around the 7th Mechanized Cavalry Brigade and the 6th
Armored Infantry Regiment at Fort Knox, a force that would be authorized 530 officers and 9329 men. Perhaps Patton had heard unofficially
that Chaffee was to take command on July 15 of a newly formed I Armored Corps, which would control the 1st Armored Division (successor to
the Mechanized Brigade) at Fort Knox and the 2d Armored Division
(successor to the Provisional Tank Brigade) at Fort Benning.

Precisely what Patton said in his letter to Chaffee toward the end of
June has been lost. No doubt, he sent his congratulations. He probably
added that people were saying good things about Chaffee's work. He may
have mentioned an observation or two from the Georgia and Louisiana
maneuvers. And he invited Chaffee to stay with the Pattons whenever he
was in Washington.

Although he may have included a jocular remark to the effect that he
wished he were helping Chaffee, Patton would not have asked for anything specific. The entire tradition and custom of the service argued
against direct pressure or subservient pleading of this sort for a favor.
The purpose of Patton's letter was to remind Chaffee, in an indirect fashion, of Patton's interest in Chaffee's endeavors and of his availability for a
new and exciting challenge.

Chaffee replied two days later. He talked about his frequent visits to
Washington and elsewhere — "I have been so busy with two trips to
Washington in the last three weeks that my head is going around. I work
all week and travel on Sunday." He thanked Patton for the invitation
— but "I usually go to the Club or to a hotel, in order to be footloose,
because my time is never my own."

Finally, he came to the heart of the matter, and what he said was probably more than Patton could have expected.

I put you on my preffered list as a brigade commander for an armored brigade. I think it is a job which you could do to the queen's

taste, and I need just such a man of your experience in command of an armored brigade. With two light armored regiments and a regiment of tanks employed in a mobile way, I think you could go to town. We have an enormous job in front of us to get this thing organized, trained, and going in a minimum of time. I hope things will work out favorably for you. I shall always be happy to know that you are around close in any capacity when there is fighting to be done. Good luck to you always and I will be seeing you soon, I hope.

This was the third event that would change Patton's career.

The fourth occurrence was the appointment early in July by President Roosevelt of Henry L. Stimson as Secretary of War. Patton immediately sent Stimson, an old friend, a congratulatory letter. Stimson acknowledged with thanks Patton's "very encouraging message which you sent me concerning my appointment." He sent affectionate good wishes to Patton and to Beatrice.

It is highly probable that Patton's note led Stimson to wonder why a proved fire-eater like George Patton was being kept at Fort Myer. And no doubt he mentioned this thought to Marshall.

Certainly there was increasing need for an officer of Patton's ability and experience. And certainly there were increasing opportunities for men of his caliber. In July 1940, the War Department activated General Headquarters, U. S. Army, under the command of General McNair to supervise the training of tactical units. In the following month, Congress would authorize the President to call National Guard units to active federal service. And in September, the President would sign the Selective Service Act permitting the induction of 630,000 draftees, would muster 270,000 National Guardsmen to the national colors, and would enlarge the Regular Army to 500,000 men. A total of 1,400,000 troops would soon be on active duty and preparing for war.

France had surrendered, and the battle of Britain had begun. The United States was finally awakening to the danger of Axis aggression.

Meanwhile, Patton left Washington on July 2 for fifteen days of leave in Massachusetts. Four days later his daughter Ruth Ellen married Lieutenant James W. Totten. The wedding was held at St. John's Church in Beverly Farms, and it was followed by a reception at Green Meadows.

As was his practice, Patton requested that his leave be extended for ten days. Permission was granted.

On July 15, while he was reading the morning newspaper at Green Meadows, he saw an item about himself. With mounting excitement, he learned that he had been assigned to the 2d Armored Division at Fort Benning, Georgia. He was going back to the tanks.

It took him several hours to restrain his joy, to compose himself, to consider the sudden turn in his career. Perhaps he made several telephone calls to Washington to confirm the information.

Letter, GSP, Jr., to Brigadier General C. L. Scott, commander 2d Armored Division, Fort Benning Georgia, July 15, 1940

My dear Scotty: You can imagine my great delight at reading in the paper this morning that I had been assigned to your outfit. I am sure that I owe the detail to you. It is probably needless for me to say that I will do my uttermost to give satisfaction.

His leave expired on July 27, he informed Scott; he would like to stay in Massachusetts at least until the 22d, but he could be at Fort Benning within 36 hours if Scott wanted him at once. He concluded: "With best regards and looking forward to a short and bloody war, I am Very sincerely."

Letter, GSP, Jr., to Brigadier General Adna R. Chaffee, Fort Knox, Kentucky, July 15, 1940

Dear General Adna: I deeply appreciate your nice letter of the 28th [of June]. In this morning's papers I note that I am to go to Benning to take one of the armored brigades. I am sure that this most happy detail was due to your efforts and I appreciate it very much indeed. You may be sure that I shall do my damndest to justify your expectations of me.

Chaffee had put Patton's name on his preferred list, but it was Scott who had the vacancy in the 2d Armored Division. Scott had selected Patton from among those whom Chaffee considered qualified and eligible for the job.

It was quickly obvious to Patton that his assignment to the 2d Armored Division would have been impossible unless Marshall approved. He therefore wrote a letter of thanks to the Chief of Staff.

Letter, Marshall to GSP, Jr., July 19, 1940

Dear Patton: I have just received your note of July 16th, thanking me for your assignment to the brigade of an armored division. I am glad this arrangement is pleasing to you, for I thought it would be just the sort of thing you would like most to do at the moment. Also, I felt that no one could do that particular job better.

I am looking forward to seeing you and having a talk with you before you leave for the South.

Hastily,

Patton arrived at Fort Benning on July 27. He moved into quarters at 601 Baltzell Avenue, and assumed command of the 2d Armored Brigade.

Two days later, the War Department revoked Patton's Mobilization Assignment — that is, the position Patton would take if the country went to war — as commanding officer of the 3d Cavalry, thereby cutting the cord that had tied him to the horse cavalry.

It must have occurred to Patton soon after his arrival at Fort Benning, if not earlier, that Pershing had probably had a hand in his transfer. It was Marshall's practice periodically to visit Pershing, who was then living permanently at the Walter Reed Hospital in Washington. With Pershing, Marshall discussed the qualities, qualifications, and capabilities of officers who could be brought along rapidly to assume positions of high command and responsibility. Certainly Pershing must have talked of Patton's success in training and leading the tankers in France.

Patton wrote to Pershing early in August. "This command," he said, "is a very fine one and I am most fortunate to have landed it." His brigade had two light tank regiments, one medium tank regiment, a field artillery regiment, and a battalion of engineers — 350 officers, 5500 men, 383 tanks, 202 armored cars, and 24 105-mm. howitzers. Some equipment was lacking, but more tanks were promised soon, and men were coming in at the rate of about 100 each day. General Scott, the division commander, was full of energy and wonderful to work for. All the officers were a carefully selected lot.

The whole thing is most interesting as most of the tactics have yet to be worked out and there is a great chance for ingenuity and leadership. As I see it we must be able to fight any place and in any manner either alone or in close association with infantry or cavalry. I think if we can get the platoons so they can fight anywhere and the men convinced that they are the best on earth and are willing to get killed to accomplish their missions, we will be a great success . . .

Just at the moment the military appearance of the men and to a degree of the officers leaves something to be desired. I am trying to set an example of being smart and soldierly and hope the rest will copy me — if they dont I will have to use stronger methods.

I seem to have inflicted a rather long letter on you but my excuse is that I am so interested in the job that I love to tell you about it.

I am quite sure that you had a lot to do with my getting this wonderful detail. Truly I appreciate it a lot and will try to be worthy of having served under you.

He added a postscript, his usual self-depreciating remark: "As my office is not yet running I had to type this my self — please excuse the mistakes."

Letter, GSP, Jr., to Pershing, August 7, 1940

Last Sunday I had a sudden impulse to turn on my radio and the very first thing I heard was some one introducing you. I heard all of your address and it was the finest and most manly statement I have ever listened to. The country is to be congratulated that it has a man like you to tell the truth and to tell it so forcefully.

Letter, Pershing to GSP, Jr., August 12, 1940

My dear Patton: Thank you very much for your kind note, which I have read with a great deal of interest. I can understand your enthusiasm for this new job, and am sure that you are going to thoroughly enjoy the experience.

Patton was on his way to fame, although probably no one, except surely himself, was aware of it. How could anyone but he know, how could anyone guess?

Hardly anyone, even in the Army, remembered that Patton had once been with tanks, that he had personified the tanks in World War I. Seemingly more important and more than apparent were his prowess as a horseman, hunter, and polo player; his attachment, his strong loyalty, to the horse cavalry; his high jinks, exuberance, and grandstanding on the polo field; his personal wealth that enabled him to keep a string of ponies and to own a yacht. He appeared to be a playboy, a socialite. His intemperate remarks outraged many persons. Some believed that he flaunted his money. Impulsive, outspoken, and aggressive, he had the facility to provoke distaste for his behavior and mode of life.

Largely forgotten were his dedication to his profession; the depth of his military knowledge and the variety of his experience; the ability he had to inspire, especially among those who worked closely with him, admiration, respect, and warm liking. Even the increasing frequency of his almost uncontrollable rages, his outbursts of temper, his periods of depression and moodiness, his extreme swings from overriding anger to abject contrition affected but slightly his friendships, never his performance of duty or his efficiency as a soldier. Georgie, his friends said, had always been eccentric.

He drove himself still, as he always had, and he realized, no doubt better than anyone else — with the single exception perhaps of Beatrice — the challenges he would face in the coming months: the challenges of his work, of the war itself, and of his personal destiny, which was coming within his reach. He would have to grasp it now, for this would be the last time he could hope to attain the glory that, in the measure he aspired to, had so far escaped him.

He was fifty-five years old, the same age that Pershing had been in 1916, the time of the Punitive Expedition into Mexico, the eve of the American entrance into the Great War. It was, then, not too late for Patton to gain achievement.

He had completed the necessary formal military education by attending the institutions of higher Army learning and succeeding in his courses with high distinction. He had served on every organizational level, from platoon to corps, both as a commander and as a staff officer. He had read far more than the average officer, had thought more deeply than most.

Yet he seemed to have moved not at all since he had left the tanks in 1920. Twenty years later, he was again with tanks, once more in command of a brigade, and still a colonel.

His classmate Devers was a brigadier general and in command of the Provisional Brigade of Washington, D.C. His classmate Eichelberger was a colonel in command of the 30th Infantry Regiment and would soon become Superintendent of the Military Academy. His friend Eisenhower, much younger than Patton, was an obscure lieutenant colonel with the 15th Infantry at Fort Lewis, Washington, and about to start his meteoric rise in rank. Mark Clark, also young, was a lieutenant colonel, an instructor at the War College, but he would soon join McNair and become his right-hand man. Omar N. Bradley was a diffident lieutenant colonel who was the Assistant Secretary of the War Department General Staff.

Fame would beckon to all of these and to others. Yet in mid-1940 it appeared to Patton that he had moved scarcely at all during the past twenty years. The two decades had been full of professional disappointment and frustration. It had taken him fourteen years to advance from major to lieutenant colonel. He had become identified with the wrong branch and the wrong bunch — the horse-cavalry men. He had backed the wrong people — Crosby and Henry, then Drum. Yet he had had the great luck to be close to Pershing, to Hines and Summerall and Craig. And finally, Stimson, Marshall, and Chaffee had smiled at him.

He had wasted time, it must have seemed to Patton, as a General Staff officer. His self-advertising at polo, sailing, hunting, and riding appeared to have backfired. The last few years of his career had been aimless, without direction.

Even the mere passage of time had changed him considerably for the worse. The two decades since the Great War had coarsened his figure — he had put on 20 pounds and weighed nearly 200. He had lost his youthful good looks.

Yet he was vigorous, energetic, and enthusiastic, even boyish. He was also somewhat chastened, less outspoken, more diplomatic, less spontaneous, more calculating. If he had had to serve the interests of the horse soldiers rather than those of the mechanized troops, to his own disadvantage, he had known how to keep rein on his impatience, to serve with loyalty, to satisfy the desires of his superiors, to practice — to an enormous extent — self-abnegation.

Patton had suffered the bitterness of the postwar years, and they had scarred and tempered him.

It was, rather, the U. S. Army that had failed to advance between the wars. The main function of tanks, as Patton had so clearly enunciated it in France, as he himself had been so largely instrumental in formulating it, was to assist the infantry. After 1918, the chiefs of the Tank Corps, of the infantry, and of the Ordnance Corps tried repeatedly to have the War Department take and support an official position on what tanks were supposed to be and what they were supposed to do. Finally, in 1922, the War Department fell back on the established rule and stated that the primary mission of tanks was "to facilitate the uninterrupted advance of the riflemen in the attack." Official doctrine in 1939 was quite the same: "As a rule, tanks are employed to assist the advance of infantry foot troops, either preceding or accompanying the infantry assault echelon."

This could not stand in 1940, not after the swift successes of the German blitzkrieg. Catching up to, overtaking, and ultimately surpassing the Germans would in large part be the work of Patton. How he would do so was quite unclear to him at the beginning of his World War II adventure at Fort Benning.

American tank production between the wars had also been gripped by inertia. Christie's tank, operating on removable tracks and also on large removable solid-rubber bogie wheels, and built on a system of independently sprung wheels, was never accepted in the United States. The infantry and the cavalry both adored the Christie tank, but the ordnance believed that it was mechanically unreliable and that its dual-purpose equipment violated good engineering practice. Controversy raged until 1938, when the convertible Christie principle was abandoned.

The Mark VIII heavy and American Renault light tanks of World War I were standard until the 1930s. From 1920 to 1935, only thirty-five tanks were built in the United States. Most were hand-tooled test models. Not until 1938 would an American designed tank be accepted and standardized. To meet the armored challenge of the age, the United States would have to design and produce a host of modern and reliable tanks quickly.

This task would belong to others. Patton's function would be to use them — to employ tanks, armored and mechanized troops, motorized infantry, self-propelled artillery, close-support aircraft, and the other elements of the combined arms team in order to out-blitzkrieg the Germans.

He would have to prove himself capable. But he had always had to do that. He had forever had to drive himself, to show himself that he was able, competent, and knowledgeable.

And now that the "next war" had come to Asia and to Europe and threatened — or, from Patton's point of view, promised — to draw in the United States, he faced the unknown with a confidence that was more apparent than real. He would reinforce his strong and vital sense of duty and devotion by his close identification with his personal destiny or fate.

It was, he was certain, his destiny or his fate to become a great captain, and he would do his uttermost, as he would have said, to make that destiny, that fate, that dream come true.

A Brief Note
on Military Terms

George S. Patton, Jr.,
His Military Chronology

A Brief Note on Military Terms

A PLATOON is a unit of about 40 soldiers and is commanded by a lieutenant, either a second lieutenant (who wears a gold bar) or a first lieutenant (silver bar).

A company — called a troop in the cavalry — consists of four platoons and is usually commanded by a captain (two silver bars).

A battalion — called a squadron in the cavalry — consists of four companies (or troops), and is under the command of a major (who wears a gold leaf) or lieutenant colonel (silver leaf).

A regiment consists of two battalions (or squadrons) and is commanded by a lieutenant colonel or a colonel (silver eagle).

A brigade is composed of two regiments and is commanded by a colonel or a brigadier general (whose insignia of rank is one star).

A division is an organization of two brigades; the commander is usually a major general (two stars).

A corps consists of two or more divisions and is commanded by a major general or a lieutenant general (three stars).

An army, sometimes called a field army, contains two or more corps and is under a lieutenant general or a general (four stars).

In the early part of the twentieth century, the U. S. Army was headed by the Secretary of War who was a member of the President's cabinet and who advised the President on military matters. The War Department, located in Washington, D.C., consisted of civilians and military men who assisted the Secretary. The top man in uniform was the Army Chief of Staff, who was the principal military adviser of the Secretary of War.

The Chief of Staff presided over the General and Special Staff Sections, each of which was headed by an officer who was responsible for a specific function, for example, Personnel, Intelligence, Plans and Operations, Supplies, Ordnance, and the like.

Staff officers were also assigned to field armies, corps, divisions, brigades, regiments, and battalions (squadrons) to help the commanders of these organizations.

There was, and is, a distinct difference between commanders and staff officers. Only commanders have the authority to direct units; only commanders bear the responsibility for unit performance. It is the commander who makes decisions and who is held responsible for success or failure. Staff officers are the commander's advisers. They help him reach his decisions, and they take action only in the name of their commander.

George S. Patton, Jr., His Military Chronology

1885 November 11	Born, San Gabriel, Los Angeles County, California
1897–1903 September–June	Student, Stephen Cutter Clark's Classical School for Boys, Pasadena, California
1903–1904 September–June	Cadet, Virginia Military Institute, Lexington, Virginia
1904 June 16	Entered U. S. Military Academy, West Point, New York
1905 June	Turned back to repeat initial year
September	Re-entered as Cadet, U. S. Military Academy
1906 June 13	Appointed Second Corporal, Cadet Corps
August 27	Apponted Sixth Corporal, Cadet Corps
1907 March 14	Appointed Second Corporal, Cadet Corps
June 14	Appointed Sergeant Major, Cadet Corps
1908 February 14	Appointed Battalion Adjutant, Cadet Corps
1909 June 11	Graduated U. S. Military Academy; commissioned Second Lieutenant, 15th Cavalry
September 12	Joined 15th Cavalry, Fort Sheridan, Illinois, and assigned to Troop K
September	Qualified as Expert Rifleman
December	Qualified as Expert Revolver Shot
1910 November 2–December 23	Commanding Officer, Machine Gun Platoon, 3d Squadron, 15th Cavalry
1911 May–November	Acting Commanding Officer, Troop K, 15th Cavalry

	December 3	Joined Troop A, 15th Cavalry, Fort Myer, Virginia
1912	March 12	Appointed Quartermaster, 1st Squadron, 15th Cavalry, Fort Myer
	June 14	Sailed for Europe to participate in Olympic Games, Stockholm, Sweden
	July 7–July 17	Participated in Modern Pentathlon, Olympic Games
	July–August	Received individual instruction in fencing at Saumur, France
	August 22	Returned to United States
1913	December 14–March 22	Temporary Duty, Office of the Chief of Staff, U. S. Army
	July 9–Sept 17	Study of Swordsmanship at Saumur, France
	September 23	Reported to Mounted Service School, Fort Riley, Kansas, as Master of the Sword and as Student, First Year Course
1914	May 8	Graduated First Year Course
	September	Master of the Sword and Student, Second Year Course
1915	June 17	Graduated Second Year Course
	September 15	Joined 8th Cavalry, Fort Bliss, Texas
	September 25	Assigned Troop D, 8th Cavalry
	October	Appointed Squadron Adjutant and Quartermaster as additional duties
1916	October 19–January 22	Stationed at Sierra Blanca, Texas
	March 13	Detached from 8th Cavalry and attached to Headquarters, Punitive Expedition, Mexico
	May 14	The Rubio Ranch Affair
	May 23	Promoted to First Lieutenant
	June 8	Transferred to 10th Cavalry, continuing duty with Headquarters, Punitive Expedition

1917	February 1	Transferred formally to 7th Cavalry, Fort Bliss, Texas
	February	Returned with Punitive Expedition from Mexico
	February 27–April 14	Commanding Officer, Troop A, 7th Cavalry
	May 15	Promoted to Captain
	May 18	Ordered to report to Pershing in Washington, D.C.; appointed Commanding Officer, Headquarters Troop, AEF
	May 28	Sailed for Europe on *Baltic* with Pershing's headquarters
	June 8	Reached Liverpool; departed for London
	June 13	Departed London; arrived Paris
	September 1	Moved with Headquarters to Chaumont
	September 13	Additional duty as Post Adjutant, Chaumont
	October 3	Requested assignment to Tank Service
	November 10	Detailed to the Tank Service
	November 18	Relinquished command of Headquarters Troop, AEF
	November 19–December 1	Observer, French Tank Center, Chamlieu
	December 16	Moved to Langres to open Light Tank Center and School
1918	January 1–January 7	Visited French and British Tank Centers
	January 23	Promoted to Major
	February 14	Formally assigned to command the Light Tanks, AEF (302d Light Tank Center)
	February 22	Moved Tank Center and School from Langres to Bourg
	March 4–March 10	Visited British Tank Center in England
	April 3	Promoted to Lieutenant Colonel

April 28	Organized 1st Light Tank Battalion with himself in command
June 6	Organized 2d Light Tank Battalion, with himself in command of the regiment
June 17–August 20	Student, General Staff College, Langres (completed course)
August 24	Organized and commanded 304th Tank Brigade (1st Tank Brigade)
September 12–September 15	St. Mihiel Offensive
September 26	Wounded near Cheppy, Meuse-Argonne Offensive
September 26–September 30	Evacuation Hospital #11
October 1–October 17	Base Hospital #49
October 17	Promoted to Colonel
October 17–October 28	Base Hospital #24
December 16	Awarded Distinguished Service Cross
1919 January 17–February 7	Detached Service, Second Army
February 26–February 28	En route to Marseille
March 2	Sailed for United States
March 17	Arrived Brooklyn, New York; to Camp Mills, Long Island, New York
March 25	To Camp Meade, Maryland
April 22	Temporary duty, Washington, D.C.
June 16	Awarded Distinguished Service Medal
September 4	Relieved from temporary duty; returned to Camp Meade
1920 June 30	Reverted to Regular grade of Captain

	July 1	Promoted to Major
	September 30	Relinquished command of 304th Tank Brigade
	October 3	Joined 3d Cavalry at Fort Myer, Virginia, as Commanding Officer, 3d Squadron
1922	December 18	Departed Fort Myer
1923	January 10	Student, Field Officers' Course, Fort Riley, Kansas
	June 3	Completed Field Officers' Course
	September	Student, Command and General Staff College, Fort Leavenworth, Kansas
1924	June 30	Honor Graduate, Command and General Staff College
	July 5	Joined First Corps Area Headquarters and assigned as Assistant Chief of Staff G-1 (Personnel)
1925	March 4	Sailed from New York for Hawaii
	March 31	Reached Hawaii; assigned G-1 and G-2, Hawaiian Division
	October 30	Detached Service, Acting G-1, Hawaiian Department
1926	September 30	G-1, G-2, and G-3, Hawaiian Division
1928	April 7	Departed Hawaii
	May 7	Joined Office of the Chief of Cavalry, Washington, D.C.
1931	September	Student, Army War College, Washington, D.C.
1932	June 2	Awarded Purple Heart for wound in 1918
	June	Distinguished Graduate, Army War College
	July 8	Executive Officer, 3d Cavalry, Fort Myer, Virginia
1934	March 1	Promoted to Lieutenant Colonel
1935	May 7	Departed Los Angeles in yacht for Hawaii
	June 8	Arrived Honolulu; assigned G-2, Hawaiian Department
1937	June 12	Departed Honolulu in yacht

July 12	Arrived Los Angeles
July 25	In hospital, Beverly, Massachusetts, with broken leg
November 4	Discharged hospital; sick in quarters
1938 February 2	Returned to duty status
February 8	Executive Officer, Academic Division of the Cavalry School and 9th Cavalry, Fort Riley, Kansas
July 1	Promoted to Colonel
July 24	Commanding Officer, 5th Cavalry, Fort Clark, Texas
December 10	Commanding Officer, 3d Cavalry, Fort Myer, Virginia
1940 April	Umpire, Spring Maneuvers, Fort Benning, Georgia
May	Control Officer, Maneuvers, Fort Beauregard, Louisiana
July 26	Commanding Officer, 2d Armored Brigade of 2d Armored Division, Fort Benning

Index

Index

Patton, General George Smith, Jr.,
(cont'd)

623; becomes post adjutant, 421;
promoted to major, 429, 430, 485–
486, 739; reputation with his men,
472, 473, 474, 525, 692; lectures
on discipline and training, 499–
504; Lt. Colonel, Tank Corps, 508,
513 (see also as Tanker, below);
and St. Mihiel offensive, 567–600;
and Meuse-Argonne offensive, 601–
617; promoted to colonel, 623–624,
644; convinced there would be another war in Western Europe, 650,
667, 920–921, 960; returns to U.S.,
post-Armistice, 681–696; postwar
years, 699–715; and Class III officers, 707–708; returns to captain,
721, 739; and Knickerbocker Theater disaster (1922), 762; and Pershing's retirement, 779–780; seeks
appointment as Commandant of
Cadets, West Point, 800, 869–870,
888, 910–912; and Bonus March
(1932), 894–900; promoted to
lieutenant colonel, 906, 959; coins
phrase "blood and gutts," 911,
912; interest in defense of Hawaii,
912–916; as brigadier general, 931,
945; and outbreak of World War
II, 943–956; his command of 2nd
Armored Division, 956–957

RELATIONSHIPS: friends, 176, 202,
447, 542, 655; and Pershing, 319–
324, 352, 369, 379, 383, 385–388,
398, 407–408, 440, 463, 480, 508,
779–780; and Rockenbach, 464–
465, 469–470, 478, 497, 511, 558;
and Joyce, 946–947

AS SPORTSMAN: 7, 8, 10, 45, 114, 118,
227–233; marksman, 31, 32, 149–
150, 154, 177, 186, 187, 191, 192,
301; horseman, 32, 142, 144, 145,
199, 203, 212, 214, 219, 226, 228,
236, 238, 240, 241, 253, 263, 344,
886, 957, 959; fisherman, 33, 184,
468; hunter, 33–34, 279, 285, 288,
348, 957, 959; sailor and yachts-

man, 33–34, 63, 887, 907, 916, 938,
959; swordsman, 34, 100, 104, 106,
107, 112–113, 142–144, 168, 177,
233–234, 245–246, 247, 248, 256–
259, 261, 263; football, 100, 103,
104, 113, 115, 120–123, 130, 131,
137, 138, 149, 151–153, 155, 177;
track, 114–115, 127, 141, 144, 145,
147, 155, 177; polo, 144, 149, 150,
203, 204, 211, 216–217, 226, 237,
253–254, 295–296, 351, 366, 369,
753–755, 763–766, 839, 957, 959;
steeplechase, 226, 227, 251, 253–
254; and Olympic Games, (1912
Stockholm) 227–233, (Berlin 1916)
278; and Army athletics program
in France (World War I), 498; fox-
hunting, 901–903

AS TANKER: 16, 213, 427, 429, 432–
435, 439–440, 444–459, 715, 716,
717, 820, 955, 957–958; on mechanization of army, 221, 799, 821–
822, 835, 840–856; and motorized
warfare, 337; seeks tank command,
427, 429; organizes and establishes
First American Tank Center, 434–
436; studies French tanks at Chamlieu, 443–459; impression of Renault tank works, 448; starts tank
school at Langres, 460–480; and
Tank Corps brassard and collar
ornament, 469; lecture on tanks at
Army school (Chaumont), 473,
475–476; and tank drill regulations, 481, 487, 493; authorized to
staff tank school, 481–482; assigned
command 1st Light Tank Center,
485; his directions for operation
of tank center and school, 490–
491; concern about shipment of
tanks, 494–495, 506; his personnel
needs, 499; requests cut-away tank
models for instruction, 508; as
Lieut. Colonel, Tank Corps, 508,
513; arrival of tanks at Bourg,
508–509, 530; and details of simulated tank combat, 517–518; first
Tank Corps maneuvers, 523–524;